SSAT® & ISEE®
FOR
DUMMIES®

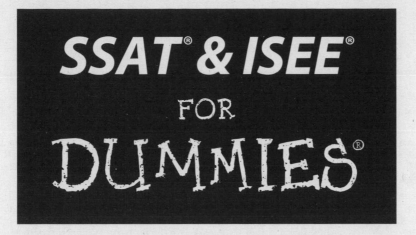

SSAT® & ISEE®
FOR
DUMMIES®

by Vince Kotchian and Curt Simmons

WILEY

John Wiley & Sons, Inc.

SSAT® & ISEE® For Dummies®

Published by
John Wiley & Sons, Inc.
111 River St.
Hoboken, NJ 07030-5774
www.wiley.com

WILEY

About the Authors

Vince Kotchian is a private test-prep tutor, admissions consultant, and freelance writer. Vince has worked with hundreds of students and has authored a variety of test-prep material for several different companies. Originally from Connecticut, Vince attended Boston College and now lives in San Diego. In his free time, he enjoys running, paddleboarding, and many other outdoor activities.

Curt Simmons is a professional educator and freelance writer. Curt holds a master's degree in education and has taught 6th through 12th grade students as well as adult learners. He's the author of numerous books about computers and technology and several test-prep titles on a variety of topics, including many *For Dummies* titles. Curt has also developed iPhone applications and has written custom courseware for several U.S. companies. When Curt isn't teaching or writing, he spends his time with his wife and two daughters and is perpetually remodeling his 100-year-old Victorian home. He lives in Texas, loves hanging out at his family cabin in Arkansas, and visits Hawaii as often as possible.

Dedication

Vince and Curt would like to dedicate this book to all the students who love learning and are constantly striving to do well in school. We're depending on you for the future!

Authors' Acknowledgments

Vince and Curt would like to thank Tracey Boggier for the green light for this project and for working so hard to bring this book to life. We owe a great debt of gratitude to Elizabeth Rea, our project editor, who gave us helpful guidance along the way and who kept everything moving in the right direction. Also, thanks to Jennette ElNaggar for the fine copyediting work and Anne Clark and Alan Gerstle for the technical review. Finally, thanks to Margot Hutchison, our literary agent, for bringing the book concept to us and for working out the details.

Publisher's Acknowledgments

We're proud of this book; please send us your comments at http://dummies.custhelp.com. For other comments, please contact our Customer Care Department within the U.S. at 877-762-2974, outside the U.S. at 317-572-3993, or fax 317-572-4002.

Some of the people who helped bring this book to market include the following:

Acquisitions, Editorial, and Vertical Websites

Project Editor: Elizabeth Rea

Acquisitions Editor: Tracy Boggier

Copy Editor: Jennette ElNaggar

Assistant Editor: David Lutton

Editorial Program Coordinator: Joe Niesen

Technical Editors: Anne Sutherland Clarke, Alan Gerstle

Editorial Manager: Michelle Hacker

Editorial Assistant: Alexa Koschier

Cover Photos: © iStockphoto.com / Steve Shepard

Cartoons: Rich Tennant (www.the5thwave.com)

Composition Services

Project Coordinator: Patrick Redmond

Layout and Graphics: Carl Byers, Carrie A. Cesavice, Joyce Haughey, Sennett Vaughan Johnson

Proofreaders: Lindsay Amones, Laura Bowman, Susan Moritz

Indexer: Potomac Indexing, LLC

Special Help: Caitlin Copple

Publishing and Editorial for Consumer Dummies

    Kathleen Nebenhaus, Vice President and Executive Publisher

    David Palmer, Associate Publisher

    Kristin Ferguson-Wagstaffe, Product Development Director

Publishing for Technology Dummies

    Andy Cummings, Vice President and Publisher

Composition Services

    Debbie Stailey, Director of Composition Services

Table of Contents

Introduction

*W*hen you first heard you needed to take either the SSAT or ISEE in order to gain admission to a private school you want to attend, your first thought probably wasn't very enthusiastic. On the other hand, you're a student, so you know a thing or two about taking tests, and you may be thinking, "Just another day, another test — no big deal."

But hang on to that thought. The SSAT and ISEE aren't like exams you're used to. The SSAT and ISEE are designed to test your achievement in school thus far — they're not subject matter exams or simply exams where you can study a few pages of notes and then hit the test with your short-term knowledge. No, the SSAT and ISEE are exams that find out how much you know about reading, writing, and math. The content can span all kinds of subjects and questions, and the goal isn't to see whether you know a block of material; the goal is to see what potential you have for success at a private school.

The good news is the SSAT and ISEE don't test little details about little details. You won't find any direct questions about science, history, music, art, and a whole host of potential topics. But don't misunderstand; the SSAT and ISEE aren't easy tests. They determine how well you read and write and how well you can solve math problems based on your grade level.

The worst thing about all of this is that you're under stringent time limits on each test, so you need some specific skills and tactics to do well. That point brings us to why we wrote this book: to help you prepare to take the test so you can do as well as possible. After all, scoring well on the test isn't just about what you know; it's about what you know about taking a test like the SSAT and ISEE. The good news is you've come to the right place to prepare. With *SSAT & ISEE For Dummies*, you discover how to tackle the test, manage your time, answer questions quickly and accurately, and get the best score possible. That, after all, is the goal.

About This Book

The SSAT and ISEE are two different exams that basically do the same thing. They're created by different companies that provide these *standardized* tests to private schools all over the United States. The exams help school officials and admissions officers determine your current ability, as compared to other students your age around the country. They then use this information to determine your likelihood of success at their school.

So what's the difference between the SSAT and the ISEE? Which one should you take? Your school may require one test over the other, so you may not even have an option. Be sure to check out the admissions requirements at your school so you know for sure. If you can take either one, you'll find that the two exams are very similar because they cover the same basic type of content: math, reading, language comprehension, and writing. You can find out more about the content on each exam in Chapter 1. So if you're on the fence about which exam you should take, check out that chapter before you do anything else in this book.

The SSAT provides lower and upper level exams, and the ISEE provides lower, middle, and upper level exams. Which exam you take depends on what grade you're in because they're designed for different grade levels. (Check out Chapter 1 for more info about the different levels of the SSAT and ISEE.)

Because the SSAT and ISEE consist of the same basic content, covering both exams in one book makes sense. We've organized this book to focus on different areas of the exam, such as reading, language, writing, and math. Throughout this book, you can find plenty of techniques, tools, and tips to help you get the best score in each section. We also include a bunch of practice questions and full-length practice exams because we believe that perfect practice makes perfect performance.

Conventions Used in This Book

To help you navigate this book, we use the following conventions:

- We use *italics* to introduce new terms. We especially use this in math and language chapters.

- **Boldface** shows you the action part of a list of steps or is used to highlight a main point or idea.

- Monofont is used to indicate a web address. If a web address is long, it may wrap to the next line in your book, but we don't include any extra dashes or anything if it breaks to a new line. In other words, just type the web address as you see it in the book, and it'll take you where you need to go.

- Some words appear in *this font*. These words are vocabulary words we've chosen to shine a spotlight on to help you prep for the exam.

- From time to time, you'll see sidebars, or blocks of text in shaded gray boxes, in various chapters. This extra info isn't critical but usually consists of additional information or stories that can help things make more sense. You can skip these sidebars if you're short on time, but do read them if you can.

Foolish Assumptions

We wrote this book for students like you, so we've assumed a few important things about you:

- You want to do well on the SSAT or ISEE, but you're not excited about having to take a standardized test. We get that (we've taken a bunch of tests over the years and aren't too excited about them either).

- You have lots of things you need to do each day, and studying for another test isn't exactly how you want to spend your time. The good news for you is we didn't fill this book with a bunch of stuff you don't need to know. If it's in here, it's important. In other words, we're not here to waste your time.

- You've taken English and math classes, and you have some writing experience, based on your grade level. With that thought in mind, our goal isn't to teach you everything there is to know about English, math, and writing (otherwise, this book would be the size of a car), but our goal *is* to show you what you need to know for the test and help you practice your skills.

- You're no dummy. In fact, we know you're already a successful student and you know a lot. You do well, and you want to continue doing well — after all, that's why you're reading this book.

How This Book Is Organized

Because this book covers two different exams that each have different levels, we took great care in organizing this book so you can make the most of it. We've organized it in such a way that you can find what you need quickly and easily. We also want this book to help you prepare for the SSAT and ISEE without wasting a second of your time, so we've included only what's really important for the exam. Here's what you'll find in this book.

Part 1: Paving the Way to Private School: Introducing the SSAT and ISEE

This part gives you an overview of the SSAT and ISEE. You find out what's on each exam, the different levels available, how to register for an exam, and some practical issues about getting ready for the test. You also discover some global test-taking skills, such as managing time limits and how to deal with questions you don't know or aren't sure about. This part gets you in on the ground floor and provides a solid foundation for the rest of your SSAT and ISEE study.

Part II: Ramping Up for the Verbal, Reading, and Essay Sections

This part explores what you need to know about the language parts of the exams. Here, you find a vocabulary primer, content chapters, and practice chapters for verbal reasoning, reading comprehension, and essay writing. The chapters explore content, how to answer questions, and how to improve your scores on these sections of the exams.

Part III: Tackling the Math Sections

If math isn't your strong suit, this section is for you. In this part, you focus on the kinds of math content you'll see on the exam, so you find content chapters and practice chapters for arithmetic, algebra, geometry, and word problems. We also help you know what kinds of math questions you'll see on the exam level you're taking, and what you can ignore, especially if you're taking a lower or middle level exam.

Part IV: SSAT Practice Exams

This part contains an upper level practice exam and two middle level practice exams for the SSAT. You find full-length exams with the exact number of questions and section time limits you'll face on the real test. Also, after each exam, we include a chapter that gives you the answers to the exam as well as an explanation for the correct answer.

Part V: ISEE Practice Exams

In this part, you find full-length practice exams for the upper, middle, and lower level ISEE. Each exam contains the exact number of questions and time limits you'll face on each section of the ISEE. We also include a chapter after each exam that contains the correct answers and an explanation for each correct answer.

Part VI: The Part of Tens

Every *For Dummies* book includes a Part of Tens. Here, you find two short chapters, each containing ten important tips about how to prepare for test day and how to calm those test jitters that affect so many of us.

Icons Used in This Book

Throughout the book, we include icons in the margin that direct your attention to content you should really pay attention to. We don't use icons just to make the page look cool, so if you see an icon, it's there for a reason — pay attention to it!

This icon points out information you should keep in mind. We often use this icon to note test-taking strategies, so be sure to pay attention when you see a paragraph accompanied by this icon.

Every standardized test has potential pitfalls in both strategy and content. We use Warning icons to alert you to common mistakes students make when they solve problems, answer questions, or even manage time limits.

Everything in the book is important, but some content is really important to remember. We add this icon next to content that you really need to remember for the test. Remember icons also accompany test-taking strategies you need to keep in mind for test day.

When you see this icon, you know you're going to practice the particular area of instruction covered in that section with a question like one you may see on the test. Each example question is followed by detailed explanations of how to most efficiently answer questions and avoid common pitfalls.

Where to Go from Here

Like every *For Dummies* book, you don't have to read this book in order from front to back cover, and you don't necessarily need to read the entire thing. Instead, you can skip around and spend more time on areas where you need additional work. For example, if you're a math whiz but you're not too great with vocabulary and answering reading comprehension questions, you can spend more time in Part II and less time in Part III. Also, because you're taking only one exam and this book covers two different exams based on different exam levels, you don't need to take every practice exam; however, the more practice you get, the better, so we recommend that you do. For example, if you're taking the upper level SSAT, consider taking the upper level ISEE practice test, too, because the exams are similar, and the extra practice certainly won't hurt.

Part I
Paving the Way to Private School: Introducing the SSAT and ISEE

"I always get a good night's sleep the day before a test so I'm relaxed and alert the next morning. Then I grab my pen, eat a banana, and I'm on my way."

In this part . . .

Part I helps you get your feet on solid ground by exploring the SSAT and ISEE as well as some study skills and techniques. We give you an idea of what to expect, how to register for an exam, and how the exam is structured, and then you explore some foundational test-taking principles and tactics that apply to all sections of the exam.

Chapter 1

Getting to Know the SSAT and ISEE

● ●

● ●

If you had a choice, you may choose a trip to the dentist over taking a standardized test like the SSAT or ISEE. Neither option is fun, but at least the dentist doesn't require you to study! Nevertheless, you're reading this book because you need to take either the SSAT or ISEE. You're taking one of these exams for entrance to a private school, and you know that your performance on the exam is important. The SSAT and ISEE aren't designed to be easy and fun, but they're important and necessary.

When you face a challenge, becoming a mini-expert on the subject is a good idea. After all, the more you know, the more likely you are to be successful. So this chapter is designed to fill you in on all the details of the tests. Before you start to study for the SSAT or ISEE, you need to know what these exams are all about, what kinds of content to expect, and how to register and prepare.

Approaching the SSAT and ISEE

When you first found out that you needed to take a test for admission to a school, you probably didn't jump for joy. No one likes taking tests, but at least at this point in your life, you're not a stranger to test days. After all, you've faced many of them in school so far.

Before you start thinking, "Great. Another test . . . ," you need to realize that the SSAT and ISEE aren't like the exams you take for a particular subject in school. In fact, these tests are very different from a typical school test, and that's why you need to ramp up your knowledge about the exams before you begin to study. In the following sections, we explain the purpose of taking the SSAT or ISEE, what to expect on either test, and how to prepare for test day.

Testing your ability

The SSAT and ISEE are different from typical school exams because they're *standardized* tests, meaning that the tests are designed to test your current ability. In other words, suppose you take a math test at school. More than likely, the math test explores several concepts and skills you've learned from a chapter or unit in your book, and therefore it tests your knowledge about those concepts. The SSAT and ISEE, however, aren't designed to test your knowledge.

The purpose of the SSAT and ISEE isn't to find out how smart you are. After all, human beings are so complex that no test really is able to measure that very well. Instead, the SSAT and ISEE help school administrators and admissions officers determine your current *ability* with a limited number of school subjects. Knowing your ability helps them determine your likelihood for success in their private school.

Unfortunately, all standardized tests (including college admission tests, like the SAT and ACT) aren't just about your current ability; they're also about your skill in test taking. To do well on the SSAT and ISEE, you have to know *how* to take the test. That's why this book is so important. We review content you need to know, but we also focus heavily on how to take the test so you can do as well as possible.

Knowing what to expect from test questions

Of course, the big question you want to know is what kinds of questions you'll see on the SSAT and ISEE. The good news is the exams are similar, and they don't test a lot of different things. The exams stick to a few basic categories: verbal, reading comprehension, math, and a writing sample. All the questions are multiple-choice except for the Writing section. This book focuses on the content you'll see, the kinds of questions you'll likely be asked, how to tackle those questions, and how to get the best score possible.

Another big question you may have is which test you should take. We answer that question this way: Suppose you're about to buy a new car. You're trying to decide between a Ford or Chevy, so which one should you pick? In truth, the decision is really yours. After all, they're both cars, and they do essentially the same thing. You just have to decide which one is best for you. In the same way, the SSAT and ISEE are both standardized tests designed to help you get into the school of your choice. They do the same thing, so it really comes down to deciding which test is best for you.

You may be applying to a school that requires one test over the other, but if you have a choice, you just need to check out the differences in the tests and make a decision. So turn to the "Getting to Know the SSAT" and "Scoping Out the ISEE" sections in this chapter to find out some specifics about each test.

Preparing yourself: Practice makes perfect

Okay, so you probably won't make a perfect score on either exam, but we wrote this book to help you do your very best. With that thought in mind, study the chapters carefully, try every practice question in every chapter, and take every practice test in the book. Additionally, you can take real practice tests from the good folks who write the SSAT and ISEE; just go to www.ssat.org and www.erblearn.org, respectively. Try the practice tests. If you have a choice of which test you can take for your desired school, try them both and see how you score on each one. You may find that you have an edge with one exam over the other, so by all means, take the test on which you perform best. However, some schools require a certain test, so be sure to check with an admissions officer at your desired school so you know what's required.

Getting to Know the SSAT

The SSAT (Secondary School Admission Test), developed by the Secondary School Admission Test Board (SSATB), explores your ability in a few distinct key areas. If you think about everything you know at this point in your life, you'll quickly realize that you've gathered massive amounts of information about all kinds of subjects. Not only that, but also you've learned to do all kinds of things. When you think about how much you really know, you'll quickly see that the SSAT tests very little of your knowledge. In fact, the SSAT focuses on a few subjects, divided into the following four basic sections:

- ✔ **Verbal:** The Verbal section tests your vocabulary mastery, verbal reasoning (also called *analogy*) skills, and your ability to relate ideas within the English language. Chapters 3 through 5 explore the Verbal section of the test and give you plenty of opportunities to practice sample questions.

- ✔ **Quantitative:** The Quantitative sections (or more easily, Math sections) test your ability to solve arithmetic, elementary algebra, and geometry problems. You answer both direct questions and word-based questions. Chapters 10 through 16 explore all these kinds of questions and present a bunch of practice questions as well.

- ✔ **Reading Comprehension:** The Reading Comprehension section of the exam tests your ability to read and understand a passage. You read a sample passage, answer a few questions about it, and then move on. You can find out about reading comprehension in Chapters 6 and 7.

- ✔ **Writing Sample:** The SSAT includes a Writing section as well. For this section, you write an essay based on the prompt, or topic, given to you. The Writing section of the test isn't scored; it's simply sent on to the school(s) to which you're applying for review. You need to do well on the Writing section because the school you want to attend is going to review it. You can find out how to ace the writing sample in Chapters 8 and 9.

That's it! The SSAT limits its questions to these four categories. You're not directly tested on your knowledge of science, social studies, art, music, technology, or anything else. The SSAT is strictly a language, math, reading, and writing exam. With the exception of the Writing section, all questions are multiple-choice.

In the following sections, we dig a little deeper into the structure of the test, how it's scored, how to register for the exam, and what you can and can't bring to the testing center on test day.

Exploring the structure of the SSAT

Each section of the SSAT has a time limit, which is common with standardized tests. If you had all the time you wanted, the test would certainly be easier because you could think more carefully and work at your own pace. But you don't have all the time in the world; for each section of the test, you have to contend with a time limit. Table 1-1 shows you how the SSAT is organized into sections and their corresponding time limits.

Table 1-1	Structure of the SSAT	
Section	*Questions*	*Time Limit*
Writing	One writing prompt	25 minutes
Quantitative	Two sections: 25 questions each, consisting of a mixture of different kinds of questions	30 minutes for each section
Reading Comprehension	One section: 40 questions based on about 7 reading passages	40 minutes
Verbal	One section: 30 synonym and 30 analogy questions	30 minutes

When you think about this table for a moment, you may get a sinking feeling. You're probably thinking, "Wait! I have 60 questions on the Verbal section and only 30 minutes? That's only 30 seconds per question!" Exactly. You may also realize that you have 40 reading comprehension questions but only one minute per question, not including the time it takes to read the passages.

As you can see, the time limit will be a struggle, but don't worry: We explore tactics in Chapters 2 and 4 and throughout the book to help you make the most of your time.

Separating the upper and lower level SSAT

The SSAT has two different versions — a lower level test and an upper level test. The only difference between these two levels is the difficulty. The lower level test questions are tailored for students currently in grades 5 through 7, and the upper level test is tailored for students currently in grades 8 through 11. Other than that, the tests are exactly the same in terms of the sections, number of questions, and time limits.

Scoring the SSAT

As we noted earlier, the Writing section of the SSAT isn't scored; your essay is simply sent to the school(s) to which you're applying for review. The rest of the exam is scored, however, and is also sent to the desired schools. The following sections explain how the questions are graded, what exactly is sent to your desired school(s), and how the schools use your scores.

How questions are graded

When you take the SSAT, you answer a series of multiple-choice questions across several different sections (described earlier in this section). Like all tests you take, the idea is to get as many questions correct as possible. However, that's where the similarity ends. Questions aren't just counted right or wrong, so it's not that simple.

Each section of the SSAT is graded in the following ways:

- For every question you answer correctly, you get 1 point.
- For each question you answer incorrectly, 1/4 point is deducted.
- Questions you leave blank aren't scored; they don't count as right or wrong.

At first glance, you may think you should answer every question you're sure about and simply avoid questions you're not sure about or don't know. However, it's not that simple because educated guessing can really help raise your score. In fact, the process of elimination in multiple-choice questions and educated guessing are both major players in getting the best score possible. We explore this technique in detail in Chapter 2.

What is sent to your school

After you finish the SSAT, your percentage of correct answers is calculated into what's called a *scaled score*. A scaled score just means that your raw score is reported in such a way that it has a meaningful relationship to the scores of others who take the test. So for the lower level test (grades 5 through 7), the three Verbal, Quantitative, and Reading Comprehension sections all receive a scaled score of 440 to 710, for a total scaled score range of 1320 to 2130.

For the upper level test (grades 8 through 11), the three Verbal, Quantitative, and Reading Comprehension sections receive a scaled score of 500 to 800, for a total scaled score range of 1500 to 2400. Naturally, you want to score as high as possible on each section in order to get the highest possible total scaled score.

In addition to your total scaled score and scaled scores for each section of the exam, the following information is also reported to your school:

- **SSAT Percentile Ranks:** The SSAT ranks your performance for each category by comparing your score to the scores of other students who've taken the SSAT in the past three years. You get a ranking of 1 to 99 percent, showing where your score falls in relation to the scores of others. For example, say your percentile rank on the Reading Comprehension is 85 percent. This score means that you scored better or equal to 85 percent of the other students on the Reading Comprehension section. Naturally, the higher your percentage score, the better.

- **Estimated National Percentile Rank (NPR):** This percentile score, provided for grades 5 through 9 only, compares your score to the national student population at large, not only students who've taken the SSAT. For example, if your estimated national percentile rank is 85 percent on the Quantitative section of the test, you're estimated to score better or equal to 85 percent of all students in your grade in the nation.

- **Predicted 12th Grade SAT Score:** This report simply guesses what you're likely to make on the SAT as a 12th grader. This information is reported for students currently in grades 7 through 10 only. This predicted score doesn't mean much because it's just a guess about your future performance, so don't let it rattle you if you don't score as high as you'd hoped to in this category.

How your school uses the score

The SSAT provides some interesting information about your performance, but in the end, the only thing that really matters is how the school you're applying to uses the information. So how does that work?

Each school has its own admission standards and methods for evaluating admission candidates. A school may look at your SSAT and look for a minimum total score. They may look for specific scores on certain sections, such as Math. They may especially look at your writing sample, too.

On the other hand, some schools use a *portfolio* approach to student admission, where your SSAT is just one piece of the puzzle. They may equally weigh your performance at your previous school, letters of recommendation, or anything else they want to see in an application.

In the end, no standard way exists for how schools use the SSAT — it's all up to the individual school. Check out the admission requirements for the school(s) you're applying to and find out whether certain SSAT scores are expected or if the SSAT score is used in a more global way for admission. How your school uses your SSAT score is completely at its discretion.

Registering for the SSAT

Several important things you need to know about registering for the SSAT include registration information, dates, and fees. Because these factors are always changing, be sure to check out www.ssat.org. Here, you can find out the latest information about registering for a test, and you can even register online.

The three types of SSAT test administrations are

- **SSAT National Test:** *National test* simply means that the test is given on a particular Saturday at many testing sites in the United States, Canada, and at other international locations. The national test is given eight different times a year; you can take the national test several times if you're trying to hit a certain score. In fact, you can take it every time it's offered. You can register for a national test by mail, fax, and online. You can also register late if space is available, although additional fees may apply.

- **SSAT Flex Test:** A *flex test* is a group of tests or an individual test given on any other date besides a national test date. A particular school or educational consultant may require you to take a flex test (it's not something you can simply choose to do on your own). If you're required to take a flex test, you can take the test only one time in a given year. See your school administrators or consultant for information about registering for a flex test.

- **SSAT Regional Flex Test:** Some regional *consortia* (a group of schools) offer the SSAT on a specific date other than the national test date. These schools may get together and offer the test one time at a particular testing location. The same flex test rules apply to a regional flex test, so get more information from your school if a flex test is required.

If you observe a Saturday Sabbath, you can register to take the test on Sunday instead of Saturday. The SSAT website provides information about how to register for a Sunday exam as well. After registration is complete, you'll receive an admission ticket, which allows you to enter the testing center.

Knowing what to bring to the SSAT testing center

When you take the SSAT, the last thing you want to do is forget something you need or bring something you shouldn't. So make sure you bring the following items with you:

- **SSAT admission ticket:** You receive your SSAT admission ticket when you register for the test. Be sure to put it in a safe place and don't forget where that is.

- **Birth certificate, Social Security card, school report card, school ID, passport, driver's license, or green card:** You need to bring only one of these items with you, which verifies your identity and shows the test administrators that you are who you say you are and not someone else taking the test for you.

- **Two sharpened #2 pencils:** Make sure the pencils are #2 (this distinction is often labeled on the box and the pencil itself) because other kinds may not be read correctly by the scoring machine.

- ✓ **A good eraser:** The last thing you want to happen is to not be able to erase an answer choice you marked incorrectly, so either make sure your pencils have good erasers on them or bring an additional one.

- ✓ **Two blue or black pens:** The test requires you to write your essay in pen, so be sure to bring a couple of blue or black pens that work well.

- ✓ **A jacket or sweater:** Because you never know what the temperature will be in the testing room, wearing a short-sleeved shirt and having a jacket or sweater to layer with is a good idea. That way, you can adjust your clothing so you're comfortable. Students who are cold or too warm often don't do as well on exams, so keep this point in mind.

Just as importantly, you want to make sure you *don't* bring any of these items to the testing center — if you do, you may be sent home:

- ✓ Books
- ✓ Calculator
- ✓ Paper (including scratch paper; the testing center provides scratch paper for the test)
- ✓ Phone
- ✓ Watch with alarm
- ✓ Any other electronic devices

Also, no visitors are allowed in the testing room, so you'll have to leave your kid brother at home.

Most exams begin at 9 a.m. and end around 12 p.m. Check your admission ticket for details and make sure you arrive at least 30 minutes early so you have plenty of time to check in and get ready for the test. You may not be allowed to take the test if you're late, so make sure you get there early!

Scoping Out the ISEE

The ISEE (Independent School Entrance Exam) is developed and administered by the Educational Records Bureau, which has existed since 1927. Like the SSAT, the ISEE is a standardized test, which means that its goal is to test your achievement level based on the performance of other students in your grade level. What's important to remember is the ISEE isn't an IQ test or anything like that. It doesn't measure how smart you are or your potential for success in the future. It's simply a tool to see how much you've achieved in school so far.

Like the SSAT and other aptitude tests, the ISEE indirectly tests your ability to perform well on a test. In other words, you not only need to know some math and English to do well on the ISEE, but you also need some skills and tactics to take the test itself. That's why we wrote this book. We review content you need to know, but we also focus heavily on how to take the test so you can do as well as possible.

In the following sections, we explore all there is to know about the ISEE, including a breakdown of the questions and sections on the test, the different levels of the ISEE, how the test is scored, how you go about registering for the exam, and what you should and shouldn't bring with you to the testing center.

Understanding what's on the ISEE

Quick — when did Cortez conquer the Aztec empire? Not sure? Don't worry; you won't see questions like this on the ISEE. Actually, the ISEE tests very little of what you already know. The exam focuses only on your ability to read and answer questions about the reading passages, to handle English language questions, to write effectively, and to solve math questions. With those ideas in mind, the ISEE is divided into four basic sections:

✔ **Verbal Reasoning:** The Verbal section tests your vocabulary mastery and your ability to relate ideas within the English language. Chapters 3 through 5 explore the Verbal section of the test and give you plenty of opportunities to practice sample questions.

✔ **Math (Quantitative Reasoning and Mathematics Achievement):** The Math sections test your ability to solve arithmetic, elementary algebra, and geometry problems. You answer both direct questions and word-based questions. The exam breaks all these concepts into two different sections so you don't have to answer every math question at one time. Chapters 10 through 16 explore all these kinds of questions and present a bunch of practice questions as well.

✔ **Reading Comprehension:** The Reading Comprehension section of the exam tests your ability to read and understand a passage. You read a sample passage, answer a few questions about it, and then move on. You can find out about reading comprehension in Chapters 6 and 7.

✔ **Essay:** The ISEE includes an Essay section as well. For this section, you write an essay based on the prompt, or topic, given to you. Like the SSAT, the Essay section of the test isn't scored; it's simply sent on to the school(s) to which you're applying for review. You need to do well on the Essay section because the school you want to attend is going to review it. You can find out how to ace the writing sample in Chapters 8 and 9.

That's it! The ISEE limits its questions to these four categories. You're not directly tested on your knowledge of science, social studies, art, music, technology, or anything else. The ISEE is strictly a language, math, reading, and writing exam. With the exception of the Essay section, all questions are multiple-choice.

Comparing the upper, middle, and lower level ISEE

The ISEE is a little different from the SSAT because it has three versions: The upper level test is for students entering grades 9 through 12; the middle level test is for students entering grades 7 and 8; and the lower level test is for students entering grades 5 and 6. So what's the difference between the three? The upper level test is more difficult and the middle and lower tests are progressively easier. The only other difference is the upper and middle level tests include *quantitative comparison questions* in the Quantitative section, which are absent from the lower level test. (Quantitative comparison questions are math questions that ask you to compare the sizes, or quantities, of two mathematical expressions.) Other than that, the tests are exactly the same in terms of the number and types of sections, although they do vary just a bit with the number of questions on each level.

Each section of the ISEE has a time limit, which is common for all standardized tests. If you had all the time you wanted, you'd probably score higher because you could work at your own pace. But you don't have all the time in the world; for each section of the test, you have to contend with a time limit. Take a look at the next three sections that show you what you can expect on each level of the ISEE. Although the time limit will be a struggle, don't worry: We explore tactics throughout the book to help you make the most of your time (check out Chapters 2 and 4 for details).

Upper level ISEE

The upper level ISEE (for grades 9 through 12) is divided into five parts with a total testing time of 2 hours and 40 minutes. Table 1-2 breaks down the sections in this test.

Table 1-2	Structure of Upper Level ISEE	
Section	**Questions**	**Time Limit**
Verbal Reasoning	40 questions	20 minutes
Quantitative Reasoning	37 questions	35 minutes
Reading Comprehension	36 questions based on about 6 reading passages	35 minutes
Mathematics Achievement	47 questions	40 minutes
Essay	One writing prompt	30 minutes

Middle level ISEE

The middle level ISEE (for grades 7 and 8) is divided into five parts with a total testing time of 2 hours and 40 minutes. Table 1-3 shows you what to expect.

Table 1-3	Structure of Middle Level ISEE	
Section	**Questions**	**Time Limit**
Verbal Reasoning	40 questions	20 minutes
Quantitative Reasoning	37 questions	35 minutes
Reading Comprehension	36 questions based on about 6 reading passages	35 minutes
Mathematics Achievement	47 questions	40 minutes
Essay	One writing prompt	30 minutes

Lower level ISEE

The lower level ISEE exam (for grades 5 and 6) is divided into five parts with a total testing time of 2 hours and 20 minutes. Check out Table 1-4 to see how many questions are in each section and what the time limits are.

Table 1-4	Structure of Lower Level ISEE	
Section	**Questions**	**Time Limit**
Verbal Reasoning	34 questions	20 minutes
Quantitative Reasoning	38 questions	35 minutes
Reading Comprehension	25 questions based on about 5 reading passages	25 minutes
Mathematics Achievement	30 questions	30 minutes
Essay	One writing prompt	30 minutes

Scoring the ISEE

As we noted earlier, the Essay section of the ISEE isn't scored, but the essay is sent to the school(s) to which you're applying for review. The rest of the exam's scores are also sent to the desired schools. The scores and writing sample may be sent to up to six schools or counselors. However, if you want to send the scores to more than six schools or counselors, you can do so for an additional fee. After the test, the scores are typically sent to schools and counselors within 7 to 10 days.

The following sections explore a few issues you need to know: how questions are graded, what exactly is sent to your desired school(s), and how schools use your scores.

How questions are graded

When you take the ISEE, you answer a series of multiple-choice questions across several different sections. Like all tests you take, the idea is to get as many questions correct as possible. The good news is the ISEE doesn't penalize you for guessing. In other words, if you answer a question incorrectly or if you skip it, you don't lose points. You only get points for questions that are answered correctly. So your best bet is to try and answer as many questions as you possibly can. Even if you don't know the exact answer to a question, you can still guess the correct answer and may earn points that way.

Because the exam is mostly a multiple-choice exam, guessing and the process of elimination are tools that can help you increase your score. We explore this technique in detail in Chapter 2.

What is sent to your school

After you finish the ISEE, your percentage of correct answers is calculated into what's called a *scaled score*. This just means that your raw score (the number of questions you answered correctly) is reported in such a way that it has a meaningful relationship to the scores of all others who take the test. ISEE scaled scores for each section of the test range from 760 to 940; the higher the score, the better.

In addition to your total scaled score and scaled scores for each section of the exam, the following information is also reported to your school:

- ✔ **ISEE Percentile Ranks:** The ISEE ranks your performance for each category by comparing your score to the scores of other students who've taken the ISEE in the past three years. You get a ranking of 1 to 99 percent, showing where your score falls in relation to the scores of others. For example, say your percentile rank on the Reading Comprehension is 85 percent. This score means that you scored better or equal to 85 percent of the other students on the Reading Comprehension section. Naturally, the higher your percentage score, the better.

- ✔ **Stanine (standard nine):** This rank is an abbreviated version of the percentile rank. With this rank, students are divided into nine possible groupings. Stanine 1 provides a percentile rank of 1 to 3 percent; stanine 2, 4 to 10 percent; stanine 3, 11 to 22 percent; stanine 4, 23 to 39 percent; stanine 5, 40 to 59 percent; stanine 6, 60 to 76 percent; stanine 7, 77 to 88 percent; stanine 8, 89 to 95 percent; and stanine 9, 96 to 99 percent. These more general rankings aren't as specific as the percentile rank, but admissions officers sometimes use them to generally compare the performance of a group of potential students.

- ✔ **Analysis:** The ISEE also provides an analysis section that reports the number of correct questions per section as well as specific results data for different types of questions.

How your school uses the score

The ISEE provides some interesting information about your performance, but in the end, the only thing that really matters is how the school you're applying to uses the information, and each school uses ISEE scoring information in different ways.

Each school has its own admission standards and methods for evaluating admission candidates. A school may look at your ISEE and look for a minimum total score. They may look for specific scores on certain sections, such as Math. They may especially look at your writing sample, too.

On the other hand, some schools use a *portfolio* approach to student admission where your ISEE is just one piece of the puzzle. They may equally weigh your performance at your previous school, letters of recommendation, or anything else they want to see in an application.

Check out the admission requirements for the school(s) you're applying to and find out whether certain ISEE scores are expected or if the ISEE score is used in a more global way for admission. How your school uses your ISEE scores is completely at their discretion.

Registering for the ISEE

Several important things you need to know about registering for the ISEE include registration information, dates, and fees. These factors are always changing, so check out www.erblearn.org/parents/admission/isee. Here, you can find out the latest information about registering for a test, and you can even register online.

The online registration allows you to locate and register for an open test site during various times throughout the year. However, some schools have closed registrations where they test their existing students or students who are applying to the school. Always check with the school you're applying to for more information about registering for a test because closed registrations must be handled by the specific school. Just start with the school's admission officer and go from there. After you register for a test, you'll be able to reschedule the test if necessary or access additional information about inclement weather, testing accommodations, and so on.

Figuring out what to bring to the ISEE testing center

When you take the ISEE, you need to bring the following items with you to the testing center:

- ✔ **ISEE admission ticket:** You receive your ISEE admission ticket when you register for the test. Be sure to put it in a safe place and don't forget where that is.

- ✔ **Birth certificate, Social Security card, school report card, school ID, passport, driver's license, or green card:** You need to bring only one of these items with you, which verifies your identity and shows the test administrators that you are who you say you are and not someone else taking the test for you.

- ✔ **Four sharpened #2 pencils:** Make sure you bring #2 pencils (this distinction is often labeled on the box and the pencil itself) because other types of pencils may not be read by the scoring machine.

- ✔ **A good eraser:** Nothing is quite as frustrating or nerve-racking as having an eraser that doesn't erase — or not having an eraser at all. Bringing a good eraser is important so you can cleanly erase any mistakes on your answer sheet.

- ✔ **Two blue or black pens:** The ISEE requires you to write your essay in pen, so be sure to bring a couple blue or black pens that work well.

- ✔ **A snack:** The ISEE provides two five-minute breaks during the test. During a break, you may eat a small snack if you want, so bring something along in case you get hungry.

- ✔ **A jacket or sweater:** Because you never know what the temperature of the testing room will be, wearing a short-sleeved shirt and having a jacket or sweater to layer with is a good idea. That way, you can adjust your clothing so you're comfortable. Students who are cold or too warm often don't do as well on exams, so keep this point in mind.

Just as importantly, you want to make sure you *don't* bring any of these items to the testing center — if you do, you may be sent home:

- ✔ Books
- ✔ Calculator
- ✔ Paper (including scratch paper; the testing center provides scratch paper for the test)
- ✔ Phone
- ✔ Watch with alarm
- ✔ Any other electronic devices

Finally, no visitors are allowed in the testing center.

Most exams begin at 9 a.m. and end around 12 p.m. Check your admission ticket for details and make sure you arrive at least 30 minutes early so you have plenty of time to check in and get ready for the test. You may not be allowed to take the test if you're late, so make sure you get there early!

Chapter 2

Picking Up Study Skills and Techniques for Testing Success

In This Chapter
▶ Watching and managing time limits
▶ Understanding the process of elimination
▶ Guessing at answers the right way

Both the SSAT and ISEE test your ability in four basic yet specific areas — verbal skills, reading, math, and writing. Within these four basic areas, a lot of variety occurs in what the test writers ask because the categories are so broad. The good news is the test writers aren't terribly creative, and they tend to stick to foundational issues within English, reading comprehension, and math. The writing sample isn't scored but is simply sent to your school for evaluation by admissions officers.

For each section of the exam, you need some specialized skills and tactics to help you perform to the best of your ability on the test, and we explore those throughout Parts II and III of this book. But you also need three global testing skills and techniques that apply to every single question of every section on the test: time management, process of elimination, and guessing. The goal of this chapter is to help you understand and use these three testing strategies so you can practice them as you continue studying for the actual test.

Clocking Your Time

One of the most frustrating things about any standardized test, such as the SSAT and ISEE (and the SAT and ACT college entrance exams), is the time limit. You have a time limit for each individual section of the test rather than an overall time limit for the entire exam.

So far in school, you most likely haven't had to worry about time limits on tests. For example, when you take a test, you often get the entire period to finish the test; if you need more time, the teacher usually gives you some leeway and lets you finish it later. So you're probably used to spending your time working on the test and focusing on doing your very best; you're likely not used to worrying about a strict time limit. Well, that's no longer the case, at least with the SSAT and ISEE: The time limit is a major player in your testing strategy, and it can determine how well you perform on the test. Getting that concept in mind right away is important.

For example, consider the Reading Comprehension section of the test. No matter whether you're taking the SSAT or ISEE or what level you're at, you have less than one minute to answer each reading comprehension question, but that time limit doesn't include actually reading the passages. If you take reading into account, you have much less than one minute to answer every question. So you can't spend much time reading the passages or answering questions — you have to move very quickly.

With this reality in mind, you need to follow a few important strategies, which we discuss in the following sections, to help you manage your time.

Practice, practice, practice

One of the best things you can do to prepare for the time limits of the actual exam is get in the habit of working through questions quickly. And you do that by practicing.

Fortunately, we give you a lot of opportunities to practice throughout the book. In Parts II and III, you find content chapters for each type of question where you can review important skills, followed by practice chapters with sample questions. When you practice, start out slowly until you get used to the testing format and managing questions, and then try answering each question as quickly as possible. In other words, stress yourself a bit by timing yourself to make sure you keep moving.

When you're ready to take the practice exams toward the back of this book, strictly follow the time limit for each section and don't let yourself run over the allotted time. Doing so helps you get familiar with how quickly you need to work on the real exam. Practicing the speed you need to work gives you a major advantage on test day, so don't waste the opportunity.

Resist the urge to finish

As a student, you probably tend to think about a test in terms of finishing the test and answering all the questions. After all, teachers typically count off, or subtract, points when you take a test. In other words, the teacher deducts a certain number of points for each question you miss and determines your final score based on how many questions you answered incorrectly.

The SSAT and ISEE don't work this way; instead, they *add* points to calculate your final score. Your score is based on the number of questions you answer correctly. Neither test counts off, or subtracts, points if you leave a question blank — that question simply doesn't count for anything. In the end, the more questions you answer correctly, the better your score, so finishing a section of the test may not be the best strategy for you.

On the SSAT and ISEE, finishing most of a section and getting many questions correct is better than finishing the entire section and getting fewer questions correct. Because skipped questions don't count against your score, finishing a section of the test doesn't necessarily mean you'll score well. You need to get as many questions correct as possible — that's how you get a good score. So break away from the answer-all-questions mentality for the SSAT and ISEE, and remember that the goal is to answer as many questions correctly as possible. If you're running out of time, deciding whether to guess at unanswered questions depends on which test you're taking. We explore guessing strategies for both tests later in this chapter.

Skip questions

Say you hit a really difficult math question on the SSAT or ISEE. You believe you may be able to solve the question and answer it correctly with a little time, but the problem is, time is something you don't really have. What should you do? *Skip it.*

Why the time limit?

In the real world, no one ever says, "Solve this problem in less than a minute." In the real world, you have a reasonable amount of time to solve problems in school and life as well. So why the time limits on standardized tests, like the SSAT and ISEE? After all, if you had more time, you'd probably score better.

Here's the deal: A standardized test works on a standard so your score is comparable to the scores of other people taking the test. This means that your score is comparable to the scores of other students who must also answer questions under the exact same time limits. Also, the test creators aren't so concerned with whether you can figure out questions; they want to see how fast you can work and how quickly you can answer questions without having time to dwell on them. Because everyone taking the test has the same stress, you end up with an accurate view of how well you can perform based on how well other students can perform. Fun? No way, but that's the reasoning behind the system.

 An easy question counts as much as a hard question. Part of your time-saving strategy should be to answer easy questions correctly and skip really difficult questions. You can always come back to hard questions and work on them if you have time, but working on a hard question when you may be able to answer two or three others correctly in the same amount of time makes little sense. You need to make a quick decision on hard questions, so as soon as you realize the question is difficult, pull the trigger and move on. Come back to it if you have time.

 Write things down. Writing down math steps, main passage ideas or key words in the reading comprehension, and so on makes your work faster and easier because you're not depending on your brain to help you remember everything. Use your pencil and make it work for you as you plow through the test.

Using the Process of Elimination

 Except for the writing sample, all questions on the SSAT and ISEE are multiple-choice. The SSAT includes five answer choices and the ISEE gives four. A typical question looks something like this:

How does the author feel about NASA's space exploration budget?

(A) The author believes that NASA wastes too much money.

(B) The author believes the space program has benefits but needs more creative fundraising methods.

(C) The author believes space exploration is more important than other governmental programs.

(D) The author doesn't state an opinion about NASA's budgeting.

(E) The author believes NASA should have more governmental funding.

As you can see, you have a question and some answer choices. Here's the reality: The answers on the SSAT and ISEE are always in front of you. One of the answers is correct. You simply need to figure out which answer choice is the right one. Of course, that's easier said than done, but one of the most powerful tools in your testing arsenal is the process of elimination.

Using the *process of elimination* simply means you very quickly rule out answer choices you know are incorrect. For example, if you have a question with five answer choices and can eliminate three of them, you're left with two choices. Maybe the two choices are similar or maybe you're not even sure of the answer, but by using the process of elimination, you give yourself a 50-50 shot of guessing the correct answer. In a nutshell, the more answer choices you eliminate, the more likely you are to answer the question correctly.

The following question is a synonym question. You see a word in capital letters, and you're given five answer choices (SSAT) or four answer choices (ISEE). You want to choose the word that's closest in meaning to the word in capital letters.

DISENCHANTED:

(A) Regroup

(B) Specious

(C) Let down

(D) Encouraged

(E) Inclined

If you know what *disenchanted* means, the question is probably easy. However, if you don't know or you're not sure, the process of elimination can help. First, notice that the word in question uses the prefix *dis-,* which means not. (See Chapter 3 for a review of common prefixes.) So you know that *disenchanted* means *not* something. Looking at the answer choices, you can eliminate Choices (A), (D), and (E), because you know that *dis-* means not, or something negative, and all these words are positive in some way. So you're left with Choices (B) and (C). The good news is if you still don't know the answer, you have at least a 50-50 shot of guessing the correct one. The correct answer is Choice **(C).** *Disenchanted* means let down. You may think, "Wait a minute! That's not technically a synonym!" And you're right. The SSAT bends the rules a bit with synonym questions while the ISEE tends to stick to exact synonym words (including words that are the same parts of speech).

In the Verbal and Reading sections of the exam, you need to find the *best* answer to the question. In other words, although you may see a couple of similar answer choices, you need to choose the best answer for the question. In order to do that, you need to consider *all* the answer choices. So typically, you may read a question, start scanning the answer choices, see that Choice (B) looks great, mark your answer sheet, and move on without considering the other options. Doing so is a mistake because Choice (D) may actually be a better answer. The process of elimination helps you avoid this mistake because you get in the habit of scanning all the answer choices in an effort to rule out ones you know are wrong and narrow in on the best one. Naturally, some answer choices will be obviously wrong, so you don't need to spend a lot of time on those, but for the answer choices that are close, make sure to always choose the best answer.

Most students read the question and try to find the correct answer in the answer choices first. Instead, read the question and quickly eliminate answers you know are incorrect. Doing so helps you focus on a few possible answers, greatly increasing your odds of answering the question correctly. The process of elimination is a powerful tool on a standardized test, so be sure to use it.

But I thought it said . . .

Students often make what teachers call *careless mistakes* on exams, meaning they answer a question incorrectly because they misread the question or misread an answer choice. We don't care for the term *careless mistake* because these types of mistakes aren't really careless. They happen because students are under stress and under a strict time limit.

Because you have to work quickly on the SSAT and ISEE, misunderstanding a question or an answer choice and answering the question incorrectly is easy. Unfortunately, there's no easy way to eliminate reading errors, and you're likely to make a few on the SSAT and ISEE. But here's a little trick: When you read a question and its answer choices, use your pencil as a pointer. Although doing so may seem a little juvenile, pointing at the words you're reading can help you reduce the likelihood of misreading and, therefore, misunderstanding a question or the answer choices.

Figuring Out a Guessing Strategy

Guessing is an important strategy that can help you increase your exam score. You'll face many questions that you're just not sure about, and guessing can help you get some of those questions right. However, you need a good strategy to make it work for you. Guessing works differently on the ISEE and SSAT, as you find out in the following sections.

Guessing on the ISEE

If you're taking the ISEE, your guessing strategy is simple. The ISEE grades your test by giving you a point for every correct answer. If you miss a question or if you leave a question blank, you get 0 points for it. In other words, on the ISEE, you're not penalized for guessing, so if you guess at a question and miss it, you don't lose any points. It's the same as if you just didn't answer the question at all.

The strategy for the ISEE is this: Guess on questions you don't know — here's how:

- ✏ If you face a question you're not sure about, use the process of elimination to give yourself the best guessing odds, and then choose an answer and move on. (Review the previous section on process of elimination.)

- ✏ If you face a question you don't have a clue about, choose a letter, such as Choice (C), and just guess. Use the same letter on any other question you don't know.

- ✏ When you're about a minute away from your time limit on a section, pick a letter and quickly bubble in all the questions you didn't have time to answer.

    Often, people say that Choice (C) is the most likely answer choice, but that's not necessarily true. However, choosing the same letter for each question you guess on is important because you increase your odds of gaining a point or two. If you randomly select different letters, the odds of getting one or two more points goes way down because you're less likely to randomly guess a correct answer from the answer choices. So choose a guessing letter and stick to it — Choice (C) works fine.

Guessing on the SSAT

The SSAT is different because you're penalized for guessing. For every question you answer correctly, you get 1 point. If you answer a question incorrectly, you lose 1/4 point. Questions you leave blank get assigned a 0, so they don't add or take away points from your score. Because you lose 1/4 point for each question you answer incorrectly, you need a targeted guessing strategy that plays the odds.

Here's how you should guess on the SSAT:

- ✔ If you face a question you're not sure about but can eliminate three answer choices, you're left with a 50-50 chance of guessing the correct answer. In this case, guessing is worth the risk.

- ✔ If you face a question you don't know very well but can eliminate at least one answer choice, you may want to guess, as long as you're sure that one answer choice is incorrect. Sometimes a gut feeling about the correct answer is right, so usually, you should guess on a question like this one. If you can eliminate an answer choice or two but don't have a gut feeling about the other answer choices, you may want to skip the question. For questions like this, you just have to make a judgment call based on how you feel about the question at the moment.

- ✔ If you face a question you don't know and you can't eliminate any answer choices, leave the question blank and move on.

- ✔ If you haven't finished a section and you're running out of time, leave all unanswered questions blank. Don't randomly fill in an answer choice for each one, because you lose points for guessing incorrectly.

In a nutshell, guessing can help you on the SSAT, but you have to play the odds. Let the process of elimination help increase your odds, but for questions you don't know or don't have time to work on, just leave them blank.

Part II

Ramping Up for the Verbal, Reading, and Essay Sections

The 5th Wave   By Rich Tennant

©RICHTENNANT

"I hate the synonyms part of this test.
I always get stumped, stymied,
and puzzled."

In this part . . .

Part II shows you how to master the Verbal, Reading, and Essay sections of the test. We give you advice on how to approach verbal questions, manage critical reading, and write a winning essay. The chapters in this part have plenty of examples as well as practice questions to let you practice your test-taking skills.

Chapter 3

Defining Your Vocabulary Skills

In This Chapter

▶ Discovering the best way to study vocabulary

▶ Recognizing the meaning of vocab words with roots, prefixes, and suffixes

▶ Memorizing common words for testing success

*N*either the SSAT nor ISEE gives you a vocabulary test. You won't see a section that asks you to choose a definition for a particular word — at least not directly. However, both the SSAT and ISEE ask you the meaning of words within the context of a reading passage (see Chapters 6 and 7). The SSAT may require you to understand some complicated words in analogy questions, and both exams require you to choose synonyms of difficult words.

So even though the exams don't provide a vocabulary test, having a good knowledge of a vast number of vocabulary words is certainly necessary. The good news: You already know a lot of vocabulary. After all, you use words every day when you speak, read, write, and even think. Instead of telling you to crack open your dictionary and start studying, we help you target your vocabulary with some specific word skills as well as review common words you may see on the exam. In this chapter, we help you build the skills you need to answer verbal questions and give you plenty of word lists to expand your vocabulary.

Studying Vocabulary

Here's a secret: You really can't study vocabulary. Sure, a teacher can give you a list of ten words and say, "Know these words for the quiz tomorrow." That's easy enough (although not much fun!). However, when you tackle an exam like the SSAT or ISEE, you don't get a list of words beforehand to memorize for the test. Instead, the test writers can ask you about any word they choose. Naturally, you can't memorize the entire dictionary, so you want to target your vocabulary study in a way that can help you decipher words you may not know, using prefixes and suffixes and even building your vocabulary skill a bit as well.

We all learn in different ways, so figure out how you most easily memorize information and take advantage of it. After all, you'll save time this way, and most importantly, you'll learn the words.

In the following sections, we outline a few different ways you can study and learn vocab words for the exam. Pick the method that works best for you and start studying!

Flipping through flashcards

The old tried-and-true method of flashcards is a great way to study and review vocabulary words. In this chapter, we provide several lists of words you should know because they have a tendency to show up on the exams. You can study the words in the chapter as they are, but you'll probably learn them faster if you grab some plain note cards, write the vocabulary word on one side, and write the definition on the other. Then, review the words and definitions until you can simply look at the word and know the definition without peeking.

Although traditional flashcards work well for many people, you may find that you learn vocabulary words more quickly by hearing the word and the definition several times, rather than looking at it in a book or on a card. If this method works for you, create an audio set of flashcards, using the voice recording feature on a phone, iPod, or your computer. Then, you can listen to yourself state the word and definition as many times as you want.

Memorizing mnemonic devices

A *mnemonic device* is something you use to help you remember something else. As you review vocabulary, you want all the help you can get, and for many people, mnemonic devices do the job with tricky concepts and vocabulary. Although a mnemonic can be virtually anything, most people use some kind of verbal cue to help remember something, such as a song, a poem, or words that rhyme with other words. For example, piano students are often taught the lines on the staff of the treble clef (EGBDF) by using the mnemonic *Every Good Boy Does Fine.* The reason is simple: You can remember this sentence much more easily than a string of letters that otherwise makes no sense.

With vocabulary, you may find that using a mnemonic device can help you remember particularly troublesome words that you just can't seem to memorize any other way. You can use any mnemonic you like, but in most cases, a defining word that rhymes with the vocabulary word or some kind of catchy phrase is often best.

For example, say you're struggling with the vocab word *suffice,* which means enough of something. A mnemonic can be something like *suffice is stuffed.* Of course, stuffed isn't the exact definition, but this little catchphrase is enough to remind you of what the word *suffice* actually means.

Mnemonics are great for troublesome words or concepts, but don't spend your time coming up with them for words you can memorize easily. A mnemonic helps you remember, so only use one when a particular vocab word, prefix, or suffix keeps leaving you stumped.

Interpreting words in context

Both the SSAT and ISEE ask you to define vocab words within context. You see a word in a sentence, and the question says something like, "What does the author most likely mean by . . . ?" Sounds easy enough, but these kinds of questions can be difficult because the English language isn't exact. In other words, the meaning of a word can change, depending on how the author uses it.

Consider this sentence: *The cruel man was arrested for mistreating the animals.*

In this sentence, what does the word *cruel* mean? By the dictionary definition, **cruel** means to cause pain or suffering. In this sentence, the man caused pain and suffering to animals, so the author means the dictionary definition of the word.

Now, consider this sentence: *The cruel waves crashed over us.*

What does the word *cruel* mean in this sentence? Waves don't experience emotion or choose to cause harm or suffering. A wave is simply water under force, so in the context of this sentence, the author is saying the waves are big, dangerous, difficult, or something like that. See how it works? A writer can alter the meaning of a word by its context, so when the exam asks you what a writer means by a certain word, it may not necessarily want the actual dictionary definition.

To answer these kinds of questions correctly, you have to read carefully and try to decipher what the author means by the word. See Chapters 6 and 7 for more information about vocabulary in context and to practice answering questions like these.

Using repetition

Think about a favorite song. You can probably sing the song in your head without any music or lyric sheet in front of you. How did you learn it? You learned the song because you listened to it over and over, and after a few times, you started singing along. Maybe you didn't know the entire song when you started singing, but because you liked the song, you kept singing it and eventually memorized it.

Vocabulary is much the same way. Using repetition to memorize is what we call *rote* memorization because you have to do it over and over to get the words and their meaning. So scanning vocabulary words doesn't help much. You need to study them over and over; you need to invest time to learn the words, prefixes, and suffixes in this chapter. So study the words, repeat, and repeat again.

Some people learn vocabulary more quickly by writing the word and definition over and over. If this applies to you, grab some scratch paper and start writing.

As you study vocabulary, try to use the words in various ways. Include them when you speak or try to write a short paragraph where you use several vocabulary words correctly. Studies show time and time again that if you can learn something and then use it in a practical way, the odds of you remembering what you learn go drastically up.

Breaking Down Vocabulary Words

Many words in the English language aren't individual units. They're made up of pieces of other words that together create their meaning. That doesn't mean that every word has various parts you can break down in order to garner the meaning of the word. However, most often, you're able to understand a part of the word that can give you at least a clue to its meaning. Being able to break down a difficult word is a powerful test tool. After all, you don't have to write the definition of a word on the test — you just need to choose the right answer from a list of choices. If you can at least get a clue as to the meaning of a word, you're more likely to answer the question correctly.

Words often contain three distinct parts — a root, a prefix, and a suffix. A word may contain a root word, a prefix, a suffix, or any combination of these parts that can help you define the word. When you know common root words, prefixes, and suffixes, which we introduce in the following sections, you can use these tools to help break down difficult vocab words you face on the exam.

Digging up roots

A *root* is the most basic form of a word that's often used within different words to convey similar meanings. For example, the root word *aqua* means water. This root is used in a number of words, such as *aquarium* and *aquifer*. Even though you may not know what both of these words technically mean, if you know they have to do with water, you have a good chance of answering the question correctly. Table 3-1 lists the most common English roots, their definition, and an example for each. Be sure to memorize this list of roots.

Table 3-1	Vocabulary: Roots	
Root	*Definition*	*Example*
aqua	water	aquarium
arch	ruler	anarchy
astro	star	astronaut
bene	good	benevolent
cap	take	capture
chrom	color	monochromatic
chron	time	chronology
circum	around	circumference
cred	believe	credible
cycl	round	unicycle
dict	say	diction
dom	home	domicile
duc	to lead	introduce
fact	to make	manufacture
fer	carry	transfer
flex	bend	flexible
fract	break	fracture
gen	birth	generation
geo	earth	geography
gram	write	telegram
gress	move	progress
ject	throw	eject
mal	bad	malware
man	hand	manicure
medi	middle	medium
min	tiny	miniature
mit	to send	transmit
mort	death	mortuary
nat	born	natural
nomen	name	nomenclature
path	pain	pathologist
ped	foot	pedicure
phil	love	philosophy
phon	sound	phonology
poli	city	metropolitan
port	carry	transport
scope	see	telescope
script	write	prescription
spec	look	inspection

Root	Definition	Example
tact	touch	contact
tend	stretch	extend
vac	empty	evacuate
ver	true	verify
voc	voice	vocal

Starting with prefixes

A *prefix* is a letter or grouping of letters placed at the beginning of a word that modifies its meaning. If you encounter words you don't know on the exam, you can look for prefixes that can give you clues about the word's meaning. In Table 3-2, we give you the prefix or collection of related prefixes, the definition, and an example word or two that uses the prefix. Memorize these prefixes.

Table 3-2	Vocabulary: Prefixes	
Prefix	**Definition**	**Example**
a-, an-	to, toward, in process of, not, without	aback, attract, adhere
ab-, abs-	away, from	abstract
ad-	to move or change	advance
ante-	before	antecedent
anti-	against	antibiotic
be-	all around or completely	bemuse
co-	to be with	confidante, confide
contra-	against	contraband
de-	down or to take away	depend, descend
dia-	across	diagonal
dis-	to remove or negate	disavow, disadvantage
en-, em-	to bring into	entangle, embrace
ex-	out	exit, extol
extra-	beyond	extracurricular
hyper-	more than normal	hyperactive
hypo-	under	hypothermia
in-	not, without, or into	inaccurate, incapable, influence
infra-	below	infrastructure
inter-	among	interact
intra-	inside	intravenous
non-	to negate or be absent	non-smoker
ob-	to block	obstruct

continued

Table 3-2 *(continued)*

Prefix	Definition	Example
peri-	around	perimeter
post-	after	postpone
pre-	before	preamble
pro-	supporting or moving forward	propulsion, prologue
re-	again	remove, review
semi-	half	semicircle
sub-	to replace or a lower position	subway, subterfuge
syn-	to act together	synchronize
trans-	across	transcontinental, translate
ultra-	extreme	ultraviolet
un-	not	unacceptable

Ending with suffixes

A *suffix* is like a prefix — it's a letter or grouping of letters — but suffixes appear at the end of words instead of at the beginning. Suffixes aren't as helpful as roots and prefixes, but they can still give you clues about the word's meaning. Table 3-3 lists the most common suffixes; be sure to memorize them as well.

Table 3-3	Vocabulary: Suffixes	
Suffix	**Definition**	**Example**
-able, -ible	capable	invincible
-acy	state or quality	adequacy
-al	act or process	denial
-ance, -ence	state	maintenance
-ate	to do or become	eviscerate
-dom	place or state	kingdom
-en	to become	brighten
-er, -or	someone who is or does something	trainer
-esque	to resemble	picturesque
-ful	noted or having much of	plentiful
-ic, -ical	pertaining to	musical
-ious, -ous	characteristic	nutritious
-ish	an inexact quality	sweetish
-ism	belief	anarchism
-ist	someone who is or does something	psychiatrist

Suffix	Definition	Example
-ity, -ty	a quality	tenacity
-ive	a certain nature	inventive
-less	without	heartless
-ment	condition of something	confinement
-ness	a state	weariness
-ship	position or condition	fellowship
-sion, -tion	a state	fulguration
-y	characteristic	fruity

Vocabulary Practice: Lower Level SSAT and Lower and Middle Level ISEE

If you're taking the lower level SSAT or the lower or middle level ISEE, these vocabulary words are for you! Here are 100 words, divided into blocks. Study these words one block at a time and make sure you know these words well before you take the test. Words like these have appeared on previous exams, and although we can't guarantee you'll see any of these words on the test, the odds are good that you'll encounter at least some of them. So study these words and use this list as a test to see how much vocabulary knowledge you already have.

Vocabulary Practice: Block 1

Word	Definition
aghast	feeling shock or surprise
beguile	to charm
bellow	to shout
blunt	not sharp; straightforward
compel	to force
debris	trash
gruesome	frightening or gory
hovel	a shack
incentive	motive
meek	passive
nomad	wanderer
pompous	arrogant or stuffy
quaint	odd or small
quell	to quiet
sequel	an addition, usually from a previous story
suffice	to be enough of something; to satisfy
wrath	extreme anger

Vocabulary Practice: Block 2

Word	Definition
amateur	nonprofessional or unskilled
bias	to show favor, often in an unfair way
buffoon	a ridiculous but entertaining person
concise	brief; to the point
deft	skillful
dispute	to argue or disagree
entice	to tempt
exquisite	beautiful
immaculate	spotlessly clean
inclement	stormy or severe
lenient	permissive or not strict
ominous	threatening
parody	an imitation meant to playfully make fun of
ransack	to messily search something
squander	to waste
torrid	very hot
zealous	intense or passionate

Vocabulary Practice: Block 3

Word	Definition
adorn	to decorate
amble	to walk slowly
benign	harmless
bounty	abundance
catastrophe	disaster
despondent	sad or depressive
fervent	enthusiastic
limber	bending or moving easily
meticulous	carefully planing or doing something
nonchalant	not concerned or interested
paradox	a contradiction
ravenous	extremely hungry
recreation	a fun or relaxing activity
robust	healthy
solicit	to request
vex	to tease or aggravate

Vocabulary Practice: Block 4

Word	Definition
atrocity	something outrageous or terrible
barrage	a flood
chronic	constant in a negative way (such as pain or a problem)
dismal	causing misery
elusive	hard to catch or understand
excursion	a short trip
heed	to pay attention to, especially a warning
jeer	to rudely make fun of
jest	a playful joke
masticate	to chew
meddle	to interfere
obscure	unclear or vague
palatable	something that tastes good
perjury	telling a lie when under oath (as in a court)
reclusive	alone; avoiding people
scarce	a small amount; hard to find
tactful	polite or discreet

Vocabulary Practice: Block 5

Word	Definition
acclaim	praise
articulate	well spoken or to speak well
banal	boring or unimportant
benefactor	a donor
devastate	to ruin or destroy
emulate	to copy
exotic	foreign or unusual
flux	a state of continual change
impasse	a blocked road or a problem with no solution
propel	to move or push forward
ratify	to approve
residue	something left behind, as when a liquid dries
stealthy	sneaky or in secret
taciturn	quiet or shy
tenacious	persistent
usurp	to take by force, usually a position

Vocabulary Practice: Block 6

Word	Definition
adhere	to stick to something
affable	agreeable
aloof	uninterested or cold in behavior
boisterous	noisy behavior
candor	open honesty
destitute	poor or lacking basic needs
entourage	a group
fickle	inconsistent
inert	inactive or not harmful
infuse	to inject
obtuse	slow intelligence.
quench	to satisfy
rancor	spite or malice
scathe	to harm or injure
tepid	lukewarm or indifferent
unanimous	all in agreement, such as in a vote or decision
voluminous	large

Vocabulary Practice: Upper Level SSAT and ISEE

All right, upper-level students, here are 100 vocabulary words, divided into blocks. Study these words a block at a time and master them before test day. Also, be sure to study the words for the lower-level exams earlier in this chapter. These words or similar words have appeared on past SSATs or ISEEs, but understand that we can't guarantee you'll see them when you take the test. However, you'll see words of similar difficulty, so this group of words is a good way to test your current vocabulary knowledge.

Vocabulary Practice: Block 1

Word	Definition
cringe	to recoil
epicure	someone who appreciates good food or drink
flout	to scorn
luminary	a person who is an exceptional expert in a given field
maverick	a rebel
narcissism	excessive love of one's self
neophyte	a novice
obfuscate	to confuse
paltry	insignificant

Word	Definition
quixotic	foolishly idealistic
raze	to completely destroy
sacrosanct	sacred
truculent	savagely brutal
unilateral	involving one side only
vacuous	lacking of ideas or substance
vocation	one's work or profession
wane	to decrease in strength

Vocabulary Practice: Block 2

Word	Definition
abrogate	to cancel
accede	to agree
bevy	a large group
bilious	bad-tempered
bilk	to cheat
blatant	obvious or noticeable
bucolic	a rural area
burnish	to polish
cadaver	a dead body
callous	insensitive
candor	open honesty
canter	a smooth and easy pace
cryptic	puzzling
niemal	relating to winter
oblivious	unaware
placid	calm or peaceful
repudiate	to shun or reject

Vocabulary Practice: Block 3

Word	Definition
abhor	to hate
apparition	a ghost
bogus	false or fake
bombastic	impressive but meaningless language
caliber	a degree of worth
credulous	gullible
engender	to cause
kindle	to start a fire
maudlin	silly or overly sentimental

continued

Vocabulary Practice: Block 3 *(continued)*

Word	Definition
mirth	amusement
nuance	a subtle difference
perfunctory	unenthusiastic
plummet	to fall suddenly
replete	full
resignation	accepting a certain fate
specious	misleading

Vocabulary Practice: Block 4

Word	Definition
absolution	forgiveness
bastion	a strong defense
besiege	to close in
blithe	carefree
bona fide	genuine or real
canvass	to survey
covert	undercover
diaphanous	transparent
panache	with much elegance
peccadillo	a minor offense
recapitulate	to review
rhetoric	the art of language usage, or over exaggeration
sardonic	mocking
serendipity	unexpected goodness or happiness
tome	a large book
usury	lending money at a high rate of interest
verdant	inexperienced

Vocabulary Practice: Block 5

Word	Definition
abasement	humiliation
abstemious	self-denying
baroque	overly decorated
bedlam	a noisy uproar
bestial	savage
brusque	abrupt in manner

Word	Definition
cogent	convincing
ensconce	to place or settle comfortably
harangue	attacking speech
lackluster	dull
obdurate	stubborn
obliterate	to destroy
plaudit	strong praise
rescind	to repeal
tenable	a position or point that can be defended
vestige	a remaining bit of something

Vocabulary Practice: Block 6

Word	Definition
abscond	to leave in secret
espy	to catch a glimpse of
evanescent	momentary
fastidious	critical or demanding attention to detail; not easy to please
gaunt	overly thin
hapless	having bad luck
illicit	improper
loquacious	talkative
risqué	near indecent or vulgar
scrupulous	careful or precise
symbiosis	working together or a mutually beneficial relationship
taciturn	not speaking much
ubiquitous	being everywhere at the same time
verbatim	word for word
vicissitudes	unexpected changes in one's life
wry	ironic or slyly amusing
zenith	the highest point or summit

Chapter 4

Talking Up Verbal Reasoning

Few things in life exist in a vacuum. In fact, most everything has a relationship with something else. Think about it: People have relationships with one another, cats prefer cats, dogs prefer other dogs, and even a pen isn't much good on its own — it needs paper to fulfill its purpose. All these relationships lead to one simple truth: Words in the English language don't stand alone. They connect and relate to other words because, in a nutshell, language helps us describe the world around us — a world full of relationships.

The SSAT and ISEE use this simple reality to test your ability to understand words and their relationships to other words. This kind of verbal reasoning tests your ability not only to understand the meaning of a word but also to understand how that meaning relates to the meaning of another word or words in a sentence. The good news is you can use some simple testing strategies to help you find the right answer quickly. This chapter shows you what to expect on the Verbal sections of the SSAT and ISEE, how the test presents verbal reasoning questions, and how to master those questions — even the tricky ones.

What Verbal Reasoning Looks Like

Knowing exactly what verbal reasoning means on the SSAT and ISEE can be a little tricky, because the tests handle this area differently. Here's a basic primer:

- ✓ **SSAT:** This exam tests your verbal reasoning skill with two types of questions: analogies and synonyms.

- ✓ **ISEE:** This exam tests your verbal reasoning skill by focusing on vocabulary and sentence usage, using synonyms and sentence completion questions only — no analogy questions.

On both the upper and lower level SSAT, you'll find 30 analogy questions and 30 synonym questions, for a total of 60 questions. You have 30 minutes to take the entire Verbal section of the test, which means you have only 30 seconds to answer each question. On the lower level ISEE, you'll find 34 questions with a time limit of 20 minutes. Both the middle and upper level ISEE exams have 40 questions with a 20-minute time limit. Don't let that stress you out, though. After all, you don't have to answer every question, and the odds are you probably won't. So like every other section of the SSAT or ISEE, your goal is to get as many questions right as possible. Keep the following overriding test tactics in mind (and be sure to check out Chapter 2 for more global testing strategies):

✔ **Answer as many questions as you can.** The SSAT deducts points for missing questions; however, guessing can be an important strategy to get more verbal questions correct. The ISEE doesn't count off or deduct points for guessing; you're not penalized for questions left blank or answered incorrectly. The ISEE gives points for the number of questions you answer correctly, so go ahead and guess at verbal questions you don't know. Be sure to check out Chapter 2, where we explore SSAT and ISEE guessing strategies.

✔ **Use the process of elimination.** Remember that the test is all about finding the right answer in a list of choices where all but one are wrong. As you search for the right answer, be sure to rule out answers you know are incorrect. That way, even if you're not sure of the right answer, you increase the odds that you'll guess the correct one. For example, if a question has four answer choices and you know that two of them are wrong, you have a 50 percent chance of guessing the right one.

✔ **Don't get bogged down.** You won't be able to solve all the questions. If you read a verbal question and just don't understand it (or know the words), move on (either skip it or guess, depending on which test you're taking). One of the worst things you can do is spend too much time on one question that you're unsure of when you may be able to answer other questions quickly and correctly.

✔ **Keep calm and cool.** If you start getting frustrated or anxious, your mental reasoning goes out the window. You'll start missing questions you actually know. Stay calm and cool and don't get frustrated. Take a breath and focus on doing your best.

Making Sense of Analogies

If you're taking either the upper or lower level SSAT, study this section carefully because you'll face analogy questions on your test, and many students consider analogies the toughest part of the exam. Analogy questions test your ability to understand the relationship between two words and then copy that same relationship to another set of words.

Keep the following in mind when dealing with analogy questions on the SSAT:

✔ The two words in the question have a relationship. Your job is to find that relationship.

✔ Choose the two words that have the *most similar* relationship.

Here's the good news: Analogy questions all follow the exact same pattern. In other words, all the test questions are structured the same way and look the same, too. This means that you need only a couple of important strategies to tackle the analogy questions because you'll simply see the same kinds of questions over and over. We provide those important strategies and a few practice questions in the following sections.

Even though the ISEE doesn't test you with analogy questions, go ahead and read this section for vocabulary practice. You don't need to worry about testing strategies for analogies because you won't see these kinds of questions on the ISEE, but you'll benefit from the vocab review.

Mapping out your strategy for analogies

When you tackle the analogy questions on the SSAT, you'll find that some analogies are simple and straightforward, some are complex in terms of the relationship between the two words, and some may seem nearly impossible if you don't know what all the words mean. So how do you attack these problems? You need a simple strategy.

Analogy questions give you isolated word groupings, and you have to find another grouping of words that have the same kind of relationship. The problem is that you don't use word groupings in an isolated way like this in your day-to-day life. In other words, you don't walk around randomly saying things like, "Anger is to emotion as distance is to measurement." That would just be weird.

Instead, you use words in relationship to other words all the time, but you do so within a context. You may say something like, "*Pac Man* is still a popular *arcade* game." The SSAT, on the other hand, would just say, "Pac Man is to arcade as . . ." and give you a list of answer choices to choose from. When you use the same words, you put them in a sentence that has context, or meaning. So when facing the analogy questions on the SSAT, you want to follow a simple, five-step strategy that takes these word groups and gives them meaning. This section helps you do just that. This section also shows you how to arrive at an answer when you're not sure what the words mean or don't understand the relationship between them.

Put the words in a sentence that shows the relationship

When you see the word pair in the question, the first thing you want to do is put the two words in a sentence that shows the relationship between the two words. For example, say the question says, "Belt is to accessory as . . ." An *accessory* is something you wear that's an extra part of your clothing or outfit. Belts, hats, jewelry, purses, and other similar items are all accessories. So create a sentence for these two words, such as, "A belt is a kind of clothing accessory."

When you create the sentence, make sure

- ✓ **It's specific but not overly specific.** For example, if you say, "A belt is an accessory," that doesn't tell you much about the belt. On the other hand, if you say, "A belt is worn around your waist as an accessory for clothing and other outfits," then the sentence has too much detail and can make things confusing. Keep it specific, but also keep it simple.

- ✓ **The sentence shows the relationship.** A common mistake students make is focusing on the meaning of the words instead of the relationship the words have with each other. For example, if you say, "A belt is worn around the waist, and an accessory is something you wear," the sentence doesn't show the relationship between the two. The analogy questions don't care about the definitions of words; they care about the relationship between them, so focus on that instead.

Plug the answer choices in to your sentence

After you have a sentence that shows the relationship of the words in the question, you simply test that relationship with the answer choices in order to find the right answer. Using the belt and accessory example, look at the entire question and answer choices:

Belt is to accessory as bean is to

(A) Food

(B) Green

(C) Vegetable

(D) Vitamins

So if you take the answer choices and plug them in to your sentence, you get the following:

(A) A *bean* is a kind of *food*.

(B) A *bean* is a kind of *green*.

(C) A *bean* is a kind of *vegetable*.

(D) A *bean* is a kind of *vitamin*.

What do you think? First, start with the process of elimination. You can rule out Choices (B) and (D) because they don't even make sense. Congratulations! You now have a 50 percent chance of guessing the right answer, even if you don't know exactly what it is. But keep working for the right answer here. Both Choices (A) and (B) are true: A bean is a kind of food and also a kind of vegetable. Remember, though, that you want to choose the answer choice that has the closest relationship to the question. Choice (A) isn't very specific while Choice (C) is more specific. The question gives you the word *belt* as a kind of accessory, rather than just saying that a belt is a kind of clothing. In other words, it's more specific. So the best answer is Choice **(C)** because a bean is a kind of vegetable and that's more specific than saying a bean is a kind of food.

As you can see, creating a sentence and then plugging the answer choices in to that sentence give these seemingly random words some context and can really make relationships come to life.

When in doubt, refine the sentence

Say you use the sentence, "A belt is a kind of accessory," but you see the following answer choices:

Belt is to accessory as

(A) Hat is to headwear

(B) Brooch is to pin

(C) Ribbon is to brush

(D) Ring is to decoration

If you take the answer choices and plug them in to your sentence, you get the following:

(A) A *hat* is a kind of *headwear*.

(B) A *brooch* is a kind of *pin*.

(C) A *ribbon* is a kind of *brush*.

(D) A *ring* is a kind of *decoration*.

Now you're running into some trouble. As you can see, Choice (C) doesn't make sense, so rule that one out, but Choices (A), (B), and (D) all fit into the sentence. What can you do? Refine the sentence and try to make it more specific, and then try the answer choices again. Certainly, a belt is an accessory, but make the sentence even more specific. What do you do with a belt? You loop it through your pants and wear it on your pants. So say it this way: "A *belt* is an *accessory* you wear on your clothes."

Now try this new sentence with the answer choices:

(A) A *hat* is *headwear* you wear on your clothes.

(B) A *brooch* is a *pin* you wear on your clothes.

(C) Eliminated.

(D) A *ring* is a *decoration* you wear on your clothes.

The only correct answer is Choice **(B)** because a brooch is a pin that you usually wear on a dress or shirt. *Belt is to accessory as brooch is to pin* is the most similar relationship out of all the choices.

When you have to get more specific with your sentence, make sure you don't get too specific. For example, if you said, "A belt is an accessory you wear on your jeans" or "A belt is an accessory made of leather," none of the answer choices would've made sense. Remember that you're not looking for items that match; you're looking for items that show the same relationship. So if the answer choices still don't work, change your sentence so it's less specific.

When you don't know a word (or several), look for clues

You may see a question that has a word or words you're just not sure about. For example, say you face a question like this:

Taciturn is to chatty as

(A) Stand is to sit

(B) Anger is to rage

(C) June is to summer

(D) Spoon is to bowl

If you know what *taciturn* means, you can easily solve this analogy. However, what if you don't know, and you're unsure of one of the word options? Try these tactics:

- ✔ **Look for opposites or synonyms.** If you don't know a word, scan the answer choices to see whether any of them stand out as possible opposites or whether they contain groups of words that are synonyms. In the preceding example question, the answer choices include one opposite match, which is Choice (A), *stand is to sit*. Because Choice (A) is an opposite match, it may be the right answer (and, in fact, it is). *Taciturn* means quiet or unwilling to speak, so *chatty* is the opposite.

  Finding an opposite or a synonym in the answer choices doesn't necessarily mean the answer is correct, but it can be a clue. Knowing this, you can easily rule out the other answer choices. Anger and rage are different intensity levels of the same emotion, June is a month during summer. And spoon and bowl are both used for eating, but neither have anything to do with the relationship in question.

- ✔ **Determine whether the relationship is positive or negative.** Sometimes you don't know the exact meaning of the word, but you may have a sense that the word is either positive or negative. For example, say you see a question that says, "Portentous is to unimportant as . . ." You know what *unimportant* means, but what about *portentous*? You may not know exactly what it means, but it sounds like something bad, or at least something important. So you can suppose that portentous is the opposite of unimportant, which is correct. Now, you can look for a similar relationship in the answer choices.

- ✔ **Look for prefixes that can give you a clue.** What if you see the word *disingenuous?* You may not know exactly what it means, but you probably know that the prefix *dis-* means not. So you know that this word means *not* something. Although you may not know what a word means, having a clue of what it *could* mean can help you construct a sentence to plug your answer choices in. Remember that even if you can't find the answer, try to rule out some answer choices to increase your odds of guessing the correct answer. (By the way, *disingenuous* means not sincere.)

- ✔ **Make a decision and move on.** In some cases, you may not know what either word in the pair really means. You likely won't see a question this hard, but say you see something like, "Quixotic is to meshuga as . . ." If you don't know either word or have a sense of their meanings, or if prefixes don't help, skip it and move on (remember wrong answers count against you on the SSAT). Don't waste time on word pairs you don't know; instead, spend your time trying to solve the ones you can figure out. By the way, both *quixotic* and *meshuga* mean senseless or impractical.

When you have trouble establishing the relationship, dig deeper

Nouns are usually easy words in analogy questions because nouns represent something concrete. When you see, "Hat is to head . . . ," you can visualize a hat sitting on someone's head, and you can easily construct a sentence that you can test out on your answer choices (in most cases).

However, other types of words, such as verbs and adjectives, and other broad categories, such as emotions and feelings, can be more challenging. For example, take a look at the following question:

Frustration is to anger as

(A) Crying is to joy

(B) Happiness is to solitude

(C) Satisfaction is to peace

(D) Stupor is to loudness

As you can see, this question is more difficult because it deals with the relationship between different kinds of feelings. When you have problems establishing relationships between words, do the following:

✔ **Try the word pairs in an actual sentence, using people or props.** For example, you may say, "She was frustrated by her low test score, but later she became angry about it." This tactic can help you refine the relationship by saying that "frustration can lead to anger." You can then try this sentence with the answer choices to see whether you can find the same relationship. In fact, you can, because *satisfaction* can lead to *peace*.

✔ **Try to match the question with words in the answer choices.** For example, consider this question:

> Hammer is to hook as carpenter is to
>
> (A) Nurse
>
> (B) Fisherman
>
> (C) Nail
>
> (D) Teacher

When you look at this question, creating a relationship between a hammer and a hook that has anything to do with the answer choices is difficult. However, if you think about it, the hammer and the hook are both tools used by professionals. Because *carpenter* is already given to you, and a carpenter uses a hammer, the best answer is Choice **(B)**, *fisherman,* because a fisherman uses a hook. This relationship is a bit more complicated, so you have to think outside the box in order to find it.

✔ **Consider an educated guess.** Like all questions on the SSAT, if you don't know and can't select a clear, right answer, make sure you don't spend too much time studying a hopeless question. Either skip the question or, if you can eliminate some answer choices, make an educated guess.

Trying your hand at analogy practice questions

Now that you have a few strategies under your belt, spend a few minutes practicing some analogy questions. In this section, we provide example analogy questions like what you'll see on the SSAT. Try to answer the questions on your own before reading the answer explanation we provide after each question.

Kitten is to cat as

(A) Bread is to butter

(B) Pig is to spider

(C) Joy is to smile

(D) Joey is to kangaroo

The question tells you that a kitten has a relationship to a cat, and your job is to choose an answer choice that presents the same kind of relationship. A kitten is a baby cat, and a joey is a baby kangaroo, so the correct answer is Choice **(D)**.

Aside from this basic question format, you may see some analogy questions that are formatted this way:

Kitten is to cat as joey is to

(A) Butter

(B) Spider

(C) Smile

(D) Kangaroo

It's the same exact question, but the test writers simply gave you part of the answer in the question itself. Otherwise, there's no difference, and like we said, all the analogy questions look the same.

Now, you're probably thinking these questions look and sound easy enough; however, that isn't always the case. Many analogy questions are more difficult than this simple example because both the words and relationships become more complex. Take a look at the next three example analogy questions, each one getting a bit more difficult.

Toy is to child as

(A) Collar is to dog

(B) Pencil is to paper

(C) Book is to library

(D) Football is to athlete

When you look at this question, you have to figure out the relationship between a toy and a child, and then find a similar relationship in the answer choices. A child plays with a toy, and in a similar way, an athlete plays with a football, so the correct answer is Choice **(D)**. When you look at the question this way, the other answer choices simply don't match up with similar relationships.

Camera is to lens as

(A) Oil is to motor

(B) Spoon is to bowl

(C) Tomato is to vine

(D) Sand is to rock

Think about the relationship for a moment. This question is a bit more difficult than the last example because the relationship isn't readily apparent. So you have to think it through. What do *camera* and *lens* have to do with each other? A camera *uses* a lens in order to take photos. After all, a camera can't work without a lens. In the same way, a motor *uses* oil in order to run, and a motor can't function without oil. So the correct answer is Choice **(A)** because it has a similar relationship.

Scorpion is to arachnid as

(A) Shoe is to pod

(B) Hereford is to bovine

(C) Foot is to leg

(D) Dog is to feline

This example is even more complicated. *Arachnid* is a family of animals that includes spiders, ticks, and scorpions, so you need an answer that shows how one thing is a part of a family of things. The correct answer is Choice **(B)** because Hereford is a kind of cow, and all cows belong to the bovine family.

Getting the Scoop on Synonyms

Both the SSAT and ISEE use synonym questions on the Verbal sections of the exams. (A *synonym* is a word that means the same thing as another word.) Synonym questions are simple in terms of the question, but of course, they may not be so simple to answer.

Synonym questions give you a capitalized word for the question, followed by several answer choices. Because these words are synonym questions, your job is to find a word that means the same thing. Some answer choices may be similar, some may be the opposite, and some you may not know well, but the goal is to simply find the closest match. We provide some strategies and practice questions in the following sections to help you ace the synonym questions.

Planning your synonym attack strategy

Because synonym questions are straightforward, your attack plan is really pretty simple. When you face synonyms, just keep this advice in mind:

✓ **Start with your own definition.** When you look at the word given to you, first quickly create your own definition of the word. Doing so keeps the answer choices from confusing or distracting you. For example, if you're given the word *annoy*, think, "Annoy means to irritate someone else."

✓ **Scan the answer choices for something similar to your definition.** Although the words provided for the synonym may not exactly match your definition of the word, look for something similar.

✓ **Rule out wrong answers.** Often, you'll quickly realize that several answer choices are completely wrong. Rule those words out quickly so you can focus on only the few that may be correct.

✓ **Choose the answer that most closely matches the word.** You may see two or more answer choices that are similar, but you want to choose the word that most closely means the same thing. You'll need to make some quick decisions because you don't have a lot of time, but always keep this simple goal in mind.

✔ **Consider the part of speech of the word(s).** On the ISEE, the word and all the answer choices stick to the same part of speech. So if the word is a verb, think in terms of action as you explore the answer choices. Sometimes, thinking about the word's part of speech can help you discover the answer.

The SSAT may or may not use the same part of speech in the answer choices. In fact, some answer choices may use more than one word that basically defines the question word. Don't let this throw you off; any of the answers can be correct, so don't rule out an answer choice because it has multiple words or isn't the same part of speech as the question word.

✔ **If the word and the answer choices are too hard (or you don't know them), make a fast decision.** If you're taking the ISEE, you're not penalized for guessing, so go ahead and guess. If you're taking the SSAT, use the guessing strategies we explore in Chapter 2 or skip the question and move on.

Checking out a few sample synonym questions

For the synonym questions in this section, look at the question and then choose the best answer choice. Remember that you want to choose the word that's closest in meaning to the capitalized word. Then, check out the paragraph following the question for the correct answer and an explanation.

COMPLETE:

(A) Undone

(B) Finish

(C) Partial

(D) Judicious

(E) Founder

In this example, *complete* means to finish something, so Choice **(B)**, *finish,* is the best answer. Choices (A) and (C) are actually *antonyms* — they mean the opposite of complete. Choices (D) and (E) are just fancy-looking words that don't have anything to do with the word *complete.*

Okay, so that seems easy enough, but as you may guess, not all synonym questions are this simple. Try another one:

BLISS:

(A) Peaceful

(B) Stressful

(C) Joy

(D) Relaxed

(E) Free

In this example, you need to find a synonym for the word *bliss.* You can rule out Choice (B) quickly because *stressful* is really the opposite of *bliss.* However, Choices (A), (C), (D), and (E) are a bit more difficult because the words are similar, at least on the surface. The word *bliss* means joy, so Choice **(C)** is the correct answer. The other choices, *peaceful, relaxed,* and *free*, may all be characteristics of joy, but they don't directly mean the same thing as bliss. In the end, the issue here is precision. You're looking for the best answer that means virtually the same thing as the word given.

INIQUITOUS:

(A) Saboteur

(B) Intrinsic

(C) Acumen

(D) Benign

(E) Criminal

The problem with this question is the word you're given is difficult, and all the answer choices are difficult, too. You may not know what the word or many of the answer choices mean. This question is basically a test of your vocabulary, so if you don't know the word or many of the answer choices, you have to make a quick decision. If you're taking the SSAT and have a hunch, you can guess. If not, skip it and don't waste your time. If you're taking the ISEE, guess because you're not penalized for guessing. By the way, *iniquitous* is a synonym for *criminal*. Both words simply mean lawless.

Filling in Sentence Completion Questions

Instead of analogy questions, the Verbal section of the ISEE uses sentence completion questions. Sentence completion questions are pretty self-explanatory: Your job is to fill in the blank(s) with the best word(s) from the answer choices given. These questions test your ability to understand the context of a sentence and then choose a word that completes the intended meaning in a sentence.

In the following sections, we provide a few basic strategies for answering the sentence completion questions as well as some sample questions to give you a chance to practice those strategies.

If you're taking the SSAT, you won't see these kinds of questions in the Verbal section on the test, but we recommend that you still review this section for the extra vocabulary practice.

Building a strategy for sentence completion

Sentence completion questions may not be easy, but many students find them less challenging than synonyms. Like with synonym questions, your attack plan for sentence completion questions is rather straightforward. Here are some tips to remember:

✔ **Pay attention to the context.** When you look at the sentence, try to insert your own word(s) into the blank(s). This way, you at least start with something to consider before you let the answer choices confuse you. In fact, some answer choices may be there to try to trick you, so start with your own word to help you escape these traps. The context of the sentence always gives you clues about what words will likely work, so make sure you read the sentence carefully and understand what the sentence is trying to communicate.

✔ **Look for positive or negative relationships.** As you consider the sentence, ask yourself whether the word you need has some kind of positive or negative meaning. Although watching for this relationship doesn't always work, sometimes it can help rule out answer choices that don't communicate in a positive or negative way.

✔ **Watch out for vocabulary.** The test may throw difficult or complex vocabulary words your way, and you may not know what all the words mean. But just because a word is complicated doesn't mean it's the right word. Sometimes a more simple word completes the meaning in the sentence, so don't fall into the trap of thinking "complex must be right."

✔ **Check out the root, prefix, and suffix of the word(s).** You may find answer choices that are difficult to decipher. Remember to look at the root, prefix, and suffix of the word, which can give you a clue about the meaning of the word and help you break down difficult vocabulary words. (See Chapter 3 for more about these vocab tricks.)

Working through a few sentence completion questions

Now that you have the scoop on answering sentence completion questions, try your hand at a few sample questions. Using the strategies we discuss in the previous section, choose an answer choice that best fits the context of the sentence, and then take a look at the answer and explanation we provide.

The teacher was very _____ by the student who kept interrupting the lesson.

(A) sublime

(B) overjoyed

(C) frustrated

(D) destroyed

(E) relaxed

Think about the context of the sentence: The student is interrupting the lesson. Because the student is posing a problem for the teacher, you're looking for a word that helps convey that meaning. Choices (A), (B), and (E) are all calm descriptive words, so you can rule those out, leaving only Choices (C) and (D). The teacher probably wasn't *destroyed* by the incident, so Choice **(C),** *frustrated,* is the best answer here to make the context of the sentence come together.

Everyone knew that Sam's _____ approach to the problem would never work.

(A) pragmatic

(B) thoughtful

(C) exact

(D) calibrated

(E) quixotic

In this example, you need to find a word that communicates within the context. Sam's idea is somehow unrealistic or impractical, so as you look at the answer choices, you can rule out Choices (A), (B), and (C) because those words all communicate a practical, logical solution. The word *calibrated* seems like an odd choice for this sentence because it means to compare something with a standard. However, the word *quixotic* means wildly romantic or impractical. Given the answer choices provided, Choice **(E)** is the best choice and the correct answer because Sam's idea is impractical in some way. This question is more difficult because you need to know the meaning of the words *calibrated* and *quixotic* to find the right choice.

Although it was a(n) _____ decision, the _____ all came together in the end.

(A) unknown . . . chances

(B) troubling . . . buoyancy

(C) rash . . . details

(D) smart . . . development

(E) trivial . . . difficulty

In some cases, you may see two blanks with answer choices containing two words. In this case, you really have to consider the context of the sentence and pick the best match that completes the sentence's intended meaning. One of the key words here is *although*. The sentence is saying that although a certain decision was made, something worked out in the end. You're looking for contrasting word choices that help communicate this meaning. If you look at the list of choices, the best answer is Choice **(C).** The decision was *rash,* or quickly made, but the *details* all worked out. In the other answer choices, either one of the words doesn't make sense in the sentence or the context keeps them from working.

Chapter 5

Practicing Verbal Reasoning

● ●

In This Chapter
▶ Practicing lower and middle level verbal reasoning
▶ Practicing upper level verbal reasoning

● ●

At best guess, more than a quarter of a million distinct English words exist, not including technical jargon, words imported from other languages, or multiple meanings of the same word (for example *dog* can mean an animal or it can mean to follow or track someone or something). As such, the SSAT and ISEE test writers have an unlimited number of words and relationships between words that they can throw your way in the Verbal sections of the tests.

In truth, you practice not to memorize all those words and relationships — you practice to hone your strategy skills that help you solve verbal reasoning questions. Then, you can apply the strategies you've learned to the test when you take the real thing (as well as the practice exams you can find later in this book).

In this chapter, you spend time practicing your verbal reasoning skills. We've divided these practice questions into different sections so you can practice analogies, synonyms, and sentence completion questions, both for lower and middle level exams as well as upper level exams. Simply flip to the sections of this chapter that apply to your test, sharpen your pencil, grab a clock or watch to time yourself, and get started!

Tackling Guided Lower Level SSAT Analogy Questions

Following are some lower level SSAT analogy questions to get you warmed up. Each question is followed by an explanation of the correct answer and how you may reach it.

1. Doberman is to dog as

   (A) Bass is to fish

   (B) Cookie is to fruit

   (C) Swim is to run

   (D) Tree is to branch

   (E) Frog is to water

A Doberman is a kind of dog, so try that sentence with the answer choices. The only match is *bass is to fish* because a bass is a kind of fish; therefore, Choice **(A)** is the correct answer.

2. Roof is to house as

    (A) Hair is to color

    (B) Table is to chair

    (C) Monkey is to banana

    (D) Sail is to boat

    (E) Cat is to milk

    Think about what a roof does for a house and also the location of the roof. A roof sits on top of a house, and a sail sits on top of a boat. This relationship is the strongest one that matches the answer choices, so the correct answer is Choice **(D).** You may have to try a few different relationship sentences to find one that works.

3. Fire is to candle as

    (A) Juice is to cup

    (B) Oven is to pan

    (C) Car is to gear

    (D) Motor is to gasoline

    (E) Computer is to mouse

    Fire burns a candle, just like a motor burns gasoline, so the correct answer is Choice **(D).** You may tend to think that the *oven to pan* option is good because an oven heats a pan, but when you refine the relationship, you see that the fire burns the candle for energy, much the same way a motor burns gasoline for energy.

4. Rock is to dirt as

    (A) Carpet is to floor

    (B) Shell is to sand

    (C) Shirt is to button

    (D) Hungry is to full

    (E) Tire is to car

    This question is all about location. You can find a rock in the dirt just as you can find a shell in the sand, so the correct answer is Choice **(B).** When you face a question like this one, just try to see a picture in your mind of a rock sitting in some dirt, and then take that same mental image and apply it to the other answer choices.

5. Fountain is to water as

    (A) Volcano is to lava

    (B) Mustard is to bottle

    (C) Grill is to fish

    (D) Lawn is to mower

    (E) Dirt is to mud

    This question is all about action. A fountain spews or ejects water just like a volcano spews or ejects lava, so the correct answer is Choice **(A).** You may think that Choice (B), *mustard is to bottle,* is a good answer. Although it's close, a bottle squirts mustard only if you make it do so. The volcano and lava option is more similar in relationship to fountain and water. Remember that you're looking for the *best* answer.

6. Ocean is to wave as

    (A) Candy is to teeth

    (B) Tire is to track

    (C) Milk is to cow

    (D) Soup is to bowl

    (E) Zoo is to monkey

This one is a bit more difficult. You may say that a wave is in the ocean or a feature of the ocean, but that still doesn't give you a matching relationship in the answer choices. You need a stronger relationship. If you say, "The ocean generates waves because of force," then you can see that "a tire creates a track because of force," so the best answer is Choice **(B)**.

7. Brain is to heartbeat as

    (A) Bat is to ball

    (B) Water is to roses

    (C) Steering wheel is to direction

    (D) Rock is to weight

    (E) Child is to school

This one is also more difficult. First, find the relationship between *brain* and *heartbeat*. Then, create a sentence, using these words that show the relationship. Make sure your example isn't too specific but specific enough that it clearly shows the relationship. The brain and heart are both part of the body, but the analogy says *heartbeat*, which is the speed of the heart. The brain controls the heart's beating, so a good relationship sentence is, "The brain controls the heartbeat." If you use this sentence and apply it to the other answer choices, you get, "The bat controls the ball," "The water controls the roses," "The steering wheel controls the direction," and "The rock controls the weight." Choice **(C)** is the correct answer because it shows the same kind of control relationship.

Practicing Lower Level SSAT Analogy Questions on Your Own

Now that you've practiced a few analogy questions, work on this set of questions on your own. Remember to use your sentence strategy to find the relationships between the pairs of words. Also, watch your time as you practice: Try to answer these 15 questions in less than 8 minutes.

1. Bowl is to spoon as

    (A) DVD is to MP3

    (B) Chair is to floor

    (C) Float is to pool

    (D) Cat is to claw

    (E) Sing is to dance

2. Sing is to dance as

    (A) Cookie is to milk

    (B) Straw is to camel

    (C) Moon is to sun

    (D) Trip is to map

    (E) Win is to lose

3. Tadpole is to frog as
    (A) Cat is to fur
    (B) Slide is to run
    (C) Cotton is to shirt
    (D) Sleep is to wake
    (E) Cry is to baby

4. School is to student as
    (A) Cry is to smirk
    (B) Port is to boat
    (C) Toast is to ketchup
    (D) Snail is to sand
    (E) Bed is to room

5. Clock is to time as
    (A) Oven is to bake
    (B) Glass is to fill
    (C) Milk is to cow
    (D) Barometer is to pressure
    (E) Summer is to winter

6. Octopus is to ink as
    (A) Mouse is to cheese
    (B) House is to alarm
    (C) Iron is to heat
    (D) Radio is to signal
    (E) Car is to radio

7. Circle is to ball as
    (A) Mug is to triangle
    (B) Stair is to step
    (C) Square is to box
    (D) Island is to ocean
    (E) Camera is to lens

8. Nurse is to doctor as
    (A) Paralegal is to dentist
    (B) Tutor is to student
    (C) Calendar is to day
    (D) Tragedy is to belonging
    (E) Actor is to stage

9. Storm is to rain as
    (A) Genius is to smart
    (B) Algae is to green
    (C) Summer is to fun
    (D) Chicken is to egg
    (E) House is to window

10. Milkshake is to milk as
    (A) Car is to paint
    (B) Waffle is to syrup
    (C) Doughnut is to jelly
    (D) Axe is to metal
    (E) Game is to play

11. Sugar is to pie as
    (A) Corn is to cook
    (B) Vanilla is to bean
    (C) Chlorine is to water
    (D) June is to July
    (E) Jump is to fall

12. Light bulb is to lamp as
    (A) Motor is to boat
    (B) Toothbrush is to water
    (C) Tomato is to sauce
    (D) Anger is to pity
    (E) Alligator is to water

13. Worry is to sleeplessness as crime is to
    (A) Passivity
    (B) Apathy
    (C) Denial
    (D) Punishment
    (E) Mischief

14. Couch is to cushions as bed is to
    (A) Horizontal
    (B) Blanket
    (C) Sleep
    (D) Night
    (E) Floor

15. Pathology is to disease as nephrology is to
    (A) Kidneys
    (B) Heart
    (C) Blood
    (D) Atoms
    (E) Skin

Answers to Lower Level SSAT Analogy Questions

1. **C.** You use a spoon to eat from a bowl, so you can create a sentence that says, "You use a spoon with a bowl." Similarly, you use a float to float in a pool. The other answer choices don't express this relationship.

2. **A.** Singing and dancing are activities often enjoyed together, so you're looking for the same kind of relationship. The best answer, Choice (A), is *cookie* and *milk* because those two food items are often enjoyed together.

3. **C.** A tadpole turns into a frog through metamorphosis. Although the answer choices aren't as specific, Choice (C) is the best answer because you can turn cotton into a shirt with manufacturing.

4. **B.** A student goes to a school or belongs to a school. In a similar relationship, a boat goes to a port or belongs to a port.

5. **D.** A clock is a device that measures time, so you're looking for a similar kind of relationship. A barometer is a device that measures atmospheric pressure, so it's the best answer.

6. **B.** An octopus can eject ink as a defense system against predators, so you can create a sentence like, "An octopus uses ink as a defense." In a similar way, a house can be equipped with an alarm, which is also a defense strategy.

7. **C.** A ball is formed in the basic shape of a circle, so you're looking for an answer that expresses the same kind of relationship. The best answer is Choice (C) because a box can be shaped in a square.

8. **B.** A nurse is someone who assists a doctor. In the same way, a tutor assists a student, so Choice (B) is the best answer.

9. **D.** A storm can *produce* rain. If you think in those terms, the best similar relationship is a chicken because a chicken can produce an egg.

10. **D.** You use milk to create a milkshake. In the same way, you use metal to create an axe. Choice (D) is the best answer.

11. **C.** Sugar is a part of a pie. Likewise, chlorine is often a part of water. Both items function as ingredients.

12. **A.** A lamp powers a light bulb, in that the light bulb can't do anything without being powered by the electricity of the lamp. Because a boat is powered by a motor, Choice (A) is the best answer.

13. **D.** Worry can lead to sleeplessness. Crime can lead to punishment. These pairs share the same kind of relationship.

14. **B.** Cushions make a couch more comfortable. In the same way, a blanket can make a bed more comfortable. Choice (B) is the correct answer.

15. **A.** Pathology is the study or treatment of disease. Nephrology is the study or treatment of the kidneys.

If you struggled (which is perfectly normal), stop for a minute and think about how you're creating your sentences. Remember that you want to create a sentence that expresses the relationship between the two words. Don't make it too specific so nothing else matches the relationship, but don't make it so general that anything goes either. Also, remember that relationships between words can be expressed in several different ways. If one doesn't work, try another — just remember to work quickly.

Tackling Guided Upper Level SSAT Analogy Questions

Following are some upper level SSAT analogy questions to get you warmed up. Each question is followed by an explanation of the correct answer and how you may reach it.

1. Abase is to degrade as

   (A) Strength is to weakness

   (B) Camel is to heat

   (C) Sunday is to Saturday

   (D) Obtuse is to acute

   (E) Strength is to might

Abase and *degrade* both mean to belittle someone or something, so the relationship here is simply sameness. You need to pick the answer choice that has two words that mean the same thing. If you check out the list of options, you can see that *strength* and *might* mean the same thing, and Choice **(E)** is the only word pair that does.

What do you do if you don't know either word in the question? Make an educated guess, or skip it and move on. (See Chapter 4 for strategies to answering analogy questions.)

2. Minute is to hour as hour is to

   (A) Day

   (B) Time

   (C) Week

   (D) Watch

   (E) Time

This question is rather simple; all you have to do is compare two distinct aspects of time. Because minute is a part of an hour, the best similar relationship is Choice **(A)** because hour is a part of a day.

3. Dreary is to mood as

    (A) Pain is to agony

    (B) Time is to watch

    (C) Bean is to green

    (D) Cucumber is to vegetable

    (E) Gum is to teeth

    The correct answer is Choice **(D).** Dreary is a kind of mood, so it's part of a group. In the same way, a cucumber is a kind of vegetable. Always think about specific and broad categories that appear in a question, which is often a tip that one item is a part of a group. Look for a similar relationship in the answer choices.

4. Hurt is to pain as

    (A) Carpet is to soft

    (B) Tired is to sleep

    (C) Geometry is to triangle

    (D) Motion is to stillness

    (E) Smile is to face

    This question is about a cause and effect relationship. If you get hurt, the wound causes pain. In the same way, if you get tired, you get sleepy. Both these analogies show a cause and effect relationship, so the best answer is Choice **(B).**

5. Limber is to bend as

    (A) Kind is to smile

    (B) Strong is to lift

    (C) Tread is to water

    (D) School is to book

    (E) Street is to surface

    This question explores the relationship of ability. If you're limber, you have the ability to bend. If you're strong, you have the ability to exert power or force, or lift something, so the correct answer is Choice **(B).**

6. Tenuous is to strength as terrestrial is to

    (A) Deep

    (B) Crazy

    (C) Water

    (D) Land

    (E) Rock

    This is a vocabulary-based question, so you need to know what the words mean to figure out the relationship. *Tenuous* means weak, which is the opposite of *strength*. So you need a word that's the opposite of *terrestrial,* which means land. The correct answer is Choice **(C),** *water.*

7. Weather is to erosion as

(A) Money is to surplus

(B) Current is to water

(C) Carelessness is to accident

(D) Wheel is to turn

(E) Summer is to sun

This question is about cause. Weather causes erosion — simple enough — so plug that relationship in to the other answer choices: "Money causes surplus," "current causes water," "carelessness causes accident(s)," "wheel causes a turn." Choices (B), (D), and (E) no longer make sense, so you can rule those out. However, both Choices (A) and (C) are possible answers. The more money you have, the more of a surplus you have, and carelessness can certainly cause accidents. So, at this point, you need to refine your sentence further so it's more specific. You can try something like, "Weather causes destructive erosion," because erosion by its nature wears away the landscape. Now, if you try to use the sentence that way, you can see that Choice **(C)** is the most similar because accidents are destructive as well.

Practicing Upper Level SSAT Analogy Questions on Your Own

Now that you've practiced a few analogy questions, work on this set of questions on your own. Remember to use your sentence strategy to find the relationships between the pairs of words. Also, watch your time as you practice: Try to answer these 15 questions in less than 8 minutes.

1. Vegan is to meat as

(A) Court is to trial

(B) Simple is to complex

(C) Smooth is to rough

(D) Cat is to water

(E) Rain is to cloud

2. Tomato is to ripen as

(A) Cookie is to flour

(B) Dog is to bark

(C) Sun is to burn

(D) Seed is to sprout

(E) Bean is to bake

3. Wood is to lumber as

(A) Salt is to season

(B) Cotton is to shirt

(C) Gasoline is to burn

(D) Leg is to jump

(E) Kidney is to blood

4. Sing is to vocal cord as

(A) Cry is to smile

(B) Street is to car

(C) Hole is to shovel

(D) Snail is to slow

(E) Animal is to species

5. Travel is to airplane as
    (A) Child is to adult
    (B) Fry is to bacon
    (C) Bread is to wheat
    (D) Computer is to play
    (E) Luggage is to coat

6. Hawaii is to ocean as
    (A) Human is to air
    (B) Cat is to fur
    (C) Coffee is to hot
    (D) TV is to signal
    (E) Key is to turn

7. Game is to strategy as
    (A) Gym is to sweat
    (B) Stair is to climb
    (C) Math is to formula
    (D) Island is to remote
    (E) Dungeon is to ground

8. Climatology is to weather as
    (A) Pharmacology is to dentist
    (B) Psychology is to mind
    (C) Kinesiology is to finger
    (D) Flower is to seed
    (E) Note is to ink

9. Drink is to swallow as
    (A) Tired is to energetic
    (B) Plant is to grow
    (C) Swim is to sweat
    (D) Bed is to sleep
    (E) Thirst is to water

10. Fear is to phobic as
    (A) Trial is to jury
    (B) Exhaustion is to exercise
    (C) Bake is to eat
    (D) Hammer is to nail
    (E) Smile is to laugh

11. Sprinkle is to flood as
    (A) Grape is to ripen
    (B) Simmer is to boil
    (C) Sleep is to rise
    (D) May is to February
    (E) Snore is to throat

12. Ruddy is to pale as tedious is to
    (A) Transit
    (B) Remember
    (C) Exciting
    (D) Boring
    (E) Singular

13. Hierarchy is to order as immaculate is to
    (A) Trite
    (B) Develop
    (C) Clean
    (D) Sweep
    (E) Tired

14. Benevolent is to hateful as bilk is to
    (A) Cheating
    (B) Lying
    (C) Honest
    (D) Friendly
    (E) Vile

15. Algid is to cold as perfunctory is to
    (A) Sincere
    (B) Tepid
    (C) Cursory
    (D) Anger
    (E) Generous

Answers to Upper Level SSAT Analogy Questions

1. **D.** A *vegan* is someone who doesn't eat animal products. So you're looking for a relationship between two words where one avoids or restricts the other. The only possible answer is *cat to water*. Of course, cats drink water, but they avoid getting wet and don't enjoy swimming or getting a bath. This answer may feel like a stretch but remember that the analogy is about a *similar* relationship. Choice (D) is the only answer choice with the same basic kind of relationship.

2. **D.** The *tomato to ripen* pairing tells you that the tomato goes through a *positive* process. A seed sprouting is also a positive process in that the seed turns into a plant.

3. **B.** Wood can be used to manufacture lumber just as cotton can be used to manufacture a shirt. The other answer choices don't express this kind of relationship.

4. **C.** Vocal cords are used to create sound. In the same way, you can use a shovel to create a hole.

5. **B.** An airplane is a method of traveling. Likewise, frying is a method for cooking bacon. The other answer choices don't have this kind of relationship.

6. **A.** This question is a bit difficult at first glance. Hawaii is a chain of islands in the South Pacific. They're *surrounded* by water. In the same way, we're constantly surrounded by air. The other answer choices don't have the same relationship.

7. **C.** You can win a game by using a strategy. In the same way, you can solve a math problem by using a formula.

8. **B.** The suffix *-ology* means the study of something, so you're looking for two words that mean the study of one thing. **Psychology** is the study of the mind, and that's the only correct answer choice here.

9. **D.** This one is a bit tricky. The purpose of drinking something is to swallow the liquid. In a similar way, the purpose of a bed is to sleep in it. You may say that the purpose of a plant is to grow, but growth isn't the plant's only purpose. Choice (D) is the best answer that's most similar to the question word pair.

10. **B.** If you're a phobic of something, you're afraid of it. So you can say that "phobia produces fear." In a similar way, exercise can produce exhaustion.

11. **B.** This question presents two different extreme states — a sprinkle and flood. So you're looking for two different extreme states of the same thing. Simmer and boil is the best answer here.

12. **C.** A ruddy complexion means that your face is red or healthy. Pale is the opposite. So you need the opposite of tedious, which is *exciting*.

13. **C.** *Hierarchy* is an *order* of something, so you need a word that means the same thing as *immaculate*. The answer is *clean*.

14. **C.** *Benevolent* means kind or harmless, which is the opposite of hateful. You need a word that means the opposite of *bilk* (cheat). The correct answer is *honest*.

15. **C.** *Algid* and *cold* mean the same thing, so you need a word that means the same thing as *perfunctory*. The correct answer is *cursory*.

Tackling Guided Lower and Middle Level Synonym Questions

Following are some lower and middle level synonym questions typical for the SSAT and ISEE. Each question is followed by an explanation of the correct answer and how you may reach it.

1. DYSFUNCTIONAL:

    (A) Nocturnal

    (B) Criminal

    (C) Edgy

    (D) Not working

    (E) Pristine

    Dysfunctional means not functional. With the prefix *dys-* in front of the word *functional,* you can probably figure out the meaning of the word, even if you're not sure. So in your word list, you're looking for the opposite of *functional,* which completes the synonym for *dysfunctional.* The best answer is Choice **(D),** *not working.*

2. DESCRIPTIVE:

    (A) Vivid

    (B) Serene

    (C) Plotless

    (D) Developmental

    (E) Dreamy

    You know that the word *descriptive* means describing something — that's easy. Yet, if you scan the answer choices, figuring out which answer is correct may be difficult. In this case, just rule out the words you know aren't correct, so you can cross off Choices (C), (D), and (E) quickly. **Serene** means peaceful, so you can rule that one out, too. Choice **(A),** *vivid,* is the best option because something vivid is highly detailed, a synonym for descriptive.

3. PASSIVE:

    (A) Hyper

    (B) Indifferent

    (C) Opinionated

    (D) Concerned

    (E) Responsive

    In this example, all but one of the answer choices are *antonyms* (opposites) of the given word. The only correct answer is Choice **(B),** *indifferent.* If you're passive, you're unconcerned or indifferent to something. All the other words carry a meaning of concern or care.

4. RELUCTANT:

(A) Astonish

(B) Aimless

(C) Demure

(D) Anxious

(E) Hesitant

The word *reluctant* means that you're hesitant to do something, so Choice **(E)** is the only correct answer here.

Remember to try and always think of your own definition to the word before you scan the answer choices. Doing so helps you stay on track and keeps you from choosing a word that simply looks good from the list.

5. COALITION:

(A) Ambiguity

(B) Destruction

(C) Disagreement

(D) Alliance

(E) Singular

A *coalition* is a group of people who work together under an agreement or for a specific purpose. Knowing that definition, the only possible synonym in the list of answer choices is Choice **(D)**, *alliance*.

Practicing Lower and Middle Level Synonym Questions on Your Own

Try this set of lower and middle level synonym questions. Because you have to work quickly on the exam, practice working with a timer and try to answer these 10 questions in only 4 minutes.

1. HANDSOME:

(A) Trying

(B) Believable

(C) Renegade

(D) Dapper

(E) Truthful

2. CONDONE:

(A) Allow

(B) Disembark

(C) Jocular

(D) Mismanage

(E) Connect

3. CONFUSING:

(A) Trite

(B) Obscure

(C) Lax

(D) Clear

(E) Pretentious

4. NIMBLE:

(A) Slow

(B) Intelligent

(C) Clumsy

(D) Agile

(E) Polished

5. TWIST:
   (A) Replace
   (B) Switch
   (C) Relocate
   (D) Move
   (E) Writhe

6. EVASIVE:
   (A) Curt
   (B) Determined
   (C) Egotistical
   (D) Avoiding
   (E) Confrontational

7. DISRESPECTFUL:
   (A) Insolent
   (B) Remarkable
   (C) Contour
   (D) Credible
   (E) Shy

8. CONGENIAL:
   (A) Taciturn
   (B) Confused
   (C) Confined
   (D) Determined
   (E) Agreeable

9. JUSTIFY:
   (A) Admire
   (B) Defend
   (C) Rectify
   (D) Blot
   (E) Compare

10. BLEND:
    (A) Merge
    (B) Hesitate
    (C) Justify
    (D) Expand
    (E) Scant

Answers to Lower and Middle Level Synonym Questions

1. **D.** *Dapper* is a synonym for handsome — both of which refer to someone who's attractive, typically a male. The other words provide some different characteristics a person may possess, but none of them are synonyms for handsome.

2. **A.** If you *condone* something, you allow it by either letting it happen or simply ignoring it. The other answer choices have nothing to do with this concept.

3. **B.** If something is confusing, it's difficult to understand. In the same way, the word *obscure* means unclear.

4. **D.** *Nimble* means dexterous, which has to do with how easily or skillfully you can move your body. The word *agile* means the same thing.

5. **E.** If you twist something, you bend or contort it in some way. The word *writhe* means the same thing.

6. **D.** The word *evasive* means someone or something that's tricky or avoids something, especially when answering a question. For example, if you asked someone, "How did you do on the test?" and that person gave you a noncommittal answer, you'd say he or she was evasive.

7. **A.** *Disrespectful* means to not respect someone or something. The word *insolent* means the same thing.

8. **E.** Both *congenial* and *agreeable* mean something along the lines of easy to get along with.

9. **B.** To *justify* means to support or prove that something is right. *Defend* means basically the same thing.

10. **A.** If you blend something, you mix different items together. The best choice in the list is *merge,* which means to put two or more things together.

Tackling Guided Upper Level Synonym Questions

Following are some upper level synonym questions typical for the SSAT and ISEE. Each question is followed by an explanation of the correct answer and how you may reach it.

1. OBFUSCATE:

    (A) Redirect

    (B) Confuse

    (C) Raze

    (D) Measure

    (E) Define

    Obfuscate means to make something complicated or confusing, so Choice **(B)** is the only synonym in the group provided.

    If you're unsure of the meaning of the word given to you, try to rule out answers you believe are incorrect.

2. BRUTAL:

    (A) Genial

    (B) Coy

    (C) Endearing

    (D) Truculent

    (E) Fixed

    The word *brutal* is easy enough, so the task is finding a synonym in the list of words provided. Once again, use the process of elimination to rule out possible options. The only synonym in the list is Choice **(D)**, *truculent,* which means savagely brutal.

3. VACUOUS:

    (A) Full

    (B) Lacking

    (C) Degenerate

    (D) Challenging

    (E) Unresponsive

    Vacuous means lacking an idea or lacking substance — something that's empty. The only possible synonym in the provided choices is simply *lacking,* Choice **(B).**

4. CABAL:

    (A) Luminary

    (B) Neophyte

    (C) Paltriness

    (D) Group

    (E) Wane

TIP A *cabal* is a small group, so Choice **(D)** is the correct answer. This question is tough because if you don't know what a cabal is, you'll have a hard time ruling out answer choices. You can try and eliminate answer choices you believe are incorrect and simply guess if you don't know the word.

5. FLIMSY:

   (A) Tenuous

   (B) Quixotic

   (C) Clammy

   (D) Barbarous

   (E) Illustrious

With this question, you have an easy word but more difficult words to choose as a synonym. The correct answer is Choice **(A)** because *tenuous* means something that's flimsy or not solid, especially when referring to an argument or a concept.

Practicing Upper Level Synonym Questions on Your Own

Try this set of upper level synonym questions similar to what you'll see on the SSAT and ISEE. Because you have to work quickly on the exam, practice working with a timer and try to answer these 10 questions in only 4 minutes or less.

1. ARROGANT:

   (A) Bumptious

   (B) Languid

   (C) Banal

   (D) Demure

   (E) Silent

2. DISASTER:

   (A) Meander

   (B) Evasiveness

   (C) Trial

   (D) Tribulation

   (E) Finesse

3. LUGUBRIOUS:

   (A) Obscure

   (B) Trite

   (C) Mournful

   (D) Placid

   (E) Mimic

4. REVERENCE:

   (A) Obeisance

   (B) Plebeian

   (C) Enactor

   (D) Quiescence

   (E) Bauble

5. CURE:

   (A) Panacea

   (B) Trinket

   (C) Banality

   (D) Mellifluousness

   (E) Vulgarity

6. CURTAIL:

   (A) Joy

   (B) Sublime

   (C) Resist

   (D) Avoid

   (E) Abbreviate

7. BUOYANT:
   (A) Nebulous
   (B) Buyable
   (C) Floatable
   (D) Selective
   (E) Redolent

8. BIBULOUS:
   (A) Messy
   (B) Absorbent
   (C) Reluctant
   (D) Noxious
   (E) Signal

9. PALLIATIVE:
   (A) Tacit
   (B) Tenacious
   (C) Tepid
   (D) Relieving
   (E) Tremorous

10. VERNACULAR:
   (A) Hope
   (B) Cauterization
   (C) Adjunct
   (D) Venerability
   (E) Speech

Answers to Upper Level Synonym Questions

1. **A.** *Arrogant* and *bumptious* mean the same thing — they both refer to negative behavior where a person has an exaggerated self opinion.

2. **D.** *Disaster* and *tribulation* mean the same thing. They both refer to destruction.

3. **C.** *Lugubrious* means overly mournful, so the synonym is basically the definition of the word.

4. **A.** *Obeisance* is a gesture of respect or reverence so this word is the only possible synonym in the list.

5. **A.** A *panacea* is something that cures everything, so in this list of answer choices, Choice (A) is the only possible synonym.

6. **E.** If you *curtail* something, you cut it short, so *abbreviate,* Choice (E), is the correct answer.

7. **C.** If something is *buoyant,* it can float in the water, so the correct synonym is simply *floatable.*

8. **B.** *Bibulous* simply means *absorbent,* so that word is the correct synonym.

9. **D.** *Palliative* refers to something that provides relief, especially from pain.

10. **E.** *Vernacular* refers to common speech or slang, so *speech* is the correct answer.

Tackling Guided Lower and Middle Level ISEE Sentence Completion Questions

Following are some lower and middle level sentence completion questions typical for the ISEE. Each question is followed by an explanation of the correct answer and how you may reach it.

Sentence completion questions are all about picking the right word or phrase in order to complete the idea or thought in the sentence.

1. Carl was _____ after failing to make even one goal in the game.

   (A) smiling

   (B) disappointed

   (C) peaceful

   (D) indifferent

   You know from the context that Carl tried to make a goal but failed. You can assume that because of failing, Carl was *disappointed,* Choice **(B)**, which is the only answer choice that completes the meaning in the sentence.

2. Mary was _____ when she was given the award because she didn't even know she was a candidate.

   (A) indifferent

   (B) furious

   (C) saddened

   (D) surprised

   Think about the context of the sentence and try to fill in the blank with your own word first. You know from the sentence that Mary received an award she didn't expect, so the most natural emotional reaction is Choice **(D)**, *surprised.*

3. When her parents suddenly told Tracy they were moving to another state, she was emotionally _____ at first.

   (A) shocked

   (B) determined

   (C) challenging

   (D) trivial

   This one is a bit more difficult. You know that Tracy wasn't expecting a move to another state, so she could have a number of different emotions. As you look at the answer choices, however, only one conveys a likely emotion or reaction, which is Choice **(A)**, *shocked.*

4. After years of neglect, the building fell into _____.

   (A) abatement

   (B) disrepair

   (C) perfection

   (D) court

   If something is neglected, such as a building, it tends to fall into *disrepair,* Choice **(B)**, because buildings require maintenance. Again, try to fill in the blank with your own word first so the answer choices don't throw you off track. Also, notice that the prefix *dis-* means not and the root word *repair* has to do with fixing something that's broken or not working. Look for word clues like these to help you choose the correct answer.

5. Even though the vacation began with _____, the constant problems soon made everyone feel _____.

   (A) frustration . . . peaceful

   (B) chaos . . . joyful

   (C) difficulty . . . resistance

   (D) promise . . . unenthusiastic

From the context, you know that the vacation began with something but ended with something else. The words _even though_ at the beginning of the sentence help you know that a change occurred. Also, because there were _constant problems,_ you can assume that the result was negative. Therefore, the best answer is Choice **(D).** The vacation began with _promise,_ but the problems made everyone _unenthusiastic._

Practicing Lower and Middle Level ISEE Sentence Completion Questions on Your Own

Try this set of lower and middle level sentence completion questions characteristic of the questions on the ISEE. Because you have to work quickly on the exam, practice working with a timer and try to answer these 10 questions in only 4 minutes or less.

1. Knowing that Mrs. Anderson was _____ with heart trouble, everyone tried to make her as comfortable as possible.

   (A) entwined

   (B) denoted

   (C) afflicted

   (D) scattered

2. The student was _____ with his performance. After all, he made straight A's for the entire school year.

   (A) overjoyed

   (B) civil

   (C) troubled

   (D) angry

3. To perform well in school, being organized and _____ is important.

   (A) obscure

   (B) resistant

   (C) antagonistic

   (D) determined

4. After the storm, the streets were littered with _____. Thankfully, no one was hurt.

   (A) rain

   (B) chaos

   (C) debris

   (D) calculations

5. The shirt was so _____ that Marcie decided to try a larger size.

   (A) loose

   (B) torn

   (C) snug

   (D) colorful

6. The entire plan was very _____. No one thought it would work.

   (A) impractical

   (B) thoughtful

   (C) directed

   (D) driven

7. She was tired of the constant _____. She decided she would not be friends with the group any longer.

   (A) peace

   (B) bickering

   (C) connotations

   (D) after effects

8. Her mother told her to clean her room, but Sarah thought it was _____ already.

   (A) tried

   (B) dirty

   (C) reticulate

   (D) immaculate

9. The student was very _____. After all, he made a pulley from some sticks and glue.

   (A) stoical

   (B) reluctant

   (C) tiresome

   (D) inventive

10. The _____ river made the canoe trip very _____.

    (A) gentle . . . awkward

    (B) treacherous . . . dangerous

    (C) dirty . . . relaxing

    (D) small . . . alert

Answers to Lower and Middle Level ISEE Sentence Completion Questions

1. **C.** Because Mrs. Anderson has heart trouble, you need a word that completes the meaning. *Afflicted* is the only word in the list that makes sense in the context of the sentence.

2. **A.** From the context, you know that the student was very happy with his performance, so the best answer that completes the meaning of the sentence is Choice (A), *overjoyed*.

3. **D.** To complete the thought, the only possible word that makes sense is *determined*. So organization and determination are keys to success in this sentence.

4. **C.** From the sentence, you know that a storm littered, or covered, the streets in something. You also know that no one was hurt, although from the context, someone could have been. Therefore, the best answer is *debris,* which means various items, such as trash, limbs, and so forth.

5. **C.** From the context, you know the shirt must have been tight because Marcie decided to try a larger size. *Snug* is the only word that completes the meaning of the sentence.

6. **A.** No one thought the plan would work, so you're looking for a word that helps convey that meaning. The word *impractical* is the best choice here.

7. **B.** Because the girl doesn't want to be friends with the group any longer, you're looking for a negative word that makes the meaning clear. *Bickering* is the best answer.

8. **D.** Sarah believes the room is already clean from the context of the sentence, so you're looking for a word that conveys this meaning. The word *immaculate* means perfectly clean, so it's the best answer.

9. **D.** Because the student made something functional from sticks and glue, the best answer choice to complete the meaning of the sentence is *inventive*.

10. **B.** When you read the sentence, you're unclear of its meaning without the missing words, so you simply need to pick two words that bring some sense to the sentence. If the river is treacherous, then the trip would be dangerous. Of the answer choices, this pair is the only one that makes sense.

Tackling Guided Upper Level ISEE Sentence Completion Questions

Following are some upper level sentence completion questions typical for the ISEE. Each question is followed by an explanation of the correct answer and how you may reach it.

Sentence completion questions are all about picking the right word or phrase in order to complete the idea or thought in the sentence.

1. The musician's _____ performance made everyone stand in applause.

   (A) noxious

   (B) saturnine

   (C) turbid

   (D) meritorious

   From the context of this sentence, you know that everyone stood in applause due to the performance. The only word that works in this sentence is Choice **(D)**, *meritorious,* which means deserving praise.

2. Although the _____ the man told the police was believable, it was later found to be untrue.

   (A) soliloquy

   (B) fluctuation

   (C) canard

   (D) vernacular

   The correct answer is Choice **(C)**, *canard,* which by definition is an untrue story. Try to rule out word choices you know are incorrect so you can narrow down the answer.

3. The _____ approach to the problem ensured that no one stopped to consider some practical implications of carrying out the solution.

   (A) pedantic

   (B) enigmatic

   (C) vituperative

   (D) defunct

   From the context, you know that you're looking for a word that conveys the meaning of something impractical or not practically considered. The only word that works is Choice **(A)**, *pedantic,* which means to be overly concerned with academic or book learning. In this context, *pedantic* means that the approach was overly *theoretical* and not so practical.

4. Because the student struggled with math, a _____ course in the basics was necessary.

   (A) research

   (B) distracting

   (C) typical

   (D) rudimentary

You're looking for the concept of basic in this sentence. The student struggled in math, so he needed a basic math course. The only word that works in this sentence is Choice **(D)**, *rudimentary,* which means basic or elementary.

5. The _____ child began to _____ his older brother.

    (A) careful . . . annoy

    (B) willful . . . acumen

    (C) loud . . . vex

    (D) distracted . . . cajole

From the context, you know that the child has a quality that does something to his older brother, although you don't know what. So find a word pair that simply makes sense within the context of the sentence. The best answer is Choice **(C)**, the *loud* child began to *vex* (annoy or bother) his older brother.

Practicing Upper Level ISEE Sentence Completion Questions on Your Own

Try this set of upper level sentence completion questions resembling questions you may see on the ISEE. Because you have to work quickly on the exam, practice working with a timer and try to answer these 10 questions in only 4 minutes or less.

1. The _____ civic club gave its leftover monies to another local group after they disbanded.

    (A) successful

    (B) defunct

    (C) affiliated

    (D) distorted

2. His convoluted discussion _____ the entire group.

    (A) plummeted

    (B) crowded

    (C) impetus

    (D) stymied

3. After hours of no accomplishment, the team became _____.

    (A) apathetic

    (B) penchant

    (C) specious

    (D) caliber

4. Her _____ speech sounded great, but everyone knew it was pointless.

    (A) engendered

    (B) bombastic

    (C) kindled

    (D) replete

5. Despite trying to make the situation better, John finally _____ himself to the inevitable fact that he would lose his job.

    (A) corrected

    (B) abhorred

    (C) removed

    (D) resigned

6. The councilman _____ the motion when he realized he didn't have adequate support.

    (A) saturated

    (B) ensconced

    (C) rescinded

    (D) masticated

7. The _____ style of the Victorian room was charming to some and tacky to others.

    (A) brusque

    (B) vestige

    (C) bedlam

    (D) baroque

8. Her _____ behavior made her even more attractive.

    (A) demure

    (B) derogatory

    (C) baroque

    (D) cryptic

9. She _____ the two pieces of art on the wall in the gallery.

    (A) invoked

    (B) characterized

    (C) subterfuge

    (D) juxtaposed

10. The _____ conversation was difficult at best, but Gina knew she could _____ the conflict in time.

    (A) entwined . . . recover

    (B) sonorous . . . abate

    (C) convoluted . . . resolve

    (D) degreed . . . resolute

Answers to Upper Level ISEE Sentence Completion Questions

1. **B. *Defunct*** means no longer functioning. Considering that the group gave its monies away before disbanding, this word completes the meaning of the sentence.

2. **D.** The word ***stymie*** means to stump or confuse. Considering the context of the sentence, this word is the only one that completes the meaning.

3. **A. *Apathetic*** means with little emotion or caring. The sentence tells the reader that after no accomplishment, the team started to lose interest and didn't care.

4. **B. *Bombastic*** means impressive but meaningless language. Within the context of the sentence, this word is the only answer that makes sense.

5. **D.** In this context, the word ***resigned*** means to accept. The sentence is saying that despite John's best efforts, he accepted the fact that he would lose his job.

6. **C.** The word ***rescind*** means to repeal, and it's the only word in the group that completes the meaning of the sentence.

7. **E. *Baroque*** means overly decorated, so within the context of the sentence, this word is the only one that completes the meaning of the sentence.

8. **A. *Demure*** means modest, and in the context of this sentence, it's the only answer choice that provides a positive characteristic.

9. **E. *Juxtapose*** means to place two items side by side, which is the only word that makes sense in this sentence.

10. **C.** You need two words that complete the meaning of the sentence. The best answer is Choice (C), so you have "the *convoluted* conversation" and "*resolve* the conflict." When you consider the other answer choices, Choice (C) is the only pair that makes sense within the context of the sentence.

Chapter 6

Comprehending Reading Comprehension

· ·

In This Chapter

▶ Discovering how to read passages on the test

▶ Looking at the different kinds of reading comprehension questions

▶ Exploring some reading comprehension strategies

· ·

All levels of the SSAT and ISEE have a Reading Comprehension section. No sweat, right? After all, you simply read a passage, answer a few questions, and move on to something else.

Not so fast! Reading comprehension on the exam isn't like relaxing in a recliner and reading the latest vampire novel. Nope, it won't be that easy. The Reading Comprehension section requires you to read quickly, move fast through a variety of questions, and then do it again, and again, and . . . well, you get the point. In fact, you'll face several reading passages and several questions on each passage, and you'll have to get through all these questions smartly and quickly in order to get a higher score.

Don't worry, though. In this chapter, we explore some easy reading and testing strategies that can help you tame the Reading Comprehension section on your test. The even better news: Unlike the popular vampire novel, the SSAT and ISEE Reading Comprehension sections won't make you deal with fangs or make you afraid of things that go *bump* in the night!

Ramping Up on Reading Passages

No, we're not going to show you how to read in this section, but tackling the SSAT and ISEE reading comprehension passages is different than reading anything else you've ever attempted. Why? The answer is all about time. If you could take all the time you want, you could carefully read each passage on the test and answer the questions. The problem is that you don't get that luxury. In fact, you don't get any luxury at all. Here's what you *do* get:

✔ The lower and upper level SSAT give you 40 reading comprehension questions with a time limit of 40 minutes.

✔ The upper and middle level ISEE give you 36 reading comprehension questions with a time limit of 40 minutes.

✔ The lower level ISEE gives you 25 questions with a time limit of 25 minutes.

In a nutshell, regardless of which test you're taking, you have about a minute to answer each question; however, that time limit doesn't take reading the passages into account. So basically you have to share your allotted time between reading the passages and answering the questions, leaving only a handful of seconds to ponder each question. How's that fair? It isn't, but welcome to standardized testing.

Because the time limit is a problem, you need to know what types of passages to expect on the Reading Comprehension section of the exam and some strategies for reading them quickly while still collecting the info you need to answer the questions. We provide that info in the following sections.

Recognizing the types of reading passages

The good news about the reading passages on the SSAT and ISEE is that they tend to run the gamut in terms of topics — meaning that you'll read about all kinds of things. The bad news is you can't really plan on seeing certain kinds of content. You'll likely encounter reading passages in the following basic categories:

- ✔ **Writing from history:** In this category, you can find historical documents, newspaper articles, speeches, historical accounts, or general historical information that you may find in a textbook. The possible topics can cover just about any historical subject. The passage may be about a person, a group, an event, a discovery, and so on.

- ✔ **Writing from science:** Science passages make great test material because they tend to be full of information. Like history, you can encounter just about anything, including information about different animals, planets, plants, natural phenomenon, and so on.

- ✔ **Persuasion or opinion pieces:** You may find passages that express an author's opinion about a subject or one that seeks to persuade the audience. Again, virtually any topic goes.

- ✔ **Fiction and poetry:** You may see a fiction passage and possibly even a poem. You may get the entire story or poem or just a segment of one.

So what should you do to prepare for the many different kinds of writing and subjects you may face on the test? Simply be aware of what to expect on the exam. In other words, you don't need to read up on history and science before test day just because it _may_ be on the test. That strategy is a complete waste of time. Instead, spend your prep time deciding _how_ you're going to read the passage because you don't really have time to read it anyway.

Reading passages on the test

If you want to do well on the Reading Comprehension section, you need to change the way you think about reading a bit. After all, you probably normally read carefully to _understand_ the content. Most likely, when you read something, you can discuss the writing and some details about it. For the SSAT and ISEE, you need to think and read in a different way.

Your goal on the Reading Comprehension section is to answer questions correctly. How much you know about a passage after the exam doesn't matter; the goal is to simply answer the questions. So you have to read with that goal in mind. Often, students get bogged down by trying to read the passages carefully and intentionally, and they run out of time. You don't want to do that. You want to move quickly so you can answer more questions correctly. In the end, reading comprehension is all about the questions.

Because you don't have a lot of time to read the passages on the test, you need a few strategies for tackling the time crunch. The good news: You don't need to remember a lot of different strategies, but three primary techniques can help you, which we discuss in the next sections.

Scanning passages instead of reading them

Because you just don't have time to carefully read the passages on the test, shift into scanning mode and quickly scan over the passage. *Scanning* means that you don't read every word or sentence carefully. Instead, you scan the passage and look for the answers to two primary questions:

- **What's the main idea of the passage?** To find the main idea, scan the passage and come up with a single sentence that provides a summary of all the ideas together. Look for repeated ideas or phrasing in a passage, which are clues about the main idea. After you scan the passage, write down the main idea because it can help you stay on track.

- **What's the author's purpose?** In other words, why did the author write the passage? Is the writer simply giving information, or is he expressing an opinion, trying to persuade the reader to do something, making an argument, refuting an idea, and so on?

Figuring out the answers to these questions can help guide you as you answer the actual questions pertaining to the passage, and the good news is you're likely to see one or both of these questions on the exam.

Circling key words, phrases, and ideas

The Reading Comprehension section is an open book test. The reading passage is in front of you, and you can look at it as much as you want when you answer the questions. Don't get bogged down in trying to remember details — they're already in front of you anyway.

You can speed up your performance by circling key words, phrases, and ideas. For example, circle names, dates, and any part of a sentence that has important information. Doing so allows you to find details quickly when you see specific content questions. So scan and circle — and do so quickly!

Don't get caught up in the comprehension

The word *comprehend* means to mentally understand something. The funny thing about reading comprehension on the exam is that how well you actually comprehend the text in the passage may not matter for many of the questions. Keep in mind that you're not writing a paper or giving a speech about the content you read. The only thing you need to do is answer as many questions correctly as possible. You don't need to necessarily understand everything about the passage.

For example, what should you do if you end up reading a passage about nuclear energy that includes some technical details about atoms and particles that you really don't understand? Don't worry about it. In

other words, don't dwell on the fact that you may not understand everything because most of the questions come from the parts of the passage that you *do* understand. If you get bogged down in some vocabulary or technical content that you have trouble reading, your progress can come to a screeching halt, wasting time that you could be using to answer questions. After all, the goal is to answer as many questions correctly as possible. So if you don't understand some passage content and you can't answer a question about it, skip it and move on. Don't let difficult content or a difficult question or two halt your progress. Skip it and keep moving!

Creating a mental outline

Another reading tactic is to create a mental outline of the passage as you scan it. By simply writing a key word or two beside each paragraph or section of the passage, you can refer to and find information more quickly. The purpose of this tactic isn't so much to help directly answer test questions but to help you find information and details you may need. The trick, of course, is to do this exercise quickly — that is, don't waste time writing a summary sentence for each paragraph, but just a word or two will do. For example, say you read an essay about dogs, and one of the paragraphs discusses several common diseases. You can write the names of the diseases beside the paragraph so you know where to find the content if you face a question about one of the diseases.

This tactic is just a tool to help keep you mentally organized and to help you bring some sense of order to the passage, because what you're reading is often an excerpt of some longer piece of writing.

Checking out a sample passage

The following is a sample passage, similar to what you'll see on the exam. Scan the passage quickly, circle key words, phrases, and ideas, and then write the main idea and author's purpose.

Saturn is the second largest planet in our solar system, yet it has the lowest density of all the planets. Made of mostly hydrogen and oxygen, Saturn is essentially a gas planet. Although Saturn is 760 times the earth's size, it's only 95 times as dense. In fact, Saturn is less dense than water, which means that if you threw Saturn into a pool, the planet would actually float.

Although the other gaseous planets — Jupiter, Neptune, and Uranus — all have rings, Saturn's are the most notable. The largest of Saturn's rings is up to 200 times the diameter of the entire planet.

Because the density of the planet is so low, Saturn isn't a place that a person can ever visit because you can't stand on it. Other reasons Saturn would never make a good vacation destination include its atmosphere, which commonly has winds that reach up to 1,100 miles per hour, and its rotation speed. Saturn turns faster than any other planet except Jupiter, making a full rotation every 10 hours. Because the planet spins so quickly, the planet doesn't stay round. Instead, it flattens at its poles, causing the planet to be about 8,000 miles wider at its equator than at the poles.

Saturn is the farthest planet visible to the naked eye. Humans have observed and speculated about it for thousands of years. In fact, the planet gets its name from the Greek god Saturn, the god of agriculture and harvest.

What's the main idea of this passage?

_____

What's the author's purpose?

_____

How'd you do? Hopefully, you read quickly and circled some key phrases, words, and ideas, such as *size, composition, rings, density, rotation,* and *observation.* For the main idea and author's purpose, your answers may vary a bit, but you should have thought of something similar to these:

✔ **Main idea:** Saturn is a gaseous, large planet that's fascinated people for centuries.

✔ **Author's purpose:** To describe several key features of Saturn.

Adopting Strategies for Answering Questions about Passages

For the Reading Comprehension section of the SSAT and ISEE, reading the passages is only part of the challenge; you then have to answer questions about what you read. Along with having a solid reading strategy (see the previous section), you also need to follow a few simple strategies for tackling the questions. Keep in mind the following global strategies that apply to all questions:

✔ **Make sure you know what the question is asking.** Because you need to work quickly, misreading a question, thus choosing the wrong answer, is easy to do. When you read a question, make sure you read every word and know exactly what the question is asking.

✔ **Use the process of elimination.** Like all test questions, use the process of elimination to weed out answer choices you know are wrong. This strategy usually helps narrow down the answer choices to just a couple to choose from, which increases your odds of getting the question right.

✔ **Find the answer.** In many cases, the answer is in the reading passage. Think of the Reading Comprehension section as an open book test. The answers are in front of you, so you just have to find them quickly.

✔ **Skip questions that are too difficult.** If you encounter a question you don't know or really don't understand, skip it and move on. You can always come back to it later if you have time. Remember that you're awarded the same number of points for every question you answer correctly, so don't spend too much time on a hard question when you can answer several other easier questions in the same amount of time.

✔ **Always find the *best* answer.** Sometimes answer choices are close in meaning, but you always want to choose the best answer. Make sure you read all the answer choices before choosing one because even if Choice (B) sounds like the right answer, Choice (D) may be even better. Also, test writers can be tricky; sometimes an answer choice sounds good, but a word or two may be wrong. If that's the case, the answer *is* wrong. A good question to ask yourself is, "Do I like *all* the words in the answer choice?" If not, that's a red flag that you're probably looking at a wrong answer.

Getting Familiar with Types of Reading Comprehension Questions

As you may imagine, both the SSAT and ISEE use several different types of reading comprehension questions. The good news is the question types are fairly predictable, so we explore them in the following sections and give you the opportunity to try your hand at a few examples.

Global content questions

Global content questions are questions about the entire passage. These questions are designed to test your overall ability to comprehend a piece of writing. Generally, global content questions ask about the purpose of a passage, its overall meaning, its overall goal, the author's purpose, the author's tone (attitude toward the subject), how the passage may be improved, and so forth.

With global content questions, the answers aren't necessarily spelled out in the passage text but instead depend on your ability to understand the entire passage.

Read the passage in the section "Checking out a sample passage" earlier in this chapter, and then try the following example questions:

This passage is primarily about

(A) The density of Saturn

(B) The size of Saturn

(C) The features of Saturn

(D) Saturn's rings

(A) The discovery of Saturn

The key word in the question is *primarily*. When you think about the passage as a whole, which answer choice is correct? The text doesn't talk about the discovery of Saturn, so you can rule out Choice (E). Choices (A), (B), and (D) are subjects the author explores in the writing, but they don't cover the entire passage. The only possible answer that explains what the passage is *primarily* about is Choice **(C),** *the features of Saturn.* Notice how we used the process of elimination to quickly find the right answer? Make sure you do the same.

How can you describe the author's tone regarding this passage?

(A) Positive

(B) Negative

(C) Condescending

(D) Unimpressed

(E) Neutral

This question is a bit more difficult. In some writings, the author has a tone toward the subject matter, which is defined as the author's attitude toward the subject. Naturally, the answer to this question isn't spelled out in the text, so you have to make a decision based on the entire passage. In this passage, the author doesn't have a positive or negative attitude toward the planet, nor does he convey a condescending or unimpressed attitude with the subject matter. He's simply relaying information about the planet, so the best answer is Choice **(E).**

What is the overall purpose of this passage?

(A) To inform

(B) To persuade

(C) To define

(D) To correct

(E) To complain

Because the passage simply gives you information about Saturn, the best answer is Choice **(A)**, *to inform.* The author isn't trying to persuade the reader to do something, to define a problem or issue, to correct errors, or to complain about a problem; he's simply providing information.

Specific content questions

Specific questions about the content in the passage are often a bit easier to answer than global content questions because the answer is in the passage — you just have to find it. Circling key ideas and words when you scan the passage helps with these questions because your circled information can help you find the answers more quickly. The mental outline trick (writing key words about each paragraph in the margin) can also help you find the content you need more quickly. (See the earlier section "Reading passages on the test" for more strategies.) Check out a few examples of specific content questions by using the Saturn passage from earlier in the chapter.

Why does the author say that a person would not be able to stand on Saturn?

(A) The planet's density is too low.

(B) The wind speed is too high.

(C) The planet's atmosphere has no oxygen.

(D) The planet spins too quickly.

(E) The planet has too much radiation.

Check the text for the answer and also use the process of elimination. The author doesn't talk about oxygen or radiation at all, so you can eliminate Choices (C) and (E). The author does mention Saturn's rotation and wind speeds, but he directly states that a person can't stand on the planet because the planet is gaseous and the density is too low. So the only correct answer is Choice **(A).** Having a good mental outline and circled key words can help you find this answer quickly because the passage directly tells you the answer.

Why does the author say that Saturn flattens at its poles?

(A) The low density does not allow Saturn to hold its shape.

(B) The wind speed creates a flattening effect.

(C) Saturn's rings create a magnetic pull.

(D) The planet spins too quickly.

(E) The lack of gravity does not allow Saturn to hold its shape.

Again, the text has the answer for you and the process of elimination can help. The author doesn't write about gravity or a magnetic pull at all, so you can eliminate Choices (C) and (E). The planet does have low density and high wind speeds, but the text directly states that the planet is flatter at its poles due to the rotation speed. So Choice **(D)** is correct.

Just because an answer choice sounds good doesn't mean it's correct, so go back to the passage and check your answer against what the passage actually says.

Word-in-context questions

Word-in-context questions give you a word from the passage and ask you what the word means *within the context of the passage.* In other words, these questions aren't simple dictionary definition questions; these questions test your understanding of what the author means by how he used the word. So you have to understand the meaning of the word within the sentence in which it appears.

For example, say you see a sentence like this, "The <u>hostile</u> sun beat down on everyone at the beach," with the following question:

What does the author most likely mean by the word *hostile?*

(A) Determined

(B) Angry

(C) Scorching

(D) Unfriendly

(E) Nagging

By definition, the word *hostile* means unfriendly or antagonistic, but does the author really mean that the sun was unfriendly? Because the sun isn't a person, it can't really be friendly or unfriendly. The author uses the word *hostile* as *personification* — a writing technique that gives human-like characteristics to things that aren't human and often heightens the meaning of a sentence. The author is simply saying that the sun was very hot, or scorching, as you can tell by the rest of the sentence, so the correct answer is Choice **(C).**

The actual dictionary definition of a word may not be the correct answer. After all, the test wants you to define the word within the context of how it's used.

"After much trial and error, Sam <u>ascertained</u> the correct answer to the problem."

What does the author most likely mean by the word *ascertained?*

(A) Relented

(B) Discovered

(C) Distressed

(D) Remarked

(E) Prevailed

In this case, you have a word whose definition you're not sure of. However, you can use the context to help find the meaning of the word. When you encounter this kind of word in a context question, do the following:

  ✔ Try to provide your own definition for the word based on the sentence context.

  ✔ Eliminate answers you know are incorrect.

  ✔ Plug the replacement word into the sentence to see whether it makes sense.

The word *ascertain* means to find out something. Of the answer choices provided, only Choice **(B),** *discovered,* means the same thing. If you plug this word back into the sentence, it reads, "After much trial and error, Sam *discovered* the correct answer to the problem." This answer choice not only makes sense in the sentence but also keeps the original meaning of the sentence the same.

What-is-true questions

A what-is-true type question is exactly what it sounds like. With these types of questions, you're given a few statements and then you have to choose which statement(s) is true according to the passage. Here's an example, using the passage about Saturn in the "Checking out a sample passage" section earlier in this chapter:

According to the passage, which of the following is true?

   I. Saturn is mostly made of oxygen and nitrogen.

  II. Saturn has less density than water.

 III. Saturn is the only planet in our solar system with rings.

(A) I only

(B) II only

(C) I and III only

(D) II and III only

(E) I, II, and III

To answer this type of question, you simply need to check the facts and determine which statement(s) is true. As you look at the statements, check them against the passage and put a check mark next to the ones that are true.

The passage states that Saturn is mostly made of oxygen and hydrogen, not nitrogen, so Statement I is false. Statement II is true because the passage says that Saturn has less density than water (and would float). Statement III is false because Saturn isn't the only planet with rings, as noted in the passage. So the correct answer is Choice **(B),** because Statement II is the only true statement.

As you work with what-is-true questions, here are a few pointers:

 ✔ **Be sure to fact-check against the passage.** As you already know, you don't have much time to ponder what's true and what isn't true, so circling key words, phrases, and ideas can help you quickly find the information you need without rereading the entire passage.

 ✔ **Don't over interpret the true/false statements.** They're typically factual and straightforward, so don't make them mean more than they do. In other words, take them at face value, and you'll do fine.

 ✔ **If part of a statement is false, then all of it is false.** In the previous example, Statement I is wrong because the word *nitrogen* is wrong. You don't get half of the answer correct because the phrase includes the word *oxygen,* which is true — the entire statement is wrong.

According to the passage, which of the following is true?

   I. Saturn has the lowest density of all planets in the solar system.

   II. Saturn is flatter at the equator due to rotation speed.

   III. Saturn is the nearest planet visible to the naked eye.

(A) I only

(B) II only

(C) I and III only

(D) II and III only

(E) I, II, and III

Checking the facts from the passage, Saturn is the lowest density planet of all planets, so Statement I is true. The second statement says that Saturn is flatter at the equator due to rotation speed, but the passage tells you that its poles are flatter, so Statement II is false. The final statement says that Saturn is the nearest planet visible to the naked eye, but the passage states that it's the farthest planet visible to the naked eye, so Statement III is also false. The correct answer is Choice **(A)**, because Statement I is the only true statement.

Elimination questions

Elimination questions often use the words *not, except,* or *least.* These questions ask you to find the wrong answer in a list of correct answers. Usually, elimination questions are specific detail questions, but you have to find the *wrong* answer instead of the right one (as if you needed more confusion to deal with).

All the following statements are true *except*

(A) Saturn has lower density than other planets.

(B) Saturn is 760 times the size of earth.

(C) Saturn has wind speeds up to 4,100 miles per hour.

(D) Saturn makes a full rotation in just over 10 hours.

(E) Saturn has been watched for thousands of years.

All these statements are found in the passage, so they're simple pieces of information. You just need to find the wrong or false statement in order to get the question right. The correct answer is Choice **(C)** because the wind speeds are 1,100 miles per hour according to the passage. So, in this case, what's wrong is right in terms of the getting credit for the question.

According to the passage, which of the following is *not* true?

(A) Saturn is named after the Roman god of agriculture.

(B) Saturn has the largest rings of any planet in the solar system.

(C) Saturn is only 95 times as dense as earth.

(D) Saturn is visible to the naked eye.

(E) Saturn has been watched for thousands of years.

This question is basically the same kind of question as the previous one: You simply need to find which statement *isn't* true. In this example, Choice **(A)** is the right answer because Saturn is named after the Greek god, not the Roman god.

When you answer elimination questions, the main thing to remember is to not get confused about the kind of question you're answering. With an elimination question, the *wrong* statement is always the right answer.

Inference questions

An inference question is a type of reading comprehension question that you'll see several times on the test. To *infer* something means to conclude or decide something, so to answer inference questions on the test, you have to understand something about the passage that it doesn't state obviously. In other words, you have to read between the lines and depend on the overall purpose of the passage. An inference question typically looks like this (refer to the passage in the earlier section "Checking out a sample passage"):

Because Saturn has been observed by the naked eye for thousands of years, it can be inferred that

(A) Saturn emits a lot of light.

(B) We know more details about Saturn than any other planet.

(C) There has been much mythology about the planet.

(D) A spacecraft could potentially land on the planet.

(E) Saturn has water.

The passage doesn't directly address any of these issues, so what you need to do first is use the process of elimination. Try to eliminate some of the answer choices immediately. First, no planet emits light, so you know that Choice (A) is incorrect. Also, the passage specifically states that a person can't stand on Saturn due to the low density, so you know Choice (D) is incorrect. Finally, the passage doesn't say anything about water (other than throwing Saturn in a pool), so Choice (E) is incorrect as well.

That leaves Choices (B) and (C). We obviously know a lot about Saturn, but you can't infer that we know more about Saturn than any other planet, so rule out Choice (B). That means Choice **(C)** is the correct answer. Because the question notes that Saturn can be viewed by the naked eye and has been observed for thousands of years, you can infer that there's been much mythology about the planet over the years. After all, the planet is named after a Greek god.

As you think about inference passages, keep these tips in mind:

- ✔ **If the question seems overly complicated, skip it.** Always keep in mind that every correct question gives you a point. A difficult question isn't worth more than an easy one, so if the question seems too hard, skip it and move on to questions you can answer quickly and easily. You can always come back to the question later if you have time.

- ✔ **You can't infer just anything about a passage.** Your inference has to be based on what the text actually says. If something seems like too much of a stretch, it's probably the wrong answer.

- ✔ **Eliminate answer choices to narrow down your choice to only a few options.** The process of elimination is especially helpful with inference questions.

Chapter 7

Practicing Reading Comprehension

*O*ne of the best things you can do to get ready for the Reading Comprehension section of the test is simply practice. You need to practice dissecting the question and finding the right answer, and you need to practice doing those things quickly. Remember that on the actual test, you have a strict time limit on reading comprehension questions, so be sure to stay within that time limit when you practice. Refer to Chapter 6 for specific time limits and strategies for reading the passages and answering questions quickly.

This chapter is divided into different sections so you can practice reading comprehension for both the lower and middle level exams and the upper level exams. Simply flip to the sections of this chapter that apply to your test, sharpen your pencil, and spend some time practicing.

Tackling Guided Lower and Middle Level Reading Comprehension Questions

Read the following passage, using the skills you explored in Chapter 6, and then answer some reading comprehension questions to get warmed up. Each question is followed by an explanation of the correct answer and how you may reach it.

A number of South Pacific islands were formed from volcanoes long ago. The Hawaiian chain, or *archipelago,* of islands is the most notable. All the Hawaiian islands — Hawaii (the Big Island), Maui, Kahoolawe, Lanai, Molokai, Oahu, Kauai, and Niihau — were formed by volcanoes, and the Big Island still has an active volcano today.

The Hawaiian Islands sit at a place where, under the earth's crust, very hot magma from the mantle flows upward, which built the islands from the ocean floor over several million years. Those areas are called *hot spots.* The Pacific Plate, which is a huge slab of the earth's crust, slides slowly toward the northwest over the hot spot, which pushes through the crust from time to time and makes a volcanic island. The crust moves on and takes the new island with it away from the hot spot. This very slow process takes thousands of years.

Currently, the hot spot resides under the southeast corner of the Big Island, and it extends another 20 miles offshore to the southeast where a new island, named Loihi, is slowly working its way up from the seabed. At some point in the future, Loihi will break the surface of the water and, over time, become an actual island. However, scientists estimate that Loihi may not break the surface for at least 10,000 more years.

1. What is the primary purpose of this passage?

    (A) To explain how the Hawaiian Islands were formed

    (B) To discuss volcanoes

    (C) To explain the birth of a new island

    (D) To discuss the features of the Hawaiian Islands

    (E) To explain why islands exist in the South Pacific

    The overall purpose of the passage is to explain how the Hawaiian Islands were formed, so the correct answer is Choice **(A).** If you look at the passage as a whole, the passage explains that all the Hawaiian Islands are volcanic, and then it gives you a brief explanation of the process. The passage ends by noting that a new island is currently being built under the sea through the volcanic process.

2. What does the word *archipelago* likely mean?

    (A) Island peaks

    (B) A group

    (C) Magma formed

    (D) Volcanic lava

    (E) Hot spot

    The word *archipelago* isn't directly defined, but it follows the words *Hawaiian chain* to help explain its meaning. An archipelago is a chain or grouping of islands, so Choice **(B)** is correct. This question is an example of a word-in-context question because you can use the context of the passage to understand its meaning.

3. According to the passage, where does hot magma come from?

    (A) The crust

    (B) The seabed

    (C) The mantle

    (D) The hot spot

    (E) The archipelago

    The passage directly states that magma comes from the mantle, so Choice **(C)** is correct. For this question, you simply need to read carefully to make sure you don't choose a wrong answer that sounds right, such as Choices (A) or (B).

4. What action begins the process of forming a volcanic island?

    (A) Moving lava

    (B) Mantle eruptions

    (C) A hot spot forms

    (D) Lava forces the Pacific Plate to form an island

    (E) Movement of the Pacific Plate

    This question is another one where you simply have to read the details carefully. The passage states that movement of the Pacific Plate pushes through the crust, releasing magma from the mantle. The correct answer is Choice **(E).**

5. According the passage, which of the following is true?

   I. All the Hawaiian Islands are an archipelago, except Kauai.

   II. Only the Big Island has an active volcano.

   III. The Hawaiian Islands sit on hot spots.

   IV. Oahu is considered a city, not an island.

   V. Loihi is unlikely to become an actual island.

(A) I only

(B) II only

(C) II and III only

(D) IV and V only

(E) All are true

Quickly check the facts from the passage and mark out the statements that aren't true. The only true statements in the list are Statements II and III, according to the passage, so Choice (C) is correct. Statement I is incorrect because all the islands are an archipelago, including Kauai. Statement IV is incorrect because Oahu is an island, not a city. Statement V is also incorrect because Loihi is likely to become an island in the future.

Practicing Lower and Middle Level Reading Comprehension Questions on Your Own

Now that we've walked you through a few reading comprehension questions and answers, take a look at the following passages and answer the questions that follow. In keeping with your time limit, you should read the following two passages and answer the 12 questions that follow in less than 12 minutes. So time yourself as you practice and answer as many of the questions correctly as possible.

Cynthia Ann Parker came from a large family of early Texas settlers. When Cynthia Ann was 9 years old, her family moved to central Texas where they built Fort Parker, in what is present-day Limestone County. The Parker family was plagued by tragedy. Cynthia Ann's brother, James, was killed on the way from Illinois to Texas when a piece of wood from a wagon wheel stabbed him in the chest. Then, on May 19, 1836, approximately 500 Comanche warriors, accompanied by Kiowa and Kichai allies, attacked the fort and killed a number of people. During the attack, the Comanches took five captives, including Cynthia Ann Parker. The other four were released after the typical ransom was paid, but Cynthia remained with the Indians for nearly 25 years. During that time, she lost all traces of her frontier life and effectively became a Comanche.

Little is known of her life during her time with the Comanches, but she had several sons and at least one daughter, Topsanna. In December 1860, Cynthia Ann and Topsanna, who was 2 years old at the time, were among a Native American party captured at the Battle of Pease River by Texas Rangers, led by Lawrence Sullivan "Sul" Ross. Cynthia Ann and her children were returned to the Parker family, yet the story was not to have a happy ending. Cynthia Ann tried to escape her new life several times and return to the Comanches. Eventually, after losing another child to influenza, she stopped eating and died in 1870.

1. What is the author's primary purpose?

    (A) To show how the Comanches assimilated captives

    (B) To explain early Texas frontier life

    (C) To describe some of the Parker family tragedies

    (D) To create sympathy for Cynthia Ann

    (E) To explain how Cynthia Ann was rescued

2. What does the author most likely mean by the word *plagued?*

    (A) To release

    (B) To infect

    (C) To be followed

    (D) To destroy

    (E) To have a disease

3. According to the passage, all the following are false *except*

    (A) The Parkers settled in southern Texas.

    (B) Cynthia Ann helped fight in the Battle of Pease River.

    (C) The Comanches released Cynthia Ann.

    (D) The Comanches were responsible for James's death.

    (E) Cynthia Ann had children.

4. Who was responsible for Cynthia Ann's return to the Parker family?

    (A) She was freely released.

    (B) Topsanna.

    (C) Kichai allies.

    (D) Kiowa allies.

    (E) Sul Ross.

5. Which of the following statements are true?

    I. The Parker family never settled in Texas after the tragedies.

    II. James was killed by a piece of wood.

    III. Cynthia Ann was captured after an attack of 500 Native Americans.

    IV. Four captives were taken during the attack.

    V. Cynthia Ann lived with the Comanches for five years.

    (A) I only

    (B) II only

    (C) IV only

    (D) II and V only

    (E) II, IV, and V only

6. What can you infer from the passage about Cynthia Ann's inability to <u>conform to life</u> after her rescue?

    (A) She could no longer speak English.

    (B) She was grieved by the death of her children.

    (C) She had lost all sense of her former life and could not adapt.

    (D) She did not remember her family.

    (E) She was unfamiliar with modern ways.

    The azure sea <u>stared</u> at the old man as he stood on the beach in the late hours of the day. There was a time in the past when he would have plunged into the cold Pacific water without a thought to catch a final wave of the day. Now, with his arthritis and recent knee surgery, about the only thing he could do was get his toes wet from the occasional <u>daring</u> wave that came in on the shore.

    As he watched the sun decline into the horizon, he felt a sense of sadness that his most active days were behind him, yet mixed with the sadness, he felt a sense of hope that happy days were still ahead.

    About that time, a young boy, maybe 10 years old or so, ran past him, picked up a small stick and tossed it toward a dog that was hot on his trail. The dog grabbed the stick and chased the boy a bit more as their evening game continued. The old man took in a deep, relaxing breath as he watched the waves and listened to them crash as the sound of the boy's laugh drifted away. In spite of it all, life was all around him, and he was still a part of it.

    As the sky grew dim, the old man slowly made his way up the beach and back toward his small house. A single lamp burned from the window, lighting his way home. Another day was coming to a close, and he knew he would follow this same routine tomorrow.

7. What does the author most likely mean by the word *stared* in this passage?

    (A) The waves made a welcoming gesture.

    (B) The ocean was in front of him.

    (C) The ocean was frightening.

    (D) The old man felt he was supposed to go in.

    (E) He knew the sea was too rough.

8. What does the author most likely mean by the word *daring* in this passage?

    (A) The wave was trying to attack the old man.

    (B) The wave had too much power.

    (C) The wave was too weak.

    (D) The wave came far onto the beach.

    (E) The wave was gentle.

9. How would you describe the overall feeling of this passage?

    (A) Melancholy

    (B) Aggressive

    (C) Sympathetic

    (D) Indifferent

    (E) Bewildered

10. The setting sun in this passage can be symbolic of what?

    (A) The boy's laughter

    (B) Weakness

    (C) Hope

    (D) Pain and suffering

    (E) The old man's life

11. What impact do the boy and dog have on the old man?

    (A) They frustrate him.

    (B) They annoy him by breaking the silence.

    (C) They make him feel old.

    (D) They make him feel unloved.

    (E) They remind him that life is happening all around him.

12. What can you infer about the last sentence in the passage?

    (A) He will consider going swimming.

    (B) He will watch the boy and dog play.

    (C) He will walk to the beach.

    (D) The old man will likely feel the same way the next day.

    (E) The old man has lost all hope.

Answers to Lower and Middle Level Reading Comprehension Questions

1. **C.** The author states that the Parker family was plagued by tragedy, and then he explains how James was killed and some of the details of Cynthia Ann's capture. Although Choice (B) may be tempting, it's too broad to accurately explain the author's purpose for this passage.

2. **C.** A *plague* is technically a disease that spreads from person to person. The author uses the word as a comparison to show that the Parker family was followed by tragedy. Though the use of the word isn't a technical definition from the dictionary, the word is used to heighten the meaning of the sentence.

3. **E.** The passage tells you that Cynthia Ann had children, so Choice (E) is the only true statement. All other statements either contradict information in the passage or the passage doesn't state the information given.

Only the passage contains the correct answers, so if the passage doesn't provide some information, assume the information is false.

4. **E.** The passage states that Sul Ross led the Texas Rangers at the Battle of Pease River, which led to Cynthia Ann's rescue.

5. **B.** The passage states that James was killed by a piece of wood from a wagon wheel. Only Statement II is correct.

6. **C.** From the passage, the best inference is that Cynthia Ann had lost all sense of her former life and simply couldn't adapt to all the changes she faced.

7. **B.** The author uses the word *stare* as a personification technique to help communicate that the ocean was in front of the old man, as if it was looking directly at him. This writing technique helps heighten the feeling of the sentence.

8. **D.** This question is another example of personification. Because a wave can't be daring, the author uses this word to communicate that some waves came far onto the beach so the old man's feet got wet.

9. **A.** When you face a question like this one, try to think of your own word first. After scanning the passage, think of one word that can describe the feeling and see whether you can find a similar word as an answer choice. This passage is about an older man who wishes he could experience life in a way that he once did. The word *melancholy* means a deep sadness. Although your word may be somewhat different, consider the passage as a whole, the description, and even the time of day (sun setting, sky growing darker); all contribute to this general feeling, and it's the only viable answer choice.

10. **E.** A *symbol* is a person, place, thing, or idea in a story that represents something else, typically a larger idea. The setting sun represents the end of a day, and that representation can be a symbol of the old man's life because he's in his twilight years.

11. **E.** You have to infer a bit with this question. When the boy and dog are around the old man, the passage tells you that he continues to feel sad yet hopeful. Of the answer choices, Choice (E) is the best one because the boy and the dog remind the old man that life is happening all around him.

12. **D.** By inference, you can tell that the last line means that the old man will follow the same routine the next day, meaning that he will feel much the same.

Remember to watch your time and scan the passages quickly. Also, remember that underlining key words and getting a mental sense of the organization of the passages can help you find answers to questions more quickly.

Tackling Guided Upper Level Reading Comprehension Questions

Read the following passage, using the skills you explored in Chapter 6, and then answer some reading comprehension questions to get warmed up. Each question is followed by an explanation of the correct answer and how you may reach it.

The Internet, or World Wide Web, is so commonplace today that users seldom give thought to its vast complexities. The Internet is effectively a global network of various servers and computers that provide information on virtually every <u>conceivable</u> topic. As the Internet has grown, so has the complexity of website and multimedia content. Yet, despite its complexities, the Internet still functions today through a primary suite of networking <u>protocols</u>, collectively referred to as Transmission Control Protocol/Internet Protocol (TCP/IP). This networking protocol enables a vast number of computers running various platforms to transmit and communicate information with each other so users can access its information through various operating systems and Internet browser software. Additionally, communication protocols within the suite of TCP/IP also enable such functionality as e-mail (POP and SMPTP), file transfers (FTP), and news protocols (NNTP). These different protocols all work together to provide the <u>myriad</u> features and options that we use on the Internet and take for granted each day.

1. What does the author most likely mean by the word *conceivable?*

    (A) Genuine

    (B) Reality

    (C) Imaginable

    (D) Trustworthy

    (E) Determined

The word *conceivable* means able to conceive or to give birth to. In this context, the author is saying that every possible topic can be found on the Internet, so the best answer is Choice **(C)**.

 With questions like this one, try to substitute your own word in place of the word in question, and then see whether you can find a word that's similar in the answer choices. Then, try that same word in place of the word in question and see whether the meaning remains the same.

2. What does the author most likely mean by the word *protocols?*

    (A) Wiring

    (B) A behavior

    (C) A language

    (D) A technical tool

    (E) A procedure

By definition, a *protocol* is a procedure or a way of doing something exactly the same every time. You can think of it as a system of rules that define how something is done. The word is commonly used when discussing computer systems and in medicine (a doctor follows a certain protocol in order to treat a specific illness). The word isn't defined for you within the text, so you have to examine its context to figure out the best definition, which is Choice **(E)** in this case.

3. What is the author's primary purpose?

    (A) To explain how TCP/IP functions

    (B) To explain how the Internet provides so much functionality

    (C) To discuss protocols

    (D) To show how multimedia functions on the Internet

    (E) To discuss the necessity of the Internet

The primary purpose is the overall idea of the passage, so you have to take the passage as a whole and make sure you don't choose an answer that's too broad or too narrow. In this passage, the author explains how various networking protocols enable computers to communicate and provide the functionality the Internet provides. The best answer that encompasses the entire meaning of the passage is Choice **(B)**.

4. The passage discusses the concept of a *suite* of protocols. What is the best explanation of this concept?

   (A) An independent collection

   (B) Various components

   (C) A group of interrelated protocols

   (D) Multiple programming languages

   (E) Compartmentalized segments

   By definition, a *suite* is a set of things that belong together. In the context of this passage, the best answer is Choice **(C)**. Some of the other answer choices sound complex and possible, but always choose the answer that provides the best (and often simplest) explanation. The passage doesn't mention anything about programming languages or segments, so make sure you avoid answers that simply sound good without additional reasons to select the answer.

5. The passage states that TCP/IP enables a "vast number of computers running on various platforms" to communicate. What is most likely meant by this statement?

   (A) The protocol makes all computers similar.

   (B) The protocol allows different networks to connect.

   (C) The protocol allows different operating systems and hardware to communicate.

   (D) The protocol creates pathways within Internet wiring.

   (E) The protocol enables communication.

   A platform refers to a way something is accomplished, and in computer operations, it specifically refers to operating systems and hardware. Of course, you may not know that information directly, but you can infer this from the passage because the Internet allows all computers to share information, regardless of brand, hardware differences, and operating systems in use. The correct answer is Choice **(C)**.

6. Which of the following statements is *not* true?

   (A) TCP/IP is an industry standard.

   (B) TCP/IP includes other protocols that enable functionality.

   (C) One protocol enables Internet functionality.

   (D) Different platforms use different protocols.

   (E) Multimedia functionality is not protocol dependant.

   With a question like this one, you simply need to find the incorrect answer by evaluating each statement carefully. The correct answer is Choice **(C)** because that statement isn't true. The passage tells you that TCP/IP is a suite, or collection, of protocols; therefore, a single protocol isn't all that's used on the Internet.

Practicing Upper Level Reading Comprehension Questions on Your Own

Now that you've practiced some comprehensive reading questions, work on this set of two passages and 12 questions on your own. Remember to scan quickly, underline key words and phrases, and work to make a mental organization of the passage so you can find answers quickly. Use a watch, phone, or iPod to give yourself a time limit of 10 minutes for this entire practice session, which mimics the same time limit you'll experience on the real exam.

A raging debate in the United States over the past several years concerns the separation of church and state in relation to public schools. In the past, schools often included religious practices, such as prayer, and in rural school areas, the Bible was often used as a textbook for reading and writing practice. In recent times, under the <u>guise</u> of separation of church and state, religious content has all but disappeared from the classroom. However, many experts feel this may not be wise.

America was founded on religious principles, and many ideas from the Constitution and even local laws are rooted in principles found in the Bible. Because so much of America's past is based on religious ideas and religious freedoms, the absence of this content from the American classroom denies some basic foundation and historical significance on which the country was founded. Some argue that basic Christian religious beliefs should be taught in public schools as a way to help students understand America's history and legal principles.

Another issue concerns freedom of speech. Many argue that a student's basic freedoms to believe in and practice a religion are actually restricted by the school system's approach to religion. If all Americans have religious freedom, how can there possibly be a true separation of church and state? In fact, some argue that the entire principle of separation of church and state is unconstitutional and virtually impossible to carry out in a practical manner.

Others argue that classes based on the tenets of various religions, such as a comparative religion course, do have a place in the global training of American students because so many modern issues in the global economy stem from differences in beliefs. To deny students this training creates a deficit in their learning and foundational understanding of not only the American culture but also the world at large.

1. What is the author's primary purpose?

   (A) To discuss differences in religion

   (B) To explain religion in America

   (C) To show why the government is anti-religion

   (D) To argue that religion has a place in public school

   (E) To show that students should be religious people

2. What does the author most likely mean by the word *guise?*

   (A) A technicality

   (B) A covering

   (C) A false appearance

   (D) A feeling

   (E) A protection

3. The author provides three reasons to support his position. How can you summarize all these positions?

    (A) Schools were better when religious content was taught.

    (B) Schools have a moral responsibility to teach religion.

    (C) Students should be religious, and schools have the responsibility to teach religion.

    (D) Religion is a part of a well-rounded education.

    (E) Religion is necessary for a stable society.

4. According to the passage, which of the following statements is *not* true?

    (A) Religion can help students have a proper historical perspective.

    (B) Separation of church and state should be abolished.

    (C) Students may not understand global issues without an understanding of religion.

    (D) Religion is foundational in American laws.

    (E) Schools may be restricting freedom of speech.

5. What would make this passage more effective?

    (A) Quotations from experts

    (B) Providing more than one specific argument

    (C) Reducing persuasive statements

    (D) Eliminating emotions

    (E) Removing difficult words

6. According to the passage, which of the following statements are true?

    I. Religion in school is not allowed due to separation of church and state.

    II. The Bible was often used in school in the past.

    III. Students morally benefit from religious training.

    IV. Religious training gives students a historical perspective.

    V. Lack of religious freedom in school may be unconstitutional.

    (A) I and II only

    (B) II and III only

    (C) I, II, III, and IV only

    (D) I, II, IV, and V only

    (E) IV and V only

The cranberry is a fruit that has become more popular in the United States in recent years. Cranberries are typically grown in northern states, such as Massachusetts, New Jersey, Oregon, Washington, and Wisconsin, because they need cooler growing environments (although the plants are not cold hardy).

Cranberries are grown and harvested in an unusual way. Like all plants, cranberries need ample sun without too much extreme heat. Yet they require a lot of water, typically an inch or more a week. For this reason, cranberry farmers must have ample access to water for growing, but water also plays an important role in harvesting the fruit. At harvest time, the cranberry plants are flooded in a *bog* and the cranberries float in the bog until they are packaged and processed. The water bog keeps the cranberries from ruining in the hot weather or even during a frost in the fall. On average, an acre of cranberries, from growth to harvest, requires about 10 feet of water.

Growing and harvesting peculiarities aside, cranberries have become more popular in recent years due to a variety of health benefits. Cranberries contain a broad spectrum of vitamins, especially vitamin C, which makes up about 24 percent of the recommended daily serving. Like other berry fruit, cranberries also contain antioxidants. Researchers have discovered that cranberries and pure cranberry juice can help prevent common health problems, such as heart disease, strokes, tooth decay, gum disease, and even stomach ulcers.

7. The author states that cranberry plants need cooler temperatures but are not cold hardy. What does this likely mean?

   (A) The plants live only in mild climates.

   (B) The plants would not survive a freeze.

   (C) The plants require ample sunshine.

   (D) The plants cannot live in temperatures above 90 degrees.

   (E) The plants require ample water.

8. The author states that cranberries are grown and harvested in unusual ways. What issue primarily makes their growth and harvest unusual?

   (A) Sunlight requirements

   (B) Nutrition requirements

   (C) Water usage

   (D) Temperature requirements

   (E) Harvest time

9. What is one reason cranberries are flooded at the time of harvest?

   (A) To kill the actual plant

   (B) To keep the fruit hydrated

   (C) To make harvesting easier

   (D) To protect the fruit against sunlight

   (E) To reduce diseases

10. What is the primary purpose of the passage?

   (A) To promote cranberry consumption

   (B) To explain nutrition and health benefits of cranberries

   (C) To explain cranberry production

   (D) To educate the reader about cranberries

   (E) To entertain

11. The passage states that cranberries have a *broad spectrum* of vitamins. What does this phrase likely mean?

   (A) Cranberries have several important vitamins.

   (B) Cranberries have minimal amounts of each vitamin.

   (C) Cranberries have three primary vitamins.

   (D) Cranberries provide limited nutrition.

   (E) Cranberries can be used in a variety of recipes.

12. According to the passage, which of the following statements are true?

   I. Cranberries are grown primarily in northern states.

   II. Cranberries require ample heat to ripen.

   III. Cranberries contain a significant source of vitamin C.

   IV. Cranberries are harvested via a bog.

   V. Cranberries require a cooling period in order to ripen.

   (A) I and II only

   (B) III and V only

   (C) I, III, and IV only

   (D) IV and V only

   (E) V only

Answers to Upper Level Reading Comprehension Questions

1. **D.** This passage is a mild persuasive essay whose overall purpose is to make an argument for including some religious training in public schools. Noting the content of each paragraph in a word or two helps you form an idea about the overall purpose of the passage and helps you answer this question more quickly, because the author provides a brief introduction and three basic arguments. The author isn't advocating a particular religion or making the argument that people should be religious, but he's arguing that some religious training promotes a well-rounded education.

With argument or persuasive passages, make sure you don't read more into what the author is saying or let your personal beliefs intertwine with the author's ideas. In other words, focus on what the author is saying and not what you personally believe.

2. **C.** A *quise* technically means a false appearance. In the context, the author is saying that keeping religious training out of schools is often hidden under the false appearance of separation of church and state. The author is trying to persuade the reader that the connection between the two issues is a false appearance.

3. **D.** To answer this question, you need a basic sentence or even phrase for each paragraph to help you gather the gist of each one. You'll notice that the common theme in each paragraph is that religion has a part in a well-rounded education, and it's a right of the student to have that education.

4. **B.** The author isn't arguing that separation of church and state should be abolished. He's arguing that connecting religion in schools with the concept of church and state may not be accurate.

5. **A.** To answer this question, you have to figure out the passage's weakness, so be careful of answers that provide global changes to the passage. Usually, this kind of question is looking for something specific because you can almost always globally change a passage in some way. So if you look at the passage, you notice that the author often uses the word *experts,* but he never names any of these experts or provides a direct quotation from them. Doing so would make the article more credible and strengthen his argument.

6. **D.** All the statements are true with the exception of Statement III. The passage doesn't say that students benefit morally from religious training. This may be an easy assumption, but because the author doesn't state this, it isn't true according to the passage.

If the passage doesn't say it, it isn't true in terms of the test question.

7. **B.** *Cold hardy* means that the plant can survive in temperatures below 32 degrees. Most plants simply go dormant during the winter months and return in the spring. If a plant isn't cold hardy, it won't survive in freezing temperatures.

8. **C.** In this question, you're looking for the issue that makes the growth and harvest of cranberries more unusual than other plants. The passage states that cranberries require a lot of water because of the growth as well as flooding for harvesting, which makes them unique from other fruit.

9. **D.** The passage directly states that fruit is kept in bogs to prevent damage from hot weather or a potential frost before packaging.

10. **D.** This question is a bit tricky. The passage explores cranberry production and health and nutrition benefits. You can rule out Choices (B) and (C) because although the passage does talk about these issues, they alone aren't necessarily the primary purpose. You need something a bit more broad, so the best answer is Choice (D). The author is simply striving to educate the reader about cranberries from both a production and a health point of view.

11. **A.** The phrase *broad spectrum* generally means that a number of ingredients or potential benefits exist, depending on how the phrase is used. Within the context of this passage, the author is saying that cranberries have many vitamins.

12. **C.** Statements II and V are incorrect because the passage doesn't state that a cooling period is required for ripening or that ample heat is required. The passage doesn't directly tell you about these conditions, so you should assume that these statements are false.

Chapter 8

Writing a Winning Essay

• •

In This Chapter

▶ Getting in the writing game
▶ Organizing a winning essay
▶ Writing and checking your work

• •

When you realized both the SSAT and ISEE require you to write a short essay, your smile probably turned to a frown, and you may have let out a long, tired sigh. Let's face it: Most students would rather scrub a bathroom with a toothbrush than write an essay. Although some students actually enjoy writing, many students struggle with it and often dread writing assignments. But writing is a big part of your school career, and it spans multiple areas of study. That the good folks who develop standardized tests, like the SSAT and ISEE, include a Writing section is no surprise because schools want to know how well you write. In short, they know good writers tend to do well in school, so they simply want to check your writing skills as a part of your admission.

The good news: A light is at the end of the tunnel. The writing sections on the SSAT and ISEE aren't as difficult as you may imagine. The writing prompts don't ask you to write about something you don't know anything about, and your essay can't be very long. With that said, a few simple guidelines and tips can help you write a winning essay. This chapter shows you what you need to know.

Exploring Essay Writing and Your Exam

Both the SSAT and ISEE approach essay writing in the same way. In a nutshell, the exams give you an essay topic, a couple of lined pages, and a total of 30 minutes to write your essay from the moment you begin. In other words, you have only half an hour to figure out what to write about based on the essay topic and then write the actual essay. Sometimes 30 minutes can feel like forever, but it really isn't a lot of time, so you're not going to be able to chew on the end of your pencil and stare into space as you think about the topic. You need to get to work right away, and you need to write quickly. Preparing yourself to write a good, solid essay starts with understanding what essay readers want to see from you and how they evaluate your finished essay. The following sections address those questions.

What do essay readers want to see?

You're probably wondering what makes a good essay. After all, essays can seem a bit subjective. As you write essays and papers for school, the teacher likely points out specific things he or she wants to see in the paper. So how in the world do you know what to do with a standardized test? Here are a few common myths and our responses about the purpose of the Writing section:

✔ **The people who evaluate your essay want you to discuss a complex topic.** Nope, not at all. In fact, the essay topics are typically pretty easy and based on your opinion and experiences.

✔ **The essay readers want the essay to be really complicated and complex.** No, actually the opposite. Essay readers want to see whether you can organize information and write in an engaging way.

✔ **The essay readers want to see how smart you are.** No, essays (or any test for that matter) don't show anyone how smart you are; instead, they show whether you can write well.

So what do the people who evaluate your essay want to see? A good SSAT or ISEE essay always contains the following:

✔ **Organized information:** Good essays present information in an organized manner. One of the primary purposes of an essay on a standardized test is to see whether you can organize thoughts and ideas.

✔ **Focused content:** Good essays stick to the topic. Can you respond to the essay prompt on the test and stay focused? Essay readers want to see focused content.

✔ **Clear and concise writing:** Essay readers don't want to see overly complicated, awkward sentences or sentences full of grammar mistakes. They also don't want you to try and impress them with over-the-top vocabulary. Make your writing clear, concise, and error free, and you'll do great!

You're probably thinking, "Wait a minute — what about the essay topic? Isn't that important?" In truth, the topic itself doesn't even make the list because the topic is really just a way to get you writing. In other words, you're evaluated on how you express yourself in writing, not on the topic. Find out more about how to address the essay topic in the "What Will You Write About?" section in this chapter.

How are essays graded?

SSAT and ISEE graders don't grade your essay. In fact, they don't even look at it. Instead, they make copies of your essay and send them along with the rest of your score report to the school(s) you're applying to. That's both good and bad. The good thing is that you don't have some stranger slapping a grade on your essay. The bad thing is trying to figure out what your school does with the essay.

A guidance counselor at the school you're applying to may be able to give you some information about how that school uses the test essay. If not, you can make any of the following three assumptions:

✔ The essay is carefully read by an admissions officer or committee who uses your writing skill as a serious aspect of your admission to the school.

✔ The essay is glanced over by an admissions officer or committee who uses your writing skill in a *portfolio* (a collection of admission materials) approach for admission to the school.

✔ The essay is barely looked at or even ignored because the admissions officer or committee is more concerned with other aspects of admission.

The odds are good that your school falls somewhere in one of these categories or even a mixture of two. So how do you know what to do? The simple answer is to do your very best on the essay writing. Because you may not entirely know how your school uses the essay for admission, you simply need to do your very best. If you do your best, you don't have to spend time worrying about how the school you want to attend grades the essay or plans to use it. Instead, use this chapter to help you learn how to write a winning essay!

What Will You Write About?

Thankfully, the SSAT and ISEE don't say, "Write about something." Instead, the exams give you a topic to use as a guide. Although the exam developers expect you to write about the topic given to you, you have a lot of leeway. In other words, the topic is really just a starting point. What you decide to write about is up to you, and here's the thing you really have to remember: The exam readers don't care *what* you write about, they just want you to write about it well. No matter what, don't forget this simple concept. As far as the exam topics are concerned, no right or wrong answer exists — it's all about how you organize and write your essay. The following sections walk you through this process.

Exploring common topics

When you get to the essay portion of the SSAT or ISEE, you're going to face something that looks similar to the following prompt, regardless of the level of exam you're taking:

You have 30 minutes to complete a brief writing sample. This writing exercise will not be scored but is used by admissions officers to assess your writing skill.

Directions: Read the following topic carefully. Take a few minutes to think about the topic and organize your thoughts before you begin writing. Be sure that your handwriting is legible and that you stay within the lines and margins.

   Topic: The best things in life are free.

Assignment: Do you agree or disagree with this topic statement? Support your position with one or two specific examples from personal experience, the experience of others, current events, history, or literature.

Think about this assignment for a moment. You're given a simple topic, and then you're told to agree or disagree with it. You need to support your position (agree or disagree) by using one or two specific examples. Here's the catch: No right or wrong answer exists, but what's important is that you take a position and then support your position. Every writing topic works in the same way. Here are a few more topic examples to consider:

   Organization is the key to success.

   A picture is worth a thousand words.

   Friends are the most important treasures in life.

   Honesty is the best policy.

Are you seeing a pattern here? All these statements are very generic. You can write about most anything, but you simply need to agree or disagree and then back up your belief with a few examples. For example, say you agree that organization is a major key to success. In your introduction, you agree with the topic, you provide a couple of paragraphs with some examples that explain why this statement is true, and then you simply wrap up the essay with a conclusion. You can use this same organizational pattern for virtually any topic on the test. (You can find more example essay topics in Chapter 9.)

In the end, the exam readers don't care about the topic or even your personal beliefs — your answer isn't right or wrong! They care about whether you can organize your thoughts and write an effective essay that supports what you believe.

If you're taking the ISEE, you may see some topics that are a bit more specific than the previous examples, such as "Describe your perfect day" or "If you could change something about your school, what would you change?" Although more specific, these topics are still very open-ended, meaning you can write about most anything as long as you stick to the topic. (You can find more example essay topics in Chapter 9.)

Figuring out how to approach a topic

If the topics are all generic, how should you approach the topic? No matter what topic you face, your approach should be the same:

1. **Read the topic.**

2. **Choose to agree or disagree.**

3. **Support what you think with two examples.**

That's it! You can approach every topic this way. The exam directions tell you to support your position with *one or two* examples, but use two — two is better than one and makes your essay much stronger.

If at all possible, use a personal experience as one of your two examples. Essay readers want to hear your voice in the essay because it helps them connect with who you are. So try to use a personal experience as the first example, and then the second example can come from someone you know or even a character in a book, a current news story, a famous person, and so on. So just think, "Choose a side and then support my side with something about me and something about someone else." If you think in that way, you'll be off to a great start.

If you find an ISEE essay topic that's more specific or even persuasive, use two personal examples instead of one. For example, if the topic asks you to write about what you would change at your school, pick an issue then provide two personal examples about that issue — that's all you need to do.

The best news of all: You can usually decide what you want to write about before the test because almost any topic can be tailored to a personal experience, something from literature, or even current events.

Here's what we mean. I (Curt) love vacationing in Hawaii, and I've had a lot of adventures and experiences there. So if I had to write an essay, I'd keep my vacations in mind because surely some experience I've had in Hawaii would work as a personal experience for one of the generic essay topics. Also because *To Kill a Mockingbird* is one of my favorite books, and I've read it a few times, I'd likely use a character's experience from the book to back up my ideas. That gives me two examples I've already thought about before I even take the exam.

How would my ideas work with the topic? Consider this example:

Topic: Courage overcomes fear.

My position: Agree

Example 1: I had to overcome my fear of boogie boarding in order to learn how. I did so by being courageous in the water.

Example 2: In *To Kill a Mockingbird,* Jem had to overcome his fear of Boo Radley in order to find out the truth about Boo. He did that through courage.

Here's another example:

Topic: The best things in life are free.

My position: Agree

Example 1: In Hawaii, one activity I did was hike the Na Pali coast. Hiking the coast is free, and this experience, though free, ended up being one of my best memories.

Example 2: In *To Kill a Mockingbird,* Jem's friends were the most important people in his life because they helped him grow as a person. Friendship is free, and Jem's friends had the biggest impact on his life.

See? I can do this over and over with basically any topic. Because the topics are so generic, I can fit these two experiences with just about any subject.

So think about what to write before you go take the test. Think about some personal experiences and something from literature, the news, or even a famous person's life that you can use as an example. Doing so helps you figure out what to write about before you even see the topic, which puts you way ahead in the writing game!

Does it matter how you really feel?

The exam often gives a well-known saying as a topic, such as "Honesty is the best policy." Because the exam writing topics are generic, agreeing with the topic is often easier than disagreeing, from a writing standpoint. For example, you may not personally believe that "experience is a hard teacher," but you may find it easier to think of examples and support the position if you agree with it.

Tip: Don't worry about what you really believe. After all, the SSAT and ISEE aren't exams that test your personal feelings. Instead, think about what you can easily write about. If you can easily agree or even disagree with a topic and provide good supporting examples, then go for it. How you really feel about the subject doesn't matter. What matters is that you write an effective essay. So don't let your personal feelings drag you down. Focus on being objective and write from a perspective that gives you the most to write about.

Organizing Your Essay from Beginning to End

The essay readers don't care *what* you write about; they just care that you write effectively. One of the most important aspects of writing an effective essay is organization. An organized essay almost always scores well. On the reverse side, a disorganized essay never does. So organization is key to doing well.

The good news: During the exam, you don't have to sit and plan how to organize your essay because you can do that in advance. Because you know what to expect in terms of the generic topic, you can already plan how to organize your essay, and your essay can be organized in the same way regardless of what topic you get.

You need a good introduction, two body paragraphs that contain your two examples, and a short conclusion. With these four paragraphs, you can write an effective, organized essay every single time.

The following sections walk you through writing each part of a good, organized essay.

Starting with an effective introduction

Many times, students are stumped with writing the introduction because they just don't know where to begin. The SSAT and ISEE essay topics help you know what you need to do. After all, you're given a topic and then you're told to agree or disagree with it. Whether you agree or disagree is the basis for your introduction, so at least the intro isn't a mystery because the exam has already told you what to do.

Organize the introduction like this:

1. **Big idea**
2. **More specific ideas**
3. **Thesis statement**

The following sections expand on these three organizational tools.

Big idea

The *big idea* is simply the exam topic that's given to you. So that means the first sentence of your introduction is basically written for you. For example, say your essay topic is "No pain, no gain." Use that phrase to start your introduction. You may say something like this:

> "No pain, no gain" is a popular saying in our culture.

With this simple, big-idea statement, you start your essay on topic, help your reader know what you're talking about, and show your reader that you're writing about the subject assigned on the exam. So far so good.

More specific ideas

Now, you just need *more specific ideas,* or a couple of sentences that help explain what the essay topic means to the reader. You may do something like the following:

"No pain, no gain" is a popular saying in our culture. This statement simply means that struggle and difficulty are normal parts of accomplishment and success. In fact, most anything that is worth accomplishing requires hard work.

As you can see, these two additional sentences simply explain the meaning of the first statement and help lead the reader to the last sentence in the introduction.

Thesis statement

The *thesis statement* is just a sentence that makes clear to the reader what you're going to talk about in the essay. Because the exam directions tell you to choose a side concerning the topic given, you need to make your position crystal clear with the thesis statement, which we've underlined in the following example. Just keep it simple.

"No pain, no gain" is a popular saying in our culture. This statement simply means that struggle and difficulty are normal parts of accomplishment and success. In fact, most anything that is worth accomplishing requires hard work. <u>In life, I believe "no pain, no gain" is an important aspect of reaching goals and being successful.</u>

With this thesis statement, the reader knows exactly what the author's position is and exactly what the rest of the essay is about.

As you think about writing thesis statements, keep these points in mind:

- **Pick a side and stick to it — don't try to play both sides of the field.** In other words, a thesis statement that says, "'No pain no gain' is a true statement sometimes, but not always" is wrong. The assignment tells you to agree or disagree, so make sure you pick a side and make it very clear in the thesis statement what your side is.

- **Keep it simple.** Your thesis statement should be short and simply help the reader know what you're talking about in the essay. It's not brain surgery, so don't make it complicated.

- **Keep it direct and formal.** Your thesis statement isn't the place to get casual and conversational with your readers. For example, don't say, "I want to talk to you about. . . ."

Developing effective body paragraphs

After you've written your introduction, you then turn your attention to the body paragraphs. As we mention earlier, you should use two different examples to support your position, so you can use a paragraph for each. Also remember that the test booklet provides only two pages to write your essay, and you're not allowed to write outside the lines, so you don't have a lot of room. Each body paragraph should be about 1/2 to 3/4 of a page. This length leaves you enough room for the introduction and conclusion but also helps you plan so you make sure you write enough. Of course, if you write really small, you won't need this much space, but if your handwriting is average in size, try to use most of the two pages given, which shouldn't be a problem because you're so organized.

For each body paragraph, start out with a topic sentence that helps the reader know what the paragraph is about. Keep it short and simple. Then use the rest of the paragraph to explain the topic sentence and support your thesis statement.

Remember that you can preplan what you want to talk about. If possible, try to use a personal experience as one of your body paragraphs. With those thoughts in mind, here's an example of an effective body paragraph, using Curt's Hawaii vacations as an example to support the thesis statement:

> I experienced "no pain no gain" first hand on a recent vacation to Hawaii. The Na Pali coast, on the island of Kauai, has the second highest sea cliffs in the world. Along the coast is the Kalalau trail, which provides a dirt path over the sea cliffs. The hike is tough and exhausting, but if you can survive the first couple of miles of the trail, you arrive at a river valley and a beach. After I started the hike, I thought about turning back several times. My legs and knees hurt, and my calves were burning with each step. I knew I wanted to make it to the beach, even though I felt all this physical pain. Each step took me closer to the beach, and I finally arrived to see a breath-taking view. If I had avoided the pain of the hike, I would have never gained the experience of reaching the beach. In the end, the pain paid off.

Notice how the topic sentence tells the reader what the paragraph proves, and then the rest of the paragraph simply provides details and information to support the topic sentence. After all, that's what a paragraph is — a unit of thought that completes an idea.

When you write the body paragraphs for your essay, make sure you keep these tips in mind:

- ✔ **Stick to the point.** Write about the details only of your topic sentence. Stay focused on proving your point. In other words, don't include details that don't apply. For example, if I were to mention a few great restaurants in Hawaii in my paragraph, I wouldn't be sticking to the point because talking about restaurants doesn't have anything to do with the topic at hand.

- ✔ **Include details.** Good writing helps the reader see what's happening. Make sure you include enough details to support your topic sentence and help the reader connect with you.

- ✔ **Make sure your content backs up your thesis statement.** Notice how I used the words *pain* and *gain* a couple of times in the paragraph? Because my topic included those words, I used the same words to show the reader that I was sticking to and proving my point.

Wrapping up with a well-crafted conclusion

When you reach the end of your essay, you need a short *conclusion*. The conclusion helps wrap things up and makes sure your reader isn't left hanging. The good news is that the conclusion can be short, and all you have to do is turn your introduction ideas upside down and use them in reverse. Just start off by restating your thesis statement and then wrap up with a few concluding statements. Here's an example:

> "No pain, no gain" is an important aspect of reaching goals and being successful. As with most things in life, if a goal is worth accomplishing, you'll likely face some difficulties along the way. Yet if you experience some gain that ends the pain, the results are well worth it.

Proofing Your Essay

After you finish your essay, spend any remaining time you have left *proofing* the essay. Proofing your essay just means that you check it over carefully for misspelled words, grammar problems, and any sentences that seem awkward. Because you write your essay in pen, and may not have one that erases easily, you can neatly cross out and correct any errors you find. Most essay readers don't expect your essay to be perfect, but you want to fix as many mistakes as possible, so proofread and correct quickly and carefully.

The following sections provide some tips to help make sure your essay is as clean and error free as possible.

Checking for common grammar problems

As you proof your essay, look for the following:

- ✓ Spelling
- ✓ Capitalization of proper nouns
- ✓ Comma usage
- ✓ Subject and verb agreement

Table 8-1 contains many commonly confused words. Try to memorize them before the test.

Table 8-1	Commonly Misused Words	
Word	*Meaning*	*Example of Correct Usage*
accept	to receive	I accepted the award.
except	to take or leave out	Everyone is going except Paul.
allusion	an indirect reference	The allusion was to Plato's writing.
illusion	something that appears real but isn't	The trick's illusion seemed real.
ascent	moving from a lower to higher state	His ascent to the presidency was slow and difficult.
assent	to agree	We assented to the contract.
breath	air inhaled or exhaled	My breath was cold.
breathe	to inhale or exhale	Can you breathe in this cold?
capital	seat of government	The Texas capital is Austin.
capitol	actual building where government officials meet	We visited the capitol.
cite	to quote	She cited several sources.
sight	vision	The sight of the wreck was scary.
site	position or place	We visited the historical site.
complement	something that completes	Her purse complemented her dress.
compliment	a praise or accolade	She blushed at the compliment.
conscience	a sense of right or wrong	My conscience stopped me from speaking.
conscious	awake	I was conscious after the accident.
council	a group that consults	I met with the council
counsel	advice	I found wise counsel.
elicit	to bring out	She elicited a response from Jim.
illicit	illegal	Illicit drugs are a problem.
eminent	respected	The eminent professor arrived.

continued

Table 8-1 *(continued)*

Word	Meaning	Example of Correct Usage
imminent	something about to happen	The clouds warned of imminent rain.
its	possessive of it	Its motor died.
it's	contraction for it is	It's cold outside.
lose	to misplace or not win	I hope we don't lose the game.
loose	not tight	The rope was too loose.
precede	to come before	The prayer preceded the speaker.
proceed	to go forward	We proceeded to class.
principal	a person in authority	I had to visit the principal's office.
principle	a general truth	I didn't understand the principle.
their	possessive of they	Their car broke down.
there	a location	My car is over there.
they're	contraction for they are	They're riding in my car.
through	finished or in / out	I'm through with this game.
threw	past tense of throw	He threw the ball.
thorough	careful or complete	Be thorough in your writing.
though	in spite of the fact	Even though he was tired, he kept running.
to	toward	I am going to town.
too	also	I am coming, too.
two	the number	There are two cats.

Watching out for sentence trouble

Reviewing every possible sentence problem that may come up is impossible (otherwise, this book would be the size of a small car!), and you wouldn't want to anyway. After all, no matter how much you prepare for the SSAT and ISEE, you need to depend on what you already know about grammar and writing. Here are a few pointers to keep in mind as you review the sentences you've written in your essay:

- **Watch out for overly long sentences.** If you see a sentence that seems really long, you may have actually connected a couple of sentences with a comma. If you're unsure, just rewrite the sentence as two sentences.

- **Watch out for wordiness.** If you can reduce the number of words in a sentence and still say the same thing, do that. This is called *concise writing* and your reader will be impressed with your ability to keep it short and to the point.

- **Watch out for pronouns, such as *he, she, they,* and especially *it*.** Make sure your pronouns actually refer to a noun in the sentence.

- **Trust your inner ear.** As you proofread, if a sentence sounds odd to you or if you have to read it a couple of times to understand its meaning, something is probably wrong with it. Don't worry about what that something is, just rewrite the sentence and move on.

Chapter 9

Practicing Writing Essays

Even though you may want to skip this chapter (after all, who wants to spend time writing an essay just because it's required for a test?), remember that practice makes perfect. So before test day, put your essay-writing skills to work and refer to Chapter 8 for tips on writing an effective essay.

In this chapter, you find upper level SSAT and ISEE writing examples and practice prompts as well as lower level SSAT and middle and lower level ISEE prompts and examples. Just turn to the section that applies to you, check out the examples, and practice a few of the writing topics provided. When you practice writing the essays, use only two sheets of notebook paper (front side only), which is about the same amount of space you have on the actual exam, and write with a pen.

Upper Level Essay

An effective essay answers the question topic and has an introduction, body, and conclusion. You need two examples to support your position, and one of those examples, although not required, should be from your own experience. If you want the best essay possible, use one of your experiences as well. Take a look at the following sample essays and example prompts for the upper level SSAT and ISEE in the following sections, and then practice writing your own essays. You have only 30 minutes to complete a brief writing sample, so time yourself as you practice.

Following the example of sample essays

Directions: Read the following topic carefully. Take a few minutes to think about the topic and organize your thoughts before you begin writing. Be sure that your handwriting is legible and that you stay within the lines and margins.

    Topic: Experience is the hardest teacher.

    Assignment: Do you agree or disagree with this topic statement? Support your position with one or two specific examples from personal experience, the experience of others, current events, history, or literature.

The following essay would get a high score from any evaluator. We explain why after the sample.

People often say that "experience is the hardest teacher." This statement means people learn from their experiences, but they especially learn from experiences that are difficult. In fact, the difficult experiences in life are often when we learn the most. As I have grown and experienced different things in life, I believe that experience is the hardest teacher.

In the novel, *To Kill A Mockingbird,* the main character, Jem, learns the most important life lesson through a difficult experience. After an African American man is accused of raping a young girl, Jem has to watch his father struggle with defending the man, who appears to be innocent. Although Jem is instructed to stay away from the trial, he sneaks into the court-room and watches the spectacle. Jem finds the racist treatment of the African American very upsetting, but this experience teaches him that people are often treated unfairly. In other words, Jem has to learn the hard lesson that truth does not always prevail. Though the lesson was difficult, Jem's experience taught him an important life lesson.

In a different way, I have also learned that experience is the hardest teacher. While vacationing in Hawaii, I decided to learn to boogie board. After practicing the basics on the sand, I tried out my new skills in the water. At first, I was doing well, but a large wave suddenly pushed me to the bottom of the ocean floor where I hit a rock. I wasn't seriously injured, but I did get a few large bruises and scrapes. Although my experi-ence was not pleasant, it helped me learn how to control the board and keep myself from further injuries. In the end, this hard experience taught me a few things about boogie boarding I never would have learned otherwise.

In my life, I have learned that experience is indeed a hard teacher. Yet, it is in the diffi-cult experiences of life that we often learn the most. After all, our experiences make us who we are as people.

This essay works well and is effective for the following reasons:

- ✔ The essay is well organized. The two body paragraphs support the thesis statement and help prove the writer's point.

- ✔ The author uses an example from literature and a personal experience. This diversity and writer's voice make the essay effective.

- ✔ The author chooses a side and sticks to the side. Everything in the essay helps support the thesis statement.

- ✔ The author stays on point and doesn't ramble or wander off topic.

- ✔ The essay is generally free from grammatical errors and awkward sentences.

Now, take a look at an essay that misses the mark. Read the following essay and note prob-lems you see. In fact, consider grabbing a pencil and marking any grammatical or spelling errors, too.

Sometimes experience can be the hardest teacher, but sometimes it isn't. In my life I have had some difficult situations Ive had to deal with. Those situations were hard, but they didn't break me from being the person I am. Its often difficult to learn from you're missteaks, but we have to go through life, right? One time I even had to learn to fly on an airplane without my parents. I was really scared at first but I had to do it. But after the flight left the ground, the flight attendant started serving peanuts and soft drinks. I even found a magazine to read to pass the time.

Overall, experiences can be hard, but they don't have to break you. You have to live in the real world and you have to try your best. Always.

This essay misses the mark for several reasons:

✔ The essay doesn't take a position on the subject. The reader isn't really sure what the author believes.

✔ The author spends most of his time talking about "experiences breaking you," which isn't the essay assignment.

✔ The essay has no clear paragraph structure. Each sentence seems disconnected from a cohesive thought.

✔ The author doesn't provide concrete examples to support his position (and we're not even really sure what the position is).

✔ The essay has several misspelled words and grammatical problems.

Responding to upper level essay practice prompts

Are you ready for a little practice on your own? The following sample prompts give you a chance to practice your essay-writing skills. Pick three of the following prompts and write an essay about each one for practice. Use only two sheets of notebook paper, one side only, and time yourself as you write.

✔ **Topic 1:** Nothing ventured, nothing gained.

Assignment: Do you agree or disagree with this topic statement? Support your position with one or two specific examples from personal experience, the experience of others, current events, history, or literature.

✔ **Topic 2:** Fear is a strong motivator.

Assignment: Do you agree or disagree with this topic statement? Support your position with one or two specific examples from personal experience, the experience of others, current events, history, or literature.

✔ **Topic 3:** What do you think is the greatest problem in America?

Assignment: Choose an issue and write about it. Support your position with one or two specific examples from personal experience, the experience of others, current events, history, or literature.

✔ **Topic 4:** Where there's a will, there's a way.

Assignment: Do you agree or disagree with this topic statement? Support your position with one or two specific examples from personal experience, the experience of others, current events, history, or literature.

✔ **Topic 5:** A rolling stone can gather no moss.

Assignment: Do you agree or disagree with this topic statement? Support your position with one or two specific examples from personal experience, the experience of others, current events, history, or literature.

Lower Level and Middle Level Essay

If you're taking the lower level SSAT or the lower or middle level ISEE, use the same paragraph structure we explore in Chapter 8, which includes an introduction, two body paragraphs, and a short conclusion. This structure helps you organize your essay and include plenty of detail. Take a look at the sample essays and example prompts in the following sections, and then practice writing your own essays. You have only 30 minutes to complete a brief writing sample, so time yourself as you practice.

Following the example of sample essays

Directions: Read the following topic carefully. Take a few minutes to think about the topic and organize your thoughts before you begin writing. Be sure that your handwriting is legible and that you stay within the lines and margins.

   Topic: All good things must come to an end.

Assignment: Do you agree or disagree with this topic statement? Support your position with one or two specific examples from personal experience, the experience of others, current events, history, or literature.

The following essay would get a high score from any evaluator. Read on and see why:

> Someone once said that "all good things must come to an end." Everything in life ends at some point because nothing lasts forever. Really, both good and bad things come to an end. The difference is the good things can always stay with us because we can remember them all of our lives. Because of our memories, good things don't really have to end.
>
> In the novel, *To Kill A Mockingbird,* the main character, Jem, had a lot of adventures with his sister, Scout. In the novel, Jem and Scout play a lot of games and they even dress up in costumes and act out plays. These good times didn't last of course because the characters went through some bad experiences in their lives. But, Jem and Scout would always be able to look back on the fun times they shared as kids. Because of this, their memories will always keep their childhood experiences alive.
>
> I also have had some "good things" in my life. While vacationing in Hawaii, I decided to learn to boogie board. After practicing the basics on the sand, I tried out my new skills in the water. At first, it was really hard. But as time went on, I learned to boogie board really well and I had so much fun. Sure, I can't stay in Hawaii and boogie board forever, but I will never forget the experience. My memory will always keep that special time alive for me.
>
> The good things in life do come to an end, but they don't really end since our memory can keep them alive. What is so great about our memories is we can forget the bad, and remember the good. In this way, the good times in life never really leave us.

This essay works well and is effective for the following reasons:

- ✔ The essay is well organized. The two body paragraphs support the thesis statement and help prove the writer's point. Even though the writer is writing against the topic, he proves his point about memories keeping good things alive.

- ✔ The author uses an example from literature and a personal experience. This diversity and writer's voice make the essay effective.

- ✔ The author chooses a side and sticks to the side. Everything in the essay helps prove the thesis statement.

- ✔ The author stays on point and doesn't ramble or wander off topic.

- ✔ The essay is generally free from grammatical errors and awkward sentences.

Now, take a look at an essay that misses the mark. Read the following essay and note problems you see. In fact, consider grabbing a pencil and marking any grammatical or spelling errors, too.

Good things don't last, but sometimes they still do. If you have something good that happens to you, you can remember it and that is a good thing. Of course, sometimes we remember things that are bad and that is not a good thing. I think we can forget some good things and still remember other good things. I remember a lot of good things that have hapened to me. One time I went on vacation in Hawaii and there were a lot of good things that happened there. I've even read many books were the main characters had good things that happened to them two. Its hard to believe, but we can remember so many good things about our lives.

This essay misses the mark for several reasons:

- ✔ The essay doesn't take a position on the subject. The reader isn't really sure what the author believes.

- ✔ The author spends most of his time talking about the contrast between good and bad things, which isn't the essay assignment.

- ✔ The essay has no clear paragraph structure. Each sentence seems disconnected from a cohesive thought.

- ✔ The author doesn't provide concrete examples to support his position (and we're not even really sure what the position is).

- ✔ The essay has several misspelled words and grammatical problems.

Responding to lower and middle level essay practice prompts

Are you ready for a little practice on your own? The following sample prompts give you a chance to practice your essay-writing skills. Pick three of the following prompts and write an essay about each one for practice. Use only two sheets of notebook paper, one side only, and time yourself as you write.

- ✔ **Topic 1:** You only live once, so make the most of it.

  Assignment: Do you agree or disagree with this topic statement? Support your position with one or two specific examples from personal experience, the experience of others, current events, history, or literature.

- ✔ **Topic 2:** Write about someone who is important in your life.

  Assignment: Choose a person and write about him or her. Support your position with one or two specific examples from personal experience, the experience of others, current events, history, or literature.

- ✔ **Topic 3:** Hard work always brings about progress.

  Assignment: Do you agree or disagree with this topic statement? Support your position with one or two specific examples from personal experience, the experience of others, current events, history, or literature.

- ✔ **Topic 4:** The hard way is the right way.

  Assignment: Do you agree or disagree with this topic statement? Support your position with one or two specific examples from personal experience, the experience of others, current events, history, or literature.

Topic 5: If an alien landed in your yard, how would you convince him to stay on earth?

Assignment: Write to persuade your reader. Support your position with one or two specific examples from personal experience, the experience of others, current events, history, or literature.

Part III
Tackling the Math Sections

The 5th Wave   By Rich Tennant

©RICHTENNANT

"The math portion of that test was so easy. I figure I've got a 7 in 5 chance of acing it."

In this part . . .

Part III is all about the Math sections of the exams. You explore math skills, like arithmetic, algebra, and geometry, and find out how to manage those pesky word problems. We focus your attention on what you really need to know, help you practice, and then let you practice on your own a bit, too.

Chapter 10

Adding Up Arithmetic

In This Chapter

▶ Revisiting the basics of arithmetic

▶ Reviewing commonly tested concepts

▶ Checking out some arithmetic tips and tricks

In this chapter, you discover the kinds of arithmetic included on the SSAT and ISEE, along with a few basic practice questions and tips. To make sure you're not a robot, the test writers get a little bit creative with the way they test math concepts. They want to see whether you can apply your math skills. The math questions on the test may sometimes seem weird or unfamiliar, but we show you how to recognize what you need to know to solve them.

Most of this chapter focuses on covering the arithmetic concepts you need to be comfortable with before you take the test. We point out which topics are more likely to appear on the ISEE than on the SSAT. As a whole, the ISEE covers more topics than the SSAT does, so if you're studying for the ISEE, make sure you check out all the topics in this chapter.

If you're not sure how to do a question after looking at it briefly, skip it and return to it after you've done all the other questions you know how to do. Always keep this testing tip in mind.

Solving Basic Arithmetic Questions

You can be sure of one thing when you're staring at a math question on the ISEE or the SSAT: It's testing a math concept — duh, right? Well, the writers of the tests like to disguise concepts you already know, so here are a few tactics you can use when staring at a funky-looking question:

✔ **Identify the concept.** Is the problem dealing with fractions? Percents? Probability?

✔ **Estimate the answer first.** Doing so helps you tell whether you did the math right. Estimation and rounding save time; just don't round too much.

✔ **Write something down.** Moving your pencil helps your brain start moving.

We provide plenty of problems for you to try these tactics in Chapter 11. In this chapter, we focus on covering the math skills you need so you can recognize those concepts when they pop up on the actual test.

Although any concept in this chapter can possibly make an appearance on any level of the ISEE or SSAT, several of the following concepts are more likely to appear on the ISEE. We let you know which ones when we get to them.

Before we begin our review, get familiar with the following math vocabulary words:

- ✔ **Positive numbers:** Numbers bigger than zero
- ✔ **Negative numbers:** Numbers smaller than zero
- ✔ **Integers:** Whole numbers, such as 2, 10, 0, and –8
- ✔ **Even numbers:** Divisible by 2 evenly, such as 4, 8, and –16
- ✔ **Odd numbers:** Not divisible by 2 evenly, such as 7, 15, and –9
- ✔ **Prime numbers:** Only divisible by themselves and 1, such as 2, 3, 7, and 31
- ✔ **Consecutive numbers:** Numbers in a row, such as 2, 3, 4, and 5
- ✔ **Exponents:** Numbers that raise other numbers to a power, like the little 2 in 5^2; $5^2 = 5 \times 5$, and $5^3 = 5 \times 5 \times 5$
- ✔ **Sum:** The result of adding
- ✔ **Difference:** The result of subtracting
- ✔ **Product:** The result of multiplying
- ✔ **Quotient:** The result of dividing

Reviewing Arithmetic

In this section, we briefly cover several arithmetic concepts and give an example of each. Because we don't write the ISEE or SSAT, we can't guarantee that all these concepts appear on the test or that others won't, but in the following sections, we review the most common arithmetic concepts you'll likely find on the ISEE and SSAT. So be sure to get familiar with any concepts you're unsure of and review others so you're prepared for whatever the test throws at you.

Rules of zero

Zero, like the masked swordsman Zorro (try Googling him), is quite a character. A few rules you want to remember about zero include the following:

- ✔ You can't divide by zero. (Math people say it's *undefined;* just don't do it.)
- ✔ Zero divided by a number is still zero. For example, $0 \div 7 = 0$.
- ✔ Zero times a number is also still zero. For example, $293 \times 0 = 0$.
- ✔ Zero is an even number (like 2, 4, or 86).
- ✔ Zero isn't positive or negative. It just never picked a side.

Order of operations

When you see a problem with a bunch of different operations, like the following, be careful. Depending on how you do it, you'll get different answers.

$(1 + 2 \times 2)^2 - 3 =$

To get the *correct* answer, you have to follow the correct *order of operations*. The order of operations tells you where to start when working a problem with different operations, like a mix of addition, multiplication, division, and operations in parentheses. To help you remember the exact order, use *PEMDAS,* which stands for:

1. **P**arentheses: $(2 + 1)$

2. **E**xponents: 4^2

3. **M**ultiplication: 5×6

4. **D**ivision: $9 \div 3$

5. **A**ddition: $20 + 18$

6. **S**ubtraction: $5 - 4$

The most common phrase to remember PEMDAS is *Please Excuse My Dear Aunt Sally,* but feel free to make up your own.

In order of operations, multiplication and division are tied. So are addition and subtraction. In other words, it doesn't matter if you do multiplication or division first, but you have to go from left to right. For example, if you have a problem like $10 - 3 + 6$, you want to do the $10 - 3$ first, and then add 6 to the result. Try using PEMDAS on the following question:

$(1 + 2 \times 2)^2 - 3 =$

(A) 78

(B) 33

(C) 22

(D) 9

(E) 3

The correct answer is Choice (C), 22. But how did you get there? PEMDAS, of course. First, look at what's inside the parentheses: $(1 + 2 \times 2)$. Multiplication comes before addition, so what's inside the parentheses becomes $(1 + 4)$. Then, $1 + 4 = 5$, so your new equation is $(5)^2 - 3 =$. The next step in the order of operations is exponents: 5^2 equals 25. The last step is to subtract: $25 - 3 = 22$.

Any time you see a question with multiple operation signs, use PEMDAS!

Number lines

Ever since you learned how to count, you've been using a *number line*. A number line is just a graph that puts numbers in order from left to right. The SSAT and ISEE use number lines to see whether you can figure out the distance between marks on a line. To figure out how much space is between unlabeled marks on a number line, you have to be comfortable using fractions, which we discuss later in this chapter.

Number lines are also used to test your knowledge of inequalities, which we cover in Chapter 12.

When in doubt on a number line question, just eyeball it. You can safely estimate because the line is drawn to scale. You can even use your answer sheet to measure. Hold your answer sheet against the question, mark a distance you know, then use that mark to measure a distance you don't know.

Here's an example of a basic number line question:

In the diagram, which number is the arrow pointing to?

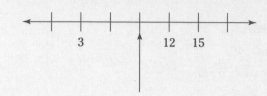

(A) 11

(B) 10

(C) 9

(D) 8

(E) 6

Because number lines on the ISEE and SSAT are drawn to scale, you can assume that the distance between each mark on the line is equal if the marks look equally spaced. Because 12 and 15 are one mark apart, each mark is 3 more than the mark to its left. The arrow is pointing to the mark before 12, so that mark is 3 less than 12, or 9, Choice **(C).**

Negative numbers

Negative numbers aren't numbers that are having a bad day; they're just lower than zero. You know you're dealing with a negative number when you see a minus sign next to it, like –3.

When solving math problems involving negative numbers, put parentheses around the negative numbers so you don't confuse the negative signs with minus signs.

If you add a negative number to another negative number, just add the two numbers and put a negative sign next to the answer. For example, $(-3) + (-4) = -7$. The sum of two negative numbers is always a negative number.

If you add a negative number to a positive number, pretend the negative sign isn't there. Then, subtract the smaller number from the bigger number. To figure out whether the answer gets a negative sign, just see which of the first two numbers is bigger. If the negative number is bigger, the answer gets a negative sign. If the positive number is bigger, the answer is positive. For example:

$(-9) + 5$ becomes $9 - 5 = 4$. The 4 gets a negative sign because 9 is bigger than 5, so the answer is –4.

$8 + (-3)$ becomes $8 - 3 = 5$. The 5 doesn't get a negative sign because 8 is bigger than 3, so the answer is 5.

Subtracting negative numbers is even easier than adding them. If you subtract a negative number from another number, cross off the negative sign and add it to the number instead. For example:

$7 - (-4) = 7 + 4 = 11$. Or $(-9) - (-6) = (-9) + 6$, which becomes $9 - 6 = 3$. The 3 gets a negative sign because 9 is bigger than 6, so the answer is –3.

If you subtract a positive number from a negative number, add the two numbers and give the answer a negative sign. For example, $(-6) - 2 = -8$.

Multiplying and dividing negative numbers is easy, too. If you multiply two negative numbers or divide two negative numbers, the answer becomes positive. For example:

$$-3 \times -3 = 9$$

$$\frac{-4}{-4} = 1$$

If you multiply or divide a positive number by a negative number or a negative number by a positive number, just multiply or divide as you normally would and the answer gets a negative sign. For example:

$$5 \times -3 = -15$$

$$\frac{8}{-2} = -4$$

Fractions

Fractions may look scary (and believe me, they scare some college graduates, too!), but you can think about them in ways that make them easier to handle. If you have the fraction $\frac{3}{4}$, it just means you have 3 out of 4 parts of something. If you had all 4 parts, you'd have the whole thing. In math terms, the *whole thing* is 1.

Another helpful thing to know about fractions is that the way they're set up tells you to divide, but you don't have to unless the test asks you to. The fraction $\frac{3}{4}$ is the same as 3 divided by 4. If you divided, you'd get 0.75, which is a decimal. It has the same value as $\frac{3}{4}$, but it's just written differently.

 Your math teacher probably wants you to know that the top number of a fraction is the *numerator* and that the bottom part is the *denominator*, but your test probably won't ever use those words. For the purpose of making things easier to remember, we just say the top part and the bottom part of the fraction we're discussing. If you do see *denominator*, think of the *d* standing for "down," because it's the bottom part of the fraction.

Here are some fraction skills you should know:

- ✔ Reducing and rewriting fractions
- ✔ Adding and subtracting fractions
- ✔ Multiplying and dividing fractions
- ✔ Comparing fractions (to see which fraction is bigger or smaller)
- ✔ Dealing with remainders

Reducing and rewriting fractions

Reducing fractions is a technique that usually makes life a little easier. If you're not sure whether a fraction can be reduced, just try it out. The easiest way to do that is to see whether a small number, like 2 or 3, can evenly divide into *both* the top and bottom parts of the fraction. For example, if you had $\frac{12}{16}$, you can check whether 2 can divide into both the top and bottom parts of the fraction. If so, do it: $\frac{12 \div 2}{16 \div 2} = \frac{6}{8}$. And then if you try it again, you get $\frac{6 \div 2}{8 \div 2} = \frac{3}{4}$, which is completely reduced. A fraction is completely reduced if nothing except for 1 can divide into both of its parts. You can divide the top and bottom parts of $\frac{3}{4}$ by 1, but that doesn't change the fraction!

Switching improper fractions to mixed numbers and vice versa is a technique that we call *rewriting fractions,* something you should also get familiar with. Both improper fractions and mixed numbers are just fractions written in different ways. A fraction like $\frac{18}{4}$ is an *improper fraction* (the top part is bigger than the bottom part). You can turn an improper fraction into a mixed number by doing the division: 18 divided by 4. The first part, or whole number part, of the mixed number is how many times 4 goes into 18, or 4. The fractional part of the mixed number, $\frac{2}{4}$, is what's left over, or the remainder: 4 goes into 18 four times with a remainder of 2. The remainder is put over the bottom part of the original fraction. So $\frac{18}{4}$ becomes $4\frac{2}{4}$. And like before, reduce: $\frac{2}{4} = \frac{2 \div 2}{4 \div 2} = \frac{1}{2}$. The final answer is $4\frac{1}{2}$.

Changing a mixed number to an improper fraction works a little differently. Say you start with $4\frac{1}{2}$. Take the bottom part of the fraction, multiply it by the whole number part of the mixed number, add the top part of the fraction, and put the result over the bottom part of the fraction. So $2 \times 4 + 1 = 9$, then put 9 over 2: $\frac{9}{2}$, which is the same as $\frac{18}{4}$ (if you had first reduced it by dividing the top and bottom by 2).

Adding and subtracting fractions

Adding and subtracting fractions with the same denominator, or bottom number, is easy. Just keep the bottom part of both fractions the same and add the top parts. For example, $\frac{1}{6} + \frac{4}{6} = \frac{5}{6}$ or $\frac{7}{9} - \frac{2}{9} = \frac{5}{9}$.

If fractions have different bottom parts, adding or subtracting them is harder. The bottom parts need to be the same, so you have to give the fractions a *common denominator.* The easiest way to do so is to multiply the bottom parts. The result is the bottom part of the new fractions.

For example, for $\frac{1}{3} + \frac{2}{7}$, the common bottom part of the new fractions is 21 (3×7): $\frac{}{21} + \frac{}{21}$. Then multiply the top part of $\frac{1}{3}$ by the bottom part of $\frac{2}{7}$, and you get $1 \times 7 = 7$. So the first new fraction is $\frac{7}{21} + \frac{}{21}$. Do the same thing for $\frac{2}{7}$: Multiply the top part by the bottom part of the other original fraction, so you end up with $\frac{6}{21}$. Now that the two fractions have a common bottom part, you can easily add them: $\frac{7}{21} + \frac{6}{21} = \frac{13}{21}$.

Subtracting fractions with different bottom parts works the same way. If the problem was $\frac{1}{3} - \frac{2}{7}$, you'd first get a common bottom part the same way you did with the addition problem, but then subtract: $\frac{7}{21} - \frac{6}{21} = \frac{1}{21}$.

Multiplying and dividing fractions

Multiplying and dividing fractions is easier than adding and subtracting them because you don't need to worry about a common denominator. When multiplying fractions, just multiply straight across. For example, if you're asked to multiply $\frac{1}{2} \times \frac{2}{3}$, just multiply straight across from left to right: $\frac{1}{2} \times \frac{2}{3} = \frac{2}{6}$, which reduces to $\frac{1}{3}$ by dividing the top and bottom by 2. If you're asked to divide $\frac{1}{2} \div \frac{2}{3}$, just flip the second fraction and multiply, like so: $\frac{1}{2} \div \frac{2}{3} = \frac{1}{2} \times \frac{3}{2} = \frac{3}{4}$.

Comparing fractions

Comparing fractions to see which is bigger or smaller usually means that you have to write the fractions the same way. In other words, you need to write both as fractions with a common bottom part. If you're asked to determine whether $\frac{1}{3}$ or $\frac{2}{7}$ is bigger, giving them a common bottom part, like when you added them, makes your job easier. After you do that, you can easily see that $\frac{7}{21}$ is bigger than $\frac{6}{21}$. A quick way to figure out which fraction in a group is biggest is to see whether any of them are bigger than one-half. For example, if you're comparing $\frac{4}{9}, \frac{15}{31}, \frac{7}{13}$, and $\frac{100}{203}$, you can quickly determine that $\frac{7}{13}$ is the biggest fraction because it's the only one that has a top part that's more than half of its bottom part (7 is more than half of 13).

Making a fraction's top part bigger makes the fraction bigger, but making a fraction's bottom part bigger makes the fraction *smaller*. For example, $\frac{8}{13}$ is bigger than $\frac{7}{13}$, and $\frac{7}{14}$ is smaller than $\frac{7}{13}$.

Dealing with remainders

Remainders are the leftovers. Before you learned what a decimal or a fraction was, you probably did long division, like this:

$$2\overline{)17} \quad \begin{array}{r} 8^{\,R1} \\ \hline 17 \\ 16 \\ \hline 1 \end{array}$$

This equation means that 2 goes into 17 eight times, with one left over. To help understand this problem, pretend someone has 17 cookies and she must put 2 cookies on each plate. She would have enough cookies to put 2 cookies on 8 plates, and then have 1 cookie — the remainder — left over. The writers of the SSAT and ISEE like to see whether you remember how to use remainders.

Decimals

Decimals are just numbers that aren't whole. Whole numbers are the numbers we use when we count: 2, 3, 4, and so on. Decimals, like fractions, are numbers that fall somewhere between two whole numbers. For example, 2.5 is between 2 and 3. And 2.5 is the same thing as $2\frac{1}{2}$.

Here are a few decimal concepts to get familiar with:

- Decimal places
- Adding, subtracting, dividing, and multiplying decimals
- Converting fractions to decimals and decimals to fractions
- Rounding and estimating

Decimal places

Knowing what places stand for when you're looking at a decimal is important. For example, take the number 762.493:

7 = hundreds place / hundreds digit

6 = tens place / tens digit

2 = ones place / ones digit

4 = tenths place

9 = hundredths place

3 = thousandths place

Adding, subtracting, dividing, and multiplying decimals

Adding and subtracting decimals is pretty simple. Just add or subtract as you normally do and remember to bring the decimal straight down into your answer. Make sure the decimal points line up when you write down the problem. For example:

$$
\begin{array}{r}
64.32 \\
+32.17 \\
\hline
96.49
\end{array}
\qquad
\begin{array}{r}
98.68 \\
-22.17 \\
\hline
76.51
\end{array}
$$

Multiplying and dividing decimals is a little harder, but here's a trick: Get rid of the decimals first. Just move the decimal points to the right until none of the numbers is a decimal any-more. Make sure you move the decimal point the same number of spots for each number.

What is 0.15 ÷ 0.03?

To make this problem easier, move the decimal point in each number two spots to the right. So 0.15 becomes 15, and 0.03 becomes 3. The resulting problem, 15 ÷ 3, is a lot easier and gives you the same answer (5) as the original problem.

Multiplying decimals can also be made easier with this technique, but when you multiply, you have to remember to move the decimal point when you have your answer.

What is 0.15 × 0.03?

Start by moving each decimal point the same number of spaces to the right until neither of the numbers is a decimal, resulting in 15 × 3. Next, do the multiplication: 15 × 3 = 45. Now, move the decimal point back to the left. To figure out how many places you need to move it, look at the original numbers (0.15 and 0.03) and count how many numbers are to the right of the decimal points: 0.15 has two (1 and 5), and 0.03 also has two (0 and 3). You have a total of four numbers to the right of the decimal points, so you move the decimal point of the answer four spots to the left, and 45 becomes 0.0045.

When counting how many numbers are to the right of the decimal point, the number 0 doesn't count if it's the last number on the right. If you'd written 0.15 as 0.150, you wouldn't count the 0 on the end as another number.

Converting fractions to decimals and decimals to fractions

Changing fractions to decimals and vice versa is also a handy skill. Converting a fraction to a decimal is easy. First, make sure the number is written as an improper fraction. For example, if you're converting $3\frac{1}{2}$ to a decimal, first write it as an improper fraction, such as $\frac{7}{2}$. Next, just do the division: 7 ÷ 2 = 3.5.

Converting a decimal into a fraction is even simpler. If one number is to the right of the decimal point, like with 0.7, then the fraction is $\frac{7}{10}$. If two numbers are to the right of the decimal point, like with 0.07, then the fraction is $\frac{7}{100}$. See the pattern? Just count how many numbers are to the right of the decimal point, take away the decimal point from the original number, and put the result over a 1 followed by as many zeroes as there were numbers to the right of the decimal point in the original number.

Rounding and estimating decimals

When you round decimals, pay attention to the answer choices to see how much rounding you may be able to do. In some problems, you can get away with rounding a decimal to a whole number to make the arithmetic easier. For example:

Which of the following is closest to 67.09 + 23.98?

(A) 88

(B) 90

(C) 91

(D) 92

(E) 95

If you round 67.09 to the nearest whole number (67) and round 23.98 to the nearest whole number (24), then the addition (67 + 24 = 91) is easier. Beware of rounding too much, though — if in this problem you had rounded 67.09 to 70 and 23.98 to 25, you'd have gotten it wrong. In general, when in doubt, round less, not more!

Percents

Percents are just how math people say how much of something there is. If you had a pizza and ate a quarter of it, you'd have three quarters left. Another way you can say this is that you ate 25 percent of the pizza, and you'd have 75 percent left. Another way to think of percent is "per 100." In the example, you would have 75 per 100 of the pizza left. In math-speak, *per* means divide, so 75 percent can be written as $\frac{75}{100}$. Here are a few percent skills to review:

  ✔ Converting decimals to percents

  ✔ Converting fractions to percents

  ✔ Taking percentages of numbers

  ✔ Percent increases and decreases (upper level SSAT; middle and upper level ISEE)

The ISEE and SSAT may ask you what percent a decimal is equal to, or vice versa. It's pretty easy if you follow these rules:

  ✔ **Percent to decimal:** Move the decimal point two numbers to the left. For example, take a look at 75 percent. In a whole number, the decimal point is to the right of the last digit, so in the number 75, it's to the right of the 5. If you move the decimal point two spots to the left, it becomes 0.75.

  ✔ **Decimal to percent:** Move the decimal point two numbers to the right. For example, start with 0.2 and move the decimal point two spots to the right. So 0.2 becomes 20.0 or 20 percent. We add a 0 because we need another spot and 0.2 only had one.

Converting fractions to percents is a little trickier. To start, we recommend that you memorize what percents some common fractions are equal to:

✓ $\frac{1}{100}$ = 0.01 = 1%

✓ $\frac{1}{10}$ = 0.1 = 10%

✓ $\frac{1}{4}$ = 0.25 = 25%

✓ $\frac{1}{3}$ = 0.33 = 33%

✓ $\frac{1}{2}$ = 0.5 = 50%

✓ $\frac{3}{4}$ = 0.75 = 75%

✓ 1 = 1 = 100%

For other, less common fraction-to-percent conversions, start by converting the fraction to a decimal, as described earlier in this chapter in the section "Converting fractions to decimals and decimals to fractions." Then convert the decimal to a percentage as we explain earlier in this section. Here's an example:

$$\frac{4}{5} = 0.8 = 80\%$$

Taking a percentage of a number just means that you multiply the number by the decimal that the percent converts into. If you're asked to take 40 percent of 120, you'd first convert 40 percent to 0.4, then multiply $120 \times 0.4 = 48$.

Using 10 percent as a baseline when taking percentages of numbers is a good way to see whether your answer makes sense. To take 10 percent of a number, just move the decimal point one spot to the left.

Using the earlier example, 40 percent of 120, if you take 10 percent of 120 first, you get 10 percent of 120 = 12. If 10 percent of 120 is 12, just double that amount to get 20 percent of 120: $12 \times 2 = 24$. And to get 40 percent, which is double 20 percent, you can just double that: $24 \times 2 = 48$. This technique is a handy way to figure out a 20 percent tip at a restaurant, too!

Similarly, you can easily take 1 percent of a number by moving the decimal point *two* spots to the left: 1 percent of 120 = 1.2. This trick is useful when trying to figure out a problem like 3 percent of 120, for example. You can either multiply 120 by 0.03 or take 1 percent of 120, which is 1.2, and multiply that by 3: $1.2 \times 3 = 3.6$.

You may also be asked to figure out a percent increase or decrease on the ISEE or SSAT. Take this problem, for example:

Yesterday, the high temperature was 80°F. Today, the high temperature was 88°F. What was the percent increase in the temperature from yesterday to today?

Percent increases and decreases use the same formula: 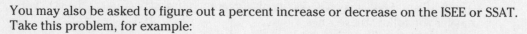 $\frac{\text{difference}}{\text{original}} \times 100$. The difference is just the difference between the two numbers. Subtract the smaller number (80) from the larger number (88) and get 8. The original is the number that you had first — the number that increased or decreased. In this problem, that number is 80. So you can write this percent increase as $\frac{8}{80} \times 100$, which simplifies to $\frac{1}{10} \times 100 = \frac{100}{10} = 10$. The percent increase is 10 percent.

Factors and multiples

Factors and multiples are terms you want to be familiar with for the ISEE and SSAT. A *factor* of a number is a number that can divide evenly into the original number. For example, the number 9 has the following positive factors: 1, 3, and 9, because these numbers all divide evenly (with nothing left over) into 9. A *multiple* is the result of *multiplying* a number by another whole number. For example, some multiples of 3 are 3 (3×1), 6 (3×2), and 9 (3×3). A *prime number* is a number with only two positive factors: 1 and itself. The numbers 2, 3, 5, 7, 11, 13, and 17 are all prime, because you can't divide any positive number into them except 1 or themselves.

The number 1 *isn't* prime; it has only one factor — itself!

The *greatest common factor* of two numbers is just the biggest factor they have in common. If you're asked to find the greatest common factor of 75 and 90, for example, just list their factors (numbers that can be divided evenly into them) and pick the biggest one they have in common, like so:

The factors of 75: 1, 3, 5, *15*, 25, 75

The factors of 90: 1, 2, 3, 5, 6, 9, 10, *15*, 18, 30, 45, 90

Therefore, the greatest common factor of 75 and 90 is 15.

When listing a number's factors, work from low to high. After 1, see whether 2 is a factor, then 3, then 4, and so on. You'll know you've found all the number's factors when you reach a number that, when multiplied by a factor you've already found, results in the number you're factoring.

For example, when finding the factors of 75, you may have done something like this:

$1 \times 75 = 75$, $3 \times 25 = 75$, $5 \times 15 = 75$, 15 . . . wait a second, you already came across 15 — you multiplied it by 5 to get 75. So you're done!

Multiples are the result of multiplying a number by another whole number. For example, 5 has the following positive multiples: 5, 10, 15, 20, 25, and so on. You get these multiples by multiplying 5 by 1 (5), by 2 (10), by 3 (15), by 4 (20), and so forth. The SSAT or ISEE may ask you whether a number is a multiple of another number. You can tell it is if the original number divides into the other number.

For example: Is 35 a multiple of 5? Yes, because 5 divides into 35 evenly. Is 36 a multiple of 7? No, because 7 doesn't divide into 36 evenly.

The *least common multiple* of two numbers is the smallest multiple that both numbers share. The easiest way to handle least common multiple questions is to just make a list of the numbers' multiples and compare them. For example, if you're asked to find the least common multiple of 6 and 9, list each of their multiples:

The multiples of 6: 6, 12, *18*, 24, 36, . . .

The multiples of 9: 9, *18*, 27, 36, 45, . . .

Therefore, the least common multiple of 6 and 9 is 18. Although 36 is also a common multiple of 6 and 9, it isn't the least common multiple.

Exponents

Exponents are just a way of saying how many times a number, the *base,* should be multiplied by itself. For example, 2^2, which is called *two squared* or *two to the second power,* means that 2 is multiplied by itself one time: $2 \times 2 = 4$. And 2^4 (two to the fourth power), where 2 is the base and 4 is the exponent, means 2 is multiplied by itself three times: $2 \times 2 \times 2 \times 2 = 16$. Here are some exponent rules to know:

- Any number to the zero power is 1. For example, $7^0 = 1$.

- Any number to the first power is itself. For example, $7^1 = 7$.

To multiply exponents with the same base, you add the exponents and keep the base the same. For example:

$2^3 \times 2^4 = 2^7$ because $3 + 4 = 7$ and the base, 2, remains the same

To divide exponents with the same base, you subtract the bottom exponent from the top one and keep the base the same. For example:

$\frac{2^6}{2^4} = 2^2$ because $6 - 4 = 2$ and the base, 2, remains the same

To raise a number with an exponent to another exponent, you multiply the exponents and keep the base the same. (You'll probably only see this on middle or upper level exams.) For example:

$(2^2)^5 = 2^{10}$ because $2 \times 5 = 10$ and the base, 2, remains the same

 Don't try to apply rules for multiplying and dividing numbers with exponents to adding and subtracting numbers with exponents, because doing so can get you into trouble. And beware of applying multiplication and division rules when the exponents have *different* bases. If the exponents have different bases, just follow PEMDAS.

 $2^3 + 2^4 = 24$, *not* 2^7! $(2 \times 2 \times 2) + (2 \times 2 \times 2 \times 2) = (8) + (16) = 24$

$3^2 \times 4^2 = 12^2$, *not* 12^4! $(3 \times 3) \times (4 \times 4) = (9) \times (16) = 144$

When in doubt, multiply it out!

Probability

Think of probability as the chances that something will happen. To illustrate, think about flipping a coin. Two possibilities exist for what side faces up when the coin lands: heads or tails. The probability that the coin will land on heads is 1 in 2, or $\frac{1}{2}$. You can also express that number as a decimal (0.5) or a percentage (50%). So to calculate probability, use this formula: What you want divided by the total number of possibilities.

For example, suppose out of a box of 24 crayons, 2 of them are red. If you close your eyes and pick a crayon, the probability of that crayon being red is 2 (what you want, because two red crayons are in the box) divided by 24 (the total number of possibilities, or crayons): $\frac{2}{24} = \frac{1}{12}$.

On tough questions, you may have to figure out the chances of two things happening together. For these types of questions, you'll multiply the two probabilities. Consider the coin example again. What's the probability that you get heads twice in a row? Think about each flip separately. You know there's a $\frac{1}{2}$ chance of heads every time you flip the coin, so just multiply the odds for each flip: $\frac{1}{2} \times \frac{1}{2} = \frac{1}{4}$.

You may also be asked what the chances are of either one thing or another thing happening. These questions are rare, but if you get one, *add* the two probabilities. For example, consider the crayons. If two red crayons and three green ones are in the box, what are the chances of picking either a red or a green crayon? You solve this problem by adding the probability of picking a red crayon and the probability of picking a green crayon: $\frac{2}{24} + \frac{3}{24} = \frac{5}{24}$.

Roots

Roots look like this: $\sqrt{}$. On the SSAT and ISEE, you'll probably use roots to take *square roots* of numbers. The square root of a number is the number that, when multiplied by itself, equals the original number. For example, the square root of 16 = 4, because $4 \times 4 = 16$. In math, you write the square root as $\sqrt{16} = 4$. The square root of 25 is 5 because $5 \times 5 = 25$: $\sqrt{25} = 5$.

Here are a few operations involving radicals and roots to know:

- ✔ Estimating roots
- ✔ Adding, subtracting, multiplying, and dividing roots
- ✔ Simplifying roots

Estimating roots

In order to estimate a root, take the root of the whole numbers lower and higher than the root and then estimate a number between the two.

For example, say you're asked to find $\sqrt{20}$. You know that $\sqrt{16} = 4$ and $\sqrt{25} = 5$, so you can guess that the answer is between 4 and 5 (something like 4.5).

Adding, subtracting, multiplying, and dividing roots

Adding and subtracting roots works like this: Add the numbers outside the roots and keep what's inside the roots the same.

$$2\sqrt{5} + 2\sqrt{5} = 4\sqrt{5}$$

$$7\sqrt{5} - 3\sqrt{5} = 4\sqrt{5}$$

Adding and subtracting roots only works when you're using the same root. When you're given a problem with different roots, be careful: You may not be able to combine them. For example, $2\sqrt{3} + 3\sqrt{4}$. In this problem, you should just leave the roots as is.

To multiply and divide roots, you perform the operation (multiplication or division) on the numbers outside the roots and then perform the operation on the numbers inside the roots. For example, $2\sqrt{5} \times 3\sqrt{4} = 6\sqrt{20}$ because $2 \times 3 = 6$ (outside the roots) and $5 \times 4 = 20$ (inside the roots).

Simplifying roots

Simplifying roots is kind of like reducing fractions — you take a number out of the root that can divide into it. The trick is to take out a number that you can take the square root of and get a whole number, like 4, 9, 16, or 25. (Simplifying roots will probably appear only on middle and upper level exams.)

For example, you're asked to reduce $\sqrt{20}$. If you rewrite it as $\sqrt{4} \times \sqrt{5}$, you can then write the $\sqrt{4}$ as 2 because $2 \times 2 = 4$. So you're left with $2\sqrt{5}$.

You also may need to simplify a root if you have a root in the bottom part of a fraction, like $\frac{2}{\sqrt{3}}$. Test writers want you to get rid of the root in the bottom part of the fraction. To do this, multiply the top and the bottom parts of the fraction by the root:

$$\frac{2}{\sqrt{3}} \times \frac{\sqrt{3}}{\sqrt{3}} = \frac{2\sqrt{3}}{\sqrt{9}} = \frac{2\sqrt{3}}{3}$$

You can even simplify roots with variables in them:

$\sqrt{x^6} = x^3$ because $x^3 \cdot x^3 = x^6$

$\sqrt{16x^8} = 4x^4$ because $4 \times 4 = 16$ and $x^4 \cdot x^4 = x^8$

If you see an operation beneath a root, like $\sqrt{16+4}$, make sure you treat the stuff beneath the root sign as if there are parentheses around it: $\sqrt{(16+4)} = \sqrt{20}$. Remember the order of operations and PEMDAS from earlier in this chapter.

Scientific notation

Scientific notation is usually used when people are dealing with numbers that are too large to write out. To make life easier, these numbers are written by using the number 10 raised to a power, or exponent. For example, 500,000,000,000 is written as 5×10^{11}, which means the number 5 followed by 11 zeroes.

The easiest way to work with scientific notation is to let the exponent tell you how many spots to move the decimal point. For example, if you're writing out 3.25×10^6, you'd take 3.25 and move the decimal point six spots to the right: 3,250,000.

If you see numbers involving scientific notation on the test, try writing them out to make them less confusing, and then proceed to work out the problem. For example: $\frac{4.5 \times 10^9}{2.3 \times 10^5} = \frac{4,500,000,000}{230,000}$.

Chapter 11

Practicing Arithmetic

In This Chapter

▶ Practicing lower and middle level arithmetic

▶ Practicing upper level arithmetic

*1*t's all well and good to *read* about how to do math questions, but to improve your skills, you're going to have to put in some serious practice. In fact, the more you practice, the better at math you're going to get, which is why your math teacher assigns 30 questions for homework instead of just 3 (as nice as that would be, it wouldn't help much).

This chapter is basically divided into sections: one section covers the lower level SSAT and the lower and middle level ISEE arithmetic, and the other section is all about the upper level SSAT and ISEE arithmetic. We guide you through several practice questions and then provide some for you to work on all your own (don't worry, though, we also provide the answers).

No matter what test you're taking, do all the lower level problems because you'll get a lot out of them even if they're easy for you. When you do the math problems in this chapter and in later chapters, remember the following tips:

✔ **Write down your steps.** Writing down your work prevents careless errors and gives your brain a break, because it won't have to do as much at once. Also draw pictures whenever possible. Get in the habit of doing these techniques now so they're second nature by the time you take the test.

✔ **Skip a question quickly if you don't *immediately* know how to do it.** All the questions are worth the same amount of points, so fight with the hard ones *after* you've done all the easier ones.

✔ **Use common sense.** Before beginning a question, take a few seconds to think logically. What do you think the answer may be? This step lets you see whether your calculated answer makes sense and can even save you from doing some or all the math on some questions.

✔ **Read the question carefully.** Although starting to calculate as quickly as possible is tempting — after all, it's a timed test — make sure you read the question *closely* and *carefully* and then read it once more before you pick an answer.

Attacking Guided Lower and Middle Level Arithmetic Questions

This section contains some arithmetic questions to practice on. Each question is followed by an explanation, but don't look for help until you've really tried to figure out the problem on your own. You'll learn much more from the exercise that way.

1. $800 - 77 \times 2 =$

    (A) 646

    (B) 664

    (C) 1,446

    (D) 1,464

    (E) 1,664

Remember PEMDAS and the order of operations! Multiplication comes before subtraction, so do $77 \times 2 = 154$, and then subtract $800 - 154 = 646$. Choice **(A)** is the correct answer. If you do the subtraction first by mistake, you end up with Choice (C).

2. To which number on the number line does the arrow point?

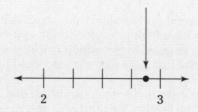

    (A) $\frac{3}{4}$

    (B) $\frac{7}{8}$

    (C) $2\frac{3}{4}$

    (D) $2\frac{7}{8}$

    (E) $2\frac{15}{16}$

Because four distances are between 2 and 3, each distance represents $\frac{1}{4}$. Just count: $2, 2\frac{1}{4}, 2\frac{1}{2}, 2\frac{3}{4}, 3$. And because the dot is halfway between $2\frac{3}{4}$ and 3, the number is $2\frac{7}{8}$, Choice **(D)**. To better understand this question, rewrite $2\frac{3}{4}$ as $2\frac{6}{8}$ and rewrite 3 as $2\frac{8}{8}$.

3. What is the sum of -4 and the product of -2 and -2?

    (A) -16

    (B) -8

    (C) 0

    (D) 8

    (E) 16

Remember, *sum* means add, and *product* means multiply. Use PEMDAS again: Do the product first: $(-2) \times (-2) = 4$ (remember that a negative number times another negative number makes a positive number). Then, $(-4) + 4 = 0$, so Choice **(C)** is correct.

4. Which is the smallest fraction?

   (A) $\frac{6}{11}$

   (B) $\frac{7}{13}$

   (C) $\frac{100}{202}$

   (D) $\frac{1}{2}$

   (E) $\frac{3}{5}$

   To compare these fractions, you can give them all a common bottom part, or denominator, or you can do the division and turn them all into decimals, but those methods take a long time. If you notice that only Choice (C) has a top part less than half its bottom part, you can save yourself some time. Choice **(C)** is correct because it's the only choice that's less than $\frac{1}{2}$.

5. Which of the following numbers is largest?

   (A) 17.0919

   (B) 17.0909

   (C) 17.1019

   (D) 17.0999

   (E) 17.0899

   This question is testing your knowledge of decimal place value. All the choices have the same tens value (1) and the same ones value (7). The answer is Choice **(C)** because its tenths value (1) is bigger than those of the other choices (which all have 0 as a tenths value). You don't even need to look at the hundredths and thousandths values of the choices at that point.

   Go from left to right when comparing numbers' sizes.

6. If Austin ate 27 of the 36 pieces of candy in a box, what percent did he eat?

   (A) 33.3%

   (B) 60%

   (C) 75%

   (D) 83.3%

   (E) 90%

   Use your common sense before doing the math; Austin ate almost all the candy. Rule out Choice (A) because it's only a third, and get rid of Choice (B) because it's just a bit over half. To find the percent, write a fraction first: $\frac{27}{36}$, which is the same as 27 out of 36. Reduce the fraction: $\frac{27}{36} = \frac{3}{4}$. Do the division to get a decimal: $\frac{3}{4} = 0.75$, then convert the decimal to a percent by moving the decimal point two spots to the right: 0.75 = 75%, Choice **(C)**.

7. Which of the following shows 45 as a product of primes?

(A) 4×5

(B) $2 \times 2 \times 5$

(C) $3 \times 3 \times 5$

(D) 5×9

(E) 1×45

Product means the result when you multiply, and prime numbers have only themselves and the number 1 as factors. Although Choices (C), (D), and (E) all make 45, only Choice **(C)** is the product of primes: Both 3 and 5 are prime numbers, and $3 \times 3 = 9$, and then $9 \times 5 = 45$.

Practicing Lower and Middle Level Arithmetic Questions on Your Own

Now that you've completed a few practice arithmetic questions, it's time to do some on your own. Review the four tips at the beginning of this chapter before starting.

1. According to the figure, what is the length of *AD?*

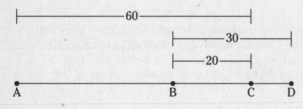

(A) 60

(B) 70

(C) 80

(D) 100

(E) 110

2. Which expression is equal to 29?

(A) $(4 + 5) + 2 + 3$

(B) $4 + 5(2) + 3$

(C) $(4 + 5) \times (2 + 3)$

(D) $4 + 5(2 + 3)$

(E) $4(5 + 2 + 3)$

3. Which of the following numbers, when multiplied by –2, is less than –10?

(A) –10

(B) –5

(C) 0

(D) 2

(E) 10

4. Which of the following is *not* true?

(A) $\frac{1}{4} = \frac{3}{12}$

(B) $\frac{2}{3} = \frac{8}{12}$

(C) $\frac{3}{4} = \frac{9}{16}$

(D) $\frac{4}{5} = \frac{8}{10}$

(E) $\frac{4}{5} = \frac{16}{20}$

5. All the following are greater than $\frac{1}{2}$ *except*

(A) $\frac{8}{17}$

(B) $\frac{2}{3}$

(C) $\frac{5}{9}$

(D) $\frac{17}{33}$

(E) $\frac{51}{100}$

6. Which number has a 3 in both the thousands place and hundredths place?

(A) 9,303.303

(B) 3,303.303

(C) 3,030.033

(D) 3,030.303

(E) 3,333.003

7. $1\frac{3}{4} \times 2\frac{3}{5} =$

    (A) $4\frac{1}{20}$

    (B) $4\frac{11}{20}$

    (C) $4\frac{19}{20}$

    (D) 5

    (E) $5\frac{1}{20}$

8. If Sarah had two hours with which to study but she watched TV for $1\frac{1}{2}$ hours, what percent of her study time was left?

    (A) 10%

    (B) 15%

    (C) 20%

    (D) 25%

    (E) 30%

9. Which number is closest to 1.33?

    (A) $\frac{9}{3}$

    (B) $1\frac{3}{10}$

    (C) $1\frac{1}{3}$

    (D) $1\frac{3}{100}$

    (E) $3\frac{1}{3}$

10. The greatest common factor of 64 and 80 is a multiple of which of the following?

    (A) 3

    (B) 4

    (C) 5

    (D) 6

    (E) 7

11. Which is equal to 10,000?

    (A) 2^5

    (B) 10^2

    (C) 10^3

    (D) 5^5

    (E) 10^4

12. If Christina spins the wheel shown in the figure, which fraction represents the probability that the arrow will land on an odd number?

    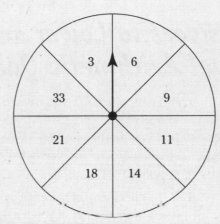

    (A) $\frac{3}{8}$

    (B) $\frac{1}{2}$

    (C) $\frac{5}{8}$

    (D) $\frac{3}{4}$

    (E) 5

13. The square root of 60 is closest to

    (A) 5

    (B) 6

    (C) 7

    (D) 8

    (E) 10

14. If Holly multiplies 896 by 149, which of the following is a good estimate of the result?

    (A) 13,500

    (B) 18,000

    (C) 135,000

    (D) 180,000

    (E) 200,000

15. What is the sum of 2.3×10^3 and 4.6?

    (A) $6\frac{9}{10}$

    (B) $27\frac{9}{10}$

    (C) $234\frac{3}{5}$

    (D) $2,304\frac{3}{5}$

    (E) $23,004\frac{3}{5}$

Answers to Lower and Middle Level Arithmetic Questions

1. **B.** To measure *AD*, you have to add *AC* (60) to *CD*. To find *CD*, take *BD* (30) and subtract *BC* (20) to get 10. And then 60 + 10 = 70.

2. **D.** If you do the math for all the choices, only Choice (D) produces 29: $4 + 5(2 + 3) = 4 + 5(5)$. Then 4 + 25 = 29. Remember PEMDAS, which is the order of operations.

3. **E.** When 10 is multiplied by –2, the result is –20, which is less than –10.

4. **C.** To check any of the choices, just see whether the fraction on the right reduces to the fraction on the left. If you try this with Choice (C), $\frac{9}{16}$ doesn't reduce to $\frac{3}{4}$; in fact, it doesn't reduce at all because nothing except 1 divides into both 9 and 16.

5. **A.** A quick way to check the choices here is to see whether any of the fractions have a top part less than half of its bottom part, because you're looking for the fraction that's less than $\frac{1}{2}$. In Choice (A), half of 17 is 8.5, and because 8 is less than 8.5, $\frac{8}{17}$ is less than $\frac{1}{2}$.

6. **C.** Only 3,030.033 has a 3 in the thousands place (**3**,030.033) and the hundredths place (3,030.0**3**3).

7. **B.** When multiplying mixed numbers, convert them to improper fractions first: $1\frac{3}{4}$ becomes $\frac{7}{4}$, and $2\frac{3}{5}$ becomes $\frac{13}{5}$. Now, multiply: $\frac{7}{4} \times \frac{13}{5} = \frac{91}{20}$. Because the answer choices are in mixed number form, convert $\frac{91}{20}$ to a mixed number: 20 goes into 91 four times with 11 left over, so the answer is $4\frac{11}{20}$.

8. **D.** Out of two hours, Sarah had a half-hour of study time left. To make that into a percent, you can think of it as $\frac{1}{4}$ of her study time because two hours have four $\frac{1}{2}$ hours. So $\frac{1}{4}$ is 25 percent.

9. **C.** You can do the division for Choice (C): $1\frac{1}{3}$ is $1 + 3\overline{)1.00}^{0.33} = 1.33$, or you may remember that the common fraction $\frac{1}{3}$ is equal to about 0.33. Don't get fooled by Choice (B): $\frac{3}{10}$ is equal to 0.3, not 0.33.

10. **B.** To figure this one out, list the factors of each number: 64 has 1, 2, 4, 8, *16*, 32, and 64, and 80 has 1, 2, 4, 5, 8, 10, *16*, 20, 40, and 80. The biggest factor they both have in common is 16, so that's the greatest common factor. Then, look at the choices to see which choice, when multiplied by a whole number, equals 16. Only Choice (B) does ($4 \times 4 = 16$).

11. **E.** $10^4 = 10 \times 10 \times 10 \times 10 = 10,000$.

12. **C.** To figure out the probability of the arrow landing on an *odd* number, count the odd numbers (3, 9, 11, 21, and 33, for a total of 5). Probability is how many of what you want to happen divided by the total possibilities. Eight numbers are on the wheel, so the answer is what you want (odd numbers = 5) divided by the total possibilities (total numbers on wheel = 8), so the answer is Choice (C), $\frac{5}{8}$.

13. **D.** Because the square root of 49 is 7 and the square root of 64 is 8, the square root of 60 must be between 7 and 8. You know it's closer to 8 than 7 because 60 is only 4 less than 64 but 11 more than 49.

14. **C.** Be careful not to round too much. Round 896 to 900 and round 149 to 150 then multiply $900 \times 150 = 135,000$.

15. **D.** Multiply first, and then add: $2.3 \times 10^3 = 2,300$, and $2,300 + 4.6 = 2,304.6$, which is the same as $2,304\frac{6}{10}$. Then, reduce the fraction to $2,304\frac{3}{5}$.

How'd it go? Any question that gave you trouble is a concept you probably need more practice with. Make sure you do several more fraction problems, for example, if you had trouble with one of the fraction questions. Repetition makes any difficult concept doable, if not easy. But remember to start with easier problems and work your way to harder ones after you've mastered the easier ones.

Tackling Guided Upper Level Arithmetic Questions

This section contains some upper level arithmetic questions for practice. Each is followed by an explanation, but make sure you don't look at the explanation until after you've attempted the problem — you'll learn more that way.

1. What is the value of the expression $\frac{4\left(4^2+4^3\right)}{16(4+12)}$?

   (A) 1

   (B) $\frac{5}{4}$

   (C) 2

   (D) 4

   (E) 16

   Do the work in parentheses first, and do exponents before adding: $\frac{4(16+64)}{16(16)}$ and simplify the (16 + 64) into (80). Then, divide the top and bottom of the fraction by 4: $\frac{4(80)}{16(16)} \div \frac{4}{4} = \frac{80}{4(16)}$. Simplify to $\frac{80}{64}$, and then reduce the fraction: $\frac{10}{8} = \frac{5}{4}$, Choice **(B)**.

2. Jill has an 18-sided die labeled 1 through 18, and Jack has a 20-sided die labeled 1 through 20. If they each roll their die twice, who has the greatest probability of rolling an odd number on both rolls?

   (A) Jill.

   (B) Jack.

   (C) Their probabilities are equal.

   (D) There is not enough information given to determine the answer.

Remember, probability is the number of things you want divided by the number of total possibilities. On her first roll, Jill has a $\frac{9}{18}$ probability of rolling an odd number, because 9 odd numbers are between 1 and 18 and 18 total numbers are between 1 and 18. On her second roll, the probability of rolling an odd number is the same, $\frac{9}{18}$. You find the probability of Jill rolling an odd number on *both* rolls by multiplying the individual probabilities (reducing fractions first): $\frac{1}{2} \times \frac{1}{2} = \frac{1}{4}$. Jack's probability of rolling an odd number on the first roll is $\frac{10}{20}$, because 10 odd numbers are between 1 and 20 and 20 total numbers are between 1 and 20. For his second roll, it's the same thing, so you just multiply the two probabilities (reducing first): $\frac{1}{2} \times \frac{1}{2} = \frac{1}{4}$. The correct answer is Choice **(C)**.

3. If Christy owns stock that was initially worth $7,500.00, what would its value be if its initial value went down by 20% then up by 20%?

   (A) $4,500.00

   (B) $6,000.00

   (C) $7,200.00

   (D) $7,500.00

   (E) $10,500.00

This question is a percent increase/decrease question. On these questions, do each percent increase or decrease *separately*. The value doesn't stay the same if it increases by 20 percent and then decreases by 20 percent, even though it may seem like it evens out. First, calculate the decrease by multiplying $7,500.00 by 0.8 (taking 80 percent of a number is the same thing as decreasing that number by 20 percent) and getting $6,000.00. Then, calculate the increase by multiplying $6,000.00 by 1.2 (taking 120 percent of a number is the same thing as increasing it by 20 percent) and you get Choice **(C)**, $7,200.00.

4. What is the value of the expression $\sqrt{16 + 25 + 36 + 49}$?

   (A) 22

   (B) $3\sqrt{14}$

   (C) $9\sqrt{14}$

   (D) 63

   (E) 126

Don't forget to treat the operations below a root sign like they're surrounded by parentheses $(16 + 25 + 36 + 49) = (126)$. To take the square root of 126, see whether you can break down the square root of 126 into two square roots where one produces a whole number. Check the answer choices for hints. Looking at Choice (A), is 22 the square root of 126 ? Nope, 22×22 is 484. Looking at Choice (B), does 14 go into 126? Yep, $14 \times 9 = 126$. So you can write $\sqrt{126} = \sqrt{9} \times \sqrt{14}$. The square root of 9 is 3, so the simplified answer is Choice **(B)**.

5. What is the value of the expression $7.9 \times 10^9 + 7.9 \times 10^9$?

   (A) 1.58×10^9

   (B) 1.58×10^{10}

   (C) 7.9×10^9

   (D) 7.9×10^{10}

   (E) 7.9×10^{18}

Beware of shortcuts; when in doubt, write it out! So 7.9×10^9 is 7,900,000,000. Add 7,900,000,000 + 7,900,000,000, and you get 15,800,000,000, which is the same thing as Choice **(B)** (1.58 with the decimal moved ten places to the right).

6. $16^8 =$

    (A) 2^{12}

    (B) 2^{16}

    (C) 2^{20}

    (D) 2^{24}

    (E) 2^{32}

The numbers in this question are *way* too big to write out in the time you have on the real test, so you need to use exponent rules. Rewrite 16^8 as $(2^4)^8$ because $2^4 = 16$. And $(2^4)^8 = 2^{32}$, which is Choice **(E).**

If you forget an exponent rule, solve a similar problem with numbers small enough to calculate, like $16^2 = 2^?$. It's easy enough to calculate 16 squared = 256, and that $2^8 = 256$. Doing this trick allows you to check whether you applied the rule correctly on the real problem.

7. All numbers that are multiples of both 4 and 7 are also multiples of

    (A) 4

    (B) 7

    (C) 11

    (D) 14

    (E) 28

Any number that is a multiple of both 4 and 7 is divisible by both 4 and 7, and looking at the answer choices, only Choice (E) fits the bill. You can also write down the multiples of each number so you have a visual. The multiples of 4 are 4, 8, 12, 16, 20, 24, *28*, 32, 36, 40, 44, 48, 52, *56,* and so on, and the multiples of 7 are 7, 14, 21, *28,* 35, 42, 49, *56,* and so on. Notice that 28 and 56 are multiples of both 4 and 7, so Choice **(E)** is correct because both 28 and 56 are multiples of 28.

Practicing Upper Level Arithmetic Questions on Your Own

Now that you've done a few practice arithmetic questions, it's time to do some on your own. Review the four tips at the beginning of this chapter before diving in.

1. Which expression does *not* result in an integer?

   (A) $\sqrt{49} + \sqrt{9}$

   (B) $\sqrt{13} \times \sqrt{13}$

   (C) $\dfrac{\sqrt{8}}{\sqrt{2}}$

   (D) $\sqrt{36 - 4}$

2. If Jordan's weight increased by 10% and then decreased by 20%, what was her final weight if her initial weight was 100 pounds?

   (A) 86 lbs

   (B) 88 lbs

   (C) 90 lbs

   (D) 92 lbs

   (E) 94 lbs

3. What is the value of the expression $\dfrac{5\left(2^3 + 3^3\right)}{\frac{1}{5}}$?

   (A) 35

   (B) 125

   (C) 875

   (D) 3,125

   (E) 15,625

4. Joe has a calendar hanging on his bedroom wall with an identically sized box for each day of the month. If the calendar is open to January (which has 31 days) and he throws a dart at the calendar, which fraction represents the probability that the dart will land on a day with at least one 1 in its number? (Assume the dart hits the calendar.)

   (A) $\dfrac{2}{31}$

   (B) $\dfrac{3}{31}$

   (C) $\dfrac{4}{31}$

   (D) $\dfrac{1}{2}$

   (E) $\dfrac{13}{31}$

5. Which value is *not* equal to $\frac{4}{3}$?

   (A) 1.33333333333

   (B) $1.\bar{3}$

   (C) $\dfrac{1}{0.75}$

   (D) $\dfrac{1}{3} + 1$

   (E) $1 \div \dfrac{2}{3}$

6. A daily lottery is played by randomly selecting one ball from a group of nine balls labeled 1 through 9. Which fraction represents the probability that the winning ball will be labeled 1 three days in a row?

   (A) $\dfrac{1}{729}$

   (B) $\dfrac{1}{81}$

   (C) $\dfrac{1}{27}$

   (D) $\dfrac{1}{9}$

   (E) $\dfrac{1}{3}$

7. Which expression is equivalent to the expression $\sqrt{0.0081}$?

   (A) 0.0009

   (B) 0.009

   (C) 0.09

   (D) 0.9

8. In a certain classroom, there are six more girls than boys. If there are 12 boys in the class, what fraction of the class is boys?

   (A) $\dfrac{1}{10}$

   (B) $\dfrac{3}{15}$

   (C) $\dfrac{1}{3}$

   (D) $\dfrac{6}{15}$

   (E) $\dfrac{7}{15}$

9. In a certain video game, a character's *power value* is calculated by multiplying his *strength value* by his *stamina value*. If a character's strength value goes from 10 to 12 and his stamina value goes from 9 to 11, by approximately what percent does his power value increase?

   (A) 27%

   (B) 37%

   (C) 47%

   (D) 57%

   (E) 67%

10. In the number 1.098237, what is the value of the digit 7?

    (A) $\frac{7}{1,000}$

    (B) $\frac{7}{10,000}$

    (C) $\frac{7}{100,000}$

    (D) $\frac{7}{1,000,000}$

    (E) $\frac{7}{10,000,000}$

11. In the following figure, what is A + B?

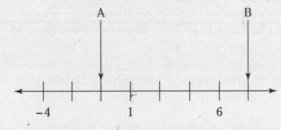

    (A) $6\frac{1}{8}$

    (B) $6\frac{1}{3}$

    (C) $6\frac{2}{3}$

    (D) $6\frac{3}{4}$

    (E) 7

12. Which operation produces the largest number?

    (A) $\frac{1}{4} + \frac{1}{4}$

    (B) $\frac{1}{4} \times \frac{1}{4}$

    (C) $\frac{1}{4} \div \frac{1}{4}$

    (D) $\left(\frac{1}{4}\right)^2$

    (E) $\left(\frac{1}{4}\right)^4$

13. What is the value of the expression $\frac{\sqrt{3^3 + 3^3 + 3^3 + 3^3}}{3}$?

    (A) $\frac{1}{3}$

    (B) $\frac{4}{3}$

    (C) 3

    (D) 9

    (E) 12

14. How many seconds are in a week?

    (A) 36,000

    (B) 86,400

    (C) 360,000

    (D) 604,800

    (E) 864,000

15. If a certain number is the sum of three consecutive integers, which of the following *must* be true?

    (A) The number is even.

    (B) The number is odd.

    (C) The number is greater than double the smallest integer.

    (D) The number is greater than the sum of any two of the integers.

    (E) None of the above.

Answers to Upper Level Arithmetic Questions

1. **D.** Choice (A) simplifies to $7 + 3 = 10$, and Choice (B) simplifies to $\sqrt{169} = 13$. For Choice (C), get rid of the root in the denominator by multiplying the top and bottom of the fraction by that root: $\frac{\sqrt{8} \times \sqrt{2}}{\sqrt{2} \times \sqrt{2}} = \frac{\sqrt{16}}{\sqrt{4}} = \frac{4}{2} = 2$. That leaves Choice (D) (which simplifies to $\sqrt{32}$, equal to about 5.7).

2. **B.** Remember to calculate percent increases and decreases one at a time. Increase 100 pounds by 10 percent: $100 \times 1.1 = 110$ lbs. Then, decrease 110 pounds by 20 percent: $110 \times 0.8 = 88$ lbs.

3. **C.** Using PEMDAS, you can simplify to $\frac{5(8+27)}{\frac{1}{5}} = \frac{5(35)}{\frac{1}{5}} = \frac{175}{\frac{1}{5}} = \frac{175}{1} \times \frac{5}{1} = 875$.

4. **E.** The number of what you want is 13, because 13 days in January have at least one 1 in their numbers (1, 10, 11, 12, 13, 14, 15, 16, 17, 18, 19, 21, 31). There are 31 total possibilities, so the probability is $\frac{13}{31}$.

5. **E.** $1 \div \frac{2}{3} = 1 \times \frac{3}{2} = 1\frac{1}{2} = 1.5$.

6. **A.** The probability of the winning ball being labeled 1 on the first day is $\frac{1}{9}$ (what you want = 1; total possibilities = 9). On the second and third days, the probability of a 1 is also $\frac{1}{9}$. To calculate the probability of a 1 on all three days, multiply the probabilities: $\frac{1}{9} \times \frac{1}{9} \times \frac{1}{9} = \frac{1}{729}$.

7. **C.** To figure out what the root of a number equals, just find the number that, when multiplied by itself, equals the number under the root: $0.09 \times 0.09 = 0.0081$.

8. **D.** If there are 12 boys and 6 more girls than boys in the classroom, then there are 18 girls. The entire class is 30 people, so the fraction of the class that's boys is $\frac{12}{30}$, which reduces to $\frac{6}{15}$.

9. **C.** The character's original power value is 90 (10×9). His new power value is 132 (12×11). The percent increase is found by dividing the difference of the two values by the original value, then multiplying the result by 100. So $132 - 90 = 42$ and $42 \div 90 = 0.467$. Multiply 0.467 by 100, and you get Choice (C), 47%.

10. **D.** In the number 1.098237, the 1 digit is ones, the 0 is tenths, the 9 is hundredths, the 8 is thousandths, the 2 is ten-thousandths, the 3 is hundred-thousandths, and the 7 is millionths. Choice (D) is 7 millionths, or $\frac{7}{1,000,000}$.

11. **E.** This problem looks easy until you realize that each mark on the line is a fractional distance from the next. After you realize that, convert every number in the problem to a fraction. So -4 becomes $\frac{-12}{3}$, 1 becomes $\frac{3}{3}$, and 6 becomes $\frac{18}{3}$. Because three distances are between $\frac{3}{3}$ and $\frac{18}{3}$, find the length of each distance by subtracting $\frac{18}{3} - \frac{3}{3} = \frac{15}{3}$ and dividing that by 3: $\frac{15}{3} \div 3 = \frac{15}{3} \times \frac{1}{3} = \frac{15}{9}$, which simplifies to $\frac{5}{3}$. Now that you know there are $\frac{5}{3}$ of distance between each mark, you can calculate that A is $-\frac{2}{3}$ and B is $\frac{23}{3}$, so $A + B = -\frac{2}{3} + \frac{23}{3} = \frac{21}{3}$, or 7.

12. **C.** Choice (A) results in $\frac{1}{2}$, Choice (B) results in $\frac{1}{16}$, Choice (C) results in 1, Choice (D) results in $\frac{1}{16}$, and Choice (E) results in $\frac{1}{256}$. So Choice (C) is the correct answer.

13. **E.** Don't take shortcuts with roots! $\frac{\sqrt{3^3 + 3^3 + 3^3} + 3^3}{3} = \frac{\sqrt{27 + 27 + 27} + 27}{3} = \frac{\sqrt{81} + 27}{3} = \frac{9 + 27}{3}$, which is $\frac{36}{3}$, or 12.

14. **D.** For this question, just multiply it out. You know that 60 seconds are in a minute, 60 minutes are in an hour, 24 hours are in a day, and 7 days are in a week, so $60 \times 60 \times 24 \times 7 = 604,800$.

15. **E.** Think about *dis*proving the choices if you see a phrase like *must be true* or *always true*. You can prove Choice (A) isn't always true by testing 2, 3, and 4 as the consecutive integers. You can prove Choice (B) isn't always true by testing 1, 2, and 3. Choice (C) isn't always true: Try –3, –2, and –1, for example. And Choice (D) can also be proven to not always be true by testing –3, –2, and –1.

Good job! Don't feel too bad if you struggled with some of these problems — at least your errors tell you what you need to work on in the days ahead. If you did make a mistake, try making up a similar problem to the one you got wrong so you can practice the concept. Also, get comfortable with all the problems here before you begin the practice test later in the book.

Chapter 12

Acing Algebra

· ·

In This Chapter

▶ Reviewing the basics of algebra

▶ Exploring different types of algebra questions

▶ Discovering methods for solving algebra problems

· ·

*I*n this chapter, we cover the building blocks of algebra. Algebra problems can seem tricky because, unlike arithmetic and geometry problems, they don't always have numbers or pictures. Instead, they usually have *variables,* which is just a math word for numbers we don't know. Don't worry — plenty of techniques for tackling algebra problems make them much more concrete and easier to understand, and we let you in on the secrets of those techniques in this chapter.

Several types of algebra problems appear on the SSAT and ISEE, and you may as well take the time to get familiar with all of them. Even if one or two of them don't show up on your test, understanding the concepts can help you in math classes and tests down the road. As usual, we note whether a certain concept is more likely to appear on the SSAT or the ISEE, but keep in mind that any concept can possibly pop up on either test.

Attacking Algebra Questions

Just like any math question on the ISEE or SSAT, an algebra question is testing a specific math skill. Before you plunge in to the math, think about the following:

✔ **What concept is being tested?** Knowing what tool to pull out of your toolbox before you start working helps you focus on the right part of the question. Do you need to find an average? Use a ratio? Or just solve an equation?

✔ **Estimation is your friend.** Using logic to guess the answer helps you determine whether you're headed in the right direction after you start working.

✔ **Move that pencil!** Writing things down gets your brain moving and helps keep you from making careless errors.

In the next chapter, we provide lots of problems for you to test these skills. But first, we take you through the categories of algebra questions that may show up on your exam. Knowing what category a problem fits into gets you one step closer to figuring it out!

Battling Basic Algebra

The following categories cover some of the types of questions students typically learn at the beginning of an algebra class. However, even if you already know how to do algebra, take the time to go through these sections to make sure your algebra foundation is rock solid. If you're new to algebra, these concepts will help you build your algebra skills.

Solving equations

You know you're looking at an algebraic equation when you see an equal sign and a variable, like x. An algebraic equation often looks something like this: $2 + x = 4$ or $3x - 3 = 9$. In algebraic equations, you usually have to break out your arithmetic skills — adding, subtracting, multiplying, and dividing — to solve for the variable.

For example, for the equation $2 + x = 4$, you need to find what number you can replace x with to make the equation true. First, get x by itself on one side of the equal sign so you can end up with $x = $ something. Because this equation has a 2 added to x, you do the *opposite* thing to *both* sides of the equation. The opposite of addition is subtraction, so because the equation originally had $x + 2$, you have to *subtract* 2 from both sides, which allows you to rewrite the equation as $x = 2$.

You have to do the same thing to *both* sides of the equation, not just one. Doing the same operation (addition or subtraction) to both sides of an algebraic equation works no matter what kind of operation is happening.

In the following equation, what does x equal?

$3x = \frac{2}{3}$

(A) $\frac{2}{9}$

(B) $\frac{1}{3}$

(C) 2

(D) $\frac{9}{2}$

(E) 6

Again, for this problem, get x by itself by doing the opposite of what's there $(3 \cdot x)$ to both sides of the equation. The opposite of multiplying x by 3 is dividing x by 3, so divide the left and right sides of the equation by 3:

$$3x \div 3 = \frac{2}{3} \div 3$$

Reminder: To divide $\frac{2}{3}$ by 3, first write 3 as a fraction: $3 = \frac{3}{1}$. Then flip $\frac{3}{1}$, making it $\frac{1}{3}$, and multiply: $\frac{2}{3} \times \frac{1}{3} = \frac{2}{9}$, so $x = \frac{2}{9}$.

If you want to check your work, just plug in the value you got for x back into the original equation. For example, does $3 \times \frac{2}{9} = \frac{2}{3}$? Just do the math to check: $3 \times \frac{2}{9} = \frac{6}{9}$, which reduces to $\frac{2}{3}$. So the correct answer is Choice **(A)**.

You may have to use the *distributive property* — multiplying each term in an expression by a number — when solving equations like the next one:

Solve for x: $4(x + 7) = 104$.

(A) 16

(B) 19

(C) 24.25

(D) 409

(E) 423

To solve this problem, you can divide both sides by 4, but you may not know whether 4 can divide into 104 evenly. Or you can distribute the 4. To *distribute* means to multiply each term in an expression — here, the expression is $x + 7$, and the terms are x and 7. Because the 4 is next to the parentheses, the stuff inside the parentheses $(x + 7)$ is multiplied by 4. You can't add x and 7 (you don't know what x is yet), so you have to distribute. Distributing the 4 results in $(4 \cdot x) + (4 \times 7)$, or $4x + 28 = 104$. From there, subtract 28 from both sides: $4x = 76$. And then divide both sides by 4: $x = 19$.

Knowing the rules of expressions

Algebraic expressions can be parts of equations, like $4x$, or they can stand alone, like $27xy + 81xy$. If an equal sign isn't involved, you can't use the do-the-same-thing-to-both-sides method you used when solving the equations in the previous section. However, following are a few things you should know about algebraic expressions:

- ✔ *Like* terms, or terms with the same variables having the same exponents, can, and should, be combined when adding and subtracting: $2x + 3x = 5x$, $81xy + 19xy = 100xy$, or $x^2y^3 + 4x^2y^3 = 5x^2y^3$.

- ✔ *Unlike* terms, or terms without the same variables and same exponents, *can't* be combined when adding and subtracting: $2x + 3y$ can't be combined (and *doesn't* equal $5xy$). Also, $2x^2 + 2x \neq 4x^2$; those terms can't be combined due to the different exponents.

- ✔ When multiplying expressions, multiply the numbers then add the exponents. For example: $3x(4x^3) = 12x^4$ or $2x(2y) = 4xy$.

- ✔ When dividing expressions, divide the numbers and subtract the larger exponent from the smaller exponent. The result stays on the part of the fraction (top or bottom) where the bigger exponent was: $\frac{4x^4}{2x^2} = \frac{2x^2}{1} = 2x^2$ or $\frac{9xy^3}{3xy} = \frac{3y^2}{1} = 3y^2$. Notice that $\frac{x}{x} = 1$ The x squared and y squared terms in these two examples stay on the tops of the fractions because that's where the bigger exponents were. The bottom parts of these fractions are 1, so just write them without fraction bars.

Note: Examples like those in the last two bullets probably won't show up on lower level tests.

If you don't see an exponent next to a number, assume its exponent is 1. Also, $x^0 = 1$.

You may have to *evaluate,* or get a number for, an expression. For example:

Evaluate $24xyz$ if $x = 1$, $y = 2$, and $z = \frac{1}{2}$.

(A) 6

(B) 12

(C) 24

(D) 48

(E) 96

To do this problem, just plug the numbers in to the equation for the variables: $24(1)(2)\left(\frac{1}{2}\right) = 24$. Therefore, the correct answer is Choice **(C)**.

You also may have to multiply expressions like $(x + 2)(x - 3)$ on the upper level tests. To do this type of multiplication, just distribute (multiply) the first expression to the second expression. So the x in the second expression gets multiplied by $(x + 2)$: $x(x + 2) = x^2 + 2x$. Then, the -3 in the second expression gets multiplied by $(x + 2)$: $-3(x + 2) = -3x + (-6)$. Now, combine the terms and get: $x^2 + 2x + (-3x) + (-6) = x^2 - x - 6$.

Solving inequalities

Some algebra questions on the SSAT and ISEE require you to know your inequality signs. Here's a recap:

- 2 < 7 means 2 is less than 7.
- 8 > 3 means 8 is greater than 3.
- $x \leq y$ means x is less than *or* equal to y.
- $x \geq y$ means x is greater than *or* equal to y.

One way to keep from confusing > and < signs is to remember that if the little part of the sign is pointing at a number or variable, that number is less because it only gets the little part of the sign; for example, 2 < 7. Because 7 is greater than 2, 7 gets the bigger part of the sign.

Now that you're familiar with inequality signs, take a look at how to use them mathematically. Inequalities are just like equations, but instead of equal signs, they have inequality signs. In algebra, you may have to solve problems like this:

Solve for x: $2x > 48$.

(A) $x > 12$

(B) $x < 12$

(C) $x > 24$

(D) $x < 24$

(E) $x > 48$

To solve this inequality, just divide both sides by 2, and you end up with $x > 24$, which means than x is any number that's bigger than 24. Easy. Correct answer: Choice **(C)**.

Inequalities can be trickier when a negative number gets involved, like this one:

Solve for x: $-3x < 27$.

(A) $x < -9$

(B) $x > -9$

(C) $x < 9$

(D) $x > 9$

(E) $x > -81$

To solve for x, you have to divide both sides by –3. However, the rule is this: Whenever you divide both sides of an inequality by a *negative number*, reverse the direction of the inequality sign. So you end up with $x > -9$. Correct answer: Choice **(B)**.

Determining absolute value

Absolute value means the distance a number is from zero. On the test, you know you're dealing with an absolute value when you see a problem like this: $|x| = 2$. Those lines on either side of x tell you that the distance of x from 0 is 2. So x can be 2, or it can be –2. If you see a variable inside an absolute value sign, there are two possible answers unless the variable equals 0.

Don't get fooled by negative numbers — their absolute values are always positive; in fact, any absolute value (except that of 0) is a positive number. For example, $|-2| = 2$, because -2 is 2 away from 0. Picturing a number line helps illustrate this concept:

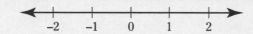

Because -2 is 2 (in terms of distance or value) away from 0, its absolute value is 2.

Absolute value inequalities are easy if you remember that you're going to end up with two answers. To figure out the two answers, start by removing the absolute value sign. Then solve the equation for the unknown. That's your first answer. Next, go back to the original absolute value equation, remove the absolute value signs again, but now flip the inequality sign and change the sign of the number to the right of the inequality sign.

$|x + 2| < 10$

(A) $x < 8$

(B) $x > 8$

(C) $x > -12$

(D) $x < -12$

(E) $-12 < x < 8$

First, remove the absolute value sign, which gives you $x + 2 < 10$. One answer is produced by solving the inequality per usual: Subtract 2 from both sides and get $x < 8$. The other solution is produced by first reversing both the inequality sign *and* the sign of the number to the right of the inequality, giving you $x + 2 > -10$.

Subtracting 2 from both sides results in $x > -12$. So your answer is $x < 8$ and $x > -12$. To check your answer, try testing a number that's less than 8 and greater than -12, which should make the inequality work. For example, try $x = 2$. Is $2 + 2 < 10$? Yep! So, the correct answer is Choice **(E)**.

Working with Statistics, Percents, and Ratios

The following categories help you develop a few more specific types of skills that you'll need for test day. Even if you've already seen these concepts in school, pay attention to what follows, because the test writers are famous for finding creative ways to test your knowledge.

Exploring mean, median, mode, and range

The *mean, median, mode,* and *range* are all ways by which people make sense of data, like finding a baseball player's batting average or determining the range of ages in a high school.

Mean means the average of a group of numbers. To find the mean, just add all the numbers in the group and divide the total by how many numbers there are.

What is the mean age of a group of friends if one is 10 years old, another is 12 years old, and the third is 13 years old?

(A) 10.9

(B) 11.5

(C) 11.7

(D) 12.3

(E) 12.7

To find the mean, just add the friends' ages and divide by 3 (total number of friends): $\frac{10+12+13}{3}$ = the mean age is $\frac{35}{3}$ = 11.7 years old, or Choice **(C)**.

If you have to find an average in a math problem, set up your average equation right away: $\frac{\text{all the numbers added up}}{\text{how many numbers there are}}$ = the average. Here's another example where this technique comes in handy:

Jim has taken three math tests, and his grades on the tests were 71, 81, and 90. What must he score on the fourth test to have an 85 average?

(A) 85

(B) 89

(C) 92

(D) 94

(E) 98

First, set up your average equation, using x for the unknown fourth test score: $\frac{71+81+90+x}{4}$ = 85. You're dividing by 4 because there are four scores counting the new one, and you know the new average has to be 85. You can solve for x by multiplying both sides by 4, which gives you 71 + 81 + 90 + x = 340. Simplify by adding: 242 + x = 340, and then subtract 242 from both sides to end up with x = 98.

Median just means the middle value. To figure out the median of a group of numbers, write them in order from lowest to highest and then find the number in the middle.

What is the median of this set (12, 4, 28, 6, and 7)?

(A) 4

(B) 6

(C) 7

(D) 9.5

(E) 12

First, write the numbers in order: 4, 6, 7, 12, and 28. Then, find the middle number, which is 7. So Choice **(C)**, 7, is the median.

Medians are a bit trickier if there isn't a middle number. If you're looking at a group of numbers with no middle number (because there's an even number of values), you have to take the *mean,* or average, of the middle two numbers.

For example, the median of 10, 11, 12, and 13 is the average of 11 and 12: $\frac{11+12}{2}$ = 11.5.

Mode means the number that appears the most often in a group of numbers. The mode of 2, 2, 2, 3, 4, 5, 6, 10, and 12 is 2, because 2 appears the most in the group. You can simply look at a group to find its mode — no math is involved except counting. If two numbers appear the same number of times, there's *no* mode in that group. The group 2, 3, 3, 4, 4, and 5 has no mode, because 3 and 4 are tied for the most appearances.

Range is the difference between the highest and lowest value in a group, or set, of numbers. To figure out what the range is, put the numbers in order, like you did to find the median. Then, subtract the lowest number from the highest one — your answer is the range of the group. For example, the range of 4, 6, 7, 12, and 28 is 28 – 4 = 24.

Calculating percentage changes

In Chapter 10, you figure out how to take percentages of numbers. Percentage changes are kind of the same thing. To solve a percentage change problem, just remember a simple formula:

$$\text{Percent change} = \frac{\text{the amount of the change}}{\text{the original amount}} \times 100$$

Yesterday, Jim made $150.00. Today, he made $175.00. What is the percent increase from yesterday to today for Jim's earnings?

(A) 10

(B) 12.5

(C) 15

(D) 17

(E) 19

The amount of the change is $25.00 and the original amount is $150.00, so the percent increase is:

$$\frac{25}{150} = 0.17$$

$$0.17 \times 100 = 17\%$$

The correct answer is Choice **(D)**.

The formula works the same way for percent decreases. Try this problem:

The high temperature yesterday was 81 degrees, and today it was 71 degrees. What is the percent decrease from yesterday to today?

(A) 6

(B) 8

(C) 10

(D) 12

(E) 14

The percent decrease is 10 (the amount of the change) ÷ 81 (the original) × 100:

$$\frac{10}{81} = 0.12$$

$$0.12 \times 100 = 12\%$$

So Choice **(D)** is the correct answer.

Using ratios and proportions

Ratios are just a way of saying how many of one thing there is compared to another thing. Ratios can be written like $\frac{a}{b}$, $a{:}b$, or a to b — they all mean the same thing. A handy way to use ratios is to write them as fractions, using the sum of their parts.

For example, if a zoo has flamingoes and rhinos, and the ratio of flamingoes to rhinos is 100 to 3, that means there are 100 flamingoes for every 3 rhinos. We don't know how many of each animal the zoo has; we just know the ratio.

The sum of the parts of this ratio is 103 (100 + 3), so you can say that in any given number of flamingoes and rhinos at that zoo, the number is going to be $\frac{100}{103}$ flamingoes and $\frac{3}{103}$ rhinos.

So if you're asked how many rhinos there are in a group of 1,090 rhinos and flamingoes, you can multiply $\frac{3}{103}$ by 1,090 = 30 rhinos. This method works because you know that in the group of 1,090 animals, $\frac{3}{103}$ of them are rhinos.

Proportions are ratios that are equal to each other. To solve, you set up a proportion and cross-multiply. In algebra problems, you use proportions in word problems like this:

The ratio of lions to tigers at a zoo is 3 to 4. If there are 12 lions, how many tigers are there?

(A) 4

(B) 8

(C) 10

(D) 12

(E) 16

To solve, set up a proportion and *cross-multiply* by multiplying the top left number in the proportion by the bottom right number, and set that product equal to the bottom left number times the top right number: $\frac{3}{4} = \frac{12}{x}$ becomes $3x = 48$. Divide both sides by 3 to get $x = 16$ tigers. Correct answer: Choice **(E)**.

On the upper level tests, you may see a question dealing with *direct* or *indirect* proportion. The best way to handle these types of questions is to understand the principle behind them:

- ✔ What happens to one number that's in direct proportion with another number happens to that other number. For example, if x and y are directly proportional and you multiply x by 2, then you also multiply y by 2.

- ✔ If numbers are *inversely* or *indirectly* proportional, then the opposite of what happens to the first number happens to the second number. If a and b are inversely proportional and you multiply a by 3, then you need to divide b by 3.

- ✔ Both indirect and direct proportions deal with multiplication and division, not addition and subtraction. So if you see x change from 3 to 15 in a proportion, think about what it was multiplied by, *not* what was added to it.

Working with Rules, Patterns, Ordering, and Counting

Words like *function, sequence, permutation,* and *matrix* may look scary, but they're just math terms for doing things like finding patterns, counting, and arranging things. This section covers a few more types of math problems you may see on the ISEE or SSAT.

Discovering the purpose of functions

We won't claim to put the *fun* in functions for you, but we can make the concept easier to handle. Functions are just rules. A simple way to understand functions is to think of them as instructions for what to do with a number. On the SSAT and ISEE, functions usually show up in what look like strange symbol problems. For example:

If $a \# b = ab + 10$, what is $3 \# 4$?

(A) 12

(B) 14

(C) 16

(D) 20

(E) 22

The # sign isn't a normal mathematical symbol, so don't feel bad if you don't recognize it. It has no meaning other than the meaning you were just given. For this problem, if any two numbers have a # between them, multiply those numbers (you know to multiply because $a \# b = ab$, which is the same as $a \cdot b$) and add 10 to the result: $3 \# 4 = 3 \times 4 + 10$ and $12 + 10 = 22$. So the answer is Choice **(E)**.

Don't make the mistake of including a and b in your answer; the a and b are just there to tell you that for any numbers with a # between them, you multiply those numbers and add 10. The test makers — especially the ISEE test writers — may get creative with the way they test functions. Just remember that a function is a rule that tells you what to do with numbers. Make sure you write everything down on function problems; they're notoriously easy to get wrong if you try to solve them in your head.

Seeing the pattern in sequences

You can think of *sequences* as patterns. After you find the pattern, you can figure out what you need to continue it. Patterns are usually found by adding a certain number to each term or multiplying each term by something. For example:

What is the missing number in the following sequence? 1, 8, 15, ___, 29?

Because you can add 7 to 1 to get 8 and 7 to 8 to get 15, the missing term must be $15 + 7$, or 22. You can check this answer by seeing whether the pattern applies to the next term: $22 + 7 = 29$. Check!

What is the missing number in this sequence? 2, 4, 16, ___, 65,536?

(A) 28

(B) 32

(C) 64

(D) 216

(E) 256

This sequence is about multiplying, but you may need to use a little trial and error to figure out what to multiply each term by. You may, at first, think each term is multiplied by 2, because the sequence starts by going from 2 to 4, but then 4×2 isn't 16. Eventually, you may realize that each term is the previous term, squared. So 4 is 2×2, 16 is 4×4, so the next term is $16 \times 16 = 256$. Check it by seeing that 256×256 is 65,536. The correct answer is Choice **(E)**.

Arranging permutations and combinations

Permutations and *combinations* are terms that define how many ways you can arrange or form groups of things. These kinds of questions may show up on the upper level tests. In the next sections, we take you through a couple common types of permutations and combinations, though there's more than one way to arrange these kinds of questions (no pun intended).

Permutations

Permutation is a big word that means how many ways a group of things can be arranged if you care about the order. For example, how many ways can you arrange the letters *A, B,* and *C?* To solve this, the best — and safest — way is to write each possibility in a careful, methodical manner. By *methodical,* we mean have a method, such as the following:

First, arrange the letters in all the ways that start with *A:* A, B, C and A, C, B

Then, do the same thing with the next letter, *B:* B, A, C and B, C, A

Finally, arrange the letters in all the ways that start with *C:* C, A, B and C, B, A.

So you can arrange the letters *A, B,* and *C* six ways.

This method is the safest way to handle permutation questions because you can visualize all the different possibilities. However, you may get a question where too many arrangements are possible to count them all, such as the following:

How many ways can you arrange the letters A, B, C, D, E, F, and G?

(A) 7

(B) 49

(C) 343

(D) 2,401

(E) 5,040

No way do you want to write all those possibilities. But you can apply a formula. First, you need to recognize that this problem is a permutation question, *not* a combination question, because you care about what order the letters are in. You can solve it by this method:

Imagine seven slots (because there are seven letters in the question): ___, ___, ___, ___, ___, ___, and ___.

The first slot has seven possible letters, so write 7, ___, ___, ___, ___, ___, ___.

The second slot has six possible letters because one is already in the first slot. So 7, 6, ___, ___, ___, ___, ___.

The third slot has five possible letters because two have been placed: 7, 6, 5, ___, ___, ___, ___.

And so on, until you have 7, 6, 5, 4, 3, 2, 1.

You get the answer by multiplying all the numbers together: $7 \times 6 \times 5 \times 4 \times 3 \times 2 \times 1 = 5{,}040$ ways, Choice **(E)**. Aren't you glad you didn't write those out?

Combinations

Combination questions ask you how many groups of two or three you can make from a bigger group of numbers. In these questions, you don't care about the order, so fewer possibilities result. As such, you can almost always write them all out (the safest option). Here's an example:

If eight players are on a field, how many groups of two people can you form?

(A) 4

(B) 8

(C) 16

(D) 28

(E) 32

Again, have a method. First, name the players A, B, C, D, E, F, G, and H so you can keep them straight. Then, start with all the groups with an A in them: AB, AC, AD, AE, AF, AG, and AH. Next, do the *B*s, but don't count BA, because that's the same two people as AB. So you have BC, BD, BE, BF, BG, and BH. Then, list the groups with the *C*s. Again, don't count CA or CB (which are the same as AC and BC): CD, CE, CF, CG, and CH. Next comes the *D*s: DE, DF, DG, and DH; then the *E*s: EF, EG, and EH; the *F*s: FG and FH; and finally, the *G*s: GH.

Notice the pattern? If you did, you can save yourself some time, but when in doubt, write it out! Now, just add: $7 + 6 + 5 + 4 + 3 + 2 + 1 = 28$, so the correct answer is Choice **(D)**.

Matching up numbers in matrices

Matrices — numbers arranged in a rectangle — are most likely going to pop up only on the upper level tests. This section shows you how to add matrices and how to multiply a matrix by a number.

To add matrices, you just add the left numbers, which form the left number in the new matrix, and then add the right numbers, which form the right number in the new matrix.

$$\begin{bmatrix} 2 & 3 \\ 4 & 5 \end{bmatrix} + \begin{bmatrix} 0 & 1 \\ 2 & 3 \end{bmatrix} =$$

(A) $\begin{bmatrix} 4 & 5 \\ 2 & 8 \end{bmatrix}$

(B) $\begin{bmatrix} 2 & 4 \\ 6 & 8 \end{bmatrix}$

(C) $\begin{bmatrix} 2 & 3 \\ 8 & 15 \end{bmatrix}$

(D) $\begin{bmatrix} 3 & 2 \\ 15 & 8 \end{bmatrix}$

(E) $\begin{bmatrix} 19 \end{bmatrix}$

The correct answer is Choice **(B).** You add the 2 in the upper left corner of the left matrix to the 0 in the upper left corner of the right matrix to form the 2 in the upper left corner of the final matrix. Then, you add the 3 in the upper right corner of the left matrix to the 1 in the upper right corner of the right matrix to form the 4 in the upper right corner of the final matrix, and so on.

Multiplying a number by a matrix is simple, too. For example, check out this matrix:

$3\begin{bmatrix} 0 & 2 \\ 3 & 1 \end{bmatrix} = \begin{bmatrix} 0 & 6 \\ 9 & 3 \end{bmatrix}$. You simple multiply the 3 to the left of the matrix by each number in

the first matrix to form a new matrix. Then 3×0 forms the upper left corner of the new matrix, 3×2 forms the upper right corner, 3×3 forms the lower left corner, and 3×1 forms the lower right corner.

Chapter 13

Practicing Algebra

No one ever learned algebra overnight. Just like arithmetic, getting good at algebra takes practice — and a lot of it. But the good news is that the more algebra problems you do, the better your skills get. You may get to the point where doing algebra problems is satisfying — and even fun. It doesn't matter whether that last sentence made you laugh or made you scowl; the fact is this: Practicing what you reviewed in Chapter 12 is important so you can be better prepared on test day.

This chapter is basically divided into two sections: One section covers the lower level SSAT and the lower and middle level ISEE algebra, and the other section is all about algebra for the upper level SSAT and ISEE. We provide several example questions and walk you through how to answer them, and then we also include practice questions that you can work on all your own, with the answers following in a separate section.

Even if you're taking an upper level test, we recommend that you complete all the problems for the lower and middle level tests. And if you think you don't really need algebra practice, go ahead and practice some of these problems anyway so you can get as familiar as possible with the way the questions are worded — which is probably quite a bit different than how the questions are worded in your math class.

Keep these four Math section pointers in mind even when you're just practicing:

✔ **Write down your steps.** Writing down your work prevents careless errors and gives your brain a break. Also draw pictures whenever possible. Get in the habit of doing these techniques now so they're second nature by the time you take the test.

✔ **Skip a question quickly if you don't *immediately* know how to do it.** All the questions are worth the same amount of points, so fight with the hard ones *after* you've done all the easier ones.

✔ **Use common sense.** Before beginning a question, take a few seconds to think logically. What do you think the answer may be? This step lets you see whether your calculated answer makes sense and can even save you from doing some or all the math on some questions.

✔ **Read the question carefully.** Although starting to calculate as quickly as possible is tempting — after all, it's a timed test — make sure you read the question *closely* and *carefully* and then read it once more before you pick an answer.

Practicing Guided Lower and Middle Level Algebra Questions

The following questions test your skills with the concepts you practiced in Chapter 12. Try your best to solve each question without looking at the explanation that follows, and read the explanation even if you get the question right.

1. What number should go in the blank to make the equation true?

   ___ – 13 + 7 = 25

   (A) 29

   (B) 31

   (C) 33

   (D) 35

   (E) 45

   Just like most algebra equations, you want to get the unknown (in this case, the blank) on one side of the equation so you can solve for it. To do that, subtract 7 from both sides and get ___ – 13 = 18. Then, add 13 to both sides and the result is ___ = 31, which is Choice **(B)**.

2. If $6 + p = 13$ and $8 + q = 13$, what is $p + q$?

   (A) 10

   (B) 11

   (C) 12

   (D) 13

   (E) 14

   Solve both equations by getting the variable on one side by itself. Start with the p equation: Subtract 6 from both sides, leaving $p = 7$. For the q equation, subtracting 8 from both sides gives you $q = 5$. Then, add $7 + 5 = 12$, Choice **(C)**.

3. A bumblebee's wings beat 180 times in two seconds. How many times do they beat in 72 seconds?

   (A) 360

   (B) 1,080

   (C) 3,600

   (D) 6,480

   (E) 6,4800

   Here, you can set up a proportion to solve the problem: $\frac{2}{180} = \frac{72}{x}$. This method works because you know the ratio of seconds to beats is $\frac{2}{180}$, and no matter how many seconds you measure, there will be 2 beats for every 180 seconds. When you set up your proportion, remember to keep the units you're measuring consistent — in this proportion, seconds are on top and beats are on the bottom. You solve it by cross-multiplying: $2x = 72 \times 180$, or $2x = 12,960$. Dividing both sides by 2 results in $x = 6,480$, making Choice **(D)** the correct answer.

4. What is the value of *x* in the output from this function machine?

In	Out
9	3
27	9
30	*x*
300	100

(A) 10

(B) 12

(C) 50

(D) 60

(E) 90

A function is just an instruction that tells you what to do with a number. In this function machine, you put in a number and get out a different number. If you notice what happens to each number that gets put in, you can figure out what *x* is. So you can divide 9 by 3 to get 3, and divide 27 by 3 to get 9, and then divide 300 by 3 to get 100, so 30 must also need to be divided by 3: 30 ÷ 3 = 10, so *x* = 10, Choice **(A)**.

Look for a *consistent* pattern in questions where you think a pattern may be going on. If you thought 6 was subtracted from 9 to get 3 in the first row, make sure it also works for the rest of the rows (it doesn't). ***Note:*** Both the ISEE and SSAT test functions, but this question is more ISEE-like.

5. Mike scored 48 total points in a basketball game that had four quarters. If the score of his highest quarter was 19, and the range of his scores was 10, which of the following could *not* have been one of his quarter scores?

(A) 8

(B) 9

(C) 10

(D) 11

(E) 12

Range is the highest value in a group minus the smallest value. You don't know Mike's lowest quarter's score, but you do know the range of scores is 10, so you can calculate his lowest score with an equation: 19 − *x* = 10 (*x* represents his lowest quarter score). Solving that equation tells you that Mike's lowest quarter score is 9, so Choice **(A)** *can't* be one of his quarter scores; otherwise, his range would be 11 (19 − 8).

6. If $\frac{1}{9} + J > 2$, which of the following could *J* be?

(A) $\frac{8}{9}$

(B) $\frac{10}{9}$

(C) $\frac{13}{9}$

(D) $\frac{15}{9}$

(E) $\frac{19}{9}$

If you know how to solve inequalities, this one is easy: Just subtract $\frac{1}{9}$ from both sides, leaving you with $J > 1\frac{8}{9}$. Then, make the comparison to the answer choices easier by converting $1\frac{8}{9}$ to an improper fraction: $\frac{17}{9}$. The only answer choice larger than $\frac{17}{9}$ is Choice **(E).** You can also solve this question by looking at the answer choices and testing them — when you test Choice (E), you end up with $\frac{20}{9}$, which makes the inequality true.

7. $4^1 = 4$, $4^2 = 16$, $4^3 = 64$, $4^4 = 256$, $4^5 = 1,024$, $4^6 = 4,096$. According to the pattern, what is the units digit for 4^{11}?

(A) 2

(B) 3

(C) 4

(D) 5

(E) 6

Although this question seems to be testing your knowledge of exponents, it's really just testing your ability to spot a pattern. Notice that whenever 4 is raised to an odd-numbered exponent, like 1, 3, or 5, the units digit of the answer is 4.

The *units digit* is the digit in a number that has a value from 0 to 9; for example, the units digit in 64 is 4 — it has a value of 4, unlike the 6 in 64, which has a value of 60. So applying that pattern to 4^{11}, the units digit must be 4, Choice **(C).** Don't worry about proving it — on the actual test, you most likely won't have time to multiply 4 by itself 10 times!

Attacking Lower and Middle Level Algebra Questions on Your Own

Good work! Now it's time to test your skills by completing some algebra questions on your own. Review the four tips at the beginning of this chapter before you begin.

1. According to the graph, if 22 students play football, how many play tennis?

Football	☺ ☺ ☺ ☺ ☺ ☺
Cheer	☺ ☺ ☺ ☺
Tennis	☺ ☺

(A) 2

(B) 4

(C) 6

(D) 8

(E) 10

2. If $\frac{3}{4} = \frac{21}{x}$ and $\frac{7}{4} = \frac{x}{16}$, what is x?

(A) 7

(B) 14

(C) 21

(D) 28

(E) 35

3. Which of the following expressions best represents the output for *x?*

In	Out
1	7
2	14
3	21
4	28
.	.
.	.
x	?

(A) $x + 7$

(B) $x + 6x$

(C) $x + 7x$

(D) $x + 8x$

(E) $2x + 5$

4. The graph of $x > -7$ is shown in which of the following number lines?

(A)

(B)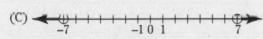

(C)

(D)

5. If a college has a student to teacher ratio of 12 to 1 and 200 teachers are at the college, how many students does the college have?

(A) 1,600

(B) 2,000

(C) 2,400

(D) 2,800

(E) 3,600

6. If $\frac{1}{5}$ of a number is greater than 35, then the number must be

(A) less than 7

(B) equal to 7

(C) less than 35

(D) equal to 175

(E) greater than 175

7. If $n \# 7 = n \div 7$, which of the following is a whole number?

(A) $2 \# 1$

(B) $4 \# 5$

(C) $5 \# 6$

(D) $6 \# 7$

(E) $7 \# 8$

8. Jack has *x* dollars, and Annie has 7 more dollars than Jack. If Annie gives Jack 12 dollars, then in terms of *x*, how many dollars does Annie then have?

(A) $x - 1$

(B) $x - 5$

(C) $x + 7$

(D) $x - 12$

(E) $x + 19$

9. Kristine has four times as many crayons as she has pencils. Which of the following can be her total number of crayons and pencils?

(A) 13

(B) 17

(C) 23

(D) 28

(E) 35

10. According to the graph, Mark's average salary for the five years from 2008 through 2012 was

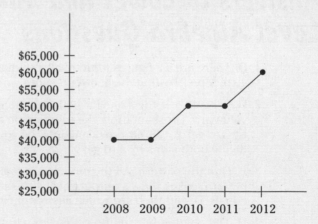

(A) $40,000

(B) $44,000

(C) $48,000

(D) $52,000

(E) $56,000

11. What is the value of x in the equation $3x + 199 = 4x$?

    (A) 28

    (B) 56

    (C) 112

    (D) 199

    (E) 224

12. Which of the following equations can be read as "three less than seven times a number is equal to nine less than the number"? (Let x represent the unknown number.)

    (A) $7x - 3 = x - 9$

    (B) $3 - 7x = 9 - x$

    (C) $3 - 7x = x - 9$

    (D) $7x - 3 = 9 - x$

    (E) $9(7x - 3) = x$

13. What is the value of n in the expression $\dfrac{16(8 + 24)}{4} = n$?

    (A) 16

    (B) 24

    (C) 32

    (D) 64

    (E) 128

14. Use the number line shown to answer the question.

    Y is the average of X and another number. What is the other number?

    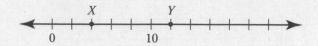

    (A) 4

    (B) 8

    (C) 12

    (D) 16

    (E) 20

15. If Sinead spent $\frac{3}{5}$ of her weekly allowance on a magazine and the remaining $2.00 on ice cream, what is her weekly allowance?

    (A) $5.00

    (B) $7.50

    (C) $10.00

    (D) $11.00

    (E) $12.50

Answers to Lower and Middle Level Algebra Questions

1. **D.** There are 5.5 figures for football. Dividing 22 by 5.5 gives you 4, so each figure represents 4 students. Testing the answer choices works well here.

2. **D.** Because x is the same for both equations, you can solve either equation to find the value of x. Cross-multiply the equation on the left to get $3x = 84$, and then divide both sides by 3 to get $x = 28$. Or cross-multiply the equation on the right to get $4x = 112$, and then divide both sides by 4 to get $x = 28$.

3. **B.** Find the pattern. All the outputs are multiples of 7 (7, 14, 21, and 28), so continuing the pattern makes the x's output equal 49. Count down to see that x is the seventh input (so it equals 7), and then see which answer choice makes 49 from an input of 7.

4. **D.** The number line in Choice (D) has a hollow circle at –7, which shows –7 isn't included on the graph, but it has all the points that are greater than –7 colored in, shown by the thick black line extending all the way through the right arrow. This thick black line tells you that the graph means all the points greater than –7.

5. **C.** Solve this question by setting up a proportion: $\frac{12}{1} = \frac{x}{200}$. The top part of the proportion represents students; the bottom represents teachers. Cross-multiply to get $x = 2,400$.

6. **E.** Set up an inequality: $\frac{1}{5}x > 35$. Solve by dividing both sides by $\frac{1}{5}$, resulting in $x > 175$. Practice your logic by thinking about Choices (A), (B), and (C) — if $\frac{1}{5}$ of a number is greater than 35, then that number is way bigger than 35.

7. **A.** The # in this particular problem means ÷, because the example tells you that $n \# 7 = n ÷ 7$. After you see that, just look at the answer choices and replace the # symbol with a ÷ sign. For Choice (A), $2 ÷ 1 = 2$, which is a whole number. Because the question asks for which of the following is a whole number, you don't need to test the other answer choices. Choice (A) is correct.

8. **B.** You can solve this question in two different ways. One: Pick a number for x and write it down. For example, pretend $x = 10$. If Jack has 10 dollars, then Annie has 17 dollars. If she gives him 12 dollars, she ends up with 5 dollars, which is $x - 5$, or Choice (B). Two: Call Jack x and Annie $x + 7$, because she has 7 more dollars than Jack. Subtracting 12 dollars from Annie gives you $x - 5$, again, Choice (B).

9. **E.** Represent Kristine's pencils by x and her crayons by $4x$, because she has four times as many crayons as pencils. Her total number of crayons and pencils is then $5x$, and only one of the answer choices can be five times a whole number: Choice (E).

TIP

Try to use just one variable when making an equation, and call the smallest quantity x. If you get stuck on a problem like Question 9, trial and error can work by guessing the number of pencils and working from there to try to match one of the choices.

10. **C.** To find the average, add all the values ($\$40,000 + \$40,000 + \$50,000 + \$50,000 + \$60,000 = \$240,000$) and divide by how many there are (5), so $\$240,000 ÷ 5 = \$48,000$.

11. **D.** To solve the equation, subtract $3x$ from both sides, which leaves you with $x = 199$.

12. **A.** "Three less than" a number means you subtract 3 from that number. For example, 3 less than 5 is 2, which is $5 - 2$. "Seven times a number" is $7x$. "Is equal to" is =, and "Nine less than the number" is $x - 9$. So the answer is $7x - 3 = x - 9$.

13. **E.** Using PEMDAS, complete the stuff in parentheses first: $(8 + 24) = (32)$. Then, $16 × 32 = 512$, and $512 ÷ 4 = 128$.

14. **E.** Looking at the number line, each mark to the right of 0 represents 2 in distance. Try using trial and error to figure out the spacing on number line questions because each line almost always represents a whole number, and the lines are almost always equally spaced. So if X is 4 and Y is 12 and Y is the average of X and another number, then the easiest thing to do is to test the choices. Choice (C) is correct because 12 is the average of 20 and 4: $\frac{20+4}{2} = 12$.

15. **A.** You don't know how much the magazine costs, but you do know that the remaining $\frac{2}{5}$ of her allowance is $\$2.00$. To solve for what you don't know (the allowance), make an equation with a variable, like x, representing the allowance. So $\frac{2}{5}$ of x is $\$2.00$ translates to $\frac{2}{5}x = 2$. Now, get x by itself by dividing both sides of the equation by $\frac{2}{5}$, and you end up with $x = \frac{10}{2}$, which simplifies to $x = 5$.

How did you do? If you had trouble with a problem, see whether you can find a way to do more of that type of question. If you made a careless mistake on any problem, don't feel bad because no one is perfect, but remember to write down all — I repeat, *all* — your steps, even when you're just practicing, so working these types of problems becomes second nature by the day of the actual test. And if you can do the problems in this chapter, congratulations — many high school students can't do what you just did.

Practicing Guided Upper Level Algebra Questions

Okay, upper level students: Here are a few questions to work through on your own. Give each question your very best effort before looking at the answers. If you're struggling with a question, try not to give up and guess until you've tried everything you can.

1. To finish a class with an A, Christy needs her test average in the class to be 95 or higher. Her scores on the first four tests were 89, 98, 92, and 96. What is the minimum score Christy needs to get on the next test to make sure she gets an A in the class? (Assume all the tests are worth the same amount.)

    (A) 85

    (B) 90

    (C) 95

    (D) 100

    (E) 105

    Testing the answer choices here may take a while, but it'll work through trial and error. Alternatively, you can set up an average equation equal to 95 and solve for x to find the missing test grade (remember that you're looking for the *minimum* test grade needed): $\frac{89+98+92+96+x}{5} = 95$. Simplify the equation by multiplying both sides by 5, which gives you $375 + x = 475$. Then subtract 375 from both sides of the equation to get $x = 100$, Choice **(D)**.

2. x is a whole number that has a remainder of 4 when divided by 5. Which of the following has a remainder of 2 when divided by 5?

    (A) $x + 2$

    (B) $x + 3$

    (C) $x + 4$

    (D) $x + 5$

    Remainder algebra problems are best solved through trial and error. In this problem, and in others like it, x has more than one value you can use, so you just have to find one that works for the initial condition. Because a number smaller than 5 doesn't have a remainder when divided by 5, start your trial and error process with 5: $\frac{5}{5} = 1$, remainder 0; $\frac{6}{5} = 1$, remainder 1; $\frac{7}{5} = 1$, remainder 2; $\frac{8}{5} = 1$, remainder 3; $\frac{9}{5} = 1$, remainder 4 — bingo! So pretend x is 9 and rewrite the answer choices: Choice (A), $9 + 2 = 11$; Choice (B) $9 + 3 = 12$; Choice (C), $9 + 4 = 13$; Choice (D), $9 + 5 = 14$. Then, test the numbers divided by 5: $\frac{12}{5} = 2$, remainder 2, so Choice **(B)** is correct.

3. For all numbers a and b, a ## b is defined as $a^2 - b^2$. Which of the following is less than $a - b$?

    (A) 2 ## 1

    (B) 3 ## 2

    (C) 1 ## 1

    (D) 1 ## 2

This question is a funny symbol function question: ## has no meaning until the question defines it for you. For example, if you have two numbers on either side of the ##, the number on the left side is a and the number on the right side is b. The ## tells you to square a and b and then subtract b^2 from a^2. Now that you know how the ## works, you can test the answer choices.

Choice (A) results in $(2 \times 2) - (1 \times 1)$, which is $4 - 1 = 3$. Is 3 less than $a - b$, or $2 - 1$? Nope. Okay, test Choice (B): $(3 \times 3) - (2 \times 2)$ simplifies to $9 - 4 = 5$. Is 5 less than $3 - 2$? No way. For Choice (C), $(1 \times 1) - (1 \times 1) = 0$, which isn't less than $1 - 1$. That leaves Choice (D): $(1 \times 1) - (2 \times 2) = 1 - 4$, or -3. Is -3 less than $1 - 2$? Yep! So Choice **(D)** is correct.

4. If $xy - 3 = ky + x$, then $y =$

   (A) $\dfrac{k + x}{x - 3}$

   (B) $\dfrac{x - 3}{x + k}$

   (C) $\dfrac{x + 3}{x - k}$

   (D) $\dfrac{x - k}{x + 1}$

The easiest, and probably the most accurate, way to tackle this type of question is by using a technique called *picking numbers for variables*. Step 1: Assign numbers to the variables in the answer choices. Suppose x is 5 and k is 10.

Don't pick 0 or 1 when picking numbers, don't pick the same number for more than one variable, and try not to use a number that you see in the problem (in this case, don't use 3).

Step 2: Get a numerical answer to the question, using your numbers. So if x is 5 and k is 10, you can rewrite the problem as $5y - 3 = 10y + 5$. Subtracting $5y$ from both sides yields $-3 = 5y + 5$, and then subtracting 5 from both sides gives you $-8 = 5y$, so $y = -\dfrac{8}{5}$.

Step 3: Plug your numbers in to the answer choices to see which one makes your number, or which answer choice equals $-\dfrac{8}{5}$. When you test Choice (C), you get 8 on the top of the fraction and -5 on the bottom, $-\dfrac{8}{5}$, so Choice **(C)** is the correct answer.

Doing this problem algebraically works too, but it's messier. The beauty of the picking numbers technique is that you can pick any numbers and Choice (C) still works. Try it!

5. If the price of a shirt is reduced by 10% during a sale, and then an employee receives a 20% discount off of the sale price, how much does the employee pay if the original price of the shirt was $30.00?

   (A) $21.00

   (B) $21.60

   (C) $22.40

   (D) $23.30

   (E) $24.50

If you see multiple percent changes in a question, don't do them both at once. In other words, you can't just take 30 percent off the original price. You have to first take 10 percent off: $30.00 × 0.1 = $3.00, so the sale price is $27.00 ($30.00 – $3.00). To take 20 percent off the sale price, you can find out what 80 percent of the sale price is by multiplying $27.00 by 0.8, which equals $21.60, or Choice **(B).** Another way to take 20 percent off of $27.00 is to figure out what 20 percent of $27.00 is, and then subtract that number from $27.00. Find out what 20 percent of $27.00 is by multiplying $27.00 by 0.2 = $5.40, and then $27.00 – $5.40 = $21.60.

6. If the temperature in Fahrenheit is F, then the temperature in Celsius is $\frac{5}{9}(F-32)$. If the Fahrenheit temperature increases from 70 degrees to 90 degrees, which is closest to the corresponding increase in the Celsius temperature?

(A) 9°

(B) 11°

(C) 13°

(D) 15°

(E) 20°

To figure out what happens to the Celsius temperature, you have to use the formula given in the question to convert Fahrenheit degrees to Celsius degrees: 70 degrees Fahrenheit turns into $\frac{5}{9}(70-32) = 21.1$ degrees Celsius; 90 degrees Fahrenheit becomes $\frac{5}{9}(90-32) = 32.2$ degrees Celsius. So the corresponding Celsius change is 32.2 – 21.1 = about 11 degrees, or Choice **(B).**

7. Which of the following inequalities is the solution of $|x| < 7$?

(A) $x < 7$

(B) $x > 7$

(C) $x < -7$

(D) $-7 < x < 7$

To solve an absolute value inequality, keep in mind that there'll be two solutions. That fact alone points to Choice **(D),** which is the answer, but do the math anyway. You can find one solution by just removing the absolute value sign: $x < 7$. Then, you can find the other solution by removing the absolute value sign, flipping the inequality sign, and changing the sign of the number on the right: $x > -7$. You can write both solutions at once, because x is greater than –7 but less than 7, so $-7 < x < 7$.

Tackling Upper Level Algebra Questions on Your Own

Now that you've worked through a few guided algebra questions, it's time to work on some by yourself. Review the four tips at the beginning of this chapter before starting. Practice good technique now so it's second nature when you have the actual test in front of you.

1. If $x* = 7x - 7$, what does $7*$ equal?

   (A) 0

   (B) 14

   (C) 42

   (D) 49

2. If $x - y = 10$, which of the following expressions is equal to y?

   (A) $10 - x$

   (B) $x - 10$

   (C) $x + 10$

   (D) $\dfrac{10}{x}$

   (E) $10x$

3. If n is a positive integer and $(x + 9)^2 = x^2 + nx + 81$, then $n =$

   (A) 0

   (B) 9

   (C) 18

   (D) 27

   (E) 81

4. The sum of the scores of Ashley's first four math tests is 372. If she gets a 98 on the next test, what is the mean of all five test scores?

   (A) 93

   (B) 94

   (C) 97

   (D) 98

   (E) The mean cannot be determined.

5. A class's test scores were compiled and are shown in the table.

Mean Score	79
Median Score	81
Mode	82
Range	27

   If the teacher adds 10 points to each test, which of the measures changes the *least*?

   (A) Mean

   (B) Median

   (C) Mode

   (D) Range

   (E) They all change by the same amount.

6. What is the result of subtracting $-8x$ from $4x$?

   (A) $-4x$

   (B) $-12x$

   (C) $4x$

   (D) $12x$

7. What is the maximum value for $5x^2$ if $-3 \geq x \geq 2$?

   (A) 20

   (B) 25

   (C) 40

   (D) 45

8. In 2009, a movie ticket cost $10.00. In 2010, the price of a movie ticket was 10% higher than in 2009. In 2011, the price of a movie ticket was 10% lower than in 2010. How much was a movie ticket in 2011?

   (A) $9.00

   (B) $9.90

   (C) $10.00

   (D) $10.10

   (E) $10.90

9. Which expression is equivalent to $2x^2y^3 + 8x^3y^2 - (3x^3y^2 - x^2y^3)$?

   (A) $x^2y^3 + 5x^3y^2$

   (B) $3x^2y^3 + 5x^3y^2$

   (C) $8x^5y^5$

   (D) $7x^5y^5$

   (E) $2x^2y^3 + 4x^3y^2$

10. For what values of x does $\dfrac{x^2 - 49}{(x+4)(x-9)} = 0$?

    (A) $x = 7$ only

    (B) $x = \pm 7$ only

    (C) $x = -4$ and $x = 9$

    (D) $x = \pm 7$, $x = -4$, and $x = 9$

    (E) $x = 0$

11. How many different arrangements of letters can be made from the letters A, B, C, and D?

    (A) 16

    (B) 20

    (C) 24

    (D) 48

    (E) 96

12. Which describes all values of x for which $|-2x - 2| < 8$?

    (A) $x < 3$

    (B) $x > 3$

    (C) $-5 < x < 3$

    (D) $x < -5$ or $x > 3$

    (E) $x > -5$

13. In the formula $x = \dfrac{10y}{z}$, y and z are always positive numbers. If one of the three variables stays the same, which of the following is true?

    (A) x increases as y decreases

    (B) x increases as z increases

    (C) x decreases as y increases

    (D) x decreases as z decreases

    (E) x increases as z decreases

14. A machine makes 600 microchips in 2 hours. How many microchips does the machine make in 60 seconds?

    (A) 5

    (B) 25

    (C) 50

    (D) 60

    (E) 120

15. At the start of an experiment, four bacteria are in a petri dish. If each bacterium divides into four bacteria after one hour, how many bacteria will be in the dish after 8 hours?

    (A) 4^8

    (B) 4^9

    (C) 4^{10}

    (D) $4 + 4^2 + 4^3 + 4^4 + 4^5 + 4^6 + 4^7 + 4^8 + 4^9$

    (E) 4^{45}

Answers to Upper Level Algebra Questions

1. **C.** The * symbol is defined as "take your number, multiply it by 7, and then subtract 7 from the result." So 7* becomes $7 \times 7 - 7$, which is $49 - 7 = 42$.

2. **B.** You can pick numbers for x and y to make the equation true. If x is, say, 20, then y would have to be 10 to make the equation true. Choice (B) results in $y = 10$ if you test your numbers in the answer choices. Alternatively, just get y by itself on one side of the equation.

3. **C.** Rewrite $(x + 9)^2$ as $(x + 9)(x + 9)$ and multiply. The result is $x^2 + 18x + 81$, so n must be 18. You can't just square both terms inside the parentheses; instead, you have to multiply the terms. So if you got $x^2 + 81$, you probably squared both terms in the parentheses.

4. **B.** Average all five scores by dividing their sum $(372 + 98)$ by how many there are (5), and the result is 94. It doesn't matter that you don't know the first four scores, because finding the mean just requires knowing the sum of the scores and how many of them there are.

5. **D.** The range is the only measure that doesn't change. If the initial range was 27, the scores may have ranged from 61 to 88 $(88 - 61 = 27)$. If all the scores go up by 10 points, the range is still 27, because they'd then go from 71 to 98 $(98 - 71 = 27)$.

6. **D.** Subtracting $-8x$ from $4x$ means $4x - (-8x)$, which is $12x$. If you got this wrong, make sure you're writing down *all* your steps!

7. **D.** Use trial and error with questions that have the words *minimum* or *maximum* in them. Using $x = -3$ results in 45.

8. **B.** Do percent changes one at a time. First, increase $10.00 by 10 percent by multiplying 10 by 1.1 = $11.00. Then, decrease $11.00 by 10 percent by multiplying 11 by 0.9 = $9.90.

9. **B.** First, distribute the negative sign in front of the parentheses and rewrite the expression as $2x^2y^3 + 8x^3y^2 - 3x^3y^2 + x^2y^3$. Combine like terms, but be careful to combine only terms where the variables and the exponents match, and the result is $3x^2y^3 + 5x^3y^2$.

10. **B.** Remember the rules of zero: Zero divided by anything is zero. Substituting either 7 or –7 for x makes the top of the fraction equal 0. You may think that putting a –4 or 9 for x makes the fraction equal 0 as well, but doing that creates a 0 in the bottom of the fraction, which is undefined, not 0.

11. **C.** If you write out the possibilities, look for a pattern. Six combinations start with A (ABCD, ABDC, ACBD, ACDB, ADBC, and ADCB). Also, six combinations start with B, six start with C, and six start with D, giving you 24 total.

    Another way to solve this permutation question is to draw four blanks (___, ___, ___, ___). The first blank has four possible letters; the second blank has three, because one has been placed in the first blank; the third blank has two possibilities (because two numbers have been placed); and the fourth blank has only one possibility. So $4 \times 3 \times 2 \times 1 = 24$.

12. **C.** You can find one solution for this absolute value inequality by taking away the absolute value sign and solving: $-2x - 2 < 8$, which equals $-2x < 10$ then $x > -5$ (remember, the inequality flips because you divided by a negative number). You can find the other solution by taking away the absolute value sign, reversing the inequality sign, and reversing the sign on the number to the right of the inequality sign: $-2x - 2 > -8$, which becomes $-2x > -6$ then $x < 3$. The two solutions can be written together as $-5 < x < 3$.

13. **E.** You can do this one logically if you think about fractions. A fraction gets bigger if its top number gets bigger, like going from $\frac{3}{7}$ to $\frac{6}{7}$. A fraction gets smaller if its bottom number gets bigger, like going from $\frac{1}{2}$ to $\frac{1}{10}$. Plug some numbers in to the problem to test your answer if you're not sure. For example, say you make $x = 20$, $y = 4$, and $z = 2$. Only Choice (E) is true; decreasing z makes x bigger. For example, if you make $z = 1$, $x = 40$.

14. **A.** Set up a proportion, because you know the machine's rate. But first, convert to a common unit, in this case, seconds: 2 hours is 120 minutes, which is 7,200 (120×60) seconds. So the machine's rate is $\frac{600}{7,200}$, which is a ratio of 600 chips made per 7,200 seconds. The proportion is $\frac{600}{7,200} = \frac{x}{60}$, because you want to discover how many chips are made in 60 seconds at that same rate. Cross-multiply to get $36,000 = 7,200x$, and divide both sides by 7,200 to get $x = 5$.

When setting up a proportion, keep the same units on the same parts of the fractions (here, the seconds are on the bottom of the fractions).

15. **B.** This question is a sequence question, so write it out until you see a pattern to apply. At the start, there are four bacteria. After one hour, each of the four bacteria turns into four bacteria, giving you 16 bacteria. After another hour, each of the 16 bacteria turns into four bacteria, making 64 bacteria. If you see that 4 is 4^1, 16 is 4^2, and 64 is 4^3, you've found your pattern. Just count eight hours, and you get to 4^9. You can also do the multiplication to check, but that takes longer.

Nice work! We included some tough problems in there. If you struggled with a certain kind of problem, do some review work with the concept and then redo the problem until you can solve it with ease.

Chapter 14

Jamming with Geometry

The nice thing about most geometry problems on the ISEE and SSAT is that you have a picture of what's going on — and if you don't, you can (and should) draw one. After working on a topic like algebra, being able to visualize what you're doing is refreshing, and using techniques, like estimating and logic, is often easier. The downside of geometry problems can be that you have to really know your formulas and geometry rules. Don't worry, though, you don't need that many, and we review the ones you do need in this chapter.

In order to make sure you have all the geometry formulas and rules you need for the ISEE and SSAT, we try to be as comprehensive as possible when we cover them. Make sure you don't just stare at the rules — you retain them better if you apply them by doing problems with them. We note whether a certain concept is more likely to appear on the SSAT or the ISEE, but keep in mind that any concept can possibly pop up on either test.

After you make your way through this review chapter, put all these formulas, facts, and figures to use on some practice questions in Chapter 15. If you get stuck on a geometry problem, you're probably just missing a concept or formula, so when you're correcting your work, make sure to go back and look up what you're missing and then do the problem from scratch.

Gearing Up for Geometry Questions

Geometry questions are usually fairly straightforward about what rule or formula you need. If a question has a circle in it, for example, you're almost definitely dealing with the circle's circumference or area. But just like any math question on the ISEE or SSAT, take a second to think about the following before you jump in to the calculations:

▸ **What rule or formula is being tested?** Jot down the formula as soon as you know.

▸ **Use estimation and logic *before* you begin.** Doing so is a good idea so you can see whether your answer makes sense. Figures are drawn to scale unless stated otherwise. For example, if one triangle *looks* bigger than another triangle, you can assume that it *is* actually bigger and use that knowledge to guide your estimates.

▸ **Start writing right away!** Draw on the figure provided and solve for whatever you can, especially if you don't know where to start.

In the next chapter, we guide you through some problems where you can use these skills. *Remember:* You have to practice a skill to be able to use it efficiently on the real test. So make your practice count by using good technique for every practice problem you do (and write down everything). In this chapter, we simply introduce you to the topics you'll likely see on the test.

Reviewing Geometry Concepts

We've broken down the geometry you're likely to encounter on the ISEE and SSAT into these categories:

- Lines, angles, and perimeter
- Triangles
- Rectangles, squares, and other polygons
- Circles
- Solid geometry
- Coordinate geometry
- Miscellaneous geometry

Most of the concepts in these categories can make an appearance on any level of the ISEE or SSAT. Rather than try to predict whether a certain concept will or won't appear on the level of the test you're taking, we recommend that you familiarize yourself with all the following concepts. With that said, it's unlikely that you'll see any of the following categories on lower level tests: triangles (except for triangle perimeter and area), circles, coordinate geometry (except for identifying coordinate points), and miscellaneous geometry.

Lines, angles, and perimeter

On the SSAT and ISEE, a *line* is identified by naming two points that the line passes through. $\overleftrightarrow{AB}$ means the line goes through points A and B. Or $\overline{AB}$ means line segment AB — in other words, the part of the line beginning with point A and ending with point B.

A line has 180 degrees on one side, and 360 degrees all the way around it. This concept is useful when you're trying to figure out the measure of an angle as part of that line — you know that the two angles have to add up to 180 degrees. For example, in Figure 14-1, angle x and angle y add up to 180 degrees, because they're around the same line.

Anytime you see a straight line on a figure on the ISEE or SSAT that's intersected by another line, forming angles, draw a *semicircle* (half a circle) around the line to help visualize that the line has 180 degrees around it.

An *angle* is where two lines meet. The symbol $\angle ABC$ indicates an angle with point B as its center, as you see in Figure 14-2.

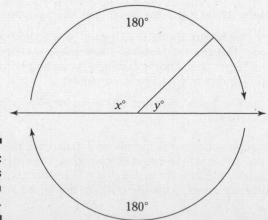

Figure 14-1:
Degrees
around a
line.

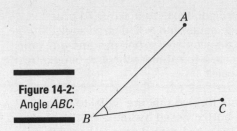

Figure 14-2:
Angle *ABC*.

When two lines intersect, the opposite angles are equal, as shown in Figure 14-3.

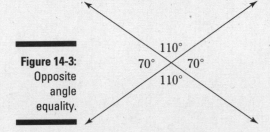

Figure 14-3:
Opposite
angle
equality.

A right angle measures 90 degrees and is designated by a square drawn in the middle of the angle, as shown in Figure 14-4. When a triangle has a right angle, it's called a *right triangle* (we discuss triangles in the next section).

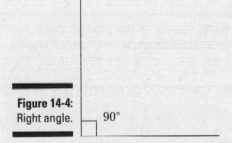

Figure 14-4:
Right angle.

Lines that don't intersect are called *parallel lines* (see Figure 14-5a). Lines that intersect and form a right angle are called *perpendicular lines* (see Figure 14-5b).

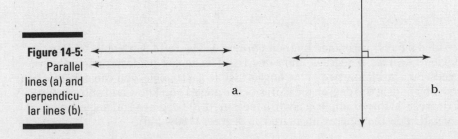

Figure 14-5:
Parallel
lines (a) and
perpendicu-
lar lines (b).

Being able to eyeball the degree measure of an angle is a good skill to master. To practice, get a protractor and draw a 90 degree angle, a 60 degree angle, and a 30 degree angle. Study them so you can make mental comparisons when you do geometry problems. And any time an angle measure is given to you on the ISEE or SSAT, use it to estimate the size of unknown angles (unless the problem says the drawing isn't to scale).

When a line crosses two parallel lines, certain angles are formed that are equal to each other. In Figure 14-6, lines ℓ and m are parallel and are both crossed by line a. Notice that the small angle line a makes with line ℓ is the same as the small angle line a makes with line m. Also notice that the large angle line a makes with line ℓ is the same as the large angle line a makes with line m.

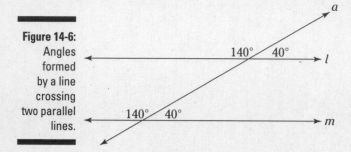

Figure 14-6:
Angles formed by a line crossing two parallel lines.

You may be asked to use this relationship to solve for missing angles in a question on the middle or upper level tests. For example, in Figure 14-6, if you didn't know the measure of the small angle line a makes with line m, you can assume it's 40 degrees because lines ℓ and m are parallel.

The *perimeter* of a shape is the sum of its sides. To find the perimeter of the triangle and rectangle in Figure 14-7, just add up their sides. The perimeter of the triangle is 18 (5 + 6 + 7), and the perimeter of the rectangle is 24 (4 + 8 + 4 + 8).

Figure 14-7:
The perimeter is the sum of a shape's sides.

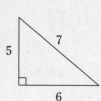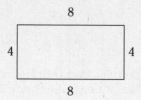

Triangles

Triangles, or three-sided figures, are named by their corners. In Figure 14-8, triangle *XYZ* has interior (inside) angles a degrees, b degrees, and c degrees. The angles inside a triangle always add up to 180 degrees. So if you know two of the angles inside of a triangle, you can solve for the angle you don't know by adding the degree measures of the angles you know and subtracting the total from 180 degrees. In this example, if angle a measured 100 degrees and angle b measured 45 degrees, you'd know that angle c measured 35 degrees (180 – 145).

Figure 14-8:
Triangle
XYZ.

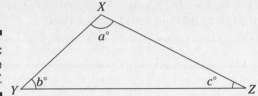

The largest angle of any triangle is opposite its longest side, and its smallest angle is opposite its shortest side. In Figure 14-9a, triangle *ABC*'s largest angle must be angle *B*, because that angle is opposite the longest side of the triangle (10). Likewise, in Figure 14-9b, you know the longest side of triangle *PQR* is side *PR*, which is the side opposite its largest angle (100 degrees).

Figure 14-9:
Finding the
largest angle
(a) and the
longest
side of tri-
angles (b).

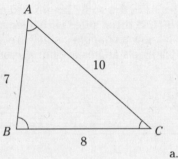

a.

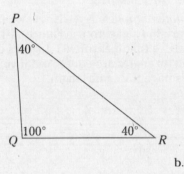

b.

Triangle questions may test your knowledge of perimeter (see the previous section and Figure 14-7) as well as the following topics, all of which will probably be on only the middle level ISEE and the upper level ISEE and SSAT except for triangle area, which can appear on any test level:

- ✔ Triangle area
- ✔ Equilateral triangles
- ✔ Isosceles triangles
- ✔ Triangle angles
- ✔ Right triangles and the Pythagorean theorem
- ✔ Special right triangles
- ✔ Similar triangles

Finding the area of a triangle

The *area* of a triangle is a measure of the space inside a triangle. The area is measured in square units, like square inches, square centimeters, or square yards. The formula for calculating a triangle's area is $\frac{1}{2}bh$, where *b* is the length of the base of the triangle, and *h* is the length of the height of the triangle. The triangle's base can be any side, but using the bottom side is usually easiest. The triangle's height is a line drawn from the base to the triangle's top corner that's *perpendicular* to the base. You know a line is perpendicular to another line if the two lines form a right angle where they meet.

In Figure 14-10, notice that the base of the triangle is 10, and the height is 8. You can find the triangle's area by multiplying 10 × 8 then taking half the result, which is 40.

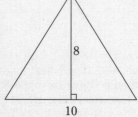

Figure 14-10:
The base and height of a triangle.

Equilateral triangles

An *equilateral triangle* is a triangle where all the sides have the same length and all the angles are the same, too. In Figure 14-11, triangle *ABC* has three sides with a length of 8 and three angles that measure 60 degrees each. So if you know a triangle's sides are equal, you know all its angles are equal. And if you know all a triangle's angles are equal, you know all its sides have the same length.

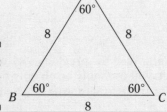

Figure 14-11:
An equilateral triangle.

Isosceles triangles

An *isosceles triangle* is a triangle with two equal sides, and the angles opposite those equal sides are also equal. For example, in Figure 14-12, triangle *ABC* has two sides measuring 7. The angles opposite those sides both measure 75 degrees. So if you know two of a triangle's sides are equal, you know the angles opposite those sides are equal. If you know a triangle has two angles that are equal, then you know the sides opposite those angles are equal.

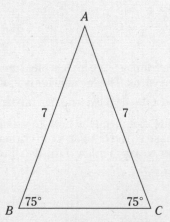

Figure 14-12:
An isosceles triangle.

Right triangles

A *right triangle* has one 90 degree angle. In a right triangle, the side opposite the right angle is called the *hypotenuse*. The hypotenuse is always the longest side of a right triangle.

The sides of a right triangle can be solved by using the *Pythagorean theorem,* a concept that may show up on the middle and upper level tests. Labeling the hypotenuse of a right triangle c and the other two sides a and b, the theorem tells us that $a^2 + b^2 = c^2$. In other words, if you know two of the sides of a right triangle, you can use that formula to solve for the third side.

In Figure 14-13, triangle *XYZ* has a hypotenuse of 5 and side lengths 3 and 4. Notice that $3^2 + 4^2 = 5^2$. If you didn't know the length of the hypotenuse, you'd have to add $9 + 16 = 25$, and then take the square root of 25. Or if you know the length of the hypotenuse is 5 and one of the sides is 3, you can find the length of the other side: $5^2 = x^2 + 3^2$, then $25 = x^2 + 9$, then $16 = x^2$. Then, take the square root of both sides to end up with $x = 4$.

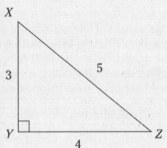

Figure 14-13: Use the Pythagorean theorem to solve questions about right triangles.

Memorize a few common *Pythagorean triples,* or common right triangle side lengths. Two popular triples are 3, 4, 5 and 6, 8, 10. Also, 5, 12, 13 and 7, 24, 25 are somewhat common. If you see a right triangle with one of those side lengths, you may be able to fill in the missing side(s) without doing any math.

Less common, but important to know for the upper level tests, are two *special* right triangles: the 45-45-90 degree right triangle and the 30-60-90 degree right triangle. In Figure 14-14, notice that in a right triangle with both smaller angles equaling 45 degrees, the sides and hypotenuse have a specific relationship: If the sides are x in length, the hypotenuse is $x\sqrt{2}$ in length. So if you had a 45-45-90 degree right triangle with a side length of 4, the hypotenuse is $4\sqrt{2}$ in length.

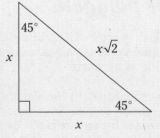

Figure 14-14: A 45-45-90 degree triangle.

In a right triangle with angles measuring 30 degrees, 60 degrees, and 90 degrees, as shown in Figure 14-15, the sides have the following relationship: If the shortest side (the one opposite the 30 degree angle) has length x, the longest side (opposite the right angle) has length $2x$, and the middle side (opposite the 60 degree angle) has length $x\sqrt{3}$. So if you have a 30-60-90 degree triangle and you know the shortest side is 2, you know the hypotenuse is 4 and the other side is $2\sqrt{3}$.

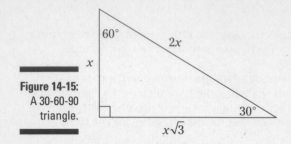

Figure 14-15:
A 30-60-90 triangle.

The great thing about special right triangles is that if you notice one, you can solve for all its sides even if you know only one of the sides. If you see a right triangle with a radical measurement as one of its sides or a right triangle with a 30 degree, 45 degree, or 60 degree angle, think about applying your special right triangle skills.

Similar triangles

Similar triangles are two triangles with the same angle measures. The useful thing about similar triangles is their common side length ratio. For example, in Figure 14-16, notice the short side of the larger triangle is double the short side of the smaller triangle. That tells you that the long side of the larger triangle is also double the long side of the smaller triangle. If you didn't know the long side of the larger triangle, you could set up a proportion to solve for it: $\frac{3}{6} = \frac{7}{x}$, knowing that the two triangles have a common side length ratio because their angles are the same.

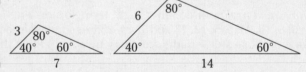

Figure 14-16:
Similar triangles.

Ratios in triangles, like any ratios, are about multiplying and dividing, not adding and subtracting. Look again at Figure 14-16: The short side of the larger triangle is 3 bigger than the short side of the smaller triangle, but don't think of it as 3 + 3; instead, think of it as 3 × 2. If you don't remember how to deal with ratios and proportions, see Chapter 12.

Rectangles, squares, and other polygons

A *rectangle* is a four-sided figure that has four right angles. A *square* is a rectangle that also has equal side lengths. Rectangles have two pairs of equal sides. Usually a rectangle's shorter side is referred to as its width and its longer side as its length.

You find the area of a rectangle by multiplying the shorter side length by the longer side length. In Figure 14-17a, the area of the rectangle is $2 \times 4 = 8$. The area of a square is found, not surprisingly, by *squaring* one of its sides. In Figure 14-17b, the area of the square is $8^2 = 64$. Because a square is also a rectangle, you can find its area by multiplying one side by the adjacent side. Again, area is expressed in square units. For example, if a rectangle has a length of 9 centimeters and a width of 3 centimeters, its area is 27 cm^2, or 27 square centimeters.

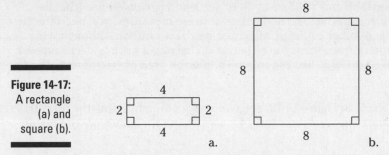

Figure 14-17:
A rectangle
(a) and
square (b).

a.

b.

A *polygon* is a shape enclosed by straight lines, so squares and rectangles are both polygons. Other polygons have different numbers of sides, and you should be familiar with what they're called. A *pentagon* (imagine home plate on a baseball field) has five sides, a *hexagon* has six (picture a honeycomb), and an *octagon* (think stop sign) has eight.

On the upper level tests, you may be asked to find the sum of the inside angles of a polygon. Remember how the angles of a triangle always add up to 180 degrees? Well, you can use that as a base to find what the angles of any polygon add up to: So if you use the total angle measure of a triangle and then add a side, add 180 degrees to the total angle measure. For example, because a rectangle has four sides, its angles add up to a triangle's plus 180 degrees, which equals 360 degrees. Because a pentagon has five sides, its angles add up to a triangle's plus two more: (180) + 180 + 180 = 540 degrees.

Try this method to find what the angles of an *octagon,* or eight-sided figure, add up to. Start with 180 degrees for the triangle plus five more sides (5 × 180), which comes to 180 + 900 = 1,080 degrees.

Circles

If you travel all the way around a circle, you travel 360 degrees. Half a circle, called a *semicircle,* contains 180 degrees, and a quarter of a circle contains 90 degrees. Another way to think of this is that 360 degrees of angles are inside a circle.

A circle is usually described by its center point. A *radius* of a circle is the length of a line drawn from its center to any point on its edge, and all *radii* (the plural of radius) are of equal length. A circle's *diameter* is the length of a line going from one side of a circle to the other, passing through its center point and splitting it in half. In Figure 14-18, Circle *K*'s radius is 4 and diameter is 8.

Figure 14-18:
A circle,
K, with a
radius of 4
and diameter of 8.

When it comes to circles, the ISEE and SSAT test you on area and *circumference* (the distance all the way around a circle's edge). To find either of these measures, you need the circle's radius and a funny little number called pi, indicated by the π symbol. Although π is equal to about 3.14, in geometry questions, you're better off leaving it as π, because answer choices are usually given in terms of π, like 24π or πx. To find the area or circumference of a circle, do the following:

✔ **Finding area:** For the circle in Figure 14-18, you can find its area by using the formula πr^2. In other words, square the circle's radius ($4 \times 4 = 16$) and then multiply the result by π: 16π.

You can also work backward: If you know a circle's area is, say, 25π, you can take the square root of the number next to π to get the circle's radius: $\sqrt{25} = 5$.

✔ **Finding circumference:** To find the circumference of the circle in Figure 14-18, use the formula $2\pi r$. Just multiply the circle's radius by 2 and then multiply the result by π. So the circle's circumference is $4 \times 2 \times \pi = 8\pi$.

If you know a circle's circumference is 20π, you can work backward to determine its radius by dividing the number next to π by 2. In this case, $20 \div 2 = $ a radius of 10.

The formulas for the area of a circle and the circumference of a circle are easy to confuse. A good way to remember them is to say, "Mmmultiply for circummmference" (you're multiplying the radius by 2) and "Squarrrre for arrrrea" (you're squaring the radius). Trust us, it works! Another way to keep the two formulas straight is to think of a circle's circumference formula as π*d*, with *d* being the circle's diameter.

Solid geometry

Solid geometry deals with 3-D shapes, like cubes, cylinders, and cones. For the purposes of the ISEE and SSAT, you need to know how to deal with only a couple of concepts: volume and surface area.

Volume

Volume means a measure of all the space inside an object. We usually measure liquids by their volumes. Next time you take a study break, open the fridge and notice that the milk jug or carton of orange juice in there has a volume, probably measured in ounces or milliliters.

On the SSAT and ISEE, volume is almost always tested with boxes. To find the volume of a box, just multiply its length by its width by its height. For example, in Figure 14-19, the box has a volume of 288 cm³, or 288 cubic centimeters. Find the volume by multiplying $4 \times 6 \times 12 = 288$. Volume questions often involve cubes, which are boxes with the same measurement for length, width, and height.

Figure 14-19:
A box with length, width, and height measurements.

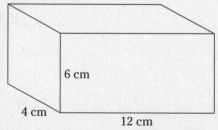

6 cm

4 cm

12 cm

Surface area

Surface area means the sum of the areas of all the sides of an object, usually a cube. To find the surface area of an object, add all the areas of all the object's sides. With a *cube* — a box with the same measurements for length, width, and height (picture a six-sided die) — find the area of one of the sides and multiply it by 6.

Coordinate geometry

Coordinate geometry deals with the *coordinate plane* — a graph formed by two perpendicular number lines known as the *x*-axis (the horizontal, or side-to-side, axis) and the *y*-axis (the vertical, or up-and-down, axis). A point on the coordinate plane is described by giving the value for its *x*-coordinate and its *y*-coordinate in what's known as a *coordinate pair,* like (8, 9). To locate or graph the point, just count over 8 units to the right and up 9 units.

The first number in a set of coordinates is the *x*-value. Write a little *x* next to the first number in a coordinate pair every time you see one on the test.

Notice that each axis has both positive and negative numbers. The two axes meet at the *origin,* which is the point (0, 0). Again, the first number in a coordinate pair is the *x*-value, or how far along the *x*-axis the point is. The second number in a coordinate pair is the *y*-value — how far up or down the *y*-axis the point is. If you see a negative number for the first number (*x*-value) of a coordinate pair, it means you're counting to the left. If you see a negative number for the second number of a coordinate pair (*y*-value), you're counting down.

In Figure 14-20, point *B* has coordinates of (5, 2), so it's 5 (five to the right) along the *x*-axis and 2 (up two) along the *y*-axis. Point *A* has coordinates (–5, –6) so it's –5 (5 to the left) along the *x*-axis and –6 (down six) along the *y*-axis.

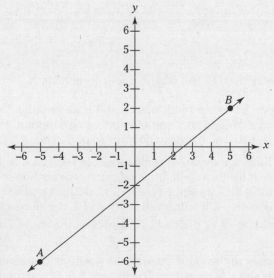

Figure 14-20:
Line *AB*.

Lines in the coordinate plane usually deal with a couple different things: the equation of the line and the slope of the line, which we discuss in the following sections.

Equation of a line

The equation of a line in the coordinate plane is often given in the following form: $y = mx + b$. In this equation, the y is the y-coordinate of any point on the line, and the x is the x-coordinate of the same point. The m is the *slope* of the line, and the b is the *y-intercept* of the line (where it hits the y-axis). Use the line's equation to graph the line or to solve for whatever part of the equation you're missing (like the y-intercept, for example).

In Figure 14-20, you can see that the line intersects the y-axis at –2, so the b in its equation is –2. To find the m, or slope, of the line, finding the line's *rise* and *run* is often easiest. A line's rise is how much you travel along the y-axis between two points on the line, and the line's run is how far along the x-axis you travel between two points on the line.

Pick two known points (points that you have the coordinates for) on the line and see how far up it is from the left point to the right point. Looking at point A, you can get to point B by going up eight along the y-axis. So the rise is 8. The run is found by noticing you travel ten to the right to get from point A to point B, so the run is 10. The slope is the rise divided by the run: $8 \div 10$, or $\frac{8}{10}$. If a line slopes downward as it goes to the right, its slope is negative. For example, to calculate the slope between the points (0, 6) and (7, 1), you have to travel *down* 5 and to the *right* 7. We think of the "down 5" as –5, so the slope is $-\frac{5}{7}$.

If a line passes through the origin (0, 0), the ISEE and SSAT may not actually tell you it does, but it's pretty obvious if a line goes through that point. Remember this because (0, 0) may be one of the two points you need to find a line's slope.

Now you have the entire equation of the line: $y = \frac{8}{10}x - 2$. You can use the equation of a line to solve for the y-coordinate of a point if you know the x-coordinate. For example, if you know the x-coordinate of a point on the line is 10 and you want to find the y-coordinate, just plug 10 into the equation for x and solve for y: $y = \frac{8}{10}(10) - 2$, then $y = \frac{80}{10} - 2$, then $y = 8 - 2$, so $y = 6$. So (10, 6) is a point on the line.

Slope of the line

Here are a couple slope rules you may need to use on the upper level tests:

- **Parallel lines have equal slopes.** In Figure 14-21, lines p and q are parallel: They both have a slope of 1. Notice on line p, you go up 2 and over 2 to go from point A to point B ($2 \div 2 = 1$), and on line q, you go up 2 and over 2 to go from point C to point D ($2 \div 2 = 1$).

- **The slopes of perpendicular lines are negative reciprocals.** In Figure 14-21, line r is perpendicular to line p because it forms a right angle where it crosses line p. Take the reciprocal of line p by dividing 1 by its slope ($1 \div 1 = 1$), and then make the result negative (–1). So the slope of line r is –1. If a line had a slope of 3, the slope of a line perpendicular to that line would be $-\frac{1}{3}$ (1 divided by 3 and then the answer made negative).

- **If a line travels upward as it goes to the right, its slope is positive. If it travels downward as it goes to the right, its slope is negative.** These facts can be useful to eliminate answer choices if you're running out of time or if you can't figure out the problem.

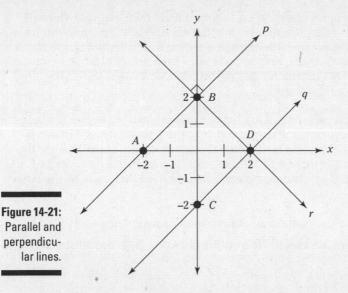

Figure 14-21:
Parallel and
perpendicu-
lar lines.

Miscellaneous geometry

On the middle or upper level ISEE or SSAT, you may encounter a strange-looking geometry
question, like this:

> Circle *X* is inscribed in a square, and the radius of Circle *X* is 3 cm, as shown in the fol-
> lowing figure. What is the area of the shaded region?

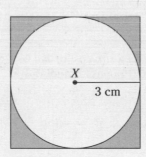

Don't panic if you encounter a question like this. The question isn't testing a geometrical
concept you haven't seen before; it's just asking you to apply what you know to a new situation. In the figure, you know the radius of the circle is 3 centimeters, so you can double that
to get the circle's diameter: $3 \times 2 = 6$ cm. If you notice that the diameter of the circle is also
the length of one of the sides of the square (because the circle is *inscribed* in the square),
you can solve for the square's area ($6 \times 6 = 36$). And after you know the square's area, the
area of the shaded region is the area of the square minus the area of the circle. Remember
the area of the circle is πr^2, so its area is 9π. The area of the shaded region is $36 - 9\pi$.

You may also see a basic trigonometry question on an upper level test. The question will probably have a picture of a right triangle and give you at least one side length of the triangle as well as one angle measure other than the right angle. You'll also probably see *sin, cos,* or *tan* in the answer choices. This type of question tests your knowledge of what's commonly known as *SOH CAH TOA*. This mnemonic helps you represent the ratios of the sine, cosine, and tangent measures of a right triangle.

In Figure 14-22, notice that the angle measures of the right triangle shown are angles *a, b,* and *c.* The **s**ine of any angle is found by dividing the **o**pposite side of the triangle by its **h**ypotenuse, hence SOH. The **c**osine of any angle is found by dividing the **a**djacent side of the triangle (in other words, the side next to the angle that *isn't* the hypotenuse) by its **h**ypotenuse, hence CAH. And the **t**angent of any angle is found by dividing the **o**pposite side from that angle by the **a**djacent side to that angle.

For example, in Figure 14-22, the sine (commonly abbreviated as *sin*) of angle *c* is $\frac{3}{5}$ (the opposite side, 3, divided by the hypotenuse, 5). The cosine of angle *c* is $\frac{4}{5}$ (the adjacent side, 4, divided by the hypotenuse, 5).

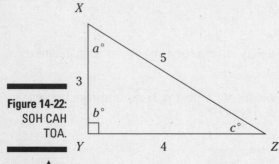

Figure 14-22:
SOH CAH
TOA.

If you see a question with a *sin, cos,* or *tan* in it on the ISEE or SSAT, you're going to be using SOH CAH TOA, so write it down immediately!

Chapter 15

Practicing Geometry

In This Chapter
▶ Practicing lower and middle level geometry
▶ Practicing upper level geometry

The more geometry problems you do, the more you realize that they're all based on the basic rules we cover in Chapter 14. Even if you come across a strange-looking figure, keep in mind that you have the tools to attack the problem. So, when in doubt, solve for something in a geometry problem, and the info will probably let you solve for something else and get the ball rolling.

This chapter is divided into two sections: One section covers the lower level SSAT and the lower and middle level ISEE geometry, and the other section includes geometry for the upper level SSAT and ISEE. We provide several example questions and walk you through how to answer them, and then we also include practice questions that you can work on all on your own, with the answers following in a separate section.

If you're taking an upper level test, we recommend that you complete all the problems for the lower and middle level tests as well. Even if you don't really need geometry practice, you want to get as familiar as possible with the way the questions are worded — which is probably quite a bit different than how the questions are worded in your math class.

Keep the following Math section pointers in mind even when you're just practicing.

✔ **Read the question carefully.** Although starting to calculate as quickly as possible is tempting — after all, it's a timed test — make sure you read the question *closely* and *carefully* and then read it once more before you pick an answer.

✔ **Skip a question quickly if you don't *immediately* know how to do it.** All the questions are worth the same amount of points, so fight with the hard ones *after* you've done all the easier ones.

✔ **Use common sense.** Before beginning a question, take a few seconds to think logically. What do you think the answer may be? This step lets you see whether your calculated answer makes sense and can even save you from doing some or all of the math on some questions.

✔ **Write down your steps.** Writing down your work prevents careless errors and gives your brain a break. Also draw pictures whenever possible. Get in the habit of doing these techniques now so they're second nature by the time you take the test.

Practicing Guided Lower and Middle Level Geometry Questions

Here are a few practice questions that let you test the geometry skills you reviewed in Chapter 14, followed by some guidance about how to find the correct answer, if you need it.

Even if you get a problem right, it's still a good idea to read the explanation that follows — you may pick up a new technique or a new way of thinking about the problem.

1. What is one way that can be used to find how many one-unit cubes make up the solid shown?

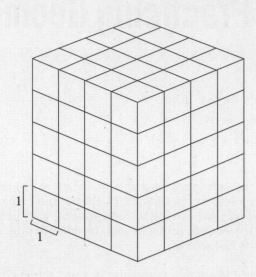

(A) $4 \times 4 \times 4$

(B) $4 \times 4 \times 5$

(C) 16×3

(D) 32×2

You can handle this counting blocks problem in a couple of ways. First, you can imagine that the figure was cut into slices. Because you can count 20 blocks on the slice facing you to the right, and there are four slices, you can calculate $20 \times 4 = 80$. Checking the answer choices, Choice **(B)** makes 80. Or you can use your volume formula for the volume of a box. The length and width of the figure are both four blocks and the height is five blocks, so $4 \times 4 \times 5$ also gives you 80, or Choice (B).

2. What is the area of the diamond in the figure?

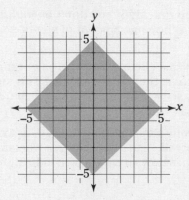

(A) 20

(B) 40

(C) 60

(D) 80

(E) 100

This problem looks tricky at first because there isn't a formula to get the area of a diamond. But notice that the diamond is made of two triangles — a triangle above the *x*-axis and a triangle below the *x*-axis. Even better, the two triangles both have a base of 10 units and a height of 4 units. Using the formula for the area of a triangle, $\frac{1}{2}bh$, the area of each triangle is $\frac{1}{2}(10)(4) = \frac{1}{2}(40) = 20$. Adding the two areas together gives you Choice **(B)**, 40.

If you forgot the formula for the area of a triangle, you can also estimate the answer by counting blocks in the figure. Although you may not get an exact answer, you can usually get close enough to narrow down the choices significantly.

3. What is the perimeter of the yard shown?

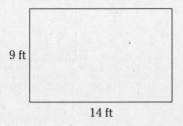

9 ft

14 ft

(A) 23 ft

(B) 46 ft

(C) 126 ft

(D) 252 ft

This perimeter problem is pretty straightforward, but be sure to write "9 feet" and "14 feet" on the two blank sides of the yard, so you remember to add them. Then, just add all four sides: 9 + 14 + 9 + 14 = 46 ft, or Choice **(B)**.

4. What are the coordinates of point *P* in the figure?

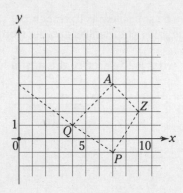

(A) (7, 1)

(B) (1, 7)

(C) (7, –1)

(D) (–1, 7)

First, measure how many units you count along the *x*-axis to get to point *P*. Because point *P* is to the right of the origin, the *x*-coordinate has a positive value. Counting over, you can see that point *P* is 7 to the right, which makes the first part of the coordinate pair 7. Next, count how far up or down the *y*-axis the point is. Because point *P* is below the *x*-axis line, it has a negative number, so its *y*-coordinate is –1. Therefore, Choice **(C)** is correct.

5. In the triangle shown, what is the value of *x?*

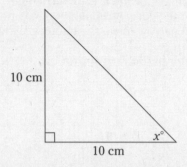

(A) 30

(B) 40

(C) 45

(D) 50

(E) It cannot be determined from the information given.

Usually, you'd be able to solve for an angle of a triangle only if you knew the other two angles — but in this case, you know only one: the right angle. However, you do know that this triangle is an *isosceles triangle* because two of its sides are equal. Therefore, you know that the angles opposite the equal sides are also equal. Because angle *x* is opposite a side measuring 10 centimeters, the top angle of the triangle is also equal to *x*, because it's also opposite a side measuring 10 centimeters. You can set up an equation, using the fact that all the angles of a triangle add up to 180 degrees: $x + x + 90 = 180$; then solve for *x*: $2x = 90$, so $x = 45$.

Another way to solve this problem is to remember that anytime a right triangle has two equal sides, it's a 45-45-90 degree right triangle; in other words, a right triangle has two 45 degree angles.

6. If *WXYZ* is a square, what is the area of the unshaded region?

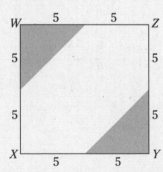

(A) 12.5

(B) 20

(C) 25

(D) 50

(E) 75

For shaded/unshaded region questions, you subtract from the total area of a shape. In this case, the total area of the square is 100, because it has a side length of 10. To figure out the area of the unshaded region, you have to subtract the area of the shaded triangles from 100.

Using the formula for the area of a triangle, the area of each triangle is $\frac{1}{2}(5)(5)=12.5$. The area of the triangles combined is 25, so the area of the unshaded region is $100-25=75$, Choice **(E)**.

7. In the figure shown, what is the value of $x + y$?

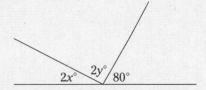

(A) 45°

(B) 50°

(C) 80°

(D) 100°

This question is tricky; you can't solve for either x or y by itself, but you can solve for $x + y$. Using the knowledge that all the angles on one side of a line add up to 180 degrees, set up an equation like this: $2x + 2y + 80 = 180$. Simplify to $2x + 2y = 100$. Dividing both sides of the equation by 2 leaves $x + y = 50$, or Choice **(B)**.

8. If the area of a square is 49 square inches, what is its perimeter?

(A) 7 in

(B) 14 in

(C) 21 in

(D) 28 in

The area of a square tells you what the length of its side are, because the area of a square is equal to one of its side lengths squared. Draw a picture of a square to help you visualize this problem, and then consider the following: What number, when squared, results in 49? Use trial and error if you need to, but the answer is 7. If the square has a side length of 7, find its perimeter by adding $7 + 7 + 7 + 7 = 28$ in, Choice **(D)**.

Attacking Lower and Middle Level Geometry Questions on Your Own

Now it's time to test your skills by completing some geometry questions on your own. Review the four tips at the beginning of this chapter (read carefully, skip quickly if you don't know how to do it, use common sense, and write down your work) before you begin.

1. What is the length of the third side of the triangle shown if its perimeter is 35 centimeters?

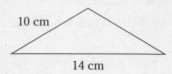

10 cm

14 cm

(A) 10 cm

(B) 11 cm

(C) 12 cm

(D) 13 cm

(E) 14 cm

2. If the perimeter of a square is 16x, what is the length of one of its sides?

(A) 4

(B) 8

(C) 4x

(D) 8x

3. The volume of the small, shaded cube is 8 cubic centimeters. What is the volume of the larger cube?

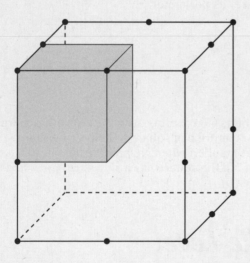

(A) 32 cm³

(B) 64 cm³

(C) 96 cm³

(D) 128 cm³

4. What is the perimeter of a rectangle that has a length of 12 inches and a width of 3 inches? (P = 2l + 2w)

(A) 15 in

(B) 18 in

(C) 28 in

(D) 30 in

5. What are the coordinates of point Z in the figure?

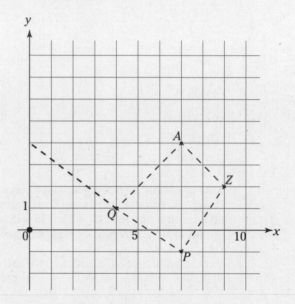

(A) (2, 9)

(B) (9, 2)

(C) (1, 9)

(D) (9, 1)

6. Each of the nine square tiles in the pattern shown has an area of 4 square inches. If the pattern is repeated 100 times to cover a floor, the portion covered with shaded tiles has an area of

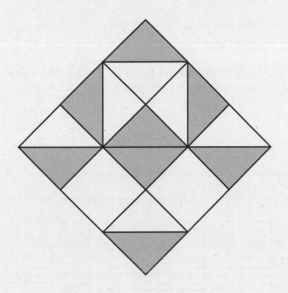

(A) 160 sq in

(B) 320 sq in

(C) 1,600 sq in

(D) 3,600 sq in

7. Which shape has a greater area: a square with a side length of 4 or a circle with a diameter of 4?

(A) The circle.

(B) The square.

(C) Their areas are the same.

(D) Not enough information is provided to answer the question.

8. If a contractor uses exactly 16 feet of fence to enclose a shape, which shape contains more area: a square or a circle?

(A) A square.

(B) A circle.

(C) The areas are the same.

(D) Not enough information is given to answer the question.

9. How many little cubes were used to make the big cube?

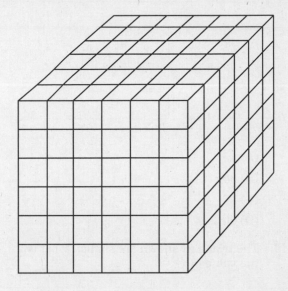

(A) 36

(B) 72

(C) 144

(D) 196

(E) 216

10. What is the slope between the points (6, 6) and (12, 0)?

(A) 1

(B) –1

(C) 2

(D) –2

11. What is the slope of the line with the equation $8x - 4y = 20$?

(A) 1

(B) –1

(C) 2

(D) –2

(E) –5

12. What is the area of triangle *ABC*?

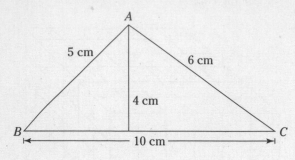

(A) 15

(B) 30

(C) 20

(D) 40

13. The triangles shown are similar. What is the value of *x*?

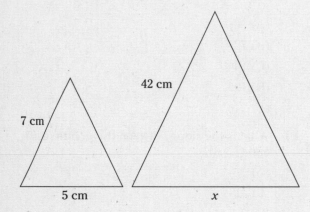

(A) 5 cm

(B) 7 cm

(C) 30 cm

(D) 40 cm

14. The surface area of a cube is 294 square centimeters. What is the volume of the cube?

(A) 343 cm³

(B) 294 cm³

(C) 49 cm³

(D) 7 cm³

15. The graph shows line *PQ*. What is the equation for the line perpendicular to line *PQ* at (5, 3)?

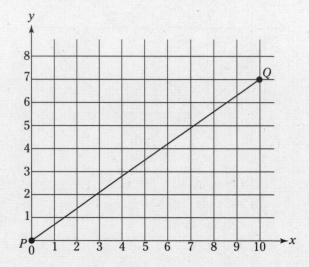

(A) $y = -\frac{10}{7}x + \frac{71}{7}$

(B) $y = -\frac{10}{7}x - \frac{71}{7}$

(C) $y = \frac{7}{10}x + \frac{71}{7}$

(D) $y = \frac{7}{10}x - \frac{71}{7}$

Answers to Lower and Middle Level Geometry Questions

1. **B.** Subtract the given two sides from 35: 35 − 14 − 10 = 11, the length of the third side.

2. **C.** Because all the sides of a square are equal, divide the perimeter by 4 to find the length of a side: $16x \div 4 = 4x$.

3. **B.** Count how many little cubes can fit inside the big cube. The markings on the big cube show that you can make a layer of four little cubes on the top layer of the big cube and another layer of four little cubes on the bottom layer of the big cube. Two layers of four equals eight little cubes, so the total area of the big cube is 64 cubic centimeters.

4. **D.** This question gives you a formula for the perimeter of a rectangle in case you don't know it, but you don't have to use it. Draw the rectangle and fill in the missing sides, and then add them together: 12 + 12 + 3 + 3 = 30.

5. **B.** Point Z is nine to the right along the x-axis, and two up along the y-axis, so its coordinates are (9, 2).

6. **C.** Count how much shaded area is in one tile. If each of the nine squares has an area of 4 square inches, then one of the shaded triangles has an area of 2 square inches. Eight shaded triangles are on one tile, so the shaded area of one tile is 16 square inches. Multiply that by 100 for 100 tiles, and you get Choice (C), 1,600 sq in.

7. **B.** Draw both shapes to get a visual. The area of the square is $4 \times 4 = 16$. The area of the circle is $\pi 2^2 = 4\pi$. Because π is about 3.14, the area of the circle is a little more than 12.

8. **B.** Draw both shapes. If the square's perimeter is 16, its side length is 4, so its area is $4 \times 4 = 16$. If the circle's perimeter is 16, its circumference is 16. To find the circle's area, you need to solve for its radius, using the fact that $16 = 2\pi r$. Solving for r gives you about 2.5. Now you can solve for the circle's area, using πr^2: $2.5 \times 2.5 = 6.25\pi$. Rounding π down to 3 and 6.25 down to 6 still gives you an area of about 18.

9. **E.** The big cube has a height of six little cubes, a width of six little cubes, and a length of six little cubes: $6 \times 6 \times 6 = 216$. Another way to solve this problem is to picture slicing the big cube up. You can count 36 little cubes in the slice closest to you, and 6 slices total, so $36 \times 6 = 216$.

10. **B.** Sketch a quick coordinate plane so you can plot both points and count the rise and run. If you draw a line connecting the points, it goes down as it goes to the right, so the slope must be negative. To get from (6, 6) to (12, 0), the rise is −6, and the run is 6. And −6 ÷ 6 = −1, Choice (B).

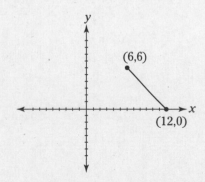

11. **C.** Get the equation into $y = mx + b$ format. Subtracting $8x$ from both sides gives you $-4y = -8x + 20$. Then, dividing both sides by −4 gives you $y = 2x - 5$. The slope is the coefficient of x when the equation is in that form, so it's 2.

12. **C.** To solve for the area of triangle *ABC*, multiply the base (10) by the height (4) and take half of the result (20).

13. **C.** Similar triangles' sides have a common ratio. You may notice that 7 is multiplied by 6 to get 42, so 5 is multiplied by 6 to get x, 30. Or set up a proportion: $\frac{7}{42} = \frac{5}{x}$ and cross-multiply to solve for x: $7x = 210$, so $x = 30$.

14. **A.** All the sides of a cube are equal, so if you know the surface area is 294 square centimeters, divide that number by 6 to get the area of one side, 49 square centimeters. This is useful because, knowing that a cube's length, width, and height are the same number, you can solve for the length of a side ($7 \times 7 = 49$) then solve for the volume: $7 \times 7 \times 7 = 343$.

15. **A.** First, find the slope of line PQ. From point P to point Q, the rise is 7 and the run is 10, so the slope is $\frac{7}{10}$. Perpendicular lines have negative reciprocal slopes, so flip $\frac{7}{10}$ to get its reciprocal, $\frac{10}{7}$, then make it negative. So far, the equation of the answer is $y = -\frac{10}{7}x + b$. To find b, or the y-intercept, you can plug in (5, 3) to the equation and solve for b, because you know the point (5, 3) is on the new line. You get $\frac{71}{7}$. But looking at Choices (A) and (B) and sketching the new line is easier; its y-intercept is clearly going to be positive, not negative. So Choice (A) is the only possible answer.

If you struggled with a certain problem, go back and try estimating to see whether you can get the answer. Estimating is particularly helpful with geometry problems on the ISEE and SSAT. And if you're missing a fact or formula, flip back and look it up, and then try the problem again. Redoing problems you got wrong is a great idea, even if it's not that much fun.

Practicing Guided Upper Level Geometry Questions

For you upper level test-takers, here are some practice questions to hone your geometry skills. Even if you don't have any trouble with certain questions, it's helpful to read their answer explanations — you'll probably learn a few new things about the test.

1. In the figure shown, what is the value of x?

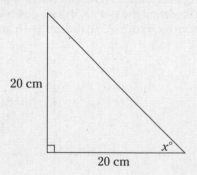

(A) 30

(B) 35

(C) 40

(D) 45

(E) It cannot be determined from the information given.

To solve for *x*, you need to realize that this triangle is an isosceles triangle. Therefore, the angles opposite the equal sides (20 cm) are the same. That tells you that the triangle's top angle and angle *x* are equal. Next, set up an equation, using the fact that 180 degrees are in a triangle: $x + x + 90 = 180$. Simplify to $2x = 90$, then divide both sides by 2 to get $x = 45$. If you recognized that this is a 45-45-90 degree triangle (because it's a right triangle with two equal sides), then bonus points for you! Either way, the answer is Choice **(D)**.

2. If a fence is built to enclose a rectangular yard with a length that is triple the yard's width and the fence is 96 feet long, what is the width of the yard?

(A) 6 ft

(B) 8 ft

(C) 10 ft

(D) 12 ft

(E) 36 ft

This is a perimeter question. Just like many word problems, you can test the answer choices here and see which one is a width that, when tripled and multiplied by 2, equals 96. Or you can make an equation. Call the width of the yard *x* and the length 3*x*. The perimeter is then 8*x*. And $8x = 96$, so $x = 12$, Choice **(D)**. If you picked Choice (E), you probably found the length of the yard instead of the width; remember to read what questions ask for carefully.

3. If an artist is cutting squares of wood that measure 5 centimeters on a side out of a piece of plywood that measures 80 centimeters by 120 centimeters, what is the greatest number of squares that can be cut?

(A) 9,600

(B) 1,920

(C) 384

(D) 192

This is an area question. You need to find the area of the big piece of wood as well as the area of the little piece of wood. Getting the area of a rectangle or square means multiplying its length by its width. The little piece is a square, so $5 \times 5 = 25$. The big piece is $80 \times 120 = 9{,}600$. Now, divide 9,600 by 25 to see how many little areas can be cut from the big area, and you get 384, Choice **(C)**. If you got Choice (B), you probably made the common mistake of getting the big area but then dividing it by the side length of the square, not by the square's area.

4. A store has circular rugs that come in three sizes: small, medium, and large. The diameter of the small rug is half the diameter of the medium rug, and the medium rug's diameter is half the diameter of the large rug. What is the ratio of the small rug's area to the large rug's area?

(A) $\frac{1}{4}$

(B) $\frac{1}{8}$

(C) $\frac{1}{16}$

(D) $\frac{1}{64}$

This problem is about area, but it's an algebra problem as well as a geometry problem. You can turn it into an arithmetic geometry problem by adding some numbers. For example, say the diameter of the small rug is 2. That makes the diameter of the medium rug 4 and the diameter of the large rug 8. Now, just calculate the areas of the small and large rugs using πr^2: The area of the small rug is π, and the area of the large rug is $\pi(4)^2 = 16\pi$. You can find the ratio of the small rug's area to the large rug's area, like so: $\frac{\text{small rug area}}{\text{large rug area}} = \frac{\pi}{16} = \frac{1}{16}$, Choice **(C)**.

5. In the figure shown, what is the length of line segment y in terms of x?

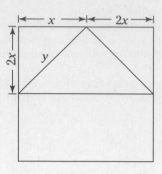

(A) $4x^2$

(B) $6x^2$

(C) $x\sqrt{5}$

(D) $x\sqrt{3}$

Like most questions with variables in the answer choices, you can use the picking-numbers-for-variables technique discussed in Chapter 14. Pick a number for the variable(s) in the choices first, and don't use 0 or 1. For example, say $x = 2$. On the figure, cross out x and write in a 2, then cross out $2x$ and write in a 4. Now, solve for y by using the Pythagorean theorem: $(2)^2 + (4)^2 = y^2$ then simplify to $y^2 = 20$. Next, $y = \sqrt{20}$. Now, break down $\sqrt{20} = \sqrt{4} \times \sqrt{5} = 2\sqrt{5}$. Now that you have a numerical answer to the question being asked, test the answer choices and see which one makes $2\sqrt{5}$ when x is 2, and you get Choice **(C)**.

6. A box has dimensions a, b, and c. If the lengths of the sides of the box are decreased by 20%, 40%, and 60%, respectively, the volume of the box decreases by about what percent?

(A) 21%

(B) 41%

(C) 61%

(D) 81%

(E) 91%

This problem is easier if you add numbers to it. Suppose the original box is $10 \times 10 \times 10$. The volume then is $10 \times 10 \times 10 = 1,000$. Decreasing 10 by 20 percent, 40 percent, and 60 percent, respectively, produces a new box with side lengths 8, 6, and 4 and a volume of 192. Use the percent increase/decrease formula $\left(\dfrac{\text{difference}}{\text{original}} \times 100 \right)$ to calculate the percent decrease. $\dfrac{1,000 - 192}{1,000} = \dfrac{808}{1,000} = 0.808$. Multiply 0.808 by 100 to get the approximate percent decrease: 81 percent, Choice **(D)**.

7. What is the minimum length of fencing needed to completely enclose a square area measuring 160 square feet?

(A) Less than 50 feet.

(B) Exactly 50 feet.

(C) More than 50 feet.

(D) There is not enough information given to determine the answer.

First, draw the square so you have a visual. It may be easiest to test the answer choices on a problem like this. Try Choice (B): If the length of the fence was exactly 50 feet, then each side would be 12.5 feet (50 ÷ 4). The area enclosed would be $12.5 \times 12.5 = 156.25$, a little bit short of what we need (160 feet), so the answer must be Choice **(C)**.

8. In the figure, which of the following distances is between 9 and 10?

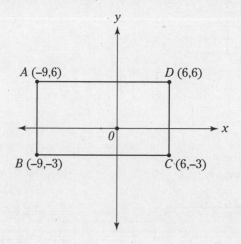

(A) *AO*

(B) *BO*

(C) *CO*

(D) *DO*

You can solve for all the lengths in the answer choices by using the Pythagorean theorem. First, draw the line segments on the figure. Then, look at the right triangles that are formed. Solve the right triangle formed with *BO* as its hypotenuse. One side is 3 (because point *B* is three down from the *x*-axis), and one side is 9 (because point *B* is nine along the *x*-axis to the left): $3^2 + 9^2 = (BO)^2$, so $(BO)^2 = 90$ and $BO = \sqrt{90}$. Knowing that the square root of 81 is 9 and the square root of 100 is 10, the square root of 90 must be between 9 and 10, so Choice **(B)** is correct.

Tackling Upper Level Geometry Questions on Your Own

Now that you've worked through a few guided practice geometry questions, it's time to do some by yourself. Review the four tips at the beginning of this chapter (read carefully, skip quickly if you don't know how to do it, use common sense, and write down your work) before you start. Practice good technique now so it's second nature when you have the actual test in front of you.

1. If the area of each grid square is 3 square centimeters, what is the area of the shaded region?

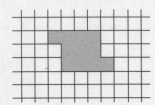

   (A) 27 cm²

   (B) 30 cm²

   (C) 33 cm²

   (D) 36 cm²

2. What is the value of $x - y$?

   (A) 0°

   (B) 30°

   (C) 40°

   (D) Not enough information is provided to answer the question.

3. A circular garden was enlarged by doubling its diameter. If the area of the original garden was M square meters, what is the area, in square meters, of the enlarged garden?

   (A) 2M

   (B) 3M

   (C) 4M

   (D) 8M

   (E) 16M

4. In the figure shown, what is the value of x?

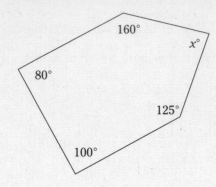

   (A) 65°

   (B) 75°

   (C) 85°

   (D) 95°

   (E) 105°

5. A high school track was designed by using a 50-meter by 100-meter rectangle with a semicircle with a 50-meter diameter on each end of the rectangle. If a runner runs two laps around the track, how many meters does she travel?

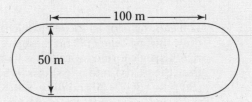

   (A) 25π m + 200 m

   (B) 50π m + 400 m

   (C) 100π m + 400 m

   (D) 200π m + 400 m

6. Which of the following is the graph of
    $y = -2x + 4$?

(A)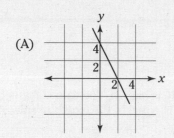

(B)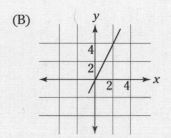

(C)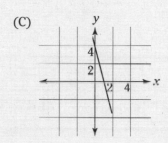

(D)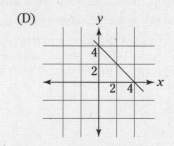

7. In the figure shown, what is the perimeter
    of rectangle *ABCD*?

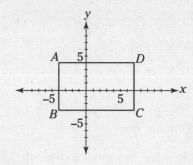

(A) 32

(B) 34

(C) 36

(D) 38

8. In the figure shown, there are four quarter
    circles, each with a radius of 2 inches, and a
    whole circle, also with a radius of 2 inches.
    What is the area of the shaded region?

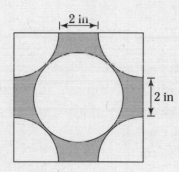

(A) $36 - 2\pi$

(B) $36 - 4\pi$

(C) $36 - 6\pi$

(D) $36 - 8\pi$

(E) $36 - 10\pi$

9. If the length of the base of a triangle is
    decreased by 20% and its height is increased
    by 30%, what happens to its area?

(A) + 2%

(B) + 4%

(C) + 6%

(D) No change

(E) – 2%

10. A rectangle has an area of 400 square inches. If the length and the width of the rectangle are measured in whole centimeters, what is the greatest possible perimeter of the rectangle?

    (A) 80 in

    (B) 100 in

    (C) 208 in

    (D) 401 in

    (E) 802 in

11. Triangle *ABC* is similar to triangle *XYZ*. What is the length of side *YZ*?

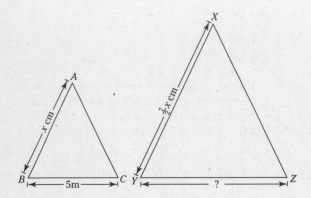

    (A) 12.5 cm

    (B) 15 cm

    (C) 17.5 cm

    (D) 20 cm

    (E) 22.5 cm

12. Which line, if graphed, would be parallel to $y = 7x - 7$?

    (A) $y = 14x - 14$

    (B) $y = 14x - 7$

    (C) $y = -\frac{1}{7}x - 7$

    (D) $y = -\frac{1}{7}x + 7$

    (E) $y = 7x$

13. Point $(-1, 5)$ is on a circle with center $(1, -1)$. What is the radius of the circle?

    (A) 6

    (B) $2\sqrt{10}$

    (C) 7

    (D) $4\sqrt{10}$

14. Triangle *ABC* is shown. The value of which expression is equal to the length of side *BC*?

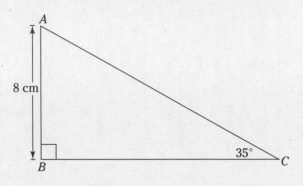

    (A) $\dfrac{8}{\tan 35°}$

    (B) $\dfrac{\tan 35°}{8}$

    (C) $\dfrac{8}{\sin 35°}$

    (D) $\dfrac{\sin 35°}{8}$

15. The formula for the volume of a cone with a circular base is $V = \frac{1}{3}\pi r^2 h$, where r is the radius of the base of the cone and h is the height of the cone. What is the volume of a cone with a height of 10 and a base with a circumference of 60π?

    (A) 600π

    (B) 900π

    (C) $3{,}000\pi$

    (D) $6{,}000\pi$

    (E) $9{,}000\pi$

Answers to Upper Level Geometry Questions

1. **C.** Count up the grid squares (there are 11) and multiply the total by 3 to get 33.

2. **A.** You don't know what either x or y is, but because the two triangles both have a 60 degree angle, and because they have the same angle where they meet, the third angles, x and y, must be equal.

3. **C.** Draw both gardens and pick a number for the original diameter that's easy to work with, like 4. The area of the original garden is then $\pi 2^2 = 4\pi$. The new garden's diameter is then 8, so its area is $\pi 4^2 = 16\pi$, or 4 times the original area.

4. **B.** The sum of the angles inside a figure is found by starting with 180 degrees — the sum of the angle measures in a triangle — then adding 180 degrees for each additional side beyond three. So for a five-sided figure, start with 180, and then add 360 because the five-sided figure has two more sides than a triangle. Subtract the known angle measures from 540, and you have 75, Choice (B).

5. **C.** First, calculate the distance around one of the semicircles by using the circle circumference formula ($2\pi r$). The radius of one of the semicircles is 25π, so the circumference is 50π if it's a whole circle. The total circumference of the two semicircles is 50π, so two laps is 100π. Count the straight sections of the track to get 400 more meters, so the correct answer is $100\pi + 400$ meters.

6. **A.** The y-intercept of the line is 4 and the slope is –2. The graph in Choice (A) checks out because its y-intercept is 4 and, if you find the slope between the points (0, 4) and (2, 0), you get –2.

7. **C.** Find the width by measuring how much of the y-axis the rectangle covers: It goes from a y-value of –3 to a y-value of 4, so its width is 7. It goes along the x-axis from –4 to 7, so its length is 11. Therefore, $7 + 11 + 7 + 11 = 36$.

8. **D.** Because the radius of each quarter circle is 2 inches and because there are 2 inches between each quarter circle, the square has a side length of 6. Its area is 36 square inches. To subtract the unshaded area: The middle circle has radius 2, so its area is 4π. Each of the quarter circles has an area of π, so they add up to 4π, making the total unshaded area equal to 8π. So, the answer is $36 - 8\pi$.

9. **B.** Put some numbers into this problem; make the base and height of the original triangle equal to 10, because taking percentages of 10 is easy. Doing so gives the original triangle an area of 50 (using $\frac{1}{2}bh$) and the new triangle a base of 8 and a height of 13, so its area is 52. The percent change from 50 to 52 is $\frac{\text{difference}}{\text{original}} \times 100 = \frac{2}{50} \times 100 = 4$ percent.

10. **E.** You may have to test the answer choices here and use a little trial and error. If you need a whole inch measurement for each side, a rectangle with a width of 1 inch and a length of 400 inches has an area of 400 square inches and a perimeter of 802 inches.

11. **C.** Similar triangles' sides have a common ratio. Find it by comparing two known sides. In the figure, you know the left sides of the triangles are x and $\frac{7}{2}x$, respectively, so the ratio of any side of the bigger triangle to the same side of the smaller triangle is $\frac{7}{2}$. So side YZ is $\frac{7}{2} \times 5 = \frac{35}{2} = 17.5$ cm.

12. **E.** Just look at the slopes of the lines: The slopes of parallel lines are equal. Because the lines are all in $y - mx + b$ form, you can see that Choice (E) and the original line both have a slope of 7.

13. **B.** Graph the points and connect them with a line, and then sketch the circle. That line is the hypotenuse of a right triangle. The bottom leg of the right triangle extends from $(-1, -1)$ to $(1, -1)$, so its length is 2. The left leg of the triangle extends up from $(-1, -1)$ to $(-1, 5)$, so its length is 6. Using the Pythagorean theorem, $2^2 + 6^2 = c^2$, so $c^2 = 40$, $c = \sqrt{40}$. Simplify: $\sqrt{40} = \sqrt{4} \times \sqrt{10} = 2\sqrt{10}$.

14. **A.** Use *SOH CAH TOA* for this problem. Because you have the opposite side from the 35 degree angle and you need to solve for the adjacent side to that angle, you have to use TOA. Tan = opposite ÷ adjacent, so $\tan 35° = \dfrac{8}{BC}$. Multiply both sides by BC and then divide both sides by $\tan 35°$, and you end up with $BC = \dfrac{8}{\tan 35°}$.

15. **C.** First, find the radius of the cone. The circumference of the base is 60π, so set that number equal to the circumference formula ($2\pi r$) and solve. The radius is 30. Now, just plug everything into the volume of a cone formula: $\dfrac{1}{3}\pi (30)^2 (10) = \dfrac{1}{3}\pi (900)(10) = \dfrac{1}{3}(9{,}000)\pi = \dfrac{9{,}000\pi}{3}$, which simplifies to $3{,}000\pi$.

If you can get through these geometry problems, you're ready for pretty much anything the ISEE or SSAT may throw at you. If you struggled with a certain kind of problem, do some review work with the concept and then redo the problem until you can figure it out more easily, so you're prepared for the practice tests later in the book and the actual test on test day.

Chapter 16

Cracking Word Problems and Quantitative Comparisons

In This Chapter

▶ Discovering ways to simplify wordy or complicated problems

▶ Reviewing the basics of word, graph, and chart problems

▶ Checking out quantitative comparison questions

The ISEE and SSAT are famous for including lots of word problems in their Math sections. In fact, when you take the test, you'll probably notice that not very many questions look like the ones your math teacher asks you to solve. Why? Well, the test-writers want to see whether you can apply the math you've learned. Whether you like word problems or not, you have to refine your skills if you want an impressive math score. Don't worry, though, we help you do that in this chapter.

Some math problems are composed solely of words. Others have charts with all kinds of information, not all of which is relevant to the problem. Still others have funky-looking graphs that you may have never seen before. You can probably bet than when you open the Math section on test day, at least one word problem will contain a setup you're unfamiliar with.

The good news: Within every word, graph, or chart problem lies a straightforward math question — you just have to dig for it. In this chapter, we guide you through the different types of word problems you'll encounter on the tests, and we help you figure out what the word problem is asking you to do and how to find the correct answer.

We review the four categories of word problems that cover the majority of those you'll see on the ISEE and SSAT:

✔ Arithmetic word problems

✔ Algebra word problems

✔ Graph and chart word problems

✔ Quantitative comparison word problems (which only appear on the middle and upper level ISEE)

Checking Out Some Basic Word Problem Strategies

Word problems can get pretty wordy — go figure! To understand what the question is asking and get started down the right path to finding the answer, follow these steps:

1. **Break it up.**

   Don't ever try to figure out a word problem all at once. Get your pencil moving and jot down relevant information as you read. Don't worry too much about *what* you write; the key is to get started and just take in a general idea of what the problem is about without figuring out everything right away. On really wordy problems, it may be useless to read the entire problem at once, because doing so will most likely overwhelm your short-term memory. On shorter ones, you may have to read the whole thing two or three times before you get it.

2. **Identify the skill.**

   Are you being asked to use a formula? Solve an equation? Remember a geometry rule? Knowing the problem category can help you select the right tool to solve the problem. Here's a quick refresher of word problem vocabulary:

   • Addition: Look for the words *sum* and *total*

   • Subtraction: Look for the words *less than* and *difference*

   • Multiplication: Look for the words *product* and *of* (*of* means *times*)

   • Division: Look for the words *per*, *percentage,* and *out of*

   • Unknowns: Look for variables such as *x* and the words *what* and *how many*

   • Equals: Look for the words *is* and *total*

3. **Estimate.**

   Just like most problems, estimating on word problems is a good idea so when you get an answer, you can tell whether your answer makes sense or is way off the mark.

4. **Start the problem!**

   If you're not sure where to start, at least do *something*. Move your pencil. Draw a picture. Solve for whatever you can. Most problems don't have irrelevant information, so chances are that the work you do will move you closer to the solution. If you just stare at the problem, you won't likely suddenly realize how to solve it. If you lose track of what you're doing, try refocusing on *what the question is asking* — which usually comes at the very end of the question.

5. **If you're still stuck, test the answer choices.**

   If the answer choices are numerical, try them out — one of them is right! In fact, this method can be easier than doing the problem like your math teacher would. Just pick a choice and test it, and if it doesn't work, test another one. This technique is particularly helpful with algebra word problems.

If you read a word problem that you just can't figure out how to do, skip it right then and there, circle it, or fill in a quick guess, and come back to it. Looking at problems with fresh eyes often makes them solvable.

A high school drama club is putting on a play at the end of the year and is planning to sell tickets for $10.00 each. The profit for the play is revenue minus cost. The cost of the play is estimated to be between $800.00 and $1,000.00 dollars. The drama club also estimates that between 500 and 600 people will attend the play. Which of the following estimates is closest to the expected profit for the play?

(A) $1,000.00

(B) $2,000.00

(C) $3,000.00

(D) $4,000.00

As you can see, that's a lot to digest! This question is about as wordy as a word problem gets, but it's a good example to break down. For this problem, you may write down "profit = rev – cost," "ticket = $10.00," "cost = about $900.00," and "number of tickets = about 550." To estimate the answer, you may not be able to guess very accurately, but you may see that selling 500 tickets at $10.00 = $5,000.00, and subtracting about $1,000.00 from that leaves about $4,000.00. You'll eventually get a more accurate answer, but having a ballpark figure helps. Make sure you estimate *before* you begin working the problem.

Calculating Arithmetic Word Problems

In arithmetic word problems, you don't have any unknowns to solve for or any geometry rules to remember. You usually just have to wade through the words to figure out what math to do. Here's an example of an arithmetic word problem:

At 6 a.m., the temperature outside the school measured 45 degrees Fahrenheit. At 9 a.m., the temperature measured 58 degrees Fahrenheit. How many degrees did the temperature outside the school increase between 6 a.m. and 9 a.m.?

Within this arithmetic word problem is a super-easy calculation (58 – 45), but that may not be completely obvious at first. A good place to focus is the numbers and what the question is asking. *How many degrees* tells you that you're looking for a number of degrees — so you can focus on the 58 and the 45. Then, you may focus on the *between 6 a.m. and 9 a.m.* and realize you're being asked about how the temperature changed.

This example is an easy one, but many arithmetic word problems are this simple when it comes down to it. Remember to focus on the numbers and what the question is asking you to find.

Ferrin had $150.00 to spend. She spent half the money on a new dress and then half of what was left on a new pair of shoes. How much money did she have left?

Again, the calculation involved here is simple: 150 ÷ 2 = 75, then 75 ÷ 2 = 37.50. Practicing turning word problems into math expressions is a valuable skill. If you get stuck, think about what operation is happening. Is something being added, subtracted, multiplied, or divided? Notice that you can translate *half the money* to $150.00 ÷ 2.

Working through Algebra Word Problems

Many word problems involve at least a little bit of algebra, which just means that the problem includes an unknown quantity. If you're going to solve the problem by writing an equation, you probably want to start with the unknown quantity and call it *x*. Often, the problem asks you to supply the unknown quantity as the answer.

Two common algebra word problems involve averages and rates of time or speed. We discuss those in the following sections.

Finding the average

When a word problem asks you to find the average of a set of numbers, the easiest way to solve the problem is to set up an *average equation,* which is the different amounts added up, divided by how many amounts there are. Here's an example:

A basketball player has played in eight games and has an average points-per-game of 10. What is the least number of points he must score in the ninth game to raise his average to 11?

(A) 12

(B) 14

(C) 16

(D) 19

Here, the unknown quantity is the number of points the basketball player has to score in the ninth game. Start off by calling that number x. Next, set up an *average equation* because the problem deals with an average.

A little trick for this average problem and those like it: Assume the basketball player scored ten points in *each* of the first eight games. You can get away with this assumption because his average is 10. It doesn't matter if he scored fewer or more points than 10 in any of the first eight games because his average is 10 either way. So your average equation should look something like this:

$$\frac{10+10+10+10+10+10+10+10+x}{9}=11$$

You add eight 10s and the x on top of the fraction to represent the first eight games and the unknown score of the ninth game. You divide by 9 because there are nine games to average, and you know that by setting the average equal to 11, it gives you the lowest number of points the player can score in the ninth game and still average 11 points.

Simplifying here means multiplying both sides of the equation by 9:

$$10 + 10 + 10 + 10 + 10 + 10 + 10 + 10 + x = 99$$

Next, add the 10s to get $80 + x = 99$ and subtract 80 from both sides to end up with $x = 19$.

You could have just tested the answer choices here. Say, for example, you thought the answer was 16. If you averaged eight 10s plus 16, you'd realize you were short of 11 and then would probably test 19 next.

Testing the middle answer choice (B or C) first can tell you whether you need to test a bigger or smaller choice and, therefore, save you time.

A key to solving this problem is recognizing what tool to use — in this case, the problem mentioned averages, so you use an average equation. Even if worse came to worst and you blanked on how to do the problem, you could have logically assumed that the player would have to score quite a few more points than 10 in the ninth game to raise his average a point, because he had eight games of 10 points weighting the average pretty heavily at 10.

Discovering the distance, rate, or time

Another common algebraic word problem type is rate. If you see a *rate,* like miles per hour, in a problem, you'll probably be using the formula *distance = rate × time*.

A car is driving down a highway. In three hours, it travels 140 miles. What is the car's approximate average speed?

(A) 40 mph

(B) 47 mph

(C) 50 mph

(D) 57 mph

Plug the numbers in to the formula: 140 miles = *rate* × 3 hours. Then, divide both sides by 3 to get the car's average speed, 46.7 miles per hour, which is closest to Choice **(B)**.

You also could have tested answer choices here. If you wanted to test 50 miles per hour as the answer, you'd multiply 50 by 3 and see whether it equaled 140. Because the answer (150) is too high, you'd probably try a smaller answer choice.

Interpreting Graph and Chart Problems

Lots of different-looking graphs can appear on the SSAT and ISEE. The ISEE, in particular, is famous for using a wide variety of graphs and charts. When it comes down to it, though, graphs and charts are just ways of displaying information to make it easier to understand. So even on the weirdest charts and graphs, keep in mind that someone thought showing the information in that way was useful!

Here are a few quick tips about charts and graphs:

- ✔ **Look at the headings of charts and the axes (the horizontal and vertical lines) of graphs.** Their labels (things like time, speed, height, and so on) give you important information about the data being displayed.

- ✔ **Notice the units being displayed.** Are the data in hours? Minutes? Seconds? Knowing the units will help you keep track.

- ✔ **Zero in on the information you're being asked to find, often, a certain number.** Don't worry about taking every single thing in.

Many charts and graphs fall into two categories: *x*- and *y*-axis graphs and tables, as we explore in the next sections.

x- and y-axis graphs

On graphs with an *x*- and *y*-axis, you usually see a title and two perpendicular lines, each labeled in a certain way. The *x*-, or horizontal, axis may measure something like time (marked off in hours or minutes) or something like quantity (marked off every 10 or 100). The *y*-axis (vertical line) may measure similar things. The data points on an *x*- and *y*-axis graph show what the *y* value is for a certain *x* value, and vice versa. Here's an example:

An airplane's altitude was measured over the course of an hour, and the data was recorded on the graph. Between which intervals did the airplane's altitude increase the most quickly?

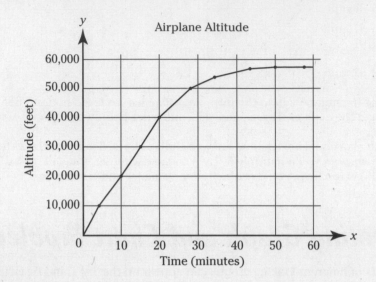

(A) 10 min and 20 min

(B) 20 min and 30 min

(C) 30 min and 40 min

(D) 40 min and 50 min

Notice the axes first: the *x*-axis displays time, and the *y*-axis displays altitude (height). The points on the graph show the time at which a certain altitude was recorded. For example, the point at (10 minutes, 20,000 feet) tells you that at 10 minutes, the altitude of the plane was 20,000 feet. The line connecting the points shows the trend of the data.

Looking at the graph, the plane goes from 20,000 feet to 40,000 feet in the interval between 10 and 20 minutes, which is the biggest change in a 10-minute interval when compared to the other answer choice intervals.

Tables

Tables are usually pretty simple. On a table, you usually see a title and data presented in labeled rows and columns. Here's an example:

Based on the data, what will be the expected temperature of the bucket in the sunny spot at 2 p.m.?

Bucket Water Temperature		
Time	*Sunny Spot*	*Shady Spot*
9 a.m.	60°F	55°F
10 a.m.	65°F	58°F
11 a.m.	70°F	61°F
12 p.m.	75°F	64°F

(A) 75°F

(B) 80°F

(C) 85°F

(D) 90°F

Paying attention to the title of the chart, "Bucket Water Temperature," is important and so is looking at the labels (to realize that the table is measuring temperature over time). Then, you need to notice the pattern of the data: The temperature of the water in the sunny spot increases by 5 degrees every hour. Knowing this, you can predict that in two hours, its temperature will increase by 10 degrees from 75 degrees Fahrenheit to 85 degrees Fahrenheit.

Answering Quantitative Comparison Word Problems

In the Quantitative Reasoning sections of the middle and upper levels of the ISEE, you'll see quantitative comparison questions, such as the following example. These questions ask you to compare numbers or expressions in two columns to determine which one is bigger.

Column A	Column B
2	3

The directions and answer choices for this type of question are always the same:

🖙 Mark Choice (A) if the quantity in Column A is greater.

🖙 Mark Choice (B) if the quantity in Column B is greater.

🖙 Mark Choice (C) if the two quantities are equal.

🖙 Mark Choice (D) if the relationship cannot be determined from the information given.

Mark Choice (A) if the quantity in Column A is *always* greater, and mark Choice (B) if the quantity in Column B is *always* greater. We say *always* because on certain questions involving unknowns, Column A is bigger if you use a certain number, but Column B is bigger if you use a different number. In those cases, the answer is Choice (D) because it depends on what number you use.

For the preceding question, 3 is obviously bigger than 2, so the correct answer is Choice **(B)**. However, things get a little trickier when variables get involved.

Column A	Column B
x	$x - x$

If you assume x is 2, the quantity in Column A is 2, and the quantity in Column B becomes $2 - 2 = 0$. If $x = 2$, Column A is bigger. However, if you chose -2 for x, Column A is -2, and Column B is $-2 - (-2) = 0$, so in that case, Column B is bigger. The correct answer for this example is Choice **(D)**.

When variables are under the columns, plug in your own numbers for the variables. The best numbers to plug in are -1, 0, and 1 because they're easy to calculate with. And in a problem like the preceding one, they expose it for the can't-be-determined question it is. Make sure you try each of the three numbers (-1, 0, and 1) in those cases to see whether you get a different result with a different number or if the result is always the same.

Mike has $0.57 in coins.

Column A	Column B
The smallest number of coins Mike can have	5

This question isn't much different than a typical ISEE question. All you have to do is find the number for Column A and compare it to the number in Column B.

If Mike has two quarters, one nickel, and two pennies, he has five coins — the smallest number of coins that can add up to $0.57. So the answer to this one is Choice **(C)**, the quantities are equal.

In some questions, using logic is better than doing all the math. Consider the following question:

Column A	Column B
-4^4	$(-4)^4$

Rather than write out $4 \times 4 \times 4 \times 4$, think about the question first. You may notice that in Column A, if you follow PEMDAS, you're going to have a negative number, because the negative is applied *after* the 4^4.

In Column B, you may remember that a negative number raised to an even exponent results in a positive number ($-2 \times -2 = 4$). So the quantity in Column B is positive. At this point, you're done with the question: A positive number is bigger than a negative number, so the answer is Choice **(B)**.

Part IV
SSAT Practice Exams

In this part . . .

Part IV provides three full-length SSAT practice exams: one upper level and two lower level exams. Each practice exam is followed by an answer chapter that gives you the answer to every question along with an explanation. Remember: Perfect practice makes perfect!

Chapter 17

SSAT Upper Level Practice Exam

• •

*T*ime for a full practice exam for you SSAT upper level students! Although taking a practice test may not sound like a lot of fun, you want to do well on the exam, and practicing the test is one of the best ways to make sure you know your stuff. To make the most of this practice exam, find yourself a quiet room, ample time, a few sharpened pencils, and some blank scratch paper. Resist the urge to play on the Internet or text your friends while you're taking the test. After all, you want to practice in the same quiet and boring conditions that you'll face on test day.

Grab a watch, an iPod, a phone, or some other way to track your time. Make sure you don't go over the time limit we've given you for each part of this practice test because you won't be allowed extra time on the actual test. You can find all the answers to this practice test in Chapter 18, but don't cheat! You'll learn more by struggling through a question than by looking up the answer. Check your answers only *after* you finish the test.

Answer Sheet

For Section 1, use two loose-leaf or lined notebook pages to write your writing sample. (On the real exam, the answer booklet contains two lined sheets.) For Sections 2 through 5 of the exam, use the following answer sheets and fill in the answer bubble for the corresponding number, using a #2 pencil.

Section 2: Quantitative, Part 1

1. Ⓐ Ⓑ Ⓒ Ⓓ Ⓔ   6. Ⓐ Ⓑ Ⓒ Ⓓ Ⓔ   11. Ⓐ Ⓑ Ⓒ Ⓓ Ⓔ   16. Ⓐ Ⓑ Ⓒ Ⓓ Ⓔ   21. Ⓐ Ⓑ Ⓒ Ⓓ Ⓔ
2. Ⓐ Ⓑ Ⓒ Ⓓ Ⓔ   7. Ⓐ Ⓑ Ⓒ Ⓓ Ⓔ   12. Ⓐ Ⓑ Ⓒ Ⓓ Ⓔ   17. Ⓐ Ⓑ Ⓒ Ⓓ Ⓔ   22. Ⓐ Ⓑ Ⓒ Ⓓ Ⓔ
3. Ⓐ Ⓑ Ⓒ Ⓓ Ⓔ   8. Ⓐ Ⓑ Ⓒ Ⓓ Ⓔ   13. Ⓐ Ⓑ Ⓒ Ⓓ Ⓔ   18. Ⓐ Ⓑ Ⓒ Ⓓ Ⓔ   23. Ⓐ Ⓑ Ⓒ Ⓓ Ⓔ
4. Ⓐ Ⓑ Ⓒ Ⓓ Ⓔ   9. Ⓐ Ⓑ Ⓒ Ⓓ Ⓔ   14. Ⓐ Ⓑ Ⓒ Ⓓ Ⓔ   19. Ⓐ Ⓑ Ⓒ Ⓓ Ⓔ   24. Ⓐ Ⓑ Ⓒ Ⓓ Ⓔ
5. Ⓐ Ⓑ Ⓒ Ⓓ Ⓔ   10. Ⓐ Ⓑ Ⓒ Ⓓ Ⓔ   15. Ⓐ Ⓑ Ⓒ Ⓓ Ⓔ   20. Ⓐ Ⓑ Ⓒ Ⓓ Ⓔ   25. Ⓐ Ⓑ Ⓒ Ⓓ Ⓔ

Section 3: Reading Comprehension

1. Ⓐ Ⓑ Ⓒ Ⓓ Ⓔ   11. Ⓐ Ⓑ Ⓒ Ⓓ Ⓔ   21. Ⓐ Ⓑ Ⓒ Ⓓ Ⓔ   31. Ⓐ Ⓑ Ⓒ Ⓓ Ⓔ
2. Ⓐ Ⓑ Ⓒ Ⓓ Ⓔ   12. Ⓐ Ⓑ Ⓒ Ⓓ Ⓔ   22. Ⓐ Ⓑ Ⓒ Ⓓ Ⓔ   32. Ⓐ Ⓑ Ⓒ Ⓓ Ⓔ
3. Ⓐ Ⓑ Ⓒ Ⓓ Ⓔ   13. Ⓐ Ⓑ Ⓒ Ⓓ Ⓔ   23. Ⓐ Ⓑ Ⓒ Ⓓ Ⓔ   33. Ⓐ Ⓑ Ⓒ Ⓓ Ⓔ
4. Ⓐ Ⓑ Ⓒ Ⓓ Ⓔ   14. Ⓐ Ⓑ Ⓒ Ⓓ Ⓔ   24. Ⓐ Ⓑ Ⓒ Ⓓ Ⓔ   34. Ⓐ Ⓑ Ⓒ Ⓓ Ⓔ
5. Ⓐ Ⓑ Ⓒ Ⓓ Ⓔ   15. Ⓐ Ⓑ Ⓒ Ⓓ Ⓔ   25. Ⓐ Ⓑ Ⓒ Ⓓ Ⓔ   35. Ⓐ Ⓑ Ⓒ Ⓓ Ⓔ
6. Ⓐ Ⓑ Ⓒ Ⓓ Ⓔ   16. Ⓐ Ⓑ Ⓒ Ⓓ Ⓔ   26. Ⓐ Ⓑ Ⓒ Ⓓ Ⓔ   36. Ⓐ Ⓑ Ⓒ Ⓓ Ⓔ
7. Ⓐ Ⓑ Ⓒ Ⓓ Ⓔ   17. Ⓐ Ⓑ Ⓒ Ⓓ Ⓔ   27. Ⓐ Ⓑ Ⓒ Ⓓ Ⓔ   37. Ⓐ Ⓑ Ⓒ Ⓓ Ⓔ
8. Ⓐ Ⓑ Ⓒ Ⓓ Ⓔ   18. Ⓐ Ⓑ Ⓒ Ⓓ Ⓔ   28. Ⓐ Ⓑ Ⓒ Ⓓ Ⓔ   38. Ⓐ Ⓑ Ⓒ Ⓓ Ⓔ
9. Ⓐ Ⓑ Ⓒ Ⓓ Ⓔ   19. Ⓐ Ⓑ Ⓒ Ⓓ Ⓔ   29. Ⓐ Ⓑ Ⓒ Ⓓ Ⓔ   39. Ⓐ Ⓑ Ⓒ Ⓓ Ⓔ
10. Ⓐ Ⓑ Ⓒ Ⓓ Ⓔ   20. Ⓐ Ⓑ Ⓒ Ⓓ Ⓔ   30. Ⓐ Ⓑ Ⓒ Ⓓ Ⓔ   40. Ⓐ Ⓑ Ⓒ Ⓓ Ⓔ

Section 4: Verbal

1. Ⓐ Ⓑ Ⓒ Ⓓ Ⓔ	13. Ⓐ Ⓑ Ⓒ Ⓓ Ⓔ	25. Ⓐ Ⓑ Ⓒ Ⓓ Ⓔ	37. Ⓐ Ⓑ Ⓒ Ⓓ Ⓔ	49. Ⓐ Ⓑ Ⓒ Ⓓ Ⓔ
2. Ⓐ Ⓑ Ⓒ Ⓓ Ⓔ	14. Ⓐ Ⓑ Ⓒ Ⓓ Ⓔ	26. Ⓐ Ⓑ Ⓒ Ⓓ Ⓔ	38. Ⓐ Ⓑ Ⓒ Ⓓ Ⓔ	50. Ⓐ Ⓑ Ⓒ Ⓓ Ⓔ
3. Ⓐ Ⓑ Ⓒ Ⓓ Ⓔ	15. Ⓐ Ⓑ Ⓒ Ⓓ Ⓔ	27. Ⓐ Ⓑ Ⓒ Ⓓ Ⓔ	39. Ⓐ Ⓑ Ⓒ Ⓓ Ⓔ	51. Ⓐ Ⓑ Ⓒ Ⓓ Ⓔ
4. Ⓐ Ⓑ Ⓒ Ⓓ Ⓔ	16. Ⓐ Ⓑ Ⓒ Ⓓ Ⓔ	28. Ⓐ Ⓑ Ⓒ Ⓓ Ⓔ	40. Ⓐ Ⓑ Ⓒ Ⓓ Ⓔ	52. Ⓐ Ⓑ Ⓒ Ⓓ Ⓔ
5. Ⓐ Ⓑ Ⓒ Ⓓ Ⓔ	17. Ⓐ Ⓑ Ⓒ Ⓓ Ⓔ	29. Ⓐ Ⓑ Ⓒ Ⓓ Ⓔ	41. Ⓐ Ⓑ Ⓒ Ⓓ Ⓔ	53. Ⓐ Ⓑ Ⓒ Ⓓ Ⓔ
6. Ⓐ Ⓑ Ⓒ Ⓓ Ⓔ	18. Ⓐ Ⓑ Ⓒ Ⓓ Ⓔ	30. Ⓐ Ⓑ Ⓒ Ⓓ Ⓔ	42. Ⓐ Ⓑ Ⓒ Ⓓ Ⓔ	54. Ⓐ Ⓑ Ⓒ Ⓓ Ⓔ
7. Ⓐ Ⓑ Ⓒ Ⓓ Ⓔ	19. Ⓐ Ⓑ Ⓒ Ⓓ Ⓔ	31. Ⓐ Ⓑ Ⓒ Ⓓ Ⓔ	43. Ⓐ Ⓑ Ⓒ Ⓓ Ⓔ	55. Ⓐ Ⓑ Ⓒ Ⓓ Ⓔ
8. Ⓐ Ⓑ Ⓒ Ⓓ Ⓔ	20. Ⓐ Ⓑ Ⓒ Ⓓ Ⓔ	32. Ⓐ Ⓑ Ⓒ Ⓓ Ⓔ	44. Ⓐ Ⓑ Ⓒ Ⓓ Ⓔ	56. Ⓐ Ⓑ Ⓒ Ⓓ Ⓔ
9. Ⓐ Ⓑ Ⓒ Ⓓ Ⓔ	21. Ⓐ Ⓑ Ⓒ Ⓓ Ⓔ	33. Ⓐ Ⓑ Ⓒ Ⓓ Ⓔ	45. Ⓐ Ⓑ Ⓒ Ⓓ Ⓔ	57. Ⓐ Ⓑ Ⓒ Ⓓ Ⓔ
10. Ⓐ Ⓑ Ⓒ Ⓓ Ⓔ	22. Ⓐ Ⓑ Ⓒ Ⓓ Ⓔ	34. Ⓐ Ⓑ Ⓒ Ⓓ Ⓔ	46. Ⓐ Ⓑ Ⓒ Ⓓ Ⓔ	58. Ⓐ Ⓑ Ⓒ Ⓓ Ⓔ
11. Ⓐ Ⓑ Ⓒ Ⓓ Ⓔ	23. Ⓐ Ⓑ Ⓒ Ⓓ Ⓔ	35. Ⓐ Ⓑ Ⓒ Ⓓ Ⓔ	47. Ⓐ Ⓑ Ⓒ Ⓓ Ⓔ	59. Ⓐ Ⓑ Ⓒ Ⓓ Ⓔ
12. Ⓐ Ⓑ Ⓒ Ⓓ Ⓔ	24. Ⓐ Ⓑ Ⓒ Ⓓ Ⓔ	36. Ⓐ Ⓑ Ⓒ Ⓓ Ⓔ	48. Ⓐ Ⓑ Ⓒ Ⓓ Ⓔ	60. Ⓐ Ⓑ Ⓒ Ⓓ Ⓔ

Section 5: Quantitative, Part 2

1. Ⓐ Ⓑ Ⓒ Ⓓ Ⓔ	6. Ⓐ Ⓑ Ⓒ Ⓓ Ⓔ	11. Ⓐ Ⓑ Ⓒ Ⓓ Ⓔ	16. Ⓐ Ⓑ Ⓒ Ⓓ Ⓔ	21. Ⓐ Ⓑ Ⓒ Ⓓ Ⓔ
2. Ⓐ Ⓑ Ⓒ Ⓓ Ⓔ	7. Ⓐ Ⓑ Ⓒ Ⓓ Ⓔ	12. Ⓐ Ⓑ Ⓒ Ⓓ Ⓔ	17. Ⓐ Ⓑ Ⓒ Ⓓ Ⓔ	22. Ⓐ Ⓑ Ⓒ Ⓓ Ⓔ
3. Ⓐ Ⓑ Ⓒ Ⓓ Ⓔ	8. Ⓐ Ⓑ Ⓒ Ⓓ Ⓔ	13. Ⓐ Ⓑ Ⓒ Ⓓ Ⓔ	18. Ⓐ Ⓑ Ⓒ Ⓓ Ⓔ	23. Ⓐ Ⓑ Ⓒ Ⓓ Ⓔ
4. Ⓐ Ⓑ Ⓒ Ⓓ Ⓔ	9. Ⓐ Ⓑ Ⓒ Ⓓ Ⓔ	14. Ⓐ Ⓑ Ⓒ Ⓓ Ⓔ	19. Ⓐ Ⓑ Ⓒ Ⓓ Ⓔ	24. Ⓐ Ⓑ Ⓒ Ⓓ Ⓔ
5. Ⓐ Ⓑ Ⓒ Ⓓ Ⓔ	10. Ⓐ Ⓑ Ⓒ Ⓓ Ⓔ	15. Ⓐ Ⓑ Ⓒ Ⓓ Ⓔ	20. Ⓐ Ⓑ Ⓒ Ⓓ Ⓔ	25. Ⓐ Ⓑ Ⓒ Ⓓ Ⓔ

Section 1

Writing Sample

Time: 25 minutes

Directions: You have 25 minutes to complete a writing sample based on the following essay topic. Use only two pages for your sample. You may use scratch paper to organize your thoughts before you begin writing.

   Topic: Discussing a disagreement is more important than solving it.

Assignment: Do you agree or disagree with this statement? Support your position with personal examples, examples of others, or examples from current news topics or history.

STOP DO NOT TURN THE PAGE UNTIL TOLD TO DO SO.
DO NOT RETURN TO A PREVIOUS TEST.

Section 2

Quantitative, Part 1

Time: 30 Minutes

Directions: You have 30 minutes to complete the following 25 questions. Work each problem in your head or in the blank space on the page. Then, look at the answer options and decide which one is best. Mark your answer to each question in the corresponding answer bubble on the answer sheet for Section 2.

1. Molly is planning a birthday party and wants to give each of the 23 guests two party favors. If the party favors come in packages of 5, how many packages does she need to buy?

    (A) 4

    (B) 5

    (C) 9

    (D) 10

    (E) 11

2. If Carl has 98 marbles and Jane has 42 marbles, how many marbles must Carl give to Jane so they have an equal number of marbles?

    (A) 16

    (B) 28

    (C) 36

    (D) 48

    (E) 56

3.

4. Kaitlin has a bag of marbles with 7 blue marbles and 28 red marbles. Bill has a bag of marbles with 8 blue marbles and 32 red marbles. Marvin has a bag with 9 blue marbles and 36 red marbles. If each person picks one marble out of his or her bag without looking, who has the greatest chance of picking a blue marble?

   (A) Kaitlin.

   (B) Bill.

   (C) Marvin.

   (D) They all have the same chance of picking a blue marble.

   (E) There is not enough information given to answer.

5. There are x more zebras than hippos at the San Diego Zoo. The zoo has two hippos. How many zebras does it have?

   (A) $x - 2$

   (B) $2 + x$

   (C) $x \div 2$

   (D) $2 - x$

   (E) $2 \div x$

6. Taylor folds several circular sheets of paper in half as shown in the following figure. Without rotating the paper, she then cuts through both layers of the folded pieces of paper with scissors to produce different shapes. When the shapes are unfolded, they can be each of the following *except*

(A)

(B)

(C)

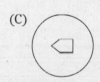

(D)

(E)

Go on to next page

7. Which of the following can be the value of Y if $\frac{2}{7} + Y < 1$?

(A) $\frac{4}{5}$

(B) $\frac{5}{7}$

(C) $\frac{3}{4}$

(D) $\frac{7}{9}$

(E) $\frac{2}{3}$

8. Fifteen tennis balls are placed in a box as illustrated in the figure. Each ball touches other balls or a side of the box in four places. If the diameter of each ball is 2.5 inches, which of the following can be the length and width of the box?

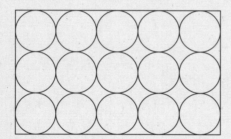

(A) 6.5 in x 11.5 in

(B) 7.5 in x 10.5 in

(C) 7.5 in x 12.5 in

(D) 9.5 in x 12.5 in

(E) 10 in x 15 in

9. Each digit is represented by a letter. In the following multiplication problem, what must be true?

$$
\begin{array}{r}
C\,D \\
\times\ A\,B \\
\hline
F\,E\,A \\
B\,H\,G\ \ \\
\hline
B\,D\,F\,A
\end{array}
$$

(A) Nine different digits appear in the calculation.

(B) $B = 1$

(C) $F + H < 10$

(D) $B = 3$

(E) $B + D + F + A < 14$

10. At Skyview High School, 245 ninth graders are waiting for buses to take them on a field trip. If at least 10 but no more than 60 students must go on each bus and no two buses have the same number of students, what is the smallest number of buses needed for the field trip?

(A) 4

(B) 5

(C) 6

(D) 7

(E) 8

11. If $X + Y = 18$ and $2Z + Y = 18$, what is the value of Z?

(A) 0

(B) 4.5

(C) 9

(D) −3

(E) It cannot be determined from the information given.

Go on to next page

12. On the coordinate plane shown, which point has an *x*-coordinate that is double the *x*-coordinate of point *A* and a *y*-coordinate that is triple the *y*-coordinate of point *A?*

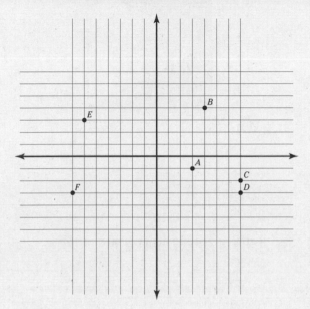

   (A) *F*

   (B) *B*

   (C) *C*

   (D) *D*

   (E) *E*

13. 98,765 ÷ 4,321 is closest to

   (A) 2.3

   (B) 3

   (C) 23

   (D) 30

   (E) 228

14. At a fruit stand, bananas are $0.50 each and apples are $0.60 each. If an equal number of apples and bananas exist and it costs $6.60 to buy all the apples and bananas, how many bananas are at the fruit stand?

   (A) 5

   (B) 6

   (C) 10

   (D) 11

   (E) 12

15. In the front yard of a school, an oak tree is 100 meters from the flagpole and a birch tree is 70 meters from the same flagpole. How many miles apart are the two trees?

   (A) 30

   (B) 60

   (C) 85

   (D) 170

   (E) It cannot be determined from the information given.

16. If half the weight of a blue whale is 75 tons, the weight of three blue whales can be calculated by multiplying 75 tons by

   (A) 0.5

   (B) 2

   (C) 3

   (D) 6

   (E) 7.5

17. Which of the following must be true if two numbers, *x* and *y*, have an average of 80 and *y* is less than *x?*

   (A) $x - 80 = 80 - y$

   (B) $x - 80 + y$

   (C) $x + y = 80$

   (D) $x - y = 40$

   (E) $x = 80$ and $y = 80$

Go on to next page

18. Each side of the cross in the figure is the same whole number of inches in length. If four square pieces, each measuring a whole number of inches in length, were added to the cross to form a square, which of the following can be the area of that square?

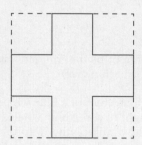

(A) 25

(B) 30

(C) 35

(D) 40

(E) 45

Questions 19–20 use the following definition:
$x^\wedge = x \div 10$

19. If $x^\wedge = 30$, then $x =$

(A) 3

(B) 10

(C) 100

(D) 300

(E) 30,000

20. $10^\wedge(10^\wedge) =$

(A) 0.001

(B) 0.01

(C) 0.1

(D) 1

(E) 10

21. If this figure is a square, what is the area of the unshaded region?

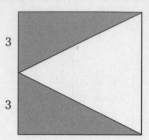

(A) 9

(B) 12

(C) 15

(D) 18

(E) 36

22. If 80% of $2y$ is 40, what is 40% of $4y$?

(A) 25

(B) 40

(C) 50

(D) 60

(E) 80

23. In the figure, if $y = 2z$, which of the following gives the value of x in terms of z?

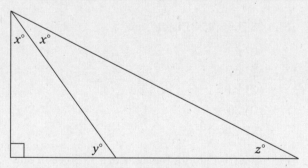

Note: Figure not drawn to scale.

(A) $\frac{z}{2}$

(B) $\frac{z}{3}$

(C) $\frac{z}{4}$

(D) $90 - 2z$

(E) $90 - \frac{z}{2}$

Go on to next page

24. If the average of six consecutive whole numbers is 11.5, what is the smallest number?

   (A) 6

   (B) 7

   (C) 8

   (D) 9

   (E) 10

25. On Saturday, a movie theater's ticket price was $12.00 and its total ticket sales totaled $12,492.00. If on Sunday, the owner wants to lower the ticket price by $3.00 but needs to make $12,492.00 or more, what is the minimum number of tickets the theater needs to sell?

   (A) 1,041

   (B) 1,042

   (C) 1,388

   (D) 1,389

   (E) 1,492

STOP DO NOT TURN THE PAGE UNTIL TOLD TO DO SO. DO NOT RETURN TO A PREVIOUS TEST.

Section 3

Reading Comprehension

Time: 40 minutes

Directions: You have 40 minutes to complete this section. Read each passage and answer the questions about the passage that follow. Mark your answer to each question in the corresponding answer bubble on the answer sheet for Section 3.

In the 1890s, railroad expansion was <u>prolific</u> in the United States because the rail system meant a new world that connected various geographic areas of the country. The expansion efforts inevitably led a rail system from Kansas City to Port Arthur, Texas, as a means to provide access to the Gulf of Mexico. This rail system led through Arkansas and notably the Ouachita Mountain range. During this time, a flat area on top of Rich Mountain, a 2,681 foot ridge, was discovered, boasting magnificent views. This area came to the attention of a group of Dutch investors who built a Victorian hotel full of the day's high-society splendor, including rich appointments, maid services, and even *water closets* — the early form of today's restrooms. The Dutch investors named the inn *Wilhelmina Inn* after the newly crowned Dutch queen. Patrons referred to the lavish structure as the *Castle in the Sky*. However, the grandeur of the inn lasted only three years. After railroad financial difficulty, the investors abandoned the inn, and it fell into disrepair over the years. Sheep and other animals even roamed throughout the hotel, and by the 1930s, only a portion of the building was still standing. Not until 1963 was a new inn built on the site and opened to the public. The area eventually became an Arkansas state park where, this day, visitors can still see the striking views and stay in the inn. The town of Mena, which sits at the base of Rich Mountain, provides access to everything else vacationers may need.

1. What is the passage's primary purpose?

   (A) To persuade readers to visit Wilhelmina Inn

   (B) To explain how early Dutch settlers remembered their heritage

   (C) To show early decline in the railroad system

   (D) To describe the history of Wilhelmina Inn

   (E) To explain how Wilhelmina Inn was rebuilt

2. What does the author most likely mean by the word *prolific?*

   (A) Expensive

   (B) Occurring often

   (C) Overly ambitious

   (D) Fast-paced

   (E) Destructive

3. Which can be considered a unique feature of the hotel?

   (A) Victorian decoration

   (B) Water closets

   (C) Expansive ballroom

   (D) Rare dining experiences

   (E) Entertainment

4. Why did the investors name the inn after Queen Wilhelmina?

   (A) She helped fund the hotel construction.

   (B) The town, Mena, was already named after her.

   (C) They were Dutch.

   (D) The hotel was decorated in the style of her palace.

   (E) The text does not say.

Go on to next page

5. Which of the following questions is answered by the passage?

   (A) How did the Wilhelmina Inn become a state park?

   (B) How did Dutch investors become wealthy?

   (C) How did the railroad change America?

   (D) Why were lavish hotels so popular in the early 1900s?

   (E) How did Arkansas attract tourism?

Satire is a form of writing that makes fun of a person or a group. Although good-natured jabbing is a common part of our culture, satirical writing has been used to explore weaknesses in political agendas and other governmental agencies for many, many years. Of course, satire is not exactly good natured in that satirical writing depends heavily on ridicule, exaggeration, sarcasm, and irony to point out weakness in action, thought, or idealism. Although satirical writing and even cartoons continue to be a part of the political <u>landscape</u> in a free society, one cannot say this form of writing is free from <u>defamation</u> because of its very nature.

6. What is the author's tone in this passage?

   (A) Neutral

   (B) Positive

   (C) Expository

   (D) Argumentative

   (E) Fearful

7. When the author uses the word *landscape*, what does he likely mean?

   (A) The nature of

   (B) The area of

   (C) The wealth of

   (D) The description of

   (E) The definition of

8. What does the author most likely mean by the term *defamation?*

   (A) Determination

   (B) Malpractice

   (C) Defunct

   (D) Maliciousness

   (E) Responsibility

9. According to the passage, all the following are true, *except*

   (A) Satirical writing is beyond good-natured fun.

   (B) Satirical writing has been used for a long time.

   (C) Satirical writing includes cartoons.

   (D) Satire is necessary in a free society.

   (E) Satire is common in a free society.

10. Which of the following statements are true according to the passage?

    I.   Satire may use irony.

    II. Satire is often political.

    III. Satire helps reform politics.

    IV. Satire is not free from responsibility.

    (A) I and II only

    (B) III only

    (C) IV only

    (D) II, III, IV only

    (E) I, II, IV only

Go on to next page

The colored part of the human eye is often considered one of the most attractive facial features. However, this area, called the *iris*, serves a much greater purpose than simple decoration. The iris controls the level of light the eye has inside at any given time. In the center of the eye, the round opening, or *pupil*, allows light to enter the eye. The iris contains a sphincter muscle around the edge of the pupil that can dilate or constrict. In bright light, the muscle contracts, which constricts the pupil and prevents too much light from entering the eye. In low light, the muscle dilates so more light enters the eye. This automatic constriction and dilation allows people to see in a variety of circumstances, from bright sunlight to very dim lighting. The iris itself is flat in shape, and the color of the iris comes from very small pigment cells called *melanin*. Although many characteristics of the iris are inherited, the actual color, texture, and even pattern of the iris are unique to each individual, in much the same way other physical characteristics are unique.

11. This passage is mainly about

(A) The pupil's function

(B) The purpose of the iris

(C) Light inside the eye

(D) Structure of the iris

(E) Unique physical characteristics

12. According to the passage, the pupil

(A) Controls incoming light

(B) Reflects incoming light

(C) Allows incoming light

(D) Processes incoming light

(E) Refracts incoming light

13. How can you simplify the sentence, "The iris contains a sphincter muscle around the edge of the pupil that can dilate or constrict"?

(A) The iris controls the pupil's function.

(B) The iris can become larger or smaller, depending on lighting conditions, as it reacts to the amount of light.

(C) A muscle in the iris enlarges or shrinks the pupil.

(D) A muscle in the iris enables it to widen or narrow around the pupil.

(E) The pupil's muscle causes it to change shape.

14. From the passage, you can infer that melanin

(A) Varies in different people

(B) Provides dark colors

(C) Provides light colors

(D) Contains muscle tissue

(E) Exists only in the iris

15. Concerning color, texture, and pattern, you can compare the iris to

(A) Eyelashes

(B) Fingerprints

(C) Toenails

(D) Skin color

(E) Hair

Go on to next page

The Maya civilization, known as a Mesoamerican civilization and found in parts of Mexico, Belize, Guatemala, and other central American countries, was one of the most advanced and interesting cultures of the time. The Mayans constructed enormously complex temples and other smaller buildings, many of which are still standing in present day. Aside from their architectural skill, the Mayans are noted for having a written language and skill in art and science, especially in astronomy. The Mayan cities reached their pinnacle of success during the Classic period, about 250 to 900 AD. The Mayans were generally ruled by a small hierarchy of leaders and priests, often ruling over cities and small geographic areas, rather than any centralized government. From Mayan pictorial text, known as <u>codices</u>, archeologists have learned that the Mayan people lived an agricultural lifestyle that centered around worship and the cycles of nature. Although a complete understanding of Mayan religious beliefs is not known, from codices, we know the Mayans practiced human sacrifice as a part of their worship of various gods. Although the civilization was very advanced, the culture declined during the eighth and ninth centuries, with most of the great cities seemingly abandoned. No definite explanation exists for the decline, but many theories have been suggested.

16. How can the Mayan system of government be characterized?

    (A) A kingdom

    (B) Democratic

    (C) Centralized leadership

    (D) Local rule and control

    (E) Township

17. According to the text, how can *codices* be explained?

    (A) Spoken language

    (B) Books

    (C) Instructional materials

    (D) Written language

    (E) Information through drawings

18. With which of the following statements would the author most likely agree?

    (A) Although skilled at architecture, the Mayans lacked skill in reading and writing.

    (B) The decline of the Mayan culture occurred over time in the same manner that other civilizations have declined.

    (C) The Mayan culture depended on slave labor.

    (D) The abrupt decline of the Mayan civilization is difficult to understand, considering the advanced nature of the society.

    (E) From codices, we know the Mayan culture was cruel.

19. According to the passage, all the following are true, *except*

    (A) The Mayan civilization was primarily agricultural.

    (B) The Mayans were skilled in astronomy.

    (C) The Mayans were skilled in architecture.

    (D) The Mayans worshipped a primary god.

    (E) The Mayans had a written language.

20. What would the author most likely discuss next?

    (A) Spanish conquests

    (B) Agricultural techniques

    (C) Specific elements of worship

    (D) Architectural details

    (E) Theories of Mayan decline

Go on to next page ⟶

The following passage is taken from the Declaration of Independence.

When, in the course of human events, it becomes necessary for one people to dissolve the political bands which have connected them with another, and to assume among the powers of the earth, the separate and equal station to which the laws of nature and of nature's God entitle them, a decent respect to the opinions of mankind requires that they should declare the causes which impel them to the separation.

We hold these truths to be self-evident, that all men are created equal, that they are endowed by their Creator with certain unalienable rights, that among these are life, liberty and the pursuit of happiness. That to secure these rights, governments are instituted among men, deriving their just powers from the consent of the governed. That whenever any form of government becomes destructive to these ends, it is the right of the people to alter or to abolish it, and to institute new government, laying its foundation on such principles and organizing its powers in such form, as to them shall seem most likely to affect their safety and happiness. Prudence, indeed, will dictate that governments long established should not be changed for light and transient causes; and accordingly all experience hath shown that mankind are more disposed to suffer, while evils are sufferable, than to right themselves by abolishing the forms to which they are accustomed. But when a long train of abuses and usurpations, pursuing invariably the same object evinces a design to reduce them under absolute despotism, it is their right, it is their duty, to throw off such government, and to provide new guards for their future security. Such has been the patient sufferance of these colonies; and such is now the necessity which constrains them to alter their former systems of government. The history of the present King of Great Britain is a history of repeated injuries and usurpations, all having in direct object the establishment of an absolute tyranny over these states.

21. Which statement best describes the meaning of the underlined passage in the first paragraph?

   (A) God entitles freedom through nature.

   (B) Human events in politics naturally unfold.

   (C) People are entitled to freedom by God and nature itself.

   (D) The God of nature entitles people.

   (E) No single person has the right to control another.

22. What is the best explanation for the term *self-evident?*

   (A) Restricted

   (B) True for all people

   (C) Needing explanation

   (D) Obvious

   (E) Needing evidence

23. What does the word *unalienable* mean in the context of this passage?

   (A) Not foreign

   (B) Inseparable

   (C) Not distinguished

   (D) Not disclosed

   (E) Without fear

24. Concerning the passage, all the following are true, *except*

   (A) The British Empire has taken away basic rights.

   (B) The colonies have an allegiance to Britain.

   (C) Governments are used to maintain the rights of people.

   (D) Political affiliations can be dissolved.

   (E) People have rights.

Go on to next page

25. What does the passage mean by the word *tyranny?*

    (A) Rule

    (B) Oppression

    (C) Governmental control

    (D) Legal status

    (E) Divine intervention

26. How can you describe the organization of this passage?

    (A) Facts, argument

    (B) Introduction, facts, conclusion

    (C) Introduction, history

    (D) Introduction, definition

    (E) Introduction, definition, action

Edgar Allan Poe was an American short story writer and poet, as well as a literary critic. He was part of the art, literary, and intellectual revolt known as the Romantic Movement, which spanned the latter half of the 18th century. Poe's work most often focused on the <u>macabre</u> and functioned as a precursor to today's horror genre, although he also wrote mystery tales. Poe was one of the first American writers to attempt to earn a living through writing alone, and his life was known for financial struggle and difficulty because of this fact. Poe's poem "The Raven" is one of his most famous works and became immediately popular after its publication. Yet the popularity of many of his works did little to truncate the poverty and tragedy that seemed to follow Poe throughout his life. His wife, Virginia, died around the age of 25 from tuberculosis. Poe died at the age of 40, and although the cause of his death is unknown, speculation included alcoholism, drug abuse, and suicide. Newspaper articles reporting his death often used phrases, such as *congestion of the brain,* as the cause, though these phrases were merely <u>euphemisms</u> of the time used to report a death of an unseemly nature. Despite the tragedy, Poe's work remained popular during his time and is still widely read today, making him one of the more notable writers of the Romantic Movement.

27. This passage is primarily about

    (A) Poe's life and death

    (B) Poe's creation of a new genre

    (C) Poe's personal problems

    (D) Poe's financial troubles

    (E) Poe's editorial work

28. From the passage, what can you infer that the word *macabre* most likely has to do with?

    (A) Overcoming failure

    (B) Spirituality

    (C) Death

    (D) Romance

    (E) Mythical beings

29. Considering Poe's financial difficulties, what can you infer from the passage?

    (A) Only newspaper writers made good money.

    (B) Writing was lucrative to only the very talented.

    (C) Most writers during the Romantic Movement made a living in other occupations.

    (D) Poe's writing was too hard to understand for the average reader.

    (E) Poe did not write enough to earn a consistent income.

30. From the passage, how can you define the word *euphemism?*

    (A) A deliberate attempt to complicate a matter

    (B) An expression for something not understood

    (C) A gentle way of saying something unpleasant

    (D) A method of stating the obvious

    (E) A speculation

Go on to next page

31. The author's attitude toward Poe can best be described as

(A) Gentle

(B) Indifferent

(C) Accusatory

(D) Celebratory

(E) Disinterested

32. What would the author most likely write about next?

(A) Additional details about Poe's financial troubles

(B) Additional details about Poe's wife

(C) Additional details about the Romantic Movement

(D) Additional theories about his death

(E) Additional details about some of Poe's more popular works

---

The following passage is taken from Ronald Reagan's first presidential inaugural address.

The business of our nation goes forward. These United States are confronted with an economic affliction of great proportions. We suffer from the longest and one of the worst sustained inflations in our national history. It distorts our economic decisions, penalizes thrift, and crushes the struggling young and the fixed-income elderly alike. It threatens to shatter the lives of millions of our people.

Idle industries have cast workers into unemployment, causing human misery and personal indignity. Those who do work are denied a fair return for their labor by a tax system which penalizes successful achievement and keeps us from maintaining full productivity.

But great as our tax burden is, it has not kept pace with public spending. For decades, we have piled deficit upon deficit, mortgaging our future and our children's future for the temporary convenience of the present. To continue this long trend is to guarantee tremendous social, cultural, political, and economic upheavals.

You and I, as individuals, can, by borrowing, live beyond our means, but for only a limited period of time. Why, then, should we think that collectively, as a nation, we are not bound by that same limitation?

We must act today in order to preserve tomorrow. And let there be no misunderstanding — we are going to begin to act, beginning today.

The economic ills we suffer have come upon us over several decades. They will not go away in days, weeks, or months, but they will go away. They will go away because we, as Americans, have the capacity now, as we have had in the past, to do whatever needs to be done to preserve this last and greatest bastion of freedom.

In this present crisis, government is not the solution to our problem.

From time to time, we have been tempted to believe that society has become too complex to be managed by self-rule, that government by an elite group is superior to government for, by, and of the people. But if no one among us is capable of governing himself, then who among us has the capacity to govern someone else? All of us together, in and out of government, must bear the burden. The solutions we seek must be equitable, with no one group singled out to pay a higher price.

Go on to next page

We hear much of special interest groups. Our concern must be for a special interest group that has been too long neglected. It knows no sectional boundaries or ethnic and racial divisions, and it crosses political party lines. It is made up of men and women who raise our food, patrol our streets, man our mines and our factories, teach our children, keep our homes, and heal us when we are sick — professionals, industrialists, shopkeepers, clerks, cabbies, and truckdrivers. They are, in short, "We the people," this breed called Americans.

33. Why does Reagan refer to the economic crisis as an affliction?

   (A) Because the problem causes pain and suffering.

   (B) It is a disease like in nature.

   (C) As a way to motivate the audience.

   (D) Because the situation is accidental.

   (E) It implies wrong doing.

34. According to the passage, what is one of the reasons for the economic problems Reagan mentions?

   (A) Big business

   (B) Lazy workers

   (C) Taxes

   (D) Angry Americans

   (E) Lack of motivation

35. How does Reagan make a point that public spending is out of control?

   (A) Individuals would not be able to live beyond their means as the government does.

   (B) He mentions wasteful programs.

   (C) He mentions a lack of oversight.

   (D) The government does not maintain a balanced budget.

   (E) The government supports too many people through public assistance.

36. Concerning government debt, who does Reagan say must be a part of the solution?

   (A) Industry

   (B) Big business

   (C) Congress

   (D) The president

   (E) The American people

37. What special interest group does Reagan refer to in this passage?

   (A) Retail

   (B) Farmers

   (C) Economists

   (D) Military

   (E) Americans

38. According to the passage, all the following are true, *except*

   (A) The economic problems occurred during the previous administration.

   (B) The economic problems are solvable.

   (C) Americans must play a part in the economic solution.

   (D) Government cannot solve the problem alone.

   (E) Taxation contributes to the problem.

39. What may you expect Reagan to discuss next in his speech?

   (A) How he will change the presidency

   (B) Administrative goals

   (C) Solutions for the present economic problem

   (D) His work with congress

   (E) A new tax law

40. Which of the following best expresses the main idea of the passage?

   (A) Economic problems abound.

   (B) The American people must work to resolve the economic problem.

   (C) The previous administration is to blame.

   (D) Taxation must be changed.

   (E) Government is the solution to the problem.

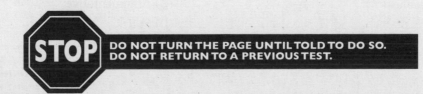

STOP DO NOT TURN THE PAGE UNTIL TOLD TO DO SO.
DO NOT RETURN TO A PREVIOUS TEST.

Section 4

Verbal

Time: 30 Minutes

Directions: You have 30 minutes to complete 30 synonym questions and 30 analogy questions. Choose the best answer for each question. Mark your answer to each question in the corresponding answer bubble on the answer sheet for Section 4.

Questions 1–30 contain one word followed by five words or phrases. Select the word or phrase whose meaning is closest to the word in capital letters.

1. BEVY:
   (A) Determination
   (B) Travel
   (C) Adjustment
   (D) Panel
   (E) Group

2. SACRED:
   (A) Whimsical
   (B) Placid
   (C) Sacrosanct
   (D) Pure
   (E) Free

3. MAVERICK:
   (A) Rebel
   (B) Alderman
   (C) Professional
   (D) Apprentice
   (E) Benefactor

4. NUANCE:
   (A) Signal
   (B) Value
   (C) Difference
   (D) Design
   (E) Disjointedness

5. REPLETE:
   (A) Repetitive
   (B) Full
   (C) Synchronized
   (D) Dejected
   (E) Cunning

6. GENUINE:
   (A) Well mannered
   (B) Kind
   (C) Replicate
   (D) Bona fide
   (E) Happy

7. PANACHE:
   (A) Tiredness
   (B) Pristine
   (C) Elegance
   (D) Furtiveness
   (E) Blasé

8. LACKLUSTER:
   (A) Dull
   (B) Shiny
   (C) Stained
   (D) Dirty
   (E) Friendly

9. BRUSQUE:
   (A) Trite
   (B) Abrupt
   (C) Argumentative
   (D) Stiff
   (E) Unfriendly

Go on to next page

10. TENABLE:
    (A) Discerning
    (B) Frustrating
    (C) Unstable
    (D) Valid
    (E) Dangerous

11. FASTIDIOUS:
    (A) Critical
    (B) Having little
    (C) To conserve
    (D) Trying
    (E) Fearful

12. GAUNT:
    (A) Disagreeable
    (B) Kind
    (C) Beneficial
    (D) Athletic
    (E) Thin

13. IMPROPER:
    (A) Immoral
    (B) Illicit
    (C) Jocund
    (D) Perilous
    (E) Prevalent

14. UNILATERAL:
    (A) Demure
    (B) Exclusive
    (C) Inclusive
    (D) One-sided
    (E) Branded

15. INSENSITIVE:
    (A) Callous
    (B) Endearing
    (C) To jeer
    (D) Respite
    (E) Formidable

16. OBVIOUS:
    (A) Blatant
    (B) Disjointed
    (C) Secretive
    (D) Expressive
    (E) Delightful

17. VACUOUS:
    (A) Insidious
    (B) Lacking
    (C) Charming
    (D) Sterile
    (E) Trustworthy

18. BILK:
    (A) Ascribe
    (B) Cheat
    (C) Frequent
    (D) Chat
    (E) Pressure

19. FAKE:
    (A) Genial
    (B) Treacherous
    (C) Bogus
    (D) Demure
    (E) Willing

20. OBDURATE:
    (A) Determined
    (B) Frustrating
    (C) Challenging
    (D) Stubborn
    (E) Willing

21. UBIQUITOUS:
    (A) Giving up
    (B) Stranded
    (C) Enormous
    (D) Large
    (E) Everywhere

Go on to next page

22. PLACID:
    (A) Calm
    (B) Unnerved
    (C) Speechless
    (D) Trivial
    (E) Extrapolative

23. PALTRY:
    (A) Detailed
    (B) Tired
    (C) Insignificant
    (D) Fitting
    (E) Remorseful

24. BLITHE:
    (A) Carefree
    (B) Diseased
    (C) Troublesome
    (D) Disastrous
    (E) Perfunctory

25. COVERT:
    (A) Finite
    (B) Critical
    (C) Undercover
    (D) Spacious
    (E) Notable

26. CANVASS:
    (A) Bright
    (B) Airy
    (C) Covering
    (D) Crowd
    (E) Survey

27. PLAUDIT:
    (A) Resistant
    (B) Praise
    (C) Trifle
    (D) Lacking hope
    (E) Mystic

28. LOQUACIOUS:
    (A) Benign
    (B) Contrary
    (C) Demanding
    (D) Talkative
    (E) Spiteful

29. RISQUÉ:
    (A) Indecent
    (B) Risky
    (C) Resilient
    (D) Random
    (E) Regulative

30. HAPLESS:
    (A) Messy
    (B) Unhappy
    (C) Unlucky
    (D) Clumsy
    (E) Carefree

Questions 31–60 ask you to find the relationships between words. For each question, choose the answer choice that has the same kind of relationship.

31. Heat is to sun as
    (A) Brush is to cat
    (B) Fish is to lure
    (C) Toaster is to oven
    (D) Steam is to locomotive
    (E) Moon is to ocean

32. Surfboard is to wave as
    (A) Street is to sign
    (B) Car is to wheel
    (C) Skateboard is to pavement
    (D) Engine is to gasoline
    (E) Icing is to doughnut

Go on to next page

33. Heater is to hot tub as
    (A) Rock is to sand
    (B) Ink is to printer
    (C) Shell is to beach
    (D) Moss is to rock
    (E) Photo is to frame

34. Smoke is to fire as
    (A) Spider is to bite
    (B) Ketchup is to bottle
    (C) Exhaust is to car
    (D) Jug is to water
    (E) Razor is to beard

35. Light bulb is to electricity as
    (A) Candy is to wrapper
    (B) Barn is to hay
    (C) Star is to constellation
    (D) Cow is to graze
    (E) Yo-yo is to string

36. Needle is to thread as
    (A) Diamond is to jeweler
    (B) Truck is to trailer
    (C) Glass is to liquid
    (D) Sign is to street
    (E) Dirt is to shoe

37. Occasional is to frequent as
    (A) Difficult is to easy
    (B) Seldom is to rarely
    (C) Chatty is to devious
    (D) Daily is to regular
    (E) Grim is to blight

38. Bombastic is to quiet as
    (A) Fearful is to anxious
    (B) Sentiment is to caring
    (C) Demure is to crass
    (D) Work is to money
    (E) Cruel is to mean

39. Switch is to light as
    (A) Wind is to current
    (B) Travel is to destination
    (C) Plan is to action
    (D) Actor is to movie
    (E) Steering wheel is to car

40. Evolve is to dismantle as
    (A) Predict is to withhold
    (B) Determine is to flee
    (C) Cringe is to retreat
    (D) Falter is to surrender
    (E) Return is to advance

41. Sugar is to gum as
    (A) Flour is to cake
    (B) Wind is to branch
    (C) Cheese is to mouse
    (D) Grass is to mower
    (E) Sun is to grass

42. Hypothesis is to test as
    (A) Cake is to bake
    (B) Track is to train
    (C) Slim is to large
    (D) Ice is to flavor
    (E) Corn is to yellow

43. Crafty is to cunning as tragic is to
    (A) Anticipation
    (B) Expected
    (C) Destination
    (D) Calamitous
    (E) Reality

44. Congenial is to agreeable as stoical is to
    (A) Difficult
    (B) Blind
    (C) Unemotional
    (D) Unending
    (E) Finite

Go on to next page

45. Treaty is to peace as exercise is to
    (A) Challenge
    (B) Stretching
    (C) Pain
    (D) Sweat
    (E) Fitness

46. Enormous is to miniscule as eradicate is to
    (A) Establish
    (B) Support
    (C) Define
    (D) Passive
    (E) Design

47. Mower is to grass as
    (A) Syrup is to pancake
    (B) Pan is to cookie
    (C) Clock is to time
    (D) Wheel is to tire
    (E) Spoon is to cup

48. Tile is to floor as book is to
    (A) Shelf
    (B) Page
    (C) Reader
    (D) Words
    (E) Author

49. Least is to most as
    (A) Doctor is to medicine
    (B) Grand is to unimpressive
    (C) Paper is to scissors
    (D) Sign is to direction
    (E) Crowd is to passengers

50. Muscle is to movement as
    (A) Dream is to wake
    (B) Drive is to notion
    (C) House is to room
    (D) TV is to picture
    (E) Battery is to watch

51. Coat is to winter as
    (A) Alligator is to teeth
    (B) Marker is to paper
    (C) Psychiatrist is to mind
    (D) Geologist is to rock
    (E) Food is to cook

52. Jury is to trial as
    (A) Mail is to delivery
    (B) Rain is to water
    (C) Battery is to engine
    (D) Hot is to pain
    (E) Chocolate is to sweet

53. Ocean is to island as glass is to
    (A) Shape
    (B) Liquid
    (C) Shatter
    (D) Bend
    (E) Clear

54. Demonstrative is to feeling as pensive is to
    (A) Altruistic
    (B) Expectant
    (C) Careless
    (D) Willful
    (E) Serious

55. Fluctuation is to interval as
    (A) Staple is to paper
    (B) Jaunt is to window
    (C) Challenge is to relationship
    (D) Stumble is to jump
    (E) Pine is to fall

56. Interloper is to guest as division is to
    (A) Reluctance
    (B) Anger
    (C) Math
    (D) Whole
    (E) Part

Go on to next page

57. Dejected is to demoralize as callous is to
    (A) Vex
    (B) Indurate
    (C) Reject
    (D) Inlay
    (E) Shear

58. Satiate is to satisfy as gregarious is to
    (A) Social
    (B) Simple
    (C) Context
    (D) Hermit
    (E) Urban

59. Ice is to cold as empathy is to
    (A) Emphatic
    (B) Caring
    (C) Memory
    (D) Usable
    (E) Sequence

60. Impulsive is to calculated as concrete is to
    (A) Antithesis
    (B) Benign
    (C) Retaliate
    (D) Subjective
    (E) Strength

STOP DO NOT TURN THE PAGE UNTIL TOLD TO DO SO.
DO NOT RETURN TO A PREVIOUS TEST.

Section 5

Quantitative, Part 2

> **Time:** 30 Minutes
>
> **Directions:** You have 30 minutes to complete 25 questions. Work each problem in your head or in the blank space on the page. Then, look at the answer options and decide which one is best. Mark your answer to each question in the corresponding answer bubble on the answer sheet for Section 5.

1. When 8,906 is divided by 403, the result is closest to
   (A) 2
   (B) 4
   (C) 10
   (D) 20
   (E) 22

2. If $0.1 \times N = 50$, then $50 + N =$
   (A) 50.1
   (B) 500
   (C) 500.1
   (D) 550
   (E) 550.1

3. $2,800 - 400 - \dfrac{2}{30} =$
   (A) $2,399\dfrac{9}{15}$
   (B) $2,399\dfrac{14}{15}$
   (C) $2,400\dfrac{9}{15}$
   (D) $2,400\dfrac{14}{15}$
   (E) $2,401\dfrac{14}{15}$

4. How many 1.25-inch pieces can a 1-foot ruler be cut into?
   (A) 8
   (B) 9
   (C) 9.6
   (D) 10.4
   (E) 10.8

5. $0.035 \times 3,500 =$
   (A) 0.125
   (B) 1.25
   (C) 12.5
   (D) 122.5
   (E) 1225

6. If $N > 25$, then $2N + 25$ can be
   (A) 0
   (B) 74
   (C) 74.99
   (D) 75
   (E) 75.01

7. $22\dfrac{3}{8} + 21\dfrac{1}{8} + 23\dfrac{7}{8} =$
   (A) $66\dfrac{3}{8}$
   (B) $66\dfrac{5}{8}$
   (C) $66\dfrac{7}{8}$
   (D) $67\dfrac{3}{8}$
   (E) $67\dfrac{5}{8}$

8. The average weight of three cars is 2,200 pounds and the average weight of two trucks is 4,300 pounds. What is the average weight of all five vehicles?
   (A) 3,000 lbs
   (B) 3,040 lbs
   (C) 3,250 lbs
   (D) 3,400 lbs
   (E) 3,650 lbs

Go on to next page

9. All the following products are equal *except*

   (A) $7 \times \frac{4}{7}$

   (B) $14 \times \frac{3}{7}$

   (C) $21 \times \frac{2}{7}$

   (D) $42 \times \frac{1}{7}$

   (E) $84 \times \frac{1}{14}$

10. 16 is 8% of

    (A) 20

    (B) 100

    (C) 120

    (D) 200

    (E) 400

11. In the number 12,345,678, how many times the value of the 8 is the 2?

    (A) 25,000

    (B) 100,000

    (C) 250,000

    (D) 1,000,000

    (E) 2,500,000

12. Alicia paid $380.00 for 100 square feet of carpet. What was her approximate cost per square inch?

    (A) $3.80

    (B) $0.38

    (C) $0.26

    (D) $0.03

    (E) $0.02

13. A taxi costs $2.50 for the first $\frac{1}{4}$ mile and $0.25 for each additional $\frac{1}{8}$ mile. How many miles can a customer go for $20.00?

    (A) 7

    (B) 8

    (C) 9

    (D) 10

    (E) 11

14. A runner took between $3\frac{1}{2}$ and 4 hours to run 26.2 miles. Which range best describes his average speed, in miles per hour?

    (A) between 5.5 and 6.5 mph

    (B) between 6 and 7 mph

    (C) between 6.5 and 7.5 mph

    (D) between 7 and 8 mph

    (E) between 7.5 and 8.5 mph

15. Mallory's average lap time, after running 8 laps of a 400-meter track, was 1 minute and 10 seconds. How long did it take her to run all 8 laps?

    (A) 4 min, 40 sec

    (B) 8 min, 40 sec

    (C) 9 min, 20 sec

    (D) 10 min, 8 sec

    (E) 12 min, 40 sec

16. In the figure, if three lines meet as shown, what is the value of $x + y$?

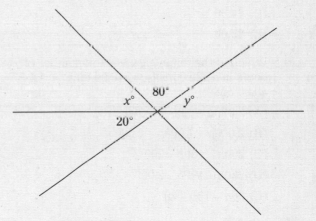

    (A) 80

    (B) 90

    (C) 100

    (D) 110

    (E) 120

Go on to next page

17. $8,624 \div 4 =$

    (A) $\dfrac{8,000}{4} \times \dfrac{600}{4} \times \dfrac{20}{4} \times \dfrac{4}{4}$

    (B) $\dfrac{8,000}{4} + \dfrac{600}{4} + \dfrac{20}{4} + \dfrac{4}{4}$

    (C) $\dfrac{8,000}{4} + \dfrac{60}{4} + \dfrac{24}{4}$

    (D) $\dfrac{8,000}{4} + \dfrac{600}{4} + 24$

    (E) $\dfrac{8,000}{4} + \dfrac{6}{4} + \dfrac{2}{4} + \dfrac{4}{4}$

18. There are 235 students in Jessica's grade. When she collected $2.50 from each student to pay for a present, she found that she had only $\dfrac{1}{3}$ of the money needed to pay for the present. How much more money must she collect from each student to pay for the present?

    (A) $3.00
    (B) $3.50
    (C) $4.00
    (D) $4.50
    (E) $5.00

19. Which of the following gives the number of cents in a $20.00 bills, b $10.00 bills, and 4 $5.00 bills?

    (A) $2,000a + 1,000b + 200$
    (B) $2,000a + 1,000b + 2,000$
    (C) $200a + 100b + 200$
    (D) $200a + 100b + 2,000$
    (E) $20a + 10b + 20$

20. A field has a perimeter of 868 feet. If the town wants to build a fence surrounding the field and each fence segment is 7 feet in length, how many fence segments are needed?

    (A) 94
    (B) 103
    (C) 114
    (D) 121
    (E) 124

21. Marty puts $18,500.00 in the bank in an account that earns 2% annual interest. How much interest will Marty earn in one year?

    (A) $3.70
    (B) $37.00
    (C) $74.00
    (D) $370.00
    (E) $740.00

22. Which of the following numbers is evenly divisible by 3?

    (A) 7,259
    (B) 7,269
    (C) 7,279
    (D) 7,289
    (E) 7,309

23. In a certain town, each of the 7,950 households owns either a computer or a television, or both. If 7,900 households own computers and 7,900 own televisions, how many households own both?

    (A) 50
    (B) 100
    (C) 7,850
    (D) 7,900
    (E) 7,950

24. Four friends split the cost of dinner and each paid $17.25. How much would each person pay if the same dinner was split between six people?

    (A) $11.50
    (B) $11.67
    (C) $12.25
    (D) $12.75
    (E) $13.75

25. If $0 < x < 1$, which of the following is greatest?

    (A) $10x$
    (B) $100x$
    (C) $\dfrac{x}{10}$
    (D) $\dfrac{x}{100}$
    (E) $\dfrac{x}{0.001}$

STOP   DO NOT TURN THE PAGE UNTIL TOLD TO DO SO.
DO NOT RETURN TO A PREVIOUS TEST.

Chapter 18

Answers to SSAT Upper Level Practice Exam

• •

*N*ow that you've finished taking the SSAT Upper Level Practice Exam, spend time reading through the answers and explanations we provide in this chapter. Doing so is a great way to find out what you missed and why. Also, reading through *all* the explanations — even for the questions you got right — only increases your learning and understanding and helps you prepare even more for test day. If you just want to do a quick check of your answers, see the abbreviated answer key at the end of this chapter.

Section 1: Writing Sample

Remember that writing samples for the SSAT don't have right or wrong answers, and with this topic (discussion is more important than a solution), you can write about a variety of issues. So don't get caught up in thinking, "Did I write what they wanted?" because truthfully, the readers of your writing sample aren't concerned about your point of view. They simply want to see that you can organize your thoughts, show your writer's voice, and write a strong essay.

With that thought in mind, the following are a few things you should have done to write a winning essay for your practice test. (For more valuable tips on writing an effective essay and some examples, check out Chapter 8.)

✔ Because the essay prompt asks you to agree or disagree with the statement, "Discussing a disagreement is more important than solving it," you should have made clear in your introduction what position you're taking — whether you agree or disagree with the statement. Simply talking about *conversations* and *solutions* won't cut it here because you're asked to agree or disagree with the provided statement.

✔ Your body paragraphs should have included specific examples that help back up or *prove* your position. These examples can be of a famous person, such as a sports star or a talented actor or singer, or a character from a book you read who realized either the art of discussion or a specific solution resolved an issue. If you use a character from a book or story on the actual test, make sure you include the name of the character and mention the name of the story or book.

✔ To really hit a home run with this essay, you should have included an example from your own life. Did you write about a time where talking about something with other people led to greater understanding, or if you disagreed with the statement, did you show how a specific solution resolved a problem or issue? Remember that the readers want to hear your voice. Including a personal story or experience is a great way to make a writing sample really come to life for the reader.

✔ You should have included a conclusion that brought your ideas together and again affirmed your position on the essay. Conclusions help show that your thoughts and ideas are organized and that you stuck with the topic, so don't forget about the conclusion when you write.

Finally, have someone else read your essay and mark misspelled words, poorly organized sentences, misplaced commas, and other grammatical problems. Doing so helps you see how many errors you made. Remember that the writing sample isn't a grammar test, and a few errors won't hurt you in the end, but overall, your sample should be well written and generally error free.

Section 2: Quantitative, Part 1

1. **D.** Because 23 people are coming and each person gets two party favors, Molly needs a total of $23 \times 2 = 46$ party favors. Because nine packages of five favors equals 45 favors ($9 \times 5 = 45$), she needs ten packages.

2. **B.** You have two ways to go about finding this answer. Either test the answer choices (probably the easier of the two approaches) or set up an equation ($98 - x = 42 + x$, where x is the number of marbles that Carl loses and also the number of marbles that Jane gains) and then solve for x. Subtracting 42 from both sides leaves $56 - x = x$; then adding x to both sides leaves $56 = 2x$. Divide both sides by 2 to end up with $x = 28$.

3. **A.** Notice that the second figure in the question is the first figure rotated one turn clockwise (or 90 degrees clockwise). Choice (A) is the third figure in the question turned 90 degrees clockwise.

4. **D.** The probability of each person picking a blue marble is found by dividing what you want (the number of blue marbles) by the total possibilities (the total number of marbles in the bag). So $\frac{7}{28}$, $\frac{8}{32}$, and $\frac{9}{36}$ all reduce to $\frac{1}{4}$, so each person has the same chance.

5. **B.** This is a variables-in-choices question. Start by picking a number for x (don't pick 0 or 1). For example, pick 23 for x. Now answer the question using your number: The zoo has 23 more zebras than hippos. It has 2 hippos, so there must be 25 zebras. Now, see which answer choice gives you the number 25 when you plug in 23 for x. Choice (B) is the only one that results in the right number ($2 + 23 = 25$).

6. **C.** The shape in Choice (C) isn't the same on both sides of the fold, and because cutting through a piece of paper that's been folded in half produces identical shapes on both sides of the fold, the figure in Choice (C) can't be one of the resulting shapes. So Choice (C) is the correct answer.

7. **E.** If you give $\frac{2}{7}$ and $\frac{2}{3}$ a common denominator, you end up with $\frac{6}{21}$ and $\frac{14}{21}$. Add them and get $\frac{19}{21}$, which is less than 1.

8. **C.** If you draw the diameters on the balls and add them up, you can see the width equals 7.5 inches (2.5×3) and the length equals 12.5 inches (2.5×5).

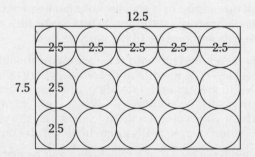

9. **C.** Adding the digits F and H (plus whatever is carried over from adding E and G) results in the digit D. Because nothing is carried over to add to B (B remains B during the final addition step), F + H must be less than 10. If F + H were 10 or more than 10, some number would be carried over to B in the final addition step, and the answer wouldn't start with B. Try assigning different digits to the numbers and experimenting if you're still confused.

10. **B.** Because you're trying to minimize the number of buses, you want to put as many students as you can on each bus. Put 60 in the first, 59 in the second, 58 in the third, 57 in the fourth, and 11 in the fifth, then add to verify: 60 + 59 + 58 + 57 + 11 = 245.

11. **E.** You know that $2Z$ is the same as X, but Z has more than one possibility. Generally, if you have two equations with three variables, there isn't a way to solve for any one variable. Similarly, if you have one equation with two variables, you can't solve for either of the variables.

12. **D.** Point A has an x-coordinate of 3 and a y-coordinate of –1. Point D has an x-coordinate of 6 (double point A's) and a y-coordinate of –3 (triple point A's).

13. **C.** Because some of the answer choices are close together, doing the long division is safest — but you can stop if you notice you've eliminated all but one of the choices. After you realize that 4,321 goes into 98,765 at least 20 times but not 30 times, Choice (C) is the only answer that can be correct.

14. **B.** Testing the answer choices is probably easiest because the number of apples and bananas is the same. For example, if you test Choice (A), you see that $5 \times \$0.50 + 5 \times \$0.60$ doesn't equal $6.60, so you try another answer choice until you find one that equals $6.60. Another way to solve this problem is to make an equation: $\$0.50x + \$0.60x = \$6.60$, where x is the number of apples and the number of bananas. Solving for x gives you the correct answer, which is 6, Choice (B).

15. **E.** Try drawing a picture to prove to yourself that many (in fact, infinite) different distances can separate the two trees. You can't assume that the trees are opposite each other.

16. **D.** This question is easier if you think about the whole weight of a whale. If half the weight of a blue whale is 75 tons, then the whale's total weight is 150 tons. Three blue whales would then weigh a total of 450 (150×3) tons. Now, see which answer choice, when multiplied by 75, equals 450; Choice (D) is correct.

17. **A.** Make life easier for yourself on this one by picking and plugging in numbers for x and y. For example, you may pick $x = 90$ and $y = 70$. Make sure the numbers you pick average 80. Then, just see which answer choice is correct, using your numbers. If you test Choice (A) with your numbers, you get $90 - 80 = 80 - 70$, which is true.

18. **A.** Only Choice (A) can be the area of a square, because of all the choices, only 25 is the result of squaring a whole number (5×5).

19. **D.** Using the definition $x^\wedge = x \div 10$, x is a number that when divided by 10 equals 30: $300 \div 10 = 30$, so $x = 300$.

20. **D.** Using the definition, $10^\wedge = 10 \div 10$, so you end up with $1(1)$, which is 1.

21. **D.** The unshaded region is a triangle, so the area is found by multiplying the base and height then dividing that number by 2. The square has a side length of 6, so the base and height of the triangle are both 6: $6 \times 6 \div 2 = 18$.

22. **B.** Solve for y with $0.80(2y) = 40$. And $40 \div 0.80 = 50$, so $y = 25$. Now, solving for 40 percent of $4y$ (100) is easier: $100 \times 0.4 = 40$.

23. **D.** Solving algebraically, substitute $2z$ for y in the left triangle, because you want everything to be in terms of z. Because the angles of a triangle add up to 180 degrees, $90 + x + 2z = 180$ degrees. Now, solve for x by subtracting $90 + 2z$ from both sides of the equation, and you're left with $x = 90 - 2z$.

24. **D.** This question is a good time to use trial and error with the answer choices. Make a few lists of six consecutive whole numbers, keeping in mind that the middle of the list should be close to 11.5. Choice (D) results in the list 9, 10, 11, 12, 13, 14, which, if averaged, results in 11.5. Algebraically, you can also set up the equation $\frac{x+x+1+x+2+x+3+x+4+x+5}{6} = 11.5$ and solve for x (x is the smallest number, $x + 1$ is the next consecutive number, and so on). You end up with $6x + 15 = 69$, which simplifies to $6x = 54$, or $x = 9$.

25. **C.** Divide $12,492.00 by $9.00 (which is the lowered ticket price because 12 − 3 = 9) to find out how many tickets need to be sold at the new price to equal $12,492.00, and you get 1,388.

Section 3: Reading Comprehension

1. **D.** The passage simply provides a summary of the historical events surrounding Wilhelmina Inn. The author doesn't dwell on a specific issue, and he isn't trying to persuade readers to visit; he's simply providing information.

2. **B.** *Prolific* means an abundance of something or that something happens often. In this passage, the author uses the basic dictionary definition of the word without any additional contextual meaning.

3. **B.** The text states that water closets were a feature of the hotel. Although Victorian decoration was present, it wasn't an unusual feature for that time period. The text doesn't say anything about the ballroom, entertainment, or dining experiences. Although these features may have been a part of the hotel, don't assume anything the text doesn't tell you.

4. **C.** This question is a basic reading question, because the text tells you that the investors were Dutch and, therefore, named the inn after the new Dutch queen.

5. **A.** You're likely to see a question or two phrased this way on the test. In order to pick the correct answer, you need to determine which question is actually answered by the reading passage. Choice (A) is correct here because the other questions provided in the answer choices are all too broad and aren't explained by the reading passage.

6. **C.** The author's tone can best be described as expository, which means to inform, explain, or describe. Although the author points out that satire can be harmful and isn't necessarily positive as a form of writing, he does so in an effort to explain and inform the reader about satire.

7. **A.** In this context, *political landscape* refers to the nature of politics in a free society. Although not the dictionary definition of *landscape,* the author uses the term within this context to extend its meaning. When you face questions like this one, try to replace the word in question with a word of your own in order to keep the intended meaning of the sentence. Doing so helps you narrow down the answer choices.

8. **D.** *Defamation* means a false accusation or a malicious misrepresentation. *Maliciousness* means an intention to do harm. The two words are related in that they both describe intended harm, so Choice (D) is correct.

9. **D.** The author doesn't say that satire is necessary in a free society. He notes that it's to be expected, but doesn't say it's necessary.

10. **E.** Statements I, II, and IV are true statements from the text. The author doesn't state that satire can help reform political issues, so Statement III is false.

11. **B.** This passage explains some basic information about the human iris. Although the passage doesn't explain everything there is to know about the iris, it gives you enough detail to understand what the iris does. You may have been tempted to choose Choice (D), but note that the passage doesn't give you many details about the structure of the iris, so overall, it isn't the primary purpose of the passage.

12. **C.** According to the passage, the pupil allows light to enter the eye. The iris constricts or dilates around the pupil in order to regulate the amount of light allowed to pass through the iris, depending on the current lighting conditions.

13. **D.** When you face a question like this one, you want to choose the answer that conveys the same meaning as the sentence in question. All the answer choices except Choice (D) alter the meaning of the sentence in some way. Choice (D) is the best answer because it doesn't change the meaning of the iris' muscle function, and it replaces the words *dilate* and *constrict* with *widen* and *narrow,* which mean the same things.

14. **A.** Although the passage doesn't directly say, you can infer that melanin varies from person to person, giving people unique eye color. The passage doesn't say anything about light or dark colors or melanin and muscle. You also can't infer that melanin exists only in the iris of the pupil.

15. **B.** The passage tells you that the color, texture, and pattern of the iris are unique to each person, so you need to choose an answer that matches this kind of unique quality. Although most every aspect of the human body has unique qualities, the best answer is Choice (B), *fingerprints,* because each person's fingerprints are unique.

16. **D.** The Mayans used local rule where a small hierarchy ruled a particular city or geographic area. According to the text, the Mayan civilization didn't have centralized leadership.

17. **E.** According to the text, *codices* were pictorial, meaning the drawings existed on buildings and other stonework. From the codices, various aspects of Mayan life were presented.

18. **D.** The passage notes the advanced nature of the Mayan society but also notes the abrupt decline that's still a mystery today. Choice (D) is an accurate reflection of the content from the passage, so the author would most likely agree with this statement.

19. **D.** The passage tells you that the Mayans worshipped many gods, but it doesn't say whether they worshipped a primary god. All other statements in this question are true.

20. **E.** If the author continued writing about the Mayans, a discussion about the theories of the decline of the civilization would be the most logical, because he ends the passage noting that several theories exist.

21. **C.** The text states that people have a right to dissolve political bands by the laws of nature as well as the God of nature, meaning that freedom from political entities is a right of people on earth. Questions like this one can be tricky, so make sure you choose the answer that best restates the *entire* meaning of the sentence(s) in question.

22. **D.** *Self-evident* means obvious, or not needing an explanation. The writers are saying that the following list of human rights don't need additional explanation for them to be true.

23. **B.** Something *alien* is foreign, but it can also mean to separate (as in *alienate*). In this context, the passage is saying that the rights can't be separated from people.

24. **B.** The passage doesn't state that the colonies have an allegiance to Britain. In fact, the purpose of the document is to show why they don't.

25. **B.** *Tyranny* means cruel or oppressive political rule.

26. **B.** The passage provides an introduction, a list of facts concerning rights and grievances, and a conclusion of how the British Empire has been oppressive.

27. **A.** This passage includes information about Poe's work, tragic life, and his popularity as an author. The best answer is Choice (A) because the passage includes information about both his life and death.

28. **C.** The word *macabre* refers to works of art that have death as the subject. Although you may not know what the word means, you can infer from the passage that Choice (C) is correct because the passage states that Poe is considered a forerunner of the modern horror genre.

29. **C.** The passage states that Poe was the first famous writer of the Romantic Movement to attempt to make a living solely from writing. You can infer from his poverty that making a living through writing alone would have been difficult during the time period, so it stands to reason that most writers would have made a living in other occupations.

30. **C.** By definition, a *euphemism* is a word or phrase that provides a gentle way of saying something that may be unpleasant or offensive.

31. **A.** *Gentle* is the best answer. The author describes a few details about Poe's life and death and concludes the passage by reminding the reader that he was one of the most popular writers of the Romantic Movement. Despite his personal tragedy, the author shows the reader that Poe's art has stood the test of time.

32. **E.** Because the author has provided an overview of Poe's life and death, the most logical topic for a new paragraph is a discussion of some of his more popular works. Because Poe is famous for being a writer, the author would naturally focus on his writing accomplishments next.

33. **A.** *Affliction* refers to pain and suffering, so Reagan uses this word to communicate how the economic problems of the day are causing pain and suffering to Americans. Be careful of over reading too much into questions like this one. Take the text at face value and work from that point.

34. **C.** In the second paragraph, Reagan mentions taxes as being a problem for workers because the system of taxation is unfair.

35. **A.** Reagan mentions public spending and then compares that spending to an individual who lives beyond his or her means in that it can be done for awhile, but not without serious consequences.

36. **E.** Reagan places the responsibility of repairing the economic problems with all American people.

37. **E.** In the last paragraph, Reagan uses the concept of special interest group to refer to the greatest special interest group: Americans.

38. **A.** The passage states that the economic problems have occurred over the past several decades, not just during the previous president's administration.

39. **C.** This passage essentially discusses the current problem, so you may expect the next portion of the speech to outline some solutions to the problem.

40. **B.** Reagan's main point is to outline the problem and show how the country, as a whole, must work together to resolve the current economic problem.

Section 4: Verbal

1. **E.** A *bevy* is a group of something, so Choice (E) is correct.

2. **C.** *Sacred* refers to something held in high regard, often in religious terms. The only term that's synonymous is *sacrosanct,* which means sacred by definition.

3. **A.** A *maverick* is a rebel by definition.

4. **C.** A *nuance* is a small difference between two items or words that appear similar at first. The word *difference* is the only correct answer.

5. **B.** *Replete* means full. When you think of the word *replete,* think complete (because it rhymes) as a clue to help you find the correct synonym.

6. **D.** *Genuine* literally means the real thing. The only possible synonym is *bona fide,* which also is a term that denotes that something is real.

7. **C.** *Panache* means with much elegance, so the synonym *elegance* is correct.

8. **A.** *Lackluster* means that something lacks luster, or shine. Therefore, the correct synonym is *dull*.

9. **B.** *Brusque* means abrupt in behavior, so Choice (B) is correct. The answer choices in this question are all rather similar, so make sure you use the process of elimination and rule out as many answer choices as possible. Remember that you're looking for the very best synonym, so evaluate the answer choices critically.

10. **D.** *Tenable* means to have a valid statement, concern, or argument, so Choice (D) is correct.

11. **A.** *Fastidious* means very critical or not easy to please. You may say, "He was fastidious in checking every detail," which means he was critical about every detail.

12. **E.** *Gaunt* means to be overly thin, so Choice (E) is the only synonym in the answer options.

13. **B.** *Illicit* means forbidden by law while *improper* means not in accordance with accepted rules and behavior. Though not exactly the same, improper is your best choice of the answer choices provided. The correct answer may not mean *exactly* the same thing, but your task is to choose the best answer choice available.

14. **D.** *Unilateral* means one-sided. Here's an example where the prefix can give you a clue; *uni-* means one, so even if you don't really know what the word means, the prefix can help you find the correct answer.

15. **A.** *Callous* means to be insensitive, so Choice (A) is correct. You may have been tempted to choose *to jeer,* which can be considered insensitive. However, this action isn't necessarily the best synonym, so always make sure you choose the best answer choice.

16. **A.** The word *blatant* means something is obvious or conspicuous, often in a negative way. Of the answer choices, Choice (A) is the only synonym.

17. **B.** *Vacuous* means to lack ideas or substance so Choice (B) is correct. If you need a mnemonic to help you, think "vacuous is a vacuum," which may help you remember the ideas of empty or lacking.

18. **B.** *Bilk* means to cheat, so Choice (B) is the correct synonym.

19. **C.** You know that *fake* refers to something that isn't real, or artificial. You need a synonym from the word list that means the same thing. The only answer is *bogus,* which means fake.

20. **D.** *Obdurate* means to be stubborn, so Choice (D) is correct. You may have found the answer choices more difficult because many of them can be characteristics of stubborn, such as *challenging* and *frustrating.* However, these words aren't the best synonym of *obdurate.* Remember to always choose the best answer.

21. **E.** *Ubiquitous* means everywhere, so Choice (E) is correct. You may have noticed that Choices (C) and (D), *enormous* and *large,* are similar words, which can make you think one of them is the answer. Don't fall for this trap. Just because two words are similar in the word list doesn't mean that one of them is necessarily the synonym.

22. **A.** *Placid* means to be calm or peaceful, so Choice (A) is correct.

23. **C.** *Paltry* means insignificant. For example, you can say, "The beggar only had a paltry meal," which means the meal was small or not a significant source of nutrition.

24. **A.** *Blithe* means carefree, so Choice (A) is correct. This word shouldn't be confused with *blight,* which means disease or destruction.

25. **C.** *Covert* means to be undercover. For example, a covert military operation is one that's done in secret.

26. **E.** *Canvass* means to survey. This word is often used in connection with political elections. You may have thought, "But you paint on a canvas," but notice the spelling: *Canvas* and *canvass* are two completely different words! Watch out!

27. **B.** *Plaudit* means to give praise to something, so Choice (B) is correct.

28. **D.** *Loquacious* is simply a big word that means talkative. The correct answer is Choice (D).

29. **A.** *Risqué* means near indecent or vulgar. Be careful of choosing a synonym simply because an answer choice sounds similar. For example, the word *risky* may sound good because *risqué* and *risky* rhyme. However, *risky* isn't a correct synonym.

30. **C.** *Hapless* means having bad luck, so Choice (C) is correct.

31. **D.** Heat is produced by the sun, so you're looking for a similar relationship where one item produces another. Under this relationship, locomotives produce steam, so Choice (D) is the best similar analogy for this question.

32. **C.** You ride a wave using a surfboard, so you're looking for a similar relationship. The only possible match is skateboard to pavement. Although you may not say that you ride pavement, the relationship of using a tool to ride something else still stands in the analogy.

33. **B.** The relationship is functionality. A hot tub requires a heater in order to function. In a similar way, a printer requires ink in order to function.

34. **C.** Fire creates smoke, so find a similar relationship that expresses the concept of create. The only possible analogy is car to exhaust because a car creates or produces exhaust.

35. **E.** A light bulb needs electricity in order to function, so you have to think of the analogy in terms of functionality. Using this relationship, a yo-yo must have a string in order to function. Without the string, the yo-yo is incapable of doing anything.

36. **B.** This one seems a bit more difficult at first. A needle pulls thread when used for sewing, so using this relationship, the only possible analogy is *truck to trailer* because a truck pulls a trailer. If no matching analogies are obvious, try different relationships until you find one that works.

37. **B.** *Occasional* means once in a while, and *frequently* means often, so the difference between once in a while and often is about the same amount of difference as *seldom,* which means once in a while, and *rarely,* which means hardly ever.

38. **C.** *Bombastic* means to be very talkative, so you're looking for two opposite relationships. *Demure* and *crass* fit this relationship as the two are opposite behaviors as well.

39. **E.** A switch controls a light, so you need the same kind of relationship that expresses one item in control of another. The only possible analogy is *steering wheel to car* because a steering wheel can be used to control a car.

40. **A.** *Evolve* means to develop gradually, and *dismantle* means to take something apart piece by piece. Although these words aren't exact antonyms, the relationship between them is opposing, so you're looking for a word pair that expresses this same kind of opposing relationship. Choice (A) is correct because *predict* means to provide information about a possible future happening, and *withhold* means to hold back. These two words express opposing actions.

41. **A.** Sugar can be an ingredient in gum, so you simply need an analogy where one item is an ingredient in another. The only possible answer is *flour to cake.*

42. **A.** You test a hypothesis to see whether it's true. Although you won't find an exact relationship like this one in the answer choices, you need something that's done to another item in order to produce a result. The only possible answer is *cake is to bake* because you bake a cake to make it usable.

43. **D.** *Cunning* and *crafty* mean the same thing, so you simply need a word that means the same thing as *tragic.* The only possible answer is *calamitous.*

44. **C.** *Congenial* and *agreeable* are synonyms, so you need another word that means the same thing as *stoical. Unemotional* is the only possible answer.

45. **E.** A treaty often leads to peace, so you need a word that completes this same relationship with the word *exercise. Fitness* is the best answer because the positive nature of fitness most closely matches the relationship of treaty and peace.

46. **A.** *Enormous* and *miniscule* are extreme opposites, so you need a word to complete the analogy that's the most extreme opposite of *eradicate.* Although *support* can work, the best choice is *establish* because it's the most extreme opposite of eradicate.

47. **C.** A mower is specifically designed to cut grass, so you're looking for a very specific relationship. Although *syrup and pancake* and *pan and cookie* may be correct analogies, they're not as specific because *syrup* and *pan* can be used for other things. The best analogy is *clock and time* because a clock is specifically designed to tell time. Remember to find the most specific relationship in questions like these.

48. **A.** Tile is put *on* a floor, so you need a word that completes the relationship with book. The only possible answer that completes the relationship is *shelf,* because a book is placed on a shelf.

49. **B.** *Least* and *most* are two extreme opposites. So you need an analogy that expresses this same kind of relationship. The best answer is *grand to unimpressive* because these two are extreme opposites of each other.

50. **E.** This relationship expresses how one item is required for another item to function. Muscles are required for movement, and the best relationship to this concept is *battery is to watch;* a watch requires a battery in order to function.

51. **B.** A coat is used in the winter, so you're looking for a relationship where one item is used specifically during or with another. The best answer is *marker and paper.*

52. **C.** A jury is a component or part of a trial. In and of itself, it doesn't create a trial, but it's a part of it. So you simply need an analogy that expresses one item as a part of something else. The best answer is *battery and engine* because the battery can be considered a part of an engine.

53. **B.** The ocean surrounds an island, so you need an item that glass can surround. The answer is *liquid* because a glass surrounds the liquid when it's put inside.

54. **E.** *Demonstrative* means showing feelings openly, so the words *demonstrative* and *feelings* are closely tied to each other. You need a word that expresses this same kind of close relationship with *pensive. Pensive* means involved in or reflecting serious thought, so *serious* expresses the same close relationship.

55. **D.** This one is difficult as well. A *fluctuation* is a random or unexpected change while an *interval* is planned or timed. So you need a relationship that says _____ is unexpected while _____ is expected. The best analogy relationship is *stumble and jump* because a stumble is something unexpected while a jump is planned or expected.

56. **D.** An *interloper* is an unwelcomed visitor while a *guest* is a welcomed visitor, so they're opposites. You need a word that's opposite of *division*, which is *whole.*

57. **B.** *Dejected* and *demoralize* mean the same thing, so you simply need a word that means the same thing as *callous.* The word *indurate* is the only possible answer because both words mean uncaring or insensitive.

58. **A.** *Satiate* and *satisfy* are synonyms, both meaning full, so you need a synonym for *gregarious,* which is *social.*

59. **B.** Cold is a characteristic of ice, so you need a characteristic of the word *empathy.* The only possible answer is *caring.* If you show empathy to a person, you show caring and concern.

60. **D.** *Impulsive* and *calculated* are opposite kinds of actions. So you need a word that communicates the opposite of *concrete* (a fact), which is *subjective* (something open to interpretation).

Section 5: Quantitative, Part 2

1. **E.** The SSAT answer choices are usually far enough apart to use rounding, so round this problem to $9{,}000 \div 400$, which results in about 22.

2. **D.** If $N \times 0.1 = 50$, you can solve for N by dividing both sides of the equation by 0.1, like so: $50 \div 0.1$ is 500 (just move the decimal place of 50 one spot to the right), and then $N + 50 = 550$.

3. **B.** First, $2,800 - 400 = 2,400$. Then, reduce $\frac{2}{30}$ to $\frac{1}{15}$. Subtracting $2,400 - \frac{1}{15}$ is easiest to do if you think about what number, when $\frac{1}{15}$ is added to it, makes 2,400. Then, just check the answer choices and see which one looks like a good fit. If you test Choice (B), adding $\frac{1}{15}$ to $2,399\frac{14}{15}$ gives you 2,400.

4. **C.** If you're faced with a problem with more than one unit of measurement, immediately convert to the unit of measurement in the answer choices. Divide 12 by 1.25 to get Choice (C), 9.6.

5. **D.** Multiplying 3,500 by 0.035 is easiest if you first multiply 3,500 by 35, then move the decimal place of the answer to the left three places (because you had to move the decimal place in 0.035 three places to the right to get 35).

6. **E.** If $N > 25$, then $2N + 25$ can't be equal to 75; it has to be higher. Choice (E) is the only number that works. In problems like this one, thinking about what happens if N was 25 (even though you know it has to be bigger) is often helpful.

7. **D.** First, add $22 + 21 + 23 = 66$. Then, $\frac{3}{8} + \frac{1}{8} + \frac{7}{8} = \frac{11}{8}$, which is $1\frac{3}{8}$. Finally, $66 + 1\frac{3}{8} = 67\frac{3}{8}$.

8. **B.** Average problems get easier if you assume, when not otherwise indicated, that everything in the problem has the same value. So if the average weight of three cars is 2,200 pounds, assume all three cars weigh 2,200 pounds. And assume both trucks weigh 4,300 pounds. When calculating the average, you have to add the weights of all five vehicles: $2,200 + 2,200 + 2,200 + 4,300 + 4,300$ and divide by 5 to get the average weight: 3,040 pounds.

9. **A.** The only fraction that doesn't reduce to 6 is Choice (A), which reduces to 4.

10. **D.** Solve by setting up an equation: *16 is 8 percent of* translates to $16 = 0.08x$. Dividing 16 by 0.08 results in Choice (D), 200. Make the division easier by moving the decimal point in 16 and in 0.08 to the right two places so you end up with $1,600 \div 8$.

11. **C.** In the number 12,345,678, the 2 represents 2,000,000 and the 8 represents plain old 8. So to figure 2,000,000 is how many times 8 translates to $2,000,000 = x \times 8$. Solve for x by dividing both sides of the equation by 8, and you get 250,000.

12. **D.** This problem is about *area*. First, get a common unit by converting the square feet in the problem to square inches. One square foot is equal to 144 square inches, because 12 inches are in a foot. (Draw a square with side length 12 inches to help visualize.) If Alicia bought 100 square feet of carpet, she bought 14,400 square inches (144×100). Divide 380 by 14,400 to see how much she paid per square inch, and you get 0.026, which rounds up to $0.03.

13. **C.** First, convert all the fractions in the problem to eighths. The first $2.50 buys $\frac{2}{8}$ of a mile, and the remaining $17.50 buys $\frac{70}{8}$ (because $17.50 \div 0.25 = 70$); $\frac{72}{8}$ reduces to 9.

14. **C.** Remember, *distance = rate × time*. To solve for rate, divide distance by time. Divide 26.2 by 4 and get 6.55; divide 26.2 by 3.5 and get 7.48.

15. **C.** Because Mallory's average lap time is 1 minute and 10 seconds, just multiply 1 minute and 10 seconds by 8 to get her total time for 8 laps, and you end up with 8 minutes and 80 seconds, which is the same thing as 9 minutes and 20 seconds.

16. **C.** To solve this one, remember that the angles on one side of a line add up to 180 degrees. If you look at the horizontal line split into x, $80°$, and y, then $x + y + 80° = 180°$, so $x + y = 100$.

17. **B.** First figure out that $8,624 \div 4 = 2,156$. Then, check the answer choices. Looking at Choice (B), $\frac{8,000}{4}$ (which is 2,000) $+ \frac{600}{4}$ (which is 150) $+ \frac{20}{4}$ (which is 5) $+ \frac{4}{4}$ (which is 1) $= 2,156$.

18. **E.** If Jessica collected $2.50 from each student and wound up with only a third of the money she needed, she should have collected three times that amount ($7.50). To get the rest of the money, she should collect $5.00 more from each student.

19. **B.** Pick numbers for *a* and *b,* such as *a* = 2 and *b* = 3. Then, calculate an answer to the question. How many cents are in two $20.00 bills? $40.00 = 4,000 cents. How many cents are in three $10.00 bills? $30.00 = 3,000 cents. And, 2,000 cents are in four $5.00 bills (or $20.00). So your total is 9,000 cents. Now, see which answer choice produces 9,000 cents if you plug in 2 for *a* and 3 for *b;* Choice (B) makes 9,000, so it's the right answer.

20. **E.** Divide the perimeter (868) by 7 (the fence segment length) and get 124, Choice (E).

21. **D.** Calculate 2 percent of 18,500 by multiplying 18,500 by 0.02 and get $370.00, Choice (D).

22. **B.** An easy way to find out whether a number is divisible by 3 is to add all its digits and see whether 3 can go into the result. If it can, the number is divisible by 3. Adding the digits in 7,269 gives you 24 (7 + 2 + 6 + 9), and because 3 evenly divides into 24 (8 times), Choice (B) is the answer. Alternatively, you can just test the answers by dividing 3 into each one.

23. **C.** The easiest way to tackle this problem is to test the choices. Testing Choice (C), if 7,850 households own both, then 50 would have to own computers (because 7,900 households own computers) and 50 would have to own televisions (because 7,900 households own televisions). So 50 + 50 + 7,850 = 7,950 (the total number of households), so Choice (C) is correct.

24. **A.** The dinner must cost $69.00 because $17.25 × 4 = $69.00. When you divide $69.00 by 6, the result is $11.50.

25. **E.** Pick a number for *x,* say 0.4. Dividing 0.4 by 0.001 is like multiplying 0.4 by 1,000, so Choice (E) always produces the largest result.

Answers at a Glance

Section 2: Quantitative, Part 1

1. D	6. C	11. E	16. D	21. D
2. B	7. E	12. D	17. A	22. B
3. A	8. C	13. C	18. A	23. D
4. D	9. C	14. B	19. D	24. D
5. B	10. B	15. E	20. D	25. C

Section 3: Reading Comprehension

1. D	9. D	17. E	25. B	33. A
2. B	10. E	18. D	26. B	34. C
3. B	11. B	19. D	27. A	35. A
4. C	12. C	20. E	28. C	36. E
5. A	13. D	21. C	29. C	37. E
6. C	14. A	22. D	30. C	38. A
7. A	15. B	23. B	31. A	39. C
8. D	16. D	24. B	32. E	40. B

Section 4: Verbal

1. E	13. B	25. C	37. B	49. B
2. C	14. D	26. E	38. C	50. E
3. A	15. A	27. B	39. E	51. B
4. C	16. A	28. D	40. A	52. C
5. B	17. B	29. A	41. A	53. B
6. D	18. B	30. C	42. A	54. E
7. C	19. C	31. D	43. D	55. D
8. A	20. D	32. C	44. C	56. D
9. B	21. E	33. B	45. E	57. B
10. D	22. A	34. C	46. A	58. A
11. A	23. C	35. E	47. C	59. B
12. E	24. A	36. B	48. A	60. D

Section 5: Quantitative, Part 2

1. E	6. E	11. C	16. C	21. D
2. D	7. D	12. D	17. B	22. B
3. B	8. B	13. C	18. E	23. C
4. C	9. A	14. C	19. B	24. A
5. D	10. D	15. C	20. E	25. E

Chapter 19

SSAT Lower Level Practice Exam 1

. . . .

*1*f you're in the 5th, 6th, or 7th grade, this practice exam is for you! You'd probably rather be doing most anything else than taking a practice exam, but as they say, practice makes perfect. To make the most of this practice exam, find yourself a quiet room, ample time, a few sharpened pencils, and some blank scratch paper. Resist the urge to blast music or watch a movie while you take this practice exam. After all, you want to practice in the same quiet and boring conditions that you'll face on test day.

Grab a watch, an iPod, a phone, or some other way to track your time. Make sure you don't go over the time limit we've given you for each part of this practice test because you won't be allowed extra time on the actual test. You can find all the answers to this practice test in Chapter 20, but don't cheat! Check your answers only *after* you finish the test.

Answer Sheet

For Section 1, use two loose-leaf or lined notebook pages to write your writing sample. (On the real exam, the answer booklet contains two lined sheets.) For Sections 2 through 5 of the exam, use the following answer sheets and fill in the answer bubble for the corresponding number, using a #2 pencil.

Section 2: Quantitative, Part 1

1. Ⓐ Ⓑ Ⓒ Ⓓ Ⓔ   6. Ⓐ Ⓑ Ⓒ Ⓓ Ⓔ   11. Ⓐ Ⓑ Ⓒ Ⓓ Ⓔ   16. Ⓐ Ⓑ Ⓒ Ⓓ Ⓔ   21. Ⓐ Ⓑ Ⓒ Ⓓ Ⓔ
2. Ⓐ Ⓑ Ⓒ Ⓓ Ⓔ   7. Ⓐ Ⓑ Ⓒ Ⓓ Ⓔ   12. Ⓐ Ⓑ Ⓒ Ⓓ Ⓔ   17. Ⓐ Ⓑ Ⓒ Ⓓ Ⓔ   22. Ⓐ Ⓑ Ⓒ Ⓓ Ⓔ
3. Ⓐ Ⓑ Ⓒ Ⓓ Ⓔ   8. Ⓐ Ⓑ Ⓒ Ⓓ Ⓔ   13. Ⓐ Ⓑ Ⓒ Ⓓ Ⓔ   18. Ⓐ Ⓑ Ⓒ Ⓓ Ⓔ   23. Ⓐ Ⓑ Ⓒ Ⓓ Ⓔ
4. Ⓐ Ⓑ Ⓒ Ⓓ Ⓔ   9. Ⓐ Ⓑ Ⓒ Ⓓ Ⓔ   14. Ⓐ Ⓑ Ⓒ Ⓓ Ⓔ   19. Ⓐ Ⓑ Ⓒ Ⓓ Ⓔ   24. Ⓐ Ⓑ Ⓒ Ⓓ Ⓔ
5. Ⓐ Ⓑ Ⓒ Ⓓ Ⓔ   10. Ⓐ Ⓑ Ⓒ Ⓓ Ⓔ   15. Ⓐ Ⓑ Ⓒ Ⓓ Ⓔ   20. Ⓐ Ⓑ Ⓒ Ⓓ Ⓔ   25. Ⓐ Ⓑ Ⓒ Ⓓ Ⓔ

Section 3: Reading Comprehension

1. Ⓐ Ⓑ Ⓒ Ⓓ Ⓔ   11. Ⓐ Ⓑ Ⓒ Ⓓ Ⓔ   21. Ⓐ Ⓑ Ⓒ Ⓓ Ⓔ   31. Ⓐ Ⓑ Ⓒ Ⓓ Ⓔ
2. Ⓐ Ⓑ Ⓒ Ⓓ Ⓔ   12. Ⓐ Ⓑ Ⓒ Ⓓ Ⓔ   22. Ⓐ Ⓑ Ⓒ Ⓓ Ⓔ   32. Ⓐ Ⓑ Ⓒ Ⓓ Ⓔ
3. Ⓐ Ⓑ Ⓒ Ⓓ Ⓔ   13. Ⓐ Ⓑ Ⓒ Ⓓ Ⓔ   23. Ⓐ Ⓑ Ⓒ Ⓓ Ⓔ   33. Ⓐ Ⓑ Ⓒ Ⓓ Ⓔ
4. Ⓐ Ⓑ Ⓒ Ⓓ Ⓔ   14. Ⓐ Ⓑ Ⓒ Ⓓ Ⓔ   24. Ⓐ Ⓑ Ⓒ Ⓓ Ⓔ   34. Ⓐ Ⓑ Ⓒ Ⓓ Ⓔ
5. Ⓐ Ⓑ Ⓒ Ⓓ Ⓔ   15. Ⓐ Ⓑ Ⓒ Ⓓ Ⓔ   25. Ⓐ Ⓑ Ⓒ Ⓓ Ⓔ   35. Ⓐ Ⓑ Ⓒ Ⓓ Ⓔ
6. Ⓐ Ⓑ Ⓒ Ⓓ Ⓔ   16. Ⓐ Ⓑ Ⓒ Ⓓ Ⓔ   26. Ⓐ Ⓑ Ⓒ Ⓓ Ⓔ   36. Ⓐ Ⓑ Ⓒ Ⓓ Ⓔ
7. Ⓐ Ⓑ Ⓒ Ⓓ Ⓔ   17. Ⓐ Ⓑ Ⓒ Ⓓ Ⓔ   27. Ⓐ Ⓑ Ⓒ Ⓓ Ⓔ   37. Ⓐ Ⓑ Ⓒ Ⓓ Ⓔ
8. Ⓐ Ⓑ Ⓒ Ⓓ Ⓔ   18. Ⓐ Ⓑ Ⓒ Ⓓ Ⓔ   28. Ⓐ Ⓑ Ⓒ Ⓓ Ⓔ   38. Ⓐ Ⓑ Ⓒ Ⓓ Ⓔ
9. Ⓐ Ⓑ Ⓒ Ⓓ Ⓔ   19. Ⓐ Ⓑ Ⓒ Ⓓ Ⓔ   29. Ⓐ Ⓑ Ⓒ Ⓓ Ⓔ   39. Ⓐ Ⓑ Ⓒ Ⓓ Ⓔ
10. Ⓐ Ⓑ Ⓒ Ⓓ Ⓔ   20. Ⓐ Ⓑ Ⓒ Ⓓ Ⓔ   30. Ⓐ Ⓑ Ⓒ Ⓓ Ⓔ   40. Ⓐ Ⓑ Ⓒ Ⓓ Ⓔ

Section 4: Verbal

1. A B C D E 13. A B C D E 25. A B C D E 37. A B C D E 49. A B C D E
2. A B C D E 14. A B C D E 26. A B C D E 38. A B C D E 50. A B C D E
3. A B C D E 15. A B C D E 27. A B C D E 39. A B C D E 51. A B C D E
4. A B C D E 16. A B C D E 28. A B C D E 40. A B C D E 52. A B C D E
5. A B C D E 17. A B C D E 29. A B C D E 41. A B C D E 53. A B C D E
6. A B C D E 18. A B C D E 30. A B C D E 42. A B C D E 54. A B C D E
7. A B C D E 19. A B C D E 31. A B C D E 43. A B C D E 55. A B C D E
8. A B C D E 20. A B C D E 32. A B C D E 44. A B C D E 56. A B C D E
9. A B C D E 21. A B C D E 33. A B C D E 45. A B C D E 57. A B C D E
10. A B C D E 22. A B C D E 34. A B C D E 46. A B C D E 58. A B C D E
11. A B C D E 23. A B C D E 35. A B C D E 47. A B C D E 59. A B C D E
12. A B C D E 24. A B C D E 36. A B C D E 48. A B C D E 60. A B C D E

Section 5: Quantitative, Part 2

1. A B C D E 6. A B C D E 11. A B C D E 16. A B C D E 21. A B C D E
2. A B C D E 7. A B C D E 12. A B C D E 17. A B C D E 22. A B C D E
3. A B C D E 8. A B C D E 13. A B C D E 18. A B C D E 23. A B C D E
4. A B C D E 9. A B C D E 14. A B C D E 19. A B C D E 24. A B C D E
5. A B C D E 10. A B C D E 15. A B C D E 20. A B C D E 25. A B C D E

Section 1

Writing Sample

Time: 25 Minutes

Directions: You have 25 minutes to complete a writing sample based on the following essay topic. Use only two pages for your sample. You may use scratch paper to organize your thoughts before you begin writing.

Topic: Practice makes perfect.

Assignment: Do you agree or disagree with this statement? Support your position with personal examples, examples of others, or examples from current news topics or history.

STOP DO NOT TURN THE PAGE UNTIL TOLD TO DO SO.
DO NOT RETURN TO A PREVIOUS TEST.

Section 2

Quantitative, Part 1

Time: 30 Minutes

Directions: You have 30 minutes to complete the following 25 questions. Work each problem in your head or in the blank space on the page. Then, look at the answer options and decide which one is best. Mark your answer to each question in the corresponding answer bubble on the answer sheet for Section 2.

1. Which one of these statements is true?

   (A) $7 \times 7 = 0$

   (B) $7 \div 7 = 0$

   (C) $7 + 7 = 0$

   (D) $7 - 7 = 0$

   (E) None of the above

2. If $9,000 - 5,000 - \Phi = 3,991$, then $\Phi =$

   (A) 9

   (B) 19

   (C) 90

   (D) 900

   (E) 4,000

3. If all the sides of the shape in the following figure have the same length and its perimeter is 30, how long is each side?

   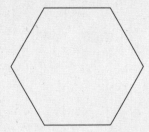

   (A) 3

   (B) 4

   (C) 5

   (D) 6

   (E) 7

4. A group of people went out to dinner, and each person paid the same amount. If the price of the dinner was $90.00, which of the following *cannot* be the amount each person contributed?

   (A) $0.25

   (B) $10.00

   (C) $15.00

   (D) $16.00

   (E) $30.00

5. P is a whole number more than 10 and less than 15. P is also more than 13 and less than 16. What is P?

   (A) 11

   (B) 12

   (C) 13

   (D) 14

   (E) 15

6. If $\frac{4}{7} = \frac{x}{63}$, then $x =$

   (A) 28

   (B) 32

   (C) 36

   (D) 40

   (E) 44

Go on to next page

7. If a small triangle represents 2 units of area in the following figure, how many units of area does the shaded part of the figure have?

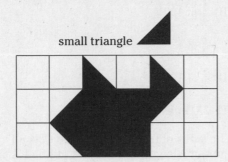

small triangle

(A) 6.5

(B) 18

(C) 26

(D) 36.5

(E) 50

8. If $8 \times n \times 100 = 0$, then $n =$

(A) 800

(B) 8

(C) 1

(D) $\frac{1}{10}$

(E) 0

9. If x is an even number, which one of these is an odd number?

(A) $x + 5$

(B) $x + 4$

(C) $2x$

(D) $3x$

(E) $4x$

10. In the following figure, what fraction of the circles is shaded?

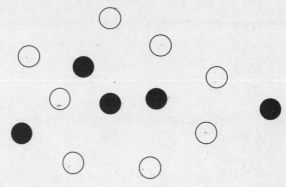

(A) $\frac{1}{4}$

(B) $\frac{4}{13}$

(C) $\frac{5}{13}$

(D) $\frac{6}{13}$

(E) $\frac{1}{2}$

Questions 11–12 refer to the following figure.

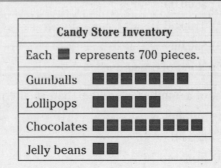

Candy Store Inventory
Each ■ represents 700 pieces.
Gumballs ■■■■■■
Lollipops ■■■■
Chocolates ■■■■■■■
Jelly beans ■■

11. How many more gumballs are there than lollipops?

(A) 2

(B) 14

(C) 700

(D) 1,400

(E) 14,000

Go on to next page

12. The number of chocolates is how many times the number of jellybeans?

    (A) $\frac{1}{4}$

    (B) 2

    (C) 4

    (D) 8

    (E) 4,200

13. All the following numbers are smaller than $\frac{1}{2}$ *except*

    (A) $\frac{49}{100}$

    (B) $\frac{3}{7}$

    (C) $\frac{100}{201}$

    (D) $\frac{5}{8}$

    (E) $\frac{24}{49}$

14. For which of the following amounts is $10.00 off more than 10% off?

    (A) $5,000.00

    (B) $500.00

    (C) $100.00

    (D) $50.00

    (E) None of the above

15. If $\frac{1}{8}$ of a number is greater than 16, then the number is

    (A) Less than 16

    (B) Equal to 16

    (C) Less than 112

    (D) Equal to 112

    (E) Greater than 112

16. Which one of the following is 0.24×121 closest to?

    (A) $\frac{1}{4}$ of 120

    (B) $\frac{1}{4}$ of 100

    (C) $\frac{1}{2}$ of 120

    (D) $\frac{1}{2}$ of 100

    (E) 25 times 12

17. The sides of triangles *ABC* and *CDA* all have the same length. If you start at point *A* and travel along the sides of the triangles, always using the shortest possible route between two points, which path is the longest?

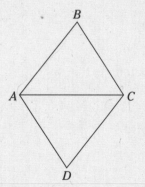

    (A) *A* to *B* to *D* to *C*

    (B) *A* to *B* to *A* to *D*

    (C) *A* to *B* to *C* to *D*

    (D) *A* to *B* to *D* to *B*

    (E) *A* to *B* to *A* to *C*

18. Mark has *x* marbles. Sophia has 3 more marbles than Mark. If Sophia gives Mark 6 marbles, then in terms of *x*, how many marbles will Sophia have?

    (A) $x - 3$

    (B) $x - 6$

    (C) $x + 3$

    (D) $x + 6$

    (E) $x - 9$

Go on to next page →

19. The can shown has a flat bottom. Which of the following pictures shows all the points where the can touches the ground?

PEAS

(A)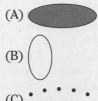

(B)

(C)

(D)

(E)

20. After taking nine history tests, Krista has a 92 average. What is the lowest score she can get on the tenth test and still have a test score average that is 90 or higher?

(A) 90

(B) 89

(C) 88

(D) 82

(E) 72

21. If $x\Omega3 = x \div 3$, which of the following is a whole number?

(A) $1\Omega3$

(B) $2\Omega3$

(C) $3\Omega3$

(D) $4\Omega3$

(E) $5\Omega3$

22. If $6(x + y) = 90$ and y is positive, then x could *not* be

(A) −15

(B) 0

(C) 5

(D) 10

(E) 15

23. 9.09 is closest to which of the following?

(A) 91

(B) 10

(C) 9.9

(D) 9.1

(E) 9

24. One of the following numbers can be written as $3x + 2$ if x is a whole number. Which one is it?

(A) 65

(B) 61

(C) 55

(D) 49

(E) 19

25. What is the value of x as shown in the following figure?

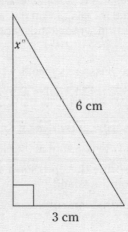

(A) 25

(B) 30

(C) 45

(D) 90

(E) The answer cannot be determined from the information given.

STOP DO NOT TURN THE PAGE UNTIL TOLD TO DO SO. DO NOT RETURN TO A PREVIOUS TEST.

Section 3
Reading Comprehension

Time: 40 Minutes

Directions: You have 40 minutes to read each passage and answer the questions about the passage that follow. Mark your answer to each question in the corresponding answer bubble on the answer sheet for Section 3.

The island of Kauai is the oldest island in the Hawaiian chain of islands. Often called the *Garden Island,* many vacationers and residents of Kauai consider it a paradise on earth. One of the most interesting aspects of Kauai is its different weather patterns. On the south side of Kauai, the town of Koloa sits near Poipu Beach, which is often called *sunny Poipu.* The beach, a popular area of the island, has short bursts of rainfall, but otherwise, the weather is almost always a sunny 80 degrees. Generally, this area gets about 30 inches of rain a year. However, the North Shore of Kauai, which includes such towns as Princeville and Hanalei, gets about 85 inches of rain a year, more than twice the amount of Poipu. These frequent, short bursts of rainfall make this side of the island full of lush, green surroundings. Finally, at the center of the island is Waialeale, which is one of the wettest spots on earth. Waialeale can get as much as 200 inches of rain a year. Although the weather patterns are diverse, the end result is a beautiful, green landscape that covers most of Kauai, making it truly the Garden Island.

1. What is the passage's primary purpose?

    (A) To prove that Kauai is a great vacation spot

    (B) To describe activities on Kauai

    (C) To show why Kauai is the Garden Island

    (D) To describe the diverse weather patterns on the island

    (E) To explore some of the major towns on Kauai

2. Why is Kauai often called the Garden Island?

    (A) Because there are many farms on Kauai

    (B) Because crops grow quickly

    (C) Because the rainfall makes the island green and lush

    (D) Because there are unusual species of plants

    (E) Because the soil is fertile

3. What Kauai beach is often the sunniest?

    (A) Koloa

    (B) Poipu

    (C) Princeville

    (D) Hanalei

    (E) Waialeale

4. Which area of Kauai would be considered the most unique?

    (A) Poipu

    (B) Koloa

    (C) North Shore

    (D) Hanalei

    (E) Waialeale

5. What does the author most likely mean by "short bursts of rainfall"?

    (A) The rain lasts only a few moments, followed by sunny weather.

    (B) The rain falls in hard bursts, followed by slow rainfall.

    (C) The rain is unpredictable.

    (D) The rain can produce flash flooding.

    (E) The rainfall is generally intense.

Go on to next page

Vacation! Every summer, that one word brings a smile to my face. Just getting on an airplane and flying to a different place for a week or so does wonders for the soul. My family loves to visit new places, so I've had the opportunity to visit a lot of exciting destinations. From beaches to mountains to large cities, I love seeing all the sights, eating new foods, and just watching the people.

When I visit a new place, I often daydream about living there. What would my life be like living in a different place? What would the schools be like? Would I make many new friends? Of course, the possibility of moving to one of these destinations is a lot like a snowstorm in July, but daydreaming about it is still fun.

For me, vacation is a time to just get away from the routine of life. On vacation, you get to sleep late and follow a completely different schedule every day. Relaxing away from home, where the daily chores and stress of school don't exist, is a lot easier. So when I'm feeling a bit tired and burned out, I stop and think about vacation for a few minutes, and it always makes me smile.

6. Why did the author write this passage?

    (A) To help the reader overcome a fear of flying

    (B) To encourage the reader to go on a vacation

    (C) To explain why vacation is so personally important

    (D) To talk about different vacations he has taken

    (E) To explain how daydreaming is fun

7. With which statement would the author agree?

    (A) Eating new foods on vacation is often frustrating.

    (B) The author enjoys a wide variety of vacation destinations.

    (C) The author prefers beach destinations.

    (D) Moving to a vacation destination is a real possibility.

    (E) The author does not enjoy air travel but does enjoy the vacation.

8. What does the author mean by the word *destination* used several times in this passage?

    (A) Different kinds of foods

    (B) A particular culture

    (C) Sightseeing

    (D) An airport

    (E) A place visited for a vacation

9. Why does the author like to daydream about living in one of the places he has visited?

    (A) As a way to cope with problems

    (B) To explore the sights of the destination

    (C) To understand the culture

    (D) To imagine how his life may be different

    (E) Because he is unhappy with his life as it is

10. The author compares living in one of the vacation spots as a "snowstorm in July." What does the author mean by this comparison?

    (A) That it is highly unlikely.

    (B) That it would be a shock.

    (C) That it is probable.

    (D) That it would be common.

    (E) That it would be exciting.

Go on to next page

The koala bear is a fascinating animal, though it is actually not a bear. The koala is a marsupial, and it keeps its young in a pouch much like the kangaroo. Like the kangaroo, koalas are native to Australia, and their population numbers are rather low. Additionally, the female koala gives birth only once a year to one baby (twins are reported but are rare). A typical koala can live up to 17 years and generally weighs around 20 pounds at maturity.

Oddly, the koala eats only eucalypt leaves and bark from the eucalypt forests in eastern and southeastern Australia. Eucalypt is poisonous to most all animals, but koalas have a digestive system that is able to detoxify the leaves. Koalas rarely drink water because eucalypt leaves are 50 percent water. However, in times of drought, koalas can and will drink water to supplement their needs.

Koalas are social animals, and they need to live around other koalas for their health — they don't do well alone. Like cats, koalas sleep about 75 percent of the day and are most active in the late evenings. During the day, they like to doze in the tops of the eucalypt trees.

When a baby koala (called a *joey*) is born, it is hairless, blind, less than 1 inch long, and weighs less than 1 gram. After birth, the baby climbs into the mother's pouch on its own and drinks milk from the mother for the next six months. After about 30 weeks, the baby koala also begins to feed on *pap,* which is a specialized dropping the mother produces. Pap helps the baby make the transition from milk to eucalypt. Eventually, the baby leaves the pouch when it becomes too large, but it rides on the mother's back and stays with the mother until the next baby koala is born.

11. Where are koalas native?

    (A) England

    (B) Australia

    (C) South America

    (D) Greenland

    (E) China

12. Which is necessary for the koala to survive?

    (A) Ample water

    (B) Eucalypt forest

    (C) Trees

    (D) Shade

    (E) Grub worms

13. How much do koalas sleep?

    (A) About 75 percent of the day

    (B) About 50 percent of the day

    (C) About 35 percent of the day

    (D) About 25 percent of the day

    (E) About 8 percent of the day

14. Why do joeys need pap?

    (A) To learn to digest eucalypt

    (B) As a vitamin supplement

    (C) To help transition from milk to eucalypt

    (D) In order to grow strong bones

    (E) In order to grow teeth

15. How long does a joey stay with its mother?

    (A) About three months

    (B) About six months

    (C) About a year

    (D) About two years

    (E) About three years

Go on to next page

If you think about the music scene in America over the past 75 years, nothing has had more of an impact to the sound and style of music than the electric guitar. The first electric guitars appeared on the music scene in the early 1930s. Few people saw any real potential for the instrument, and even guitar players did not realize the possible sounds an electric guitar could produce. Yet, as the era of rock and roll music started changing the <u>musical landscape</u>, the electric guitar became the defining instrument that created the sound for a new generation of music lovers.

Acoustic and electric guitars are similar in that they both have six strings that are tuned with tuning pegs. Also, both instruments have frets along the neck. However, the similarities end at the body of the guitar. An acoustic guitar has a hollow body that allows sound from the strings to resonate within the hollow cavity and generate sound. Electric guitars typically have a thinner, solid body because the sound is not generated within the guitar itself. Instead, when you pluck a string on an electric guitar, magnetic pickups controlled by knobs found on the body produce the sound. The pickups generate a signal sent through a cord or wireless controller to an amplifier and speaker. Because of the electrical and magnetic component, electric guitars are capable of producing many different sounds, including distortion effects. These kinds of power effects are <u>pervasive</u> in so many different kinds of music today.

16. What is the primary purpose of this passage?

(A) To explain how an electric guitar works

(B) To describe musical qualities of rock and roll

(C) To encourage the reader to learn to play guitar

(D) To show why electric guitars are better than acoustic guitars

(E) To explain how amplifiers work

17. According to the passage, all the following are true *except*

(A) The electric guitar is a defining instrument of modern rock and roll music.

(B) Electric guitars typically have a thinner, solid body.

(C) Acoustic guitars have a hollow body.

(D) Electric guitars need only an amplifier.

(E) Many people did not think electric guitars were important in the 1930s.

18. What does the author most likely mean by the phrase *musical landscape?*

(A) The music scene across the country

(B) The music scene in California

(C) Country music

(D) Popular radio

(E) The decorative appearance of music album art

19. What does the author most likely mean by the word *pervasive?*

(A) Unlikely to happen

(B) Everywhere

(C) A move or go forward

(D) To be inventive

(E) To cause frustration

20. With which statement would the author most likely agree?

(A) Electric guitars are better than acoustic guitars.

(B) Electric guitars changed music in America.

(C) Electric guitars are more difficult to play.

(D) Electric guitars are more attractive.

(E) Electric guitars have many negative aspects.

Go on to next page

An alternator is part of a car's engine that works with the battery to generate electricity for various parts of the car's electrical system, such as the headlights, interior cabin lighting, dashboard lighting, and so forth. The term *alternator* comes from alternating current, or AC. The alternator is usually located toward the front of the engine, and the AC power that the alternator generates comes from electromagnetism. As the engine runs, a rotor turns inside the alternator, generating the electricity. The current is sent to the battery, and the battery uses its power to run various parts of the vehicle as noted. In effect, when the car is running, the alternator works to charge the battery. Without the alternator, the battery cells would quickly be <u>depleted</u> because the charge would be used up by the car's different components that need electrical power.

21. What is the author's main point?

   (A) To describe how an alternator helps power a car's electrical components

   (B) To explain how an alternator is a part of the engine

   (C) To explain electromagnetism

   (D) To explore various power sources

   (E) To define AC current within the car's electrical system

22. How did the alternator get its name?

   (A) From the inventor's last name

   (B) From battery power

   (C) From electromagnetism

   (D) From the electrical system nature of the device

   (E) From *alternating current*

23. What can you infer about the rotor?

   (A) It generates electromagnetism.

   (B) It is magnetic.

   (C) It works to create DC current.

   (D) It is the only moving part of the alternator.

   (E) It wears out easily.

24. What does the alternator do?

   (A) Stops electrostatic interference

   (B) Runs the dashboard lighting

   (C) Runs the headlights

   (D) Charges the battery

   (E) Runs cabin lighting

25. If the alternator stops working, what happens to the car?

   (A) The car builds up static interference.

   (B) The dashboard lighting will not work.

   (C) The headlights will not work.

   (D) The cabin lighting will not work.

   (E) The battery runs down.

26. What does the word *depleted* mean in this passage?

   (A) Ruined

   (B) Run down

   (C) Weakened

   (D) Destroyed

   (E) Burned

Go on to next page

A public speaker depends on an effective speaking voice, but in reality, so much of a public speaker's communication ability comes from nonverbal means. When a speaker stands in front of an audience, he must effectively use a number of nonverbal communication behaviors that most of us take for granted every single day. This <u>kinesic</u> behavior helps convey the message the speaker wants to communicate to the audience.

One of the most important aspects of this nonverbal communication is eye contact and facial expression. When we talk to people, we give our words additional meaning and force by the eye contact and facial expressions we use. For example, a person can say, "I am happy," but conflicting facial expressions and eye contact can make the words have a <u>sarcastic</u> meaning.

In a similar way, hand gestures and body posture also communicate to the audience. With hand gestures, the speaker can emphasize key words, concepts, and ideas. Effective body posture also communicates interest and attention. Without effective gestures and posture, the speaker often appears disinterred or even afraid.

When you put all these issues together, you can quickly see that public speaking is more than just the sound of a speaker's voice.

27. What does the word *kinesic* most likely mean in this passage?

   (A) Eye contact

   (B) Communication with the body

   (C) Facial expressions

   (D) Posture

   (E) Physical work

28. What is the author's main idea?

   (A) A speaker's meaning can be misunderstood.

   (B) Humans communicate in several ways.

   (C) Nonverbal communication is important for the public speaker.

   (D) Posture is important.

   (E) Eye contact is necessary.

29. In the passage, what does the word *sarcastic* mean?

   (A) Ironic

   (B) Confused

   (C) Empathetic

   (D) Snide

   (E) Difficult

30. According to the passage, what can posture communicate?

   (A) Interest

   (B) Disinterest

   (C) Fear

   (D) A and C

   (E) A, B, and C

31. What do hand gestures most often do?

   (A) Create a physical connection.

   (B) Distract the audience.

   (C) Make the speaker more interesting.

   (D) Emphasize key concepts.

   (E) Give the speaker more animation.

32. When the author says that we take nonverbal communication for granted, what does he mean?

   (A) Most people do not know how to nonverbally communicate.

   (B) Most people know how to nonverbally communicate.

   (C) We use nonverbal communication all the time and do not focus on it.

   (D) We do not appreciate nonverbal communication.

   (E) We do not understand nonverbal communication.

Go on to next page

One of the most unusual breeds of cats is the Sphynx. The Sphynx is a larger, <u>domesticated</u> cat that is virtually hairless. Aside from a lack of fur, the cats also have no eyelashes or whiskers. Adding to the odd appearance are its <u>exceptionally</u> large ears and a long tail.

Sphynx cats are social animals and enjoy both humans and other cats. Most Sphynx owners describe the cats as being similar to dogs because they enjoy being near their owners, instead of having the typical solitary nature that most cats exhibit. Sphynx cats are playful and adept climbers. They are generally easy to manage, although their energetic nature can be difficult at times.

Most owners describe the Sphynx's skin as a warm peach. The cats are rather soft, and their skin often has many wrinkles. A cat's normal body temperature is 102 degrees Fahrenheit, so Sphynx cats are warm to the touch because there is no barrier of fur. Oddly, even though their body temperature is warmer than humans, the Sphynx cats particularly enjoy warm rooms and digging under blankets for a nap. They enjoy lying on warm surfaces, such as clothes dryers, or near the heating vents of refrigerators.

Generally, the Sphynx is a healthy breed and most owners experience few health problems or difficulties. Like most cats, the Sphynx lives for around 18 years.

33. How could you describe the author's attitude toward Sphynx cats?

   (A) The author believes they are good pets.

   (B) The author believes they are good pets for only certain kinds of people.

   (C) The author believes their unusual behavior keeps them from being good pets.

   (D) The author believes only specially skilled people should own the cats.

   (E) The author is neither positive nor negative toward the cats.

34. What does the word *domesticated* mean?

   (A) Non trainable

   (B) Bred for life with humans

   (C) Accessible

   (D) Captured from the wild

   (E) Disease free

35. The author believes all the following characteristics make the Sphynx an interesting pet *except*

   (A) Long tail

   (B) No whiskers

   (C) No eyelashes

   (D) Small eyes

   (E) No hair

36. What does the word *exceptionally* mean in the passage?

   (A) Average

   (B) To an unusual degree

   (C) Like many others

   (D) Similar

   (E) With a usual appearance

37. The author calls the cats *adept climbers*. What does this phrase likely mean?

   (A) With slowness

   (B) With difficulty

   (C) With power

   (D) With force

   (E) With skill

38. The author states that the Sphynx's energetic nature can be difficult at times. What does he probably mean by this?

   (A) The Sphynx does not behave.

   (B) The Sphynx is too aggressive.

   (C) The Sphynx destroys household furniture.

   (D) The Sphynx is too friendly to strangers.

   (E) The Sphynx can be difficult to manage as an indoor pet.

Go on to next page

39. Why does the author mention the Sphynx's body temperature if it is common in all cats?

    (A) The Sphynx may be too hot for some people.

    (B) The Sphynx may require treatment.

    (C) The Sphynx needs a cool environment.

    (D) Because the Sphynx is hairless, the elevated body temperature is noticeable.

    (E) The Sphynx can become sick.

40. Why do Sphynx cats enjoy lying on clothes dryers?

    (A) They like the heat coming from the dryer.

    (B) They enjoy the higher surface.

    (C) They enjoy the sound of the motor.

    (D) They enjoy the vibration of the motor.

    (E) They are naturally curious.

STOP DO NOT TURN THE PAGE UNTIL TOLD TO DO SO. DO NOT RETURN TO A PREVIOUS TEST.

Section 4

Verbal

Time: 30 Minutes

Directions: You have 30 minutes to complete 30 synonym questions and 30 analogy questions. Choose the best answer for each question. Mark your answer to each question in the corresponding answer bubble on the answer sheet for Section 4.

Questions 1–30 contain one word followed by five words or phrases. Select the word or phrase whose meaning is closest to the word in capital letters.

1. CONTRARY:
   (A) Single
   (B) Docile
   (C) Frustrated
   (D) Difficult
   (E) Fun

2. INERT:
   (A) Vanishing
   (B) Not dangerous
   (C) Fearful
   (D) Trial
   (E) Challenging

3. IMPRACTICAL:
   (A) Not helpful
   (B) Not honest
   (C) Not boastful
   (D) Not willful
   (E) Not challenging

4. ASSET:
   (A) Craft
   (B) Valuable
   (C) Benign
   (D) Multiples
   (E) Balance

5. TRINKET:
   (A) Rope
   (B) Chain
   (C) Bells
   (D) Ornament
   (E) Jewel

6. CAPABLE:
   (A) Crescent
   (B) Unable
   (C) Degenerate
   (D) Unwilling
   (E) Competent

7. NONCHALANT:
   (A) Interested
   (B) Concerned
   (C) Careless
   (D) Secretive
   (E) Blasé

8. GENIAL:
   (A) Sad
   (B) Fearful
   (C) Stubborn
   (D) Eager
   (E) Friendly

9. CANTANKEROUS:
   (A) Quarrelsome
   (B) Sympathetic
   (C) Miserly
   (D) Jocund
   (E) Stoical

Go on to next page ⟶

10. BENIGN:
    (A) Agile
    (B) Sincere
    (C) Forgetful
    (D) Harmless
    (E) Dangerous

11. AFFLUENT:
    (A) Doomed
    (B) Wealthy
    (C) Celebratory
    (D) Tricky
    (E) Worrisome

12. IMMACULATE:
    (A) Spotless
    (B) Kind
    (C) Beautiful
    (D) Tenuous
    (E) Keen

13. BLIGHT:
    (A) Storm
    (B) Growth
    (C) Disease
    (D) Trial
    (E) Travel

14. PAUPER:
    (A) Timidity
    (B) Moodiness
    (C) Sleeper
    (D) Intelligence
    (E) Poor person

15. ADAPT:
    (A) Exert
    (B) Fatigued
    (C) Adjust
    (D) Eat
    (E) Anger

16. ANALYSIS:
    (A) Explanation
    (B) Income
    (C) Juncture
    (D) Joviality
    (E) Confusion

17. ANNOY:
    (A) Expose
    (B) Sadden
    (C) Retreat
    (D) Fight
    (E) Frustrate

18. PIOUS:
    (A) Silent
    (B) Eager
    (C) Quiet
    (D) Pretty
    (E) Religious

19. VIGOR:
    (A) Small
    (B) Triteness
    (C) Strength
    (D) Violence
    (E) Viciousness

20. STOICAL:
    (A) Unaffected
    (B) Emotional
    (C) Reasonable
    (D) Victorious
    (E) Challenging

21. TRIVIAL:
    (A) Studious
    (B) Angry
    (C) Callous
    (D) Not important
    (E) Serious

Go on to next page

22. NOVICE:
    (A) Beginner
    (B) Leader
    (C) Spectator
    (D) Expert
    (E) Professor

23. JEST:
    (A) Tranquility
    (B) Woefulness
    (C) Cherishable
    (D) Joke
    (E) Hurt

24. DESTRUCT:
    (A) Sublime
    (B) Conquer
    (C) Tear apart
    (D) Rebuild
    (E) Transition

25. SYMPATHETIC:
    (A) Understanding
    (B) Critical
    (C) Coaching
    (D) To ignore
    (E) Laughable

26. DEMURE:
    (A) Sneaky
    (B) Sly
    (C) Silly
    (D) Loud
    (E) Shy

27. FLUCTUATION:
    (A) Tremble
    (B) Change
    (C) Gain
    (D) In tatters
    (E) Separation

28. CYCLE:
    (A) Introduction
    (B) Repeating series
    (C) Trip
    (D) Procedure
    (E) Mileage

29. AMBIGUOUS:
    (A) Determined
    (B) Silent
    (C) Large
    (D) Unclear
    (E) Surprising

30. EXTOL:
    (A) Recall
    (B) Aggress
    (C) Prod
    (D) Correct
    (E) Praise

Questions 31–60 ask you to find the relationships between words. For each question, choose the answer choice that has the same kind of relationship.

---

31. Roof is to house as
    (A) Hair is to color
    (B) Table is to chair
    (C) Monkey is to banana
    (D) Sail is to boat
    (E) Trash is to can

32. Fire is to candle as
    (A) Juice is to cup
    (B) Oven is to pan
    (C) Car is to gear
    (D) Motor is to diesel
    (E) Picture is to frame

Go on to next page

33. Rock is to dirt as
    (A) Carpet is to floor
    (B) Shell is to sand
    (C) Shirt is to button
    (D) Hungry is to full
    (E) Printer is to ink

34. Coward is to brave as
    (A) Volcano is to lava
    (B) Heat is to cold
    (C) Grill is to fish
    (D) Lawn is to mower
    (E) Music is to note

35. Moon is to Milky Way as
    (A) Candy is to teeth
    (B) Key is to keyboard
    (C) Rubber is to texture
    (D) Soup is to bowl
    (E) Shoe is to foot

36. Coffee is to mug as
    (A) Ring is to finger
    (B) Fin is to fish
    (C) Ice is to cooler
    (D) Signal is to traffic
    (E) Chair is to table

37. Window is to light as
    (A) Screen is to wind
    (B) Car is to lane
    (C) Triangle is to shape
    (D) Lake is to boat
    (E) Sun is to moon

38. Rude is to polite as
    (A) Sleep is to wake
    (B) Kindness is to gentleness
    (C) Fun is to smile
    (D) Work is to money
    (E) Cruel is to mean

39. Monkey is to primate as
    (A) Airplane is to speed
    (B) Trip is to plan
    (C) Grape is to fruit
    (D) Pen is to paper
    (E) Dog is to cat

40. Suit is to lawyer as
    (A) Scream is to mouth
    (B) Sugar is to coffee
    (C) Scrubs is to nurse
    (D) Drill is to bit
    (E) Pool is to water

41. Building is to architect as
    (A) Garden is to landscaper
    (B) Corn is to bird
    (C) Chemical is to plant
    (D) Grass is to mower
    (E) Plant is to seed

42. Christmas is to December as
    (A) October is to weather
    (B) Glass is to juice
    (C) Snow is to Colorado
    (D) Anger is to honesty
    (E) January is to heat

43. Sentence is to paragraph as word is to
    (A) Meaning
    (B) Communication
    (C) Letter
    (D) Sentence
    (E) Speaking

44. Summer is to winter as reserved is to
    (A) Cordial
    (B) Bombastic
    (C) Simmer
    (D) Benign
    (E) Finite

Go on to next page

45. Trite is to banal as content is to
    (A) Challenge
    (B) Pious
    (C) Gratify
    (D) Frank
    (E) Shine

46. Running is to fatigue as eating is to
    (A) Food
    (B) Chew
    (C) Swallow
    (D) Digestion
    (E) Full

47. Page is to book as
    (A) Yolk is to egg
    (B) Pen is to write
    (C) Chair is to room
    (D) Desk is to chair
    (E) Penny is to money

48. Barn is to cow as coop is to
    (A) Monkey
    (B) Donkey
    (C) Chicken
    (D) Alligator
    (E) Bird

49. Actor is to script as
    (A) Carpenter is to saw
    (B) Mechanic is to engine
    (C) Program is to computer
    (D) Dentist is to drill
    (E) Doctor is to x-ray

50. Refuge is to safety as
    (A) Cage is to freedom
    (B) Cave is to home
    (C) Bunker is to bomb
    (D) Anger is to soothing
    (E) Predicament is to difficulty

51. Geologist is to rock as
    (A) Botanist is to animal
    (B) Lawyer is to client
    (C) Psychiatrist is to mind
    (D) Psychologist is to blood
    (E) Farmer is to field

52. Vegetables is to stew as
    (A) Sugar is to cake
    (B) Mud is to ground
    (C) Water is to liquid
    (D) Sweet is to tooth
    (E) Poison is to vanilla

53. Fish is to gill as kangaroo is to
    (A) Lung
    (B) Air
    (C) Hop
    (D) Fur
    (E) Pouch

54. Boil is to steam as motor is to
    (A) Noise
    (B) Turn
    (C) Gasoline
    (D) Exhaust
    (E) Power

55. Hair is to head as
    (A) Moss is to rock
    (B) Milk is to butter
    (C) Grass is to seed
    (D) Corn is to field
    (E) Virus is to food

56. Bone is to leg as frame is to
    (A) Chair
    (B) Bench
    (C) Stand
    (D) House
    (E) Beam

Go on to next page

57. Fortunate is to prosperity as despondent is to
    - (A) Crisis
    - (B) Dejected
    - (C) Derogatory
    - (D) Exuberant
    - (E) Vanity

58. Sane is to insane as cajole is to
    - (A) Coax
    - (B) Jab
    - (C) Demand
    - (D) Offend
    - (E) Redistribute

59. Recycle is to preserve as waste is to
    - (A) Relinquish
    - (B) Save
    - (C) Reduce
    - (D) Use
    - (E) Squander

60. Book is to series as link is to
    - (A) Metal
    - (B) Unit
    - (C) Circle
    - (D) Chain
    - (E) Strength

STOP DO NOT TURN THE PAGE UNTIL TOLD TO DO SO.
DO NOT RETURN TO A PREVIOUS TEST.

Section 5

Quantitative, Part 2

Time: 30 Minutes

Directions: You have 30 minutes to complete 25 questions. Work each problem in your head or in the blank space on the page. Then, look at the answer options and decide which one is best. Mark your answer to each question in the corresponding answer bubble on the answer sheet for Section 5.

1. Which of these shapes can be folded into a square, using only one fold?

   (A)

   (B)

   (C)

   (D)

   (E)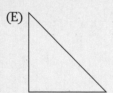

2. 2,000 – 209 =

   (A) 1,791
   (B) 1,709
   (C) 1,701
   (D) 1,691
   (E) 1,601

3. Alyssa had 24 different baseball cards in her collection. Alexis gave her 7 new cards, but Alyssa already had 4 of the new cards. How many different cards did Alyssa then have?

   (A) 24
   (B) 25
   (C) 26
   (D) 27
   (E) 31

4. If 3 is subtracted from a number, the result is 15. If the same number is multiplied by 3, the result is

   (A) 9
   (B) 36
   (C) 45
   (D) 54
   (E) 57

5. $\dfrac{2+3+4}{1+2+3} =$

   (A) $\dfrac{2}{3}$

   (B) $\dfrac{3}{4}$

   (C) $\dfrac{4}{5}$

   (D) $1\dfrac{1}{4}$

   (E) $1\dfrac{1}{2}$

Go on to next page

6. At midnight, the temperature was 20 degrees below zero. If the temperature had risen 40 degrees by 3 p.m., the temperature at 3 p.m. was

   (A) 60 degrees below zero

   (B) 20 degrees below zero

   (C) 0 degrees

   (D) 20 degrees

   (E) 40 degrees

7. Using the following graph, about how much time did Masha spend studying for history?

   Masha's 7 Hours of Study Time

   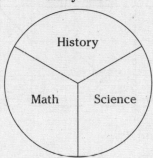

   (A) 1.25 hours

   (B) 1.33 hours

   (C) 2 hours

   (D) 2.33 hours

   (E) 3 hours

8. If $x + 2 = 18$, then 2 more than $2x =$

   (A) 20

   (B) 30

   (C) 32

   (D) 34

   (E) 36

9. If the perimeter of the shape in the figure is 31, what is x?

   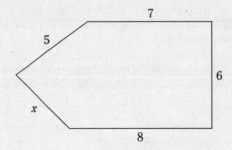

   (A) 3

   (B) 4

   (C) 5

   (D) 6

   (E) 7

10. If $2 \times 3 \times 4 \times 5 \times y = 120$, then $y =$

    (A) 0

    (B) 1

    (C) 2

    (D) 3

    (F) 4

Go on to next page

11. A radio signal comes out of a station in the center of the wall, as shown in the figure. If the signal cannot go through the wall and it can be picked up for 100 miles, which picture shows the area where the signal can be picked up?

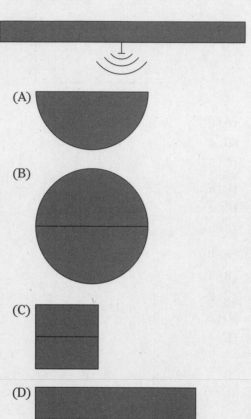

(A)

(B)

(C)

(D)

(E)

12. A classroom of students had three times as many girls as boys. Which of the following could be the total number of students in the classroom?

(A) 18

(B) 20

(C) 22

(D) 26

(E) 30

13. If the shape drawn on the paper shown in the following illustration is folded along the dotted line, which two points will be on top of each other?

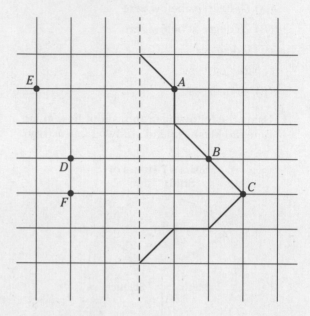

(A) *A* and *B*

(B) *A* and *E*

(C) *B* and *D*

(D) *B* and *F*

(E) *C* and *F*

14. If $\frac{1}{6}p = 6$, then $\frac{1}{4}p =$

(A) 1

(B) 6

(C) 9

(D) 12

(E) 36

Go on to next page

15. According to the following graph, Paul's average number of points per game was

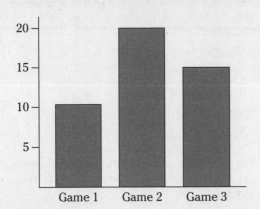

(A) 5

(B) 10

(C) 15

(D) 20

(E) 45

Questions 16–18 refer to the following definition.

For all real numbers x and y, $x \triangle y = (x - y) + (x + y)$

Example: $4 \triangle 3 = (4 - 3) + (4 + 3) = 1 + 7$

---

16. $7 \triangle 2 =$

(A) 4

(B) 10

(C) 12

(D) 14

(E) 16

17. If $p \triangle 3 = 22$, then $p =$

(A) 8

(B) 11

(C) 12

(D) 14

(E) 19

18. If x does not equal 0, which of the following must be true?

   I. $x \triangle y = y \triangle x$

   II. $x \triangle 0 = 2x$

   III. $x \triangle \frac{1}{x} = 2x$

(A) I only

(B) II only

(C) III only

(D) I and II

(E) II and III

19. Julia painted a house from 6 a.m. to 10 a.m. and finished $\frac{1}{3}$ of the house. She has to be done painting the house by 8 p.m. If she paints at the same rate, what is the latest time she can start painting again to make sure she finishes by 8 p.m.?

(A) 10 a.m.

(B) 11 a.m.

(C) 12 p.m.

(D) 1 p.m.

(E) 2 p.m.

20. Which one of the following is closest to 5% of $17.95?

(A) $0.50

(B) $0.75

(C) $0.90

(D) $1.00

(E) $1.80

Go on to next page

21. Of the following figures, which one *cannot* be drawn without lifting the pencil or tracing over a line already drawn?

    (A)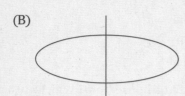

    (B)

    (C)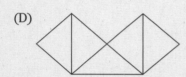

    (D)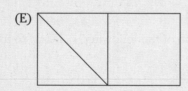

    (E)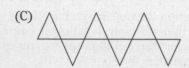

22. If 0.698 is about $\frac{x}{10}$, which of the following is closest to *x?*

    (A) 0.6

    (B) 0.7

    (C) 6

    (D) 7

    (E) 69.8

23. The population of antelope in the wild was reported to be 2.5 million in 2008. This number is 900,000 more than the number reported in 2001. What was the 2001 number?

    (A) 590,000

    (B) 880,000

    (C) 1,500,000

    (D) 1,600,000

    (E) 3,400,000

24. Seven consecutive whole numbers average to 14. What is the largest number in the group?

    (A) 14

    (B) 15

    (C) 16

    (D) 17

    (E) 18

25. In the problems shown, $x + y =$

    $$13\overline{)x}^{\,12 \text{ remainder } 12} \qquad 13\overline{)y}^{\,13}$$

    (A) 335

    (B) 336

    (C) 337

    (D) 338

    (E) 339

STOP DO NOT TURN THE PAGE UNTIL TOLD TO DO SO.
DO NOT RETURN TO A PREVIOUS TEST.

Chapter 20

Answers to SSAT Lower Level Practice Exam 1

• •

*N*ow that you've finished taking the SSAT Lower Level Practice Exam 1, spend time reading through the answers and explanations provided in this chapter. Doing so is a great way to find out what you missed and why. Also, reading through *all* the explanations — even for the questions you got right — only increases your learning and understanding and helps you prepare even more for test day. If you just want to do a quick check of your answers, see the abbreviated answer key at the end of this chapter.

Section 1: Writing Sample

Remember that writing samples for the SSAT don't have right or wrong answers, and with this topic (practice makes perfect), you can write about a variety of issues. So don't get caught up in thinking, "Did I write what they wanted?" because, truthfully, the readers of your writing sample don't care what you write about. They simply want to see that you can organize your thoughts, show your writer's voice, and write a strong essay.

With that thought in mind, the following are a few things you should have done to write a winning essay for your practice test. (For more valuable tips on writing an effective essay and some examples, check out Chapter 8.)

✔ Because the essay prompt asks you to agree or disagree with the statement, "Practice makes perfect," you should have made clear in your introduction what position you're taking — whether you agree or disagree with the statement. Simply talking about *practice* won't cut it here because you're asked to agree or disagree with the idea that practice makes perfect.

✔ Your body paragraphs should have included specific examples that help back up or *prove* your position. These examples can be of a famous person, such as a sports star or a talented actor or singer, or a character from a book you read who learned how to do something well after practicing. If you use a character from a book or story on the actual test, make sure you include the name of the character and mention the name of the story or book.

✔ To really hit a home run with this essay, you should have included an example from your own life. Did you write about a time where you learned to do something well after a lot of practice? Or if you disagreed with the statement, did you show how excessive practice actually caused you not to do well? Remember that the readers want to hear your voice. Including a personal story or experience is a great way to make a writing sample really come to life for the reader.

✔ You should have included a conclusion that brought your ideas together and again affirmed your position on the essay. Conclusions help show that your thoughts and ideas are organized and that you stuck with the topic, so don't forget about the conclusion when you write.

Finally, have someone else read your essay and mark misspelled words, poorly organized sentences, misplaced commas, and other grammatical problems. Doing so helps you see how many errors you made. Remember that the writing sample isn't a grammar test, and a few errors won't hurt you in the end, but overall, your sample should be well written and generally error free.

Section 2: Quantitative, Part 1

1. **D.** 7 minus 7 is 0.

2. **A.** First, subtract 5,000 from 9,000: 9,000 – 5,000 = 4,000. If you subtract Φ from 4,000, the result is 3,991. To figure out what Φ is, subtract 3,991 from 4,000: 4,000 – 3,991 = 9.

3. **C.** We know that the sides are equal in length. Because the six sides add up to 30, each side must be 5 in length (30 ÷ 6 = 5).

4. **D.** If everyone paid the same amount, then just check the answer choices to see which one doesn't divide evenly into 90. The best answer is Choice (D), because 90 ÷ 16 = 5.625. Some people would have to pay $5.62 and some would pay $5.63, because you can't split pennies.

5. **D.** First, write down the possibilities for the first statement: 11, 12, 13, and 14. Then, write down the possibilities for the second statement: 14 and 15. Choice (D) is the correct answer because 14 is the only number that can fit into both statements.

6. **C.** You can cross-multiply here: $4 \times 63 = 7x$; $252 = 7x$. Then, $252 \div 7 = x$, so $x = 36$. Or because you may notice that 7 multiplied by 9 is 63, you can do the same thing to 4 ($4 \times 9 = 36$).

7. **C.** Just count up the small triangles. A square is two small triangles put together, so a square equals 4 units and a small triangle equals 2 units.

8. **E.** Any number multiplied by 0 is 0. If $8 \times 0 = 0$, then $0 \times 100 = 0$.

9. **A.** Pick a number to represent x to make this problem easier; just make sure you pick an even number (for example, say $x = 6$). Choice (A) is the only answer choice that results in an odd number (6 + 5 = 11).

10. **C.** Out of the 13 circles, 5 are shaded; so $\frac{5}{13}$ of the circles are shaded.

11. **D.** If one shaded box equals 700 pieces, then the answer is 1,400 because the gumballs row has two more shaded boxes than the lollipops row.

12. **C.** The chocolates row has eight shaded boxes, and the jellybeans row has two, so 8 is 4 times 2. Checking the answer choices is the easiest way to find the correct one. You can also set up the equation as $8 = 2x$ and solve for x by dividing both sides by 2.

13. **D.** An easy way to check whether a number is smaller than $\frac{1}{2}$ is to see whether the top part of the fraction is less than half of the bottom part. For $\frac{5}{8}$, 5 is *more* than half of 8, so you know that $\frac{5}{8}$ is bigger than $\frac{1}{2}$.

14. **D.** The correct answer is Choice (D) because $10.00 off of $50.00 is $40.00 ($50.00 – $10.00 = $40.00), but 10 percent off of $50.00 = $45.00. To find 10 percent of a number, multiply the number by 0.1: $50.00 \times 0.1 = 5.00, then $50.00 – $5.00 = $45.00.

15. **E.** Check the answer choices. First, take $\frac{1}{8}$ of 16, which is $\frac{16}{8} = 2$, so the number is much bigger than 16. Then, try the other number given, 112; $\frac{112}{8} = 14$, so the number is greater than 112.

16. **A.** If you round 0.24 up to 0.25 (same thing as $\frac{1}{4}$) and round 121 down to 120, then the answer is closest to Choice (A).

17. **D.** A to B = 1, B to D = 2, and D to B = 2 (1 + 2 + 2 = 5). All the other paths are shorter.

18. **A.** If Mark has x marbles, then Sophia has $x + 3$ marbles, because she has 3 more than Mark's amount (which is x). If she gives away 6 marbles, subtract 6 from $x + 3$. So $x + 3 - 6 = x - 3$. Or you can pick a number for x. For example, if you say that $x = 10$, then Mark has 10 marbles and Sophia has 13. If she gives him 6 of her 13 marbles, she has 7 left ($13 - 6 = 7$). Then, check the answer choices, substituting 10 for x, and only Choice (A) produces 7. Keep this strategy in mind when you see variables in the answer choices for any question.

19. **A.** The bottom of the can is a circle just like the top, so all the points where it touches the ground are also a circle. Because the bottom is flat, all the points on and inside the circle touch the ground, so the picture of the shaded circle represents all those points.

20. **E.** If you think about it, you may realize that it'd take a pretty low grade to reduce a 92 average to a 90, because Krista basically has nine test grades of 92. It's always a good idea to estimate first on questions like this so you have an idea of what the answer may be. So if you take a look at the lowest score in the answer choices, 72, you can average nine 92s and one 72 to get $\frac{9 \times 92 + 72}{10} = 90$.

21. **C.** Because the Ω symbol is representing a division sign, only Choice (C) produces a whole number: $\frac{3}{3} = 1$.

22. **E.** Simplify this equation first by dividing both sides by 6: $(x + y) = 15$. Then, check the answer choices. For Choice (E), if x is 15 and y is positive, then there's nothing y could be to make the equation true.

23. **D.** 9.09 is closest to 9.1, because 0.09 rounds up to 0.1. It's also only one hundredth away from 9.1 ($9.09 + 0.01 = 9.1$).

24. **A.** For this problem, you have to check the answer choices. For Choice (A), to find out whether 65 can be written as $3x + 2$, set it equal to that expression: $3x + 2 = 65$. Then simplify: $3x = 63$, so $x = 21$. Because 21 is a whole number, you know that Choice (A) is correct.

25. **B.** This right triangle is a special right triangle: a 30-60-90 right triangle (the degree measures of the inside angles are 30 degrees, 60 degrees, and 90 degrees). You can prove this because the hypotenuse (the side opposite the right angle) is twice as long as the shortest side. The shortest angle of a triangle is opposite its shortest side. Because you know the angles are 30, 60, and 90 degrees, and x is opposite the side measuring 3 centimeters, x must be 30 degrees.

Section 3: Reading Comprehension

1. **D.** Although the passage mentions that Kauai is a great vacation spot, the goal and overall purpose of the passage is to describe some of the different weather patterns on the island, specifically the rainfall levels in different areas of the island.

2. **C.** Kauai is called the *Garden Island* because the rainfall makes the island lush and green. The passage doesn't say anything about crops, farms, or soil, so you can rule out Choices (A), (B), and (E). Although many unusual species of plants may in fact be on the island, the passage doesn't mention this either, so rule out Choice (D) as well.

3. **B.** The only beach mentioned in the passage is Poipu, and the passage notes that Poipu is often called *sunny Poipu*. The other answer choices are all towns in Kauai.

4. **E.** To answer this question, ask yourself what the most unusual feature mentioned in the passage is. Waialeale is one of the wettest spots on earth, so Choice (E) is correct. Although the passage mentions rainfall percentages and sunny locations for some of the other answer choices, these features aren't necessarily unique from many other places in the world.

5. **A.** The author doesn't expressly define what is meant by the phrase *short bursts of rainfall,* so you have to *infer* (decide) the meaning from the passage. Judging from what the author wrote, it rains for a short period of time and then the sun comes out, so Choice (A) is your best option. The author doesn't say anything about lingering rain showers, so Choice (B) is incorrect. The author also doesn't say anything about flash flooding, unpredictable weather, or intense rainstorms, so you can rule out Choices (C), (D), and (E). Remember that an answer choice may sound good, but if the author doesn't talk about it, the answer choice is most likely wrong.

6. **C.** The author uses this passage to explain why vacations are so enjoyable to him, so Choice (C) is the best answer. He doesn't talk about a fear of flying, encourage the reader to go on vacation, explore different vacations he's taken, or even explain why daydreaming is fun, so you can rule out the other choices.

7. **B.** From the passage, you can infer that the author has enjoyed a wide variety of vacation destinations, including beaches, mountains, and even cities. Choice (B) is the only correct statement in the list of answer choices; you can check each answer choice by simply scanning the reading passage.

8. **E.** A *destination* is a place, so the best answer is Choice (E). The author uses the word to denote a place he has visited for a vacation.

9. **D.** The author daydreams as a way to imagine how his life may be different if he lived in one of the vacation destinations, and he uses examples in the passage, such as wondering how school may be different. The author doesn't say anything about using daydreaming as an escape from his life or problems or as a way to understand the sights or culture, so you can rule out all the other answer choices.

10. **A.** The comparison is a *simile,* which is a way of comparing two dissimilar things in order to heighten meaning. Because a snowstorm in July is highly unlikely in most areas of the world, the author is saying that moving to a vacation destination is highly unlikely as well. Choice (A) is your best answer.

11. **B.** The passage tells you that the koalas are native to Australia.

12. **B.** The koalas need a eucalypt forest for food as well as social survival. Although the koalas need water, they get most of their water from the eucalypt leaves and rarely drink it.

13. **A.** The passage tells you that koalas sleep about 75 percent of the day, so Choice (A) is the only correct answer.

14. **C.** The pap helps the koala joey begin a transition from milk to eucalypt, so Choice (C) is the best answer. Choice (A) is close, but the passage doesn't say that pap helps the joey learn to digest eucalypt. Make sure the answer choice you choose is precise — sometimes the wrong answer appears correct at a first glance.

15. **C.** The passage tells you that a joey stays with its mother until the next joey is born. The female koala can have one joey per year, so on average, the joey stays with his mother for about a year before becoming independent.

16. **A.** The primary purpose of this passage is to explain how electric guitars work. The author gives you a brief introduction to explain why electric guitars are important, but the main purpose of the passage is to explain how they work.

17. **D.** According to the passage, an electric guitar needs both an amplifier and a speaker to produce sound.

18. **A.** The word *landscape* often refers to outside areas, such as yards, gardens, and parks. However, *landscape* can also refer to the appearance of something figurative. The author uses this word in relation to popular music to show how music across America looked in a figurative sense.

19. **B.** *Pervasive* means that something has spread or is spreading everywhere. Using this word, the author is saying that electric guitars are *everywhere* in the music industry.

20. **B.** The passage explains that electric guitars changed the music industry, especially with the popularity of rock and roll. The author doesn't allude to or suggest any of the ideas presented in the other answer choices.

21. **A.** The main point of the passage is to describe how an alternator helps power a car's electrical system. Make sure you don't select an answer choice that's too specific when you encounter a question like this one.

22. **E.** The passage tells you that the name comes from *alternating current,* or *AC.*

23. **A.** The *rotor* is a moving part within the alternator, so the best explanation is that it generates electromagnetism. The text doesn't explicitly say so, but Choice (A) is the best answer.

24. **D.** The passage tells you that the current is sent to the battery in order to charge the battery.

25. **E.** Because the alternator charges the battery, the car's battery runs down without it. Choices (B), (C), and (D) happen after the battery runs down, not because the alternator stops working. A bit tricky, but you'll see questions like this one!

26. **B.** The word *depleted* simply means run down, as in, the battery is drained of its power.

27. **B.** The word *kinesic* means communication with the body. Although the passage doesn't directly define the word, it uses the word to describe the rest of the nonverbal communication behaviors in the passage.

28. **C.** The author explains how nonverbal communication is important to the public speaker.

29. **A.** *Sarcastic* describes something ironic.

30. **E.** Posture can communicate interest, disinterest, and fear according to the passage.

31. **D.** According to the passage, hand gestures help the speaker nonverbally emphasize key concepts.

32. **C.** People use nonverbal communication all the time in their day-to-day lives, which is why the author says that we take it for granted.

33. **A.** The author is positive about the Sphynx cats and writes in such a way that helps the reader believe the cats are good pets.

34. **B.** *Domesticated* animals are animals that have characteristics and/or are bred for compatibility with humans.

35. **D.** The author doesn't mention that Sphynx cats have small eyes.

36. **B.** The author uses the word *exceptionally* to communicate that the Sphynx cats have long tails and big ears — much more so than typical domesticated cats.

37. **E.** The word *adept* means to have skill, so Choice (E) is the best answer.

38. **E.** Without giving you details, the author tells you that the cats are energetic, which can create some problems in terms of their level of activity. He doesn't directly say anything about the issues pointed out in Choices (A) through (D); therefore, Choice (E) is the best answer.

39. **D.** The author tells you that a typical cat has a body temperature of 102 degrees. He points this out because you don't notice the heat level on a typical cat due to the layer of fur.

40. **A.** The author talks about clothes dryers in terms of the cats liking warm areas.

Section 4: Verbal

1. **D.** *Contrary* means difficult or hard to get along with. A contrary person is someone who you may struggle working or playing with. You may say, "Sam was so contrary that we couldn't even finish the game."

2. **B.** *Inert* means harmless, so the best answer choice is Choice (B), *not dangerous.* The word often describes chemicals or gasses that don't react to other chemicals or gasses, or chemicals or gasses that pose no threat to people. If you say, "An inert gas was venting into the room," you're saying that the gas was harmless.

3. **A.** *Impractical* means not helpful or unwise to implement. For example, "The homework was impractical because the teacher didn't explain how to solve the problems."

4. **B.** An *asset* is something that has value. People refer to their bank accounts, homes, cars, jewelry, and other valuable items as assets.

5. **D.** The word *trinket* can actually mean several things, such as an ornament or even a very inexpensive piece of jewelry. Of the answer options provided, only *ornament,* Choice (D), is a correct synonym. For example, "At the gift shop, I bought a small trinket." Note that Choice (E), *jewel,* is something expensive. A jewel is not the same as *jewelry,* though, because jewelry doesn't have to have any real jewels.

6. **E.** The word *capable* means that you're able to do something or are *competent* in some way. If you said, "The boy was a capable swimmer," you're saying that he's able to swim with skill, or in a competent way.

7. **C.** *Nonchalant* means unconcerned, careless, cool, casual, and so on. Of the available answer choices, only Choice (C), *careless,* is correct. You may have thought that *blasé,* Choice (E), was correct, but this term means indifferent toward some excitement or pleasure because of repeated enjoyment. You can say, "Jim was blasé about the roller coaster because he had ridden it 12 times." Blasé doesn't mean the same as nonchalant, however. For example, "Jim was nonchalant about the roller coaster, even though he had ridden it before." This sentence means that Jim was unconcerned, or cool, about the upcoming experience. There's a fine difference between these two ideas, but you'll see questions like this one on the exam. Remember to always pick the best answer choice.

8. **E.** The word *genial* means friendly. For example, "The old man was kind and genial."

9. **A.** *Cantankerous* means quarrelsome or difficult to get along with, so Choice (A) is your best answer for this question. For example, "The cantankerous chairman argued with everyone during the meeting."

10. **D.** The word *benign* means harmless. This word often describes a potential illness or threat that turns out not to be so. For example, a doctor may say, "The tumor was benign," which just means that the tumor wasn't cancerous or harmful.

11. **B.** *Affluent* means having a lot of material possessions, or more simply, *wealthy.* For example, "The affluent business woman provided several helpful scholarships."

12. **A.** The word *immaculate* means perfectly clean, so *spotless,* Choice (A), is your best answer. For example, "The apartment was immaculate after my mother cleaned for hours."

13. **C.** The word *blight* means harmful, such as in a disease or destructive force. For example, "The farmer realized the blighted crops were worthless," which means that a disease had spread through the crops, destroying them or their value.

14. **E.** A *pauper* is simply a poor person. For example, "The pauper begged for a loan from the neighborhood bank."

15. **C.** *Adapt* means to change or adjust to something. You can say, "The cows adapted to the colder weather by growing thicker hair," which means that they adjusted to the change in climate.

16. **A.** An *analysis* is an explanation for something, usually noting a detailed explanation. This word is often used in science to explain the outcome of an experiment. For example, "After months of research, the biologist provided a detailed analysis of his findings."

17. **E.** The word *annoy* means to frustrate or aggravate, so the best answer is Choice (E). For example, "The constantly talking child was very annoying."

18. **E.** *Pious* simply means religious. For example, "The pious man folded his hands in prayer."

REMEMBER

19. **C.** The word *vigor* means strength or toughness. You may say, "The weightlifting routine was vigorous," which means it was a tough routine. Notice that two of the answer choices, Choice (D), *violence,* and Choice (E), *viciousness,* also begin with the letter *v.* In some cases, test-writers use words for answer choices that start with the same letter or even sound similar to the word in the question (*vigor* in this case) as a way of distracting your attention to the correct answer. People tend to want to group words that sound alike, even though their meanings may not be similar at all. Don't fall for this trap!

20. **A.** The word *stoical* means unaffected. This word often describes someone who doesn't show emotion in a situation where emotion is expected. For example, "Although everyone was crying at the funeral, the young man remained stoical."

21. **D.** The word *trivial* means something that is unimportant. For example, "Her complaint was trivial," which means that no one thought the complaint was important.

22. **A.** A *novice* is someone who's new to something and is, therefore, a beginner. For example, "Judging by his swing, the golfer was a novice." This sentence means that the golfer was obviously new to the game because he didn't have a good swing.

23. **D.** *Jest* is simply a joke. For example, "The comment was meant as a jest," means the remark wasn't serious but said in a joking manner.

24. **C.** *Destruct* means to completely destroy something or tear apart.

25. **A.** *Sympathetic* means understanding, especially toward someone else's problems or difficulties. For example, "When my friend broke his arm, I was sympathetic because I had broken mine last year."

26. **E.** *Demure* simply means shy. For example, "The demure girl stood by the door during the school dance."

27. **B.** The word *fluctuation* means a change. You may say, "The weather fluctuation from warm to cool during the spring is frustrating." This sentence just means that the weather temperature keeps going up and down.

28. **B.** This one is a bit tricky. The word *cycle* means a series that occurs in a certain order and often in a repeating fashion. For example, the seasons are cyclical because they occur in the same order each year. You may be tempted to choose Choice (D), *procedure,* but a *procedure* is a set of instructions for performing a task and isn't necessarily a cycle.

29. **D.** The word *ambiguous* means unclear. In other words, something that's ambiguous can be taken or understood in different ways. For example, "The instructions for the assignment were so ambiguous that no one knew exactly what to do." This sentence means that the instructions could be taken in different ways, so no one knew what was expected or how to proceed.

30. **E.** The word *extol* means to praise. For example, "The mayor extolled the city employees for a fine job on the project."

31. **D.** A roof sits on top of a house and a sail sits on top of a boat. Choice (D) is the strongest relationship out of all the answer choices.

32. **D.** Fire burns a candle, just like a motor burns diesel fuel. You may tend to think that the oven to pan option is good because an oven heats a pan, but when you refine the relationship, you see that the fire uses the candle for energy, much the same way a motor uses diesel for energy.

33. **B.** This question is fairly simple — you commonly find rocks in dirt just as you can find a shell in the sand. The relationship has to do with location. Now, if you picked Choice (E), you probably got the order of the words mixed up: You can find ink in a printer, but a printer isn't in ink.

34. **B.** This question gives you an opposite relationship because a *coward* by definition is someone who isn't brave. So you need to choose an answer option that is opposite. The best answer is Choice (B) because heat isn't cold.

35. **B.** The moon is part of the Milky Way galaxy, so this analogy expresses a relationship where the first item is part of the second. The only possible answer is Choice (B) because a key is part of a keyboard.

36. **C.** A mug holds coffee and keeps it warm. In a similar way, a cooler holds ice and keeps it cold.

37. **A.** A window allows light into a room, and a screen allows wind (air flow) to come in.

38. **A.** Rude is the opposite of polite, just like sleep is the opposite of being awake.

39. **C.** A monkey belongs to the primate family, so saying that a monkey is a kind of primate establishes the relationship. If you think about one item belonging to a group or family, you can see that Choice (C) is the best answer because a grape is a kind of fruit.

40. **C.** A lawyer wears a suit just as a nurse wears scrubs.

41. **A.** An architect is someone who designs buildings; a landscaper is someone who designs gardens and other kinds of landscape features.

42. **C.** For this tricky question, just find the best relationship sentence. "Christmas occurs in December" like "snow occurs in Colorado." You could also look at the answer this way: December is *known* for Christmas while Colorado is *known* for snow and snow-related activities. Choice (C) is the best answer.

43. **D.** A sentence is a part of a paragraph like a word is a part of a sentence.

44. **B.** In this question, the vocabulary can cause you problems. Summer and winter are opposites, so that part is easy. Now, you need an opposite word for *reserved. Bombastic,* which means overly (and annoyingly) loud or talkative, is the opposite of *reserved.* Remember that when in doubt, use the process of elimination to rule out other options.

45. **C.** Again, the vocabulary can cause you trouble discovering the relationship. *Trite* and *banal* both mean something overly used or said. So the relationship is two words that mean the same thing. What you need is a word that means the same thing as *content,* so your only option is *gratify.*

46. **E.** Running causes fatigue, so you're looking for a relationship where eating causes something. The only possible answer is Choice (E), which is *full.* When you eat, you become full, which causes you to stop eating. The same way, running causes fatigue, which causes you to stop running.

47. **A.** A page is a part of a book — it contributes to the whole. In the same way, a yolk is a part of an egg, contributing to the whole egg. The other answer choices don't have this kind of relationship.

48. **C.** A barn is a place where a cow can be kept for feeding and safety. You need the same kind of relationship with the word *coop,* which is *chicken.*

49. **E.** This one is a bit more difficult. An actor follows a script in order to interpret the character's lines so he or she can act the part. In the same way, a doctor interprets the meaning of an x-ray so he or she can take action to treat the patient.

50. **E.** *Refuge* is a place of safety. In the same way, if you're in a predicament, you're in a place of difficulty. This relationship is the only similar one in the answer choices provided.

51. **C.** A *geologist* is a person who studies rocks and other aspects of the earth, so you're looking for someone who studies something in the list. Choice (C) is the only answer choice that works because a psychiatrist is someone who studies the human mind.

52. **A.** You use vegetables when you make a stew. In the same way, you use sugar as an ingredient in a cake. None of the other answer choices match this relationship because you don't use mud to make ground, water to make liquid, sweet to make tooth, or poison to make vanilla.

53. **A.** A fish breathes by using a gill. A kangaroo breathes by using a lung. The other answer choices provide characteristics of the kangaroo, but only lung has the same kind of relationship as gill.

54. **D.** When water boils, it produces steam. When a motor burns gas or diesel, it produces exhaust. The other answer choices don't express this kind of cause and effect relationship.

55. **A.** Hair grows on your head. In a similar way, moss can grow on a rock, so Choice (A) is the best answer. The other answer choices don't have this grows *on* kind of relationship.

56. **D.** A bone provides structure and support for your leg — without it, your leg wouldn't have the shape it does. In the same way, a frame supports the structure of a house. Just like flesh covers the bone in your leg, you don't see the frame of a house, but it exists under other coverings, such as bricks.

57. **B.** This question tests your vocabulary knowledge. *Prosperity* means to be prosperous or fortunate, so the relationship here is synonyms. *Despondent* means to feel dejected. The other answer choices don't express this same kind of relationship.

58. **C.** *Sane* and *insane* are opposites, so you need to choose a word that expresses the opposite of *cajole*. If you *cajole* someone, you try to gently persuade him with flattery and kindness. The opposite of this action is to demand, so Choice (C) is the correct answer.

59. **E.** Recycling preserves resources, so you're looking for a similar relationship with the word *waste*. Wasting resources squanders them, so Choice (E) is the correct answer.

60. **D.** A book is a part of a series of books, so you're looking for a part of whole relationship. In the same way, a link is a part of a chain, so Choice (D) is the correct answer.

Section 5: Quantitative, Part 2

1. **C.** Folding the triangle part to the left forms a square.

2. **A.** $2,000 - 209 = 1,791$.

3. **D.** Alyssa received seven cards from Alexis, but she already had four of them. In other words, she only got $(7 - 4) = 3$ new ones, so $24 + 3 = 27$.

4. **D.** You can write the first sentence as $x - 3 = 15$, then $x = 18$. When you multiply 18 by 3, you get 54.

5. **E.** First, add up the top and bottom of the fraction: $2 + 3 + 4 = 9$, and $1 + 2 + 3 = 6$. And $\frac{9}{6}$ converts to $1\frac{1}{2}$.

6. **D.** This one is a simple addition question. Just add 40 to -20, which is 20.

7. **D.** The circle graph has three equal parts. So $\frac{1}{3}$ of 7 hours is about 2.33 ($7 \div 3 = 2.33$).

8. **D.** Solving for x, you first have to subtract 2 from both sides of the equation to get $x = 16$. The phrase *2 more than 2x* is the same thing as $16 \times 2 + 2$, which is 34.

9. **C.** Add all the known sides: $5 + 7 + 6 + 8 = 26$. If the perimeter is 31, the missing side (x) must be 5, because $26 + 5 = 31$.

10. **B.** The correct answer is 1 because $2 \times 3 = 6$, $6 \times 4 = 24$, $24 \times 5 = 120$, and $120 \times 1 = 120$.

11. **A.** Choice (A) shows an area that extends an equal distance in every direction from the station (except the wall, because the signal can't go through the wall).

12. **B.** If the number of girls is three times the number of boys, then you can say the number of boys is x and the number of girls is $3x$. So to figure out the total number of students, add the number of boys to number of girls: $x + 3x = 4x$. Only Choice (B) is equal to four times a whole number ($4x = 20$), and because the number of kids can't be a fraction, it must be correct!

13. **C.** An easy way to check this answer is to count how far each dot will be from the fold. Both dot B and dot D are two units away from the fold, so they'll be on top of each other when the paper is folded.

14. **C.** First, solve for p: $p = 6 \div \frac{1}{6} = 36$. Then, $\frac{1}{4}$ of $36 = 36 \div 4 = 9$.

15. **C.** To find the average, add all the values ($10 + 20 + 15 = 45$) and divide by how many values there are (3): $45 \div 3 = 15$.

16. **D.** When you follow the instructions, you get $7 \Delta 2 = (7 - 2) + (7 + 2)$, which equals $5 + 9 = 14$.

17. **B.** When you follow the instructions, $(p - 3) + (p + 3) = 22$. That simplifies to $2p = 22$, so $p = 11$.

18. **E.** This problem is a difficult one, so we'll walk you through it step by step. The key is to pick numbers and then test them. For Option I, if you plug in 2 for x and 3 for y, you end up with $(2 - 3) + (2 + 3) = -1 + 5 = 4$. But if you use 3 for x and 2 for y, you get $(3 - 2) + (3 + 2) = 1 + 5 = 6$. So you *can't* say Option I must be true.

    For Option II, if you plug in any number for x, you get $2x$. For example, if you plug in -7 for x, you get $(-7 - 0) + (-7 + 0) = -14$, which can also be written as $2x$, or 2×-7. So Option II must be true.

    For Option III, if you plug in any number for x, you get $2x$. For example, plugging in 10 for x gives you $\left(10 - \frac{1}{10}\right) + \left(10 + \frac{1}{10}\right) = \left(9\frac{9}{10} + 10\frac{1}{10}\right) = 20$, which is $2x$, or 2×10. So Option III must be true.

    Both Options II and III must be true because they work for any numbers that we plugged in.

19. **C.** Because it takes Julia four hours to complete $\frac{1}{3}$ of the house, it'll take her four more hours to be $\frac{2}{3}$ done and four *more* hours on top of that to be $\frac{3}{3}$ done (completely done). If she kept painting without taking a break, she'd finish at 6 p.m. (eight hours later than 10 a.m.). But she has until 8 p.m. to finish, so she can wait as late at 12 p.m. and then paint for eight hours.

20. **C.** The easiest thing to do here is to round up $17.95 to $18.00. Then, either multiply $18.00 by 0.05 to see what 5 percent of it is or use your percent skills (see Chapter 10): 10 percent of $18.00 is $1.80, so 5 percent of $18.00 is half of that ($0.90).

21. **A.** On scrap paper, try to redraw the figure in Choice (A) without retracing or picking up your pencil to prove that you can't do it.

22. **D.** Solve the equation $\left(0.698 = \frac{x}{10}\right)$ by multiplying both sides by 10 or just move the decimal one spot to the right, so 0.698 becomes 6.98, which is closest to 7. You can do this simple multiplication when multiplying any number by 10, or even 100 (just move the decimal two places to the right).

23. **D.** Don't let the big numbers scare you here. If 2.5 million is 900,000 more than another number, then that number is simply 2.5 million minus 900,000. So $2,500,000 - 900,000 = 1,600,000$, or 1.6 million.

24. **D.** If 14 is the average of seven consecutive whole numbers, it's in the exact middle of them: 11, 12, 13, 14, 15, 16, and 17. So 17 is the largest.

    You can also solve this problem by setting up an average equation: $\dfrac{x+x+1+x+2+x+3+x+4+x+5+x+6}{7}=14$, which simplifies to $\dfrac{7x+21}{7}=14$ then $7x+21=14\times7$, which turns into $7x+21=98$. So $7x=77$, and $x=11$. If $x=11$, then the largest number is $x+6$, which is 17.

25. **C.** Finding the value of y first is easier, because it's just a number that 13 can go into 13 times with nothing left over. To find that number, multiply 13 by 13, which is 169. To find x, ask yourself, "What number can 13 go into only 12 times and have a remainder of 12?" Because you already figured out what y is, you know that x must be close to 169. To figure the value of x, you can do some trial and error or, hopefully, realize that if the remainder were 13, it'd divide in one more time. Therefore, x is 168, y is 169, and 168 + 169 = 337.

Answers at a Glance

Section 2: Quantitative, Part 1

1. D	6. C	11. D	16. A	21. C
2. A	7. C	12. C	17. D	22. E
3. C	8. E	13. D	18. A	23. D
4. D	9. A	14. D	19. A	24. A
5. D	10. C	15. E	20. E	25. B

Section 3: Reading Comprehension

1. D	9. D	17. D	25. E	33. A
2. C	10. A	18. A	26. B	34. B
3. B	11. B	19. B	27. B	35. D
4. E	12. B	20. B	28. C	36. B
5. A	13. A	21. A	29. A	37. E
6. C	14. C	22. E	30. E	38. E
7. B	15. C	23. A	31. D	39. D
8. E	16. A	24. D	32. C	40. A

Section 4: Verbal

1. D	13. C	25. A	37. A	49. E
2. B	14. E	26. E	38. A	50. E
3. A	15. C	27. B	39. C	51. C
4. B	16. A	28. B	40. C	52. A
5. D	17. E	29. D	41. A	53. A
6. E	18. E	30. E	42. C	54. D
7. C	19. C	31. D	43. D	55. A
8. E	20. A	32. D	44. B	56. D
9. A	21. D	33. B	45. C	57. B
10. D	22. A	34. B	46. E	58. C
11. B	23. D	35. B	47. A	59. E
12. A	24. C	36. C	48. C	60. D

Section 5: Quantitative, Part 2

1. C	6. D	11. A	16. D	21. A
2. A	7. D	12. B	17. B	22. D
3. D	8. D	13. C	18. E	23. D
4. D	9. C	14. C	19. C	24. D
5. E	10. B	15. C	20. C	25. C

Chapter 21

SSAT Lower Level Practice Exam 2

. . . .

All right, 5th, 6th, and 7th graders, here's another practice exam for you. Just like the first practice exam in Chapter 19, you should make the most of this test. Find yourself a quiet room, ample time, a few sharpened pencils, and some blank scratch paper. Resist the urge to blast music or watch a movie while you take this practice exam. After all, you want to simulate the same conditions you'll find on test day.

Grab a watch, an iPod, a phone, or some other way to track your time. Make sure you don't go over the time limit we've given you for each part of the test because you won't be allowed extra time on test day. You can find all the answers to this practice test in Chapter 22, but don't cheat! Check your answers only *after* you finish the test.

Answer Sheet

For Section 1, use two loose-leaf or lined notebook pages to write your writing sample. (On the real exam, the answer booklet contains two lined sheets.) For Sections 2 through 5 of the exam, use the following answer sheets and fill in the answer bubble for the corresponding number, using a #2 pencil.

Section 2: Quantitative, Part 1

1. Ⓐ Ⓑ Ⓒ Ⓓ Ⓔ   6. Ⓐ Ⓑ Ⓒ Ⓓ Ⓔ   11. Ⓐ Ⓑ Ⓒ Ⓓ Ⓔ   16. Ⓐ Ⓑ Ⓒ Ⓓ Ⓔ   21. Ⓐ Ⓑ Ⓒ Ⓓ Ⓔ
2. Ⓐ Ⓑ Ⓒ Ⓓ Ⓔ   7. Ⓐ Ⓑ Ⓒ Ⓓ Ⓔ   12. Ⓐ Ⓑ Ⓒ Ⓓ Ⓔ   17. Ⓐ Ⓑ Ⓒ Ⓓ Ⓔ   22. Ⓐ Ⓑ Ⓒ Ⓓ Ⓔ
3. Ⓐ Ⓑ Ⓒ Ⓓ Ⓔ   8. Ⓐ Ⓑ Ⓒ Ⓓ Ⓔ   13. Ⓐ Ⓑ Ⓒ Ⓓ Ⓔ   18. Ⓐ Ⓑ Ⓒ Ⓓ Ⓔ   23. Ⓐ Ⓑ Ⓒ Ⓓ Ⓔ
4. Ⓐ Ⓑ Ⓒ Ⓓ Ⓔ   9. Ⓐ Ⓑ Ⓒ Ⓓ Ⓔ   14. Ⓐ Ⓑ Ⓒ Ⓓ Ⓔ   19. Ⓐ Ⓑ Ⓒ Ⓓ Ⓔ   24. Ⓐ Ⓑ Ⓒ Ⓓ Ⓔ
5. Ⓐ Ⓑ Ⓒ Ⓓ Ⓔ   10. Ⓐ Ⓑ Ⓒ Ⓓ Ⓔ   15. Ⓐ Ⓑ Ⓒ Ⓓ Ⓔ   20. Ⓐ Ⓑ Ⓒ Ⓓ Ⓔ   25. Ⓐ Ⓑ Ⓒ Ⓓ Ⓔ

Section 3: Reading Comprehension

1. Ⓐ Ⓑ Ⓒ Ⓓ Ⓔ   11. Ⓐ Ⓑ Ⓒ Ⓓ Ⓔ   21. Ⓐ Ⓑ Ⓒ Ⓓ Ⓔ   31. Ⓐ Ⓑ Ⓒ Ⓓ Ⓔ
2. Ⓐ Ⓑ Ⓒ Ⓓ Ⓔ   12. Ⓐ Ⓑ Ⓒ Ⓓ Ⓔ   22. Ⓐ Ⓑ Ⓒ Ⓓ Ⓔ   32. Ⓐ Ⓑ Ⓒ Ⓓ Ⓔ
3. Ⓐ Ⓑ Ⓒ Ⓓ Ⓔ   13. Ⓐ Ⓑ Ⓒ Ⓓ Ⓔ   23. Ⓐ Ⓑ Ⓒ Ⓓ Ⓔ   33. Ⓐ Ⓑ Ⓒ Ⓓ Ⓔ
4. Ⓐ Ⓑ Ⓒ Ⓓ Ⓔ   14. Ⓐ Ⓑ Ⓒ Ⓓ Ⓔ   24. Ⓐ Ⓑ Ⓒ Ⓓ Ⓔ   34. Ⓐ Ⓑ Ⓒ Ⓓ Ⓔ
5. Ⓐ Ⓑ Ⓒ Ⓓ Ⓔ   15. Ⓐ Ⓑ Ⓒ Ⓓ Ⓔ   25. Ⓐ Ⓑ Ⓒ Ⓓ Ⓔ   35. Ⓐ Ⓑ Ⓒ Ⓓ Ⓔ
6. Ⓐ Ⓑ Ⓒ Ⓓ Ⓔ   16. Ⓐ Ⓑ Ⓒ Ⓓ Ⓔ   26. Ⓐ Ⓑ Ⓒ Ⓓ Ⓔ   36. Ⓐ Ⓑ Ⓒ Ⓓ Ⓔ
7. Ⓐ Ⓑ Ⓒ Ⓓ Ⓔ   17. Ⓐ Ⓑ Ⓒ Ⓓ Ⓔ   27. Ⓐ Ⓑ Ⓒ Ⓓ Ⓔ   37. Ⓐ Ⓑ Ⓒ Ⓓ Ⓔ
8. Ⓐ Ⓑ Ⓒ Ⓓ Ⓔ   18. Ⓐ Ⓑ Ⓒ Ⓓ Ⓔ   28. Ⓐ Ⓑ Ⓒ Ⓓ Ⓔ   38. Ⓐ Ⓑ Ⓒ Ⓓ Ⓔ
9. Ⓐ Ⓑ Ⓒ Ⓓ Ⓔ   19. Ⓐ Ⓑ Ⓒ Ⓓ Ⓔ   29. Ⓐ Ⓑ Ⓒ Ⓓ Ⓔ   39. Ⓐ Ⓑ Ⓒ Ⓓ Ⓔ
10. Ⓐ Ⓑ Ⓒ Ⓓ Ⓔ   20. Ⓐ Ⓑ Ⓒ Ⓓ Ⓔ   30. Ⓐ Ⓑ Ⓒ Ⓓ Ⓔ   40. Ⓐ Ⓑ Ⓒ Ⓓ Ⓔ

Section 4: Verbal

1. Ⓐ Ⓑ Ⓒ Ⓓ Ⓔ   13. Ⓐ Ⓑ Ⓒ Ⓓ Ⓔ   25. Ⓐ Ⓑ Ⓒ Ⓓ Ⓔ   37. Ⓐ Ⓑ Ⓒ Ⓓ Ⓔ   49. Ⓐ Ⓑ Ⓒ Ⓓ Ⓔ
2. Ⓐ Ⓑ Ⓒ Ⓓ Ⓔ   14. Ⓐ Ⓑ Ⓒ Ⓓ Ⓔ   26. Ⓐ Ⓑ Ⓒ Ⓓ Ⓔ   38. Ⓐ Ⓑ Ⓒ Ⓓ Ⓔ   50. Ⓐ Ⓑ Ⓒ Ⓓ Ⓔ
3. Ⓐ Ⓑ Ⓒ Ⓓ Ⓔ   15. Ⓐ Ⓑ Ⓒ Ⓓ Ⓔ   27. Ⓐ Ⓑ Ⓒ Ⓓ Ⓔ   39. Ⓐ Ⓑ Ⓒ Ⓓ Ⓔ   51. Ⓐ Ⓑ Ⓒ Ⓓ Ⓔ
4. Ⓐ Ⓑ Ⓒ Ⓓ Ⓔ   16. Ⓐ Ⓑ Ⓒ Ⓓ Ⓔ   28. Ⓐ Ⓑ Ⓒ Ⓓ Ⓔ   40. Ⓐ Ⓑ Ⓒ Ⓓ Ⓔ   52. Ⓐ Ⓑ Ⓒ Ⓓ Ⓔ
5. Ⓐ Ⓑ Ⓒ Ⓓ Ⓔ   17. Ⓐ Ⓑ Ⓒ Ⓓ Ⓔ   29. Ⓐ Ⓑ Ⓒ Ⓓ Ⓔ   41. Ⓐ Ⓑ Ⓒ Ⓓ Ⓔ   53. Ⓐ Ⓑ Ⓒ Ⓓ Ⓔ
6. Ⓐ Ⓑ Ⓒ Ⓓ Ⓔ   18. Ⓐ Ⓑ Ⓒ Ⓓ Ⓔ   30. Ⓐ Ⓑ Ⓒ Ⓓ Ⓔ   42. Ⓐ Ⓑ Ⓒ Ⓓ Ⓔ   54. Ⓐ Ⓑ Ⓒ Ⓓ Ⓔ
7. Ⓐ Ⓑ Ⓒ Ⓓ Ⓔ   19. Ⓐ Ⓑ Ⓒ Ⓓ Ⓔ   31. Ⓐ Ⓑ Ⓒ Ⓓ Ⓔ   43. Ⓐ Ⓑ Ⓒ Ⓓ Ⓔ   55. Ⓐ Ⓑ Ⓒ Ⓓ Ⓔ
8. Ⓐ Ⓑ Ⓒ Ⓓ Ⓔ   20. Ⓐ Ⓑ Ⓒ Ⓓ Ⓔ   32. Ⓐ Ⓑ Ⓒ Ⓓ Ⓔ   44. Ⓐ Ⓑ Ⓒ Ⓓ Ⓔ   56. Ⓐ Ⓑ Ⓒ Ⓓ Ⓔ
9. Ⓐ Ⓑ Ⓒ Ⓓ Ⓔ   21. Ⓐ Ⓑ Ⓒ Ⓓ Ⓔ   33. Ⓐ Ⓑ Ⓒ Ⓓ Ⓔ   45. Ⓐ Ⓑ Ⓒ Ⓓ Ⓔ   57. Ⓐ Ⓑ Ⓒ Ⓓ Ⓔ
10. Ⓐ Ⓑ Ⓒ Ⓓ Ⓔ   22. Ⓐ Ⓑ Ⓒ Ⓓ Ⓔ   34. Ⓐ Ⓑ Ⓒ Ⓓ Ⓔ   46. Ⓐ Ⓑ Ⓒ Ⓓ Ⓔ   58. Ⓐ Ⓑ Ⓒ Ⓓ Ⓔ
11. Ⓐ Ⓑ Ⓒ Ⓓ Ⓔ   23. Ⓐ Ⓑ Ⓒ Ⓓ Ⓔ   35. Ⓐ Ⓑ Ⓒ Ⓓ Ⓔ   47. Ⓐ Ⓑ Ⓒ Ⓓ Ⓔ   59. Ⓐ Ⓑ Ⓒ Ⓓ Ⓔ
12. Ⓐ Ⓑ Ⓒ Ⓓ Ⓔ   24. Ⓐ Ⓑ Ⓒ Ⓓ Ⓔ   36. Ⓐ Ⓑ Ⓒ Ⓓ Ⓔ   48. Ⓐ Ⓑ Ⓒ Ⓓ Ⓔ   60. Ⓐ Ⓑ Ⓒ Ⓓ Ⓔ

Section 5: Quantitative, Part 2

1. Ⓐ Ⓑ Ⓒ Ⓓ Ⓔ   6. Ⓐ Ⓑ Ⓒ Ⓓ Ⓔ   11. Ⓐ Ⓑ Ⓒ Ⓓ Ⓔ   16. Ⓐ Ⓑ Ⓒ Ⓓ Ⓔ   21. Ⓐ Ⓑ Ⓒ Ⓓ Ⓔ
2. Ⓐ Ⓑ Ⓒ Ⓓ Ⓔ   7. Ⓐ Ⓑ Ⓒ Ⓓ Ⓔ   12. Ⓐ Ⓑ Ⓒ Ⓓ Ⓔ   17. Ⓐ Ⓑ Ⓒ Ⓓ Ⓔ   22. Ⓐ Ⓑ Ⓒ Ⓓ Ⓔ
3. Ⓐ Ⓑ Ⓒ Ⓓ Ⓔ   8. Ⓐ Ⓑ Ⓒ Ⓓ Ⓔ   13. Ⓐ Ⓑ Ⓒ Ⓓ Ⓔ   18. Ⓐ Ⓑ Ⓒ Ⓓ Ⓔ   23. Ⓐ Ⓑ Ⓒ Ⓓ Ⓔ
4. Ⓐ Ⓑ Ⓒ Ⓓ Ⓔ   9. Ⓐ Ⓑ Ⓒ Ⓓ Ⓔ   14. Ⓐ Ⓑ Ⓒ Ⓓ Ⓔ   19. Ⓐ Ⓑ Ⓒ Ⓓ Ⓔ   24. Ⓐ Ⓑ Ⓒ Ⓓ Ⓔ
5. Ⓐ Ⓑ Ⓒ Ⓓ Ⓔ   10. Ⓐ Ⓑ Ⓒ Ⓓ Ⓔ   15. Ⓐ Ⓑ Ⓒ Ⓓ Ⓔ   20. Ⓐ Ⓑ Ⓒ Ⓓ Ⓔ   25. Ⓐ Ⓑ Ⓒ Ⓓ Ⓔ

Section 1
Writing Sample

Time: 25 Minutes

Directions: You have 25 minutes to complete a writing sample based on the following essay topic. Use only two pages for your sample. You may use scratch paper to organize your thoughts before you begin writing.

Topic: The early bird catches the worm.

Assignment: Do you agree or disagree with this statement? Support your position with personal examples, examples of others, or examples from current news topics or history.

STOP DO NOT TURN THE PAGE UNTIL TOLD TO DO SO.
DO NOT RETURN TO A PREVIOUS TEST.

Section 2

Quantitative, Part 1

Time: 30 Minutes

Directions: You have 30 minutes to complete the following 25 questions. Work each problem in your head or in the blank space on the page. Then, look at the answer choices and decide which one is best. Mark your answer to each question in the corresponding answer bubble on the answer sheet for Section 2.

1. Tracy has 18 brownies, and Sarah has 26. How many brownies must Sarah give to Tracy so they each have the same number?

   (A) 3

   (B) 4

   (C) 5

   (D) 6

   (E) 8

2. $5 \times \frac{1}{5} \times 250 =$

   (A) 5

   (B) 25

   (C) 50

   (D) 250

   (E) 500

3.

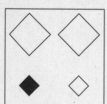 is to 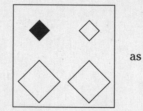 as

 is to

(A)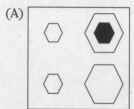

(B)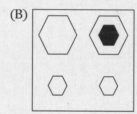

(C)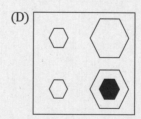

(D)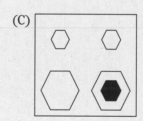

(E)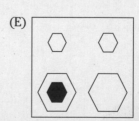

Go on to next page

4. By spinning which of these arrows would you have the *least* chance of landing on an odd number?

(A)

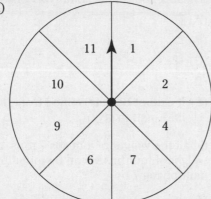

(B)

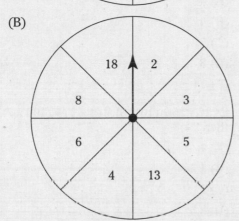

(C)

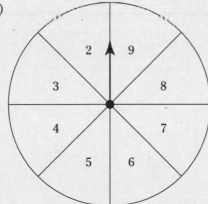

(D)

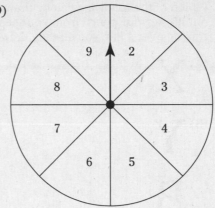

(E)

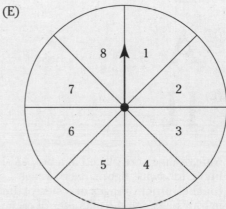

5. Peter has 26 dogs. He plans to buy enough dog bones to give each dog one bone. The bones are sold in packages of 4. How many packages must he buy?

(A) 5

(B) 6

(C) 7

(D) 8

(E) 9

6. Twenty-four people are waiting to be seated at a restaurant. If at least two but no more than seven people can sit at each table and no two tables have the same number of people, what is the smallest number of tables needed to seat all the people?

(A) 3

(B) 4

(C) 5

(D) 6

(E) 7

Go on to next page

7. Which of the following can be drawn without lifting your pencil from your paper or tracing over a line you already drew?

(A) X

(B) Y

(C) B

(D) A

(E) H

8. Nine oranges are placed in a box, as shown in the following figure. Each orange touches other oranges or a side of the box in four places. If the diameter of each orange is 3 inches, which of the following can be the length and width of the box?

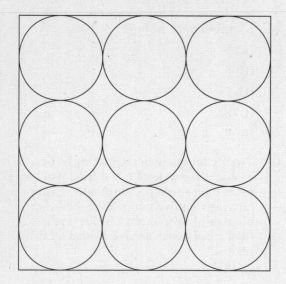

(A) 6 in x 6 in

(B) 7 in x 7 in

(C) 8 in x 8 in

(D) 9 in x 9 in

(E) 12 in x 12 in

9. Sinead lives 5 miles from the park and Tommy lives 12 miles from the same park. What is the distance, in miles, between Sinead's house and Tommy's house?

(A) 7

(B) 11

(C) 12

(D) 17

(E) It cannot be determined from the information given.

10. If half the weight of a bus is 7 tons, the weight of four buses can be found by multiplying 7 by

(A) $\frac{1}{2}$

(B) 4

(C) 7

(D) 8

(E) 14

11. If $227 + 36 = (10 \times 6) + (3 \times 1) + (100 \times ?)$, then $? =$

(A) 1

(B) 1.5

(C) 2

(D) 2.5

(E) 3

Go on to next page

12. The following illustration is a square piece of sheet metal that four identical square pieces have been cut out of. If the total area of the missing pieces is 16 square inches, which of the following could have been the area of the original piece of metal before the pieces were removed?

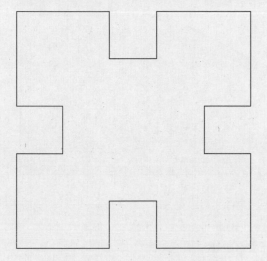

Note: Figure not drawn to scale.

(A) 20 square inches

(B) 26 square inches

(C) 30 square inches

(D) 32 square inches

(E) 36 square inches

13. Christine folds pieces of paper in half as shown. She then cuts through both layers of the folded pieces with scissors to make different shapes. When the pieces are unfolded, they can look like each of the following *except*

(A)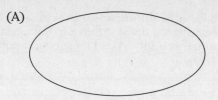

(B)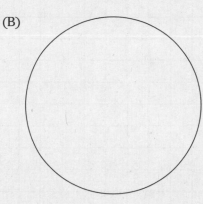

(C)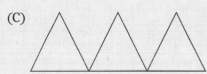

(D)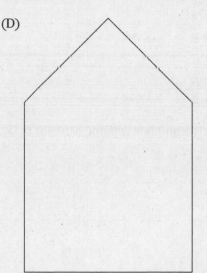

(E)

Go on to next page

14. On the grid shown, a star is at (4, 3). Which letter should the star move to if its first number is doubled and its second number is tripled?

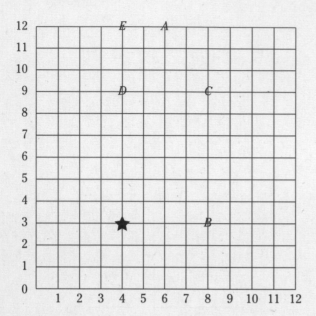

(A) *A*

(B) *B*

(C) *C*

(D) *D*

(E) *E*

15. On the number line, the arrow points to

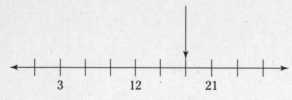

(A) $12\frac{1}{2}$

(B) 14

(C) 16

(D) 18

(E) 20

16. What is the area of the shaded region pictured in the figure if *GHIJ* is a square?

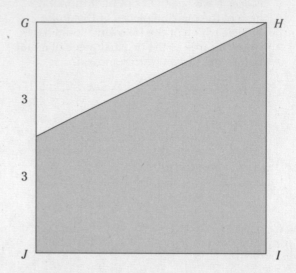

(A) 3

(B) 9

(C) 18

(D) 27

(E) 36

17. The water in a swimming pool is 17 inches below the halfway mark at 10 a.m. If the water level rises 23 inches by 3 p.m., then the water level will be

(A) 6 inches below the halfway mark

(B) At the halfway mark

(C) 3 inches above the halfway mark

(D) 6 inches above the halfway mark

(E) 16 inches above the halfway mark

18. If 30% of *n* is 10, what is 15% of 2*n*?

(A) 5

(B) 7.5

(C) 10

(D) 12.5

(E) 15

Go on to next page

19. 95,284 ÷ 2,105 is closest to which of the following?

    (A) 90,000

    (B) 45,000

    (C) 4,500

    (D) 45

    (E) 4.5

20. A store sells all-terrain vehicles with three wheels (trikes) and all-terrain vehicles with four wheels (quads). The number of trikes and quads in the store is equal. If the number of trike wheels plus the number of quad wheels equals 35, how many quads are in the store?

    (A) 3

    (B) 4

    (C) 5

    (D) 6

    (E) 7

21. A store offers a 25% discount on all computers. If a computer has an original price of $995.00, which of the following is closest to the price after the discount is taken?

    (A) $250.00

    (B) $700.00

    (C) $750.00

    (D) $800.00

    (E) $900.00

22. A go-kart track has an average of 300 customers per day. To increase business, the owner plans to reduce the regular price of a rental from $7.50 to $5.00 before 5 p.m. If 200 people pay $7.50, how many people must pay $5.00 for the daily sales to remain the same as before the discount was offered?

    (A) 150

    (B) 155

    (C) 160

    (D) 175

    (E) 200

23. The figure shows a solid block made of cubes. How many cubes were used to make the block?

    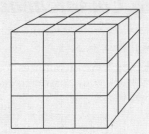

    (A) 9

    (B) 15

    (C) 21

    (D) 27

    (E) 35

24. If $\frac{1}{5} + K > 1$, which of the following could be the value of K?

    (A) $\frac{1}{2}$

    (B) $\frac{2}{3}$

    (C) $\frac{3}{4}$

    (D) $\frac{4}{5}$

    (E) $\frac{5}{6}$

25. When a pie is cut into 16ths instead of 12ths, which of the following must be true?

    (A) Four fewer pieces of pie exist.

    (B) Each piece of the pie is bigger.

    (C) Some pieces of pie are larger than others.

    (D) Four more pieces of pie exist.

    (E) Some of the pieces of pie have a different shape than others.

STOP DO NOT TURN THE PAGE UNTIL TOLD TO DO SO. DO NOT RETURN TO A PREVIOUS TEST.

Section 3

Reading Comprehension

Time: 40 Minutes

Directions: You have 40 minutes to read each passage and answer the questions about the passage that follow. Mark your answer to each question in the corresponding answer bubble on the answer sheet for Section 3.

The armadillo is a mammal that originated in South America but can now be found in many southern states in the United States. The striking feature of the armadillo, of which about 20 <u>distinct</u> species exist, is the leathery, hard shell that looks like armor. This unique shell not only protects the armadillo against potential predators but also prevents the armadillo from being flexible.

Armadillos eat a variety of roots, plants, and insects. They find food primarily by digging. Armadillos have short, strong legs and tough claws, enabling them to dig quickly. Because of this ability, they often wreak <u>havoc</u> in gardens, fields, and even yards in residential areas. Because of the damage they can do in a short period of time, armadillos aren't a popular animal among southern state residents. Regardless, the armadillo is a <u>resilient</u> animal that will continue to call these areas home for a long time in the future.

1. What is the passage's primary purpose?

   (A) To explain agricultural benefits of armadillos

   (B) To explain why the armadillo is disliked

   (C) To describe the armadillo

   (D) To explore southern state animals

   (E) To explain why armadillos have claws

2. What does the author mean by the word *distinct* in this passage?

   (A) Unique

   (B) Common

   (C) Basic

   (D) Determined

   (E) Functional

3. What does the author mean by *havoc* in this passage?

   (A) Damage

   (B) Confusion

   (C) Frustration

   (D) Denial

   (E) Specific

4. What does the author mean by *resilient* in this passage?

   (A) Able to survive

   (B) Intrusive

   (C) Contorted

   (D) Renewable

   (E) Destructive

5. Concerning the passage, which of the following statements can be considered an opinion?

   (A) The armadillo has short legs.

   (B) The armadillo has sharp claws.

   (C) The armadillo is disliked.

   (D) The armadillo eats insects.

   (E) There are no opinions in this passage.

Go on to next page

In the <u>contemporary</u> world, the need for everyone to focus on recycling is more important now than ever. As people consume more and more, they should also strive to recycle waste products to avoid overfilling landfills and contributing to overall pollution. One way that everyone can easily reduce pollution is to avoid plastic bags at stores. When the option is available, choose paper bags that are easily recycled, or better yet, buy your own reusable bags and simply take them with you to the store. If everyone did this, imagine how much plastic pollution could be reduced in a year. Each person has a responsibility to preserve the environment and to do his or her part to save resources, reduce pollution, and recycle waste products.

6. How can you describe this passage?

   (A) A passage of facts

   (B) A passage of opinions

   (C) A passage to describe a product

   (D) A passage explaining how something works

   (E) A passage describing a detail

7. Why does the author believe that avoiding plastic bags can help the environment?

   (A) Because people do not take care of them.

   (B) Because they are too wasteful.

   (C) Because they are difficult to recycle.

   (D) Because they are not strong.

   (E) The author does not say.

8. What is the author's ultimate goal for his reader?

   (A) Take action.

   (B) Believe him.

   (C) Understand his point of view.

   (D) Discuss the topic with others.

   (E) Nothing.

9. What does the author mean by *contemporary* in this passage?

   (A) The world with automobiles

   (B) The world with computing technology

   (C) The world with electricity

   (D) The world after 1900

   (E) The world the way it is now

10. What could the author do to make this passage better?

   (A) Reorganize the passage.

   (B) Include more instruction for the readers to take action.

   (C) Describe how plastic is made.

   (D) Explain where to buy reusable bags.

   (E) Explore other issues of the contemporary world.

Go on to next page

A number of states in the United States experience the dangerous and destructive forces of tornadoes each year. A tornado forms when cool, dry polar air from Canada meets warm air from Mexico. These conditions typically occur from April to June, which is often simply called *tornado season.* A particular area susceptible to tornadoes, called *Tornado Alley,* stretches from areas of Texas across Oklahoma and Kansas, though tornadoes can certainly occur in other areas as well. When the cool air hits the warm air, a circular air pattern forms, often traveling at speeds up to 500 miles per hour. This circulating, fast-moving air is so strong that it can drive a straw into a piece of wood or even a piece of wood into metal. With that power, no wonder tornadoes can be so destructive to homes and property. Although many people believe the low pressure formed within tornadoes makes them so deadly and destructive, experts report that it is simply the wind speed.

11. Why are tornados so destructive?

   (A) Low pressure

   (B) Wind speed

   (C) Circular pattern

   (D) Air masses

   (E) Lightening

12. Which state would most likely experience a tornado?

   (A) California

   (B) North Dakota

   (C) Colorado

   (D) Texas

   (E) Oregon

13. What is the primary cause of tornadoes?

   (A) Low pressure

   (B) Wind patterns

   (C) Dry conditions

   (D) Hot and cold air

   (E) The article does not say

14. In which month would a tornado most likely occur?

   (A) October

   (B) August

   (C) December

   (D) January

   (E) May

15. What is the maximum wind speed of a tornado?

   (A) 100 mph

   (B) 200 mph

   (C) 300 mph

   (D) 400 mph

   (E) 500 mph

Go on to next page

Although Shane and Allyson were <u>furious</u>, they didn't <u>exhibit</u> any behavior that would give their emotional state away. Instead, they chose to simply grin and bear the insults that almost everyone around them spoke. After all, as two overachievers, they were used to feeling singled out. Yet as they walked home from school that afternoon, they couldn't deny a feeling of deep sadness. Why did things always have to be so complicated! They worked hard and studied every day, so why shouldn't they <u>reap</u> the benefits of their labor? In the end, however, there was no way to make the name calling and insults go away, proving yet again that the old saying, "Sticks and stones may break my bones but words will never harm me," was utter and complete nonsense. In fact, Shane and Allyson would both say that words were the most painful things of all.

16. What does the word *furious* mean in the passage?

    (A) Fighting

    (B) Unable to think clearly

    (C) With regret

    (D) Extremely angry

    (E) Skeptical

17. What does the author mean by the word *exhibit?*

    (A) To resort to name calling

    (B) To cause a scene

    (C) To show or display emotion

    (D) To run away

    (E) To sneer

18. What does the author mean by the word *reap?*

    (A) To use a small amount

    (B) To refrain

    (C) To indict

    (D) To have or own

    (E) To plow

19. What does the author mean by the phrase *grin and bear?*

    (A) To stop moving

    (B) To show frustration

    (C) To carry a weight with pride

    (D) To act like nothing had happened

    (E) To smile with joy

20. How could you rephrase the last sentence of the passage?

    (A) Sometimes people talk in a way that is not understood.

    (B) People talk too much.

    (C) Words do not physically hurt people and can be ignored.

    (D) Words are like stones.

    (E) The things people say can be very hurtful.

Go on to next page

Abraham (Abe) Lincoln is one of the most <u>notable</u> American historical figures. Certainly, Lincoln had many accomplishments in his career and presidency, but also a number of myths, or folklore, exist about him. First, Abe Lincoln is often portrayed as a simple country lawyer who later became president. Yet, in fact, Lincoln was known as a very successful lawyer in his home state, and he represented numerous companies, including large railroads. Secondly, it is often rumored that Lincoln was gravely ill when he was assassinated. In truth, although Lincoln was very thin, doctors of the time reported that Lincoln was very healthy when he was shot, which explained why it took him nine hours to <u>succumb</u> to death after he was wounded. Finally, people have reported that Lincoln was very modest and shy. Although we can't entirely say whether this is true, we do know that Lincoln sat for more painters and sculptors than any other U.S. president as an <u>act of free will</u>. This fact alone seems to <u>debunk</u> this myth.

21. What is the author's main point?

    (A) To refute some common Lincoln myths

    (B) To explain the nature of folklore

    (C) To describe the myths about Lincoln

    (D) To present an accurate view of Lincoln

    (E) To explore Lincoln's life

22. What does the author mean by the word *notable?*

    (A) Written about

    (B) Remarkable

    (C) Common

    (D) Truthful

    (E) Defined

23. What does the author mean by the word *succumb?*

    (A) To argue

    (B) To create style

    (C) To fail to resist

    (D) To fight

    (E) To disgust

24. What does the author mean by the word *debunk?*

    (A) To show as false

    (B) To prove as true

    (C) To define a belief

    (D) To argue a position

    (E) To demoralize

25. How could you best define the concept of *myth?*

    (A) A belief that can be proven

    (B) A belief that is not grounded in facts

    (C) A concept of immortality

    (D) A superhero

    (E) A character with larger-than-life characteristics

26. The author uses the phrase *an act of free will.* In the context of this writing, what does the author mean?

    (A) Lincoln hoped for better.

    (B) Lincoln believed he could make a difference.

    (C) Lincoln did it for the good of the country.

    (D) Lincoln was forced.

    (E) Lincoln chose to do it without any influence.

Go on to next page

Iceland is a large island in the North Atlantic, close to the Arctic Circle. Often considered the youngest continent, Iceland has some of the most active volcanoes in the world. Helka, which lies in the southern portion of Iceland, has erupted 16 times, providing black lava fields and spouting sulfur vents. Yet the island is not just a volcanic wonder. Other areas of the island boast blue geysers, green valleys, beautiful coastal regions, and several water-falls. This contrast creates a most unique island. The capital city, Reykjavik, is a bustling metropolitan city where more than half the residents of Iceland live. Although an old city, it is still vibrant. Because of the variety of natural wonders as well as an active capital city, Iceland is a popular tourist destination.

27. What does the word *boast* most likely mean in this passage?

    (A) Determination
    (B) Unusual behavior
    (C) To have a desirable feature
    (D) Bragging rights
    (E) Determined

28. What is the author's purpose?

    (A) To explore unique qualities of Iceland's population
    (B) To explain volcanic activity
    (C) To describe some basic features of Iceland
    (D) To encourage vacationing activity
    (E) To describe coastal regions

29. What can you infer is evidence that Iceland is a young continent?

    (A) Green valleys
    (B) Geysers
    (C) Varying landscape
    (D) Low population
    (E) Volcanic activity

30. How many times has Helka erupted?

    (A) 10
    (B) 12
    (C) 16
    (D) 18
    (E) 20

31. What does the author mean by the word *contrast?*

    (A) The different landscape features make the island interesting.
    (B) Different features exist in small areas.
    (C) The island has different temperature extremes.
    (D) There are numerous island areas.
    (E) Much of the island is the same.

32. What does the author mean by the word *vibrant?*

    (A) Colorful
    (B) Full of life
    (C) Diverse
    (D) Unappreciated
    (E) Difficult to travel

Go on to next page

Sam knew he was in trouble. As the canoe <u>swiftly</u> tipped over, he found himself <u>plunging</u> into the cold water of the river. The current immediately separated him from the boat and even though he was wearing a lifejacket, a sickening fear grabbed him, <u>like someone was squeezing his stomach</u>. <u>Instinctively</u>, he started swimming for the edge of the river bank, but the current kept him from making much progress. The greater problem is Sam knew the river and what was coming.

Just down the river, a sharp bend would turn the <u>raging water</u> on a near 90 degree angle, forcing it to conform to the river path by slamming it into a massive rock wall. Sam knew he would face the same fate as the water: The <u>rock wall was coming</u> for him as well.

He had to take action. As the water continued to move him down the river, Sam used all his strength to begin swimming toward the edge. He had to make it to a place along the edge of the river where he could at least touch the ground if he had any hope of getting out before the turn came his way.

In times of fear and danger, the body and mind can do amazing things. In spite of the current, Sam swam harder than he ever had. Only a few hundred feet before the river turned, his foot grazed the bottom of the river bed, and with a few more hard thrusts, he was able to touch, grab onto a large rock, and hoist himself to safety. He collapsed against the bank exhausted and thinking that the hard feeling of the rocks was perhaps the best thing he had ever touched.

33. What does the author mean by the word *swiftly?*
    (A) Happening quickly
    (B) Moving with the current
    (C) Without warning
    (D) In expectation
    (E) With predicted behavior

34. What does the word *plunging* mean?
    (A) To fall unexpectedly
    (B) To be harmed
    (C) To enter quickly
    (D) To collapse
    (E) To be weakened

35. When the author says *like someone was squeezing his stomach,* what kind of writing technique is he using?
    (A) Foreshadowing
    (B) Irony
    (C) Personification
    (D) Metaphor
    (E) Simile

36. What does the word *instinctively* mean in this passage?
    (A) A fearful thought
    (B) A mood
    (C) A behavior that is planned
    (D) A reaction that doesn't require thought
    (E) By nature

37. When the author says that Sam knew the river and what was coming, what writing technique is he using?
    (A) Foreshadowing
    (B) Irony
    (C) Personification
    (D) Metaphor
    (E) Simile

38. What does the author mean by *raging* water?
    (A) Deep
    (B) With current
    (C) Willful
    (D) Dangerous
    (E) Angry

Go on to next page

39. The author states that the rock wall *was coming* for the character. Because the rock wall wasn't technically coming, what is the author trying to communicate?

    (A) Attitude

    (B) Frustration

    (C) Possibilities

    (D) Landscape features

    (E) Danger

40. Why does the character enjoy the feeling of the rocks at the end of the passage?

    (A) They represent safety.

    (B) They are cool.

    (C) They helped his footing.

    (D) They were comfortable.

    (E) He enjoys rocks.

STOP DO NOT TURN THE PAGE UNTIL TOLD TO DO SO.
DO NOT RETURN TO A PREVIOUS TEST.

Section 4

Verbal

Time: 30 Minutes

Directions: You have 30 minutes to complete 30 synonym questions and 30 analogy questions. Choose the best answer for each question. Mark your answer to each question in the corresponding answer bubble on the answer sheet for Section 4.

Questions 1–30 contain one word followed by five words or phrases. Select the word or phrase whose meaning is closest to the word in capital letters.

1. EXTRAORDINARY:
   (A) Several
   (B) Frustrated
   (C) Singular
   (D) Unusual
   (E) Detailed

2. CALLOUS:
   (A) Happy
   (B) Unwilling
   (C) Uncaring
   (D) Unilateral
   (E) Fearful

3. SOLITARY:
   (A) Defensive
   (B) Plural
   (C) Argumentative
   (D) Alone
   (E) Frequent

4. ELUDE:
   (A) Remember
   (B) Escape
   (C) Fall
   (D) Deny
   (E) Determine

5. AWKWARD:
   (A) Clumsy
   (B) Skillful
   (C) Confusing
   (D) Genuine
   (E) Renewing

6. CONSTRAIN:
   (A) Give
   (B) Bind
   (C) Hide
   (D) Develop
   (E) Compel

7. DECEPTIVE:
   (A) Forthcoming
   (B) Caring
   (C) Honest
   (D) Truthful
   (E) Wily

8. COMPLY:
   (A) Complain
   (B) Confer
   (C) Cooperate
   (D) Calculate
   (E) Consider

9. DEBUNK:
   (A) Act poorly
   (B) Determine
   (C) Devalue
   (D) Disinfect
   (E) Expose

Go on to next page

10. SUPPORT:

    (A) Sustain

    (B) Enlighten

    (C) Try

    (D) Fear

    (E) Hope

11. TRADITIONAL:

    (A) Trite

    (B) Rich

    (C) Conventional

    (D) New

    (E) Serious

12. INQUIRY:

    (A) Pain

    (B) Request

    (C) Demand

    (D) Stoic

    (E) Insight

13. UNCLEAR:

    (A) Ambiguous

    (B) Tenacious

    (C) Jocund

    (D) Predictable

    (E) Trivial

14. UNCOMMON:

    (A) Tractional

    (B) Tenuous

    (C) Sleepy

    (D) Secretive

    (E) Rare

15. EQUIVALENT:

    (A) Actual

    (B) Intrinsic

    (C) Unscrupulous

    (D) Equal

    (E) Relative

16. DISAGREEMENT:

    (A) Animosity

    (B) Cooperation

    (C) Revitalization

    (D) Pander

    (E) Synchronization

17. NOTORIOUS:

    (A) Famous from acting

    (B) Famous to most all people

    (C) Famous to only a small group

    (D) Famous in a positive way

    (E) Famous in a negative way

18. INFURIATED:

    (A) Silent

    (B) Angry

    (C) Quiet

    (D) Still

    (E) Mournful

19. SLAPHAPPY:

    (A) Tenacious

    (B) Frustrated

    (C) Angry

    (D) Silly

    (E) Scolded

20. TRUNCATED:

    (A) Powerful

    (B) Shortened

    (C) Deliberate

    (D) Demure

    (E) Refined

21. OPERATE:

    (A) Calculate

    (B) Sting

    (C) Develop

    (D) Procure

    (E) Work

Go on to next page

22. RETROSPECT:
    (A) To return
    (B) To ignore
    (C) To look back
    (D) To stylize
    (E) To satisfy

23. SYMPATHIZE:
    (A) Translate
    (B) Remember
    (C) Pity
    (D) Inundate
    (E) Reject

24. INTERPRET:
    (A) Translate
    (B) Deny
    (C) Follow
    (D) Found
    (E) Renumber

25. CANNON:
    (A) Surround
    (B) Destruct
    (C) Inflect
    (D) Discharge
    (E) Resurge

26. JAUNT:
    (A) To make fun of
    (B) Laughter
    (C) Trip
    (D) Preliminary
    (E) Not serious

27. STRICKEN:
    (A) Perilous
    (B) Flexible
    (C) To gain
    (D) To hit
    (E) Sick

28. POTENT:
    (A) Bad
    (B) Strong
    (C) Dangerous
    (D) Destructive
    (E) Well-mannered

29. INCONSEQUENTIAL:
    (A) Unimportant
    (B) Unequal
    (C) Challenging
    (D) Unhelpful
    (E) Failing

30. PREVAIL:
    (A) Prefer
    (B) Overcome
    (C) Define
    (D) Act
    (E) Challenge

Questions 31–60 ask you to find the relationships between words. For each question, choose the answer choice that has the same kind of relationship.

31. Tree is to forest as
    (A) Hair is to head
    (B) Kitchen is to house
    (C) Peel is to banana
    (D) Cow is to herd
    (E) Piece is to puzzle

32. Heart is to body as
    (A) Apple is to stomach
    (B) Glass is to cabinet
    (C) Processor is to computer
    (D) Clothes are to dryer
    (E) Dream is to memory

Go on to next page

33. Paper is to printer as
    (A) Page is to book
    (B) Detergent is to washer
    (C) Frame is to picture
    (D) Pool is to water
    (E) Bulb is to light

34. Zipper is to luggage as
    (A) Glue is to paper
    (B) Shelf is to bottle
    (C) Fin is to fish
    (D) Blade is to grass
    (E) Diamond is to ring

35. Moon is to planet as
    (A) Sugar is to chocolate
    (B) Milk is to coffee
    (C) Satellite is to earth
    (D) Mill is to wood
    (E) Key is to lock

36. Image is to television as
    (A) Camera is to picture
    (B) Ad is to sign
    (C) June is to July
    (D) Street is to car
    (E) Carpet is to room

37. Thermometer is to heat as
    (A) Jacket is to winter
    (B) Clock is to time
    (C) Dream is to night
    (D) Sail is to boat
    (E) Water is to lake

38. Degree is to college student as
    (A) Pond is to fish
    (B) Anger is to strife
    (C) Super Bowl is to football player
    (D) Money is to debt
    (E) Credit is to shopping

39. Keyboard is to computer as
    (A) Luggage is to clothing
    (B) Rain is to sleet
    (C) Steering wheel is to car
    (D) Simple is to complex
    (E) Dog is to collar

40. Bandage is to nurse as
    (A) Service is to plumber
    (B) Leash is to dog
    (C) Summer is to heat
    (D) Paper is to writer
    (E) Comma is to sentence

41. Dream is to reality as
    (A) Water is to land
    (B) Apple is to worm
    (C) Movie is to sleep
    (D) Flower is to sun
    (E) Midnight is to dark

42. Alligator is to river as
    (A) Bird is to tree
    (B) Ant is to grass
    (C) Dog is to snow
    (D) Fun is to sadness
    (E) Bird is to nest

43. Trial is to error as workout is to
    (A) Effort
    (B) Energy
    (C) Time
    (D) Repetition
    (E) Growth

44. Fun is to laugh as seed is to
    (A) Flower
    (B) Sun
    (C) Water
    (D) Soil
    (E) Germination

Go on to next page

45. Smile is to frown as gargantuan is to
    (A) Immobile
    (B) Vicious
    (C) Tiny
    (D) Silent
    (E) Silky

46. Detail is to specific as adulation is to
    (A) Deafen
    (B) Renew
    (C) Cajole
    (D) Laud
    (E) Smart

47. Liner is to pool as
    (A) Shell is to egg
    (B) Bottle is to label
    (C) House is to lot
    (D) Green is to tree
    (E) Wicked is to flattery

48. Saw is to blade as bread is to
    (A) Color
    (B) Water
    (C) Heat
    (D) Yeast
    (E) Crust

49. Denial is to deny as
    (A) Renew is to reuse
    (B) Comprehension is to understand
    (C) Complain is to pacify
    (D) Dentist is to tooth
    (E) Calculate is to confuse

50. Brick is to mortar as
    (A) Bird is to sunlight
    (B) Cup is to water
    (C) Pavement is to stone
    (D) Depression is to night
    (E) Sing is to note

51. Formula is to solution as
    (A) Animal is to fur
    (B) Ruler is to measurement
    (C) Pencil is to lead
    (D) Blood is to oxygen
    (E) Tractor is to tire

52. Jump is to gravity as
    (A) Air is to tank
    (B) Bench press is to weight
    (C) Shirt is to cloth
    (D) Sing is to voice
    (E) Drift is to anchor

53. Fear is to terror as happy is to
    (A) Furious
    (B) Tricky
    (C) Ecstatic
    (D) Neutral
    (E) Careless

54. Jocular is to funny as reticent is to
    (A) Quiet
    (B) Bland
    (C) Jumpy
    (D) Juvenile
    (E) Happy

55. Fork is to drawer as
    (A) Bird is to cage
    (B) Coin is to purse
    (C) Pen is to page
    (D) Store is to people
    (E) Money is to table

56. Calculate is to guess as deceptive is to
    (A) Specious
    (B) Truthful
    (C) Trying
    (D) Filtering
    (E) Innumerable

Go on to next page

57. Angst is to peace as impeccable is to
    (A) Error
    (B) Clean
    (C) Stoic
    (D) Deny
    (E) Anxiety

58. Job is to pay as book is to
    (A) Relax
    (B) Cover
    (C) Read
    (D) Information
    (E) Page

59. Accelerator is to speed as fatigue is to
    (A) Sleep
    (B) Sunburn
    (C) Work
    (D) Relaxation
    (E) Food

60. Gallant is to courageous as emphatic is to
    (A) Hopeless
    (B) Forceful
    (C) Dreamy
    (D) Tiring
    (E) Trivial

STOP DO NOT TURN THE PAGE UNTIL TOLD TO DO SO.
DO NOT RETURN TO A PREVIOUS TEST.

Section 5

Quantitative, Part 2

Time: 30 Minutes

Directions: You have 30 minutes to complete 25 questions. Work each problem in your head or in the blank space on the page. Then, look at the answer choices and decide which one is best. Mark your answer to each question in the corresponding answer bubble on the answer sheet for Section 5.

1. $7,902 - 407 =$

    (A) 6,495

    (B) 6,496

    (C) 7,495

    (D) 7,496

    (E) 7,595

2. If $50 \times N = 50$, then $50 + N =$

    (A) 0

    (B) $\frac{1}{50}$

    (C) 1

    (D) 50

    (E) 51

3. $200 - 4\frac{2}{30} =$

    (A) $195\frac{9}{15}$

    (B) $195\frac{14}{15}$

    (C) $196\frac{9}{15}$

    (D) $196\frac{14}{15}$

    (E) $197\frac{14}{15}$

4. A string that is $5\frac{1}{2}$ feet long can be cut into how many 6-inch pieces?

    (A) 9

    (B) 10

    (C) 11

    (D) 12

    (E) 13

5. $0.025 \times 500 =$

    (A) 0.125

    (B) 1.25

    (C) 12.5

    (D) 125

    (E) 1,250

6. If an integer $N > 5$, then $2N + 4$ could be

    (A) 12

    (B) 13

    (C) 14

    (D) 15

    (E) 16

7. $2\frac{7}{8} + 1\frac{3}{8} =$

    (A) 4.05

    (B) 4.15

    (C) 4.25

    (D) 4.35

    (E) 4.5

8. The average weight of three dogs is 50 pounds, and the average weight of two cats is 10 pounds. What is the average weight of all five animals?

    (A) 30 lbs

    (B) 34 lbs

    (C) 40 lbs

    (D) 44 lbs

    (E) 45 lbs

Go on to next page

9. All the following are equal *except*

   (A) $2 \times \frac{2}{3}$

   (B) $4 \times \frac{1}{3}$

   (C) $8 \times \frac{1}{6}$

   (D) $16 \times \frac{1}{12}$

   (E) $32 \times \frac{1}{20}$

10. 8 is 25% of

    (A) 4

    (B) 16

    (C) 24

    (D) 32

    (E) 40

11. In the number 77,777, how many times the value of the rightmost 7 is the leftmost 7?

    (A) 1,000

    (B) 7,000

    (C) 10,000

    (D) 70,000

    (E) 100,000

12. Yvonne paid $810.00 for a rectangle of fabric that was 60 inches long by 45 inches wide. What was her cost per square inch?

    (A) $0.03

    (B) $0.30

    (C) $3.00

    (D) $3.33

    (E) $8.10

13. A taxi costs $2.00 for the first $\frac{1}{4}$ mile and $0.75 for each additional $\frac{1}{4}$ mile. How many miles can a customer go for $5.00?

    (A) $\frac{3}{4}$

    (B) 1

    (C) $1\frac{1}{4}$

    (D) $1\frac{1}{2}$

    (E) $1\frac{3}{4}$

14. A race-car driver took between $3\frac{1}{2}$ and 4 hours to drive 500 miles on a track. His average speed, in miles per hour, must have been between

    (A) 125 and 143 mph

    (B) 143 and 158 mph

    (C) 158 and 167 mph

    (D) 167 and 181 mph

    (E) 181 and 200 mph

15. Bill took 2 hours and 24 minutes to run a marathon. Fred took four times as long to walk the same distance. How much time did Fred spend walking?

    (A) 8 h 48 min

    (B) 9 h 32 min

    (C) 9 h 36 min

    (D) 10 h 32 min

    (E) 10 h 36 min

16. In the figure, if three lines meet as shown, what is the value of $x + 3y$?

    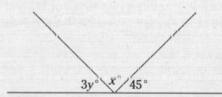

    (A) 90

    (B) 105

    (C) 120

    (D) 135

    (E) 150

17. $624 \div 4 =$

    (A) $\frac{600}{4} \times \frac{20}{4} \times \frac{4}{4}$

    (B) $\frac{600}{4} + \frac{20}{4} + \frac{4}{4}$

    (C) $\frac{60}{4} + \frac{24}{4}$

    (D) $\frac{600}{4} + 24$

    (E) $\frac{6}{4} + \frac{2}{4} + \frac{4}{4}$

Go on to next page

18. Alex's class has 35 students. When she collected $0.50 from each student to pay for a present, she found that she had only $\frac{1}{4}$ of the money needed to pay for the present. How much more money must she collect from each student to pay for the present?

    (A) $0.50

    (B) $0.75

    (C) $1.25

    (D) $1.50

    (E) $1.75

19. Which of the following gives the number of dollars in a $50.00 bills, b $20.00 bills, and six $5.00 bills?

    (A) $\frac{a}{50} + \frac{b}{20} + 30$

    (B) $\frac{50}{a} + \frac{20}{b} + 30$

    (C) $50a + 20b + 30$

    (D) $50a + 20b + 6$

    (E) $50a + 20b + 5$

20. If a polygon has a perimeter of 128 and its sides all measure 8 in length, how many sides does it have?

    (A) 15

    (B) 16

    (C) 17

    (D) 18

    (E) 1,024

21. If Will's savings earn 4% interest for a year, how much interest is earned annually for every dollar he saves?

    (A) 0.04 cents

    (B) 0.4 cents

    (C) 4 cents

    (D) 40 cents

    (E) 400 cents

22. Which of the following numbers is evenly divisible by 3?

    (A) 725

    (B) 726

    (C) 727

    (D) 728

    (E) 730

23. In a certain classroom, each of 30 students owns either a computer or a cellphone or both. If 25 students in the classroom own cellphones and 25 own computers, how many students own both?

    (A) 10

    (B) 15

    (C) 20

    (D) 25

    (E) 30

24. Two people shared the cost of a taxi to the airport, and each paid $9.00. How much would each person have paid if a third person shared the cost equally with them?

    (A) $5.00

    (B) $5.50

    (C) $6.00

    (D) $6.50

    (E) $7.00

25. If $x > 2$, which of the following is greatest?

    (A) $2x + 1$

    (B) $x + 1$

    (C) $x - 1$

    (D) $\frac{x}{2}$

    (E) 5

STOP DO NOT TURN THE PAGE UNTIL TOLD TO DO SO. DO NOT RETURN TO A PREVIOUS TEST.

Chapter 22

Answers to SSAT Lower Level Practice Exam 2

• •

Now that you've finished taking the SSAT Lower Level Practice Exam 2, spend time reading through the answers and explanations provided in this chapter. Doing so is a great way to find out what you missed and why. Also, reading through *all* the explanations — even for the questions you got right — only increases your learning and understanding and helps you prepare even more for test day. If you just want to do a quick check of your answers, see the abbreviated answer key at the end of this chapter.

Section 1: Writing Sample

Remember that writing samples don't have right or wrong answers, and with this topic (the early bird catches the worm), you can write about a variety of issues. You want to choose a side — whether you agree or disagree — to this statement and support your position with examples.

Following are a few things you should have done to write a winning practice essay:

✔ Because the essay prompt asks you to agree or disagree with the statement, "The early bird catches the worm," you should have made clear in your introduction what position you're taking — whether you agreed or disagreed with the statement.

✔ Your body paragraphs should have included specific examples that help back up or *prove* your position. These examples can be of a famous person, such as a sports star or a talented actor or singer, or a character from a book you read who was successful as the early bird who caught the worm. If you use a character from a book or story on the actual test, make sure you include the name of the character and mention the name of the story or book.

✔ To really hit a home run with this essay, you should have included an example from your own life. Did you write about a time where you succeeded (or not) because you were first or early? Remember that the readers want to hear your voice. Including a personal story or experience is a great way to make a writing sample really come to life for the reader.

✔ You should have included a conclusion that brought your ideas together and again affirmed your position on the essay. Conclusions help show that your thoughts and ideas are organized and that you stuck with the topic, so don't forget about the conclusion when you write.

Finally, have someone else read your essay and mark misspelled words, poorly organized sentences, misplaced commas, and other grammatical problems. Doing so helps you see how many errors you made. Remember that the writing sample isn't a grammar test, and a few errors won't hurt you in the end, but overall, your sample should be well written and generally error free.

Section 2: Quantitative, Part 1

1. **B.** Check the answer choices and see which one results in the same number: $18 + 4 = 22$ and $26 - 4 = 22$. Or, if you like algebra, you can set up an equation: $18 + x = 26 - x$, where x is the number of brownies given, and then solve: $2x = 8$, so $x = 4$.

2. **D.** To work this problem, you simply have to do the math, starting with the first part of the equation: $5 \times \frac{1}{5} = 1$ or $\left(\frac{5}{1} \times \frac{1}{5} = \frac{5}{5} = 1 \right)$ then 1×250 is 250.

3. **E.** You need to notice what changed in the example figures, and then apply that change to the new figure — kind of like an analogy. In the example, each little diamond changed places with the big diamond above it, so the correct answer is a picture where each little hexagon changed places with the big hexagon above it.

4. **B.** The wheel for Choice (B) has only three odd numbers out of eight total numbers, so the probability of spinning an odd number on that wheel is $\frac{3}{8}$ (remember, *probability* is how many of what you want divided by the total number of possibilities). All the other wheels have four odd numbers, so they have a greater chance $\left(\frac{4}{8} \right)$ of spinning an odd number.

5. **C.** If Peter buys seven packages, he'll have two bones left over. If he buys six packages, he'll have only 24 bones, which isn't enough for each dog to have one. So Choice (C) is the best answer.

6. **C.** Draw a picture so you can visualize the tables.

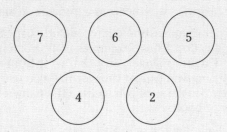

Because you need the *smallest* number of tables, each table should be maxed out. If the first table has seven people, the next gets six (because you can't have the same number at any table). The third gets five, the fourth gets four, and the fifth gets the rest of the people (two): $7 + 6 + 5 + 4 + 2 = 24$.

7. **C.** Try drawing the letters. You can draw a B without lifting your pencil or retracing. Don't worry if you need to use a little trial and error!

8. **D.** If you draw the diameters on the oranges, you can see that the box is 9 inches by 9 inches.

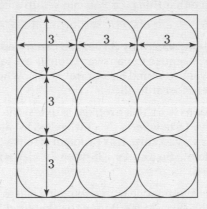

9. **E.** Try drawing this one, too, to prove to yourself that there's no way to tell for sure. For example, if you draw both of their houses due north of the park, they'll be only seven miles apart, but if one is north of the park and one is south of the park, then they'll be 17 miles apart.

10. **D.** It may be easiest to think about this question if you're dealing in whole buses rather than half buses. If half a bus is 7 tons, then a whole bus is 14 tons. Four whole buses are then $14 \times 4 = 56$ tons, which is 7×8 (check the choices or divide 56 by 7).

11. **C.** First add 227 + 36 to get 263, which is the number the other side of the equation must equal. Then multiply the numbers in parentheses: $10 \times 6 = 60$; $3 \times 1 = 3$. Add those two numbers: $60 + 3 = 63$; so you need 200 more to make 263. Therefore, *?* equals 2 because $100 \times 2 = 200$.

12. **E.** The trick to solving this question is to realize that only one of the answer choices can be the area of a square. Only Choice (E) is the result of multiplying a number by itself ($6 \times 6 = 36$).

13. **E.** The key to this question is to realize that if you fold a piece of paper in half and then cut something out of it, both sides of the unfolded paper are mirror images of each other. Only Choice (E) *isn't* symmetrical.

14. **C.** If the star is located at (4, 3), then the 4 represents four lines to the right and the 3 represents three lines up. If you double the first number, 4 becomes 8 ($4 \times 2 = 8$). If you triple the second number, 3 becomes 9 ($3 \times 3 = 9$). Look for the point eight lines to the right and nine lines up, which is *C*. So Choice (C) is the correct answer.

15. **D.** If the marks on a number line look equally spaced, you can assume they are. So if there are three marks between 3 and 12, each one of those distances must be 3 in length (3, 6, 9, 12). After you figure that out, you just have to fill in the missing marks: 3, *6, 9,* 12, *15, 18,* and 21. The arrow points at 18. Trial and error works pretty well on this question, too — the correct choice makes the distance between marks the same number.

16. **D.** Shaded region problems are usually about finding the whole area and subtracting what you don't want. You can find the area of the square by multiplying its length by its width: $6 \times 6 = 36$, because a square has equal sides. Then, subtract the area of the triangle. The area of a triangle is $\frac{1}{2}$ (*base* $\times$ *height*). This triangle's base is 3 and its height is 6 (or vice versa, it doesn't matter which is base and which is height as long as they're perpendicular to each other), so $\frac{1}{2}(3 \times 6) = \frac{1}{2}(18) = 9$. Then $36 - 9 = 27$.

17. **D.** If the water is 17 inches below the halfway mark, then it'd be at the halfway mark if it rose 17 inches. But it rises 23 inches, so it goes above the halfway mark by $23 - 17 = 6$ inches.

18. **C.** If you're a math whiz, you may know that 30 percent of something is the same thing as 15 percent of twice that thing. Or you can set up an equation: $0.30n = 10$, so $n = \frac{10}{0.3} = 33.33$. Then solve for 15 percent of $2n$ by setting up $2(33.3)(0.15) = 9.99$, which is basically 10.

19. **D.** Instead of dividing 95,284 by 2,105, you can round the numbers down to make this problem a little easier, because the answer choices are fairly far apart (if they were really close together, you'd want to round less or not at all). When you divide 95,000 by 2,100, you end up with an answer closest to 45.

20. **C.** The easiest way to work this problem is to test the choices; when you get to Choice (C), you notice that five trike wheels (5×3 wheels = 15) and five quad wheels (5×4 wheels = 20) equal 35. Another way to solve this problem is to make an equation, calling the number of each type of vehicle x. So $3x + 4x = 35$, then $7x = 35$, and dividing both sides of that equation by 7 results in $x = 5$.

21. **C.** This problem is another one where rounding makes your life easier. Round the price of the computer from $995.00 to $1,000.00 and then subtract 25 percent of $1,000.00 from $1,000.00 (you can figure out 25 percent of $1,000.00 by multiplying: $1,000.00 \times 0.25 = $250.00), so $1,000.00 - $250.00 = $750.00.

22. **A.** You can find the daily sales before the discount by multiplying the number of people by the price ($300 \times $7.50 = $2,250.00). You can then find the first part of the new daily sales by multiplying the number of people paying the old price by the old price ($200 \times $7.50 = $1,500.00). Then, subtract $1,500.00 from $2,250.00 to find out how much money the discount price must make up for: $2,250.00 - $1,500.00 = $750.00. Finally, divide $750.00 by $5.00 to see how many people need to pay $5.00 to make up the difference: $750.00 ÷ $5.00 = 150 people.

23. **D.** Using a little visualization helps with this one. Try imagining the cube is split up into three equal slices from top to bottom. You can see that nine blocks are in the top slice, and because the cube is solid, nine blocks must be in each slice: ($9 \times 3 = 27$).

24. **E.** If $\frac{1}{5} + K > 1$, then K has to be bigger than $\frac{4}{5}$, because $\frac{1}{5} + \frac{4}{5} = 1$. Checking the choices, only $\frac{5}{6}$ is bigger than $\frac{4}{5}$. Remember, you can compare the size of fractions accurately by giving them a common denominator, or bottom part. You can check your answer by adding $\frac{1}{5}$ and $\frac{5}{6}$: $\frac{1}{5} + \frac{5}{6} = \left(\frac{1 \times 6}{5 \times 6}\right) + \left(\frac{5 \times 5}{6 \times 5}\right) = \frac{6}{30} + \frac{25}{30} = \frac{31}{30} = 1\frac{1}{30}$, which is greater than 1.

25. **D.** For this problem, you may want to draw a picture to give yourself a visual. Then, count the pieces: 16 is four more than 12, so Choice (D) is the only answer choice that works. Also, more pieces mean each piece is smaller. And because the pie is divided into 16ths, each piece is exactly $\frac{1}{16}$ of the whole pie, so they're all the same size.

Section 3: Reading Comprehension

1. **C.** Remember that the overall purpose of a passage describes what the piece of writing accomplishes. As such, be careful of being too general or too specific with the answer. This passage describes the armadillo's features.

2. **A.** *Distinct* simply means unique. The author is saying that 20 unique species of the armadillo exist.

3. **A.** By definition, *havoc* means chaos or disorder. In this context, the author simply means that the armadillo causes problems, or damage, in planted areas.

4. **A.** *Resilient* means to recover from problems or hardship. In this passage, the author is saying the armadillo is able to survive.

5. **C.** The author states that many southern residents dislike the armadillo because they can be destructive. This statement is an opinion because no facts actually determine that southern residents generally dislike the animal. When you face a question like this one, look at what answer choices can be easily proven. For example, you can easily prove that armadillos have short legs with facts about leg length. Rule out answer choices that are factual to help find the answer choice that is an opinion, something typically not based on facts.

6. **B.** This paragraph is an opinion paragraph. The writer offers an opinion about the environment, but he provides no facts or details. Therefore, Choice (B) is your best answer.

7. **C.** The author implies that plastic bags are a pollutant, unlike paper bags that don't pollute the environment. The author states that paper bags are easier to recycle.

8. **A.** The author wants the reader to take action. The example given is to use paper bags instead of plastic as a way to reduce plastic pollution. Although the author obviously wants you to understand what he's writing about, his primary goal is that you'll take an action in response to what he's written.

9. **E.** In this passage, the word *contemporary* refers to the current state of the world. The author uses this word to establish his idea that pollution and recycling are important for everyone alive at the moment.

10. **B.** In this passage, the author gives the reader only one action, despite how complex the problem of pollution and recycling is in the modern world. If more examples of actions were added, the article would be stronger. The other answer choices would provide more details, but not necessarily more details that are helpful to the purpose of the article.

11. **B.** The text specifically points out that tornadoes are destructive because of the wind speed.

12. **D.** Tornadoes can occur anywhere but are more concentrated in the Tornado Alley states. Of the answer choices provided, Texas is the only state in Tornado Alley, so Choice (D) is the correct answer in terms of likelihood.

13. **D.** The article explains that hot and cold air create tornado conditions.

14. **E.** The article states that tornado season is April to June, so the best answer is May, because a tornado is most likely to occur during seasonal months.

15. **E.** The article states that tornadoes can have wind speeds up to 500 mph, so that's the maximum speed.

16. **D.** *Furious* means full of fury — or extremely angry.

17. **C.** *Exhibit* means to show or display something, so in this passage, the characters didn't show or display any emotion.

18. **D.** *Reap* means to have or own something you deserve.

19. **D.** *Grin and bear* is a slang phrase, meaning to act like nothing is wrong in times of difficulty.

20. **E.** If you face a question like this, look at the sentence in question and then find a sentence that means the same thing or further explains the meaning. What the author is saying is that the things people say can be very hurtful.

21. **A.** The purpose of the article is to refute three common myths about Lincoln. The article briefly describes each myth and provides evidence to disprove each myth.

22. **B.** *Notable* means remarkable or noteworthy. This word often describes someone famous or who's made some great accomplishment.

23. **C.** The word *succumb* means to fail to resist — often used to describe someone failing to resist a disease or injury that ends in death.

24. **A.** The word *debunk* means to prove that something is false. This term is often used when someone proves an idea, belief, or myth to be false.

25. **B.** A myth is something believed to be true, but it isn't grounded in any factual evidence. The concepts of myths and folklore are often used interchangeably.

26. **E.** The phrase means that Lincoln chose to sit for paintings and sculptures without any outside influence. In other words, he chose to do it himself.

27. **C.** The word *boast* can mean different things, including a negative human behavior. In this context, it means to possess or own desirable features.

28. **C.** The overall purpose of the passage is to describe some basic features of Iceland, including the landscape, cities, and culture.

29. **E.** You can infer that Iceland is a young continent because of the volcanic activity that likely formed the island. This clue is the strongest one the text gives you.

30. **C.** This question is a simple recall question from the passage, which tells you Helka has erupted 16 times.

31. **A.** The author is saying that the different landscape features, from volcanoes to waterfalls, make the island interesting.

32. **B.** *Vibrant* means full of life. The author is saying that although the city is old, it's still a lively city.

33. **A.** The word *swiftly* simply means that something happens quickly. When you encounter a question like this one, don't read more into the meaning than the author intends. You may be tempted to choose *without warning,* considering the circumstances of the canoe accident, but the word simply means that the incident happened quickly, so be sure to stick to the simplest explanation for a word.

34. **C.** The word *plunge* means to enter something quickly. The author is saying the character was thrown out of the canoe and quickly into the water.

35. **E.** A *simile* is a comparison between two often dissimilar things using the words *like* or *as.*

36. **D.** An *instinct* is something animals do without having to be taught. The author uses the word here to describe an action that the character does without thinking about it.

37. **A.** *Foreshadowing* is a literary technique where the author gives clues about what will happen or a potential outcome. In this passage, the author uses this technique to build suspense.

38. **D.** The word *raging* means to have extreme anger. Of course, water doesn't experience emotions, so in this case, the author uses this word to communicate danger. This phrase is an example of personification.

39. **E.** The author is using personification to make the reader feel that the rock wall is a danger or threat to the character.

40. **A.** The rocks felt good to the character because they represent safety.

Section 4: Verbal

1. **D.** *Extraordinary* means beyond what's normal. The best answer is *unusual* because the two words refer to something that doesn't happen normally.

2. **C.** *Callous* means harsh, cold, uncaring, or unfeeling, so Choice (C), *uncaring,* is the correct answer.

3. **D.** *Solitary* means to be alone, so Choice (D) is the only answer that works.

4. **B.** The word *elude* means to avoid, evade, or escape. Choice (B), *escape,* is the only word that means the same thing.

5. **A.** *Awkward* means clumsy, or it can also refer to something embarrassing. *Clumsy* is the only word in the list that can be a synonym, so Choice (A) is the correct answer.

6. **B.** If you *constrain* something, you bind it or hold it back in some way. Choice (B) is the only synonym for this word.

7. **E.** Someone who's *deceptive* is untruthful or avoids the complete truth. The word *wily* means the same thing. The other answer choices are all *antonyms,* meaning they're the opposite.

8. **C.** *Comply* means to cooperate or do something that you're asked to do, so Choice (C) is correct. Don't let the other answer choices that sound similar fool you. Just because two words sound alike doesn't mean they're similar in meaning.

9. **E.** The word *debunk* means to prove or expose something false. You can say, "The theory was debunked by several other scientists." Choice (E) is the only synonym.

10. **A.** If you *support* something, you uphold or sustain it. For example, if you want to support your school team, you cheer it on and speak well of it. The word *sustain* means the same thing.

11. **C.** Something *traditional* holds to commonly accepted beliefs or practices. The word *conventional* means the same thing.

12. **B.** An *inquiry* is a question or request. For example, "John made an inquiry about the process for a driver's license."

13. **A.** In this problem, you have an easy word for the question, but the answer choices are more difficult. The word *ambiguous* means unclear, so Choice (A) is the correct answer.

14. **E.** The word *uncommon* means unusual or rare. In other words, an uncommon event rarely ever happens. Based on this definition, Choice (E) is correct.

15. **D.** The word *equivalent* simply means equal. You can say, "2 + 2 is equivalent to 5 – 1."

16. **A.** *Animosity* means *disagreement* or even hate in some cases. Of the answer choices provided, it's the only possible synonym.

17. **E.** *Notorious* means famous but for a negative reason. For example, you can say, "The bank robber was notorious."

18. **B.** To be *infuriated* means you're furious or angry.

19. **D.** The word *slaphappy* simply means silly.

20. **B.** The word *truncated* means shortened. For example, "The boat tour was truncated because of the bad weather."

21. **E.** The word *operate* technically means to work. If your MP3 player operates, it works.

22. **C.** The word *retrospect* means to look back or remember. This question is an example of how a prefix can give you a clue. The prefix *retro-* means in the past. So always look for prefixes and suffixes that lead you in the right direction.

23. **C.** The word *sympathize,* from the word *sympathy,* means to have compassion for someone or to feel pity for someone. For example, "I sympathized with you on this problem."

24. **A.** If you *interpret* something, you translate it into greater meaning. For example, if you interpret a math problem, you give it greater meaning. In the same way, if someone speaks a foreign language and you translate it, you interpret for them, or give their words greater meaning to someone who doesn't know the language.

25. **D.** *Cannon* can refer to an actual cannon ball, or it can also be used as a verb, as it is in this question, meaning discharge. For example, "The soldiers cannoned the shells over the wall."

26. **C.** A *jaunt* is a short trip, so Choice (C) is the correct answer.

27. **E.** *Stricken* means sick in some way. For example, "Sam was stricken with a stomach virus."

28. **B.** *Potent* means strong. This word can describe someone who's physically strong, but it often describes a drink or even a medicine. For example, "The potent antibiotic was needed to cure the disease."

29. **A.** This question is another example of where you need to look for words within the word. You may realize the word *inconsequential* comes from the word *consequence*. The prefix *in-* means not, so the literal meaning is not of consequence, which is the same thing as not important, or *unimportant*.

30. **B.** The word *prevail* means to overcome an obstacle or problem of some kind. Of the provided answer choices, Choice (B) is the only synonym.

31. **D.** A forest is made up of trees, so a single tree is a *unit* of a forest. As you look at the answer choices, the only two that express this relationship are Choices (D) and (E). However, an important difference exists between these two choices: A forest is made up of a *group* of trees just as a herd is made up of a *group* of cows, but a *group* of puzzle pieces don't make a puzzle — it takes unique pieces fitting together to create the whole. Choice (D) is correct because it expresses the same relationship as the question.

Always choose the *best* answer that has the closest relationship to the analogy given.

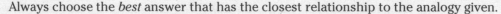

32. **C.** A heart is a part of the body, so it's a part of the whole. Additionally, the body requires the heart to operate, so you're looking for similar relationships. The only answer that expresses the same relationship is a *processor to a computer* because the processor is a part of the whole, and the computer can't operate without a processor. You may have started off thinking, "The heart is in the body." However, the other answer choices have the same relationship as well. This is a case where you begin with one relationship, but you may have to define it more or at least be more specific to find the right answer.

33. **B.** A printer uses paper to perform the job it was designed to perform. In the same way, a washer uses detergent to perform the job it was designed to perform. Always remember that you're not looking for the same kind of analogy but one that expresses the same kind of relationship.

34. **A.** A zipper can hold a piece of luggage together, so you need a similar relationship. The best answer is glue to paper, because glue can hold two pieces of paper together.

35. **C.** This one is rather straightforward. The moon orbits the earth, so first consider that relationship. A satellite orbits the earth, so it expresses a similar relationship.

36. **B.** A television displays an image. In the same way, a sign displays an ad. Choice (B) is the best similar relationship.

37. **B.** A thermometer measures temperature. In a similar way, a clock measures time.

38. **C.** A college student goes to college to get a degree, so you can say that a degree is the goal of the college student. Looking for a similar kind of relationship, the best match is the *football player and Super Bowl.* The ultimate goal of a football player is to play in the Super Bowl, so Choice (C) expresses the same basic relationship.

39. **C.** This one is rather straightforward; just remember to keep the concept of *relationship* in mind. You use a keyboard to manage or control a computer like you use a steering wheel to manage or control a car.

40. **D.** Here's another fairly easy analogy. A bandage is a tool that a nurse uses, so you're specifically looking for a tool and someone who uses it. Under this construction, Choice (D) is the only possible answer because a paper is a tool that a writer uses.

41. **A.** This one is a bit more complicated. A dream *isn't* reality, but if you use this kind of sentence, every answer choice can work. Instead, think a bit deeper and realize that a dream is the opposite of reality — it seems real even though it isn't. If you think in terms of opposites, the only possible answer that has the same kind of relationship is Choice (A). Water and land are opposites in a similar way. It's a bit of a stretch, but you'll encounter these kinds of test questions. Remember to look for the *best* answer.

42. **E.** The relationship here is easy: An alligator lives in a river. Using a similar relationship, you have two possible answers: Choices (A) and (E). In this case, you need to choose the best answer. A bird's home is a nest, which is often in a tree, but birds can also build nests in other locations as well. So Choice (E) is the best answer.

43. **E.** You can say that trial leads to error — if you try certain things, some will fail. You're given the word *workout,* so you need a word that shows what working out can lead to. The best answer is Choice (E), *growth,* because a workout gives your skills and strength the opportunity to grow.

44. **A.** Fun can lead to a laugh. In the same way, a seed can eventually lead to a flower of some kind. Choice (A) is the best relationship from the available answer choices.

45. **C.** For this question, the first analogy concerns an opposite relationship (smile to frown). You simply need to find the word that means the opposite of gargantuan. *Gargantuan* means extremely large, so the only possible answer is Choice (C), *tiny*.

46. **D.** A detail is something specific, so you're looking for a basic synonym of the word *adulation,* which means to praise. The only possible answer is *laud,* which means the same thing.

47. **A.** A liner is what gives a pool its shape or contains the water. In the same way, a shell contains an egg or gives it the shape.

48. **D.** This one is a bit more difficult. A saw is able to saw because of a blade. In other words, the blade is what makes the saw function. In a similar way, yeast is what makes bread rise; without yeast, bread wouldn't cook to become bread as we know it.

49. **B.** *Denial* and *deny* are basically the same word used in different ways, but the meaning is the same. So you simply need a relationship between two words that mean the same thing. Choice (B), *comprehension is to understand,* is the only answer with two words that mean the same thing.

50. **B.** Mortar is used to hold bricks in place, such as in a brick wall. In a similar way, a cup is used to hold water in place.

51. **B.** A formula is used to find a solution to a problem. In a similar way, you can use a ruler to find a particular measurement. In this question, you can also look at the formula and ruler as tools that can be used for these purposes.

52. **B.** In order to jump, you have to overcome gravity. In a similar way, if you want to do a bench press exercise, you have to overcome the weight in order to be able to lift it.

53. **C.** Terror is a greater degree of fear, so you need a word that expresses a greater degree of being happy. *Ecstatic* is the only possible answer because it means extreme happiness.

54. **A.** *Jocular* means funny, so the two words have the same meaning. You simply need a word that means the same as *reticent. Reticent* means bashful or quiet, so Choice (A) is correct.

55. **B.** A fork is stored in a drawer, so you need a relationship that expresses a location where something is stored. The best answer is Choice (B) because coins can be stored in a purse. You may be tempted to choose bird and cage, but a bird isn't stored in a cage. You want to get as close to the primary relationship as possible.

56. **B.** *Calculate* and *guess* are opposites of each other, so you simply need to choose a word that expresses an opposite relationship of *deceptive*. The correct answer is *truthful*.

57. **A.** *Angst* means to be fearful, which is the opposite of peace. So you need a word that's the opposite of impeccable. *Impeccable* means flawless, so the opposite word you need is *error*.

58. **D.** You receive pay from a job, so you need a relationship that shows what you receive from a book. The only possible answer is Choice (D), *information*.

59. **A.** If you press down on the accelerator of a car, the car speeds up. So you're looking for a cause and effect relationship between the word *fatigue,* which means to be exhausted or tired, and another word. The only possible answer is Choice (A), *sleep*. Fatigue causes sleep because you sleep when you're very tired.

60. **B.** *Gallant* and *courageous* mean the same thing, so you simply need to choose a word that means the same thing as *emphatic*. The correct answer is Choice (B), *forceful*.

Section 5: Quantitative, Part 2

1. **C.** $7{,}902 - 407 = 7{,}495$.

2. **E.** If $50 \times N$ is 50, then N must be 1, because $50 \times 1 = 50$. So $50 + N = 50 + 1$, which is 51.

3. **B.** First, figure out the whole number, $200 - 4 = 196$, then subtract the fraction $196 - \frac{2}{30} = 195\frac{28}{30}$ or $195\frac{14}{15}$. If you convert the answer choices to 30ths, you can easily see that subtracting $\frac{2}{30}$ from 196 leaves $195\frac{28}{30}$. Alternatively, you can go backward and see which answer choice you can add $\frac{2}{30}$ to and get 196.

4. **C.** Converting to a common unit of measurement is usually a good idea. So if you convert feet to inches, the string is $5 \times 12 = 60$ inches long, plus half a foot (6 inches) = 66 inches. Then, divide by 6: $\frac{66}{6} = 11$.

5. **C.** Multiplying 500 by 0.025 is the same thing as multiplying 500 by 25 (move the decimal point in 0.025 three spots to the right to give yourself a whole number and then move the decimal back three spots to the left). So do it the normal way ($500 \times 0.025 = 12.5$) or try $500 \times 25 = 12{,}500$, and then move the decimal 3 spots to the left to get 12.5.

6. **E.** If $N > 5$, then make $N = 6$, because N is an integer, or whole number, and $2N$ would then equal 12. So $12 + 4 = 16$. If N were 5, then the answer could be Choice (D), 15, but because N has to be greater than 5, the only answer that can work is Choice (E).

7. **C.** First, add the whole numbers: $2 + 1 = 3$. Then, add the fractions: $\frac{7}{8} + \frac{3}{8} = \frac{10}{8}$, which reduces to $\frac{5}{4}$. To figure out what that is as a decimal, divide 5 by 4 and get 1.25. So the answer is $3 + 1.25 = 4.25$.

8. **B.** Average problems get easier if you assume — when not otherwise indicated — that everything in the problem has the same value. So if the average weight of three dogs is 50 pounds, assume that they *all* weigh 50 pounds, and that *both* cats weigh 10 pounds. Now, add all the values ($50 + 50 + 50 + 10 + 10 = 170$) and divide by 5 to get the average: $\frac{170}{5} = 34$.

9. **E.** The only one that doesn't end up as $\frac{4}{3}$ is Choice (E): $32 \times \frac{1}{20} = \frac{32}{20}$, which reduces to $\frac{8}{5}$.

10. **D.** Just check the answer choices and think about which number 8 is 25 percent, or a quarter, of. To see whether you're right, divide the number by 8 ($32 \div 8 = 4$, so 8 is 25 percent of 32). Algebraically, you can write 8 is 25 percent of what number as $8 = 0.25x$ then solve for x by dividing both sides of the equation by 0.25: $8 \div 0.25 = 32$.

11. **C.** In the number 77,777, the leftmost 7 has a value of 70,000, and the rightmost 7 has a value of 7. So $70{,}000 = 7 \times 10{,}000$; in other words, 70,000 has a value that is 10,000 times 7.

12. **B.** This problem is about *area*. To find the area of the piece of fabric, multiply its length by its width: $60 \times 45 = 2{,}700$ square inches. Because Yvonne paid \$810.00 for the fabric, divide \$810.00 by 2,700 to see how much she paid for each square inch: $810 \div 2{,}700 = \$0.30$.

13. **C.** If the customer has \$5.00, the first $\frac{1}{4}$ mile costs \$2.00, leaving \$3.00. The next $\frac{1}{4}$ mile costs \$0.75, leaving \$2.25. Then a $\frac{1}{4}$ mile more = \$1.50 left, a $\frac{1}{4}$ mile more than that = \$0.75 left, and the final $\frac{1}{4}$ mile = \$0.00 left. Add the miles and you get $1\frac{1}{4}$ total miles.

14. **A.** To figure out the driver's average speed, remember the formula *distance = rate × time*. Dividing both sides of that equation by time gives you the driver's rate, or speed: $\frac{500}{3.5} =$ about 143 and $\frac{500}{4} = 125$, so if the driver's time was between $3\frac{1}{2}$ and 4 hours, his average speed must have been between 125 and 143 mph.

15. **C.** To figure out what 2 hours and 24 minutes × 4 is, first figure out the hours: 2 × 4 = 8. Then figure out the minutes: 24 × 4 = 96 minutes. Because 60 minutes are in an hour, the 96 minutes adds one more hour (so the total is now 9), with 36 minutes left over (96 − 60 = 36). So, in total, the answer is 9 hours and 36 minutes.

16. **D.** To solve this one, remember that the angles on one side of a line add up to 180 degrees. So 45 + x + 3y = 180 degrees. To find out what x + 3y equals, subtract 45 from both sides: x + 3y = 135.

17. **B.** For this problem, first simply do the math: 624 ÷ 4 = 156. Choice (B) is the correct answer: $\frac{600}{4}(150) + \frac{20}{4}(5) + \frac{4}{4}(1) = 156$.

18. **D.** One way to do this is to multiply 35 by $0.50 to figure out how much money Alex initially received: 35 × 0.5 = $17.50. If $17.50 paid for only $\frac{1}{4}$ of the present, the entire present must cost 4 times that: $17.50 × 4 = $70.00. You can then subtract $17.50 from $70.00 to see how much money is still needed and divide that number by 35 to see how much each student must contribute: $70.00 − $17.50 = $52.50, $52.50 ÷ 35 = $1.50. Or, logically, if a $0.50 contribution was $\frac{1}{4}$ of what was needed, then you can figure out what number $0.50 is a quarter of: $\frac{1}{4}x$ = $0.50. Dividing both sides by $\frac{1}{4}$ equals x = $2.00, and because $0.50 was already given, $1.50 is still needed from each student.

19. **C.** The six $5.00 bills are easy to calculate: 6 × 5 = 30. Because 50 dollars are in every $50.00 bill and there are a $50.00 bills, 50 × a gives you the number of dollars in a $50.00 bills. Say you had four $50.00 bills, 50 × 4 = 200, which is the amount of dollars in four $50.00 bills. Similarly, 20 dollars are in each $20.00 bill, so 20 × b gives you that amount.

20. **B.** If all the sides in the polygon have a length of 8, you can find out how many sides there are by dividing: 128 ÷ 8 = 16.

21. **C.** Here, 4 percent is 4 per *cent*, and *cent* in the word *percent* means 100. So Will earns 4 cents interest for every dollar, because 100 cents are in a dollar. Alternatively, you can multiply the 100 cents in the dollar by 0.04 (the decimal that 4 percent converts to) to find out how much interest is earned.

22. **B.** An easy way to find out whether a number is divisible by 3 is to add all its digits and see whether 3 can go into the result. Adding the digits in 726 gives you 15 (7 + 2 + 6), and because 3 goes into 15, that's the answer. Or you can just test the answers by dividing 3 into each one.

23. **C.** The easiest way to tackle this problem is to test the choices. For example, if you test Choice (A), 10 students own both cellphones and computers. If that were true, 15 students would have to own *only* cellphones to make a total of 25 students with cellphones (15 with just cellphones, 10 with both cellphones and computers). And then 15 students would own *only* computers (to make a total of 25 students with computers). Because that choice results in 40 total students, it can't be correct — the question says there are 30 students! However, if you test Choice (C) and assume that 20 students have both, then 5 students have only cellphones and 5 have only computers, giving you a total of 30 students.

24. **C.** If each person paid $9.00, together they paid $18.00 total. Adding a third person would mean that the $18.00 is split three ways: $18.00 ÷ 3 = $6.00.

25. **A.** Assuming x is 2 can be useful here (so you don't have to deal with decimals); just don't forget it has to be a little higher. Choice (A) would equal 5 (2 × 2 + 1 = 5), but because x is greater than 2, imagine that Choice (A) is a number a little higher than 5. The only other answer that's close to Choice (A) is Choice (E), so Choice (A) has to be bigger.

Answers at a Glance

Section 2: Quantitative, Part 1

1. B	6. C	11. C	16. D	21. C
2. D	7. C	12. E	17. D	22. A
3. E	8. D	13. E	18. C	23. D
4. B	9. E	14. C	19. D	24. E
5. C	10. D	15. D	20. C	25. D

Section 3: Reading Comprehension

1. C	9. E	17. C	25. B	33. A
2. A	10. B	18. D	26. E	34. C
3. A	11. B	19. D	27. C	35. E
4. A	12. D	20. E	28. C	36. D
5. C	13. D	21. A	29. E	37. A
6. B	14. E	22. B	30. C	38. D
7. C	15. E	23. C	31. A	39. E
8. A	16. D	24. A	32. B	40. A

Section 4: Verbal

1. D	9. E	17. E	25. D	33. B
2. C	10. A	18. B	26. C	34. A
3. D	11. C	19. D	27. E	35. C
4. B	12. B	20. B	28. B	36. B
5. A	13. A	21. E	29. A	37. B
6. B	14. E	22. C	30. B	38. C
7. E	15. D	23. C	31. D	39. C
8. C	16. A	24. A	32. C	40. D

41. A	45. C	49. B	53. C	57. A
42. E	46. D	50. B	54. A	58. D
43. E	47. A	51. B	55. B	59. A
44. A	48. D	52. B	56. B	60. B

Section 5: Quantitative, Part 2

1. C	6. E	11. C	16. D	21. C
2. E	7. C	12. B	17. B	22. B
3. B	8. B	13. C	18. D	23. C
4. C	9. E	14. A	19. C	24. C
5. C	10. D	15. C	20. B	25. A

Part V
ISEE Practice Exams

The 5th Wave   By Rich Tennant

"It's an ISEE testing center, but it operates half the year as a meatpacking plant."

In this part . . .

Part V includes three full ISEE practice exams: one upper level, one middle level, and one lower level exam. After each exam, we provide a chapter with the answers to every question as well as an explanation for each correct answer. So get some ISEE practice and do your best!

Chapter 23

ISEE Upper Level Practice Exam

*T*ime to get to work, ISEE upper level students! Practice exams are never fun, and although you may be tempted to make a half-hearted effort, remember that practice makes perfect, so treat this practice test like an actual ISEE exam and give it your all. To make the most of this practice exam, find yourself a quiet room, ample time, a few sharpened pencils, and some blank scratch paper. Resist the urge to play on the Internet or text your friends while you're taking the test. After all, you want to practice in the same quiet and boring conditions that you'll face on test day.

Grab a watch, an iPod, a phone, or some other way to track your time. Make sure you don't go over the time limit we've given you for each part of this practice test because you won't be allowed extra time on the actual test. You can find all the answers to this practice test in Chapter 24, but don't cheat! Check your answers only *after* you finish the test.

Answer Sheet

For Sections 1 through 4 of the exam, use the following answer sheets and fill in the answer bubble for the corresponding number, using a #2 pencil.

Section 1: Verbal Reasoning

1. Ⓐ Ⓑ Ⓒ Ⓓ Ⓔ	11. Ⓐ Ⓑ Ⓒ Ⓓ Ⓔ	21. Ⓐ Ⓑ Ⓒ Ⓓ Ⓔ	31. Ⓐ Ⓑ Ⓒ Ⓓ Ⓔ
2. Ⓐ Ⓑ Ⓒ Ⓓ Ⓔ	12. Ⓐ Ⓑ Ⓒ Ⓓ Ⓔ	22. Ⓐ Ⓑ Ⓒ Ⓓ Ⓔ	32. Ⓐ Ⓑ Ⓒ Ⓓ Ⓔ
3. Ⓐ Ⓑ Ⓒ Ⓓ Ⓔ	13. Ⓐ Ⓑ Ⓒ Ⓓ Ⓔ	23. Ⓐ Ⓑ Ⓒ Ⓓ Ⓔ	33. Ⓐ Ⓑ Ⓒ Ⓓ Ⓔ
4. Ⓐ Ⓑ Ⓒ Ⓓ Ⓔ	14. Ⓐ Ⓑ Ⓒ Ⓓ Ⓔ	24. Ⓐ Ⓑ Ⓒ Ⓓ Ⓔ	34. Ⓐ Ⓑ Ⓒ Ⓓ Ⓔ
5. Ⓐ Ⓑ Ⓒ Ⓓ Ⓔ	15. Ⓐ Ⓑ Ⓒ Ⓓ Ⓔ	25. Ⓐ Ⓑ Ⓒ Ⓓ Ⓔ	35. Ⓐ Ⓑ Ⓒ Ⓓ Ⓔ
6. Ⓐ Ⓑ Ⓒ Ⓓ Ⓔ	16. Ⓐ Ⓑ Ⓒ Ⓓ Ⓔ	26. Ⓐ Ⓑ Ⓒ Ⓓ Ⓔ	36. Ⓐ Ⓑ Ⓒ Ⓓ Ⓔ
7. Ⓐ Ⓑ Ⓒ Ⓓ Ⓔ	17. Ⓐ Ⓑ Ⓒ Ⓓ Ⓔ	27. Ⓐ Ⓑ Ⓒ Ⓓ Ⓔ	37. Ⓐ Ⓑ Ⓒ Ⓓ Ⓔ
8. Ⓐ Ⓑ Ⓒ Ⓓ Ⓔ	18. Ⓐ Ⓑ Ⓒ Ⓓ Ⓔ	28. Ⓐ Ⓑ Ⓒ Ⓓ Ⓔ	38. Ⓐ Ⓑ Ⓒ Ⓓ Ⓔ
9. Ⓐ Ⓑ Ⓒ Ⓓ Ⓔ	19. Ⓐ Ⓑ Ⓒ Ⓓ Ⓔ	29. Ⓐ Ⓑ Ⓒ Ⓓ Ⓔ	39. Ⓐ Ⓑ Ⓒ Ⓓ Ⓔ
10. Ⓐ Ⓑ Ⓒ Ⓓ Ⓔ	20. Ⓐ Ⓑ Ⓒ Ⓓ Ⓔ	30. Ⓐ Ⓑ Ⓒ Ⓓ Ⓔ	40. Ⓐ Ⓑ Ⓒ Ⓓ Ⓔ

Section 2: Quantitative Reasoning

1 Ⓐ Ⓑ Ⓒ Ⓓ	9 Ⓐ Ⓑ Ⓒ Ⓓ	17 Ⓐ Ⓑ Ⓒ Ⓓ	25 Ⓐ Ⓑ Ⓒ Ⓓ	33 Ⓐ Ⓑ Ⓒ Ⓓ
2. Ⓐ Ⓑ Ⓒ Ⓓ	10. Ⓐ Ⓑ Ⓒ Ⓓ	18. Ⓐ Ⓑ Ⓒ Ⓓ	26. Ⓐ Ⓑ Ⓒ Ⓓ	34. Ⓐ Ⓑ Ⓒ Ⓓ
3. Ⓐ Ⓑ Ⓒ Ⓓ	11. Ⓐ Ⓑ Ⓒ Ⓓ	19. Ⓐ Ⓑ Ⓒ Ⓓ	27. Ⓐ Ⓑ Ⓒ Ⓓ	35. Ⓐ Ⓑ Ⓒ Ⓓ
4. Ⓐ Ⓑ Ⓒ Ⓓ	12. Ⓐ Ⓑ Ⓒ Ⓓ	20. Ⓐ Ⓑ Ⓒ Ⓓ	28. Ⓐ Ⓑ Ⓒ Ⓓ	36. Ⓐ Ⓑ Ⓒ Ⓓ
5. Ⓐ Ⓑ Ⓒ Ⓓ	13. Ⓐ Ⓑ Ⓒ Ⓓ	21. Ⓐ Ⓑ Ⓒ Ⓓ	29. Ⓐ Ⓑ Ⓒ Ⓓ	37. Ⓐ Ⓑ Ⓒ Ⓓ
6. Ⓐ Ⓑ Ⓒ Ⓓ	14. Ⓐ Ⓑ Ⓒ Ⓓ	22. Ⓐ Ⓑ Ⓒ Ⓓ	30. Ⓐ Ⓑ Ⓒ Ⓓ	
7. Ⓐ Ⓑ Ⓒ Ⓓ	15. Ⓐ Ⓑ Ⓒ Ⓓ	23. Ⓐ Ⓑ Ⓒ Ⓓ	31. Ⓐ Ⓑ Ⓒ Ⓓ	
8. Ⓐ Ⓑ Ⓒ Ⓓ	16. Ⓐ Ⓑ Ⓒ Ⓓ	24. Ⓐ Ⓑ Ⓒ Ⓓ	32. Ⓐ Ⓑ Ⓒ Ⓓ	

Section 3: Reading Comprehension

1. Ⓐ Ⓑ Ⓒ Ⓓ	13. Ⓐ Ⓑ Ⓒ Ⓓ	25. Ⓐ Ⓑ Ⓒ Ⓓ
2. Ⓐ Ⓑ Ⓒ Ⓓ	14. Ⓐ Ⓑ Ⓒ Ⓓ	26. Ⓐ Ⓑ Ⓒ Ⓓ
3. Ⓐ Ⓑ Ⓒ Ⓓ	15. Ⓐ Ⓑ Ⓒ Ⓓ	27. Ⓐ Ⓑ Ⓒ Ⓓ
4. Ⓐ Ⓑ Ⓒ Ⓓ	16. Ⓐ Ⓑ Ⓒ Ⓓ	28. Ⓐ Ⓑ Ⓒ Ⓓ
5. Ⓐ Ⓑ Ⓒ Ⓓ	17. Ⓐ Ⓑ Ⓒ Ⓓ	29. Ⓐ Ⓑ Ⓒ Ⓓ
6. Ⓐ Ⓑ Ⓒ Ⓓ	18. Ⓐ Ⓑ Ⓒ Ⓓ	30. Ⓐ Ⓑ Ⓒ Ⓓ
7. Ⓐ Ⓑ Ⓒ Ⓓ	19. Ⓐ Ⓑ Ⓒ Ⓓ	31. Ⓐ Ⓑ Ⓒ Ⓓ
8. Ⓐ Ⓑ Ⓒ Ⓓ	20. Ⓐ Ⓑ Ⓒ Ⓓ	32. Ⓐ Ⓑ Ⓒ Ⓓ
9. Ⓐ Ⓑ Ⓒ Ⓓ	21. Ⓐ Ⓑ Ⓒ Ⓓ	33. Ⓐ Ⓑ Ⓒ Ⓓ
10. Ⓐ Ⓑ Ⓒ Ⓓ	22. Ⓐ Ⓑ Ⓒ Ⓓ	34. Ⓐ Ⓑ Ⓒ Ⓓ
11. Ⓐ Ⓑ Ⓒ Ⓓ	23. Ⓐ Ⓑ Ⓒ Ⓓ	35. Ⓐ Ⓑ Ⓒ Ⓓ
12. Ⓐ Ⓑ Ⓒ Ⓓ	24. Ⓐ Ⓑ Ⓒ Ⓓ	36. Ⓐ Ⓑ Ⓒ Ⓓ

Section 4: Mathematics Achievement

1. Ⓐ Ⓑ Ⓒ Ⓓ	13. Ⓐ Ⓑ Ⓒ Ⓓ	25. Ⓐ Ⓑ Ⓒ Ⓓ	37. Ⓐ Ⓑ Ⓒ Ⓓ
2. Ⓐ Ⓑ Ⓒ Ⓓ	14. Ⓐ Ⓑ Ⓒ Ⓓ	26. Ⓐ Ⓑ Ⓒ Ⓓ	38. Ⓐ Ⓑ Ⓒ Ⓓ
3. Ⓐ Ⓑ Ⓒ Ⓓ	15. Ⓐ Ⓑ Ⓒ Ⓓ	27. Ⓐ Ⓑ Ⓒ Ⓓ	39. Ⓐ Ⓑ Ⓒ Ⓓ
4. Ⓐ Ⓑ Ⓒ Ⓓ	16. Ⓐ Ⓑ Ⓒ Ⓓ	28. Ⓐ Ⓑ Ⓒ Ⓓ	40. Ⓐ Ⓑ Ⓒ Ⓓ
5. Ⓐ Ⓑ Ⓒ Ⓓ	17. Ⓐ Ⓑ Ⓒ Ⓓ	29. Ⓐ Ⓑ Ⓒ Ⓓ	41. Ⓐ Ⓑ Ⓒ Ⓓ
6. Ⓐ Ⓑ Ⓒ Ⓓ	18. Ⓐ Ⓑ Ⓒ Ⓓ	30. Ⓐ Ⓑ Ⓒ Ⓓ	42. Ⓐ Ⓑ Ⓒ Ⓓ
7. Ⓐ Ⓑ Ⓒ Ⓓ	19. Ⓐ Ⓑ Ⓒ Ⓓ	31. Ⓐ Ⓑ Ⓒ Ⓓ	43. Ⓐ Ⓑ Ⓒ Ⓓ
8. Ⓐ Ⓑ Ⓒ Ⓓ	20. Ⓐ Ⓑ Ⓒ Ⓓ	32. Ⓐ Ⓑ Ⓒ Ⓓ	44. Ⓐ Ⓑ Ⓒ Ⓓ
9. Ⓐ Ⓑ Ⓒ Ⓓ	21. Ⓐ Ⓑ Ⓒ Ⓓ	33. Ⓐ Ⓑ Ⓒ Ⓓ	45. Ⓐ Ⓑ Ⓒ Ⓓ
10. Ⓐ Ⓑ Ⓒ Ⓓ	22. Ⓐ Ⓑ Ⓒ Ⓓ	34. Ⓐ Ⓑ Ⓒ Ⓓ	46. Ⓐ Ⓑ Ⓒ Ⓓ
11. Ⓐ Ⓑ Ⓒ Ⓓ	23. Ⓐ Ⓑ Ⓒ Ⓓ	35. Ⓐ Ⓑ Ⓒ Ⓓ	47. Ⓐ Ⓑ Ⓒ Ⓓ
12. Ⓐ Ⓑ Ⓒ Ⓓ	24. Ⓐ Ⓑ Ⓒ Ⓓ	36. Ⓐ Ⓑ Ⓒ Ⓓ	

Section 5: Essay

For Section 5, use two loose-leaf or lined notebook pages to write your essay. (On the real exam, the answer booklet contains two lined sheets.)

Section 1

Verbal Reasoning

Time: 20 Minutes

Directions: You have 20 minutes to complete the following 40 questions. Look at the answer options and decide which answer is best. Mark your answer to each question in the corresponding answer bubble on the answer sheet for Section 1.

Questions 1–24 contain a capitalized word and four answer choices. Choose the word that is the closest in meaning to the capitalized word.

1. CANDOR:
   (A) Quiet
   (B) Honesty
   (C) Challenge
   (D) Peace

2. RAZE:
   (A) Travel
   (B) Plead
   (C) React
   (D) Destroy

3. MIRTH:
   (A) Wishfulness
   (B) Amusement
   (C) Destruction
   (D) Passive

4. ABHOR:
   (A) Emphasize
   (B) Hate
   (C) Critique
   (D) Connect

5. BASTION:
   (A) Defense
   (B) Group
   (C) Trial
   (D) Renege

6. ABASE:
   (A) Condemn
   (B) Distracted
   (C) Humiliate
   (D) Plead

7. BOGUS:
   (A) Separate
   (B) Carnal
   (C) Fake
   (D) Brutish

8. BEDLAM:
   (A) Chaos
   (B) Difficulty
   (C) Population
   (D) Evil

9. VERBATIM:
   (A) Detailed
   (B) Venerable
   (C) Distraught
   (D) Exact

10. SCRUPULOUS:
    (A) Sinister
    (B) Enigmatic
    (C) Selfish
    (D) Careful

Go on to next page

11. NEOPHYTE:
    (A) Beginner
    (B) Minor
    (C) Conservative
    (D) Apprentice

12. BILIOUS:
    (A) Bendable
    (B) Angry
    (C) Artificial
    (D) Bountiful

13. BLATANT:
    (A) Obvious
    (B) Belligerent
    (C) Cyclic
    (D) Punishable

14. WANE:
    (A) Imagine
    (B) Fail
    (C) Synchronize
    (D) Thrust

15. BUCOLIC:
    (A) Trendy
    (B) Alleviative
    (C) Rural
    (D) Stifling

16. RECOIL:
    (A) Cringe
    (B) Jump
    (C) Slow
    (D) Degenerate

17. MISLEADING:
    (A) Specious
    (B) Studious
    (C) Cryptic
    (D) Altruistic

18. SARDONIC:
    (A) Vexing
    (B) Cheating
    (C) Sadistic
    (D) Mocking

19. BLITHE:
    (A) Studious
    (B) Carefree
    (C) Careful
    (D) Willing

20. SERENDIPITY:
    (A) Anemic
    (B) Calculated
    (C) Confused
    (D) Happy

21. RESCIND:
    (A) Remind
    (B) Repeal
    (C) Recalculate
    (D) Renumber

22. ABROGATE:
    (A) Afflict
    (B) Argue
    (C) Cancel
    (D) Anger

23. CREDULOUS:
    (A) Benign
    (B) Stoical
    (C) Stealthy
    (D) Gullible

24. PLUMMET:
    (A) Flail
    (B) Burgeon
    (C) Fall
    (D) Brag

Go on to next page

For Questions 25–40, choose the best word that completes the meaning of the following sentences.

25. His art was considered to be of a high _____; people often paid a lot of money for his paintings.
    (A) caliber
    (B) splendor
    (C) bedlam
    (D) junket

26. Everyone considered him a _____. He was an exceptional expert in his field.
    (A) novice
    (B) amateur
    (C) luminary
    (D) proselyte

27. Although the councilman offered many ideas, everyone considered him _____, so no one paid him any attention.
    (A) quixotic
    (B) jaded
    (C) practical
    (D) bucolic

28. The campfire was difficult to _____ because it had rained most of the night.
    (A) kindle
    (B) corral
    (C) besiege
    (D) challenge

29. His _____ behavior made everyone smile with amusement.
    (A) predictable
    (B) fastidious
    (C) wry
    (D) bombastic

30. Her _____ smile appeared and quickly disappeared, but he still knew what it meant.
    (A) vestigial
    (B) taciturn
    (C) hapless
    (D) evanescent

31. The hikers reached the _____ just before midday.
    (A) peccadillo
    (B) bastion
    (C) zenith
    (D) plaudit

32. The parade moved along at a slow _____.
    (A) saunter
    (B) vector
    (C) bevy
    (D) mirth

33. The mayor spoke in difficult, complex terms in order to _____ the issue.
    (A) abrogate
    (B) obfuscate
    (C) articulate
    (D) banter

34. The _____ excuses the team offered did not support their defense of weak sportsmanship.
    (A) irreverent
    (B) maudlin
    (C) sacrosanct
    (D) paltry

35. He _____ the proposal because it was full of potential problems.
    (A) ensconced
    (B) converted
    (C) repudiated
    (D) initiated

Go on to next page ⟹

36. Although no one wanted to consider it, the idea was _____.

    (A) tenable

    (B) fastidious

    (C) nuanced

    (D) flustered

37. The _____ nature of the tornado made everyone _____.

    (A) destructive . . . tremulous

    (B) abusive . . . destitute

    (C) naive . . . regretful

    (D) frustrating . . . despiteful

38. The criminal sought _____ for his crimes, but the court handed down a maximum _____ anyway.

    (A) bedlam . . . punishment

    (B) absolution . . . verdict

    (C) renunciation . . . recapitulation

    (D) generosity . . . antidote

39. The lofty _____ the president used in the speech did not _____ the voters.

    (A) constructions . . . anticipate

    (B) harangue . . . excite

    (C) ideas . . . inundate

    (D) rhetoric . . . impress

40. Because of their _____ relationship, the two scientists found a solution to the problem much _____.

    (A) hapless . . . easier

    (B) symbiotic . . . faster

    (C) loquacious . . . easier

    (D) difficult . . . faster

STOP DO NOT TURN THE PAGE UNTIL TOLD TO DO SO.
DO NOT RETURN TO A PREVIOUS TEST.

Section 2

Quantitative Reasoning

Time: 35 Minutes

Directions: You have 35 minutes to complete 37 questions. Work each problem in your head or in the blank space on the page. Then, look at the answer options and decide which one is best. Mark your answer to each question in the corresponding answer bubble on the answer sheet for Section 2.

1. If $n* = 5n + 2$, what is the value of $7*$?

   (A) 7
   (B) 35
   (C) 37
   (D) 39

2. If $m - n = 2$, which expression is equal to n?

   (A) $m + 2$
   (B) $m - 2$
   (C) $-m + 2$
   (D) $-m - 2$

3. If the sum of all integers from 2 to 2,000, inclusive, is p, which expression represents the sum of all integers from 2 to 1,998, inclusive?

   (A) $p - 3,999$
   (B) $p - 2,999$
   (C) $p + 2,999$
   (D) $p + 3,999$

4. If the length of a rectangle is increased by 10% and the width of the rectangle is decreased by 10%, what is the percent decrease in the area of the rectangle?

   (A) 0%
   (B) 1%
   (C) 10%
   (D) 11%

5. If n is a positive integer and $(x + 9)^2 = x^2 + nx + 81$, what is the value of n?

   (A) 0
   (B) 9
   (C) 18
   (D) 27

6. A zookeeper is planning to calculate the mean number of monkeys at the zoo, which has five different monkey habitats. He doesn't know how many monkeys are in each of the first four habitats, but he knows that the sum of the monkeys in the first four habitats is 80. If 15 monkeys are in the fifth habitat, what is the mean number of monkeys at the zoo?

   (A) 17
   (B) 18
   (C) 19
   (D) 20

7. A rectangle has a perimeter of 40 inches. If the length and width of the rectangle are measured in whole inches, what is the least possible area of the rectangle?

   (A) 19
   (B) 36
   (C) 51
   (D) 64

Go on to next page

8. A can of soda at room temperature is placed in a freezer with a temperature of 32 degrees Fahrenheit for one hour. Which graph best shows what happens to the temperature of the soda during the hour?

(A)

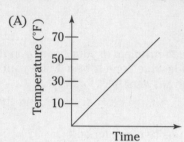

(B)

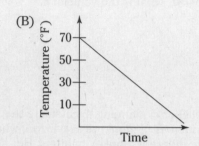

(C)

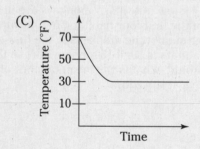

(D)

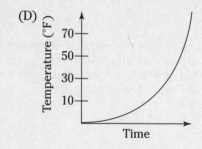

9. Triangle *ABC* is similar to triangle *DEF*. What is the length of side *DF*?

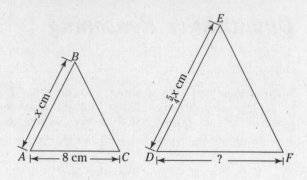

(A) 8 cm

(B) 10 cm

(C) 8*x* cm

(D) 10*x* cm

10. What is the value of the expression $\dfrac{4\left(4^2 + 4^3\right)}{16\left(4 + 16\right)}$?

(A) 0

(B) 1

(C) 4

(D) 16

Go on to next page

11. The graph shows how far Tom was from school as a function of time during a walk home from school. At one point in the walk, Tom stopped for several minutes to talk with a friend. How far from school was Tom when he stopped to talk with his friend?

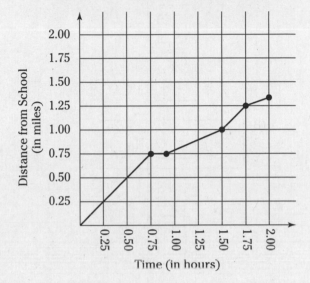

(A) 0.50 miles

(B) 0.75 miles

(C) 1.00 miles

(D) 1.50 miles

12. Mr. Bannon graded the quizzes of his 25 students. He then calculated the mean, median, mode, and range of the quiz scores. The following table gives the value of each measure.

Measure	Value
Mean	80
Median	85
Mode	85
Range	43

Mr. Bannon decided to add five points to each of his students' scores, and then he recalculated the values of each measure. Which of the measures changed the least?

(A) mean

(B) median

(C) mode

(D) range

13. Jeremy and Corinne are playing a game with dice. Each of them rolls two dice, numbered 1 through 6, and then they write down the sum of their two rolls. If Jeremy's sum is 8, he wins the game. If Corinne's sum is 12, she wins the game. Who has a greater probability of winning the game?

(A) Jeremy.

(B) Corinne.

(C) They have the same chance of winning.

(D) There is not enough information given to determine the answer.

14. A basketball statistician collects data for a high school basketball team. He finds that both the mean and median of the total points per game statistic are equal to 58, and the data are symmetric about this value. He begins creating the graph shown but does not finish the graph. If the range of the data is 20 and the maximum value of the data is 98, how many data points fall above the value 58?

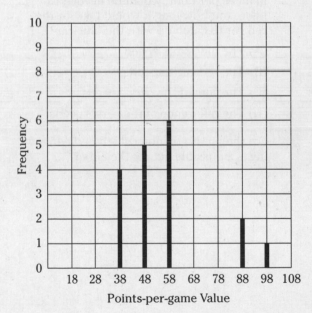

(A) 3

(B) 9

(C) 10

(D) 12

Go on to next page

15. What is the maximum value for x if $x = 3x^2 + 2$ for $-3 \leq x < 1$?

    (A) 5

    (B) 6

    (C) 27

    (D) 29

16. If a is a factor of 16 and b is a factor of 27, which is the least value that ab must be a factor of?

    (A) 1

    (B) 6

    (C) 144

    (D) 432

17. A red car and a blue car were driving on the same highway, and the red car was traveling at a faster speed than the blue car. When the red car started driving, the blue car had already traveled 5 miles. Which one additional piece of information, in miles per hour, would be needed to figure out how long it would take for the red car to catch up with the blue car?

    (A) The blue car's speed

    (B) The red car's speed

    (C) The sum of the cars' speeds

    (D) The difference of the cars' speeds

18. For the pictured cube, which of the following is a possible net for the cube?

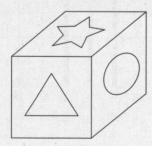

(A)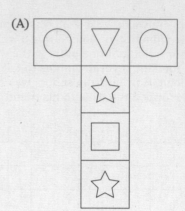

(B)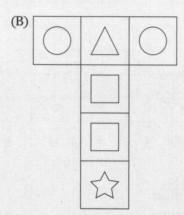

(C)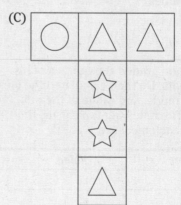

(D)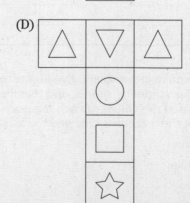

Go on to next page

19. A box has three dimensions: length, width, and height. If the length is increased by 20%, the width is increased by 30%, and the height is increased by 40%, the volume increases by approximately what percent?

    (A) 90%

    (B) 100%

    (C) 120%

    (D) 220%

20. Michael knows that x is an integer greater than 7 and less than 11, and Jill knows that x is an integer greater than 8 and less than 13. If they share their information about x, they know that x must be

    (A) Exactly one number

    (B) One of two possible numbers

    (C) One of three possible numbers

    (D) One of four possible numbers

21. If n is an even integer, which of the following *cannot* be an integer?

    (A) $n + 1$

    (B) $2n + 1$

    (C) $\frac{n}{3}$

    (D) $\frac{n+1}{2}$

22. If a 99-inch piece of string were cut into two pieces so one piece was 45 inches longer than the other, what would be the length, in inches, of the longer piece?

    (A) 27

    (B) 45

    (C) 72

    (D) 80

23. The formula for converting degrees Fahrenheit (F) to degrees Celsius is $\frac{5}{9}(F - 32)$. If the Fahrenheit temperature decreases from 95° to 77°, then the corresponding decrease in the Celsius temperature is

    (A) 10°

    (B) 14°

    (C) 18°

    (D) 19°

Directions: Using the information given in Questions 24–37, compare the quantity in Column A to the quantity in Column B. All the following questions have these answer choices:

(A) The quantity in Column A is greater.

(B) The quantity in Column B is greater.

(C) The two quantities are equal.

(D) The relationship cannot be determined from the information given.

24.

Rectangle M

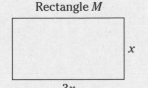

$3x$

Rectangle N

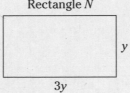

$3y$

Note: Figures not drawn to scale.

The area of Rectangle M is 48 in².
The perimeter of rectangle N is 40 cm.

Column A	Column B
x	y

25.

Column A	Column B
$6 + 2 \times (7 + 2)$	24

26.

Column A	Column B
$(a - b)(a^2 + ab + b^2)$	$a^3 - b^3$

Go on to next page

27. At a fruit stand, pears cost $0.25 and apples cost $0.10. Buying all the pears and apples at the stand would cost $5.50, and there are three times as many apples as there are pears.

Column A	Column B
The total value of apples	$3.00

28.

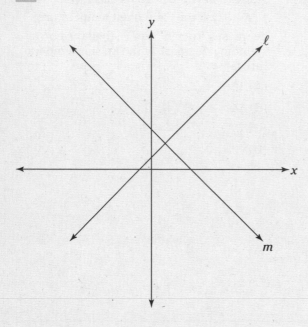

Line ℓ is the graph of $y = x + 1$. Line m is perpendicular to line ℓ.

Column A	Column B
The slope of line m	−1

29. The perimeter of a rectangle is 60 inches.

Column A	Column B
The area of the rectangle	200 in²

30.

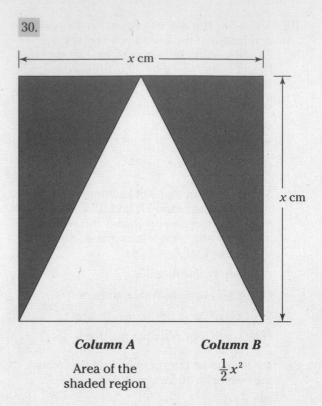

Column A	Column B
Area of the shaded region	$\frac{1}{2}x^2$

31. The sum of four consecutive integers is 106.

Column A	Column B
The largest of the four integers	30

32.

Column A	Column B
$10x - 10$	$10(x - 10)$

Go on to next page

33.

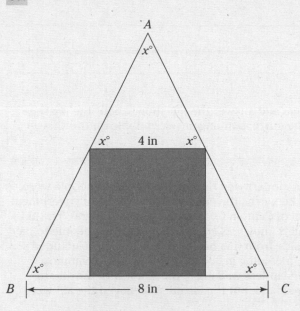

Note: Figure not drawn to scale.

Column A	Column B
The perimeter of triangle *ABC*	Twice the perimeter of the square

34.

Column A	Column B
The probability of flipping a coin twice and getting heads both times	The probability of rolling a six-sided die and rolling either a 2 or a 5

35. A jar contains ten buttons: six black buttons and four white buttons. One button, at random, is removed from the jar and then replaced. Then a second button is removed at random from the jar.

Column A	Column B
The probability that both buttons are black	The probability that the first button is white

36. The histogram shows the number of coins in several different people's coin collections.

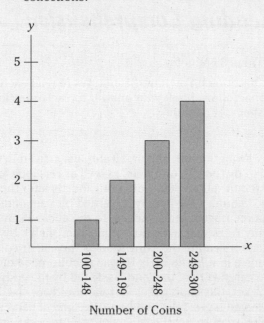

Number of Coins

Column A	Column B
The median number of coins	The range of the number of coins

37. Halfway through the school year, Brian's math grade was 90. Two-thirds of the way through the year, Brian's grade dropped 10% from the halfway point, but by the end of the year, his grade had risen 10% from what it was two-thirds of the way through the year.

Column A	Column B
Brian's grade at the end of the year	90

STOP DO NOT TURN THE PAGE UNTIL TOLD TO DO SO. DO NOT RETURN TO A PREVIOUS TEST.

Section 3

Reading Comprehension

Time: 35 Minutes

Directions: You have 35 minutes to read each passage and answer the questions about the passage that follow. Mark your answer to each question in the corresponding answer bubble on the answer sheet for Section 3.

From the time the first Tahitians arrived in what is modern-day Hawaii, the Hawaiian people were ruled by the *alii,* or chiefs, as well as religious leaders known as the *kahuna.* This system of government lasted for about 800 years until shortly after the arrival of Captain Cook to the island of Kauai. The alii and kahuna were largely governed by a set of moral rules known as *kapu,* which required people to pay a percentage of their income to the alii and kahuna. Aside from this basic system, the kapu included many rules that were potentially punishable by death, including men eating with women, common islanders eating the same food as the alii, or common islanders walking in the shadow of the alii, to name a few. In the early Hawaiian culture, no one owned land, but the islanders believed the alii were the caretakers of the land, assigned by the gods.

Yet, this kapu belief system would not last. When Captain Cook arrived in Kauai, the Hawaiians believed he was the god Lono, the god of harvest. His pale skin, strange ship, and tools that were unheard of to the Hawaiians only increased this belief, and Cook did not correct the false assumption. Cook and his men traded with the Hawaiians, often unfairly, and his men often took advantage of the Hawaiian women. One of the items the Hawaiians wanted from Cook was nails because they were so helpful with construction and the Hawaiians had none of their own. However, this simple item would reveal Cook's lie. On a later visit to Kauai, some Hawaiians who were seeking more nails tried to steal one of Cook's ships, which resulted in a fight. Although the historical details are sketchy, it is commonly believed that Cook was injured, and the Hawaiians, upon seeing Cook's blood, realized he was a human and not a god. Caught in the lie, the Hawaiians killed him.

Cook's visits, however, changed the islands. After seeing some of the weapons and tactics Cook used in battle, Kamehameha I, a warrior who longed to bring all the islands under one rule, waged war on all islands, eventually becoming the first king of Hawaii. Although warfare and difficult times followed, historical accounts note that Kamehameha I became a <u>benevolent</u> king in his later years and made many positive changes that helped the Hawaiian people, including the termination of the often unfair kapu system.

1. What is the primary purpose of this passage?

   (A) To explain the kapu system

   (B) To explain how Cook's arrival changed Hawaiian government

   (C) To explain how Cook died

   (D) To explain the early religious beliefs of the Hawaiian people

2. According to the passage, what is a *kahuna?*

   (A) Religious leader

   (B) Chief

   (C) Moral law

   (D) The god of harvest

3. What deterred people from walking in the shadow of an alii?

   (A) Kahuna

   (B) Kapu

   (C) Lono

   (D) Cook

Go on to next page

4. What can you infer about Cook and his men from this passage?

    (A) They were fascinated with the Hawaiian culture.

    (B) They wanted peace between the islands.

    (C) They saw the Hawaiians as people they could exploit.

    (D) They tried to assume control of the islands.

5. What does the author most likely mean by the word *benevolent?*

    (A) Devoted

    (B) Interfering

    (C) Kind

    (D) Constructive

6. With which of the following statements would the author agree?

    (A) The Alii ruled in conjunction with the kapu.

    (B) The kapu system was often unfair but necessary.

    (C) The Hawaiians expected Cook to reform Kauai.

    (D) Cook inadvertently brought change to Hawaii.

The atom was first proposed as the smallest unit of matter and was first considered by early Greek philosophers, though they had no proof of its existence. In fact, the word *atom* comes from the Greek language meaning indivisible. However, in the 19th and 20th centuries, scientists discovered that the atom was, in fact, divisible into smaller components, namely the nucleus, electrons, protons, and neutrons.

The atom consists of a central nucleus surrounded by negatively charged electrons. The nucleus itself contains positively charged protons and electrically neutral neutrons. Atoms are classified according to the protons and neutrons in the nucleus. The number of protons in the nucleus determines the chemical elements, and the number of neutrons determines the isotope (which has to do with different chemical forms) of the element.

Because of continued study, scientists realized that atoms contain an isotope that is unstable and, therefore, subject to radioactive decay. Because of this, nuclear fission can occur by splitting the atom, releasing energy, heat, and radiation. This basic concept is the foundation for both nuclear energy and nuclear weapons. Certainly, the Greek philosophers who first imagined the concept of the atom had no idea of its complicated nature or its power.

7. What would be an appropriate title for this article?

    (A) A Basic Understanding of the Atom

    (B) The Nucleus

    (C) Basics of Nuclear Fission

    (D) Understanding Atomic Charges

8. Concerning the nucleus, which statement is true?

    (A) Positive and neutral charges exist.

    (B) Positive and negative charges exist.

    (C) Negative and positive charges exist.

    (D) Negative and neutral charges exist.

9. How are atoms classified, according to the passage?

    (A) According to the number of electrons and their charge

    (B) By radioactive elements

    (C) By isotope

    (D) According to the number of charged protons and neutrons

10. What is the foundational element of nuclear fission?

    (A) Unstable radioactivity

    (B) Unstable isotope

    (C) Neutrons

    (D) Electrons

Go on to next page

11. What can you infer about nuclear fission?

    (A) Splitting creates nuclear heat.

    (B) Splitting atoms interacts with the radio-active isotope.

    (C) Only certain kinds of atoms can be split.

    (D) Energy requires radioactive decay.

12. How is the isotope of an element determined?

    (A) Electrical charges

    (B) Number of electrons

    (C) Number of protons

    (D) Number of neutrons

The first few years of the 20th century were a time of marked prosperity and modern scientific developments in many areas of the world. Technological advances were growing at an amazing rate and many societies felt this new world was an unstoppable force. No singular marvel represented this ideal-ism more than the ocean liner *Titanic*.

The *Titanic* was generally considered one of the largest and well-appointed steam ships ever designed, so much so that it was considered an unsinkable ship. Able to carry more than two thousand people, the *Titanic* had 16 water-tight doors, or compartments, built into the design of the ship. The idea was that the compartments could not only withstand any impact but also isolate flooding so no matter what happened on a voyage, the number of water-tight compartments would keep the ship from sinking. This idea, however, was a tragic mistake.

On April 14, 1912, during its maiden voyage, the *Titanic* hit an iceberg that punctured several areas along the side of the ship, flooding five of the water-tight compartments at the same time. This massive flooding caused the ship to start sinking rapidly. Woefully unprepared for such an event, crew person-nel attempted to evacuate passengers to lifeboats, filling a number of them only partially. Of the 2,223 passengers onboard, only 706 survived the tragedy.

Newspapers around the world brought the shocking news that the unsinkable ship had not even survived its maiden voyage. In many ways, the sinking of the *Titanic* served as a symbol for a hard lesson — man's industrial savvy was still no match for Mother Nature.

13. Which statement expresses the main idea of the passage?

    (A) The *Titanic* represents a failure of technology.

    (B) The *Titanic* disaster was a freak acci-dent that never should have happened.

    (C) The *Titanic* disaster was easily preventable.

    (D) Disasters and technological failures are a natural part of a technological age.

14. Considering the tone of the passage, with which statement would the author agree?

    (A) Many people in the early 20th century placed too much faith in technology.

    (B) The early 20th century ushered in a new understanding of the world.

    (C) The *Titanic* symbolized mankind's advancement over poverty.

    (D) The *Titanic* was proof of the arrival of a new world order.

15. In the first sentence of the passage, the author mentions *marked prosperity*. What does this most likely mean?

    (A) Inappropriate advancement

    (B) Noticeable gain

    (C) Common judgment

    (D) Illegal business

16. Why was the *Titanic* labeled an unsinkable ship?

    (A) Steel construction

    (B) Water-tight doors

    (C) Massive size

    (D) Anti-rolling features

Go on to next page

17. The author states that the crew was woefully unprepared for a disaster. What can you infer from the passage as the mostly likely reason why?

    (A) The crew had no concern for passenger safety.

    (B) The crew was unfamiliar with the new ship.

    (C) The crew was not trained.

    (D) The crew did not believe the ship could sink.

18. What does the author most likely mean when he says that the *Titanic* is a symbol?

    (A) The ship represents new hope.

    (B) The ship represents the people of the time.

    (C) The ship represents the failure of the idealism of the day.

    (D) The ship represents the lack of knowledge in an early technological age.

The mystery genre is similar to other genres of fiction but with some substantial differences. All fiction revolves around characters, settings, plots, and themes, but within particular genres, certain elements must be present or take place for the literature to work. The mystery genre is a good example because a mystery story contains the standard elements of any piece of fiction but with added features.

A good mystery revolves around a central character, typically a detective, who works to solve the crime or series of crimes that have taken place in the story. Typically, the mystery story begins with a crime as a way of *hooking* readers into the story. From that point, the detective becomes the central character.

The mystery story foundationally functions on logic. The detective must uncover clues that lead him or her, and effectively, the readers, to the solution of the crime. As such, the mystery writer has to think carefully about not only what the crime is but also how the crime is logically solved. Mystery stories that do not follow a sound logical conclusion most often fail with readers because they expect a logical conclusion.

Aside from the detective and the logic of the mystery (which drives the direction of the plot), an effective mystery story has to have some other important elements as well. First, the crime must be sufficient in order to gain the readers' attention and warrant an actual story. In the same way, the culprit must be capable of committing the crime and both the crime and culprit must be believable. Believability is extremely important to the mystery enthusiast, so the stories have to seem plausible. Another important aspect of the mystery is the revelation. After the mystery is solved, the story quickly ends, so the writer must be careful not to give away too many clues so readers do not solve the mystery before the main character manages to solve it. Finally, the readers are all-important, so readers must be respected. Accidental solutions, supernatural intervention, evil twin constructions, and other improbable solutions are unsatisfying and tend to anger readers.

19. This passage is primarily about

    (A) Specific details of genres of literature

    (B) What makes a mystery story effective

    (C) How mystery stories are plot-driven

    (D) The nature of logic within a mystery story

20. In this passage, the word *genre* most likely means

    (A) Characterization techniques

    (B) A logical plot

    (C) An argument

    (D) A particular kind

21. The passage states that a mystery story often begins with the crime in order to *hook* readers. What does this most likely mean?

    (A) Introduce the main character.

    (B) Grab the reader's attention.

    (C) Explain the plot to the reader.

    (D) Help guide the revelation of the story.

22. According to the passage, what is one of the most foundational elements of an effective mystery story?

    (A) Theme

    (B) Characters' points of view

    (C) Logic

    (D) Crime scene

Go on to next page

23. The author mentions that the crime must be *sufficient*. What does the author most likely mean?

    (A) A crime of passion

    (B) A crime of hate

    (C) An actual crime

    (D) Provide enough interest

24. Which of the following does the author point out as one specific issue that the mystery writer must handle with care in order to not ruin the story?

    (A) Using static characters

    (B) Letting the revelation come too quickly

    (C) Using subplots

    (D) Having more than one culprit

25. What does the author suggest in the last paragraph that is important for the mystery writer to have concerning his or her readers?

    (A) Respect

    (B) Plenty of details

    (C) Improbable solutions

    (D) Hooks for a new story

26. The author does all the following in this passage *except*

    (A) Warns writers against potential pitfalls

    (B) Examines character and culprit

    (C) Provides genre classifications

    (D) Discusses logic in mystery stories

The cockroach is one of the most hated insects. Scientists estimate that cockroaches have existed for millions of years, and despite modern man's best efforts to eradicate them, they continue to be a growing force in homes, neighborhoods, and cities. In fact, one scientist even remarked that the cockroach would be the only thing to survive a nuclear blast.

It's no wonder cockroaches have survived and thrived. Although many different kinds of cockroaches exist, most of them have the same basic features and resistance to eradication. After all, consider these basic facts: The average cockroach can live a month without food and two weeks without water. A cockroach can even live for a week without its head! Cockroaches can hold their breath for up to 40 minutes and run up to 3 miles in an hour. A single pair of cockroaches in a home can result in more than a million in less than a year. On top of these staggering facts, many female cockroaches mate only once but stay pregnant for life.

In addition to these issues, the cockroach eats virtually anything, from food crumbs, toothpaste, soap, paper, and even the feces of other cockroaches. In other words, you can't starve them out of your home; they will always find something to eat.

When you see cockroaches in your home, a pest control service can treat your home, but a single treatment is unlikely to rid the house of all cockroaches. Often, treatments are repeated and several kinds are used at once. Many sprays will kill the cockroach on contact, but this method isn't effective because of the rapid reproduction rate of the entire family. So pesticides that render the cockroach sterile are often effective because the poison is passed through feces, on which other roaches feed, also becoming sterile. This approach works over time but be forewarned: Should your home become invaded, eradication is difficult and often costly.

27. According to the passage, all the following are true, *except*

    (A) Cockroaches drown easily.

    (B) Cockroaches are fast.

    (C) Cockroaches eat both food and non-food items.

    (D) Cockroaches rapidly reproduce.

28. How would you characterize the last sentence of the first paragraph?

    (A) Exaggeration

    (B) Fact

    (C) Illustration

    (D) Evidence

Go on to next page

29. From the passage, what would you say is the greatest reason infestations are such a problem?

    (A) Lack of natural predators

    (B) Places to hide

    (C) Availability of food

    (D) Rapid reproduction

30. According to the passage, what pesticide feature is often effective?

    (A) Removal of water sources

    (B) Removal of food sources

    (C) Sterilization

    (D) Kill-on-contact poisons

31. According to the passage, if a homeowner needs a pesticide service, what should he expect?

    (A) Multiple treatments

    (B) Fast eradication

    (C) Food control options

    (D) Water control options

The following passage is taken from the Constitution of the United States.

Section 3 – The Senate

The Senate of the United States shall be composed of two Senators from each State, *(chosen by the Legislature thereof,)* (The preceding words in parentheses superseded by 17th Amendment, section 1.) for six Years; and each Senator shall have one Vote.

Immediately after they shall be assembled in Consequence of the first Election, they shall be divided as equally as may be into three Classes. The Seats of the Senators of the first Class shall be vacated at the Expiration of the second Year, of the second Class at the Expiration of the fourth Year, and of the third Class at the Expiration of the sixth Year, so that one third may be chosen every second Year; *(and if Vacancies happen by Resignation, or otherwise, during the Recess of the Legislature of any State, the Executive thereof may make temporary Appointments until the next Meeting of the Legislature, which shall then fill such Vacancies.)* (The preceding words in parentheses were superseded by the 17th Amendment, section 2.)

No person shall be a Senator who shall not have attained to the Age of thirty Years, and been nine Years a Citizen of the United States, and who shall not, when elected, be an Inhabitant of that State for which he shall be chosen.

The Vice President of the United States shall be President of the Senate, but shall have no Vote, unless they be equally divided.

The Senate shall chuse their other Officers, and also a President pro tempore, in the absence of the Vice President, or when he shall exercise the Office of President of the United States.

The Senate shall have the sole Power to try all Impeachments. When sitting for that Purpose, they shall be on Oath or Affirmation. When the President of the United States is tried, the Chief Justice shall preside: And no Person shall be convicted without the Concurrence of two thirds of the Members present.

Judgment in Cases of Impeachment shall not extend further than to removal from Office, and disqualification to hold and enjoy any Office of honor, Trust or Profit under the United States: but the Party convicted shall nevertheless be liable and subject to Indictment, Trial, Judgment and Punishment, according to Law.

Go on to next page

32. The passage states (regarding senators), "consequence of the first election." How can you rephrase this statement?

    (A) With elected status

    (B) After election

    (C) After voting

    (D) Prior to election

33. In the case of a vacancy of a senator's seat, who fills the vacancy?

    (A) Voters

    (B) Legislature

    (C) President

    (D) Governor of that state

34. How old must a person be before becoming a senator?

    (A) 25

    (B) 30

    (C) 35

    (D) There is no age restriction.

35. All the following statements are true, *except*

    (A) Senators serve a three-year term.

    (B) The Vice President is the President of the senate.

    (C) The President of the senate has no vote except when the senate is equally divided on a vote.

    (D) Senators must be citizens of the United States for at least nine years before taking office.

36. In terms of impeachment, what power does the senate have should the president or member of congress be found guilty?

    (A) Removal from office

    (B) Fines levied

    (C) Prison sentencing

    (D) None of the above

STOP DO NOT TURN THE PAGE UNTIL TOLD TO DO SO.
DO NOT RETURN TO A PREVIOUS TEST.

Section 4

Mathematics Achievement

Time: 40 Minutes

Directions: You have 40 minutes to answer the following 47 mathematics achievement questions. Mark your answer to each question in the corresponding answer bubble on the answer sheet for Section 4.

1. The area of each grid square is 6 cm². What is the area of the shaded region?

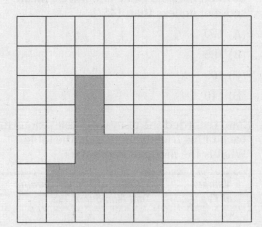

   (A) 42 cm²

   (B) 48 cm²

   (C) 54 cm²

   (D) 60 cm²

2. A box contains 50 red buttons, 60 blue buttons, and 80 white buttons. If one button is chosen randomly and then put back in to the box and then a second button is chosen at random, what is the probability that both of the buttons are blue?

   (A) $\frac{6}{19}$

   (B) $\frac{12}{19}$

   (C) $\frac{1}{10}$

   (D) $\frac{36}{361}$

3. What is the value of the numerical expression $4.9 \times 10^6 + 3.7 \times 10^4$?

   (A) 4.937×10^5

   (B) 4.937×10^6

   (C) 4.937×10^7

   (D) 4.937×10^{10}

4. Which value is *not* equal to $\frac{1}{3}$?

   (A) $\frac{33}{99}$

   (B) $0.\bar{3}$

   (C) $\frac{3}{10}$

   (D) $\frac{0.5}{1.5}$

5. If $(7.95 + 2.05)x = x$, then $x =$

   (A) 10

   (B) 1

   (C) 0.1

   (D) 0

6. For what value of y is the equation $\frac{y-3}{3-y} = 0$ true?

   (A) 3

   (B) 0

   (C) All real numbers

   (D) There are no values for y that would make the equation true.

Go on to next page

7. What is the value of the numerical expression $\sqrt{36+64}$?

   (A) 10

   (B) 12

   (C) 14

   (D) 100

8. The bar graph shown represents the scores of six different athletes at a snowboarding competition. What is the median score?

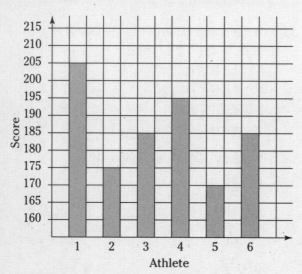

   (A) 175

   (B) 185

   (C) 185.83

   (D) 190

9. When the two of them pick carrots, Peter picks three times as many carrots as Judy does. If Peter and Judy picked a total of 28 carrots yesterday, how many carrots did Judy pick?

   (A) 7

   (B) 14

   (C) 21

   (D) 28

10. Jared has bowled three games so far in a tournament, and his scores are 131, 169, and 171. What is the lowest score he can bowl on his final game and have a mean score of no less than 145?

    (A) 100

    (B) 105

    (C) 109

    (D) 110

11. Paul recorded the number of televisions in each of his friends' houses in the table. What is the mode of Paul's data?

Number of TVs	Number of Friends Owning That Number of TVs
1	2
2	3
3	4
4	5
5	2

    (A) 1

    (B) 2

    (C) 3

    (D) 4

Go on to next page

12. If x and y are prime numbers, what is the least common multiple of $2x$, $3xy$, and $4x^2$?

    (A) $6xy$

    (B) $6x^2y$

    (C) $12xy$

    (D) $12x^2y$

13. If $7x - 7 = xy - y$ and $x \neq 1$, what is the value of y?

    (A) -7

    (B) -1

    (C) 1

    (D) 7

14. Which expression is equivalent to the expression $6m^5n^3 + 7m^3n^5 - (5m^3n^5 - 4m^5n^3)$?

    (A) $2m^5n^3 + 2m^3n^5$

    (B) $4m^5n^3$

    (C) $10m^5n^3 + 2m^3n^5$

    (D) $13m^5n^3 - 9m^3n^5$

15. For what value(s) of x does $\dfrac{x^2 - 81}{(x+4)(x-5)} = 0$?

    (A) $x = 9$ only

    (B) $x = -4$ and $x = 5$

    (C) $x = 9$ and $x = -9$

    (D) $x = -4$, $x = 5$, $x = 9$, and $x = -9$

16. Which expression is equivalent to the expression $(x - 4)(x + 5)$?

    (A) $x^2 - 9$

    (B) $x^2 - 20$

    (C) $x^2 + x - 20$

    (D) $x^2 - x - 20$

17. The graph of a line is shown. What is the slope of the line?

    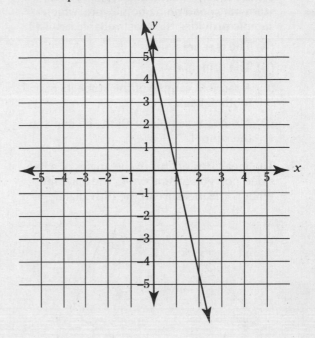

    (A) 5

    (B) -5

    (C) $\dfrac{1}{5}$

    (D) $-\dfrac{1}{5}$

18. Point $(3, 10)$ is on a circle with center $(-3, 2)$. What is the radius of the circle?

    (A) 8 grid units

    (B) 9 grid units

    (C) 10 grid units

    (D) 11 grid units

Go on to next page

19. If a researcher is surveying people in a school to find the average number of hours students spend doing homework, which sample provides the most reliable results?

    (A) The teachers

    (B) The principal

    (C) A random sample of the students at a football game

    (D) A random sample of all the students in the school

20. The measures of four of the angles of a five-sided polygon are shown in the diagram. What is the measure of the fifth angle?

    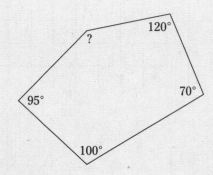

    (A) 90°

    (B) 120°

    (C) 145°

    (D) 155°

21. If a golf team has seven members and only four can play in a tournament, how many four-person groups can be made from the entire team?

    (A) 24

    (B) 28

    (C) 35

    (D) 70

22. The grid shows three vertices of a parallelogram. Which of the following can be the coordinates of the fourth vertex?

    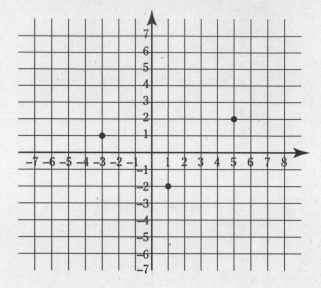

    (A) (1, 5)

    (B) (5, 1)

    (C) (1, 4)

    (D) (7, −1)

23. Which describes all values of x for which $|3x − 6| \leq 12$?

    (A) $x \leq 6$

    (B) $x \geq 2$

    (C) $-2 \leq x \leq 6$

    (D) $x \leq -2$ or $x \geq 6$

24. Which of the following numbers is irrational?

    (A) 0

    (B) π

    (C) $0.\overline{3}$

    (D) $\sqrt{1}$

Go on to next page

25. The graph shows the number of pets owned by the students in a ninth-grade class. The numbers on the horizontal axis represent the number of pets owned, and the height of the bar represents the number of students who own this number of pets. What is the mean number of pets owned?

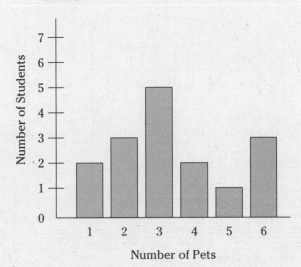

Number of Students

Number of Pets

(A) 3.250

(B) 3.375

(C) 3.5

(D) 4

26. A solution set is graphed on the number line shown. Which inequality is graphed?

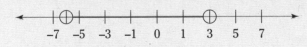

(A) $|x-1.5| > 4.5$

(B) $|x-1.5| < 4.5$

(C) $|x+1.5| < 4.5$

(D) $|x+1.5| > 4.5$

27. A six-sided die is rolled twice and the sum of the two rolls is recorded. Which of the following sums has the greatest probability of occurring?

(A) 3

(B) 4

(C) 6

(D) 10

28. There are 0.000305 kilometers in one foot. There are 5,280 feet in 1 mile. A runner is traveling at a speed of 0.5 kilometers per minute. Which expression has a value equal to the runner's speed in miles per hour?

(A) $\dfrac{0.5 \times 60}{0.000305 \times 5,280}$

(B) $\dfrac{0.5 \times 60 \times 0.000305}{5,280}$

(C) $\dfrac{60}{0.5 \times 0.000305 \times 5,280}$

(D) $\dfrac{0.5 \times 0.000305 \times 5,280}{60}$

29. As shown in the diagram, at 2 p.m., a 30-foot flagpole casts a 50-foot shadow. If the 30-foot flagpole is replaced with a 50-foot flagpole, how long will the shadow be?

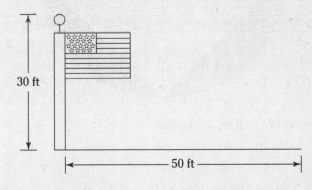

30 ft

50 ft

(A) 70 ft

(B) 80 ft

(C) 83.3 ft

(D) 86.7 ft

Go on to next page

30. When measuring the weight of an apple, which is the most reasonable unit to use?

    (A) Grams

    (B) Kilograms

    (C) Tons

    (D) Centimeters

31. Which numerical expression does *not* represent an integer?

    (A) $\sqrt{9} - \sqrt{36}$

    (B) $\sqrt{9} \times \sqrt{36}$

    (C) $\sqrt{36 - 9}$

    (D) $\sqrt{9 \times 36}$

32. A square is inscribed in a circle with a diameter of 20 centimeters, as shown. What is the area of the shaded region?

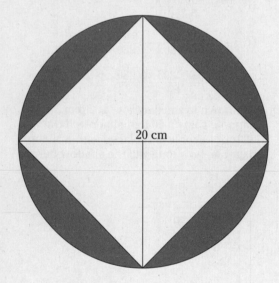

20 cm

    (A) $(200\pi - 200)$ cm^2

    (B) $(200\pi - 100)$ cm^2

    (C) $(100\pi - 200)$ cm^2

    (D) $(100\pi - 100)$ cm^2

33. The height of the cylinder shown is 1.5 times its diameter. The formula used to calculate the volume of a cylinder is $V = \pi r^2 h$, where r is the radius of the cylinder and h is the height of the cylinder. If the diameter of the cylinder is 12 inches, what is its volume, in inches^3?

12 in

    (A) 648π

    (B) 216π

    (C) 144π

    (D) 96π

34. The box-and-whisker plot represents the highest quiz score for every quiz throughout the year in a difficult computer science class. What is the range of the data?

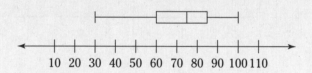

10 20 30 40 50 60 70 80 90 100 110

    (A) 77

    (B) 70

    (C) 30

    (D) 28

Go on to next page ⇨

35. A bag contains 17 pennies, 14 nickels, 10 dimes, and 8 quarters. Katie randomly removes one coin from the bag and keeps it. George then randomly removes a coin from the bag. If the coin that Katie removed from the bag was a nickel, what is the probability that the coin George removed from the bag was a quarter?

    (A) $\frac{8}{49}$

    (B) $\frac{1}{6}$

    (C) $\frac{8}{49} \times \frac{1}{6}$

    (D) $\frac{8}{49} + \frac{1}{6}$

36. Which expression is equivalent to the expression $\sqrt{64x^{36}}$?

    (A) $8x^6$

    (B) $8x^{18}$

    (C) $4x^6$

    (D) $4x^{18}$

37. Triangle ABC is shown. The length of AC is 18 centimeters. The measure of angle ABC is 36 degrees. The value of which of the following expressions is equal to the length of side AB?

    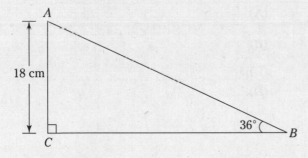

    (A) $\dfrac{18}{\sin 36°}$

    (B) $\dfrac{\sin 36°}{18}$

    (C) $\dfrac{18}{\cos 36°}$

    (D) $\dfrac{\cos 36°}{18}$

38. Which graph represents the solution set of the inequality $2 \le 3x - 3 \le 7$?

    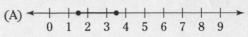

    (A)
    (B)
    (C)
    (D)

39. The stem-and-leaf plot shown represents the high temperatures in degrees Fahrenheit, measured at a location over the course of several days. What is the median temperature for the days measured?

Stem	Leaf
4	7 9
5	1 3 3 3 6 7
6	1 2 2 5 5 6 7 8 8
7	0 1 1 2 3

    (A) 61°

    (B) 62.5°

    (C) 63.5°

    (D) 65°

Go on to next page

40. What is the solution set for $x^2 + 100 = 0$?

(A) 10

(B) −10

(C) ±10i

(D) 10i

41. What is the result of the expression
$$\begin{pmatrix} 1 & 0 \\ 0 & 1 \end{pmatrix} + \begin{pmatrix} 1 & 0 \\ 0 & 1 \end{pmatrix}?$$

(A) $\begin{pmatrix} 1 & 0 \\ 0 & 1 \end{pmatrix}$

(B) $\begin{pmatrix} 2 & 0 \\ 0 & 2 \end{pmatrix}$

(C) $\begin{pmatrix} 1 & 1 \\ 1 & 1 \end{pmatrix}$

(D) $[2]$

42. The formula for the volume of a sphere is $V = \frac{4}{3}\pi r^3$. A bowling ball has a volume of 972π cm^3. What is the radius of the bowling ball?

(A) 2 cm

(B) 3 cm

(C) 6 cm

(D) 9 cm

43. Which of the following inequalities is the solution of $|x - 2| < 3$?

(A) $x < 5$

(B) $x > 5$

(C) $x > -1$

(D) $-1 < x < 5$

44. During a 150-minute sports game on television, $\frac{1}{4}$ of the time was used for commercials. If the commercials averaged 30 seconds each, how many commercials were shown during the game?

(A) 37.5

(B) 50

(C) 75

(D) 95

45. When −8x is subtracted from −8x, the result is:

(A) −16x

(B) −8x

(C) 0

(D) 16x

46. $\sqrt{25x^{36}} =$

(A) $5x^6$

(B) $5x^{18}$

(C) $5x^{36}$

(D) $25x^6$

47. A varies directly with B and inversely with C. If B is tripled and C is divided by 4, A is how many times its original value?

(A) $\frac{1}{12}$

(B)

(C) 3

(D) 12

STOP DO NOT TURN THE PAGE UNTIL TOLD TO DO SO. DO NOT RETURN TO A PREVIOUS TEST.

Section 5

Essay

Time: 30 Minutes

Directions: You have 30 minutes to complete a writing sample based on the following essay topic. Use only two pages for your essay. You may use scratch paper to organize your thoughts before you begin writing.

Topic: As a method of training and experience, do you believe high school students should perform a certain number of community service hours each year as a requirement for high school graduation?

Assignment: What is your position on this idea? Support your position with personal examples, examples of others, or examples from current news topics, or from history.

STOP DO NOT TURN THE PAGE UNTIL TOLD TO DO SO.
DO NOT RETURN TO A PREVIOUS TEST.

Chapter 24

Answers to ISEE Upper Level Practice Exam

· ·

Now that you've finished taking the ISEE Upper Level Practice Exam, spend time reading through the answers and explanations we provide in this chapter. Doing so is a great way to find out what you missed and why. Also, reading through *all* the explanations — even for the questions you got right — only increases your learning and understanding and helps you better prepare for test day. If you just want to do a quick check of your answers, see the abbreviated answer key at the end of this chapter.

Section 1: Verbal Reasoning

1. **B.** *Candor* means open honesty, so Choice (B) is the correct answer. If you had at least some idea about the answer, you may have been tempted to choose *quiet,* but the word *candor* has to do with honesty.

2. **D.** *Raze* means to completely destroy, so Choice (D) is the best answer choice.

3. **B.** *Mirth* means amusement, so Choice (B) is the synonym in this list. Remember to use the process of elimination if you're unsure of the meaning of a word — you may at least be able to rule out a couple of answer choices, thereby increasing your guessing odds.

4. **B.** *Abhor* means to hate, so Choice (B) is the correct answer.

5. **A.** *Bastion* means a strong defense, so Choice (A) is the best answer. *Renege* means to go back on a promise.

6. **C.** *Abase* means to humiliate, so Choice (C) is correct.

7. **C.** *Bogus* means false or fake, so Choice (C) is correct. You could say, "The boy gave a bogus answer when the teacher asked him about his homework," which means the boy gave a false response.

8. **A.** *Bedlam* means a noisy uproar. Although you don't have an exact match in the answer choices, the best answer is Choice (A), *chaos.* Remember that you need to find the word that has the closest meaning, but the two words may not be entirely identical or synonymous.

9. **D.** *Verbatim* means word for word, so the best answer is Choice (D), *exact.* You could say, "The paper was copied verbatim," which means it was copied word for word.

10. **D.** *Scrupulous* means careful or precise, so Choice (D) is the correct answer. Be careful of choosing an answer choice that rhymes or sounds similar, such as *selfish.* Similar-sounding words may or may not be a synonym, so don't fall for this trap.

11. **A.** A *neophyte* is a novice or someone who is unskilled. The best answer is Choice (A), *beginner.* An *apprentice* is someone who is being trained by a professional, so this choice isn't a correct synonym for *neophyte.*

12. **B.** *Bilious* means bad temper, so although the exact meaning isn't present in the answer choices, *angry* is the best answer. Remember the synonym you choose should be the closest in terms of meaning, but it may not always be exact.

13. **A.** *Blatant* refers to something that's noticeable or obvious. This word is often used with a negative connotation, such as "Robert's blatant poor behavior was a problem for the teacher."

14. **B.** *Wane* means to lose strength. An exact word match doesn't appear in the list, but the word with the closest meaning is *fail*.

15. **C.** *Bucolic* refers to the pleasurable aspects of country life. The correct answer is Choice (C). Again, the synonym isn't exact, but it's your best option of the provided answer choices.

16. **A.** *Recoil* means to *cringe* or move away from something out of fear, so Choice (A) is correct.

17. **A.** *Misleading* means directing something or someone away from the truth. *Specious* means the same thing. You may have chosen *cryptic,* but this word means secret or hidden, so it isn't the best synonym.

18. **D.** *Sardonic* refers to something that is mocking or making fun of, so Choice (D) is correct.

19. **B.** *Blithe* means *carefree,* so Choice (B) is correct. You could say, "Her blithe attitude made everyone feel at ease."

20. **D.** *Serendipitous* means happy because of a chance event, so Choice (D) is the correct answer. Although the synonym isn't exact in terms of the definition, it's the best answer choice available.

21. **B.** To *rescind* means to take back or *repeal,* so Choice (B) is correct. All the answer choices sound similar (they all begin with *re-*), but don't let that throw you off track. Use the process of elimination if you're unsure of the answer.

22. **C.** *Abrogate* means to cancel, so Choice (C) is correct.

23. **D.** *Credulous* means *gullible,* or refers to someone who believes anything. The correct answer is Choice (D). You could say, "Steve was credulous even though the truth was all around him," meaning that Steve easily believed an untruth.

24. **C.** *Plummet* simply means to fall, so Choice (C) is the correct answer. *Burgeon* means to grow rapidly, so that answer choice is incorrect.

25. **A.** *Caliber* refers to the worth or quality of something, so it's the only word that completes the meaning of the sentence. If you get stumped, try inserting your own word into the sentence, and then see if you can find an answer choice that matches your word.

26. **C.** A *luminary* is someone who's an exceptional expert in a given field, so Choice (C) is correct.

27. **A.** *Quixotic* means foolishly idealistic, so of the answer choices, it's the only word that completes the meaning of the sentence. *Bucolic* is a more difficult word choice; it has to do with a countryside or its people, so it's not the correct answer.

28. **A.** *Kindle* means to start a fire, so Choice (A) is the correct answer. *Corral* means to control or contain.

29. **C.** *Wry* means slyly amusing, so it's the best answer. You may have considered *bombastic,* but it refers to annoying speech that's loud or pointless, and it doesn't complete the meaning of the sentence.

30. **D.** *Evanescent* means momentary and is the only word that completes the meaning of the sentence. *Vestigial* refers to a very small part of something that was once greater or noticeable. *Taciturn* means reserved or having very little to say.

31. **C.** A *zenith* is the highest point or pinnacle of something, so it's the correct answer. A *peccadillo* is a minor offense.

32. **A.** *Saunter* is a slow, easy pace, so Choice (A) is correct. The other answer choices don't have anything to do with movement or pacing, so you can use the process of elimination with this question.

33. **B.** *Obfuscate* means to confuse. The sentence tells you that the mayor spoke in complicated terms, so you know you need a word that completes the meaning or result of his action. Choice (B) is the answer choice that does that. *Articulate* means to make something clear or easy to understand, so this word is the antonym of the word you need.

34. **D.** *Paltry* means insignificant, so of the answer choices, it's the only word that completes the meaning of the sentence. This question is a bit more difficult because some of the other words will fit in the sentence, such as *irreverent* or even potentially *sacrosanct*. It's important to look at the sentence and make sure you understand the intended meaning to answer these questions correctly. In this question, the team had some kind of excuse that didn't work as an excuse for their bad sportsmanship. The only word that completes this meaning is *paltry*. In other words, the team offered a weak or insignificant excuse.

35. **C.** *Repudiate* means to reject, so in the context of the sentence, it completes the meaning. The word *ensconced* is a more difficult word choice as well; it means to establish someone in a safe or protected place.

36. **A.** *Tenable* means having a valid position or point, so in the context of this sentence, Choice (A) is the best answer. Again, keep in mind the intended meaning of the sentence. The sentence is saying, in effect, "The idea was valid, even though no one wanted to consider it."

37. **A.** First, consider the answer choices and the intended meaning of the sentence. You know that a tornado is destructive in nature, so Choice (A) seems like the best option. A natural result of something destructive is fear, so this pair of words completes the meaning of the sentence.

38. **B.** *Absolution* means forgiveness, so in the context of this sentence, the criminal sought *forgiveness*, but the jury handed down a strict *verdict* (decision or judgment) anyway. These two words complete the meaning of the sentence.

39. **D.** *Rhetoric* refers to speech or writing, but it can refer to over exaggeration in speech. In this case, the *rhetoric* did not *impress* the voters, and this combination of words completes the intended meaning of the sentence.

40. **D.** *Symbiotic* technically refers to biological organisms that have a close and often long-term relationship. In a less technical way, this word often refers to being cooperative or working together or having an interdependent relationship. In this case, the two scientists worked together well so they found a solution much faster. These two words complete the meaning of the sentence.

Section 2: Quantitative Reasoning

1. **C.** The problem tells you that for any number with a * next to it, multiply it by 5 and then add 2 to the result. So $7* = 5 \times 7 + 2$, which equals 37.

2. **B.** Pick numbers for the variables in the answer choices. For example, say $m = 5$, so n would have to be 3. Next, get a numerical answer to the question. Easy: $n = 3$. Which answer choice is true if you use those numbers for the variables? Only Choice (B): $3 = 5 - 2$.

3. **A.** The sum of the integers from 2 to 1,998 is the same thing as the sum of the integers from 2 to 2,000 minus two integers: 1,999 and 2,000. So the sum of the integers from 2 to 1,998 is $p - 3,999$. The 3,999 is $1,999 + 2,000$.

4. **B.** Add numbers to this problem so you can test it; the easiest numbers to work with on percentage problems are either 10 or 100. If the original rectangle has a length of 10 and a width of 10, increasing the length by 10 percent is done by multiplying $10 \times 1.1 = 11$. Decreasing the width of 10 by 10 percent is done by multiplying $10 \times 0.9 = 9$. The original area was $10 \times 10 = 100$, and the new area is $11 \times 9 = 99$ — a decrease of 1 percent.

5. **C.** FOILing the expression $(x + 9)^2$ gives you $x^2 + 9x + 9x + 81$, which simplifies to $x^2 + 18x + 81$. Therefore, n is 18.

6. **C.** Even though you don't know the number of monkeys in any of the first four habitats, you can assume that the number in each is equal to the average of all four. Because 80 monkeys are in the first four habitats, the average number in each of the first four habitats is 20. To get the average of all five habitats, add all the monkeys and divide by the number of habitats: $\frac{20 + 20 + 20 + 20 + 15}{5} = 19$.

7. **A.** The words *least possible* tell you to use some trial and error. Use the answer choices for clues, and when in doubt, test the smallest choice, because you're looking for the least possible value. Can you draw a rectangle with 19 as an area? Sure — make the width 1 and the length 19. Add the sides to make sure the perimeter is 40, and you're done!

8. **C.** The correct graph, Choice (C), shows what happens to the temperature of the can of soda as time passes. At the beginning, the temperature is 70 degrees Fahrenheit, and as time passes, the temperature drops down to the temperature of the freezer, 32 degrees Fahrenheit, and stays there.

9. **B.** Similar triangles' side lengths are proportional. So if the little triangle's left side is x centimeters and the big triangle's left side is $\frac{5}{4}x$ centimeters, that's the proportion: $\frac{\text{a side of the big triangle}}{\text{the same side of the small triangle}} = \frac{\frac{5}{4}}{1}$. Knowing that proportion, you can set up an equation: $\frac{x}{8} = \frac{5}{4}$, where x is the side of the big triangle you're looking for. Cross-multiply to get $4x = 40$, and simplify to $x = 10$.

10. **B.** You can simplify this expression in more than one way, but try starting by dividing the top and bottom by 4, leaving $\frac{\left(4^2 + 4^3\right)}{4(4 + 16)}$. Then, distribute the 4 in the bottom part of the fraction: $\frac{\left(4^2 + 4^3\right)}{16 + 64}$. You may, at this point, notice that the top and bottom parts of the fraction are the same, or that they both are equal to 80, so the fraction simplifies to 1.

11. **B.** You can easily tell when Tom stopped to talk to his friend because during the time he was stopped, his distance from school stayed the same. Looking at the graph, Tom's distance from school (0.75 miles) stayed the same from 0.75 hours to about 0.85 hours.

12. **D.** Adding five points to each quiz score has no effect on the range of the scores, which is calculated by subtracting the lowest score from the highest score. If the low and high scores were initially 50 and 93, the range would be 43. If Mr. Bannon added five points to each score, producing 55 and 98 as the new low and high scores, the range would still be 43.

13. **A.** Don't bother calculating the probabilities exactly here unless you need to in order to see the logic. Corinne can win in only one way — if she rolls a 6 on both rolls. Jeremy can get a sum of 8 in several ways: a 2 on the first roll and a 6 on the second, a 3 on the first roll and a 5 on the second, and so on. So the probability (the number of what you want divided by the number of total possibilities) is much higher for Jeremy.

14. **D.** Complete the graph so you can count the points. Because the graph is symmetrical about the value at 58, the left and right halves of the graph should be mirror images of each other. Looking at the values above 58, five values are at 68 (because the frequency is 5 there), four at 78, two at 88, and one at 98, giving you a total of 12 data points above 58.

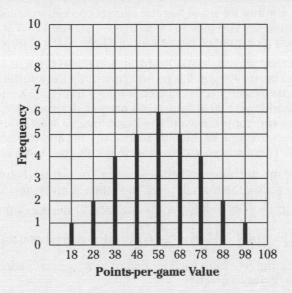

15. **D.** On questions like this one, test values until you're confident you've found the maximum value. Although it may seem odd, –3 produces the greatest value $[3(-3)^2 + 2 = 3(9) + 2 = 29]$.

16. **C.** The ISEE defines *factor* as a number that can divide evenly into another number, but it doesn't consider any number to be a factor of itself. For example, the biggest factor of 10 (on the ISEE) would be 5, not 10, even though 10 divides evenly into 10. Because you're looking for the smallest number that *ab* can be a factor of, consider the biggest number that *ab* can be. The biggest factor of 16 is 8, and the biggest factor of 27 is 9. So the biggest number that *ab* can be is 72. And 144 is the *least* value that *ab* must be a factor of, because 72 divides into both 432 and 144, but 144 is smaller.

17. **D.** Knowing the difference between the two speeds is the only option that lets you compare the speeds. For example, if you knew the difference was one mile per hour, you'd know that the red car gains one mile every hour on the blue car.

18. **B.** The net of the cube, when folded, forms the three-dimensional cube. The star at the bottom of Choice (B) becomes the top of the pictured cube, and the circle to the right of the triangle becomes the right side of the pictured cube.

19. **C.** This problem is easier if you imagine the box as a cube with side length 10. Because all the dimensions (length, width, and height) of a cube are the same, find the volume of the initial cube by multiplying (*length*) × (*width*) × (*height*): $10 \times 10 \times 10 = 1,000$. Increase the length by 20 percent by multiplying $10 \times 1.2 = 12$, the length of the new box. Increase the width by 30 percent by multiplying $10 \times 1.3 = 13$, the width of the new box. And increase the height by 40 percent by multiplying $10 \times 1.4 = 14$, the height of the new box. Find the volume of the new box by multiplying $12 \times 13 \times 14 = 2,184$. Now, find the percent increase with the formula $\frac{\text{difference}}{\text{original}} \times 100$. The difference between 2,184 and 1,000 is 1,184. So $1,184 \div 1,000 = 1.184$, and $1.184 \times 100 = 118.4$, which is closest to Choice (C).

20. **B.** Write down Michael's possibilities: If he knows the integer is greater than 7 and less than 11, it must be either 8, 9, or 10. Then write down Jill's possibilities: If she knows the integer is more than 8 but less than 13, it must be either 9, 10, 11, or 12. Looking at both lists of numbers, 9 and 10 are common, so the integer can be one of two numbers.

21. **D.** Pick a number for n and test the answer choices to see which one *can't* make an integer. For example, say you pick 10 for n: 10 + 1 = 11, and 11 ÷ 2 is 5.5, which isn't an integer. As long as you pick an even number for n, Choice (D) will never make an integer.

22. **C.** The easiest way to do this problem, and those like it, is to test the answer choices to see which one must be right. If you test Choice (C), the shorter piece must be 27 inches long, because the longer piece is 45 inches longer than the shorter piece (72 – 45 = 27). Because 27 and 72 add up to 99, Choice (C) is correct. Alternatively, you can set up an equation, calling the shorter piece x and the longer piece $x + 45$. Added together, the two pieces equal 99: $x + x + 45 = 99$. Simplify to $2x + 45 = 99$, and then $2x = 54$. Divide both sides by 2 to get $x = 27$. Then, subtract 27 from 99 to get 72, the length of the longer piece.

23. **A.** To find the decrease in Celsius, you can convert the Fahrenheit degree temperatures to Celsius (using the formula given) and then subtract them: 95 degrees Fahrenheit is $\frac{5}{9}(95-32)=\frac{5}{9}(63)=\frac{63\times5}{9}=\frac{315}{9}=35$; and 77 degrees Fahrenheit is $\frac{5}{9}(77-32)=\frac{5}{9}(45)=\frac{5\times45}{9}=\frac{225}{9}=25$. So the corresponding Celsius decrease is 35 – 25 = 10.

24. **C.** Distributing $(a-b)$ to each term in $a^2 + ab + b^2$ results in $a^3 - a^2b + a^2b - ab^2 + ab^2 - b^3$, which simplifies to $a^3 - b^3$.

25. **C.** Using PEMDAS, first add 7 + 2 and get 9, then multiply 9 by 2 and get 18, finally add 6 to 18 and get 24. The two columns are the same.

26. **B.** Solve for x. The area of rectangle M (48 square inches) is found by multiplying its length by its width: $3x \cdot x = 48$, so $3x^2 = 48$. Divide both sides by 3 and get $x^2 = 16$. Then, take the square root of both sides, leaving $x = 4$. For rectangle N, the perimeter is found by adding all the sides. Two sides measure $3y$, and two measure y, so the perimeter is $8y$. You know that the perimeter is 40, so $8y = 40$, and $y = 5$.

27. **C.** This problem requires algebra, so start with the unknowns and assign variables to them. For example, say the number of pears is x and the number of apples is $3x$ (because you know the number of apples is three times the number of pears). You also know that buying all the pears and apples costs $5.50, so setting up the equation, $0.25x + $0.10(3x) = 5.50, lets you solve for x: $0.25x + $0.30x = 5.50, then $0.55x = 5.50. Divide both sides by $0.55 to get $x = 10$. So, the number of apples ($3x = 3 \times 10$) is 30, and the total value of the apples is $3.00 ($0.10 \times 30$).

28. **C.** The slope of line ℓ is 1, which you can tell by looking at its equation because the equation is in slope-intercept form (the slope of the line is the coefficient of x). Perpendicular lines have negative reciprocal slopes. The reciprocal of 1 is just 1 (1 ÷ 1 = 1), so the negative reciprocal of 1 is –1. Therefore, line m has a slope of –1.

29. **D.** Draw a few rectangles with perimeters of 60 inches but different lengths and widths. You can make a rectangle with a perimeter of 60 inches that has an area bigger than 200 square inches, and you can make one with an area smaller than 200 square inches. For example, if the length and width of the rectangle were 16 inches by 14 inches, the area would be 224 square inches, and if the two long sides were both 29 and the two short sides were 1, the area would be only 29 square inches — so the answer can't be determined.

30. **C.** Find the area of the shaded region by subtracting the area of the triangle from the area of the square. The area of the square is x^2, and the area of the triangle is $\frac{1}{2}x^2$, so $x^2 - \frac{1}{2}x^2 = \frac{1}{2}x^2$.

31. **B.** For this problem, either guess and check or make an equation. If you guess, think about which four consecutive integers may add to 106, and you'll eventually figure out what the integers are through trial and error. However, setting up an equation is faster: $(x) + (x + 1) + (x + 2) + (x + 3) = 106$, which simplifies to $4x + 6 = 106$. Then, x turns out to be 25, so the largest integer, $(x + 3)$, must be 28.

32. **A.** Always test numbers on problems like this one; the best numbers to test are 1, 0, and –1. But whatever number you test for this particular problem, Column A is bigger.

33. **B.** The perimeter of the square is 16 (side length is 4), so twice its perimeter is 32. Triangle *ABC* is *equilateral,* because its angles are all equal to *x* degrees. Because you know the bottom side is 8 inches, its other sides must also be 8 inches, so its perimeter is 24.

34. **B.** The probability of flipping a coin twice and getting heads both times is found by multiplying the probability of getting heads on the first flip by the probability of getting heads on the second flip. Because probability is (the result you want) ÷ (the total number of possibilities), each flip has a $\frac{1}{2}$ probability of being heads (because the coin has only one heads out of the two sides). Multiplying the two probabilities gives you $= \frac{1}{2} \times \frac{1}{2} = \frac{1}{4}$. For the die, the probability is two of what you want (rolling a 2 or a 5), divided by six total possibilities, giving you a $\frac{1}{3}$ probability (when simplified).

35. **B.** The probability of selecting a black button for both buttons is the probability of selecting a black button once $\frac{6}{10}$ by the probability of selecting a black button the second time $\frac{6}{10} = \frac{36}{100}$. The probability of selecting a white button is $\frac{4}{10}$. Comparing the two fractions, Column B is bigger.

36. **D.** The range of the number of coins is some number between 200 (if at least one of the four collectors who has between 249 and 300 coins has 300 coins and if at least one of the collectors who has between 100 and 148 coins has 100 coins) and 101 (if at least one of the four collectors who has between 249 and 300 coins has only 249 coins and if at least one of the collectors who has between 100 and 148 coins has 148 coins).

The median of the numbers of coins is found by writing a list in order. One collector has between 100 and 148 coins, so the first item in the list is a number between 100 and 148, the next two items in the list are numbers between 149 and 199 (because two collectors have between 149 and 199 coins). When the list is entirely written out, its two middle numbers are both between 200 and 248. Because all you know is that those two numbers are *between* 200 and 248, they can both be 200 or both be 248 or somewhere in between. And because the range can be 200, the values in Column A and Column B may be equal or different.

37. **B.** Always calculate percentage changes one at a time. If the grade drops 10 percent from 90, it becomes $(90 \times 0.9) = 81$. If the grade rises 10 percent from 81, it becomes $(81 \times 1.1) = 89.1$.

Section 3: Reading Comprehension

1. **B.** Although the passage talks about several issues related to Hawaiian history, notice that the one theme mentioned in the first paragraph is how Cook's arrival was a pivotal shift for the Hawaiians. The rest of the passage explains how the government worked, what happened when Cook arrived, and how government was centralized after Cook's death.

2. **A.** The passage tells you that *kahuna* refers to religious leaders.

3. **B.** The *kapu system* was a group of moral laws that governed the people. According to the passage, one of the rules that could be punishable by death was walking in the shadow of an alii.

4. **C.** You can infer from the events in the passage that Cook and his men saw the Hawaiians as a primitive people they could exploit for both their own needs and pleasure, as noted by unfair trading practices, Cook's denial of the truth about Lono, and how Cook's men took advantage of local women.

5. **C.** *Benevolent* means kind or generous, so Choice (C) is correct.

6. **D.** According to the passage, Cook was partially responsible for bringing change to the Hawaiian Islands, although indirectly.

7. **A.** When you face a question like this, be sure to think about everything the passage tells you. In this short article, a brief background of beliefs, reality about the atom's makeup, and a short bit of information about nuclear fission is provided for the reader. Taking all of this into account, the best title is *A Basic Understanding of the Atom*. The other answer choices are too specific for this passage.

8. **A.** The text tells you that particles in the nucleus have positive and neutral charges. Particles outside the nucleus have negative charges.

9. **D.** The text tells you that classification is assigned by the number of protons and neutrons and related charges in the nucleus.

10. **B.** The text tells you that atoms have an unstable isotope that can lead to radioactive decay.

11. **B.** This question is a bit tricky because all the answer choices sound good. With a question like this one, go with what you know. Read the text and choose the answer that the text actually supports. Be careful of selecting an answer you can't infer or prove with the text.

12. **D.** The text tells you directly that the number of neutrons in the nucleus determines the isotope.

13. **A.** The passage presents the *Titanic* as a symbol, representing technology and industrialism that failed to solve the world's problems. You may have been tempted to select Choice (D), but the tone of the passage doesn't support the idea that tragedies like the *Titanic* should be expected. Remember to always select the best answer.

14. **A.** This question requires you to consider the passage as a whole and the author's overall tone, or attitude, toward the subject. You know from the passage that the author believes that the *Titanic* is a symbol of some ideological failures of the early 20th century, so you have to consider the answer choices with that thought in mind. Considering the entire passage, Choice (A) is the only possible answer because many people placed too much faith in technology and advancements in the early 20th century.

15. **B.** In this passage, *marked prosperity* means that the changes, advancements, or gains in society were noticeable. In this context, the word *marked* means that something is important and obvious.

16. **B.** The passage tells you that the ship's designers believed the water-tight doors would prevent the ship from sinking because a few areas could flood and the *Titanic* would still stay afloat.

17. **D.** Considering the passage as a whole, the most likely explanation is Choice (D). Because the ship was considered an unsinkable ship, perhaps the crew wasn't prepared for a sinking disaster as a real possibility. You need to speculate a bit to answer this question, but considering all the answer choices, Choice (D) is the most likely.

18. **C.** A *symbol* is something that represents something larger than itself. In this case, the author believes that the *Titanic* is a symbol of the failure of the idealism of the day that modern technology would solve all the world's problems.

19. **B.** Should you see a question that asks what the passage is primarily about, look for an answer choice that sums up the entire passage. For this question, Choice (B) is correct because the entire passage is about *what makes a mystery story effective*. Be careful not to choose an answer choice that focuses on smaller details of the passage without supporting the entire passage. Choice (A) sounds good because it uses the word *genre,* but this answer choice is much too broad to describe what the passage is primarily about.

20. **D.** The word *genre* means a category of art, music, or writing that conforms to a particular form or style. You don't have to know exactly what genre means to answer this question — just use the process of elimination as you consider the answer choices. From the first paragraph of the passage, you know the writer is talking about different kinds of fiction, so that should have been a clue to follow as you looked for the answer.

21. **B.** A *hook* is a method for grabbing the reader's attention so readers become interested in the story. For this reason, many mystery stories begin with the crime.

22. **C.** The passage states that logic is of utmost importance in a mystery story because the mystery must be logical as well as solved through logical means.

23. **D.** The passage doesn't directly define the concept of sufficient crime, so you need to infer the meaning based on the rest of the passage. In this passage, the author uses this phrasing as he writes about readers' attention, so you can infer that the crime must be sufficient enough to make readers interested in the story. In other words, the theft of a gum machine wouldn't be sufficient for a typical mystery story but a murder at city hall would be.

24. **B.** The author mentions that the readers shouldn't be able to solve the mystery without the writer's help, so Choice (B) is correct. The passage doesn't directly mention the other answer choices.

25. **A.** The author of the passage recommends that the mystery writer have respect for his or her readers. In other words, don't disrespect readers with improbable solutions to the mystery.

26. **C.** The author mentions genres in the first paragraph but doesn't write about different classifications or details concerning various literary genres.

27. **A.** The passage states that cockroaches can hold their breath for up to 40 minutes, so they're not easily drowned.

28. **A.** Although the statement may hold some truth, the idea that cockroaches can survive a nuclear blast is most likely exaggeration used to make a point that cockroaches are extremely hardy.

29. **D.** Although all the choices can be factors for infestation, the greatest problem is the rate of reproduction. Because cockroaches reproduce so quickly, homeowners may have a difficult time eradicating them.

30. **C.** Because removing food and water sources from your home is virtually impossible, Choices (A) and (B) are incorrect. Kill-on-demand products aren't as effective as sterilization pesticides, so Choice (C) is the correct answer.

31. **A.** The text tells you that multiple treatments are often necessary, including different kinds of treatments used in conjunction with each other.

32. **B.** The text is saying that the senators will be assembled after their election. If you face a question similar to this one, choose the answer that best completes the thought in the simplest way.

33. **B.** The passage tells you in the second paragraph that the legislature fills vacancies.

34. **B.** The passage tells you in the third paragraph that a candidate must be at least 30 years of age.

35. **A.** The passage tells you in the second paragraph that senators serve a six-year term, not three.

36. **A.** The passage tells you that the senate may impeach the president or another member of congress, but all they can do is remove the person from office if found guilty. However, the convicted person may still be liable for crimes under the law, but the senate has no power to levy sentencing and fines.

Section 4: Mathematics Achievement

1. **C.** All you have to do is count the number of shaded squares and multiply by 6. Nine squares are shaded, so the total area of the shaded region is 54 square centimeters.

2. **D.** To find the probability of two things *both* happening, multiply the probability of one event happening by the probability of the other event happening. The probability of picking a blue button on the first pick is $\frac{60}{190} = \frac{6}{19}$, and the probability of picking a blue button on the second pick is the same. Multiplying the two probabilities gives you $\frac{6}{19} \times \frac{6}{19} = \frac{36}{361}$.

3. **B.** Convert from scientific notation to standard notation to make the addition easier: $4.9 \times 10^6 = 4,900,000$ and $3.7 \times 10^4 = 37,000$, so adding the numbers gives you 4,937,000. Convert back to scientific notation by moving the decimal point to the left until just one digit is to the point's left (4.937), and count how many places the decimal moved (six places). Your answer is 4.937×10^6.

4. **C.** $\frac{3}{10} = 0.3$, and $\frac{1}{3} = 0.\bar{3}$, which means 0.3 repeating (0.3333333333333333333 . . .).

5. **D.** Test the answer choices. The only choice that can make the equation true is $x = 0$.

6. **D.** You may think that 3 works, giving you $\frac{0}{0}$, but anything divided by 0 is undefined, even 0 itself. So no values for y make the equation true.

7. **A.** The plus sign under the root means you have to treat the operation below the root as if it were surrounded by parentheses. So first add 36 and 64, and then take the square root of the answer (100) to get 10.

8. **B.** To find the median, write all the numbers in order from least to greatest: 170, 175, 185, 185, 195, and 205. In a list with an even number of values, the median is the average of the middle two values. In this case, the middle two values are both 185, so the median is 185.

9. **A.** Test the answer choices or make an equation. If you test Choice (A), Peter picks $3 \times 7 = 21$ carrots, which, when combined with Judy's 7, makes 28. Or $3x + x = 28$ (Peter is $3x$ and Judy is x). Solving for x gives you 7.

10. **C.** Make an average equation: $\frac{131 + 169 + 171 + x}{4} = 145$. Solving for x produces 109. Or just test the answer choices until you find one that, when averaged with Jared's first three scores, equals 145.

11. **D.** The greatest number of Paul's friends own four TVs (the graph shows that five of his friends own four TVs), so the mode of the data is 4. The mode is just the number that appears most often in the data.

12. **D.** First, find the least common multiple of the coefficients (2, 3, and 4). The lowest number they all divide into evenly is 12, narrowing your choices down to Choices (C) and (D). Now, find the least common multiple of the variables. They all divide evenly into x^2y, making Choice (D) the correct answer.

13. **D.** If you noticed that the first expression looks a lot like the second expression, you're off to a good start. Both expressions are written as x times a number minus that same number. Putting in 7 for y makes the expressions exactly alike. If you didn't notice that, you could factor a 7 out of the first expression, $7(x - 1)$, and factor a y out of the second expression, $y(x - 1)$, so you're left with $7(x - 1) = y(x - 1)$. Dividing both sides by $(x - 1)$ leaves $7 = y$.

14. **C.** Combine only terms with the same exponents to the same powers. And to avoid confusion, distribute the negative sign in front of the parentheses by multiplying each term inside the parentheses by -1. First, you have $6m^5n^3 + 7m^3n^5 - 5m^3n^5 + 4m^5n^3$. Next, combine like terms to get $10m^5n^3 + 2m^3n^5$.

15. **C.** Either 9 or –9 makes the top of the fraction equal 0, thus making the whole thing equal to 0. Watch out: Putting a –4 or a –5 in for x makes the bottom of the fraction equal 0, thus making the whole thing *undefined,* not 0.

16. **C.** Distributing $(x - 4)$ to each term in $(x + 5)$ results in $x^2 - 4x + 5x - 20$, which simplifies to Choice (C).

17. **B.** Use $\frac{\text{rise}}{\text{run}}$ to find the slope, and count from a point on the line that you know, like (0, 5). Moving to the point (1, 0) is a rise of –5 and a run of 1, so the slope is $\frac{-5}{1}$, or –5.

18. **C.** If you know the formula for the equation of a circle, you may as well use it here. But drawing the circle and figuring it out by using the Pythagorean theorem is probably easier and safer. Notice that you can make a right triangle with the radius as the hypotenuse of the triangle. You know the bottom leg of the triangle is six grid units because it goes from the x-coordinate of the circle center (–3) to the x-coordinate of the point on the circle (3). The other leg of the triangle is eight grid units because it goes from the y-coordinate of the circle center (2) to the y-coordinate of the point on the circle (10). Solving with the Pythagorean theorem gives you $6^2 + 8^2 = c^2$, which simplifies to $c = 10$.

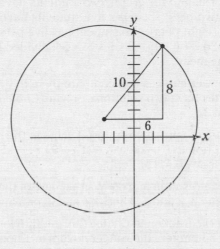

19. **D.** The answer to this problem is simple logic — the best way to get the average number of hours of homework done per student is to survey all the students. But because that isn't one of the choices, Choice (D) is the best answer because it's closest and takes the entire school into account.

20. **D.** To find the total measure of the interior angles of a polygon, use the formula $180(n - 2)$, where n is the number of sides. So the total measure of the five-sided figure's angles is $180(5 - 2)$, which equals 540 degrees. Now, add all the angles you know and subtract the total from 540 degrees to find the measure of the missing angle.

21. **C.** You can write all the combinations (but on this problem, doing so is time-consuming), or you can use the following formula: $\frac{n!}{r!(n-r)!}$, where n is the total number of things, and r is the number of things in the group. The ! sign means factorial. So 7! means $7 \times 6 \times 5 \times 4 \times 3 \times 2 \times 1$. Using the formula, $\frac{7!}{4!(7-4)!} = \frac{7 \times 6 \times 5 \times 4 \times 3 \times 2 \times 1}{4 \times 3 \times 2 \times 1(3 \times 2 \times 1)} = \frac{7 \times 6 \times 5}{6} = 35$.

Most of the time, on both the ISEE and SSAT, methodically writing out all the combinations is safer than using a formula.

22. **A.** Plot all the answer choices as points on the grid, and draw what the parallelogram would look like for each. To see which point is correct, count rise over run to find the slopes of each side of the parallelograms. The correct point, (1, 5), when connected with the point (–3, 1), forms a line with a slope of 1, parallel to the line between the other two points (1, –2) and (5, 2).

23. **C.** To solve this absolute value inequality, write two equations. You form the first by taking away the absolute value sign, leaving $3x - 6 \leq 12$. Solving the equation gives you $x \leq 6$. You form the second equation by removing the absolute value signs, then reversing both the direction of the inequality and the sign of the number to the right of the inequality, giving you $3x - 6 \geq -12$. Solving for x gives you $x \geq -2$. The answer is the combination of both solutions: $-2 \leq x \leq 6$.

24. **B.** An irrational number is any number than can't be expressed as an integer divided by another integer. So 0 can be expressed as $\frac{0}{2}$, $0.\overline{3} = \frac{1}{3}$, and $\sqrt{1} = 1$, which can be expressed as $\frac{7}{7}$, for example.

25. **B.** To find the mean, you have to count all the pets and then divide by how many students there are. According to the graph, two students have one pet (so that's two pets), three students have two pets (six pets), five students have three pets (15 pets), two students have four pets (eight pets), one student has five pets (five), and three students have six pets (18 pets). So 2 + 6 + 15 + 8 + 5 + 18 = 54, divided by the number of students (16) gives you 3.375 as the mean.

26. **C.** Solve the answer choices and compare them to the graph. Remember that absolute value inequalities have two solutions. Solving Choice (C) results in $-6 < x < 3$, or all values between –6 and 3.

If you're not sure of your answer, test a value in the range of the answer choice you think is correct. For Choice (C), you can test $x = 0$ or $x = -5$ and see whether the inequality is still true. For $x = 0$, is $|x + 0| < 4.5$? Yep!

27. **C.** A sum of 6 can result in more ways than any of the other choices. To have a sum of 6, one can roll 1 and 5, 2 and 4, 3 and 3, 4 and 2, or 5 and 1.

28. **A.** In the top of the fraction in Choice (A), multiplying 0.5 kilometers by 60 minutes tells you how many kilometers the runner covers in 1 hour ($0.5 \times 60 = 30$). In the bottom of the fraction in Choice (A), multiplying 0.000305 kilometers by 5,280 feet tells you how many kilometers are in one mile ($0.000305 \times 5,280 =$ about 1.6). Dividing 30 by 1.6 converts kilometers to miles. Another way to approach this question is to look at all the choices and see which produces a realistic number for a runner's speed.

29. **C.** Set up a proportion: $\frac{30 \text{ ft}}{50 \text{ ft}} = \frac{50 \text{ft}}{x}$ and cross-multiply to solve for x. Doing so lets you apply the ratio of the height of the first flagpole to its shadow to the height of the second flagpole so you can solve for the length of the second flagpole's shadow.

30. **A.** This question may seem easy, but it's a good place to remind you to read questions carefully and, before you select an answer, reread exactly what the question is asking for. A kilogram is 2.2 pounds — way too heavy for an apple — so grams are a better measurement.

31. **C.** Choice (A) results in $3 - 6$, or –3; Choice (B) results in 3×6, or 18; and Choice (D) can be rewritten as $\sqrt{9} \times \sqrt{36}$, making it the same expression as Choice (B). Choice (C) results in $\sqrt{27}$, which is approximately 5.2, and isn't an integer.

32. **C.** Find the area of the circle using πr^2, and then subtract the area of the square, leaving the area of the shaded region. The radius of the circle is 10 centimeters, so its area is 100π. The area of the square is easiest to calculate if you divide it into two equal triangles, each with a base of 20 centimeters and height of 10 centimeters. Using $\frac{1}{2}bh$, the area of the triangles is 100 cm² + 100 cm² = 200 cm².

33. **A.** Multiply the diameter (12 inches) by 1.5 to find the height (18 inches). Then, square the radius (6) to get $36\pi \times 18 = 648\pi$.

34. **B.** The range of the data is found by subtracting the lowest score (30) from the highest score (100), giving you a range of 70. The low and high values of a box-and-whisker plot are the ends of the line graphed.

35. **B.** If Katie removes one coin, 48 coins are left in the bag. Find the probability of George taking a quarter by dividing (how many there are of what you want) by (the total number of possibilities). Because there are 8 of what you want (quarters) and 48 possible coins, the probability is $\frac{8}{48} = \frac{1}{6}$.

36. **B.** Split up the expression for easier understanding: $\sqrt{64x^{36}} = \sqrt{64} \times \sqrt{x^{36}}$. Then ask yourself: What times itself equals 64? The answer is 8. What times itself equals $\sqrt{x^{36}}$? The answer is x^{18}, so the correct answer is Choice (B).

37. **A.** Use the mnemonic *SOH CAH TOA* to solve for side lengths of a right triangle, using basic trigonometry. Because you need to find the hypotenuse of the triangle and you know the side length opposite from the angle you know, use SOH, which stands for sin = $\frac{\text{opposite}}{\text{hypotenuse}}$. Filling in what you know, $\sin 36° = \frac{18 \text{ cm}}{\text{hypotenuse}}$. Because you need to solve for AB (the hypotenuse), multiply both sides by the hypotenuse and then divide both sides by $\sin 36°$ to arrive at Choice (A).

38. **A.** Split up the inequality into $2 \le 3x - 3$ and $3x - 3 \le 7$ and solve both separately, resulting in two solutions: $\frac{5}{3} \le x$ and $x \le \frac{10}{3}$. Choice (A) shows all the values of x that fit both of those inequalities.

39. **C.** To find the median temperature, make a list of all the temperatures. The "Stem" section of the chart represents the tens digit in the temperature and the "Leaf" section represents the ones digit. So the temperatures are 47, 49, 51, 53, 53, 53, 56, 57, 61, 62, 62, 65, 65, 66, 67, 68, 68, 70, 71, 71, 72, and 73. Because an even number of temperatures (22) exists, find the mean of the middle two values (62 and 65).

40. **C.** Simplify the equation: $x^2 = -100$, $x = \sqrt{-100}$. The square root of -100 can be rewritten as $\sqrt{-1} \times \sqrt{100}$. The square root of -1 is the imaginary number i and the square root of 100 is ± 10, so the answer is Choice (C).

41. **B.** Adding these two matrices forms a new matrix with the same number of rows and columns. The upper left corner of the left matrix (1) gets added to the upper left corner of the right matrix (1) to form the upper left corner of the new matrix (2). Repeat this process to find the values of the other corners of the new matrix.

42. **D.** Set up an equation: $972\pi \text{ cm}^3 = \frac{4}{3}\pi r^3$. Divide both sides by $\frac{4}{3}$, resulting in $729\pi \text{ cm}^3 = \pi r^3$. Now, check the answer choices: Which number, when cubed, gives you 729? Choice (D) is the correct radius.

43. **D.** Absolute value inequalities usually have two answers. To find the first, remove the absolute value signs and solve the inequality: $x - 2 < 3$, so adding 2 to both sides gives you $x < 5$. For the second solution, remove the absolute value signs from the original and solve but reverse the inequality sign and make 3 negative: $x - 2 > -3$. To solve, add 2 to both sides: $x > -1$. Write both solutions as $-1 < x < 5$.

44. **C.** Divide 150 by 4 to find out how much of the 150-minute telecast was commercials: $150 \div 4 = 37.5$. If 37.5 minutes were commercials and the commercials averaged 30 seconds each, you need to find out how many 30-second commercials fit into 37.5 minutes. First, convert seconds to minutes, because you're dividing into 37.5 minutes: 30 seconds is 0.5 minutes. Then, divide: $37.5 \div 0.5 = 75$.

45. **C.** When subtracting a negative number from another number, just remove the negative sign and *add* the numbers. So $-8x - (-8x)$ is the same thing as $-8x + 8x$, which equals 0.

46. **B.** Split up the root to make this easier: $\sqrt{25x^{36}} = \sqrt{25} \times \sqrt{x^{36}}$. The square root of 25 is 5, and the square root of x^{36} is found by thinking what number, when multiplied by itself, equals x^{36}. The answer is x^{18} because, using exponent rules, $x^{18} \times x^{18} = x^{36}$. So $5 \times x^{18} = 5x^{18}$.

47. **D.** A varies *directly* with B, so when B is multiplied by 3, A is, too, resulting in $3A$. A varies *inversely* with C, so when C is divided by 4, A is multiplied by 4, resulting in $12A$.

Section 5: Essay

Remember that writing samples for the ISEE don't have right or wrong answers, and with this topic about community service, you can write about a variety of issues. So don't get caught up in thinking, "Did I write what they wanted?" because truthfully, the readers of your writing sample aren't concerned about your point of view. They simply want to see that you can organize your thoughts, show your writer's voice, and write a strong essay.

With that thought in mind, the following are a few things you should have done to write a winning essay for your practice test. (For more valuable tips on writing an effective essay and some examples, check out Chapter 8.)

✔ Because the essay prompt asks you to agree or disagree with the concept of high school students being required to complete community service hours as a part of graduation, you should have made clear in your introduction what position you're taking — whether you agree or disagree with the statement. Simply talking about positives and negatives of both sides of the issue won't cut it here because you're asked to agree or disagree with the idea.

✔ Your body paragraphs should have included specific examples that help back up or *prove* your position. These examples can be of a famous person, such as a sports star or a talented actor or singer, or a character from a book you read who realized helping other people was beneficial. If you use a character from a book or story on the actual test, make sure you include the name of the character and mention the name of the story or book.

✔ To really hit a home run with this essay, you should have included an example from your own life. Did you write about a time where helping someone else helped you? Or if you disagreed, did you provide reasons why students should be required to perform community service? Remember that the readers want to hear your voice. Including a personal story or experience is a great way to make a writing sample really come to life for the reader.

✔ You should have included a conclusion that brought your ideas together and again affirmed your position on the essay. Conclusions help show that your thoughts and ideas are organized and that you stuck with the topic, so don't forget about the conclusion when you write.

Finally, have someone else read your essay and mark misspelled words, poorly organized sentences, misplaced commas, and other grammatical problems. Doing so helps you see how many errors you made. Remember that the writing sample isn't a grammar test, and a few errors won't hurt you in the end, but overall, your sample should be well written and generally error free.

Answers at a Glance

Section 1: Verbal Reasoning

1. B	9. D	17. A	25. A	33. B
2. D	10. D	18. D	26. C	34. D
3. B	11. A	19. B	27. A	35. C
4. B	12. B	20. D	28. A	36. A
5. A	13. A	21. B	29. C	37. A
6. C	14. B	22. C	30. D	38. B
7. C	15. C	23. D	31. C	39. D
8. A	16. A	24. C	32. A	40. D

Section 2: Quantitative Reasoning

1. C	9. B	17. D	25. C	33. B
2. B	10. B	18. B	26. B	34. B
3. A	11. B	19. C	27. C	35. B
4. B	12. D	20. B	28. C	36. D
5. C	13. A	21. D	29. D	37. B
6. C	14. D	22. C	30. C	
7. A	15. D	23. A	31. B	
8. C	16. C	24. C	32. A	

Section 3: Reading Comprehension

1. B	9. D	17. D	25. A	33. B
2. A	10. B	18. C	26. C	34. B
3. B	11. B	19. B	27. A	35. A
4. C	12. D	20. D	28. A	36. A
5. C	13. A	21. B	29. D	
6. D	14. A	22. C	30. C	
7. A	15. B	23. D	31. A	
8. A	16. B	24. B	32. B	

Section 4: Mathematics Achievement

1. C	11. D	21. C	31. C	41. B
2. D	12. D	22. A	32. C	42. D
3. B	13. D	23. C	33. A	43. D
4. C	14. C	24. B	34. B	44. C
5. D	15. C	25. B	35. B	45. C
6. D	16. C	26. C	36. B	46. B
7. A	17. B	27. C	37. A	47. D
8. B	18. C	28. A	38. A	
9. A	19. D	29. C	39. C	
10. C	20. D	30. A	40. C	

Chapter 25

ISEE Middle Level Practice Exam

• •

*T*his practice exam is for ISEE middle level students — those seeking entrance to grades 7 and 8. Taking practice tests can help you perform better on test day, so when you sit down to practice this test, make sure you give it your all. To make the most of this practice exam, find yourself a quiet room, ample time, a few sharpened pencils, and some blank scratch paper. Resist the urge to play on the Internet or text your friends while you're taking the test. After all, you want to practice in the same quiet and boring conditions that you'll face on test day.

Grab a watch, an iPod, a phone, or some other way to track your time. Make sure you don't go over the time limit we've given you for each part of this practice test because you won't be allowed extra time on the actual test. You can find all the answers to this practice test in Chapter 26, but don't cheat! Check your answers only *after* you finish the test.

Answer Sheet

For Sections 1 through 4 of the exam, use the following answer sheets and fill in the answer bubble for the corresponding number, using a #2 pencil.

Section 1: Verbal Reasoning

1. Ⓐ Ⓑ Ⓒ Ⓓ Ⓔ	11. Ⓐ Ⓑ Ⓒ Ⓓ Ⓔ	21. Ⓐ Ⓑ Ⓒ Ⓓ Ⓔ	31. Ⓐ Ⓑ Ⓒ Ⓓ Ⓔ
2. Ⓐ Ⓑ Ⓒ Ⓓ Ⓔ	12. Ⓐ Ⓑ Ⓒ Ⓓ Ⓔ	22. Ⓐ Ⓑ Ⓒ Ⓓ Ⓔ	32. Ⓐ Ⓑ Ⓒ Ⓓ Ⓔ
3. Ⓐ Ⓑ Ⓒ Ⓓ Ⓔ	13. Ⓐ Ⓑ Ⓒ Ⓓ Ⓔ	23. Ⓐ Ⓑ Ⓒ Ⓓ Ⓔ	33. Ⓐ Ⓑ Ⓒ Ⓓ Ⓔ
4. Ⓐ Ⓑ Ⓒ Ⓓ Ⓔ	14. Ⓐ Ⓑ Ⓒ Ⓓ Ⓔ	24. Ⓐ Ⓑ Ⓒ Ⓓ Ⓔ	34. Ⓐ Ⓑ Ⓒ Ⓓ Ⓔ
5. Ⓐ Ⓑ Ⓒ Ⓓ Ⓔ	15. Ⓐ Ⓑ Ⓒ Ⓓ Ⓔ	25. Ⓐ Ⓑ Ⓒ Ⓓ Ⓔ	35. Ⓐ Ⓑ Ⓒ Ⓓ Ⓔ
6. Ⓐ Ⓑ Ⓒ Ⓓ Ⓔ	16. Ⓐ Ⓑ Ⓒ Ⓓ Ⓔ	26. Ⓐ Ⓑ Ⓒ Ⓓ Ⓔ	36. Ⓐ Ⓑ Ⓒ Ⓓ Ⓔ
7. Ⓐ Ⓑ Ⓒ Ⓓ Ⓔ	17. Ⓐ Ⓑ Ⓒ Ⓓ Ⓔ	27. Ⓐ Ⓑ Ⓒ Ⓓ Ⓔ	37. Ⓐ Ⓑ Ⓒ Ⓓ Ⓔ
8. Ⓐ Ⓑ Ⓒ Ⓓ Ⓔ	18. Ⓐ Ⓑ Ⓒ Ⓓ Ⓔ	28. Ⓐ Ⓑ Ⓒ Ⓓ Ⓔ	38. Ⓐ Ⓑ Ⓒ Ⓓ Ⓔ
9. Ⓐ Ⓑ Ⓒ Ⓓ Ⓔ	19. Ⓐ Ⓑ Ⓒ Ⓓ Ⓔ	29. Ⓐ Ⓑ Ⓒ Ⓓ Ⓔ	39. Ⓐ Ⓑ Ⓒ Ⓓ Ⓔ
10. Ⓐ Ⓑ Ⓒ Ⓓ Ⓔ	20. Ⓐ Ⓑ Ⓒ Ⓓ Ⓔ	30. Ⓐ Ⓑ Ⓒ Ⓓ Ⓔ	40. Ⓐ Ⓑ Ⓒ Ⓓ Ⓔ

Section 2: Quantitative Reasoning

1. Ⓐ Ⓑ Ⓒ Ⓓ	9. Ⓐ Ⓑ Ⓒ Ⓓ	17 Ⓐ Ⓑ Ⓒ Ⓓ	25. Ⓐ Ⓑ Ⓒ Ⓓ	33. Ⓐ Ⓑ Ⓒ Ⓓ
2. Ⓐ Ⓑ Ⓒ Ⓓ	10. Ⓐ Ⓑ Ⓒ Ⓓ	18. Ⓐ Ⓑ Ⓒ Ⓓ	26. Ⓐ Ⓑ Ⓒ Ⓓ	34. Ⓐ Ⓑ Ⓒ Ⓓ
3. Ⓐ Ⓑ Ⓒ Ⓓ	11. Ⓐ Ⓑ Ⓒ Ⓓ	19. Ⓐ Ⓑ Ⓒ Ⓓ	27. Ⓐ Ⓑ Ⓒ Ⓓ	35. Ⓐ Ⓑ Ⓒ Ⓓ
4. Ⓐ Ⓑ Ⓒ Ⓓ	12. Ⓐ Ⓑ Ⓒ Ⓓ	20. Ⓐ Ⓑ Ⓒ Ⓓ	28. Ⓐ Ⓑ Ⓒ Ⓓ	36. Ⓐ Ⓑ Ⓒ Ⓓ
5. Ⓐ Ⓑ Ⓒ Ⓓ	13. Ⓐ Ⓑ Ⓒ Ⓓ	21. Ⓐ Ⓑ Ⓒ Ⓓ	29. Ⓐ Ⓑ Ⓒ Ⓓ	37. Ⓐ Ⓑ Ⓒ Ⓓ
6. Ⓐ Ⓑ Ⓒ Ⓓ	14. Ⓐ Ⓑ Ⓒ Ⓓ	22. Ⓐ Ⓑ Ⓒ Ⓓ	30. Ⓐ Ⓑ Ⓒ Ⓓ	
7. Ⓐ Ⓑ Ⓒ Ⓓ	15. Ⓐ Ⓑ Ⓒ Ⓓ	23. Ⓐ Ⓑ Ⓒ Ⓓ	31. Ⓐ Ⓑ Ⓒ Ⓓ	
8. Ⓐ Ⓑ Ⓒ Ⓓ	16. Ⓐ Ⓑ Ⓒ Ⓓ	24. Ⓐ Ⓑ Ⓒ Ⓓ	32. Ⓐ Ⓑ Ⓒ Ⓓ	

Section 3: Reading Comprehension

1. Ⓐ Ⓑ Ⓒ Ⓓ
2. Ⓐ Ⓑ Ⓒ Ⓓ
3. Ⓐ Ⓑ Ⓒ Ⓓ
4. Ⓐ Ⓑ Ⓒ Ⓓ
5. Ⓐ Ⓑ Ⓒ Ⓓ
6. Ⓐ Ⓑ Ⓒ Ⓓ
7. Ⓐ Ⓑ Ⓒ Ⓓ
8. Ⓐ Ⓑ Ⓒ Ⓓ
9. Ⓐ Ⓑ Ⓒ Ⓓ
10. Ⓐ Ⓑ Ⓒ Ⓓ
11. Ⓐ Ⓑ Ⓒ Ⓓ
12. Ⓐ Ⓑ Ⓒ Ⓓ

13. Ⓐ Ⓑ Ⓒ Ⓓ
14. Ⓐ Ⓑ Ⓒ Ⓓ
15. Ⓐ Ⓑ Ⓒ Ⓓ
16. Ⓐ Ⓑ Ⓒ Ⓓ
17. Ⓐ Ⓑ Ⓒ Ⓓ
18. Ⓐ Ⓑ Ⓒ Ⓓ
19. Ⓐ Ⓑ Ⓒ Ⓓ
20. Ⓐ Ⓑ Ⓒ Ⓓ
21. Ⓐ Ⓑ Ⓒ Ⓓ
22. Ⓐ Ⓑ Ⓒ Ⓓ
23. Ⓐ Ⓑ Ⓒ Ⓓ
24. Ⓐ Ⓑ Ⓒ Ⓓ

25. Ⓐ Ⓑ Ⓒ Ⓓ
26. Ⓐ Ⓑ Ⓒ Ⓓ
27. Ⓐ Ⓑ Ⓒ Ⓓ
28. Ⓐ Ⓑ Ⓒ Ⓓ
29. Ⓐ Ⓑ Ⓒ Ⓓ
30. Ⓐ Ⓑ Ⓒ Ⓓ
31. Ⓐ Ⓑ Ⓒ Ⓓ
32. Ⓐ Ⓑ Ⓒ Ⓓ
33. Ⓐ Ⓑ Ⓒ Ⓓ
34. Ⓐ Ⓑ Ⓒ Ⓓ
35. Ⓐ Ⓑ Ⓒ Ⓓ
36. Ⓐ Ⓑ Ⓒ Ⓓ

Section 4: Mathematics Achievement

1. Ⓐ Ⓑ Ⓒ Ⓓ
2. Ⓐ Ⓑ Ⓒ Ⓓ
3. Ⓐ Ⓑ Ⓒ Ⓓ
4. Ⓐ Ⓑ Ⓒ Ⓓ
5. Ⓐ Ⓑ Ⓒ Ⓓ
6. Ⓐ Ⓑ Ⓒ Ⓓ
7. Ⓐ Ⓑ Ⓒ Ⓓ
8. Ⓐ Ⓑ Ⓒ Ⓓ
9. Ⓐ Ⓑ Ⓒ Ⓓ
10. Ⓐ Ⓑ Ⓒ Ⓓ
11. Ⓐ Ⓑ Ⓒ Ⓓ
12. Ⓐ Ⓑ Ⓒ Ⓓ

13. Ⓐ Ⓑ Ⓒ Ⓓ
14. Ⓐ Ⓑ Ⓒ Ⓓ
15. Ⓐ Ⓑ Ⓒ Ⓓ
16. Ⓐ Ⓑ Ⓒ Ⓓ
17. Ⓐ Ⓑ Ⓒ Ⓓ
18. Ⓐ Ⓑ Ⓒ Ⓓ
19. Ⓐ Ⓑ Ⓒ Ⓓ
20. Ⓐ Ⓑ Ⓒ Ⓓ
21. Ⓐ Ⓑ Ⓒ Ⓓ
22. Ⓐ Ⓑ Ⓒ Ⓓ
23. Ⓐ Ⓑ Ⓒ Ⓓ
24. Ⓐ Ⓑ Ⓒ Ⓓ

25. Ⓐ Ⓑ Ⓒ Ⓓ
26. Ⓐ Ⓑ Ⓒ Ⓓ
27. Ⓐ Ⓑ Ⓒ Ⓓ
28. Ⓐ Ⓑ Ⓒ Ⓓ
29. Ⓐ Ⓑ Ⓒ Ⓓ
30. Ⓐ Ⓑ Ⓒ Ⓓ
31. Ⓐ Ⓑ Ⓒ Ⓓ
32. Ⓐ Ⓑ Ⓒ Ⓓ
33. Ⓐ Ⓑ Ⓒ Ⓓ
34. Ⓐ Ⓑ Ⓒ Ⓓ
35. Ⓐ Ⓑ Ⓒ Ⓓ
36. Ⓐ Ⓑ Ⓒ Ⓓ

37. Ⓐ Ⓑ Ⓒ Ⓓ
38. Ⓐ Ⓑ Ⓒ Ⓓ
39. Ⓐ Ⓑ Ⓒ Ⓓ
40. Ⓐ Ⓑ Ⓒ Ⓓ
41. Ⓐ Ⓑ Ⓒ Ⓓ
42. Ⓐ Ⓑ Ⓒ Ⓓ
43. Ⓐ Ⓑ Ⓒ Ⓓ
44. Ⓐ Ⓑ Ⓒ Ⓓ
45. Ⓐ Ⓑ Ⓒ Ⓓ
46. Ⓐ Ⓑ Ⓒ Ⓓ
47. Ⓐ Ⓑ Ⓒ Ⓓ

Section 5: Essay

For Section 5, use two loose-leaf or lined notebook pages to write your essay. (On the real exam, the answer booklet contains two lined sheets.)

Section 1
Verbal Reasoning

Time: 20 Minutes

Directions: You have 20 minutes to complete the following 40 questions. Look at the answer options and decide which answer is best. Mark your answer to each question in the corresponding answer bubble on the answer sheet for Section 1.

Questions 1–24 contain a capitalized word and four answer choices. Choose the word that is the closest in meaning to the capitalized word.

1. OMINOUS:
    (A) Frustrating
    (B) Tiring
    (C) Confusing
    (D) Threatening

2. BIAS:
    (A) Favor
    (B) Determine
    (C) Catapult
    (D) Capture

3. BENIGN:
    (A) Uncommon
    (B) Typical
    (C) Harmless
    (D) Direct

4. ADORN:
    (A) Decorate
    (B) Manage
    (C) Justify
    (D) Fail

5. MEDDLE:
    (A) Defend
    (B) Disagree
    (C) Interfere
    (D) Lie

6. OBSCURE:
    (A) Unclear
    (B) Large
    (C) Simple
    (D) Repetitive

7. ARTICULATE:
    (A) Argumentative
    (B) Clear
    (C) Wordy
    (D) Unusual

8. RESIDUE:
    (A) Compound
    (B) Sediment
    (C) Leftover
    (D) Poison

9. ALOOF:
    (A) Rude
    (B) Uninterested
    (C) Desperate
    (D) Demure

10. INERT:
    (A) Harmless
    (B) Destructive
    (C) Vanishing
    (D) Free

Go on to next page

11. QUENCH:
    (A) Kill
    (B) Satisfy
    (C) Regroup
    (D) Belittle

12. POMPOUS:
    (A) Friendly
    (B) Arrogant
    (C) Beautiful
    (D) Carefree

13. DEBRIS:
    (A) Deflection
    (B) Ownership
    (C) Container
    (D) Trash

14. QUAINT:
    (A) Common
    (B) Typical
    (C) Odd
    (D) Reduced

15. DEFT:
    (A) Crisp
    (B) Defeated
    (C) Dry
    (D) Skillful

16. CONCISE:
    (A) Famous
    (B) Inexpensive
    (C) Brief
    (D) Instructional

17. TORRID:
    (A) Hot
    (B) Illegal
    (C) Frustrating
    (D) Fierce

18. TACTFUL:
    (A) Angry
    (B) Reserved
    (C) Polite
    (D) Sharp

19. HEED:
    (A) Attention
    (B) Warning
    (C) Deference
    (D) Detour

20. STEALTHY:
    (A) Clumsy
    (B) Sneaky
    (C) Quick
    (D) Energetic

21. ROBUST:
    (A) Healthy
    (B) Large
    (C) Functional
    (D) Gifted

22. EMULATE:
    (A) Create
    (B) Design
    (C) Cancel
    (D) Copy

23. BOISTEROUS:
    (A) Rude
    (B) Noisy
    (C) Single
    (D) Gullible

24. RANCOR:
    (A) Odor
    (B) Spite
    (C) Disagreement
    (D) Defense

Go on to next page

For Questions 25–40, choose the best word that completes the meaning of the sentence.

25. The movie star left the event with a(n) _____ of friends.
    (A) entourage
    (B) treaty
    (C) conundrum
    (D) dormant

26. John is _____; he always goes along with what everyone wants to do.
    (A) affable
    (B) agitated
    (C) integrated
    (E) customary

27. The tape would not _____ to the paper.
    (A) correlate
    (B) scathe
    (C) invent
    (D) adhere

28. The storm _____ the crops in the entire region.
    (A) reattributed
    (B) devastated
    (C) usurped
    (D) propelled

29. Even though the team lost, the fans gave _____ applause.
    (A) reticent
    (B) fastidious
    (C) fervent
    (D) annoying

30. The meaning was _____; the report was difficult to understand.
    (A) bestial
    (B) loquacious
    (C) spatial
    (D) elusive

31. The student was very _____; he would not stop until he answered every question on the test.
    (A) tenacious
    (B) sincere
    (C) slow
    (D) obtuse

32. Her _____ behavior made her difficult to talk to because she would rarely speak.
    (A) dismal
    (B) bombastic
    (C) taciturn
    (D) tenacious

33. Although the joke was meant in _____, he still took offense.
    (A) predominance
    (B) jest
    (C) punctuality
    (D) paradox

34. Although the first movie was not great, the _____ was much better.
    (A) sequel
    (B) chapter
    (C) prologue
    (D) epilogue

35. Because she was so _____, she did not reply to the insult.
    (A) ensconced
    (B) meek
    (C) fastidious
    (D) angular

36. The apartment did not have much space, but Jim knew it would _____.
    (A) entice
    (B) squander
    (C) disclose
    (D) suffice

Go on to next page

37. After forgetting his lunch and not eating all day, the man was _____ when he got home.

    (A) spiteful

    (B) immobile

    (C) ravenous

    (D) jocund

38. Even though the trip was supposed to be fun, her _____ behavior told everyone she was not having a good time.

    (A) immaculate

    (B) nonchalant

    (C) ominous

    (D) lenient

39. The two parties had a major _____ over the details of the contract.

    (A) dispute

    (B) harangue

    (C) fluctuation

    (D) rhetoric

40. The vacation had very few problems because Sally _____ planned every detail.

    (A) ravenously

    (B) symbiotically

    (C) immaculately

    (D) meticulously

STOP DO NOT TURN THE PAGE UNTIL TOLD TO DO SO.
DO NOT RETURN TO A PREVIOUS TEST.

Section 2

Quantitative Reasoning

Time: 35 Minutes

Directions: You have 35 minutes to complete 37 questions. Work each problem in your head or in the blank space on the page. Then, look at the answer options and decide which one is best. Mark your answer to each question in the corresponding answer bubble on the answer sheet for Section 2.

1. The graph shows the total snowfall for five months in City Z. According to the graph, what is the mean monthly snowfall?

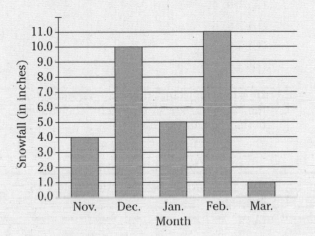

   (A) 5.7 in

   (B) 6.2 in

   (C) 6.8 in

   (D) 11 in

2. A set of nine numbers has a mean of 11. What additional number must be included in this set to create a new set with a mean that is two less than the mean of the original set?

   (A) –7

   (B) –9

   (C) –14

   (D) –18

3. Jenna has 12 coins, all of which are pennies and nickels. If her pennies were nickels and her nickels were pennies, her coins would total 8 cents more. How many pennies does Jenna have?

   (A) 5

   (B) 6

   (C) 7

   (D) 9

4. A cook at a restaurant had nine same-sized cups filled with milk. For the first recipe, he used $\frac{1}{5}$ of each cup of milk. For the next recipe, he used $\frac{1}{6}$ of each cup of milk. Approximately how many cups of milk did he have left?

   (A) 3 cups

   (B) 3.5 cups

   (C) 5.5 cups

   (D) 6.5 cups

Go on to next page

5. The area of the entire rectangle shown is 450 square centimeters. What is the area of the shaded region?

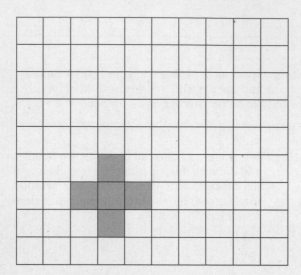

   (A) 4 sq cm

   (B) 25 sq cm

   (C) 40 sq cm

   (D) 45 sq cm

6. Which number is closest to the square root of 170?

   (A) 12

   (B) 13

   (C) 14

   (D) 15

7. The figures show two cubes whose volumes (V) are proportional. What is the ratio of the side length of the cube in Figure 1 to the side length of the cube in Figure 2?

   Figure 1   Figure 2

           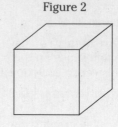

   $V = 64$ in^3 $V = 343$ in^3

   (A) 1 to 4

   (B) 2 to 5

   (C) 1 to 2

   (D) 4 to 7

8. On a certain island, there is no money, but the natives trade with objects. The values of the objects are as shown:

   1 flower = 3 apples

   4 bananas = 2 flowers

   How many apples would it take to buy 16 bananas?

   (A) 8

   (B) 16

   (C) 21

   (D) 24

Go on to next page

9. The graph shows the relationship between the number of items ordered and the total cost of the order. Using the line of best fit, what is the average cost of a single item when 700 items are ordered?

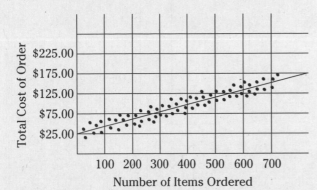

(A) $0.11

(B) $0.21

(C) $149

(D) $150

10. If $15x + 9 = 54$, what does $30x + 18$ equal?

(A) 3

(B) 5

(C) 54

(D) 108

11. Mark's longest long jump at a track competition after the first heat was 8 feet. After the second heat, his longest long jump had gone up by 125%. What was Mark's longest long jump after the second heat?

(A) 10 ft

(B) 12 ft

(C) 18 ft

(D) 20 ft

12. George has a six-sided die marked 1 through 6. He rolls it once, notices what number it shows, then rolls it again. What is the probability that both rolls are 5?

(A) $\frac{1}{5}$

(B) $\frac{1}{12}$

(C) $\frac{1}{25}$

(D) $\frac{1}{36}$

Go on to next page

13. The pattern shown can be folded into a polyhedron. Which polyhedron would result from correctly folding the pattern?

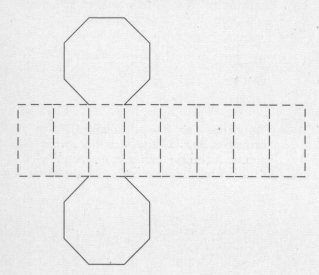

(C)

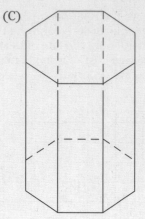

(D)

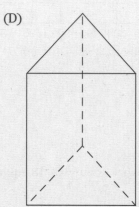

(A)

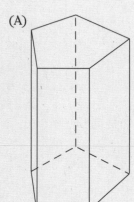

(B)

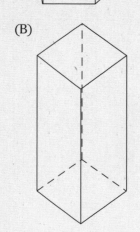

14. In a certain game, points are awarded according to the pattern shown in the table. A player scored 1,024 points. How many shots in a row did he make?

Number of Shots Made in a Row	Points
2	4
3	16
4	64
5	256

(A) 5

(B) 6

(C) 7

(D) 8

Go on to next page

15. The large cube shown was built using smaller cubes. How many small cubes were used to build the large cube?

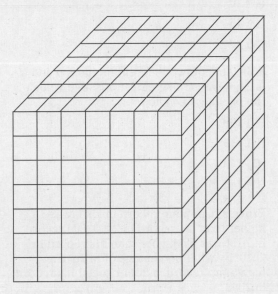

   (A) 49

   (B) 216

   (C) 300

   (D) 343

16. In a certain country, watches always cost $20.00, and there is an 8% sales tax added to any purchase, along with a standard fee that is the same for each purchase. The table gives the total cost, including the fee, for four different orders. What is the amount of the standard fee?

Number of Watches	Total Cost of Each Order
1	$26.00
2	$47.60
3	$69.20
4	$90.80

   (A) $4.00

   (B) $4.20

   (C) $4.40

   (D) $5.40

17. For which function does the y value decrease at the greatest rate as the x value increases?

(A)

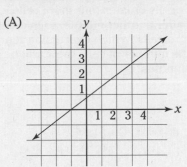

(B)

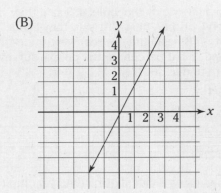

(C)

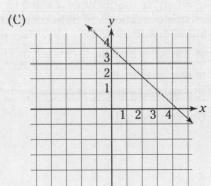

(D)

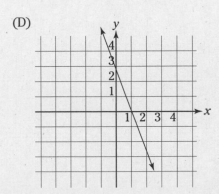

Go on to next page

18. After one minute of being placed in a nutrient solution, a certain cell creates four other cells. After another minute, each of the four cells creates four more cells, which, after another minute, each create four more cells. Which expression represents the number of cells there will be after seven minutes?

    (A) $1 + 4^6$

    (B) $1 + 4^7$

    (C) $4^1 + 4^2 + 4^3 + 4^4 + 4^5 + 4^6 + 4^7$

    (D) $1 + 4 + 4^2 + 4^3 + 4^4 + 4^5 + 4^6 + 4^7$

19. In a survey of 800 people, 439 said they liked Option A best, 201 said they liked Option B best, and the rest were undecided. What percent of the people surveyed were undecided?

    (A) 16%

    (B) 20%

    (C) 25%

    (D) 28%

20. When using a calculator, Jeremy multiplied by 0.9 when he should have divided by 0.9. Which one operation will both correct the error and divide by 0.9?

    (A) Multiplying by 0.81

    (B) Multiplying by 0.9

    (C) Dividing by 0.9

    (D) Dividing by 0.81

21. If $x + 7$ is 7 more than y, then $x + 17$ is how much more than y?

    (A) 7

    (B) 10

    (C) 15

    (D) 17

22. If the sum of two different integers a and b is 24, what is the greatest possible value of the product of a and b?

    (A) 108

    (B) 119

    (C) 143

    (D) 144

23. Bruce's high-jump record in 2010 was 10% higher than his record in 2009. His record in 2011 was 5% higher than his record in 2010. By what percentage did Bruce's high-jump record in 2011 exceed his record in 2009?

    (A) 15%

    (B) 15.5%

    (C) 50%

    (D) 55%

Go on to next page

Directions: Using the information given in Questions 24–37, compare the quantity in Column A to the quantity in Column B. All the following questions have these answer choices:

(A) The quantity in Column A is greater.

(B) The quantity in Column B is greater.

(C) The two quantities are equal.

(D) The relationship cannot be determined from the information given.

24. $y = 9x - 2$

Column A	**Column B**
The value of x when y is 7	The value of y when x is 1

25. Craig received $1.98 in quarters, dimes, and pennies only.

Column A	**Column B**
The smallest number of coins that Craig could have received	12

26.
Column A	**Column B**
$\sqrt{100 + 44}$	$\sqrt{100} + \sqrt{44}$

27.
Column A	**Column B**
-8^8	$(-8)^8$

28. The original price of a car was $10,000.00.

Column A	**Column B**
The amount saved after a 40% discount	The amount saved after two separate discounts of 20% and 20%

29. Aaron can go to school by bicycle for 5 miles at an average speed of 10 miles per hour, or he can take the bus, which takes a longer route, for 10 miles at an average speed of 15 miles per hour.

Column A	**Column B**
Average time the trip takes by bicycle	Average time the trip takes by bus

30.
Column A	**Column B**
The slope of $6x - 4y = 15$	The slope between $(2, 3)$ and $(4, 6)$

31. In a poll before a school election, 40% of the girls at a school and 60% of the boys said that they would vote for Candidate A in the election. The poll showed 80 *yes* votes from the girls surveyed and 120 *yes* votes from the boys surveyed.

Column A	**Column B**
The number of girls in the school	The number of boys in the school

32.

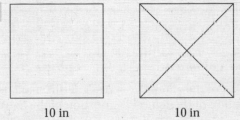

10 in   10 in

Column A	**Column B**
The perimeter of the square	The combined length of the square's diagonals

Go on to next page

33. The distance from point *A* to point *B* is 12 centimeters. The distance from point *B* to point *C* is 15 centimeters. The distance from point *C* to point *D* is 18 centimeters.

Column A	*Column B*
The distance from point *A* to point *C*	The distance from point *B* to point *D*

34.

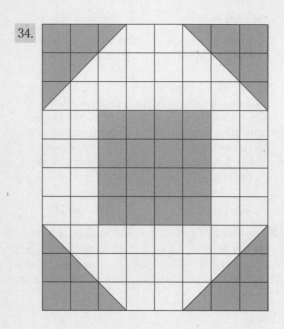

Column A	*Column B*
Area of the shaded portion of the figure	Area of the unshaded portion of the figure

35. A wall clock has a battery that is running out.

Column A	*Column B*
The probability that the hour hand will stop between 12 and 3	The probability that the hour hand will stop between 9 and 12

36. Eleven pieces of paper labeled 1 through 11 are put into a hat.

Column A	*Column B*
Probability of choosing an even number	Probability of choosing an odd number

37. *A* and *B* are points on line *ℓ*. *S* (not shown) is a point on line *ℓ* to the right of *B*.

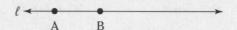

Column A	*Column B*
The distance between *A* and *B*	The distance between *B* and *S*

STOP   DO NOT TURN THE PAGE UNTIL TOLD TO DO SO.
DO NOT RETURN TO A PREVIOUS TEST.

Section 3
Reading Comprehension

Time: 35 Minutes

Directions: You have 35 minutes to read each passage and answer the questions that follow. Mark your answer to each question in the corresponding answer bubble on the answer sheet for Section 3.

Wisdom teeth may not make you feel wise, but they can certainly cause you pain and a lot of aggravation. Wisdom teeth, technically known as *third molars,* are the last teeth to appear and typically make their way through the gums in the late teen years or early twenties. They usually appear on both the top and bottom of the mouth, although some people have one or more that never makes its way to the surface. Because the other 28 teeth are already in place, often wisdom teeth do not have much room to break through the gums and fit as the final set of teeth in an already full mouth. The end result for many people is their wisdom teeth are impacted, meaning they cannot come in all the way or at the correct angle.

Because of the spacing issue, wisdom teeth may be impacted in several ways. First, these third molars may have a *mesial impaction,* meaning they grow in at an angle toward the front of the mouth. *Vertical impaction* means the tooth comes in straight but gets stuck against the tooth next to it. *Horizontal impaction* means the tooth grows horizontally instead of vertically, pushing against the tooth in front of it. Finally, *distal impaction* is where the wisdom tooth grows away from the tooth in front of it and gets stuck in that position. As you can imagine, any of these impacted positions often results in pain, swelling gums, and even damage to the teeth in front of the third molars. For this reason, many people choose to have their wisdom teeth removed by an <u>oral surgeon</u>. Although recovery can be a bit <u>trying</u> and painful, most patients feel much better after a few days and are happy to have the troubling teeth removed. In the end, the wisdom of wisdom teeth is often to have them removed as soon as possible.

1. What can you infer about an oral surgeon?

    (A) A doctor who treats infections

    (B) A doctor who treats areas outside of the body

    (C) A doctor who specializes in problems with the mouth

    (D) A doctor who specializes in anesthesia

2. Of the types of impactions discussed in the article, which is the most painful?

    (A) Horizontal.

    (B) Vertical.

    (C) Mesial.

    (D) The passage does not say.

3. According to the passage, all the following are true, *except*

    (A) Wisdom teeth appear only on the bottom.

    (B) Wisdom teeth often do not have enough room to come in correctly.

    (C) Wisdom teeth are third molars.

    (D) Wisdom teeth often appear in the late teen years.

4. Concerning removal of wisdom teeth, you can infer that

    (A) They should always be removed.

    (B) They are necessary teeth.

    (C) They need to be removed in some people.

    (D) They typically do not need to be removed.

5. What does the author most likely mean by the word *trying?*

   (A) Emotional

   (B) Interested

   (C) Frustrating

   (D) Hard work

6. Which would be a good title for this passage?

   (A) Understanding Wisdom Teeth

   (B) Types of Impactions

   (C) Oral Surgeon to the Rescue

   (D) A Surprise at 20

A calorie is a measurement of energy that is stored in food, and this measurement helps people know how much food they are eating or not eating in terms of the energy that food provides. Technically, a calorie is a measurement of energy required to raise the temperature of one gram of water one degree centigrade. As you can imagine, different types of food have more calories than others. For example, one cup of chocolate cake has many more calories than one cup of celery. Also, because a calorie is a unit of measurement, there are not different types of calories, as some diet books claim. In other words, a fat calorie has the same amount of energy as a protein calorie because the calorie itself simply measures the amount of energy.

Of course, eating fatty foods is not the same in terms of nutrition as eating protein-dense foods, but the distinction should be made concerning the nutrition of the food and not the calories in and of themselves. Depending on your age, height, and weight, you have a recommended daily caloric intake, which is simply a measurement of how much energy your body needs to function properly. If you eat too many calories (too much energy), your body can store the excess as fat. If you eat too few calories (too little energy), your body must burn fat stores in order to make up the difference in its energy requirement. This simple measurement fact is the basis for all diets. In the end, a healthy diet consists of enough calories for your body to burn with the right nutrition to fuel your body's many systems and functions.

7. According to the passage, which of the following statements is true?

   (A) A fat calorie is less dense.

   (B) A calorie is not food.

   (C) A protein calorie is less dense.

   (D) Calories create fat.

8. Why does the author state that a fat calorie is the same as a protein calorie?

   (A) Because both are stored as fat by the body

   (B) Because they both weigh the same

   (C) Because a calorie is only a unit of measurement

   (D) Because fat has the same nutritional content as protein

9. What is a *recommended daily caloric intake?*

   (A) The amount of energy needed to maintain basic body functions

   (B) The calories you burn per day

   (C) The amount of calories your body needs per day

   (D) The amount of calories you need to gain weight

10. According to the passage, which of the following causes weight loss?

    (A) Eating more fat calories

    (B) Consuming fewer calories than your body needs

    (C) Eating more protein calories

    (D) Eating calorie dense foods in small portions

Go on to next page

11. How are the number of calories a person should consume each day calculated?

   (A) Age, weight, height

   (B) Weight, height

   (C) Age, weight

   (D) The passage does not say.

12. When the author states that a fat calorie is the same as a protein calorie in terms of energy, but not the same otherwise, what does he mean?

   (A) They are different kinds of fats.

   (B) They are different kinds of proteins.

   (C) They are different kinds of calories.

   (D) They are not the same nutritionally.

Teachers often state that English is a very difficult language to learn for students who grew up speaking another language. One reason for the difficulty concerns language rules. Like all languages, English functions through the use of letters, words, sentences, and ultimately groups of sentences that complete a thought. The problem is that the English language often does not <u>adhere to its own standards</u>.

Consider the simple idea of plural words. A word that is plural refers to two or more. In most cases, you simply add an *s* to the end of the word to make the word plural. For example, the word *dog* is singular and refers to one dog, while the word *dogs* refers to two or more dogs. That's easy enough, yet this little rule often isn't true. For example, to form the plural of some words, you must add an *es* on the end. Other words have more unusual plural forms. The word *child* means one child, but to form the plural, you must add a *ren* (children) to the end of the word. To make matters worse, plural forms of pronouns often do not follow a particular pattern. For example, singular pronouns such as *I, me, he, she,* and *it* have different plural forms, such as *we, us, they,* and *them*. The pronoun *you* can be both singular and plural, depending on how it is used. As you can see, these differences can be <u>dizzying</u> to the student who is learning English as a second language.

13. What is the primary purpose of this passage?

   (A) To discuss different language complexities

   (B) To explain a reason why English is hard to learn for non-English speakers

   (C) To explain plural forms

   (E) To explain problems in English teaching

14. How can you simplify the phrase *adhere to its own standards?*

   (A) Explain how it works

   (B) Consider its forms

   (C) Follow its rules

   (D) Challenge rule authority

15. How does the author explain why various plural forms exist?

   (A) English has been made more complicated than necessary.

   (B) Certain words cannot be changed for plural forms.

   (C) Certain words need certain plural letters.

   (D) The author does not explain it.

16. What does the author most likely mean by the word *dizzying?*

   (A) Very sickening

   (B) Very confusing

   (C) Very untruthful

   (D) Very benign

Go on to next page

17. The tone of this passage is

    (A) Argumentative

    (B) Explanatory

    (C) Cheerful

    (D) Indecisive

18. Why does the author mention the issue of *you* being both singular and plural?

    (A) To provide a complete view of plural pronoun usage

    (B) To confuse the reader's understanding

    (C) To provide another example of singular and plural form confusion

    (D) To begin a new conversation

In any computer application where text is used, you can generally choose from a variety of fonts for that text. A font is a group of characters (such as letters) and other symbols that contain certain style features, making up a family. When you choose a particular font, you know that all the text, numbers, and symbols you type will conform to the same style. This style or design is called a *typeface.*

Fonts can be used to stylize a document or any creation that uses text, numbers, or symbols, but they also ensure a consistent style and readability. The size of a font is either a pitch size or point size, depending on whether the font is considered a fixed space font or proportional font. A *fixed space font* means that each character has the same width. In a fixed space font, the letter *c* takes up as much width as the letter *h* and so on. In a fixed space font family, the *pitch* specifies the number of characters that print within one inch of horizontal type. For example, a 10 point fixed space font prints 10 characters per inch while a 12 point fixed space font prints 12 characters per inch and so on. In *proportional fonts,* every character has a different width, depending on the shape of the character. In this case, *point size* refers to the height of the character rather than the width.

Fonts may also be characterized as serif fonts or sans serif fonts. *Serif fonts* have little decorative attachments added to areas of certain letters. For example, *E* shown here is a serif font — notice the little curves at the bottom line, middle line, and top line? A *sans serif font* does not have these decorative additions added to letters. *Verdana* is a popular sans serif font. Both serif and sans serif fonts are effective in terms of readability, so the choice often comes down to style for a particular document.

19. Which statement best defines the concept of font?

    (A) A set of styles used for letters, numbers, and symbols

    (B) Serif features applied to letters, numbers, and symbols

    (C) Sans serif features applied to letters, numbers, and symbols

    (D) A group of letters, symbols, and numbers

20. What is the main purpose of this passage?

    (A) To discuss san serif fonts

    (B) To define the concept of typeface

    (C) To explain the concept of fonts

    (D) To discuss computer applications

21. According to the passage, why are fonts important to a document?

    (A) Width spacing

    (B) Style and readability

    (C) Height spacing

    (D) Serif readability

22. This passage can best be described as

    (A) Factual

    (B) Persuasive

    (C) Emotional

    (D) Distant

Go on to next page

23. In an 8 point fixed space font, how many characters print per horizontal inch?

    (A) 4

    (B) 6

    (C) 8

    (D) 10

24. Which statement is true concerning a proportional font?

    (A) Every character is the same width.

    (B) Every character is the same height.

    (C) Characters have different widths.

    (D) Characters are all sans serif.

25. What signifies a serif font?

    (A) Font height

    (B) Lack of decorative additions to characters

    (C) Font width

    (D) Decorative additions to characters

26. Why does the author mention the concept of typeface?

    (A) To explain font types

    (B) To help the reader understand the concept of a font family

    (C) To make fonts seem less important

    (D) To explain the reason multiple fonts are necessary for a document

Chronemics is the study of how people communicate through the use of time. Chronemics, sometimes called *chronemic communication,* is a form of nonverbal communication. *Nonverbal communication* refers to communication other than spoken language, and it includes behaviors such as eye contact, gestures, posture, the pitch and speed of your voice, how you dress, and many others. Chronemics belongs to the nonverbal communication family because this area of study explores people's use of time, approach to time management, and related behaviors both in individuals as well as different cultures.

Researchers who study chronemics often focus on different kinds of nonverbal time behaviors in different geographic locations, cultures, and even countries. Researchers have noted that these groups approach time and react to it in different ways. Researchers often explore issues, such as punctuality, rate of speaking, and even willingness to listen. Also, researchers consider *time anxiety* across different cultures. For example, some cultures are very time specific while others are not. In a time-specific culture, a meeting at 8 a.m. means the meeting will occur precisely at that time. In other cultures, an 8 a.m. meeting simply means the meeting will occur at some time in the morning. Cultures that are very time specific may also experience more anxiety about late meetings or events, delays, or having to wait for other people.

Chronemics researchers generally classify cultures in two different ways: monochromic and polychromic. In a monochromic culture, time is broken into units of tasks that are managed one at a time, and events that operate outside of the limits are considered late. In this approach, the day is very scheduled. An example of this approach is most U.S. schools. In a typical school day, a number of different subjects are each given a particular time slot, and each day, a teacher for the subject teaches in that time slot so the period always begins and ends at the same time.

Yet some cultures are considered polychromic. In a polychromic culture, multiple activities may happen at the same time and those activities may not be given equal <u>weight</u>. For example, in a polychromic school, a set schedule may not be followed every day. If the math teacher feels like students need more time to complete an assignment, math class could last twice as long that day and other classes may not meet at all. In other words, in a polychromic culture, time is seen as more fluid rather than something to be managed by the hours in a day.

Go on to next page

27. According to the passage, all the following are true *except*

    (A) Nonverbal communication includes many different behaviors.

    (B) Different cultures use chronemics in different ways.

    (C) Monochromic cultures often accomplish more than polychromic cultures.

    (D) Chronemics applies to both individuals as well as different cultures.

28. The main point of the passage is that

    (A) The way humans communicate nonverbally is very complex.

    (B) Chronemics is often misunderstood across different cultures.

    (C) The way people communicate with time management varies from person to person as well as culture to culture.

    (D) Chronemics is a nonverbal communication behavior that is less known than other communication behaviors.

29. According to the passage, why would some cultures have less time anxiety?

    (A) Because some cultures perform multiple tasks at the same time

    (B) Because people in some cultures do not care about time management

    (C) Because time allotments in many cultures are not as specific

    (D) Because some people do not live in a polychromic manner

30. What does the author most likely mean by the word *weight* in this passage?

    (A) Specific

    (B) Time allotment

    (C) Importance

    (D) Heaviness

31. Concerning the passage, which of the following statements is true?

    (A) The author is biased toward monochromic cultures.

    (B) The author is biased toward polychromic cultures.

    (C) The author does not write with a bias.

    (D) The author believes both monochromic and polychromic cultures are flawed.

The following passage is an excerpt from Franklin D. Roosevelt's Inaugural Address.

Happiness lies not in the mere possession of money; it lies in the joy of achievement, in the thrill of creative effort. The joy and moral stimulation of work no longer must be forgotten in the mad chase of evanescent profits. These dark days will be worth all they cost us if they teach us that our true destiny is not to be ministered unto but to minister to ourselves and to our fellow men.

Recognition of the falsity of material wealth as the standard of success goes hand in hand with the abandonment of the false belief that public office and high political position are to be valued only by the standards of pride of place and personal profit; and there must be an end to a conduct in banking and in business which too often has given to a sacred trust the likeness of callous and selfish wrongdoing. Small wonder that confidence languishes, for it thrives only on honesty, on honor, on the sacredness of obligations, on faithful protection, on unselfish performance; without them it cannot live.

Restoration calls, however, not for changes in ethics alone. This Nation asks for action, and action now.

Go on to next page

Our greatest primary task is to put people to work. This is no unsolvable problem if we face it wisely and courageously. It can be accomplished in part by direct recruiting by the Government itself, treating the task as we would treat the emergency of a war, but at the same time, through this employment, accomplishing greatly needed projects to stimulate and reorganize the use of our natural resources.

Hand in hand with this we must frankly recognize the overbalance of population in our industrial centers and, by engaging on a national scale in a redistribution, endeavor to provide a better use of the land for those best fitted for the land. The task can be helped by definite efforts to raise the values of agricultural products and with this the power to purchase the output of our cities. It can be helped by preventing realistically the tragedy of the growing loss through foreclosure of our small homes and our farms. It can be helped by insistence that the Federal, State, and local governments act forthwith on the demand that their cost be drastically reduced. It can be helped by the unifying of relief activities which today are often scattered, uneconomical, and unequal. It can be helped by national planning for and supervision of all forms of transportation and of communications and other utilities which have a definitely public character. There are many ways in which it can be helped, but it can never be helped merely by talking about it. We must act and act quickly.

32. This passage can be described as

(A) A summary of problems

(B) A discussion of success

(C) A call to action

(D) An attempt to challenge

33. What does the author most likely mean by *evanescent?*

(A) Dependable

(B) Vanishing

(C) Calculated

(D) Suddenly

34. According to the passage, what is the most important task the government faces?

(A) Working together

(B) Policies

(C) War

(D) Employment

35. The passage states, "Confidence . . . thrives on honesty." What does the author most likely mean by this statement?

(A) Everyone should be honest with the government.

(B) Confidence is always needed.

(C) Confidence has to be based on reality.

(D) People like people who are honest.

36. Considering the final paragraph, what seems to be a major focus Roosevelt has?

(A) Saving small farms and other agricultural businesses

(B) Helping unemployed city dwellers find work in factories

(C) Expanding the federal government

(D) Increasing taxes to support programs

STOP DO NOT TURN THE PAGE UNTIL TOLD TO DO SO.
DO NOT RETURN TO A PREVIOUS TEST.

Section 4

Mathematics Achievement

Time: 40 Minutes

Directions: You have 40 minutes to answer the following 47 mathematics achievement questions. Mark your answer to each question in the corresponding answer bubble on the answer sheet for Section 4.

1. What is the sum of 82,398 + 23,987?

    (A) 106,385

    (B) 107,385

    (C) 108,385

    (D) 110,385

2. Which expression has the greatest value?

    (A) $(4 \times 5) + 6 - 7$

    (B) $4 \times (5 + 6) - 7$

    (C) $4 \times 5 + (6 - 7)$

    (D) $4 \times (5 + 6 - 7)$

3. The circle shown is divided into equal parts. What part of the circle is shaded?

    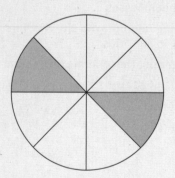

    (A) $\frac{1}{8}$

    (B) $\frac{1}{6}$

    (C) $\frac{1}{4}$

    (D) $\frac{1}{3}$

4. Which number has no positive factors except itself and 1?

    (A) 25

    (B) 33

    (C) 39

    (D) 41

5. In a certain country, fruit is used for money. If 5 cherries are worth 3 peaches and 1 peach is worth 15 bananas, how many bananas is 1 cherry worth?

    (A) 6

    (B) 7

    (C) 8

    (D) 9

6. Gina scored an average of 20 points in her first five basketball games. If her lowest score was 12 points and the range of her scores was 22, what was her highest score?

    (A) 26

    (B) 29

    (C) 34

    (D) 36

Go on to next page

7. A student checked the hourly temperature outside his house during a snowstorm and displayed the results on the graph shown. What was the difference between the highest and lowest temperatures recorded?

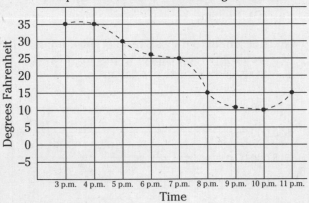

Temperature at Each Hour During a Snowstorm

(A) 20°

(B) 25°

(C) 30°

(D) 35°

8. If $P = 2 \times (L + W)$, what is P when L is 19 inches and W is 7 inches?

(A) 26 in

(B) 42 in

(C) 52 in

(D) 56 in

9. What is the closest estimate of the answer for the expression $(48 \times 62) \div 600$?

(A) 4

(B) 5

(C) 40

(D) 50

10. A student made a table to keep track of the price of a can of soda at the grocery store for four weeks. How much did the price of a can of soda increase each week?

Price of a Can of Soda	
Week	*Price*
1	$0.62
2	$0.74
3	$0.86
4	$0.98

(A) $0.02

(B) $0.08

(C) $0.12

(D) $0.24

11. Which is equivalent to the expression $\dfrac{80(27+23)}{4}$?

(A) 1,000

(B) 1,500

(C) 2,000

(D) 2,500

12. Last year, the price of a gallon of gasoline was 1.5 times what it is today. By what percent did the price decrease from last year to this year?

(A) 25%

(B) 33%

(C) 50%

(D) 100%

Go on to next page

13. In this figure, a square is inscribed inside a circle. What is the area of the shaded region? (area of a circle = πr^2)

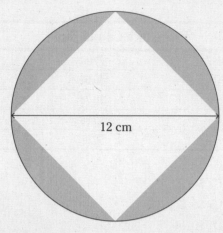

12 cm

   (A) $36\pi - 72$
   (B) $36\pi - 36$
   (C) $72\pi - 72$
   (D) $72\pi - 36$

14. A box has eight more apples than oranges. If 12 apples are in the box, what fraction of the fruit in the box is oranges?

   (A) $\frac{1}{8}$
   (B) $\frac{1}{6}$
   (C) $\frac{1}{4}$
   (D) $\frac{1}{3}$

15. The number of liters of oxygen, l, used by an exercising adult depends on the number of minutes, m, the adult spends exercising, according to the formula $l = 10m + 8$. What is the meaning of 10 in this formula?

   (A) For every 10 minutes that are spent exercising, 8 liters are used.
   (B) For every 8 minutes that are spent exercising, 10 liters are used.
   (C) For every 1 minute that is spent exercising, 10 liters are used.
   (D) When 0 minutes are spent exercising, 80 liters are used.

16. On a map, 3 inches equals 1,000 miles. If two cities are 10.5 inches apart on the map, what is their actual distance apart?

   (A) 1,500 mi
   (B) 1,750 mi
   (C) 3,000 mi
   (D) 3,500 mi

17. According to the scatter plot, how much would a person expect to pay for a car that averaged 40 miles per gallon?

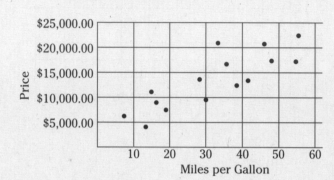

   (A) $5,000.00
   (B) $10,000.00
   (C) $15,000.00
   (D) $25,000.00

18. A bag contains 20 blue chips, 40 white chips, and 10 red chips. What is the probability of selecting either a white or red chip?

   (A) $\frac{2}{7}$
   (B) $\frac{3}{7}$
   (C) $\frac{4}{7}$
   (D) $\frac{5}{7}$

19. What is the value of n in the equation $1\frac{1}{7} \div 1\frac{3}{8} = n$?

   (A) $\frac{8}{11}$
   (B) $\frac{64}{77}$
   (C) $1\frac{4}{7}$
   (D) $1\frac{64}{77}$

Go on to next page

20. Triangle *RST* is similar to triangle *XYZ*. What is the ratio of the length of a side of triangle *RST* to the corresponding side of triangle *XYZ*?

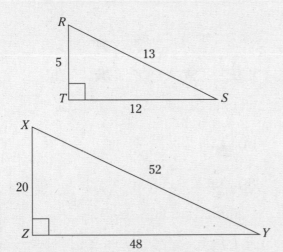

(A) 1 to 3

(B) 1 to 4

(C) 3 to 1

(D) 4 to 1

21. In the equation $\frac{N}{90} = \frac{6}{18}$, what is the value of *N*?

(A) 3

(B) 13

(C) 30

(D) 300

22. What is the slope of the line $6x - 8y = -16$?

(A) $-\frac{3}{4}$

(B) $-\frac{4}{3}$

(C) $\frac{3}{4}$

(D) $\frac{4}{3}$

23. A certain box has three red balls, four green balls, and five purple balls. One ball of each color is marked with a gold star. If a person randomly picks a ball of each color without looking, what is the probability that she will pick the ball with the gold star for each color?

(A) $\frac{1}{60}$

(B) $\frac{1}{20}$

(C) $\frac{1}{12}$

(D) $\frac{3}{5}$

24. Stina conducted a survey in her grade to find out the number of people who played baseball, basketball, or football. She displayed the results in the circle graph shown. Which data correspond to the sample of people surveyed?

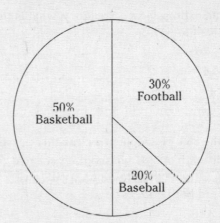

(A) 10 basketball players, 8 football players, 6 baseball players

(B) 20 basketball players, 12 football players, 8 baseball players

(C) 30 basketball players, 16 football players, 12 baseball players

(D) 40 basketball players, 24 football players, 12 baseball players

Go on to next page

25. The expression $\dfrac{x}{y}\left(\dfrac{y}{x} - \dfrac{x}{z}\right)$ is equivalent to which expression?

    (A) $1 - \dfrac{x}{yz}$

    (B) $1 - \dfrac{x^2}{yz}$

    (C) $\dfrac{x}{y}\left(\dfrac{yz - 2x}{xz}\right)$

    (D) $\dfrac{x}{y}\left(\dfrac{yz - x}{z}\right)$

26. If the temperature outside is −15 degrees Fahrenheit, how many degrees must the temperature increase to reach 30 degrees Fahrenheit?

    (A) 15

    (B) 30

    (C) 45

    (D) 60

27. In the expression $x - 8 + 12 = y$, what is the value of $(x - y)$?

    (A) −20

    (B) −4

    (C) 4

    (D) 20

28. Of the 85% of people in a class that passed their math quiz, $\dfrac{4}{5}$ passed their science quiz as well. What fraction of the class passed both quizzes?

    (A) $\dfrac{3}{5}$

    (B) $\dfrac{17}{25}$

    (C) $\dfrac{3}{4}$

    (D) $\dfrac{5}{6}$

29. The figure shows the first five elements of a pattern. What is the sixth element of this pattern?

Go on to next page

30. The graph shows the changes in altitude (height) of four different airplanes. Which airplane had the greatest increase in altitude per minute?

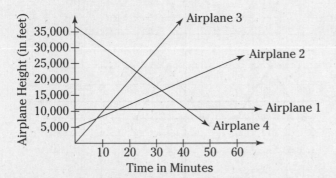

(A) Airplane 1

(B) Airplane 2

(C) Airplane 3

(D) Airplane 4

31. If $\frac{7}{8}$ of a bucket can be filled in one minute, about how many minutes will it take to fill the rest of the bucket at the same rate?

(A) 0.08

(B) 0.125

(C) 0.14

(D) 1.125

32. A coin has two sides: heads and tails. Jake has three coins. If he drops all three coins onto a table, what is the probability that all three coins land on heads?

(A) $\frac{1}{12}$

(B) $\frac{1}{8}$

(C) $\frac{1}{3}$

(D) $\frac{1}{2}$

33. What type of quadrilateral is *ABCD?*

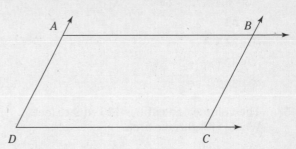

(A) Rhombus

(B) Square

(C) Parallelogram

(D) Rectangle

34. Which of the following is equivalent to $x = \frac{2y}{3} + 3$?

(A) $3x = 2y + 9$

(B) $3x = 2y - 9$

(C) $2y = 3x + 9$

(D) $y = x - 3$

35. An isosceles triangle (a triangle with two equal sides) is being plotted on the coordinate system shown. If two of the triangle's vertices are points *A* and *B*, which of the following could be the coordinates of the third vertex?

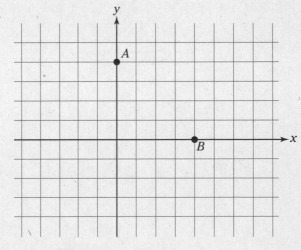

(A) (–4, 0)

(B) (–3, 0)

(C) (0, –3)

(D) (8, 3)

Go on to next page

36. What is the value of the expression 4.29 + 5.3 + 6.4 + 7.5 + 8.61?

    (A) 32

    (B) 32.1

    (C) 32.11

    (D) 32.2

37. The volume of a cube is 125 square feet. What is its surface area?

    (A) 25 sq ft

    (B) 100 sq ft

    (C) 125 sq ft

    (D) 150 sq ft

38. Which of the following expressions is the equivalent to $\dfrac{4\left(\sqrt{100}+10x\right)}{\sqrt{36}}$?

    (A) $\dfrac{20+5x}{3}$

    (B) $\dfrac{20+20x}{3}$

    (C) $\dfrac{40+40x}{36}$

    (D) $\dfrac{40+40x}{9}$

39. The triangles shown are similar. What is the value of x?

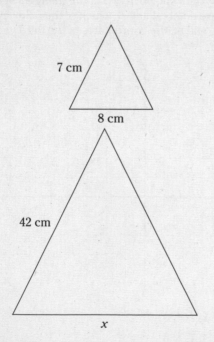

    (A) 42 cm

    (B) 48 cm

    (C) 52 cm

    (D) 56 cm

40. Triangle *XYZ* has been transformed. What type of transformation was performed?

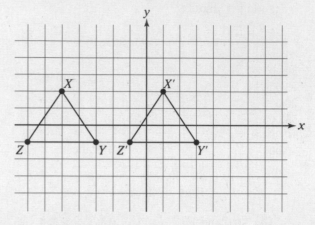

    (A) Reflection

    (B) Rotation

    (C) Slide

    (D) Turn

41. A hot dog vendor is planning to sell hot dogs for 30 days. His profit is his revenue minus his cost. Buying the hot dogs costs between $400.00 and $600.00, and he expects to sell an average of 20 hot dogs per day. If the hot dogs sell for $2.00 each, what is the vendor's approximate expected profit for the 30 days?

    (A) $250.00

    (B) $700.00

    (C) $1,200.00

    (D) $1,400.00

Go on to next page

42. The graph shows line *FG*. What is the equation for the line parallel to *FG*?

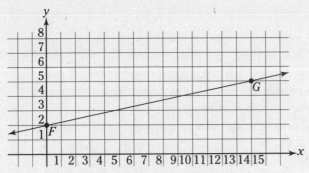

(A) $y = \frac{3}{14}x + 14$

(B) $y = \frac{4}{14}x + 14$

(C) $y = \frac{1}{9}x + 2$

(D) $y = \frac{1}{12}x + 2$

43. A rectangular garden was enlarged by tripling the width and increasing the length by $\frac{1}{2}$. If the area of the original garden was *x* square feet, what is the area, in square feet, of the enlarged garden?

(A) 1.5*x*

(B) 2.5*x*

(C) 3.5*x*

(D) 4.5*x*

44. Karlyn received grades of 80, 84, and 93 on her first three math tests of the year. What will she have to score on the fourth test to have an 89 test average, assuming all the tests count equally toward the average?

(A) 89

(B) 93

(C) 95

(D) 99

45. A 33-foot tall building stands next to a 60-foot tall tree. If the tree casts a shadow that is 80 feet long, how long is the building's shadow, in feet?

(A) 36

(B) 38

(C) 44

(D) 48

46. For all integers *a* and *b*, *a*#*b* is defined as $2a - 2b$. Which of the following has the greatest value?

(A) 4#5

(B) 5#4

(C) 4#–5

(D) –5#4

47. If $x < 0 < y$, which of the following must be true?

(A) $x^2 < y^2$

(B) $x^3 > y^3$

(C) $-x > y$

(D) $y - x > 0$

STOP DO NOT TURN THE PAGE UNTIL TOLD TO DO SO.
DO NOT RETURN TO A PREVIOUS TEST.

Section 5

Essay

Time: 30 Minutes

Directions: You have 30 minutes to complete an essay based on the following topic. Use only two pages for your essay. You may use scratch paper to organize your thoughts before you begin writing your essay.

Topic: If you could travel anywhere in the world, where would you go and why?

Assignment: Write about the place you would visit and include details and information about your trip. Be sure to explain why you want to visit the place you have chosen.

STOP DO NOT TURN THE PAGE UNTIL TOLD TO DO SO.
DO NOT RETURN TO A PREVIOUS TEST.

Chapter 26

Answers to ISEE Middle Level Practice Exam

● ●

*N*ow that you've finished taking the ISEE Middle Level Practice Exam, spend time reading through the answers and explanations we provide in this chapter. Doing so is a great way to find out what you missed and why. Also, reading through *all* the explanations — even for the questions you got right — only increases your learning and understanding and helps you prepare even more for test day. If you just want to do a quick check of your answers, see the abbreviated answer key at the end of this chapter.

Section 1: Verbal Reasoning

1. **D.** *Ominous* means threatening, so Choice (D) is correct. *Ominous* is often used to describe something that appears dangerous, such as a storm cloud.

2. **A.** *Bias* means to show favor toward a person or group and is often used in reference to someone or something showing unfair favor.

3. **C.** *Benign* means harmless. Often, people in the medical field use this word to describe a condition that's harmless, such as a growth or tumor.

4. **A.** *Adorn* means to decorate. It can be used to describe a decorated object, or it can refer to jewelry and other clothing accessories, too.

5. **C.** *Meddle* means to interfere and is often used to describe someone who interferes in someone else's business.

6. **A.** *Obscure* means unclear. This word can describe something that's hard to understand or see. For example, glass that you can't see through, such as a shower door, is called obscured glass.

7. **B.** *Articulate* often describes someone who speaks clearly and is easy to understand. You could say, "The teacher was very articulate," meaning she spoke clearly and used sentences that were clear and easily understood.

8. **C.** *Residue* refers to something left behind, something left over. For example, if you allow a dark liquid to dry on a counter, the stain left behind is considered residue.

9. **B.** *Aloof* means uninterested and is often used in reference to a person's behavior. Typically, this word is used in a negative way, such as, "No one enjoyed her company because she seemed so aloof."

10. **A.** *Inert* means harmless or having little or no activity or power. For example, a harmless gas is often referred to as inert.

11. **B.** *Quench* means to satisfy. If you quench your thirst with water, you're no longer thirsty.

12. **B.** *Pompous* refers to a person who's arrogant in his or her behavior. The correct answer is Choice (B), *arrogant*. For example, "The mayor's pompous behavior angered everyone at the meeting." This sentence means the mayor acted in an arrogant manner.

13. **D.** *Debris* simply means trash or litter. For example, you can say, "After the storm, our yard was full of debris."

14. **C.** *Quaint* means odd or unusual. This word is often used in a positive way. For example, if you said, "We visited a quaint little town," you mean the town was odd or unusual, but in a pleasing way.

15. **D.** *Deft* refers to quick, neat, or skillful. You can say, "The deft sprinter won the race."

16. **C.** *Concise* means brief or to the point. If you said, "The teacher gave a concise answer," then the answer was short without a lot of extra details.

17. **A.** *Torrid* means very hot. For example, "The torrid weather was miserable."

18. **C.** *Tactful* refers to someone who's polite, often referring to situations where a person could be rude. For example, "The waiter tactfully asked the rude man to leave the restaurant." In other words, the waiter handled the situation in a polite manner.

19. **A.** *Heed* means pay close attention to something, such as a warning. For example, "Make sure you heed the road signs," means to pay attention to them.

20. **B.** *Stealthy* means sneaky. For example, "The stealthy soldier captured the village."

21. **A.** *Robust* means full of health and strength. You could say, "The robust athlete dominated the competition."

22. **D.** *Emulate* means to copy something or someone. For example, you can say, "I try to emulate my favorite football player when I play the game."

23. **B.** *Boisterous* means to be noisy, loud, and lacking restraint and discipline. For example, "The boisterous kindergarteners gave the teacher a headache." This sentence means the children were loud and difficult to control.

24. **B.** *Rancor* means spite or malice. For example, "Her response was full of rancor," means she had a spiteful or malicious attitude or answer.

25. **A.** An *entourage* refers to a group of people who often travel together or with one specific person. This is the only word that completes the group concept in the sentence.

26. **A.** *Affable* means agreeable, so within the context of the sentence, this word is the only one that completes the meaning. When you consider the answer choices, be sure to look back at the sentence for a definition for the word you need. In this case, the second part of the sentence basically provides a definition for *affable*. Use the sentence to help you find clues!

27. **D.** *Adhere* means to stick, so Choice (D) is the only word that completes the meaning of the sentence.

28. **B.** *Devastate* means to completely destroy. Within the context of the sentence, this word is the only one that makes sense. This question is a bit more difficult because the sentence really doesn't give you any context clues. However, you know from the sentence that the subject is a storm, so a good working assumption is that the verb will be a negative action on the crops.

29. **C.** *Fervent* means enthusiastic, so in the context of the sentence, the fans applauded with enthusiasm even though their team lost. Use the process of elimination to help eliminate choices you know are wrong. Even if you didn't know the meaning of *fervent*, you could probably eliminate at least two answer choices, giving yourself a 50-50 shot at answering the question correctly.

30. **D.** *Elusive* means hard to understand, so in the context of the sentence, Choice (D) can be the only correct answer. Again, the second half of the sentence basically provides a definition for the word you need, so be sure to let the sentence help you find the right answer.

31. **A.** *Tenacious* means persistent. Considering that the student wouldn't stop until he'd completed the test, *tenacious* is the only answer choice that fits.

32. **C.** *Taciturn* means shy or quiet, so within the context of the sentence, this word is the only one that makes sense. Also, the sentence provides a definition of the word because the sentence tells you that she "would rarely speak."

33. **B.** *Jest* is a playful joke — not something meant to be harmful. This sentence begins with the word *although*, which is a clue that there'll be a contrast in meaning. The second part

of the sentence tells you, "he took offense," so you're looking for a word that has to do with a playful joke. Let context clues like this help you.

34. **A.** *Sequel* is a second part of something, often used to note a second part of a movie.

35. **B.** *Meek* means passive. Considering that the woman in the sentence didn't say anything after being insulted, this word completes the meaning of the sentence.

36. **D.** *Suffice* means to be enough of something. In the context of the sentence, this word is the only one that completes the meaning because even though the apartment was small, it would still be enough.

37. **C.** *Ravenous* means extremely hungry. This word is the only answer choice that completes the meaning of the sentence.

38. **B.** *Nonchalant* means not concerned or interested. This word typically refers to someone who has a cool or easy detachment from something, so the word can be used in a positive or negative way, depending on the meaning of the sentence.

39. **A.** *Dispute* means argument or disagreement, so Choice (A) is the correct answer. You may have considered Choice (B), *harangue*, but this word means a long pompous speech.

40. **D.** *Meticulously* means being extremely careful about details. This word can be used in a positive or negative sense, depending on its use in a sentence.

Section 2: Quantitative Reasoning

1. **B.** To find the mean, add all the values and divide by how many values there are: $(4 + 10 + 5 + 11 + 1) = 31 \div 5 = 6.2$.

2. **B.** If the set of numbers has a mean of 11, assume that all nine numbers are 11. To figure out which additional number would lower the mean by two, set up an average equation with the current nine numbers added to the new number, divided by 10 (because with the new number, there are ten values). The equation should equal 9 (a mean two less than the original): $\frac{11+11+11+11+11+11+11+11+11+x}{10} = 9$, which simplifies to $99 + x = 90$, so $x = -9$.

3. **C.** Test the answer choices. Looking at Choice (C), Jenna currently has seven pennies and five nickels for a total of 32 cents. If the coin types switched, she'd have five pennies and seven nickels for a total of 40 cents.

4. **C.** For the first recipe, the cook used $\frac{9}{5}$ cups of milk. For the next recipe, he used $\frac{9}{6}$ cups of milk. Add the two fractions for the total amount of milk used: $\frac{9}{5} + \frac{9}{6} = \frac{54}{30} + \frac{45}{30} = \frac{99}{30}$, which is about $3\frac{1}{3}$ cups. Because the cook started with nine cups, he has about $5\frac{2}{3}$ cups left, so the closest answer choice is Choice (C).

5. **B.** Notice that the rectangle is nine rows by ten columns, so it has 90 little squares. To find the area of each little square, divide the total area (450) by 90 and get 5. Because the rectangle has five shaded squares, the area of the shaded region is $5 \times 5 = 25$.

6. **B.** Test the answer choices; 13 squared is 169, so the square root of 170 is very close to 13.

7. **D.** If you know the volume of a cube, you can find its side length by figuring out what number when cubed (multiplied by itself two times) equals the volume. Use trial and error: The little cube is 64 cubic inches, which is $4 \times 4 \times 4$, so its side length is 4. The big cube is 343 cubic inches, which is $7 \times 7 \times 7$, so its side length is 7. So the ratio is 4 to 7.

8. **D.** To compare, convert everything to bananas because that's what the problem is asking about. According to the values provided, if 4 bananas = 2 flowers, then 2 bananas = 1 flower. And 1 flower = 3 apples, so 3 apples = 2 bananas. Because multiplying 2 bananas × 8 = 16 (the number of bananas the question asks for), you want to also multiply the number of apples (3) by 8 to keep the proportion the same (which equals 24).

9. **B.** The *line of best fit* just means the line that comes closest to going through the greatest number of points, just like a best guess. Looking at the line at 700 items ordered, the total cost of the order is about $150.00. Find the average cost of an item by dividing $150.00 by 700, which equals about $0.21.

10. **D.** For this problem, you can solve the first equation for x and then plug that value into the expression, or you can simply notice that $30x$ is double $15x$ and that 18 is double 9. So the answer, 108, is double 54.

11. **C.** To increase 8 by 125 percent, multiply it by 2.25. Consider that if you increased 8 by 100 percent, you'd double it and get 16. Then, you can add 25 percent of 8 (a quarter of 8 is 2) to get to 18.

12. **D.** The probability of rolling a 5 on the first roll is found by dividing the number of what you want (1, because there's only one desired result) by the total number of possibilities (6, because there are six numbers on the die). To find the probability of two things *both* happening, multiply the probabilities of each of them happening: $\frac{1}{6} \times \frac{1}{6} = \frac{1}{36}$.

13. **C.** The top of the pattern is an octagon, which matches the octagon in Choice (C).

14. **B.** Notice the pattern in the table: 2 shots = 4 points, 3 shots = 4×4 (16) points, 4 shots = $4 \times 4 \times 4$ (64) points, and 5 shots = $4 \times 4 \times 4 \times 4$ (256) points. So 6 shots is $4 \times 4 \times 4 \times 4 \times 4 =$ 1,024 points.

15. **D.** The large cube is seven little cubes by seven little cubes by seven little cubes. Finding the volume of a cube means multiplying its side length by its side length by its side length: $7 \times 7 \times 7 = 343$. You also may notice that the front face of the cube has $7 \times 7 = 49$ little cubes, and that the big cube has seven layers of 49 little cubes ($7 \times 49 = 343$).

16. **C.** First, consider buying one watch. The price is $20.00. To figure out 8 percent sales tax on $20.00, multiply $20.00 \times 0.08 = $1.60. Now, find the fee by subtracting $21.60 from the total cost ($26.00) to get $4.40.

17. **D.** To find the function in which the y value is decreasing at the greatest rate, begin by eliminating Choices (A) and (B), because, in both of those choices, the y value increases as the x value increases. In Choice (C), the y value goes down by one for every one increase in the x value, but in Choice (D), the y value goes down by about three for every one increase in x value, so Choice (D) has the greatest rate of y value decrease.

18. **D.** Write out what happens until you see a pattern. At first, only one cell exists, which makes four cells (1 + 4). The four new cells each make four new cells (1 + 4 + 16, or $1 + 4^1 + 4^2$). Choice (D) follows this pattern.

19. **B.** To find the percent of people who were undecided, first find out how many people were undecided: 439 + 201 = 640 people were decided, so 800 – 640 = 160 people were undecided. To get the percent, divide 160 by 800, which equals 0.2, and multiply by 100 to convert to a percentage: $0.2 \times 100 = 20$ percent.

20. **D.** Instead of doing this problem theoretically, add a number (try using 9 for the initial number). When you multiply 9 by 0.9, you get 8.1. You *should have* divided 9 by 0.9 to get 10. Now, test the answer choices: Which one, when applied to the mistake (which resulted in 8.1) gives you the answer you should have gotten (10)? Testing Choice (D), 8.1 ÷ 0.81 gives you 10.

21. **D.** Make this problem more concrete by picking a number for x. If x is 20, then $x + 7$ is 27. Because $x + 7$ is 7 more than y (or 27 is 7 more than y) y must be 20. Then, $x + 17$ turns into 37 (because x is 20). How many more than 20 is 37? Simply subtract to find out: 37 – 20 = 17, or Choice (D).

22. **C.** The phrase *greatest possible* means you'll probably be doing some trial and error. Write number pairs that add up to 24 and start multiplying them until you see a pattern. You'll notice that the closer the two numbers are together, the higher their product. The highest product of two integers that add to 24 is 144, but that would mean multiplying 12 by 12, and the problem says the integers must be different. So 11×13 produces the greatest product (143) among different numbers that add to 24.

23. **B.** Assuming the first high-jump record is 100 makes this problem easier because it involves calculating a percentage. If the record in 2009 was 100 and 10 percent higher in 2010, increase 100 by 10 percent by multiplying it by 1.1: $100 \times 1.1 = 110$. Then, because the record was 5 percent higher in 2011, increase 110 by 5 percent by multiplying it by 1.05: $110 \times 1.05 = 115.5$. To find the percent increase, use the formula $\frac{difference}{original} \times 100$. The difference is found by subtracting the 2009 value (100) from the 2011 value (115.5): $\frac{115.5 - 100}{100} \times 100 = \frac{15.5}{100} \times 100 = \frac{1550}{100} = 15.5$. **Remember:** Percent changes must be calculated one at a time. If you chose Choice (A), you may have done both at once.

24. **B.** In Column A, x is 1 if y is 7 (plug in 7 for y and solve). In Column B, y is 7 when x is 1. Write down the value you get for each column to avoid careless errors; Column B is greater (7 > 1).

25. **C.** To find the smallest number of coins, use as many quarters as possible first: seven quarters is $7 \times 0.25 = \$1.75$. Then, use as many dimes as possible: two dimes brings the total to $\$1.75 + 2(\$0.10) = \$1.95$. Now, add three pennies to get to $\$1.98$. Because 12 coins is the lowest number of coins possible, the quantities are equal.

26. **B.** Treat the operation(s) under a root sign as if they're in parentheses. In Column A, add $100 + 44 = 144$, and then take the square root and get 12. In Column B, the square root of 100 is 10, and the square root of 44 is between 6 (6 squared is 36) and 7 (7 squared is 49). Even 10 + 6 is easily bigger than 12.

27. **B.** Following PEMDAS, in Column A, you must complete the exponent operation before making the answer negative. Don't do all the math; just notice that the answer is a negative number. In Column B, remember that a negative number raised to an even exponent becomes positive ($-2 \times -2 = 4$). Again, you don't have to do all the math to notice that the answer is a positive number, so Column (B) is larger.

28. **A.** Multiply $\$10,000.00$ by 0.6 to take 40 percent off and get $\$6,000.00$. So the amount saved in Column A is $\$4,000.00$. In Column B, make sure you take the discounts one at a time. Take 20 percent off by multiplying $\$10,000.00$ by 0.8 and get $\$8,000.00$, then take 20 percent off $\$8,000.00$ by multiplying $\$8,000.00$ by 0.8 and get $\$6,400.00$. The total amount saved in Column B is only $\$3,600.00$.

29. **B.** Using *distance = rate × time* (or $d = rt$), in Column A, 5 mi = 10 mph × *time*. Dividing both sides of that equation by 10 gives a time of 0.5 (half an hour). In Column B, 10 mi = 15 mph × *time*. Dividing both sides of that equation by 15 gives a time of about 0.67, so Column B is bigger.

30. **C.** To get the slope of the line in Column A, isolate y. Subtract $6x$ from both sides, and then divide both sides by -4, resulting in $y = \frac{6}{4}x - \frac{15}{4}$, so the slope is $\frac{6}{4}$. In Column B, find the slope by putting the change in y ($3 - 6 = -3$) over the change in x ($2 - 4 = -2$), and you get $\frac{3}{2} = \frac{6}{4}$, so the slopes are the same.

31. **C.** You can find how many girls there are because you know 40 percent of the girls equals 80. So set up an equation and solve for x (number of girls): $0.4x = 80$, and $x = 80 \div 0.4 = 200$. To figure out how many boys there are, set up another equation. You know that 60 percent of the boys equals 120, so $0.6y = 120$, and $y = 120 \div 0.6y = 200$. So the quantities are equal.

32. **A.** The perimeter of the square is $4s = 40$. Rather than calculate the length of the square's diagonals, notice that a diagonal connecting two sides is always shorter than the combined length of those two sides, and so the length of both diagonals must be less than the length of four sides. So Column A is larger.

33. **D.** Draw the points and experiment enough to convince yourself that, depending on how you draw them, either Column A or Column B can be bigger.

34. **B.** The entire figure is ten rows by eight columns, which equals 80 little squares. Sixteen shaded squares are in the middle. Notice that each corner block of 9 squares is divided into half shaded, half unshaded, so each corner has 4.5 shaded squares. Adding all four corners + the center block = 34 shaded. There are $80 - 34 = 46$ unshaded, so Column B is larger.

35. **C.** The distances between 12 and 3 and between 9 and 12 are equal, so the probabilities are the same.

36. **B.** Because six odd numbers (1, 3, 5, 7, 9, and 11) and five even numbers (2, 4, 6, 8, and 10) are between 1 and 11, a higher probability exists of choosing an odd number.

37. **D.** Draw a few different scenarios to prove.

Section 3: Reading Comprehension

1. **C.** An *oral surgeon* is someone who specializes in surgical procedures of the mouth. The word *oral* means mouth, so that could have been a clue for you to find the right answer.

2. **D.** The passage doesn't state whether one kind of impaction is more painful than another.

3. **A.** Typically, people get four wisdom teeth — two on top and two on bottom — however, for one or more not to appear isn't unusual.

4. **C.** You can infer from the passage that many people have trouble with wisdom teeth, so you know the answer is either Choice (A) or Choice (C). The passage doesn't explicitly state the answer, so the best inference is Choice (C), because very seldom do all situations or problems apply to all people.

5. **C.** In the context of the passage, the word *trying* means frustrating or difficult. In other words, the author is saying that wisdom teeth are frustrating and painful.

6. **A.** When you face a title question, choose a title that covers the entire content of the passage and is clear yet simple. This passage simply explains what wisdom teeth are and the types of impactions, and it includes a brief bit of info about having them removed. *Understanding Wisdom Teeth* is the most encompassing, clear title option.

7. **B.** According to the article, a calorie is a unit of measurement, so it isn't food in and of itself. Noting this fact from the article, all other statements are false, so Choice (B) is the only correct statement.

8. **C.** Because a calorie is just a measurement of energy, the author states that different kinds of calories don't exist. A fat calorie and a protein calorie are the same in terms of the energy measurement.

9. **C.** *Daily caloric intake* refers to the number of calories your body needs every day, based on your age, weight, and height. The number includes the basic amount of energy your body needs to stay alive but also enough calories for other activities.

10. **B.** If you consume fewer calories than your body needs, your body burns calories stored as fat to make up the difference.

11. **A.** The number of calories a person needs per day is calculated by the person's age, weight, and height.

12. **D.** The author is noting that fat calories and protein calories are the same in terms of energy, but they're not nutritionally the same.

13. **B.** The author states that English is a difficult language to learn as a second language and provides one reason why in the rest of the passage.

14. **C.** The author uses a complicated phrase to communicate a simple idea: English often doesn't follow its own rules. If you face a question like this one, be sure to find the simplest explanation for the phrase — after all, that's what the question has asked you to do.

15. **D.** The author doesn't offer any explanation as to why the different plural forms exist in the English language.

16. **B.** In the context of the passage, the author is saying that the differences in English can be very confusing to a new learner. Although this isn't what the word *dizzy* means, remember that you need to define the word based on the context of how it's used. Keep in mind that context is important while literal definitions aren't.

17. **B.** Because a particular tone in this passage doesn't stand out (the author simply provides information), *explanatory* is the best answer.

18. **C.** The author uses the concept of *you* to further support and enforce the idea that plural forms are confusing in the English language. Think of this statement as an additional form of proof to back up what the author is saying.

19. **A.** The best definition is a group of style features applied to letters, numbers, and symbols. Choices (B), (C), and (D) are all wrong because they're not specific enough to function as a definition. When you choose a definition for a word or concept, make sure you choose a definition that's specific enough but not so specific that the answer doesn't define the actual word.

20. **C.** The overall purpose of the passage is to explain some basic information about fonts. Always think about the entire passage when you answer this kind of question.

21. **B.** Fonts are important because they affect the style and readability of a document.

22. **A.** This passage can best be described as factual. The author is simply providing facts and information about fonts.

23. **C.** In an 8 point fixed space font, eight characters print per horizontal inch.

24. **C.** In a proportional font, characters can have different widths because they're not *fixed space,* according to the text.

25. **D.** Serif fonts have small decorative additions, typically to the ends of lines in letters, symbols, and numbers.

26. **B.** Typeface is mentioned because the author has defined the concept of a font family. A *font family,* which applies styles to all letters, numbers, and symbols, is a typeface, so the author includes the term he's explained to the reader.

27. **C.** The author doesn't make any judgment calls about monochromic or polychromic cultures; he simply presents information, so the statement in Choice (C) is false. Be careful of reading more into the passage than it actually says. Because the passage doesn't make this statement or even infer it in any way, the answer has to be false.

28. **C.** This passage explores how time communication is used with different individuals as well as different cultures. When you face a question like this one, be sure to choose the best answer that encompasses the point of the entire passage.

29. **C.** You can infer from the passage that time anxiety occurs in cultures where appointments are very time specific. In cultures where this is less the case, less anxiety exists because lateness isn't as much of an issue.

30. **C.** The word *weight* in the context of the passage means importance. The author is saying that every class may not be given the same amount of importance from a time perspective.

31. **C.** Bias means an author unfairly favors one idea, person, or thing over others. In this article, the author provides information about monochromic and polychromic cultures but doesn't seem to favor one over the other. In other words, he writes without a bias.

32. **C.** Roosevelt's main purpose in this passage is to call people to action that will help restore the economy. He does this by addressing the definition of success and then talking about the need to get people back to work in order to get the economy moving forward.

33. **B.** The passage doesn't define the word *evanescent,* but within the context, Roosevelt is talking about the loss of money. The best answer is Choice (B), *vanishing.* **Evanescent** means brief, temporary, or vanishing.

34. **D.** The passage states that the most important task is getting people back to work, or employment, as stated in the third paragraph.

35. **C.** Roosevelt is saying that people can only be confident when the government is honest with them about the current conditions as well as the action it intends on taking.

36. **A.** The final paragraph discusses the need to save small farms and keep agricultural industries growing.

Section 4: Mathematics Achievement

1. **A.** Add 'em — but don't rush just because it's simple math.

2. **B.** Test the answer choices. In Choice (B), you get $4 \times 11 = 44 - 7 = 37$.

3. **C.** Notice that the circle is divided into eight pieces. Two of those pieces are shaded, so a quarter of the circle is shaded.

4. **D.** If you're not sure which of the numbers is prime, try dividing the one(s) you're not sure about by small numbers (like 2 and 3) to test them.

5. **D.** Convert everything to cherries because that's what the question is asking for: 5 cherries = 3 peaches, so 1 peach = $\frac{5}{3}$ cherries. One peach also equals 15 bananas, so 15 bananas = $\frac{5}{3}$ cherries. Divide both sides of that equation by $\frac{5}{3}$; 9 bananas = 1 cherry.

6. **C.** Find the range by subtracting the lowest score from the highest. Because you know the range is 22, 22 = (the highest score) – 12. Add 12 to both sides to get a highest score of 34.

7. **B.** Looking at the graph, the highest temperature is 35 degrees Fahrenheit, and the lowest is 10 degrees Fahrenheit, so the difference is $35 - 10 = 25$ degrees Fahrenheit.

8. **C.** Find P by plugging the given values for L and W into the formula (using the formula for finding the perimeter of a rectangle): $(19 + 7) \times 2 = 52$.

9. **B.** Round 48 to 50 and 62 to 60, and then multiply $(50 \times 60 = 3{,}000)$. Then divide: $300 \div 600 = 5$.

10. **C.** Notice the pattern. An increase of $0.12 occurs between each week.

11. **A.** First, add $27 + 23 = 50$. Then, multiply $50 \times 80 = 4{,}000$, and then divide by 4 to get 1,000.

12. **B.** Make this numberless problem easier by adding numbers to it. Say, for example, the price last year was $1.50 and the price this year is $1.00. Find the percent decrease by calculating *difference* ÷ *original* × 100. So $50 \div 150 = 0.33$, and $0.33 \times 100 = 33$. Also, think about how much $1.50 decreased to get to $1.00 — it decreased $0.50, or a third of $1.50, and one-third equals 33 percent.

13. **A.** Find the area of the shaded region by calculating the area of the circle and then subtracting the area of the square. The area of the circle is found with πr^2, where r is the radius of the circle. The circle's diameter is 12, so its radius is half that number, or 6. So the area of the circle is 36π. Finding the area of the square is easiest by noticing that it's split into two congruent (equal) triangles. The height of each triangle is the radius of the circle, and the base of each triangle is 12. The area of one of the triangles is $\frac{1}{2}bh = \frac{1}{2}(12 \times 6) = 36$, so the area of both triangles is 72, making the correct answer $36\pi - 72$.

14. **C.** Because 12 apples are in the box and there are 8 more apples than oranges, there are 4 oranges. Then, $12 + 4 = 16$ total pieces of fruit. The fraction of the total that is oranges is $\frac{4}{16} = \frac{1}{4}$.

15. **C.** You can figure out what the m means by process of elimination or logic. Logically, the more minutes someone spends exercising, the greater the amount of oxygen used, so it makes sense that m is a number that, as it increases, increases l.

16. **D.** Try solving this question with a proportion, because the ratio of inches to miles is always 3 to 1,000: $\frac{3}{1{,}000} = \frac{10.5}{x}$. Cross-multiply and divide both sides by 3 to get 3,500.

17. **C.** Looking at the points where 40 miles per gallon is on the graph and checking the answer choices, $15,000.00, is the best option to be closest to the greater number of dots.

18. **D.** Find the probability by dividing the number of what you want (40 white chips + 10 red chips = 50) by the total possibilities $(20 + 40 + 10) = 70$. You get $\frac{50}{70} = \frac{5}{7}$.

19. **B.** Dividing these numbers is easier if you first convert them to improper fractions: $1\frac{1}{7} = \frac{8}{7}$ and $1\frac{3}{8} = \frac{11}{8}$. Now, divide by flipping the second fraction and multiplying: $\frac{8}{7} \times \frac{8}{11} = \frac{64}{77}$.

20. **B.** If two triangles are similar, their sides share a common ratio. Notice that the smallest side of the small triangle is 5 and the smallest side of the large triangle is 20, so the ratio is 5 to 20, which reduces to 1 to 4.

21. **C.** Cross-multiply: $18N = 540$, and then divide both sides by 18 to get $N = 30$.

22. **C.** To find the slope, isolate y. Subtract $6x$ from both sides to get $-8y = -6x - 16$. Then, divide both sides by -8 to get $y = \frac{-6x}{-8} - \frac{16}{-8}$. So the slope is $\frac{-6}{-8} = \frac{6}{8} = \frac{3}{4}$.

23. **A.** The probability of picking a gold-starred ball for each color is found by multiplying all the individual probabilities of picking a gold-starred ball. The probabilities of picking a gold-starred ball from the red, green, and purple balls are $\frac{1}{3}, \frac{1}{4}$, and $\frac{1}{5}$, respectively. Multiplying these probabilities gives you $\frac{1}{3} \times \frac{1}{4} = \frac{1}{12} \times \frac{1}{5} = \frac{1}{60}$.

24. **B.** Checking the choices, only Choice (B) has numbers that reduce to the same ratio as the graph (5 to 3 to 2). Divide all the numbers in Choice (B) by 4 to check.

25. **B.** The easiest way to handle many problems with variables in the answer choices is to pick numbers for those variables. For example, pick 2 for x, 3 for y, and 4 for z. Then, plug those numbers in to the initial expression: $\frac{2}{3}\left(\frac{3}{2} - \frac{2}{4}\right) = \frac{2}{3}\left(\frac{6}{4} - \frac{2}{4}\right) = \frac{2}{3}\left(\frac{4}{4}\right) = \frac{2}{3}$. Now, see which answer choice makes $\frac{2}{3}$ when you plug those numbers into the answer choices. Testing Choice (B), you get $1 - \frac{2^2}{12} = 1 - \frac{4}{12} = 1 - \frac{1}{3} = \frac{2}{3}$.

26. **C.** It takes an increase of 15 degrees to get to zero and then an increase of another 30 degrees to get to 30 degrees Fahrenheit, giving you a total increase of 45 degrees.

27. **B.** To find what $x - y$ is equal to, isolate that as an expression. Subtract y from both sides to get $x - y - 8 + 12 = 0$, which simplifies to $x - y + 4 = 0$. Subtract 4 from both sides to end up with $x - y = -4$.

28. **B.** To find the fraction of people who passed both quizzes, you have to take $\frac{4}{5}$ of 85 percent. The easiest way to do this is to convert 85 percent to a fraction, $\frac{85}{100}$, and then multiply by $\frac{4}{5}$: $\frac{85}{100} \times \frac{4}{5} = \frac{340}{500} = \frac{17}{25}$.

29. **C.** Following the pattern, the first two elements have one star, but they're different colors. The third and fourth elements have two stars, and the colors there also alternate. Following this pattern, the sixth element should have three black stars.

30. **C.** When you compare the airplane lines, you may notice that the line for Airplane 3 gains the most altitude in the shortest amount of time when compared to the other airplanes.

31. **C.** To solve this problem, find out how long it takes to fill $\frac{1}{8}$ of the bucket, because that's the remaining quantity. If filling the bucket $\frac{7}{8}$ takes one minute, $\frac{1}{8}$ will take $\frac{1}{7}$ minutes (divide both $\frac{7}{8}$ and one minute by 7). Divide 1 by 7 to convert to a decimal, and you get about 0.14.

32. **B.** To find the probability of *all* the coins landing on heads, multiply the probabilities of each of the coins landing on heads. Because a coin has two sides, the probability of landing on heads is $\frac{1}{2}$. Multiply all the probabilities: $\frac{1}{2} \times \frac{1}{2} \times \frac{1}{2} = \frac{1}{8}$.

33. **C.** The two little arrows on each parallel-looking pair of lines indicate that those lines are parallel. A four-sided figure with two sets of parallel lines is a parallelogram.

34. **A.** Pick numbers for variables. Try 6 for y. Then, x would have to be 7. Plugging those numbers in to the answer choices, only Choice (A) is true.

35. **A.** Test the answer choices by plotting them as points on the graph. Because isosceles triangles have two equal sides, only the point in Choice (A) makes an isosceles triangle. To prove this, notice that to get to point A from $(-4, 0)$, you go up four and over four, and that to get to point B from point A, you go down four and over four, so the distances are the same.

36. **B.** For this problem, you simply have to add. Tack on a zero to 5.3, 6.4, and 7.5, making them 5.30, 6.40, and 7.50, to make lining up the numbers easier.

37. **D.** If the volume of a cube is 125, its side length is a number that, when multiplied by itself twice, equals 125. Do some trial and error, and you find that $5 \times 5 \times 5 = 125$. If the side length of the cube is 5, the surface area of one face is $5 \times 5 = 25$. A cube has six faces, making the total surface area $25 \times 6 = 150$.

38. **B.** Simplify the roots: The square root of 100 is 10, and the square root of 36 is 6. Then, distribute the 4 to the numerator of the fraction, resulting in $\frac{40 + 40x}{6}$. Divide each term by 2 to get $\frac{20 + 20x}{3}$.

39. **B.** Because similar triangles have a common ratio among their corresponding side lengths, find the ratio by comparing the left side of the small triangle to the left side of the big triangle: The ratio is 7 to 42, which reduces to 1 to 6. Therefore, each side of the big triangle is 6 times the corresponding side of the small triangle, so x is $6 \times 8 = 48$.

40. **C.** The triangle on the right is in the same orientation as the triangle on the left because the vertices are in the same order, so it's a *slide* — picture it sliding over to the right.

41. **B.** Use some estimation for this problem. For example, use $500.00 for the cost. If the vendor sells 20 hot dogs per day for 30 days, he sells 600 hot dogs $\times$ $2.00 = $1,200.00. When the cost is subtracted from $1,200.00, the vendor is left with a $700.00 profit.

42. **A.** Parallel lines have equal slopes. Find the slope of the line on the graph by picking two points on it: $(0, 2)$ and $(14, 5)$. Find the change in y $(5 - 2 = 3)$, and write it over the change in x $(14 - 0 = 14)$ to get $\frac{3}{14}$. Now, just look at the answer choices and find a line with a matching slope.

43. **D.** Pretend the original garden is a square (a square is a rectangle) measuring 10 by 10, and draw a picture to give yourself a visual. Find the original area by multiplying length by width $(10 \times 10) = 100$. At this point, you've picked a number for x (100). Draw the new garden by tripling the width $(10 \times 3) = 30$ and multiplying the length by 1.5 to increase the length by $\frac{1}{2}$: $10 \times 1.5 = 15$. Find the area of the new garden by multiplying $30 \times 15 = 450$, which is the answer to the question as a number. Now, just see which answer choice makes that number by plugging in your x (100) into the choices. Testing Choice (D), $4.5 \times 100 = 450$.

44. **D.** Test the answer choices by picking a choice as the score for the fourth test and seeing what the average would be. Testing Choice (D), $\frac{80 + 84 + 93 + 99}{4} = 89$.

45. **C.** The ratio of the tree's height to its shadow is the same as the ratio of the building's height to its shadow. Set up a proportion to solve: $\frac{60}{80} = \frac{33}{x}$, and then cross-multiply to solve: $60x = 2,640$. Divide both sides by 60 to solve for x: $2,640 \div 60 = 44$.

46. **C.** This question gives you instructions to follow when two numbers are on either side of the #. So $a\#b = 2a - 2b$ means that you have to multiply both numbers by 2 and subtract 2 times the second number from 2 times the first number. When you test the answer choices, Choice (C) turns into $2(4) - 2(-5)$, which equals $8 - (-10) = 18$. All the other choices produce lower numbers.

47. **D.** Only Choice (D) will *always* produce a number greater than 0. Because x is less than 0, x is negative. Because y is more than zero, y is positive. If a negative number is subtracted from a positive number, it's the same thing as taking away the negative sign and adding the numbers; a positive number added to another positive number will be greater than 0. So $y - x > 0$.

Section 5: Essay

Remember that writing samples for the ISEE don't have right or wrong answers, and with this topic (if you could travel anywhere in the world, where would you go and why), you can write about a wide variety of topics. So don't get caught up in thinking, "Did I write what they wanted?" because truthfully, the readers of your writing sample don't care what you write about. They simply want to see that you can organize your thoughts, show your writer's voice, and write a strong essay.

With that thought in mind, the following are a few things you should have done in order to write a winning essay for your practice test. (For more valuable tips on writing an effective essay and some examples, check out Chapter 8.)

✔ Because the essay prompt clearly wants you to choose *one* place you'd visit and write about it, you should have made clear in your introduction what that one place is, and you shouldn't talk about several different places.

✔ Your body paragraphs should have included specific reasons why you'd visit this place. You should have included characteristics of the place you want to visit and especially focused on why you want to visit. What would you do? What would you see? What activities would you involve yourself in while visiting this place? Be sure to discuss what you'd do at the location you chose and not simply provide a statement. For example, if you said, "I would go boogie boarding at the beach," you should have explained why this activity is important to you or why you want to try it.

✔ You should have included a conclusion that brought your ideas together and again mentioned the place you want to visit. Conclusions help show that your thoughts and ideas are organized and that you stuck with the topic, so don't forget about the conclusion when you write.

Finally, have someone else read your essay and mark misspelled words, poorly organized sentences, misplaced commas, and other grammatical problems. Doing so helps you see how many errors you made. Remember that the writing sample isn't a grammar test, and a few errors won't hurt you in the end, but overall, your sample should be well written and generally error free.

Answers at a Glance

Section 1: Verbal Reasoning

1. D	9. B	17. A	25. A	33. B
2. A	10. A	18. C	26. A	34. A
3. C	11. B	19. A	27. D	35. B
4. A	12. B	20. B	28. B	36. D
5. C	13. D	21. A	29. C	37. C
6. A	14. C	22. D	30. D	38. B
7. B	15. D	23. B	31. A	39. A
8. C	16. C	24. B	32. C	40. D

Section 2: Quantitative Reasoning

1. B	9. B	17. D	25. C	33. D
2. B	10. D	18. D	26. B	34. B
3. C	11. C	19. B	27. B	35. C
4. C	12. D	20. D	28. A	36. B
5. B	13. C	21. D	29. B	37. D
6. B	14. B	22. C	30. C	
7. D	15. D	23. B	31. C	
8. D	16. C	24. B	32. A	

Section 3: Reading Comprehension

1. C	9. C	17. B	25. D	33. B
2. D	10. B	18. C	26. B	34. D
3. A	11. A	19. A	27. C	35. C
4. C	12. D	20. C	28. C	36. A
5. C	13. B	21. B	29. C	
6. A	14. C	22. A	30. C	
7. B	15. D	23. C	31. C	
8. C	16. B	24. C	32. C	

Section 4: Mathematics Achievement

1. A	11. A	21. C	31. C	41. B
2. B	12. B	22. C	32. B	42. A
3. C	13. A	23. A	33. C	43. D
4. D	14. C	24. B	34. A	44. D
5. D	15. C	25. B	35. A	45. C
6. C	16. D	26. C	36. B	46. C
7. B	17. C	27. B	37. D	47. D
8. C	18. D	28. B	38. B	
9. B	19. B	29. C	39. B	
10. C	20. B	30. C	40. C	

Chapter 27

ISEE Lower Level Practice Exam

This practice exam is for ISEE lower level students (grades 5 and 6). Taking practice tests can help you perform better on test day, so when you sit down to practice this test, make sure you give it your all. To make the most of this practice exam, find yourself a quiet room, ample time, a few sharpened pencils, and some blank scratch paper. Resist the urge to play on the Internet or text your friends while you're taking the test. After all, you want to practice in the same quiet and boring conditions that you'll face on test day.

Grab a watch, an iPod, a phone, or some other way to track your time. Make sure you don't go over the time limit we've given you for each part of this practice test because you won't be allowed extra time on the actual test. You can find all the answers to this practice test in Chapter 28, but don't cheat! Check your answers only *after* you finish the test.

Answer Sheet

For Sections 1 through 4 of the exam, use the following answer sheets and fill in the answer bubble for the corresponding number, using a #2 pencil.

Section 1: Verbal Reasoning

1. Ⓐ Ⓑ Ⓒ Ⓓ	13. Ⓐ Ⓑ Ⓒ Ⓓ	25. Ⓐ Ⓑ Ⓒ Ⓓ
2. Ⓐ Ⓑ Ⓒ Ⓓ	14. Ⓐ Ⓑ Ⓒ Ⓓ	26. Ⓐ Ⓑ Ⓒ Ⓓ
3. Ⓐ Ⓑ Ⓒ Ⓓ	15. Ⓐ Ⓑ Ⓒ Ⓓ	27. Ⓐ Ⓑ Ⓒ Ⓓ
4. Ⓐ Ⓑ Ⓒ Ⓓ	16. Ⓐ Ⓑ Ⓒ Ⓓ	28. Ⓐ Ⓑ Ⓒ Ⓓ
5. Ⓐ Ⓑ Ⓒ Ⓓ	17. Ⓐ Ⓑ Ⓒ Ⓓ	29. Ⓐ Ⓑ Ⓒ Ⓓ
6. Ⓐ Ⓑ Ⓒ Ⓓ	18. Ⓐ Ⓑ Ⓒ Ⓓ	30. Ⓐ Ⓑ Ⓒ Ⓓ
7. Ⓐ Ⓑ Ⓒ Ⓓ	19. Ⓐ Ⓑ Ⓒ Ⓓ	31. Ⓐ Ⓑ Ⓒ Ⓓ
8. Ⓐ Ⓑ Ⓒ Ⓓ	20. Ⓐ Ⓑ Ⓒ Ⓓ	32. Ⓐ Ⓑ Ⓒ Ⓓ
9. Ⓐ Ⓑ Ⓒ Ⓓ	21. Ⓐ Ⓑ Ⓒ Ⓓ	33. Ⓐ Ⓑ Ⓒ Ⓓ
10. Ⓐ Ⓑ Ⓒ Ⓓ	22. Ⓐ Ⓑ Ⓒ Ⓓ	34. Ⓐ Ⓑ Ⓒ Ⓓ
11. Ⓐ Ⓑ Ⓒ Ⓓ	23. Ⓐ Ⓑ Ⓒ Ⓓ	
12. Ⓐ Ⓑ Ⓒ Ⓓ	24. Ⓐ Ⓑ Ⓒ Ⓓ	

Section 2: Quantitative Reasoning

1. Ⓐ Ⓑ Ⓒ Ⓓ Ⓔ	11. Ⓐ Ⓑ Ⓒ Ⓓ Ⓔ	21. Ⓐ Ⓑ Ⓒ Ⓓ Ⓔ	31. Ⓐ Ⓑ Ⓒ Ⓓ Ⓔ
2. Ⓐ Ⓑ Ⓒ Ⓓ Ⓔ	12. Ⓐ Ⓑ Ⓒ Ⓓ Ⓔ	22. Ⓐ Ⓑ Ⓒ Ⓓ Ⓔ	32. Ⓐ Ⓑ Ⓒ Ⓓ Ⓔ
3. Ⓐ Ⓑ Ⓒ Ⓓ Ⓔ	13. Ⓐ Ⓑ Ⓒ Ⓓ Ⓔ	23. Ⓐ Ⓑ Ⓒ Ⓓ Ⓔ	33. Ⓐ Ⓑ Ⓒ Ⓓ Ⓔ
4. Ⓐ Ⓑ Ⓒ Ⓓ Ⓔ	14. Ⓐ Ⓑ Ⓒ Ⓓ Ⓔ	24. Ⓐ Ⓑ Ⓒ Ⓓ Ⓔ	34. Ⓐ Ⓑ Ⓒ Ⓓ Ⓔ
5. Ⓐ Ⓑ Ⓒ Ⓓ Ⓔ	15. Ⓐ Ⓑ Ⓒ Ⓓ Ⓔ	25. Ⓐ Ⓑ Ⓒ Ⓓ Ⓔ	35. Ⓐ Ⓑ Ⓒ Ⓓ Ⓔ
6. Ⓐ Ⓑ Ⓒ Ⓓ Ⓔ	16. Ⓐ Ⓑ Ⓒ Ⓓ Ⓔ	26. Ⓐ Ⓑ Ⓒ Ⓓ Ⓔ	36. Ⓐ Ⓑ Ⓒ Ⓓ Ⓔ
7. Ⓐ Ⓑ Ⓒ Ⓓ Ⓔ	17. Ⓐ Ⓑ Ⓒ Ⓓ Ⓔ	27. Ⓐ Ⓑ Ⓒ Ⓓ Ⓔ	37. Ⓐ Ⓑ Ⓒ Ⓓ Ⓔ
8. Ⓐ Ⓑ Ⓒ Ⓓ Ⓔ	18. Ⓐ Ⓑ Ⓒ Ⓓ Ⓔ	28. Ⓐ Ⓑ Ⓒ Ⓓ Ⓔ	38. Ⓐ Ⓑ Ⓒ Ⓓ Ⓔ
9. Ⓐ Ⓑ Ⓒ Ⓓ Ⓔ	19. Ⓐ Ⓑ Ⓒ Ⓓ Ⓔ	29. Ⓐ Ⓑ Ⓒ Ⓓ Ⓔ	
10. Ⓐ Ⓑ Ⓒ Ⓓ Ⓔ	20. Ⓐ Ⓑ Ⓒ Ⓓ Ⓔ	30. Ⓐ Ⓑ Ⓒ Ⓓ Ⓔ	

Section 3: Reading Comprehension

1. Ⓐ Ⓑ Ⓒ Ⓓ Ⓔ   11. Ⓐ Ⓑ Ⓒ Ⓓ Ⓔ   21. Ⓐ Ⓑ Ⓒ Ⓓ Ⓔ
2. Ⓐ Ⓑ Ⓒ Ⓓ Ⓔ   12. Ⓐ Ⓑ Ⓒ Ⓓ Ⓔ   22. Ⓐ Ⓑ Ⓒ Ⓓ Ⓔ
3. Ⓐ Ⓑ Ⓒ Ⓓ Ⓔ   13. Ⓐ Ⓑ Ⓒ Ⓓ Ⓔ   23. Ⓐ Ⓑ Ⓒ Ⓓ Ⓔ
4. Ⓐ Ⓑ Ⓒ Ⓓ Ⓔ   14. Ⓐ Ⓑ Ⓒ Ⓓ Ⓔ   24. Ⓐ Ⓑ Ⓒ Ⓓ Ⓔ
5. Ⓐ Ⓑ Ⓒ Ⓓ Ⓔ   15. Ⓐ Ⓑ Ⓒ Ⓓ Ⓔ   25. Ⓐ Ⓑ Ⓒ Ⓓ Ⓔ
6. Ⓐ Ⓑ Ⓒ Ⓓ Ⓔ   16. Ⓐ Ⓑ Ⓒ Ⓓ Ⓔ
7. Ⓐ Ⓑ Ⓒ Ⓓ Ⓔ   17. Ⓐ Ⓑ Ⓒ Ⓓ Ⓔ
8. Ⓐ Ⓑ Ⓒ Ⓓ Ⓔ   18. Ⓐ Ⓑ Ⓒ Ⓓ Ⓔ
9. Ⓐ Ⓑ Ⓒ Ⓓ Ⓔ   19. Ⓐ Ⓑ Ⓒ Ⓓ Ⓔ
10. Ⓐ Ⓑ Ⓒ Ⓓ Ⓔ   20. Ⓐ Ⓑ Ⓒ Ⓓ Ⓔ

Section 4: Mathematics Achievement

1. Ⓐ Ⓑ Ⓒ Ⓓ Ⓔ   11. Ⓐ Ⓑ Ⓒ Ⓓ Ⓔ   21. Ⓐ Ⓑ Ⓒ Ⓓ Ⓔ
2. Ⓐ Ⓑ Ⓒ Ⓓ Ⓔ   12. Ⓐ Ⓑ Ⓒ Ⓓ Ⓔ   22. Ⓐ Ⓑ Ⓒ Ⓓ Ⓔ
3. Ⓐ Ⓑ Ⓒ Ⓓ Ⓔ   13. Ⓐ Ⓑ Ⓒ Ⓓ Ⓔ   23. Ⓐ Ⓑ Ⓒ Ⓓ Ⓔ
4. Ⓐ Ⓑ Ⓒ Ⓓ Ⓔ   14. Ⓐ Ⓑ Ⓒ Ⓓ Ⓔ   24. Ⓐ Ⓑ Ⓒ Ⓓ Ⓔ
5. Ⓐ Ⓑ Ⓒ Ⓓ Ⓔ   15. Ⓐ Ⓑ Ⓒ Ⓓ Ⓔ   25. Ⓐ Ⓑ Ⓒ Ⓓ Ⓔ
6. Ⓐ Ⓑ Ⓒ Ⓓ Ⓔ   16. Ⓐ Ⓑ Ⓒ Ⓓ Ⓔ   26. Ⓐ Ⓑ Ⓒ Ⓓ Ⓔ
7. Ⓐ Ⓑ Ⓒ Ⓓ Ⓔ   17. Ⓐ Ⓑ Ⓒ Ⓓ Ⓔ   27. Ⓐ Ⓑ Ⓒ Ⓓ Ⓔ
8. Ⓐ Ⓑ Ⓒ Ⓓ Ⓔ   18. Ⓐ Ⓑ Ⓒ Ⓓ Ⓔ   28. Ⓐ Ⓑ Ⓒ Ⓓ Ⓔ
9. Ⓐ Ⓑ Ⓒ Ⓓ Ⓔ   19. Ⓐ Ⓑ Ⓒ Ⓓ Ⓔ   29. Ⓐ Ⓑ Ⓒ Ⓓ Ⓔ
10. Ⓐ Ⓑ Ⓒ Ⓓ Ⓔ   20. Ⓐ Ⓑ Ⓒ Ⓓ Ⓔ   30. Ⓐ Ⓑ Ⓒ Ⓓ Ⓔ

Section 5: Essay

For Section 5, use two loose-leaf or lined notebook pages to write your essay. (On the real exam, the answer booklet contains two lined sheets.)

Section 1

Verbal Reasoning

Time: 20 Minutes

Directions: You have 20 minutes to complete the following 34 questions. Look at the answer options and decide which answer is best. Mark your answer to each question in the corresponding answer bubble on the answer sheet for Section 1.

Questions 1–17 contain a capitalized word and four answer choices. Choose the word that is the closest in meaning to the capitalized word.

1. PALTRY:
   - (A) Important
   - (B) Caky
   - (C) Insignificant
   - (D) Great

2. CRYPTIC:
   - (A) Deep
   - (B) Puzzling
   - (C) Unimpressive
   - (D) Neutral

3. OBLIVIOUS:
   - (A) Uneasy
   - (B) Unreasonable
   - (C) Uncaring
   - (D) Unaware

4. BILK:
   - (A) Cheat
   - (B) Ruin
   - (C) Specify
   - (D) Challenge

5. BEVY:
   - (A) Powder
   - (B) Knife
   - (C) Jar
   - (D) Group

6. BOGUS:
   - (A) Fake
   - (B) Fearful
   - (C) Fancy
   - (D) Friendly

7. REPLETE:
   - (A) Full
   - (B) Clear
   - (C) Known
   - (D) Defined

8. COVERT:
   - (A) Glamorous
   - (B) Itchy
   - (C) Undercover
   - (D) Tiring

9. GAUNT:
   - (A) Thin
   - (B) Gruesome
   - (C) Simple
   - (D) Tender

10. INCONSIDERATE:
    - (A) Easy
    - (B) Wishful
    - (C) Rude
    - (D) Happy

Go on to next page

11. PREDICTABLE:

    (A) Sloppy

    (B) Understood

    (C) Collective

    (D) Smart

12. ARROGANT:

    (A) Proud

    (B) Helpful

    (C) Beautiful

    (D) Stunted

13. DEFEND:

    (A) Detract

    (B) Fund

    (C) Protect

    (D) Lie

14. SCRUFFY:

    (A) Unkempt

    (B) Old

    (C) Tired

    (D) Neat

15. STEALTHY:

    (A) Cheerful

    (B) Quick

    (C) Sneaky

    (D) Relaxed

16. GENEROUS:

    (A) Judgmental

    (B) Unselfish

    (C) Caring

    (D) Quick

17. DISTRACTED:

    (A) Unhappy

    (B) Inattentive

    (C) Careless

    (D) Wishful

For Questions 18–34, choose the best word that completes the meaning of each sentence.

18. She found the problem _____ because she could not find a correct answer.

    (A) challenging

    (B) calculated

    (C) genial

    (D) irreverent

19. The river ride was very _____. We had difficulty staying on the boat.

    (A) sublime

    (B) treacherous

    (C) simple

    (E) restful

20. We climbed to the _____ of the mountain, which was the highest point.

    (A) limb

    (B) mount

    (C) crevice

    (D) zenith

21. He copied the teacher's notes _____; they were an exact copy.

    (A) reactively

    (B) cryptically

    (C) verbatim

    (D) gingerly

22. He was _____ after his team lost due to many blunders.

    (A) exasperated

    (B) infinite

    (C) quaint

    (D) jovial

23. Carl felt _____ by the team because all the other boys were bigger.

    (A) tributary

    (B) latitudinal

    (C) intrigued

    (D) intimidated

Go on to next page

24. Everyone thought her remarks at the funeral were _____. She was very insensitive.

    (A) callous
    (B) appropriate
    (C) dismissive
    (D) terminal

25. His whole speech was _____; he really had nothing important to say.

    (A) critical
    (B) timid
    (C) loquacious
    (D) vacuous

26. The troops _____ the entire village until there was nothing left.

    (A) razed
    (B) synchronized
    (C) meandered
    (D) instituted

27. A _____ of steps had to be completed in order.

    (A) spectacle
    (B) challenge
    (C) conglomerate
    (D) sequence

28. Although Jack was aware of the _____, he cheated on the test anyway.

    (A) cadaver
    (B) luminary
    (C) consequences
    (D) nuance

29. Tim felt like there should have been a red light at the traffic _____.

    (A) junction
    (B) mirth
    (C) wane
    (D) vestige

30. The _____ of the wave was almost ten feet tall.

    (A) trail
    (B) power
    (C) crest
    (D) spout

31. Because of its _____, the meteor hit the field with tremendous force.

    (A) velocity
    (B) acoustic
    (C) peccadillo
    (D) aptitude

32. The whole conversation was _____. No one even cared.

    (A) disputed
    (B) trivial
    (C) concise
    (D) docile

33. After all the hiking, the team was weak and in need of _____.

    (A) regurgitation
    (B) sustenance
    (C) semaphore
    (D) actuality

34. The man _____ his pack over the ravine.

    (A) abhorred
    (B) stymied
    (C) drifted
    (D) catapulted

STOP DO NOT TURN THE PAGE UNTIL TOLD TO DO SO.
DO NOT RETURN TO A PREVIOUS TEST.

Section 2

Quantitative Reasoning

Time: 35 Minutes

Directions: You have 35 minutes to complete 38 questions. Work each problem in your head or in the blank space on the page. Then, look at the answer options and decide which one is best. Mark your answer to each question in the corresponding answer bubble on the answer sheet for Section 2.

1. The largest triangle shown is divided into small triangles. What fraction of the largest triangle is shaded?

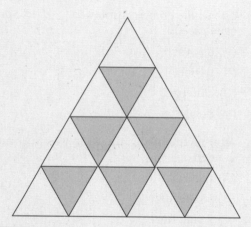

(A) $\frac{5}{16}$

(B) $\frac{3}{8}$

(C) $\frac{1}{2}$

(D) $\frac{5}{8}$

2. Which story best fits the equation 40 ÷ 8 = 5?

(A) I have 40 books. After giving 8 books away, how many books do I have left?

(B) I want to share 40 books with 8 friends. How many books does each person get?

(C) I have 40 boxes with 8 books in each. How many books do I have all together?

(D) I have 40 books, and my friend has 8 books. How many books would I have to give him so we have the same number of books?

3. Judy has more than 9 cookies but fewer than 13 cookies. The number of cookies she has is also greater than 11 but less than 15. How many cookies does Judy have?

(A) 10

(B) 11

(C) 12

(D) 13

4. The perimeter of the triangle is 68 centimeters. The lengths of two of the sides are shown. What is the length of the third side?

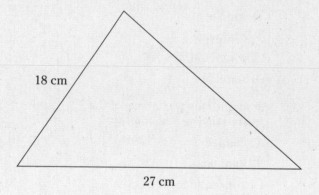

(A) 20 cm

(B) 23 cm

(C) 88 cm

(D) 91 cm

Go on to next page

5. Use the following equations to answer the question:

$$7 - p = 2$$

$$9 - q = 3$$

What is the sum of $p + q$?

(A) 5

(B) 6

(C) 11

(D) 12

6. Use the diagram to answer the question. Which piece would complete the diagram to make a square?

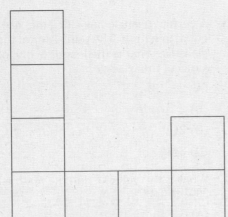

(A)

(B)

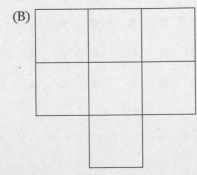

(C)

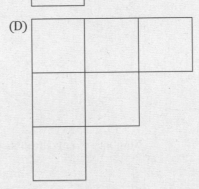

(D)

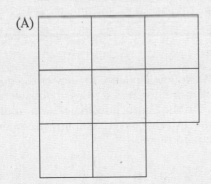

7. Adela and Zariah were jogging along a track at the same speed. It took Adela 30 minutes to jog 2 miles. How long did it take Zariah to jog 3 miles?

(A) 15 min

(B) 25 min

(C) 35 min

(D) 45 min

8. Which is the largest fraction?

(A) $\frac{8}{15}$

(B) $\frac{9}{19}$

(C) $\frac{10}{21}$

(D) $\frac{11}{23}$

9. If x can be divided by both 5 and 7 without leaving a remainder, then x can also be divided by which number without leaving a remainder?

(A) 3

(B) 12

(C) 21

(D) 35

Go on to next page

10. Use the Venn diagram to answer the question. What number can be found in the shaded part of the Venn diagram?

Numbers smaller than 10

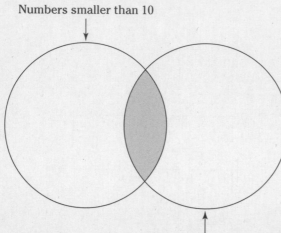

Numbers evenly divisible by 3

(A) 6

(B) 7

(C) 8

(D) 12

11. A class measured the temperature at which a pot of water boiled and then began adding salt to the pot and recording how the boiling point changed. The class recorded the data in the following table. According to the pattern from the data, what would be the predicted boiling point of the water after 6 teaspoons of salt were added?

No salt	212° F
1 tsp salt	213° F
2 tsp salt	215° F
3 tsp salt	218° F
4 tsp salt	222° F
5 tsp salt	227° F

(A) 227° F

(B) 230° F

(C) 232° F

(D) 233° F

12. Use the table to determine the rule for the function.

Input	Output
Φ	Λ
3	10
9	16
17	24

(A) $\Phi \times 3 + 1 = \Lambda$

(B) $\Phi \times 2 - 2 = \Lambda$

(C) $\Phi + 6 = \Lambda$

(D) $\Phi + 7 = \Lambda$

13. A certain triangle has sides that are all equal in length. The perimeter of the triangle is 6s. What is the length of one of the sides of the triangle?

(A) 2

(B) 3

(C) 2s

(D) 3s

14. What is the value of n in the math equation $20 = 4n + 4$?

(A) 3

(B) 4

(C) 5

(D) 6

15. Use the following figure to answer the question. If more horizontal rows of dots were added to the figure, how many dots would the seventh row have, assuming the same pattern continues?

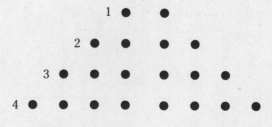

(A) 10

(B) 12

(C) 14

(D) 16

Go on to next page

16. Use the pattern to help answer the question.

$$2^2 + 2^2 = 2^3$$
$$3^3 + 3^3 + 3^3 = 3^4$$
$$4^4 + 4^4 + 4^4 + 4^4 = 4^5$$

What is the solution to $7^7 + 7^7 + 7^7 + 7^7 + 7^7 + 7^7 + 7^7$?

(A) 7^5

(B) 7^6

(C) 7^7

(D) 7^8

17. A survey of 200 students' favorite colors is shown in the circle graph. About what fraction of the students chose purple as their favorite color?

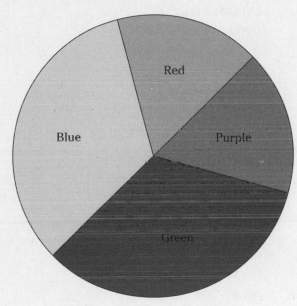

(A) $\frac{1}{10}$

(B) $\frac{1}{6}$

(C) $\frac{1}{4}$

(D) $\frac{1}{3}$

18. A lion had a litter of five cubs. Two of the cubs weighed $10\frac{1}{2}$ ounces each, and the other three cubs each weighed 11 ounces. What is the mean weight of the cubs from the litter?

(A) $10\frac{8}{10}$ ounces

(B) 11 ounces

(C) $11\frac{1}{2}$ ounces

(D) 12 ounces

19. Use the number line to answer the question. Which two numbers are the vertical arrows pointing to on the number line?

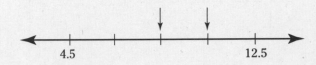

(A) 8, 10

(B) 8.5, 10.5

(C) 9, 11

(D) 9.5, 11.5

20. The lengths of line segments RS and TU are both x and the length of line segment RT is y. What is the length of line segment SU?

(A) y

(B) $y + x$

(C) $x - y$

(D) $2x - y$

21. A box has 892 matchbooks with 27 matches in each book. Which expression gives the best estimate of the total number of matches in the box?

(A) 89×30

(B) 90×30

(C) 800×30

(D) 900×30

Go on to next page

22. The volume of the small, shaded cube is 1 unit³. What is the volume of the larger cube?

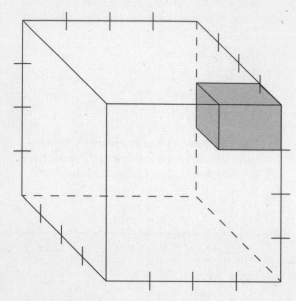

   (A) 16 units³
   (B) 32 units³
   (C) 64 units³
   (D) 128 units³

23. Jar 1 and Jar 2 each hold 1 cup of water when filled to the top. The jars shown are not completely filled to the top. If the liquids in the two jars are combined, approximately how much liquid will there be altogether?

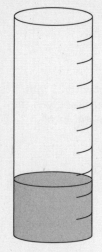

   (A) $\frac{3}{4}$ cup
   (B) 1 cup
   (C) $1\frac{3}{4}$ cups
   (D) 2 cups

24. The figure shown may be folded along one or more of the dotted lines. Which line or pair of lines will make the shapes connect to form a diamond?

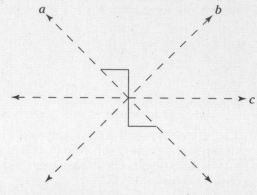

   (A) Line *a* only
   (B) Line *b* only
   (C) Line *c* only
   (D) Both line *a* and line *b*

25. The ingredients in the recipe were evenly mixed and divided into 7 bags.

   9 cups of chocolate candies

   8 cups of peanut butter cups

   6 cups of marshmallows

   4 cups of gummy bears

   1 cup of gumballs

   Approximately how many cups of the mixture were placed in each bag?
   (A) $3\frac{1}{2}$
   (B) 4
   (C) $4\frac{1}{2}$
   (D) 5

26. The scale on Andrew's map shows that 1.8 inches represents 1,000 miles. How many inches would it take to represent 3,500 miles?

   (A) 5.0 in
   (B) 5.8 in
   (C) 6.3 in
   (D) 7.0 in

Go on to next page

27. Mr. McElroy put all his black pens and red pens in a box. The probability that he pulls a red pen out of the box at random is 4 out of 15. If 44 black pens are in the box, how many red pens are in the box?

    (A) 8

    (B) 16

    (C) 32

    (D) 44

28. Use the diagram of the cube to answer the question. How many small cubes are used to build the large cube?

    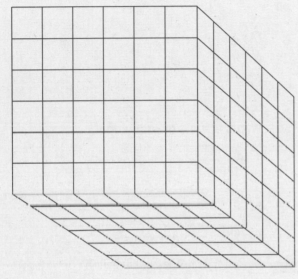

    (A) 36

    (B) 64

    (C) 216

    (D) 432

29. Four students recorded the number of minutes spent working on homework for one night in the graph shown. Based on this graph, which conclusion is true about the number of minutes spent doing homework?

    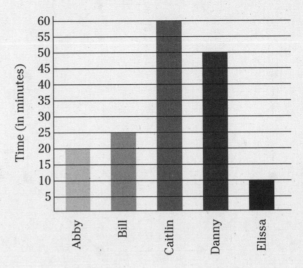

    (A) The mean is between 30 and 40.

    (B) Bill worked more minutes than Abby and Elissa combined.

    (C) The range is greater than the number of minutes Danny worked.

    (D) Caitlin worked the same number of minutes as Abby, Bill, and Elissa combined.

30. Which equation can be read as "4 less than 7 times a number is equal to 10 more than the number"? Let x represent the unknown number.

    (A) $4 - (7 \cdot x) = x + 10$

    (B) $(7 \cdot x) - 4 = x + 10$

    (C) $4 - (7 \cdot x) = 10x$

    (D) $(7 \cdot x) - 4 = 10x$

Go on to next page

31. Use the figure shown to answer the question. How many triangular regions can be made in the figure by drawing line segments only from vertex Q to the other vertices?

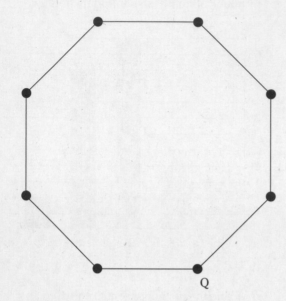

Q

(A) 5

(B) 6

(C) 7

(D) 8

32. Rosemary has a box full of jars containing six different kinds of spices, one kind per jar: cinnamon, sage, thyme, parsley, pepper, and clove. The probability of choosing a jar of thyme is 2 out of 11. Which combination of jars is possible?

(A) 2 jars of thyme and 11 others

(B) 4 jars of thyme and 11 others

(C) 2 jars of thyme and 13 others

(D) 4 jars of thyme and 18 others

33. Peter did the problem shown with his calculator: $\frac{89 \times 246}{35}$. What is a reasonable estimation for this answer?

(A) Between 400 and 500

(B) Between 500 and 600

(C) Between 600 and 700

(D) Between 700 and 800

34. What is the value of n in the expression $\frac{40(16+64)}{4} = n$?

(A) 200

(B) 400

(C) 800

(D) 1600

35. Use the number line shown to answer the question. P is the average of Q and another number. What is the other number?

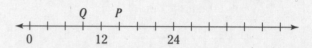

(A) 3

(B) 9

(C) 15

(D) 21

36. Which is the largest fraction?

(A) $\frac{6}{9}$

(B) $\frac{12}{18}$

(C) $\frac{3}{4}$

(D) $\frac{101}{200}$

37. A pool that holds 20,000 gallons of water is $\frac{3}{4}$ full. How many gallons of water are in the pool?

(A) 5,000

(B) 12,000

(C) 14,000

(D) 15,000

38. If 5 bips equals 3 bops, then 5 bips + 3 bops = how many bips?

(A) 5

(B) 8

(C) 10

(D) 13

STOP DO NOT TURN THE PAGE UNTIL TOLD TO DO SO.
DO NOT RETURN TO A PREVIOUS TEST.

Section 3
Reading Comprehension

Time: 25 Minutes

Directions: You have 25 minutes to read each passage and answer the questions about the passage that follow. Mark your answer to each question in the corresponding answer bubble on the answer sheet for Section 3.

Nature is often <u>thrifty</u>, meaning it uses and reuses its own natural resources. One example of this <u>phenomenon</u> is the hermit crab. The hermit crab, technically called a *decapod crustacean* of the Paguroidea family, is an ocean crab of which more than 1,100 species exist. Hermit crabs are different than typical crabs that have a hard shell, which protects the abdomen area; a hermit crab's shell is soft, leaving the animal easily exposed to attacks. So the hermit crab does something industrious to protect itself: It uses a discarded shell that once belonged to another ocean animal, often a snail. The hermit crab finds an empty shell it can fit into, and then simply carries this shell around as if it were his own. The hermit crab always finds a shell that he can completely retract into during times of threat or attack. As the crab grows, he has to abandon the shell and find a new, larger one to <u>accommodate</u> his body. This behavior is why the hermit crab is named such. A *hermit* is someone who lives alone.

1. What does the author mean by the word *thrifty?*

   (A) Not wasteful

   (B) Careful

   (C) Smart

   (D) Sharing

2. What does the author most likely mean by the word *phenomenon?*

   (A) Tested

   (B) Event

   (C) Unnatural

   (D) Direct action

3. Which of the following words can you use to replace the word *accommodate* in this passage?

   (A) Expose

   (B) Style

   (C) Design

   (D) Fit

4. According to the passage, what kind of shell does the hermit crab often use?

   (A) Snail

   (B) Blue crab

   (C) Octopus

   (D) Another hermit crab's shell

5. All the following are true *except*

   (A) More than 1,100 species of hermit crabs exist.

   (B) Hermit crabs kill other animals in order to take their shell.

   (C) Hermit crabs outgrow shells and have to replace them.

   (D) Hermit crabs have a soft abdomen.

Go on to next page

Amelia Earhart, born July 24, 1897, is considered an American aviation <u>pioneer</u>. As a pilot, Earhart received numerous awards, including the U.S. Distinguished Flying Cross for flying solo across the Atlantic Ocean. She was the first woman to ever receive this award. Additionally, Earhart authored two bestselling books about her flying experiences, and she helped start *The Ninety-Nines,* an organization for women pilots. Along with flying, Earhart joined the faculty at Purdue University in 1935 as a visiting faculty member.

On July 2, 1937, Earhart disappeared over the Pacific Ocean during an attempted flight around the world. She was legally declared dead in 1939, but her disappearance is still a subject of conversation today. Most historians believe she either crashed at sea or on a small island. Other theories say she managed to land the plane but was captured by islanders, and one theory even states that the entire disappearance was staged so Earhart could take on an assumed identity. Because her body was never recovered, the world will most likely never know for certain what happened to her.

6. What does the author mean by the word *pioneer?*

   (A) Aircraft developer

   (B) First to do something

   (C) A dangerous job

   (D) A researcher

7. Why did Earhart receive the U.S. Distinguished Flying Cross?

   (A) Because she was the first woman pilot

   (B) Because she could fly faster than most other aviators

   (C) Because she flew across the Atlantic Ocean

   (D) Because she wrote two bestsellers

8. Which of the following would be an effective title for this passage?

   (A) Who is Amelia Earhart?

   (B) Famous Pilots

   (C) Flying across the Ocean

   (D) Theories about Earhart's Disappearance

9. According to the passage, all the following are true *except*

   (A) She disappeared over the Atlantic.

   (B) She was a professor at Purdue.

   (C) No one really knows what happened to Earhart.

   (D) Earhart wrote two bestsellers.

10. What is the most likely reason so many theories exist about Earhart's disappearance?

    (A) She wanted to escape her life.

    (B) Some people were chasing her.

    (C) Her body or plane was never found.

    (D) The disappearance was strange.

Go on to next page

> The following passage is from Aesop's Fables. A fable is a fictional story, often about animals, that has a moral point.

A Man and his son were once going with their Donkey to market. As they were walking along by its side a countryman passed them and said: "You fools, what is a Donkey for but to ride upon?"

So the Man put the Boy on the Donkey and they went on their way. But soon they passed a group of men, one of whom said: "See that lazy youngster, he lets his father walk while he rides."

So the Man ordered his Boy to get off, and got on himself. But they hadn't gone far when they passed two women, one of whom said to the other: "Shame on that lazy lout to let his poor little son trudge along."

Well, the Man didn't know what to do, but at last he took his Boy up before him on the Donkey. By this time they had come to the town, and the passers-by began to jeer and point at them. The Man stopped and asked what they were scoffing at. The men said: "Aren't you ashamed of yourself for over-loading that poor donkey of yours and your hulking son?"

The Man and Boy got off and tried to think what to do. They thought and they thought, till at last they cut down a pole, tied the donkey's feet to it, and raised the pole and the donkey to their shoulders. They went along amid the laughter of all who met them till they came to Market Bridge, when the Donkey, getting one of his feet loose, kicked out and caused the Boy to drop his end of the pole. In the struggle the Donkey fell over the bridge, and his fore-feet being tied together he was drowned. "That will teach you," said an old man who had followed them: "Please all, and you will please none."

11. Why did the boy and the man try different combinations of riding and leading the donkey?

    (A) They didn't understand the donkey.

    (B) The journey was long.

    (C) The donkey was uncomfortable.

    (D) They listened to the advice of others.

12. Why was the man criticized for letting his child ride the donkey while he walked alongside?

    (A) The donkey should be carrying more.

    (B) The child was ungrateful.

    (C) The child was being lazy.

    (D) The donkey was too small.

13. Why did the donkey drown?

    (A) The man held him under the water.

    (B) His feet were tied.

    (C) He could not swim.

    (D) The story does not say.

14. When the man and his son both rode the donkey, why were they criticized?

    (A) For making a public scene

    (B) For not watching where they were going

    (C) For being lazy

    (D) For overloading the donkey

15. The moral of the story is found in the last sentence. How can you rephrase this moral?

    (A) Never try to please other people.

    (B) Don't take everyone's advice.

    (C) Do whatever you want to do.

    (D) No one knows what a donkey needs.

Go on to next page

> *The following passage is taken from Harry S. Truman's inaugural address.*

Each period of our national history has had its special challenges. Those that confront us now are as momentous as any in the past. Today marks the beginning not only of a new administration, but of a period that will be eventful, perhaps <u>decisive</u>, for us and for the world.

It may be our lot to experience, and in large measure to bring about, a major turning point in the long history of the human race. The first half of this century has been marked by <u>unprecedented</u> and brutal attacks on the rights of man, and by the two most frightful wars in history. The supreme need of our time is for men to learn to live together in peace and harmony.

The peoples of the earth face the future with grave uncertainty, composed almost equally of great hopes and great fears. In this time of doubt, they look to the United States as never before for good will, strength, and wise leadership.

It is fitting, therefore, that we take this occasion to proclaim to the world the essential principles of the faith by which we live, and to declare our aims to all peoples.

The American people stand firm in the faith which has inspired this Nation from the beginning. We believe that all men have a right to equal justice under law and equal opportunity to share in the common good. We believe that all men have the right to freedom of thought and expression. We believe that all men are created equal because they are created in the image of God.

From this faith we will not be moved.

16. What does the author most likely mean by the word *decisive?*

    (A) Crucial

    (B) Spontaneous

    (C) Reverent

    (D) Impossible

17. Which expresses the main idea of the passage?

    (A) The United States can stop future wars.

    (B) The world has many problems and will have many more.

    (C) Weapons must be reduced.

    (D) Peace and harmony are needed around the world.

18. What does the word *unprecedented* most likely mean in this passage?

    (A) Typical

    (B) Never happening before

    (C) An unworthy praise

    (D) A fearful outlook

19. Based on the passage, the author would most likely agree with which statement?

    (A) Freedom is not as important as justice.

    (B) Freedom is something most people cannot have.

    (C) The whole world is free, but people just do not know it yet.

    (D) Freedom is a right everyone should have.

20. How could you rephrase the last line of the passage?

    (A) We have to keep trying.

    (B) We are stronger than everyone else in every way.

    (C) No one will stop us from believing what we believe.

    (D) We will never give up.

Go on to next page

The tarantula is one of the most fearsome-looking spiders and one that most people go to great lengths to avoid. The tarantula is a large spider (often 3 inches long and 3 inches tall) with hairy legs and a hairy body, often dark red to black in color. Even spookier, tarantulas have eight eyes in two groups of four (although tarantulas do not see very well). The mouth sits below the eyes with two larger fangs. Near the fangs are two *pedipalps,* which are little leg-like appendages that help push food into the mouth. Like most spiders, tarantulas can produce silk, and they have eight legs.

About 850 species of tarantulas exist in various locations around the world, including North and South America, Australia, New Zealand, Africa, Madagascar, as well as many others. Tarantulas tend to live in drier regions and make their homes in the ground, often around the roots of trees which offer camouflage and protection. Like other spiders, tarantulas eat insects. As frightening as tarantulas are, they are not harmful to humans and can be good pets as they become tame with handling. Most tarantulas in North America have venomous hairs on their abdomen and can even use their legs to throw the hairs onto predators, but these hairs are harmless to humans. Of course, a tarantula can bite you, but other than some pain and discomfort, similar to a wasp or bee sting, tarantula bites are not dangerous.

21. Which is a fact about the tarantula's eyes?

    (A) They have no eyelids.

    (B) Their vision is poor.

    (C) They rotate counterclockwise.

    (D) All eight are in a row.

22. According to the passage, what are pedipalps?

    (A) Fangs

    (B) Additional short legs

    (C) Poisonous hairs

    (D) Appendages near the mouth

23. According to the passage, all the following statements are true *except*

    (A) Tarantulas are not dangerous to humans.

    (B) Tarantulas are not poisonous.

    (C) Tarantulas eat insects.

    (D) Tarantulas make silk.

24. Why do some people have tarantulas as pets?

    (A) They reduce insects in the home.

    (B) The owners are immune to the venom.

    (C) They tame easily.

    (D) They are friendly to other pets.

25. When the author says that tarantula bites are not dangerous, what does he most likely mean?

    (A) Their poison has a numbing effect.

    (B) There is no pain with a bite.

    (C) They do not cause permanent harm.

    (D) They cannot break the skin.

STOP DO NOT TURN THE PAGE UNTIL TOLD TO DO SO. DO NOT RETURN TO A PREVIOUS TEST.

Section 4

Mathematics Achievement

Time: 30 Minutes

Directions: You have 30 minutes to answer the following 30 mathematics questions. Mark your answer to each question in the corresponding answer bubble on the answer sheet for Section 4.

1. Use the triangle to answer the question. What is the perimeter of the triangle? ($P = s + s + s$)

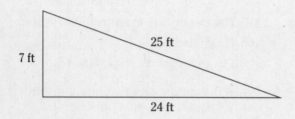

(A) 54 ft

(B) 56 ft

(C) 58 ft

(D) 60 ft

2. A total of 48 students were asked which one of three colors — pink, orange, or turquoise — they liked best. If 23 students said they preferred turquoise and 9 students said they preferred pink, how many students said they preferred orange?

(A) 10

(B) 12

(C) 14

(D) 16

3. What is the name of a six-sided figure with sides of equal length?

(A) Pentagon

(B) Hexagon

(C) Octagon

(D) Sphere

4. What is the standard form for one million eighty-nine thousand twenty-seven?

(A) 189,027

(B) 189,270

(C) 1,089,027

(D) 1,890,027

5. Use the number line to answer the question. What number is represented by point P on the number line?

(A) 54

(B) 56

(C) 58

(D) 59

6. What is the value of the expression 298 + 694?

(A) 982

(B) 992

(C) 1,002

(D) 1,012

7. Which expression is equal to 30?

(A) $(4 \times 8) + 8 - 10$

(B) $4 \times (8 \times 8) - 10$

(C) $4 \times 8 + (-10)$

(D) $4 \times (8 + 8 - 10)$

Go on to next page

8. A class planted a bean in three different pots to watch the beans grow. One pot was put in a sunny spot outside, another pot was put in a shady spot outside, and the third pot was kept indoors. The table shows the data collected. At eight weeks, how much taller was the bean sprout in the sunny pot than the bean sprout in the shady pot?

Start	Sunny Pot	Shady Pot	Indoor Pot
1 week	2 inches	1 inch	1 inch
2 weeks	6 inches	3 inches	2 inches
3 weeks	9 inches	7 inches	2 inches
4 weeks	12 inches	9 inches	4 inches
5 weeks	16 inches	10 inches	5 inches
6 weeks	21 inches	11 inches	7 inches
7 weeks	24 inches	13 inches	8 inches
8 weeks	27 inches	14 inches	8 inches

(A) 7 inches

(B) 12 inches

(C) 13 inches

(D) 19 inches

9. Which fraction is equivalent to 0.02?

(A) $\frac{1}{2}$

(B) $\frac{2}{10}$

(C) $\frac{2}{100}$

(D) $\frac{2}{1,000}$

10. What is the value of the expression $9,000 - 175$?

(A) 8,725

(B) 8,825

(C) 8,875

(D) 8,925

11. If $4 \times (^\wedge + 3) = 44$, what number does $^\wedge$ stand for?

(A) 6

(B) 7

(C) 8

(D) 9

12. Jennifer buys five items that cost $4.51, $8.99, $10.52, $3.01, and $4.99. What is the estimated total cost of Jennifer's items?

(A) Between $20.00 and $25.00

(B) Between $25.00 and $30.00

(C) Between $30.00 and $35.00

(D) Between $35.00 and $40.00

Go on to next page ⟹

13. The graph shows the numbers of animals at a zoo. How many more flamingoes are there than hummingbirds?

Population of Animals at the Zoo

Lions	☆
Hummingbirds	☆☆☆☆
Lizards	☆☆☆
Hippos	☆
Flamingoes	☆☆☆☆☆☆

☆ = 15 animals

(A) 3

(B) 15

(C) 30

(D) 45

14. Country Z has an area of 39,102 square miles. Which country has an area closest to $\frac{1}{4}$ that of Country Z?

(A) Country A, which has an area of 9,987 mi²

(B) Country B, which has an area of 11,802 mi²

(C) Country C, which has an area of 13,013 mi²

(D) Country D, which has an area of 13,907 mi²

15. If 8 black checkers and 12 red checkers are in a bag and one checker is taken out of the bag at random, what is the chance that it will be a black checker?

(A) 1 out of 5

(B) 1 out of 4

(C) 2 out of 5

(D) 2 out of 3

16. A diver received scores from ten judges for her dive at a competition. The ten scores were 7.9, 7.9, 8.1, 8.2, 8.4, 8.4, 8.4, 8.8, 9.1, and 9.2. What is the mode of the set of scores?

(A) 7.9

(B) 8.4

(C) 8.44

(D) 1.3

17. Use the set of numbers shown to answer the question.

{2, 13, 17, 29, 41, . . .}

Which of the following describes this set of numbers?

(A) Odd numbers

(B) Even numbers

(C) Prime numbers

(D) Irrational numbers

18. If the area of a triangle is 10 square centimeters, which equation can be used to determine the height of that triangle? ($A = \frac{1}{2}bh$, where A = Area, l = length, and w = width)

(A) $h = \frac{20}{b}$

(B) $h = \frac{b}{20}$

(C) $h = 20 - b$

(D) $h = b - 20$

19. Which fraction is between $\frac{1}{4}$ and $\frac{3}{4}$?

(A) $\frac{1}{5}$

(B) $\frac{2}{9}$

(C) $\frac{2}{3}$

(D) $\frac{4}{5}$

20. Use the number sequence to answer the question.

3, 6, 10, 15, 21, 28, _____

What is the next number in the sequence?

(A) 29

(B) 35

(C) 36

(D) 41

Go on to next page ⟹

21. When it is 9 a.m. in Boston, it is 6 a.m. in San Diego, because San Diego is in a different time zone than Boston. An airplane leaves Boston at 8 a.m. and arrives in San Diego six hours later. What time is it in San Diego when the airplane lands?

    (A) 11 a.m.

    (B) 2 p.m.

    (C) 5 p.m.

    (D) 8 p.m.

22. What is the sum of 5.8 and 2.3?

    (A) $7\frac{9}{10}$

    (B) $8\frac{1}{10}$

    (C) $9\frac{1}{10}$

    (D) $9\frac{3}{10}$

23. What is the perimeter of a rectangle that has a length of 11 inches and a width of 9 inches?

    (A) 20 in

    (B) 30 in

    (C) 40 in

    (D) 99 in

24. If a plank of wood measures $9\frac{7}{8}$ feet and $4\frac{1}{4}$ feet are cut off, how long is the piece of wood that remains?

    (A) $5\frac{1}{2}$ ft

    (B) $5\frac{5}{8}$ ft

    (C) $5\frac{7}{8}$ ft

    (D) $6\frac{1}{8}$ ft

25. Use the coordinate grid to answer the question. What are the coordinates of point P in the figure?

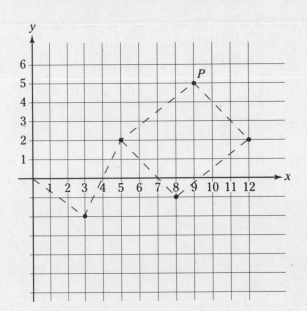

    (A) (5, 9)

    (B) (9, 5)

    (C) (6, 9)

    (D) (9, 6)

26. What is the sum of 19 and the product of 19 and 2?

    (A) 40

    (B) 57

    (C) 363

    (D) 399

27. The square root of 79 is closest to

    (A) 7

    (B) 8

    (C) 9

    (D) 40

Go on to next page

28. What is the volume of a box measuring 6 inches by 8 inches by 10 inches?

    (A) 24 sq in
    (B) 48 sq in
    (C) 140 sq in
    (D) 480 sq in

29. If Victoria has read 39 out of 60 books in a series, what percentage of the books has she read?

    (A) 40%
    (B) 55%
    (C) 65%
    (D) 80%

30. Which of the following is equivalent to 1.6 hours?

    (A) 1 hr and 6 min
    (B) 1 hr and 36 min
    (C) 1 hr and 48 min
    (D) 1 hr and 56 min

STOP DO NOT TURN THE PAGE UNTIL TOLD TO DO SO. DO NOT RETURN TO A PREVIOUS TEST.

Section 5

Essay

Time: 30 Minutes

Directions: You have 30 minutes to complete an essay based on the following essay topic. Use only two pages for your essay. You may use scratch paper to organize your thoughts before you begin writing.

    Topic: Write about someone who has made a difference in your life.

Assignment: Write about this person and be sure to include details about how this person has made a difference in your life.

Chapter 28

Answers to ISEE Lower Level Practice Exam

....

*N*ow that you've finished taking the ISEE Lower Level Practice Exam, spend time reading through the answers and explanations we provide in this chapter. Doing so is a great way to find out what you missed and why. Also, reading through *all* the explanations — even for the questions you got right — only increases your learning and understanding and helps you prepare even more for test day. If you just want to do a quick check of your answers, see the abbreviated answer key at the end of this chapter.

Section 1: Verbal Reasoning

1. **C.** *Paltry* means insignificant or unimportant, therefore Choice (C) is correct. For example, "The paltry snack was not enough food for the hungry child." In this sentence, *paltry* tells the reader the snack was insignificant or not substantial enough.

2. **B.** *Cryptic* means puzzling or difficult to understand. For example, "No one could understand the cryptic message," means the message was confusing or difficult. Choice (B) is the best answer.

3. **D.** *Oblivious* means to be unaware, or more simply, you just don't know what's going on around you. For example, you could say, "The child was oblivious to the homework assignment," which means the child was unaware of it. The correct answer is Choice (D).

4. **A.** *Bilk* means to cheat. You may say, "He bilked the bank out of millions of dollars."

5. **D.** A *bevy* is a group of something. You can use this word to refer to both people as well as animals. For example, you could say, "A bevy of birds landed in our yard." The correct answer is Choice (D).

6. **A.** *Bogus* means fake or false, so the correct answer is Choice (A). For example, "The bogus diamond necklace didn't fool anyone." This means the necklace was a fake.

7. **A.** *Replete* means full; therefore, the correct answer is Choice (A). For example, "The replete sound of the orchestra filled the auditorium," means the sound was full or complete.

8. **C.** *Covert* means undercover. For example, "The covert operation was planned carefully," meaning the operation was a secret or an undercover operation. Notice that Choices (A) and (B) sound similar to *covert.* Just because another word sounds similar doesn't mean the word means the same thing, so make sure you don't fall for this trap.

9. **A.** *Gaunt* means to be overly thin. For example, "The old man was rather gaunt," which means he was very thin. The correct answer is Choice (A).

10. **C.** *Inconsiderate* means rude or uncaring. In other words, someone who's inconsiderate doesn't consider the needs of others. For example, "The inconsiderate waitress made the dinner less than enjoyable." This means the waitress was rude.

11. **B.** *Predictable* means able to predict or understand the outcome of something or how someone may act. For example, "Because reviewed the material so carefully, the math test was predictable." This means one could guess what content would be on the test.

12. **A.** Someone who's arrogant thinks more of himself than he should. The best answer is *proud.*

You need to find the word that's closest to the capitalized word, but you may not find a word that technically defines the word in question, so just find the closest match.

13. **C.** *Defend* means to protect or stand up for someone or something. For example, "His older brother defended him against the bully."

14. **A.** *Scruffy* means unkempt or messy. For example, "The cat's scruffy appearance made him look like a stray."

15. **C.** *Stealthy* means sneaky or secretive, so the correct answer is Choice (C). For example, "No one noticed the stealthy dog approaching." In other words, the dog was sneaky.

16. **B.** *Generous* means to give freely or to be unselfish. For example, "The generous woman donated several thousand dollars to the school."

17. **B.** *Distracted* means to not pay attention or to be *inattentive.* For example, "The distracted student didn't hear the teacher's instructions." This means the student wasn't paying attention to what the teacher was saying.

18. **A.** The problem was *challenging* or difficult because she couldn't find a correct answer. Choice (A) is the best word that completes the meaning of the sentence.

19. **B.** The best answer is *treacherous,* which means dangerous or difficult. This word completes the meaning of the sentence. For example, you could say, "The hiking trail was treacherous," which means it was difficult or even dangerous.

20. **D.** *Zenith* means the highest point, so Choice (D) is correct. For example, "The climbers reached the zenith before noon," which means they reached the highest point of the climb.

21. **C.** *Verbatim* means exact copy or word for word, so the correct answer is Choice (C). For example, "The student took the statement verbatim from the book," which means the statement was an exact copy.

22. **A.** *Exasperated* means very irritated. After losing a game because of blunders, being exasperated would be an appropriate emotion.

23. **D.** *Intimidated* means to feel fearful due to a lack of some needed quality, often relating to other people. In this sentence, Carl feels intimated because the other boys are bigger.

24. **A.** *Callous* means insensitive, so Choice (A) is correct and the only word that completes the meaning of the sentence. For example, you could say, "His callous remarks angered all his friends," which means his comments were insensitive and, therefore, upsetting.

25. **D.** *Vacuous* means lacking ideas or substance. This word is the only one that makes sense within the context of the sentence. For example, "The speaker's talk was vacuous at best," means the speech lacked any real ideas or good content.

26. **A.** *Razed* means to completely destroy and is the only word that makes sense within the context of the sentence. For example, "The hurricane razed the entire area." This means everything was completely destroyed.

27. **D.** *Sequence* means a certain order of things. Because you know from the sentence that a series of steps had to be completed in order, *sequence* is the best word that completes the meaning of the sentence.

28. **C.** The only word that makes sense for this sentence is *consequences.* A consequence is a result. For example, you could say, "The consequence of not studying is often a bad grade."

29. **A.** A *junction* is a place where traffic routes cross, so in this sentence, only the word *junction* completes the meaning. For example, "We came to a junction in the road before we arrived at our destination."

30. **C.** *Crest* means highest point and is the only word that completes the meaning of this sentence. For example, you could say, "The crest of the wave was ten feet tall."

31. **A.** *Velocity* has to do with the speed and direction of a moving object. It's the only word that makes sense in the sentence. For example, "The velocity of the wind made our hike very difficult." This means the wind speed was fast and the direction of the wind was against the hikers.

32. **B.** *Trivial* means of little or no importance. This word is the only one that makes sense within the context of the sentence. For example, "The information the booklet provided was trivial" means the information wasn't important or helpful.

33. **B.** *Sustenance* means food and drink — the sentence is saying the team needed food.

34. **D.** *Catapult* means to hurl or throw something, so this word is the only one that makes sense within the context of the sentence. For example, "The hunter catapulted the spear into the air" means the hunter threw the spear.

Section 2: Quantitative Reasoning

1. **B.** Count the little triangles — there are 16 of them. Because six triangles are shaded, the fraction that's shaded is $\frac{6}{16}$, which reduces to $\frac{3}{8}$.

2. **B.** Sharing 40 books with 8 friends would mean dividing 40 by 8, which equals 5.

3. **C.** Because Judy has more than 9 cookies but fewer than 13, she can have 10, 11, or 12 cookies. If her number of cookies is greater than 11 but less than 15, she can have 12, 13, or 14 cookies. Only a total of 12 cookies makes both statements true.

4. **B.** To figure out the missing side, guess and check: See which answer choice, when added to the given sides ($18 + 27 = 45$), gives you 68. Or you can add the given sides and subtract the total from the perimeter ($68 - 45 = 23$).

5. **C.** Solve the first equation to find p (What number when subtracted from 7 results in 2? 5). Then find q (What number when subtracted from 9 gives you 3? 6). Then, $5 + 6 = 11$.

6. **A.** Use your visualization skills here. Better yet, sketch a complete square on the original drawing and look at the shape that's missing from the original. Check your answer by counting how many little squares are in between the original and the added piece. Because the original has four little squares on a side, the completed square should have 16 little square in total.

7. **D.** On problems like this one, seeing what happens in one of the things being measured can be helpful. In this case, find out how many minutes it takes Adela to go 1 mile. She goes 2 miles in 30 minutes, so divide 30 by 2 to get 15 minutes for 1 mile. And because Zariah runs the same speed, multiply 15 minutes by 3 miles to find how long it takes her to run 3 miles ($15 \times 3 = 45$).

8. **A.** The easiest way to do this problem is to notice that only one of the answer choices has a fraction larger than $\frac{1}{2}$. If a fraction is equal to $\frac{1}{2}$, its numerator is exactly one-half of its denominator. So if the numerator of a fraction is *more* than one-half of its denominator, it's larger than $\frac{1}{2}$. For Choice (A), 8 is more than half of 15. If you didn't know that, you can just divide 15 by 2 and get 7.5.

9. **D.** Pick a number for x to make this easier; just make sure you pick a number that both 5 and 7 go into evenly. An easy way to get one is to multiply $5 \times 7 = 35$; 35 can be divided by 35 with no remainder, so that's the answer. This technique works with any number for x that you pick, as long as 5 and 7 go into it (try 70, for example).

10. **A.** Check the answer choices. You need a number that's *both* of the following things: smaller than 10 and evenly divisible by 3. Only Choice (A), *6,* fits both categories.

11. **D.** Notice the pattern: At 1 teaspoon of salt, the boiling point went up 1 degree; at 2 teaspoons, it went up 2 degrees; at 3 teaspoons, it was up 3 degrees. Following the pattern, at 6 teaspoons, the boiling point will go up 6 degrees from where it was at 5 teaspoons: 227 + 6 = 233 degrees Fahrenheit.

12. **D.** Find the pattern: If you input 3, you get an output of 10, which is 7 more than 3. If you input 9, you get an output of 16, which is 7 more than 9. If you input 17, you get 24 (7 more than 17). So Choice (D), which adds 7 to the input, explains the rule.

13. **C.** If the triangle's sides are all equal and its perimeter is 6*s,* then you can divide 6*s* by 3 to get the length of one of the sides: $6s \div 3 = 2s$.

14. **B.** Either guess and check by plugging in the answer choices for *n* until you find one that works, or subtract 4 from both sides of the equation, giving you 16 = 4*n*. Then divide both sides by 4 to get *n* = 4.

15. **C.** Your best bet is to draw in the fifth, sixth, and seventh rows and then count the dots in the seventh row. Doing so can help you notice or confirm the pattern: Each additional row adds two dots to the number in the previous row. The fourth row has 8 dots; the fifth row, 10; the sixth, 12; and the seventh, 14.

16. **D.** Notice the pattern here: The exponent on the answer goes up one each time. Following this pattern, the exponent on the 7 equation should be 8.

17. **B.** You've got to estimate this one. You may notice that if you combine the red and purple sections, the circle divides into thirds; then, you can estimate that the purple section is half of a third, or one-sixth.

18. **A.** To find the mean (average) weight, set up an average equation: $\dfrac{10\frac{1}{2}+10\frac{1}{2}+11+11+11}{5} = mean$. Adding all the weights and dividing by 5 results in $54 \div 5 = 10.8$, which is the same as $10\frac{8}{10}$ ounces. You can also simply notice that the mean *must* be less than 11 because three cubs weigh 11 ounces and two weigh less. Only Choice (A) is a number less than 11.

19. **B.** On number line questions, use some trial and error to fill in the unlabeled marks. Because the marks on this number line are evenly spaced, you find that a distance of 2 separates each mark. So the arrows are pointing at 8.5 and 10.5. Testing the answer choices can work well on questions like this one.

20. **A.** Because *RS* and *TU* are both *x* in length, the distance from *R* to *T* must be the same as from *S* to *U.* Put some numbers into the problem to illustrate. For example, say *x* is 3. So *RS* and *TU* are both 3. Then, say *ST* is 9, so *RT,* or *y,* is 12. Now, just add *ST* to *TU*: 9 + 3 = 12, or *y*.

21. **D.** Round 892 to 900 and 27 to 30, so Choice (D) shows the best estimate.

22. **C.** Notice the marks on the side of the larger cube. You can fit four small cubes down the front right corner of the large cube, and you can fit four small cubes along the top front edge of the large cube. So 16 small cubes can fit against the front face of the large cube. And because you can fit four small cubes along the top right side of the large cube, you can make four layers of 16 cubes: $4 \times 16 = 64$.

23. **B.** This problem is a good one to estimate on rather than add the fractions. Notice that the skinny jar has ten sections. Because its water level goes up to between the second and third mark, it's about $\frac{1}{4}$ full. Because the entire skinny jar holds one cup, you can estimate that it has $\frac{1}{4}$ cup of water in it. The fat jar is $\frac{3}{4}$ full, because three of the four sections contain water. Therefore, it has about $\frac{3}{4}$ cup of water in it. Adding $\frac{1}{4}$ cup to $\frac{3}{4}$ cup equals 1 cup.

24. **B.** Try redrawing the figure on a see-through piece of paper to prove to yourself, if you can't visualize it, that only by folding the paper along line *b* forms a diamond.

25. **B.** Add all the amounts: $9 + 8 + 6 + 4 + 1 = 28$. Then, divide 28 by 7 bags to get 4 cups per bag.

26. **C.** If 1.8 inches is 1,000 miles, then double that ($1.8 + 1.8 = 3.6$) is 2,000 miles. Another 1.8 ($1.8 + 3.6 = 5.4$) would be 3,000 miles. To figure out the extra 500 miles, just divide $1.8 \div 2 = 0.9$. Add 0.9 to 5.4 to get 6.3 inches for 3,500 miles. Alternatively, set up a proportion: $\frac{1.8}{1,000} = \frac{x}{3,500}$ and solve for x by cross-multiplying.

27. **B.** If the probability of picking a red pen is 4 out of 15, that means that for every 15 pens, 4 of them are red, so 11 of the 15 are black. Now you can set up a proportion because you know the ratio of red to black pens is 4 to 11: $\frac{4}{11} = \frac{x}{44}$. Cross-multiply to get $11x = 176$, and then divide both sides by 11 to end up with $x = 16$.

28. **C.** The large cube is six little cubes across by six little cubes down by six little cubes deep: $6 \times 6 \times 6 = 216$. You can also think of the large cube as having six layers of 36 cubes (count the cubes in the front face and multiply by 6).

29. **A.** The mean, or average, is found by adding all the data and dividing that number by how many data there are. Adding $20 + 25 + 60 + 50 + 10$ gives you 165, and $165 \div 5 = 33$, so the mean is between 30 and 40.

30. **B.** The words "4 less" are the tricky part: They mean the number minus 4, *not* 4 minus the number. So "4 less than 7 times a number" is $7x - 4$, and "10 more than the number" is just $x + 10$. Choice (B) gets both parts right.

31. **B.** Draw a line from point Q to each vertex (the ones immediately to the left and right of Q don't count, because those lines are part of the octagon). Now, count the triangles that are formed.

32. **D.** If the probability of choosing thyme is 2 out of 11, you know that for every two jars of thyme, there are nine other jars. Now, you know the ratio of jars of thyme to other jars is 2 to 9. Looking at the answer choices, Choice (D) is 4 to 18, which reduces (divide both numbers by 2) to 2 to 9.

33. **C.** Round 89 to 90, 246 to 250, and *don't* round 35 (rounding too much isn't a good thing; when in doubt, round less). Then solve: $90 \times 250 = 22,500$, and $22,500 \div 35 =$ about 642.

34. **C.** Following PEMDAS, add the numbers in the parentheses first ($16 + 64 = 80$), and then make sure you multiply by 40. In PEMDAS, multiplication and division are technically tied, but work from top to bottom (and left to right). So $80 \times 40 = 3,200$, and $3,200 \div 4 = 800$.

35. **D.** Use trial and error to figure out the distance between the marks. Because three marks are between 0 and 12, you find that the missing marks are 3, 6, and 9. So Q is 9 and P must be 15. Now, you can set up your average equation: 15 is the average of 9 and another number, or $\frac{9 + x}{2} = 15$. Multiply both sides of that equation by 2 to simplify and get $x + 9 = 30$. Then, subtract 9 from both sides to end up with $x = 21$.

36. **C.** To compare the fractions, first reduce where you can. Choice (A) reduces to $\frac{2}{3}$ like so: $\frac{6 \div 3}{9 \div 3} = \frac{2}{3}$; so does Choice (B): $\frac{12 \div 6}{18 \div 6} = \frac{2}{3}$. Choice (D) can round to $\frac{100}{200} = \frac{1}{2}$, so it's out because the other choices are more than $\frac{1}{2}$. By process of elimination, Choice (C) is correct because it's more than Choices (A) and (B).

37. **D.** To find out how many gallons of water are in the pool, multiply $20,000 \times \frac{3}{4} = \frac{60,000}{4} = 15,000$.

38. **C.** Because you're being asked for the total in bips, convert everything to bips. If 3 bops equals 5 bips, rewrite the question as 5 bips + 5 bips = how many bips? Doing so makes it easier to see the answer is 10.

Section 3: Reading Comprehension

1. **A.** *Thrifty* means to save or not be wasteful, so Choice (A) is correct. The author uses this word to show how nature reuses sea shells.

2. **B.** A *phenomenon* is an event you can see or observe. The author mentions that nature is thrifty and then uses the hermit crab as an example of the phenomenon of nature being thrifty.

3. **D.** *Accommodate* means to have enough space for something. The only replacement word in the list of options is *fit*. In other words, the hermit crab has to find a shell that fits his body.

4. **A.** The passage tells you that snail shells are often used, so you simply need to find this answer in the passage.

5. **B.** The hermit crab doesn't kill other animals to get shells. It simply finds a shell that's already empty.

6. **B.** The word *pioneer* refers to someone who's first to do something, so the passage is saying that Earhart is an aviation pioneer or a first person to fly.

7. **C.** Earhart received the award for flying across the Atlantic Ocean. She was the first woman to accomplish this, but she didn't receive the award because she was a woman.

8. **A.** This passage gives you a short overview of Earhart's life, so the best title is simply *Who is Amelia Earhart?* The other title options are either too general or too specific for this passage.

9. **A.** Earhart disappeared over the Pacific Ocean, not the Atlantic Ocean, so Choice (A) is false. All the other statements are true.

10. **C.** Because neither Earhart nor her plane were ever found, a lot of ideas have formed about what may have happened to her. If she had been found, people would have less interest in theories or ideas, but because she was never found, this fact makes the disappearance even more mysterious.

11. **D.** Numerous people offered advice about who should ride the donkey. The man and his son listened to everyone's advice and kept trying to do what other people wanted.

12. **C.** The man is criticized for letting the child be lazy. The passerby said the child should be walking and the man should be riding the donkey.

13. **B.** The donkey's feet were tied together when he fell into the river, which caused him to drown.

14. **D.** They were criticized for overloading the donkey.

15. **B.** The moral of the story is stated as, "Please all, and you will please none." This means that if you try to please everyone, no one will be happy. In the answer choices, the best and closest meaning to this phrase is Choice (B), *Don't take everyone's advice.*

16. **A.** Decisive means that something is the deciding factor or the most crucial or important factor. For example, if you said, "Your argument was the most decisive in the debate," you're saying the argument was the most important.

17. **D.** The passage primarily promotes the concept that peace and harmony are the most important need of the day, as noted in the last line of the second paragraph. The rest of the passage focuses on this need.

18. **B.** *Unprecedented* means having no precedent or never happening before. For example, if you said, "The cold temperature was unprecedented in this part of the country," you mean the weather had never been that cold in the past.

19. **D.** The author mentions the importance of freedom several times in the passage and how he believes everyone in the world should have that right. Of the answer choices, Choice (D) is the best selection.

20. **C.** The statement, "From this faith we will not be moved," means that we won't give in, give up, or be stopped. To *not be moved* means to stand firm. So, of the answer choices provided, only Choice (C) contains the same meaning.

21. **B.** With this kind of question, you have to go on a quick fact-checking expedition. Just look at the statements and see which ones you can verify with the text. Of these answer choices, only Choice (B) is supported by the passage.

    As you're taking the test, don't read more into the questions and answer choices than what they say. If the passage doesn't verify a statement as true, then consider it to be false.

22. **D.** A *pedipalp* is an appendage near the tarantula's mouth that helps the spider eat.

23. **B.** Tarantulas do have poisonous hairs that cause pain and irritation to predators, but they're generally harmless to humans.

24. **C.** Tarantulas can make good pets because they tame easily with handling. Most tarantula owners can hold and pet the spider.

25. **C.** The author is saying that tarantula bites don't cause permanent harm. They do hurt, much like a wasp or bee sting, but a tarantula bite isn't serious, in that you wouldn't need medical help.

Section 4: Mathematics Achievement

1. **B.** Add the sides to get the perimeter: $7 + 24 + 25 = 56$.

2. **D.** The number of students who picked orange is equal to the total number of students (48) minus the students who picked turquoise and pink ($23 + 9 = 32$), so $48 - 32 - 16$.

3. **B.** Hexagons are six-sided figures. Pentagons have five sides; octagons have eight. A sphere is shaped like a ball.

4. **C.** Split this one up if you're not sure. First, write one million: 1,000,000. Below it, write eighty-nine thousand: 89,000. Below that, write twenty-seven: 27. Now, add the numbers, giving you 1,089,027.

5. **B.** Use trial and error to figure out that each of the marks between 60 and 70 is another 2. So one mark to the left of 60 is 58; two marks to the left of 60 is 56.

6. **B.** Add 'em up: $298 + 694 = 992$. Don't rush, even though it's basic arithmetic.

7. **A.** You have to test the choices here. Looking at Choice (A), PEMDAS tells you to multiply the numbers in the parentheses first ($4 \times 8 = 32$). Then, work from left to right: $32 + 8 = 40$, and $40 - 10 = 30$.

8. **C.** Compare the value for the sunny pot at eight weeks (27 inches) to the value for the shady pot at eight weeks (14 inches). Subtract to get the difference: $27 - 14 = 13$.

9. **C.** This question is simple enough: 0.02 is $\frac{2}{100}$. If you weren't sure of that, remember that 0.2 is $\frac{2}{10}$, so 0.02 is 10 times smaller than that.

10. **B.** Just subtract. You can check your answer by adding 175 to the result if you're not sure you did the subtraction correctly.

11. **C.** You can check the answer choices to see which one works. Plugging 8 in for the $^\wedge$ results in $4 \times (11) = 44$. Or simplify the equation by dividing both sides by 4, resulting in $(^\wedge + 3) = 11$. Then, subtract 3 from both sides to get $^\wedge = 8$.

12. **C.** Round the item costs to $4.50, $9.00, $10.50, $3.00, and $5.00, then add to get $32.00, which is between $30.00 and $35.00.

13. **C.** Count the flamingoes by multiplying 7 stars by 15 to get 105. Then, count the humming-birds by multiplying 5 stars by 15 to get 75. Subtract to get how many more flamingoes there are: 105 – 75 = 30.

14. **A.** Round 39,102 to 40,000. Looking at Choice (A), 9,987 can be rounded to 10,000. And 40,000 ÷ 10,000 = 4, so Country A has about a quarter of the area of Country Z.

15. **C.** Find the chance by realizing that 20 checkers are in the bag. The chance of picking a black checker is 8 out of 20. Then, reduce the fraction: $\frac{8}{20} = \frac{4}{10} = \frac{2}{5}$.

16. **B.** To find the mode, just look and see whether a number appears more often than any of the others. Three scores are 8.4, so 8.4 is the mode.

17. **C.** All the numbers in the set can be evenly divided only by themselves and 1, so they're all *prime*.

18. **A.** Set up the equation: 10, the area, $= \frac{1}{2}bh$. Next, divide both sides of the equation by $\frac{1}{2}$ to get 20 = bh. Now, look at the answer choices: They're written as h = something. So isolate h by dividing both sides by b to get $h = \frac{20}{b}$.

19. **C.** Convert all the fractions in the problem to a common denominator so you can compare them more easily. Looking at Choice (C), you need to find a number for a common denominator that both 3 and 4 divide into — the smallest number that they both go into is 12. Rewriting the fractions results in the following: $\frac{1}{4} = \frac{3}{12}$, $\frac{2}{3} = \frac{8}{12}$, $\frac{3}{4} = \frac{9}{12}$.

20. **C.** Notice that 3 + **3** = 6, 6 + **4** = 10, 10 + **5** = 15, 15 + **6** = 21, and 21 + **7** = 28. Following the pattern of adding a number that's one greater each time, add **8** to 28 to get 36.

21. **A.** The time in San Diego is three hours *earlier* than the time in Boston. A good trick for this problem is to imagine a person on the airplane wearing a watch. The person's watch says 8 a.m. when the plane takes off and then 2 p.m. (six hours later) when the plane lands, because the flight was six hours long. However, the person then needs to turn her watch *back* three hours, because San Diego is three hours earlier than Boston. Three hours earlier than 2 p.m. is 11 a.m.

22. **B.** Add the decimals: 5.8 + 2.3 = 8.1. Turning 8.1 into a fraction is easy; the 8 means eight ones and the 0.1 means one-tenth. So 8.1 is eight and one-tenth, or $8\frac{1}{10}$.

23. **C.** To find the perimeter, add all the sides. You may want to draw the rectangle so you can see what you're doing. Your drawing should have two sides measuring 11 inches and two sides measuring 9 inches: 11 + 11 + 9 + 9 = 40.

24. **B.** Give the fractions in the problem a common denominator so you can subtract them. Looking at $\frac{7}{8}$ and $\frac{1}{4}$, the denominator of the second fraction goes into the denominator of the first fraction evenly, so use 8 as the common denominator. So $4\frac{1}{4} = 4\frac{2}{8}$. Now, you can subtract more easily: $9\frac{7}{8} - 4\frac{2}{8} = 5\frac{5}{8}$.

25. **B.** To find the first number of the answer, count how many right from zero the point is (9). To figure out the second number, count how many up from zero it is (5). The answer is (9, 5).

26. **B.** *Sum* means add and *product* means multiply. So the sum of 19 and the product of 19 and 2 means 19 + 19 × 2. Remember PEMDAS and do the multiplication first: 19 × 2 = 38, and 19 + 38 = 57.

27. **C.** If you square the answer choices, you can easily see which one, when squared, is closest to 81. Choice (C) is the closest: $9 \times 9 = 81$.

28. **D.** To find the volume of a box, just multiply the length $\times$ the width $\times$ the height: $6 \times 8 = 48$, and $48 \times 10 = 480$.

29. **C.** To help think about how to calculate this percentage, you can use a fraction to show how many books Victoria has read: $\frac{39}{60}$. To find the percentage, divide 39 by 60: $39 \div 60 = 0.65$, which converts to 65 percent.

30. **B.** To answer this question, convert 0.6 hours to minutes. Because 1 hour is 60 minutes, you can simply multiply 60 by 0.6 to get 36 minutes, which is 0.6 of an hour. So the answer is 1 hour and 36 minutes.

Section 5: Writing Sample

Remember that writing samples for the ISEE don't have right or wrong answers, and with this topic (write about someone who has made a difference in your life), you can write about many different things. So don't get caught up in thinking, "Did I write what they wanted?" because truthfully, the readers of your writing sample don't care what you write about. They simply want to see that you can organize your thoughts, show your writer's voice, and write a strong essay.

With that thought in mind, the following are a few things you should have done in order to write a winning essay for your practice test. (For more valuable tips on writing an effective essay and some examples, check out Chapter 8.)

✔ Because the essay prompt asks you to write about a person who's made a difference in your life, you should have chosen one person and explained in your essay *why* and *how* that person made a difference. When you write the introduction, make sure you're very clear about who you're writing about. For example, including a statement such as, "My grandfather is a person who has made a big difference in my life," helps the reader get a clear understanding of who you're writing about.

✔ Your body paragraphs should have included specific examples that help back up or explain why and how this person made a difference to you. These examples can be personal experiences that prove how this person made a difference. To make this essay really work, you should have explained your own feelings about this person. Remember that the readers want to hear your voice. Including a personal story or experience is a great way to make a writing sample really come to life for the reader.

✔ You should have included a conclusion that brought your ideas together and again affirmed your position on the essay. Conclusions help show that your thoughts and ideas are organized and that you stuck with the topic, so don't forget about the conclusion when you write.

Finally, have someone else read your essay and mark misspelled words, poorly organized sentences, misplaced commas, and other grammatical problems. Doing so helps you see how many errors you made. Remember that the writing sample isn't a grammar test, and a few errors won't hurt you in the end, but overall, your sample should be well written and generally error free.

Answers at a Glance

Section 1: Verbal Reasoning

1. C	8. C	15. C	22. A	29. A
2. B	9. A	16. B	23. D	30. C
3. D	10. C	17. B	24. A	31. A
4. A	11. B	18. A	25. D	32. B
5. D	12. A	19. B	26. A	33. B
6. A	13. C	20. D	27. D	34. D
7. A	14. A	21. C	28. C	

Section 2: Quantitative Reasoning

1. C	9. D	17. B	25. B	33. C
2. B	10. A	18. A	26. C	34. C
3. C	11. D	19. B	27. B	35. D
4. B	12. D	20. A	28. C	36. C
5. C	13. C	21. D	29. A	37. D
6. A	14. B	22. C	30. B	38. C
7. D	15. C	23. B	31. B	
8. A	16. D	24. B	32. D	

Section 3: Reading Comprehension

1. A	6. B	11. D	16. A	21. B
2. B	7. C	12. C	17. D	22. D
3. D	8. A	13. B	18. B	23. B
4. A	9. A	14. D	19. D	24. C
5. B	10. C	15. B	20. C	25. C

Section 4: Mathematics Achievement

1. B	7. A	13. C	19. C	25. B
2. D	8. C	14. A	20. C	26. B
3. B	9. C	15. C	21. A	27. C
4. C	10. B	16. B	22. B	28. D
5. B	11. C	17. C	23. C	29. C
6. B	12. C	18. A	24. B	30. B

Part VI
The Part of Tens

The 5th Wave   By Rich Tennant

"I went around to all the businesses in town collecting new words for the vocabulary part of the SSAT. I learned a lot of new words related to not being annoying."

In this part . . .

Part VI provides a couple of quick reference lists to help you get ready for test day. Here, you'll find ten quick tips to prepare for the day of the test and ten helpful ways to calm the test-day jitters. Just tuck these tips into your hat so you keep them on top of your head.

Chapter 29

Ten Tips for Test Day

· ·

In This Chapter

▶ Getting organized and ready for the big day

▶ Giving yourself a competitive edge

▶ Taking care of number one — you!

· ·

You've taken plenty of tests at this point in your student career. So the idea of taking the SSAT or ISEE may not seem like a big deal because test taking is nothing new. However, as we stress throughout the book, taking a standardized test is a lot different than taking an exam for a class at school. As such, you need to study and prepare differently (hence, this book's existence), and you also need to do a little bit of self-preparation to give you the edge you need for test day. The ten tips in this chapter go beyond just showing you how to answer the questions; they help you prepare for the actual day of the test, from getting everything ready the night before to the moment you pick up your pencil to fill in that first answer bubble.

Get Organized

Okay, you've heard over and over that you need to be organized for most things in life, so you're probably tempted to skip this tip, but don't! The good news about getting organized for the SSAT or ISEE is that you don't need a lot of items for test day. Likely, you need only a few pencils, a couple of pens, an admission ticket, a form of ID, and maybe a snack (see the next section and check out Chapter 1 for a list of what to bring to each test). So although you don't have much stuff to worry about, you'd be shocked at how often students forget to bring something they really need — even pencils!

Make it easy on yourself and do this: The evening before your test, check the list of things you need in Chapter 1, and then round up those items and put them together in a place where you won't forget them, such as on a chair in your bedroom or even on the kitchen table. This way, when you're getting ready to leave the next morning for your test, everything is organized and ready to go. Sounds simple, but when you're still trying to force yourself to eat breakfast and someone is yelling, "We have to leave in five minutes!" you won't have to worry about getting your stuff together.

Pack a Snack

You get a short break during the exam, and although you'll probably use that time to hit the restroom and get some water, you should also try to eat a quick snack. You can take a small snack to the testing center with you. Even if you think you won't need a snack, being prepared is better than realizing you're hungry with nothing to eat.

Your best bet is to take a protein bar, quality granola bar, or something like that. You want your snack to be easy, portable, quick to eat, and something that actually has real food in it. Studies have shown that good, nutritious food helps fuel the body and your brain. In short, you're likely to perform better if your system has good nutrition running through it. Strive for a snack that has a good protein-to-carb balance, which is why protein bars, energy bars, or even granola bars are a good choice. Most of these bars have a good mix of the nutrition you need. Doughnuts and candy are out, so leave those kinds of things at home.

Catch Plenty of Zzz's

The SSAT or ISEE may take place on a Saturday morning, and, let's face it: No one wants to go to bed early on a Friday night. But here's the deal: You need at least eight hours of uninterrupted sleep to give yourself the best competitive edge. Studies show time and time again that students who get a good night's sleep before a test do better than those who don't.

So the night before the test, get to bed on time — no movies, texting, or late night Internet surfing — and make sure you get a full night's sleep. After all, you've done the hard work of prepping for this test, and you don't want to let lack of sleep cause you to miss test questions.

Rise and Shine

You get up early and get ready for school nearly every day of your life, so why do we need to include a tip for rise and shine? One simple reason: Murphy's Law. This law basically states that if something can possibly go wrong on exam day, it probably will. To overcome Murphy's Law, you need to allow yourself extra time.

Plan to get up at least 30 minutes earlier than you normally get up. Doing so gives you a bit of extra time to overcome any morning obstacles you may face. Also, the extra time keeps you from having to rush around and feeling flustered by the time you reach the testing center.

Eat a Good Breakfast

If you're naturally a breakfast eater, you'll have no problem with this tip, but if you're not, you'll likely gag. Studies show that students who eat a nutritious breakfast perform better on tests than those who don't. The simple fact is your body and brain run on fuel that you give it. When you get up in the morning, your body has used all the available fuel you ate from the evening before. You need to feed your body and brain to help them perform well when you take the test, even if you don't normally like to eat breakfast.

So what should you eat? The day of the test isn't the day to have a chocolate doughnut or two. Instead, choose protein and complex carbohydrate foods, such as quality cereals, eggs, oatmeal, fruit, yogurt, and other foods that actually have real nutritional value. Eat, but don't overdo it — test day isn't the best time to eat a stack of pancakes at your favorite restaurant because they may make you feel tired and sluggish.

Resist the Urge to Study

If you're really industrious, getting up at 5 a.m. and studying for a while before you go take the test may sound like a good idea. *Wrong!* Time and time again, educational studies show that students who cram before a test often don't do as well. If you cram, you're actually causing your brain and eyes additional work before you even get to the testing center. This cramming leads to fatigue, and when you get tired, you start missing questions. When you cram, you cause your brain and body to begin the test after already expending some of its resources. So your best bet is to study on the days before the exam and let your brain rest on the morning of the test, making sure it's fresh for the actual exam. Your brain cells will thank you.

Review the Test Order

Although you shouldn't cram for the exam the morning of the test, reviewing the different sections and the number of questions you'll face on the test is a good idea. Doing so gives you a quick mental reminder of how the test is structured and what to expect. You don't need to spend more than five minutes reviewing the test order, so don't make this easy exercise hard. Check out Chapter 1 for more info about the sections and numbers of questions you'll see on the exam.

Get out the Door on Time

Because you have all your stuff rounded up and your snack packed, you should be able to get out the door and on the way to the testing center with ease. That said, make sure you know where the testing center is and how long it'll take to get there, factoring in time for traffic. In short, the day of the test isn't the day to be running late, so know before you go to bed exactly when you must leave your house. Then, plan your morning so you're able to get out the door on time and with ease.

Arrive a Bit Early

Along with getting out the door on time, arriving a bit early (ideally 30 minutes) to the testing center is helpful. Getting there early gives you plenty of time to check in and go to the restroom before the test begins. Also, the extra few minutes gives you some time to relax and mentally get ready for the test to begin. The SSAT or ISEE is one occasion where you don't want to show up fashionably late.

Depending on the time of year you take the test and where you live, you may also need to factor the weather into your arrival time. Snowy or stormy conditions can certainly slow down a commute, so always make plans to arrive early. If you're a bit too early, that's fine, but you can't be a bit too late. (If you're late, you may not be able to take the exam.) It's always better to be safe than sorry!

Take a Deep Breath and Dive In

When you're ready to start to take the test, take a deep breath and begin. Each section of the test is timed so you need to work quickly and smartly. The good news is you've used this book to practice, so you're familiar with the kinds of questions you'll see and working under pressure. Don't forget the many tips and tactics you've explored as you've studied. Success is all about working efficiently and carefully, so do your best and keep your cool.

If you think you'll feel a bit nervous (which many students do), be sure to check out Chapter 30. That chapter gives you ten tried and true tips for calming test-day nerves!

Chapter 30

Ten Ways to Calm Your Nerves

You don't need us to tell you that test taking can be nerve wracking. The SSAT and ISEE may be even more so because you're using one of these tests to help you get into a school you want to attend. With that issue on the line, feeling a bit nervous is only natural.

Many times, people try to control nervousness by simply willing it away or pretending it's not there. Yet how often have you been able to simply will a problem away or pretend it's not there? Instead of focusing on *not* being nervous, which doesn't work, focus on reducing the symptoms of nervousness so you can spend your time getting all those test answers correct. We show you how to calm your test-day nerves in this chapter with ten easy tips.

Check Your Breathing

When you get nervous, your body and mind naturally want to breathe in a more erratic and shallow manner. This reaction is part of your nervous system's *fight or flight* response. The problem is when you take short, shallow breaths, you increase your body's oxygen levels, creating a host of other symptoms, such as shaky hands and the jitters in general. To control your breathing, try taking slow, steady breaths, even though you may not feel very steady. Just by breathing normally, you reduce a number of other nervous symptoms, which, in turn, helps you focus on the test.

Do Some Pacing

When you're nervous, your body creates more energy than you need as part of the fight or flight system. Because you're probably not going to be physically fighting or running during your test (at least let's hope not), you need to try to burn some of the extra energy your body has created due to nervousness.

Arriving at the testing center a bit early can help calm your nerves. After you check in, find an area, such as a hallway, to simply pace before you're seated for the test. Doing so helps you burn energy so you don't have as much pent-up energy to deal with when you're sitting and staring at that first question.

Use the Muscle Tension/Relaxation Technique

After you're seated for the test, you'll probably have a few moments before the test actually begins. You can use this time to burn a bit more energy and relax in an easy and inconspicuous way. This technique, known as the Muscle Tension/Relaxation Technique, can help you calm those test-day nerves. Starting with your legs, simply tense your calves as hard as you can for ten seconds and then relax them for ten seconds. Then, do the same thing again. Next, move to your thighs and do the same thing. Continue the pattern up your body, tensing and relaxing each major muscle group. Then, do the entire process again.

Your body requires energy to hold a muscle in a tensed state, so this simple technique helps you burn additional energy you don't need. When you're nervous and you purposefully burn energy, you help your body relax. Try it — it works!

Sing a Song (To Yourself Anyway!)

Bursting out into your favorite top-40 hit song for everyone to hear isn't a good idea (unless you want to get ushered out of the testing center), but you can sing a favorite song in your mind just before you start taking the test, which can help calm your nerves.

This trick is basically a distraction technique because you force your mind to focus on something other than being nervous. Also, you're focusing on something you enjoy and that makes you happy, and this mental exercise can help break down the cycle of nervousness because you're forcing yourself to focus on something relaxing.

Use Your Pencil as a Pointer

When you're nervous, your brain naturally wants to work quickly. That's actually a good thing because you need to move fast on the test anyway. However, if your brain is moving too quickly, you can easily misread questions and even skip over words. Working too quickly can cause you to misunderstand what a question is asking, which in turn can cause you to choose the wrong answer.

To combat this fact, use your pencil as a pointer and simply point to each word in the question and the answer choices. This little technique can help your brain slow down and focus on each word, making sure you read and understand the question correctly.

Slow Down

The SSAT and ISEE are both timed exams, so why do we suggest slowing down? Because nervous energy can put you in lightning mode where you're actually going too fast, you can misread and miss questions you'd otherwise answer correctly. The trick? Occasionally, just tell yourself to slow down. Sure, you need to be aware of the time limit, and you need to work quickly, but you don't want to work so quickly that you miss questions. In the end, just watch your pace and slow down if you feel like you're working too quickly.

Skip a Question

You won't know the answer to every question on the test — just accept that fact. However, a question you don't know can really turn your brain into soup and flood your system with frustration and nervousness. The problem is if you let a single question rattle you, the odds are good that you'll end up missing a question you'd probably be able to figure out. A simple trick to avoid this situation is to skip a question if you don't know how to answer it.

 You want to answer as many questions correctly as you can in order to get the best score, and dwelling on a question you can't figure out just wastes your time and makes you feel more nervous. The key is to know when to skip: If you just don't have any clue about the question, skip it and move on. If you have time, you can always come back to it after you answer the other questions in that section of the test.

Stretch Your Neck

When you're nervous, you have a tendency to tense your neck muscles. The problem with tense neck muscles is that they can give you a headache, so here's what you need to do periodically: Rotate your neck from side to side and stretch those muscles. When you stretch your neck, you release tension in those muscles. If you don't relieve that tension, the nervous energy causing you to tense up in the first place will only get worse. So remember to stretch your neck from time to time as you're taking the test.

Move Your Feet

An easy way you can absent-mindedly alleviate stress and energy as you answer test questions is to move your feet a bit. This movement helps your subconscious have something to do while you're focused on the task at hand. Of course, you shouldn't do a dance under your seat or you'll distract everyone else, but you can wiggle your feet and toes around some to burn excess energy.

Keep Everything in Perspective

Naturally, you'll be nervous because you're taking a test. That fact is a given. Yet as you think about the test and your performance, keeping everything in perspective is also important. The test, in the end, is just a test; it isn't a measurement of who you are as a person, how smart you are, or your chances to make all your dreams come true. Try to approach the test as simply something you need to do, but don't let it define who you are. Just remembering this simple truth can help you keep the test in perspective and, in the end, help you relax as you take the exam.

Index